FRACTIONAL AND DECIMAL EQUIVALENTS

Fractional Notation	Decimal Notation	Percent Notation
$\frac{1}{10}$	0.1	10%
$\frac{1}{8}$	0.125	12.5% or $12\frac{1}{2}$%
$\frac{1}{6}$	$0.16\bar{6}$	$16.6\bar{6}$% or $16\frac{2}{3}$%
$\frac{1}{5}$	0.2	20%
$\frac{1}{4}$	0.25	25%
$\frac{3}{10}$	0.3	30%
$\frac{1}{3}$	$0.333\bar{3}$	$33.3\bar{3}$% or $33\frac{1}{3}$%
$\frac{3}{8}$	0.375	37.5% or $37\frac{1}{2}$%
$\frac{2}{5}$	0.4	40%
$\frac{1}{2}$	0.5	50%
$\frac{3}{5}$	0.6	60%
$\frac{5}{8}$	0.625	62.5% or $62\frac{1}{2}$%
$\frac{2}{3}$	$0.666\bar{6}$	$66.6\bar{6}$% or $66\frac{2}{3}$%
$\frac{7}{10}$	0.7	70%
$\frac{3}{4}$	0.75	75%
$\frac{4}{5}$	0.8	80%
$\frac{5}{6}$	$0.83\bar{3}$	$83.3\bar{3}$% or $83\frac{1}{3}$%
$\frac{7}{8}$	0.875	87.5% or $87\frac{1}{2}$%
$\frac{9}{10}$	0.9	90%
$\frac{1}{1}$	1	100%

Business Mathematics for College Students

THIRD EDITION

Business Mathematics for College Students

THIRD EDITION

MARVIN L. BITTINGER
Indiana University—Purdue University at Indianapolis

WILLIAM B. RUDOLPH
Iowa State University

▲ ADDISON-WESLEY PUBLISHING COMPANY

Reading, Massachusetts • Menlo Park, California
Don Mills, Ontario • Wokingham, England • Amsterdam
Sydney • Singapore • Tokyo • Madrid • Bogotá
Santiago • San Juan

Sponsoring Editor	Susan Zorn
Production Supervisor	Susanah H. Michener
Copy Editor	Margaret Hill
Text Designer	Geri Davis, Quadrata
Illustrator	Robert C. Forget
Production Coordinator	Marcia Strykowski
Manufacturing Supervisor	Ann E. DeLacey
Cover Photo	Marshall Henrichs

PHOTO CREDITS   Chapter title photographs for Chapters 12 and 14 are by Bruce Anderson. All other photographs are by Rick Haston, Latent Images, Carmel, Indiana.

Library of Congress Cataloging-in-Publication Data

Bittinger, Marvin L.
  Business mathematics for college students.

  Rev. ed. of: Business mathematics. 2nd ed. 1984.
  Includes index.
  1. Business mathematics.   I. Rudolph, William B., 1938–
II. Bittinger, Marvin L. Business mathematics.   III. Title.
HF5691.B58   1986   513'.93   86-14184
ISBN 0-201-11212-4

ABCDEFGHIJ-MU-89876

PREFACE

Business Mathematics for College Students has been designed to help students and consumers learn the mathematics needed to perform business operations effectively and efficiently. This is an arithmetic-based text with a heavy applications emphasis and includes chapters on taxes, depreciation, statistics, insurance, investments, and analyzing financial statements.

NEW TO THIS EDITION

- **Calculator Chapter**   Calculator usage is becoming commonplace in business and daily living. For this reason, we have included a brief chapter at the beginning of the book on the basic operation of a calculator. Interspersed throughout the text and the exercise sets are problems clearly marked for using a calculator. The instructor may wish to have students use the calculator as needed throughout the textbook.

- **Skill Maintenance Features**   The need to reinforce previously learned materials is of great importance in acquiring new concepts and skills. Skill maintenance exercises are provided at the end of each exercise set beginning with Section 1.2. These problems will provide the student with the practice necessary to retain a good knowledge of previous materials.

- **More Applications**   Many more real-life applications have been included throughout the text and exercise sets. The problems have been personalized to be more relevant to students' experiences and to help motivate them to learn the concepts involved. The basic mathematics in this text has been presented from a nonalgebraic viewpoint; therefore, no algebra is needed.

- **Glossary of Business Terms**   A glossary has been added for easy reference as the reader progresses through the text. Each glossary item is highlighted with bold italics the first time it appears in the text.

- **Shortened Text** The arithmetic review has been condensed and algebra references deleted to allow more time for the mastery of essential business concepts.

FEATURES

- **Chapter Openers** Each chapter begins with a photograph and descriptive paragraph of a businessperson who uses the mathematics developed in this textbook. These allow students to see how concepts covered in the chapter can be used, motivating them to learn the material. Information on salary, personal characteristics, academic background, and job description provide a background for students on possible careers.

- **Objectives** Each section begins with carefully developed objectives stated in the margin and marked with domino symbols. Sections of text, problems in the exercise sets, and Review Tests are keyed to the objectives so that the student is always able to find the correct review material when experiencing difficulty in working problems.

- **Real and Personalized Problems** Many new exercises have been added to this edition. These include problems that occur frequently in business and in our daily lives. Ads, forms, graphs, diagrams, charts, and art provide motivation and a realistic setting for the material presented.

- **Color Highlights** The use of color emphasizes important material. When reviewing, many students will benefit by examining the highlighted concepts.

- **Exercise Sets** Problems in the exercise sets have been carefully developed to parallel those presented in the text. Exercise set items are keyed to objectives and their development in the text. Students may use this device to secure help when needed in solving a problem. All exercise sets appear on tearout pages for easy removal and checking.

- **Skill Maintenance Exercises** These exercises occur at the end of every exercise set beginning with Section 1.2. Previously learned concepts are continually reviewed throughout the textbook. This provides the student with a continuous review of previously learned material.

- **Review Tests** These tests appear at the end of each chapter. Items are carefully indexed to the objectives by domino symbols. All review tests may be removed for easy checking. All answers to the Review Tests are given at the back of the textbook. Three alternate forms of each test are provided in the Instructor's Resource Guide.

WAYS TO USE THIS BOOK

Business Mathematics for College Students has been carefully designed so that its format is flexible. The text can be used in the following ways.

- When instructors use the book as an *ordinary textbook*, they may lecture on the material and assign problems to be done outside of class. The marginal exercise format greatly enhances the student's ability to read and study alone.

- When instructors use the book for a *modified lecture*, they present the material and have students do marginal exercises at the appropriate time in class.

- When the book is used in a *nonlecture class*, the students study on their own, marking trouble spots and exercises they cannot do. The use of class time is then maximized by spending it solely to work on student difficulties, eliminating the need to lecture on anything the students can learn on their own.

- When the book is used as a *self-study textbook*, the user progresses at his or her own pace. Materials are very readable and the format encourages a user immediately to check progress toward the study objective.

ACKNOWLEDGMENTS

The authors of *Business Mathematics for College Students*, Third Edition, have many people to thank for their help, advice, and cooperation.

We especially want to thank those who consented to having their photographs appear as chapter openers. Their names will not be listed here since they appear with the photographs, but we are deeply grateful. To ensure the relevance of the applied materials, the authors have consulted with many persons in the business world. We wish to thank them for giving so generously of their time and advice. They are as follows: Paul W. Poppe, Toshiba America, Inc.; Lois Poppe, Cytronics, Inc.; Robert J. Ertle, Iowa–Des Moines National Bank; Bill Strickler, State Farm Insurance Co.; Andrew Engel, Certified Public Accountant; Clarence W. Schnicke, Stockbroker; and Barton L. Kaufman, CLU, General Agent, Indianapolis Life Insurance Co.

We also wish to thank Larry Bittinger, Susan Eichner, Virginia McCarthy, Marcia Montag, and Cheri Weinheimer for their meticulous proofreading of the manuscript and checking of the answers. Special thanks to Virginia McCarthy, Jane Ringwald, and Joanne Van Dyke for their assistance in the preparation of the Instructor's Resource Guide. We would like to thank Professor David Wheaton of Terra Technical College for allowing us to use his transparency and handout masters for the Instructor's Resource Guide.

The textual presentation has been improved considerably by the valuable comments and suggestions from users of the second edition. We thank these individuals and the following reviewers: Jim Broussard, American Institute of Business; James C. Carstens, Mesa College; Ray E. Collings, Tri-County Technical College; John Drury, Columbus Technical Institute; Mary Robertson, Midlands Technical College; Steven A. Schmidt, Butte Community College; Martha Sklar, Los Angeles City College; John Snyder, Sinclair Community College; and David Wheaton, Terra Technical College.

M. L. B.
W. B. R.

SUPPLEMENTS

- **Annotated Teacher's Edition** The *Annotated Teacher's Edition* contains the answers to all marginal exercises, all problems in the exercise sets, and all Review Test problems. These answers are provided in color for easy identification and are located adjacent to the statement of the problem.

- **Instructor's Resource Guide** The *Instructor's Resource Guide* contains three alternate forms of each test, answers for these tests, teaching suggestions, and more. For each section, alternate examples are included for the instructor to use in developing the textbook material as well as additional items that may be used as a short quiz to check student progress daily. Problems more difficult than those presented in the text are provided to challenge students. The transparency masters may be displayed on an overhead projector or copied for distribution to the students.

- **Audio Tapes and Video Tapes and Instructional Software** Audio cassettes, video tapes, and instructional software are available for those who wish to use this media to review the materials developed in Chapters 1 and 2.

- **Software Tables** Because interest rates have been so erratic in recent years, it is difficult to prepare tables that remain current. Thus, we have programmed software on a diskette for use with Apple computers. One simply enters the interest rate, the total number of compounding periods, and the kind of compounding, and an appropriate table can be printed. These tables can be produced as simple interest; interest compounded annually, semiannually, quarterly, monthly, and daily; interest compounded continuously; present value of compound interest; and present value of annuities.

CONTENTS

0

CALCULATOR BASICS   1

0.1 Calculator basics   2
    Review test   5

PART ONE

BASICS

1

WHOLE NUMBERS, FRACTIONS, AND DECIMALS   7

1.1 Addition and subtraction of whole numbers   8
1.2 Multiplication and division of whole numbers   13
1.3 Fractions and mixed numerals   19
1.4 Multiplying and dividing using fractional notation   23
1.5 Addition and subtraction using fractional notation   29
1.6 Adding and subtracting using decimals   37
1.7 Multiplication and division using decimals   45
1.8 Rounding   51
1.9 Exponents and order of operations   55
    Review test   59

2

RATIO AND PERCENT   61

2.1 Ratio and proportion   62
2.2 Percent   67
2.3 More problem solving   75
    Review test   83

PART TWO

PERSONAL FINANCE

3

INTEREST 85

3.1 Simple interest 86
3.2 Simple interest computation methods 91
3.3 Simple interest tables 97
3.4 Compound interest 103
3.5 Nominal and effective interest rates 111
3.6 Present value 115
    Review test 119

4

CHECKING, SAVINGS, AND MONEY MARKET ACCOUNTS 121

4.1 Paying by check 122
4.2 Reconciling a bank statement with a check record 133
4.3 Other financial transactions 139
    Review test 143

5

LOANS AND ANNUITIES 147

5.1 Notes and discounts 148
5.2 Partial payment of notes 155
5.3 Annuities 163
5.4 Present value of an annuity 171
    Review test 177

6

INSTALLMENT AND CONSUMER CREDIT 179

6.1 The annual percentage rate (APR) 180
6.2 Finding the payment amount 187
6.3 More on interest 193
6.4 Charge cards 201
    Review test 209

7

STOCKS AND BONDS   211

7.1   Stocks and commissions   212
7.2   Stocks: Yield and price-earnings ratio   217
7.3   Bonds and commissions   221
     Review test   227

8

INSURANCE   229

8.1   Business and homeowner's insurance   230
8.2   Automobile insurance   239
8.3   Life insurance   245
     Review test   253

9

TAXES   255

9.1   Sales tax   256
9.2   Property tax   261
     Review test   265

PART THREE

RETAILING/ ACCOUNTING

10

FINANCIAL STATEMENTS   267

10.1   Profit and loss   268
10.2   Income statements   273
10.3   Balance sheets   279
     Review test   287

11

PURCHASING AND INVENTORY   291

11.1   Discount and price   292
11.2   More trade and cash discounts   297
11.3   Inventory   303
     Review test   309

12

DEPRECIATION 311

12.1 Depreciation: The straight-line method 312
12.2 Depreciation: The declining-balance method 317
12.3 Depreciation: The sum-of-the-years'-digits method 321
12.4 Depreciation: ACRS and federal taxes 325
Review test 329

13

PRICING 331

13.1 Pricing goods: Cost price basis 332
13.2 Pricing goods: Selling price basis 337
13.3 Markdown 343
Review test 349

14

PAYROLL 351

14.1 Hourly and piecework wages 352
14.2 Salary and commission 357
14.3 Federal withholding and social security withholding 365
14.4 Payroll 371
14.5 Federal income tax 377
Review test 389

PART FOUR

STATISTICS

15

STATISTICS AND GRAPHS 393

15.1 Averages, medians, and modes 394
15.2 Bar graphs and frequency distributions 399
15.3 Line graphs and circle graphs 403
Review test 411

APPENDIX: THE METRIC SYSTEM   413

TABLES   T–1

GLOSSARY   G–1

ANSWERS   A–1

INDEX   I–1

Contents

O

CALCULATOR BASICS

CAREER: CERTIFIED PUBLIC ACCOUNTANT This is Maria Gamboa Farrell. She is a certified public accountant (CPA). To become a CPA you must work for a few years as an accountant and then pass a CPA exam. The financial rewards for becoming a CPA are great, as CPA's can earn an annual salary of $30,000 or more.

MARIA GAMBOA FARRELL

Knowing how to use a calculator is useful for almost everyone, but it is essential to anyone who works with numbers as Maria does. Maria has always enjoyed math and has a firm background in the subject. This allows her to make confident and informed decisions regarding financial statements, investments, and taxes. Maria is more qualified mathematically than most CPA's. She has a BS in Mathematics, an MS in Accounting, and a Master's in Business Administration.

Maria believes that computers will be increasingly used in the field of accounting to improve productivity. She advises anyone considering accounting as a career to take as many computer courses as possible.

Add.

1. $987 + 573.76$

2. $593 + 456.12 + 47$

ANSWERS ON PAGE A-1

Calculator Basics

Throughout this book you will find it to your advantage to use a calculator. Many of the rather lengthy calculations in this book can be done easily and rapidly on a calculator. We include this chapter so you may have the skill needed to operate a calculator.

• ADDING

Turn on your calculator and push the clear C key.

This assures that any entries made previously will not appear in your calculations.

Example 1 Add: $465 + 397.17$.

Solution

Enter	Display	Comments
C	0	Clears calculator
465	465	Enters first number
+	465	
397.17	397.17	Enters second number
=	862.17	Answer for $465 + 397.17$

Example 2 Add: $42.9 + 56 + 329$.

Solution

Enter	Display	Comments
C	0	Clears calculator
42.9	42.9	Enters first number
+	42.9	
56	56	Enters second number
+	98.9	Answer for $42.9 + 56$
329	329	Enters third number
=	427.9	Answer for $42.9 + 56 + 329$

DO EXERCISES 1 AND 2.

∴ SUBTRACTING

Subtraction may be readily done using a calculator.

Example 3 Subtract: $872 - 498.75$.

Solution

Enter	Display	Comments
C	0	Clears calculator
872	872	Enters first number
−	872	
498.75	498.75	Enters second number
=	373.25	Answer for $872 - 498.75$

DO EXERCISE 3.

∴ MULTIPLYING

Two or more numbers may be quickly multiplied using a calculator.

Example 4 Multiply: 329×47.

Solution

Enter	Display	Comments
C	0	Clears calculator
329	329	Enters first number
×	329	
47	47	Enters second number
=	15463	Answer for 329×47

Example 5 Multiply: $38 \times 461 \times 7$.

Solution

Enter	Display	Comments
C	0	Clears calculator
38	38	Enters first number
×	38	
461	461	Enters second number
×	17518	Answer for 38×461
7	7	Enters third number
=	122626	Answer for $38 \times 461 \times 7$

DO EXERCISES 4 AND 5.

Subtract.

3. $795 - 326.19$

Multiply.

4. 875×94

5. $49 \times 115 \times 38$

ANSWERS ON PAGE A-1

Divide.

6. $42483 \div 867$

Find.

7. $(14.1)^2$

ANSWERS ON PAGE A-1

⠒ DIVIDING

Example 6 Divide: $3915 \div 29$.

Solution

Enter	Display	Comments
C	0	Clears calculator
3915	3915	Enters first number
÷	3915	
29	29	Enters second number
=	135	Answer for $3915 \div 29$

DO EXERCISE 6.

⠓ RAISING TO A POWER

Raising to a power is useful in compound interest, present value, and annuity problems.

Example 7 Find $(1.02)^3$.

Solution

Enter	Display	Comments
C	0	Clears calculator
1.02	1.02	Enters number in parentheses
y^x	1.02	Some calculators use different keys for this operation
3	3	Enters second number (called the exponent)
=	1.061208	Answer for $(1.02)^3$

Without a y^x or similar key example 7 is done as follows.

Example 8 Find $(1.02)^3$.

Solution

Enter	Display	Comments
C	0	Clears calculator
1.02	1.02	Enters number in parentheses
×	1.02	
= =	1.061208	Answer for $(1.02)^3$

DO EXERCISE 7.

Calculator use makes skills such as rounding and estimating increasingly important. These topics are developed in this book.

NAME:

CLASS/SECTION: DATE:

All of these exercises should be done using a calculator.

|•| Add.

1. 98.7 49.9	**2.** 87.6 19.9	**3.** 47.6 29.0	**4.** 86.5 99.0
5. 143.6 428.9	**6.** 985.7 914.9	**7.** 846.7 593.6	**8.** 481.9 795.9
9. 45 86 62	**10.** 68 49 59	**11.** 98.9 86.9 294.7	**12.** 112.87 347.90 664.80
13. 456.98 385.47 35.80 14.30	**14.** 472.36 997.78 48.70 29.70	**15.** 871.46 972.36 89.97 63.70	**16.** 993.68 714.94 38.83 59.75

|••| Subtract.

17. 45.8 − 6.1	**18.** 65.7 − 9.9	**19.** 69.3 −45.8	**20.** 98.4 −63.9
21. 145.80 − 35.62	**22.** 475.82 − 27.40	**23.** 478.92 −135.86	**24.** 872.95 −482.70
25. 1457.8 − 826.5	**26.** 4527.93 − 378.90	**27.** 9834.6 −7315.9	**28.** 4901.26 −3761.49
29. 2894.82 − 982.40	**30.** 5693.0 − 796.4	**31.** 9847.0 − 378.9	**32.** 6843.15 −4999.90

ANSWERS

1.
2.
3.
4.
5.
6.
7.
8.
9.
10.
11.
12.
13.
14.
15.
16.
17.
18.
19.
20.
21.
22.
23.
24.
25.
26.
27.
28.
29.
30.
31.
32.

∴ Multiply.

33. 478 × 63 **34.** 985 × 98 **35.** 568 × 87

36. 873 × 49 **37.** 328 × 135 **38.** 147 × 981

39. 453.1 × 38 **40.** 567.5 × 67 **41.** 356.1 × 37.2

42. 985.1 × 36.9 **43.** 45 × 36 × 9 **44.** 58 × 95 × 31

45. 35.2 × 23 × 12.5 **46.** 65.4 × 29 × 68.5

⠿ Divide.

47. 2405 ÷ 37 **48.** 5488 ÷ 56 **49.** 6305 ÷ 97

50. 1596 ÷ 28 **51.** 8568 ÷ 126 **52.** 7011 ÷ 369

53. 37.8 ÷ 4.5 **54.** 23.14 ÷ 8.9 **55.** 10115.74 ÷ 568.3

56. 3835.26 ÷ 128.7

⠿ Find.

57. $(4)^3$ **58.** $(7)^3$ **59.** $(2.1)^4$ **60.** $(3.2)^4$

61. $(2)^7$ **62.** $(3)^7$ **63.** $(5)^8$ **64.** $(7)^8$

PART ONE
BASICS

1

WHOLE NUMBERS, FRACTIONS, AND DECIMALS

CAREER: RESTAURANT MANAGEMENT This is Ho Ming Hsia. He is the manager of a restaurant, which uses modern business methodology and fast food production techniques to produce take-out Chinese food.

HO MING HSIA

The ability to manipulate whole numbers, fractions, and decimals is essential to Ho's business. Anytime he rings up a sale, or makes change, he must add or subtract whole numbers and decimals. When Ho directs his cooks to prepare food, they use fractions to measure ingredients. Actually, most of the mathematics in this book is relevant to the operation of a restaurant. On a day-to-day basis a restaurant owner must deal with interest charges on business loans, checking accounts, insurance charges, taxes, financial statements, purchasing, inventory, depreciation, pricing, and payroll.

The restaurant business is demanding. To be successful one has to look at it as a long-term career, rather than a short-term job. A restaurant manager must enjoy working with all kinds of people, and has to make providing good service a priority. Of utmost importance is integrity in all phases of the business operation.

Salaries in the restaurant business are variable. Fast-food restaurant managers can make $25,000 per year plus bonuses. The salaries for managers of other types of restaurants can range from $20,000–$70,000 or more.

Ho immigrated to the United States from Taiwan. Before leaving, he earned a BS in Public Administration from Cheng Chi University as well as an MS in Anthropology. His hobbies include Chinese herb medicine and food medicine. In particular, he likes to show how to use such medicines to cure canker sores and lower back pains.

Write a word name.

1. 220,456,203

2. 88

Addition and Subtraction of Whole Numbers

In this chapter we review addition, subtraction, multiplication, and division of whole numbers and decimals together with related problem solving.

▫ **PLACE VALUE AND WORD NAMES**

Recently the United States government owned

   $11,718,123,786

worth of gold. To find a word name for this number we use a place value chart.

Billions			Millions			Thousands			Ones			← Period
Hundreds	Tens	Ones	Hundreds	Tens	Ones	Hundreds	Tens	Ones	Hundreds	Tens	Ones	← Place
1	1	,	7	1	8	,	1	2	3	,	7 8 6	← Digit

Each comma represents a *period*. We write out the word names in each period.

Example 1 Write word names for 11,718,123,786 and 97.

Solution

a) Eleven **billion,** seven hundred eighteen **million,** one hundred twenty-three **thousand,** seven hundred eighty-six.

b) Ninety-seven (most two-digit numbers have word names that contain hyphens).

DO EXERCISES 1 AND 2 (IN THE MARGIN).

▪▪ **ADDITION**

The whole numbers are 0, 1, 2, 3, 4, 5, 6, 7, 8, 9, 10, 11, and so on. To add whole numbers we add the ones first, then the tens, then the hundreds, and so on.

Example 2 Add: 8765 + 6495.

Solution

a)
```
    1
  8 7 6 5
+ 6 4 9 5
─────────
        0
```
Add ones. Write a 0 in the ones column. Carry a 1 above the tens column. Why? Because 5 + 5 = 10 = 1 ten + 0 ones.

b)
```
  1 1
  8 7 6 5
+ 6 4 9 5
─────────
      6 0
```
Add tens. Write a 6 in the tens column. Carry a 1 above the hundreds column. Why? Because 1 ten + 6 tens + 9 tens = 16 tens or 1 hundred + 6 tens.

c)

$$
\begin{array}{r}
\overset{1}{8}\,\overset{1}{7}\,\overset{1}{6}\,5 \\
+6\,4\,9\,5 \\
\hline
2\,6\,0
\end{array}
$$

Add hundreds. Write a 2 in the hundreds column. Carry a 1 above the thousands column.

d)

$$
\begin{array}{r}
\overset{1}{8}\,7\,\overset{1}{6}\,\overset{1}{5} \\
+6\,4\,9\,5 \\
\hline
1\,5\,2\,6\,0
\end{array}
$$

Add thousands.

> Write only this:
> $$
> \begin{array}{r}
> 8\,7\,6\,5 \\
> +6\,4\,9\,5 \\
> \hline
> 1\,5{,}2\,6\,0
> \end{array}
> $$

DO EXERCISES 3–5.

We use the following terminology with addition:

$$8765 \quad + \quad 6495 \quad = 15{,}260$$

Addend Addend **Sum**

••• SUBTRACTION

To subtract whole numbers we subtract the ones first, then the tens, then the hundreds, and so on. Sometimes we need to borrow one unit from the column to the left.

Example 3 Subtract: $647 - 395$.

Solution

a)

$$
\begin{array}{r}
6\,4\,7 \\
-3\,9\,5 \\
\hline
2
\end{array}
$$

Subtract ones.

b)

$$
\begin{array}{r}
6\,4\,7 \\
-3\,9\,5 \\
\hline
?\,2
\end{array}
$$

Subtract tens, if possible.
Think: $40 - 90$ is not a whole number.

c)

$$
\begin{array}{r}
\overset{5}{\cancel{6}}\,\overset{14}{4}\,7 \\
-3\,9\,5 \\
\hline
2
\end{array}
$$

Borrow 1 hundred. Write 5 above the hundreds column and 14 above the tens because 4 tens + 1 hundred = 4 tens + 10 tens = 14 tens.

d)

$$
\begin{array}{r}
\overset{5}{\cancel{6}}\,\overset{14}{4}\,7 \\
-3\,9\,5 \\
\hline
5\,2
\end{array}
$$

Subtract tens.

e)

$$
\begin{array}{r}
\overset{5}{\cancel{6}}\,\overset{14}{\cancel{4}}\,7 \\
-3\,9\,5 \\
\hline
2\,5\,2
\end{array}
$$

Subtract hundreds.

> Write only this:
> $$
> \begin{array}{r}
> \overset{5}{\cancel{6}}\,\overset{14}{\cancel{4}}\,7 \\
> -3\,9\,5 \\
> \hline
> 2\,5\,2
> \end{array}
> $$

DO EXERCISES 6 AND 7.

We use the following terminology with subtraction:

$$647 \quad - \quad 395 \quad = \quad 252$$

Minuend **Subtrahend** **Difference**

3. $8436 + 2351$

4.
$$
\begin{array}{r}
9956 \\
+4988 \\
\hline
\end{array}
$$

5. $7377 + 881$

Subtract.

6.
$$
\begin{array}{r}
718 \\
-240 \\
\hline
\end{array}
$$

7. $529 - 439$

ANSWERS ON PAGE A-1

Subtract.

8.   907
      −128

9.   5004
      −3768

10. 9000
      −5613

11. 7052 − 2467

12. It takes an average of 993 kWh of electricity to operate a clothes dryer for a year. It takes 103 kWh for a washing machine and 4219 kWh for a water heater. How much electricity does it take to run all three?

13. Sara Freel has $902 in a checking account and writes checks for $84 and $77. How much is left in the account?

ANSWERS ON PAGE A-1

Example 4 Subtract: 8001 − 3654.

Solution

$$\begin{array}{r} {}^{7}\;{}^{9}\;{}^{9}\;{}^{11} \\ 8\,0\,0\,1 \\ -\,3\,6\,5\,4 \\ \hline 4\,3\,4\,7 \end{array}$$

8001 is 8 thousands + 1 one, or 800 tens + 1 one. We borrow 1 ten, leaving 799 tens. Then we subtract ones, tens, hundreds, and thousands.

DO EXERCISES 8–11.

⠿ **PROBLEM SOLVING**

Certain problems can be solved using addition.

Example 5 It takes an average of 1761 kilowatt-hours (kWh) of electricity to operate a frostfree freezer for one year. It takes 1217 kWh for a frostfree refrigerator and 455 kWh for a range. How much electricity does it take to run all three?

Solution

$$\begin{array}{ccccccc} \text{Electricity} & & \text{Electricity} & & \text{Electricity} & & \text{Electricity} \\ \text{for all} & = & \text{for} & + & \text{for} & + & \text{for} \\ \text{three} & & \text{freezer} & & \text{refrigerator} & & \text{range} \\ & = & 1761 & + & 1217 & + & 455 \end{array}$$

We add as follows:

$$\begin{array}{r} {}^{1}\;{}^{1}\;{}^{1} \\ 1\,7\,6\,1 \\ 1\,2\,1\,7 \\ +\,\;\;4\,5\,5 \\ \hline 3\,4\,3\,3 \end{array}$$

It takes 3433 kWh to operate all three appliances for one year.

DO EXERCISE 12.

Certain problems can be solved using subtraction.

Example 6 A consumer has $876 in a checking account and writes checks for $89 and $46. How much is left in the account?

		PLEASE BE SURE TO **DEDUCT** ANY PER CHECK CHARGES OR SERVICE CHARGES THAT MAY APPLY TO YOUR ACCOUNT					
CHECK NO	DATE	CHECKS ISSUED TO OR DESCRIPTION OF DEPOSIT	(−) AMOUNT OF CHECK	✓ T	(−) CHECK FEE (IF ANY)	(+) AMOUNT OF DEPOSIT	BALANCE
							876 00
279	4/16/87	Sally's Sport Shop	89 00				
280	4/16/87	Joe's Snaks Heaven	46 00				?

Solution

$$\begin{array}{ccccccc} \text{Amount} & = & \text{Original} & - & \text{Amount of} & - & \text{Amount of} \\ \text{left} & & \text{amount} & & \text{first check} & & \text{second check} \\ & = & \$876 & - & \$89 & - & \$46 \end{array}$$

We subtract 89 from 876, and then 46 from that answer.

$$\begin{array}{rr} {}^{\;\;16}_{7\;\;6\;16} & \\ 8\,7\,6 & \quad 7\,8\,7 \\ -\;\;8\,9 & \quad -\;\;4\,6 \\ \hline 7\,8\,7 & \quad 7\,4\,1 \end{array}$$

There is $741 left in the account. (This problem could also have been done by adding 89 and 46 and subtracting that answer from 876.)

DO EXERCISE 13.

EXERCISE SET 1.1

⬚ Write a word name.

1. 13

2. 38

3. 56,789

4. 18,235,872,234

⬚⬚ Add.

5.
```
  888
+222
```

6.
```
  769
+488
```

7.
```
  909
+101
```

8.
```
  7819
+1490
```

9.
```
  9118
+1996
```

10.
```
  8866
+6645
```

11.
```
  9999
+7648
```

12.
```
  54,879
+23,787
```

13. ▦
```
  67,443
+10,898
```

14.
```
  98,786
+67,786
```

15. ▦
```
  88,543
+34,686
```

16.
```
  863
  596
  412
+333
```

17.
```
  992
  203
  847
+214
```

18. ▦
```
   923
  2037
    77
+3348
```

19.
```
  7819
    19
  6230
+ 376
```

⬚⬚⬚ Subtract.

20. 678 − 106

21. 798 − 403

22. 734 − 708

23.
```
  725
-317
```

24. ▦
```
  953
-246
```

25.
```
  932
-747
```

26.
```
  8431
-4420
```

27.
```
  9887
-9456
```

28.
```
  6345
-2859
```

29.
```
  580
-279
```

30.
```
  690
-325
```

31.
```
  7002
-1328
```

32.
```
  68,070
-29,691
```

33. ▦
```
  50,680
-17,387
```

34.
```
  79,411
-56,856
```

⠒ Solve.

35. It takes an average of 363 kWh of electricity to operate a dishwasher for a year. It takes 83 kWh to run a deep-fat fryer. How much electricity does it take for both?

36. It takes an average of 860 kWh of electricity to operate a room air conditioner for a year. It takes 163 kWh to run a humidifier. How much electricity does it take for both?

37. Jill Lake has assets of $9876 in real estate, $2190 in a savings account, and $4200 in stock. What are her total assets?

38. Kim Lee has assets of $10,780 in real estate, $3745 in a checking account, and $4898 in municipal bonds. What are her total assets?

39. Recently average annual costs for students at a four-year public college were $1242 for tuition and fees, $2473 for room and board, $373 for books and supplies, $836 for personal items, and $390 for transportation. What was the total cost?

40. ▤ Recently average annual costs for students at a four-year private college were $5418 for tuition and fees, $2781 for room and board, $384 for books and supplies, $694 for personal items, and $382 for transportation. What was the total cost?

41. ▤ In a recent month the number of cars sold by the five divisions of General Motors were 148,344 Chevrolets, 76,943 Pontiacs, 100,137 Oldsmobiles, 76,262 Buicks, and 27,592 Cadillacs. What were total sales?

42. In a recent month the number of cars sold by the two divisions of Ford Motor Company were 120,610 Fords, and 64,913 Lincoln-Mercurys. What were total sales?

43. Misty's Books has an inventory of 6704 books. During one week 1985 books are sold and 789 new books are received from suppliers. How many books were in the inventory at the end of the week?

44. Charlton's had 2590 suits in stock. One week 879 suits are sold and 1240 new suits are received from suppliers. How many suits were in stock at the end of the week?

45. First Trust has a cash balance of $34,567,980. It pays out $18,567,876 and receives $12,788,984. What is the new cash balance?

46. A Lockheed L-1011 TriStar has 1,285,000 rivets and fasteners. Of these, 580,000 are titanium fasteners and 5000 are stainless-steel fasteners. The rest are aluminum rivets. How many aluminum rivets are there?

47. Recent monthly sales of cars manufactured in the United States were 744,764. In the comparable period in the previous year sales were 603,463. What was the difference?

48. Recent monthly sales for Honda cars manufactured in the United States were 33,620. In the comparable period in the previous year sales were 28,019. What was the difference?

49. Canadian steel-ingot production was 280,103 metric tons in a recent week, down from 282,800 metric tons the previous week. By how many metric tons did steel-ingot production decrease?

50. ▤ On the New York Stock Exchange 94,480,000 shares traded on a recent day. Trading was 85,510,000 the previous day. What was the increase in the number of shares traded?

1.2

Multiplication and Division of Whole Numbers

In this section we review multiplication and division of whole numbers and related problem solving.

• MULTIPLICATION

Example 1 Multiply: 396×824.

Solution

a)

```
      1 2
    8 2 4
  ×   3 9 6
    4 9 4 4
```
Multiply 6 times 824 and get 4944.

b)

```
      2 3
      1 2
    8 2 4
  ×   3 9 6
    4,9 4 4
  7 4,1 6 0
```
Multiply 90 times 824 and get 74,160.

c)

```
        1
      2 3
      1 2
      8 2 4
  ×     3 9 6
      4,9 4 4
    7 4,1 6 0
  2 4 7,2 0 0
  3 2 6,3 0 4
```
Multiply 300 times 824 and get 247,200.
Add.

DO EXERCISES 1 AND 2.

We can also use a dot "·" for multiplication rather than "×". That is,

$396 \times 824 = 396 \cdot 824$

We use the following terminology with multiplication:

$$396 \quad \times \quad 824 \quad = 326,304$$
$\uparrow$ $\uparrow$ $\uparrow$
Multiplier   *Multiplicand*   *Product*

We also say 396 and 824 are *factors* of 326,304.

Example 2 Multiply: 408×139.

Solution

```
        1 3 9
  ×     4 0 8
      1,1 1 2
    5 5,6 0 0
    5 6,7 1 2
```
$408 = 4$ hundreds $+ 8$ ones.
Multiply 8 times 139 and get 1112.
Multiply 400 times 139 and get 55,600.
(Write 00 and then multiply 4 times 139.)
Add.

DO EXERCISES 3 AND 4.

Multiply.

1.
```
    8 5 7
  ×   3 9
```

2.
```
    9 1 8
  × 4 6 3
```

Multiply.

3.
```
    8 7 4
  × 3 0 2
```

4.
```
    8 3 4 4
  × 6 0 0 7
```

ANSWERS ON PAGE A-1

Divide.

5. $1\overline{)29468}$

6. $2\overline{)7847}$

• • DIVISION

Example 3 Divide: $8322 \div 38$.

Solution

a)

$$\begin{array}{r} 2 \\ 38\overline{)8322} \\ 76 \\ \hline 72 \end{array}$$

Consider $83 \div 38$; 38 is about 40 and 83 is about 80. Then $80 \div 40$ is 2.

b)

$$\begin{array}{r} 21 \\ 38\overline{)8322} \\ 76 \\ \hline 72 \\ 38 \\ \hline 34 \end{array}$$

Think of this as $70 \div 40$, which is 1.

c)

$$\begin{array}{r} 219 \\ 38\overline{)8322} \\ 76 \\ \hline 72 \\ 38 \\ \hline 342 \\ 342 \\ \hline 0 \end{array}$$

Think of this as $340 \div 40$, which would be 8, but $8 \times 38 = 304$, and

$$\begin{array}{r} 342 \\ -304 \\ \hline 38 \end{array}$$

We see that this estimate is too small, so we increase the 8 to 9.

The answer is 219. The number 0 is the remainder. We do not write 0 remainders in answers.

DO EXERCISES 5 AND 6.

The following terminology is used with division:

$$8322 \div 38 = 219$$

Dividend   *Divisor*   *Quotient*

$$\begin{array}{r} 219 \\ 38\overline{)8322} \end{array}$$

Example 4 Divide: $20{,}733 \div 28$.

Solution

a)

$$\begin{array}{r} 7 \\ 28\overline{)20{,}733} \\ 196 \\ \hline 113 \end{array}$$

Estimate $210 \div 30$, which is 7.

b)

```
           7 4
    2 8 ) 2 0,7 3 3
          1 9 6
          ─────
          1 1 3
          1 1 2
          ─────
              1 3
```

Estimate this as $110 \div 30$, which is 3, but $3 \times 28 = 84$, and

```
    1 1 3
  −   8 4
  ───────
      2 9
```

We see that this estimate is too small, so we increase the 3 to 4.

c)

```
           7 4 0
    2 8 ) 2 0,7 3 3
          1 9 6
          ─────
          1 1 3
          1 1 2
          ─────
              1 3
```

There are no 28's in 13. We write a 0.

The answer is 740 R 13. The quotient is 740. The remainder is 13.

DO EXERCISE 7.

⦿⦿⦿ PROBLEM SOLVING

Certain problems can be solved using multiplication.

Example 5 What is the total cost of three tickets from Indianapolis to Boston and seven tickets from Indianapolis to San Francisco?

FROM INDIANAPOLIS TO:	MON-THURS SUPERSAVER
Albany	$284
Boston	$215
San Francisco	$410
Tucson	$409
Tulsa	$283
Washington	$245

Solution

Cost = Cost of Boston tickets + Cost of San Francisco tickets

= (Number of tickets) × (Cost per Boston ticket)

+ (Number of tickets) × (Cost per San Francisco ticket)

= 3 × $215 + 7 × $410   See the advertisement.

When multiplications and additions occur in the same sentence, the multiplications are to be done first, followed by the additions.

We multiply as follows:

```
    2 1 5          4 1 0
  ×     3        ×     7
  ───────        ───────
    6 4 5          2 8 7 0
```

We then add as follows:

```
      6 4 5
  + 2 8 7 0
  ─────────
    3 5 1 5
```

The total cost of the tickets is $3515.

DO EXERCISE 8.

Divide.

7.
```
  1 4 ) 7 8 4 0
```

8. What is the total cost of eight tickets from Indianapolis to Tucson and six tickets from Indianapolis to Washington? (See the advertisement.)

ANSWERS ON PAGE A-1

9. How many 16-ounce bottles can be filled by 3475 ounces of soda? How many ounces will be left over?

10. There are 167 employees in RTE Corporation. One month $181,696 in salaries is paid. What is the average salary of each employee?

Certain problems can be solved using division.

Example 6 How many 12-ounce bottles of soda can be filled by 3475 ounces of soda? How many ounces of soda will be left over?

Solution

$$\begin{array}{c} \text{Number of} \\ \text{bottles} \end{array} = \begin{array}{c} \text{Number of} \\ \text{ounces} \end{array} \div \begin{array}{c} \text{Amount in} \\ \text{each bottle} \end{array}$$
$$= \quad 3475 \quad \div \quad 12$$

We divide as follows:

```
        2 8 9
  1 2 ) 3 4 7 5
        2 4
        ─────
        1 0 7
          9 6
          ─────
          1 1 5
          1 0 8
          ─────
              7
```

Thus 289 bottles can be filled. There will be 7 ounces left over.

DO EXERCISE 9.

Example 7 There are 248 employees in ARD Corporation. One month $314,216 in salaries is paid. What is the average salary of each employee?

Solution

$$\text{Average salary} = \frac{\text{Total amount paid in salaries}}{\text{Number of employees}}$$
$$= \frac{\$314,216}{248}$$

We divide as follows:

```
            1 2 6 7
  2 4 8 ) 3 1 4,2 1 6
          2 4 8
          ───────
            6 6 2
            4 9 6
            ───────
            1 6 6 1
            1 4 8 8
            ───────
              1 7 3 6
              1 7 3 6
              ───────
                    0
```

The average salary is $1267.

DO EXERCISE 10.

EXERCISE SET 1.2

• Multiply.

1. 8 5 6
    × 7 2

2. 9 7 4
    × 3 9

3. 8 8 8
    × 8 8

4. 3 3 4
    × 3 4

5. 6 0 8
    × 3 0 4

6. 4 0 2
    × 7 5 0

7. 4 5 9
    × 2 0 6

8. 3 8 4
    × 5 0 2

9. 6 4 3 2
    × 1 0 5

10. 7 4 0 8
    × 1 0 7

11. ▦ 2 0 0 9
    × 4 0 0 3

12. 6 7 0 0
    × 5 0 0 6

13. 9 9 9 9
    × 1 1

14. 3 3 3 5
    × 2 2

15. 9 8 7 6
    × 2 3 3 4

16. ▦ 7 8 8 4
    × 1 9 8 4

•• Divide.

17. 4 0) 9 7 5

18. 5 0) 8 8 7

19. 2 1) 6 8 8

20. 5 3) 8 4 7

21. 5 5) 2 5 3 0

22. 9 8) 2 3 5 2

23. 7 8) 9 0 5 7

24. 6 4) 8 4 4 4

25. 3 8) 3 4 , 2 0 0

26. 6 1) 1 8 , 3 0 0

27. 1 1 2) 2 8 0 7

28. 1 0 9) 2 6 2 0

29. 3 2 5) 2 2 7 5

30. 4 6 8) 4 2 1 2

31. 2 1 8) 4 0 , 4 5 9

32. 3 2 6) 5 0 , 7 6 4

ANSWERS

1. _____
2. _____
3. _____
4. _____
5. _____
6. _____
7. _____
8. _____
9. _____
10. _____
11. _____
12. _____
13. _____
14. _____
15. _____
16. _____
17. _____
18. _____
19. _____
20. _____
21. _____
22. _____
23. _____
24. _____
25. _____
26. _____
27. _____
28. _____
29. _____
30. _____
31. _____
32. _____

●●● Solve.

33. A Ford Escort gets 37 miles per gallon for highway driving. How far can it go on 56 gallons of gasoline?

34. A Honda Civic gets 42 miles per gallon for highway driving. How far can it go on 56 gallons of gasoline?

35. Maria Zanatta makes $6 per hour for 40 hours and $9 per hour for 16 hours of overtime. How much does Maria earn?

36. Rizzo's car wash makes $3 for washing a sedan and $5 for washing a station wagon. How much does Rizzo's earn washing 16 cars and 12 wagons?

37. TKR Corporation pays each of its 2116 employees a salary of $13,458 one year. What was the total amount paid?

38. ▦ If the national debt were paid off, each of the 236 million people in this country would owe $7627. What is the national debt?

39. A one-year lease for an apartment specifies $356 rent each month. How much will be spent for rent in the next 12 months?

40. A one-year lease for an automobile specifies a $225 payment each month. How much will be spent in the next 12 months for this lease?

41. A student is to pay off a $3744 loan in 24 equal payments. How much is each payment?

42. A student is to pay off a $5339 loan in 25 equal payments. How much is each payment?

43. ▦ A winner of a state lottery is to be paid $1,500,000 over the next 25 years in monthly payments. How much is each payment?

44. The starting annual salary for a systems analyst who is a recent college graduate was $29,232. What was the monthly salary?

✔ **SKILL MAINTENANCE**

This symbol indicates that the following exercises are *Skill Maintenance Exercises* which review skills previously studied in the text. You can expect such exercises in almost every exercise set.

Write a word name.

45. 14,583

46. 457,982

Subtract.

47. 4592 − 2896

48. 10,923 − 4685

1.3

Fractions and Mixed Numerals

• FRACTIONS

The study of arithmetic begins with the whole numbers

0, 1, 2, 3, 4, 5, 6, 7, 8, 9, 10, 11, and so on.

The need soon arises for halves, thirds, fourths, and so on. These numbers are called **fractions.** The following numbers are fractions:

$$\frac{1}{2}, \frac{3}{4}, \frac{8}{5}, \frac{11}{23}.$$

This way of writing number names is called *fractional notation*. The top number is called the **numerator** and the bottom number is called the **denominator.** In $\frac{3}{4}$, 3 is the numerator and 4 is the denominator. There are several ways to think of a fraction. One way is as part of an object.

Example 1 What part is shaded?

Solution

$\frac{3}{4}$ of a dollar

The object is divided into 4 parts of the same size, and 3 of them are shaded. This is $3 \cdot \frac{1}{4}$, or $\frac{3}{4}$. Thus, $\frac{3}{4}$ (*three-fourths*) of the object is shaded.

DO EXERCISES 1–5.

We also use fractions to indicate parts of a set in which the individual parts are not equal.

Example 2 In Dana Corporation three out of every four people are technicians. What fraction are technicians?

Solution

$\frac{3}{4}$ are technicians.

DO EXERCISE 6.

What part is shaded?

1. $1

2. 1 mile

3.
1 gallon

4.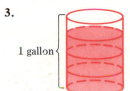

5.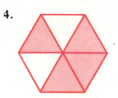

6. You have three pennies, four dimes, seven quarters, and five nickels. What fraction of the total number of coins is pennies? What fraction is dimes?

ANSWERS ON PAGE A-1

Convert to a mixed numeral.

7. $\dfrac{65}{8}$

8. $\dfrac{19}{4}$

9. $\dfrac{89}{16}$

Convert to fractional notation.

10. $2\dfrac{1}{3}$

11. $3\dfrac{7}{8}$

12. $10\dfrac{14}{15}$

• • MIXED NUMERALS

Below we see a drawing representing the fraction $\dfrac{11}{4}$.

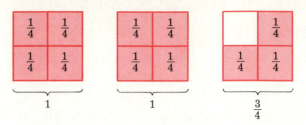

This is also $2 + \dfrac{3}{4}$. We can write this as a **mixed numeral.**

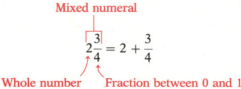

Mixed numeral

$$2\dfrac{3}{4} = 2 + \dfrac{3}{4}$$

Whole number   Fraction between 0 and 1

Example 3 Convert to a mixed numeral: $\dfrac{77}{8}$.

Solution

$$\begin{array}{r} 9 \\ 8\overline{)7\,7} \\ 7\,2 \\ \hline 5 \end{array} \qquad \dfrac{77}{8} = 9\dfrac{5}{8}$$

Keep the denominator.

DO EXERCISES 7–9.

Example 4 Convert to fractional notation: $3\dfrac{4}{5}$.

Solution

$$3\dfrac{4}{5} = \dfrac{(3 \times 5) + 4}{5}$$

a) Multiply the whole number and the denominator of the fraction.

b) Add the numerator.

c) Keep the denominator.

$$= \dfrac{15 + 4}{5}$$

$$= \dfrac{19}{5}$$

DO EXERCISES 10–12.

• • • DIVISION BY ZERO

We cannot divide by zero or have 0 for a denominator in fractional notation. Suppose 4 could be divided by 0. Then, if □ were the answer, $4 \div 0 = \square$ and so $4 = \square \cdot 0 = 0$, which is false. Moreover, $0 \div 0$ would give us any number: for example, $0 \div 0 = 7$ because $0 \cdot 7 = 0$; $0 \div 0 = 13$ because $0 \cdot 13 = 0$; and so on. We avoid all the preceding difficulties by agreeing to exclude division by 0.

• Write fractional notation.

1. By weight, 2 parts out of 3 of the human body are water. What **fraction** is water? What fraction is not water?

2. At present, 1 out of 3 food dollars is spent in a restaurant. What fraction is this? By 1990, 1 out of 2 food dollars will be spent in a restaurant. What fraction is this?

3. There are 8760 hours in a year. The average TV set is in operation 2200 of these hours. What fraction of the hours in a year is this?

4. By area, 3 out of every 4 square miles of the earth's surface are water. What fraction is this?

5. Farrafluids spends 2 out of every 5 dollars of revenues for research. What fraction of revenues is spent for research?

6. In a recent year 3 out of every 5 marriages ended in divorce. What fraction of marriages ended in divorce?

• • Write a mixed numeral.

7. $18 + \dfrac{8}{9}$

8. $24 + \dfrac{2}{3}$

9. $59 + \dfrac{11}{12}$

10. $67 + \dfrac{14}{25}$

Convert to a mixed numeral.

11. $\dfrac{9}{5}$

12. $\dfrac{9}{7}$

13. $\dfrac{19}{8}$

14. $\dfrac{5}{4}$

15. $\dfrac{47}{10}$

16. $\dfrac{63}{10}$

17. $\dfrac{55}{6}$

18. $\dfrac{62}{9}$

19. $\dfrac{347}{6}$

20. $\dfrac{225}{8}$

21. $\dfrac{879}{100}$

22. $\dfrac{5677}{1000}$

ANSWERS

1. _____
2. _____
3. _____
4. _____
5. _____
6. _____
7. _____
8. _____
9. _____
10. _____
11. _____
12. _____
13. _____
14. _____
15. _____
16. _____
17. _____
18. _____
19. _____
20. _____
21. _____
22. _____

Convert to fractional notation.

23. $1\frac{1}{3}$

24. $2\frac{1}{8}$

25. $7\frac{2}{5}$

26. $5\frac{4}{6}$

27. $9\frac{3}{10}$

28. ▦ $9898\frac{2121}{8877}$

29. $99\frac{44}{100}$

30. $78\frac{999}{1000}$

31. $14\frac{8}{9}$

32. $15\frac{6}{7}$

33. ▦ $4567\frac{1267}{8910}$

34. $57\frac{11}{16}$

35. $14\frac{7}{10}$

36. ▦ $79\frac{36}{127}$

37. $24\frac{13}{15}$

38. ▦ $97\frac{72}{328}$

●●● Divide, if possible. If not possible, write "impossible."

39. $\frac{6}{0}$

40. $\frac{14}{7}$

41. $\frac{0}{7}$

42. $\frac{8}{16-16}$

✓ **SKILL MAINTENANCE**

Add.

43. $5783 + 786$

44. $2978 + 3458$

Divide.

45. $1624 \div 29$

46. $42{,}900 \div 123$

1.4

Multiplying and Dividing Using Fractional Notation

•   MULTIPLYING AND SIMPLIFYING USING FRACTIONAL NOTATION

> **To multiply:**
>
> a)   Convert to fractional notation, if necessary.
> b)   Multiply numerators.
> c)   Multiply denominators.
> d)   Do not carry out the products in numerators and denominators.

After multiplying you can often simplify. To simplify, we remove common factors greater than 1 and convert to a mixed numeral, if possible.

Example 1   Multiply and simplify: $\frac{2}{3} \cdot \frac{5}{8}$.

Solution

$$\frac{2}{3} \cdot \frac{5}{8} = \frac{2 \cdot 5}{3 \cdot 8} = \frac{2 \cdot 5}{3 \cdot 2 \cdot 4} = \frac{2}{2} \cdot \frac{5}{3 \cdot 4} = \frac{5}{12}$$

DO EXERCISE 1.

Example 2   Multiply and simplify: $4\frac{1}{5} \cdot 6\frac{2}{3}$.

Solution

$$4\frac{1}{5} \cdot 6\frac{2}{3} = \frac{21}{5} \cdot \frac{20}{3} = \frac{21 \cdot 20}{5 \cdot 3} = \frac{3 \cdot 7 \cdot 4 \cdot 5}{5 \cdot 3} = \frac{5 \cdot 3}{5 \cdot 3} \cdot \frac{7 \cdot 4}{1} = 28$$

DO EXERCISE 2.

Example 3   Multiply and simplify: $4\frac{1}{3} \cdot 5\frac{6}{7}$.

Solution

$$4\frac{1}{3} \cdot 5\frac{6}{7} = \frac{13}{3} \cdot \frac{41}{7} = \frac{13 \cdot 41}{3 \cdot 7} = \frac{533}{21} = 25\frac{8}{21}$$

DO EXERCISE 3.

• •   DIVISION USING FRACTIONAL NOTATION

Two numbers whose product is 1 are called **reciprocals.** Thus, $\frac{4}{5}$ and $\frac{5}{4}$ are reciprocals, and 6 and $\frac{1}{6}$ are reciprocals.

> **To find the reciprocal of a number in fractional notation, interchange the numerator and denominator.**

After finishing Section 1.4, you should be able to:

•	Multiply using fractional notation or mixed numerals, and simplify.
• •	Divide using fractional notation or mixed numerals, and simplify.
• • •	Solve problems involving multiplication and division of fractions.

Multiply and simplify.

1. $\frac{3}{4} \cdot \frac{8}{9}$

Multiply and simplify.

2. $5\frac{1}{3} \cdot 1\frac{1}{8}$

Multiply and simplify.

3. $4\frac{1}{2} \cdot 5\frac{2}{3}$

ANSWERS ON PAGE A-2

Find the reciprocal.

4. $\dfrac{3}{4}$

5. $\dfrac{6}{5}$

Divide.

6. $\dfrac{2}{5} \div \dfrac{3}{4}$

Divide.

7. $\dfrac{7}{8} \div \dfrac{1}{3}$

Divide.

8. $\dfrac{3}{8} \div 24$

ANSWERS ON PAGE A-2

Example 4 Find the reciprocal of $\dfrac{7}{8}$.

Solution

$$\dfrac{7}{8} \diagdown \dfrac{8}{7} \qquad \text{The reciprocal of } \dfrac{7}{8} \text{ is } \dfrac{8}{7}.$$

DO EXERCISES 4 AND 5.

> **To divide:**
>
> a) **Convert to fractional notation, if necessary.**
> b) **Multiply the dividend by the reciprocal of the divisor.**
> c) **Simplify, if possible. When the numerator is larger than the denominator, convert to a mixed numeral.**

Example 5 Divide: $\dfrac{2}{3} \div \dfrac{4}{5}$.

Solution

$$\dfrac{2}{3} \div \dfrac{4}{5} = \dfrac{2}{3} \cdot \dfrac{5}{4} \qquad \text{The reciprocal of } \dfrac{4}{5} \text{ is } \dfrac{5}{4}.$$

$$= \dfrac{2 \cdot 5}{3 \cdot 4} = \dfrac{2 \cdot 5}{3 \cdot 2 \cdot 2} = \boxed{\dfrac{2}{2}} \cdot \dfrac{5}{3 \cdot 2} = \dfrac{5}{6}$$

$$\text{Check: } \dfrac{5}{6} \cdot \dfrac{4}{5} = \dfrac{5 \cdot 4}{6 \cdot 5} = \dfrac{4}{6} = \dfrac{2}{3}$$

DO EXERCISE 6.

Example 6 Divide: $\dfrac{3}{5} \div \dfrac{1}{8}$.

Solution

$$\dfrac{3}{5} \div \dfrac{1}{8} = \dfrac{3}{5} \cdot 8 \qquad \text{The reciprocal of } \dfrac{1}{8} \text{ is } 8.$$

$$= \dfrac{3}{5} \cdot \dfrac{8}{1}$$

$$= \dfrac{3 \cdot 8}{5 \cdot 1} = \dfrac{24}{5} = 4\dfrac{4}{5}$$

DO EXERCISE 7.

Example 7 Divide: $\dfrac{4}{5} \div 16$.

Solution

$$\dfrac{4}{5} \div 16 = \dfrac{4}{5} \cdot \dfrac{1}{16} \qquad \text{The reciprocal of } 16 \text{ is } \dfrac{1}{16}.$$

$$= \dfrac{4 \cdot 1}{5 \cdot 16} = \dfrac{4 \cdot 1}{5 \cdot 4 \cdot 4} = \boxed{\dfrac{4}{4}} \cdot \dfrac{1}{5 \cdot 4} = \dfrac{1}{20}$$

DO EXERCISE 8.

Chapter 1 **Whole Numbers, Fractions, and Decimals**

Example 8 Divide: $8\frac{2}{3} \div 5\frac{7}{9}$.

Solution

$$8\frac{2}{3} \div 5\frac{7}{9} = \frac{26}{3} \div \frac{52}{9}$$

$$= \frac{26}{3} \cdot \frac{9}{32}$$

$$= \frac{26 \cdot 9}{3 \cdot 52}$$

$$= \frac{13 \cdot 3 \cdot 2}{13 \cdot 3 \cdot 2} \cdot \frac{3}{2}$$

$$= \frac{3}{2}$$

$$= 1\frac{1}{2}$$

DO EXERCISE 9.

●●● PROBLEM SOLVING

Example 9 An employee earns $55 for a full work day. How much would the employee earn working $\frac{1}{4}$ of the work day?

Solution

$$\begin{pmatrix} \text{Amount earned} \\ \text{in } \frac{1}{4} \text{ of the day} \end{pmatrix} = \begin{pmatrix} \text{Amount earned} \\ \text{in a full day} \end{pmatrix} \text{ times } \begin{pmatrix} \text{Fraction of} \\ \text{a work day} \end{pmatrix}$$

$$= \qquad \$55 \qquad \cdot \qquad \frac{1}{4}$$

Think of the word "of" translating to "times."

We multiply as follows:

$$55 \cdot \frac{1}{4} = \frac{55}{1} \cdot \frac{1}{4} = \frac{55 \cdot 1}{1 \cdot 4} = \frac{55}{4} = 13\frac{3}{4}.$$

The employee would earn $13\frac{3}{4}$ working $\frac{1}{4}$ of the work day.

DO EXERCISE 10.

Example 10 A long-playing record makes $33\frac{1}{3}$ revolutions per minute. It plays 12 minutes. How many revolutions does it make?

Solution We translate and solve as follows:

$$\begin{pmatrix} \text{Revolutions} \\ \text{per minute} \end{pmatrix} \cdot \begin{pmatrix} \text{Number of} \\ \text{minutes played} \end{pmatrix} = \begin{pmatrix} \text{Total number} \\ \text{of revolutions} \end{pmatrix}$$

$$33\frac{1}{3} \qquad \cdot \qquad 12 \qquad =$$

This tells us what to do. We multiply:

$$33\frac{1}{3} \cdot 12 = \frac{100}{3} \cdot \frac{12}{1} = \frac{1200}{3} = 400.$$

It makes 400 revolutions in 12 minutes.

DO EXERCISE 11.

Divide.

9. $2\frac{1}{3} \div 1\frac{3}{4}$

10. How much steak would it take to serve 50 people if each gets $\frac{2}{3}$ lb of steak?

11. A car travels on an interstate highway at 55 mph for $3\frac{1}{2}$ hours. How far does it travel?

ANSWERS ON PAGE A-2

12. How many jars, each containing $\frac{3}{4}$ lb, can be filled with 600 lb of peanuts?

13. A car travels 302 miles on $15\frac{1}{10}$ gallons of gas. How many miles per gallon did it get?

ANSWERS ON PAGE A-2

Example 11 A car travels 406 miles on $20\frac{3}{10}$ gallons of gasoline. How many miles per gallon does it get?

Solution

$$\frac{\text{Miles per}}{\text{gallon}} = \frac{\text{Total miles}}{\text{driven}} \div \frac{\text{Gallons of}}{\text{gasoline used}}$$

"per" means "for each"

$$= 406 \div 20\frac{3}{10}$$

We divide as follows:

$$406 \div 20\frac{3}{10} = 406 \div \frac{203}{10} = 406 \cdot \frac{10}{203} = \frac{406}{1} \cdot \frac{10}{203}$$

$$= \frac{203 \cdot 2 \cdot 10}{1 \cdot 203} = \frac{203}{203} \cdot \frac{2 \cdot 10}{1} = 20.$$

DO EXERCISE 12.

Example 12 A long-playing record makes $33\frac{1}{3}$ revolutions per minute. It makes 500 revolutions. How long does it play?

Solution The division that corresponds to the situation is

$$500 \div 33\frac{1}{3} = \text{Time}.$$

This tells us what to do. We divide:

$$500 \div 33\frac{1}{3} = \frac{500}{1} \div \frac{100}{3} = \frac{500}{1} \cdot \frac{3}{100} = \frac{1500}{100} = 15.$$

It plays 15 minutes.

DO EXERCISE 13.

Chapter 1   **Whole Numbers, Fractions, and Decimals**

• Multiply and simplify.

1. $\frac{2}{3} \cdot \frac{1}{2}$

2. $\frac{1}{4} \cdot \frac{2}{3}$

3. $\frac{8}{9} \cdot \frac{5}{12}$

4. $\frac{15}{16} \cdot \frac{4}{5}$

5. $18 \cdot \frac{5}{6}$

6. $12 \cdot \frac{3}{4}$

7. $360 \cdot \frac{1}{4}$

8. $120 \cdot \frac{1}{3}$

9. $\frac{3}{5} \cdot 10$

10. $\frac{2}{3} \cdot 24$

11. $3\frac{1}{5} \cdot 3\frac{3}{4}$

12. $4\frac{1}{2} \cdot 2\frac{2}{3}$

13. $3\frac{2}{5} \cdot 1\frac{1}{4}$

14. $1\frac{3}{5} \cdot 3\frac{1}{3}$

15. $6\frac{3}{10} \cdot 5\frac{7}{10}$

16. $8\frac{1}{10} \cdot 2\frac{9}{10}$

17. $28 \cdot 5\frac{1}{4} \cdot \frac{4}{7}$

18. $40 \cdot 3\frac{5}{8}$

19. $1\frac{5}{8} \cdot \frac{2}{3} \cdot \frac{12}{26}$

20. $6\frac{2}{3} \cdot \frac{1}{4}$

•• Divide. Simplify, if possible.

21. $\frac{3}{5} \div \frac{3}{4}$

22. $\frac{6}{7} \div \frac{3}{5}$

23. $\frac{9}{8} \div \frac{1}{3}$

24. $\frac{10}{9} \div \frac{1}{2}$

25. $\frac{12}{7} \div 4$

26. $\frac{8}{7} \div 2$

27. $7 \div \frac{1}{5}$

28. $10 \div \frac{1}{4}$

29. $\frac{7}{8} \div \frac{7}{8}$

30. $\frac{5}{3} \div \frac{5}{3}$

31. $\frac{8}{15} \div \frac{4}{5}$

32. $\frac{6}{13} \div \frac{3}{26}$

33. $4\frac{1}{3} \div 26$

34. $5\frac{1}{2} \div 22$

35. $2\frac{1}{2} \div 1\frac{1}{4}$

36. $3\frac{1}{2} \div 2\frac{2}{3}$

ANSWERS

1. _____
2. _____
3. _____
4. _____
5. _____
6. _____
7. _____
8. _____
9. _____
10. _____
11. _____
12. _____
13. _____
14. _____
15. _____
16. _____
17. _____
18. _____
19. _____
20. _____
21. _____
22. _____
23. _____
24. _____
25. _____
26. _____
27. _____
28. _____
29. _____
30. _____
31. _____
32. _____
33. _____
34. _____
35. _____
36. _____

37. $4\frac{3}{8} \div 2\frac{5}{6}$

38. $6\frac{7}{8} \div 1\frac{2}{3}$

39. $7\frac{3}{10} \div 5\frac{9}{10}$

40. $6\frac{1}{10} \div 2\frac{1}{10}$

41. $16\frac{1}{3} \div 70$

42. $20\frac{1}{5} \div 10$

43. $11\frac{1}{4} \div 2\frac{1}{2}$

44. $10\frac{1}{3} \div 3\frac{2}{5}$

••• Solve.

45. Debra Voelker earns $68 for a full work day. How much would Debra earn working $\frac{1}{5}$ of the work day?

46. Stuart Krupnick earns $563 one week and donates $\frac{1}{10}$ to charity. How much was donated?

47. Laura Smith purchases 100 shares of Chrysler stock at $36\frac{5}{8}$ per share. What was the total amount invested?

48. Derek Mazula purchases 100 shares of IBM stock at $126\frac{3}{4}$ per share. What was the total amount invested?

49. On a map 1 inch represents 240 miles. How much does $\frac{2}{5}$ inch represent?

50. On a map 1 inch represents 180 miles. How much does $\frac{3}{4}$ inch represent?

51. In a recent year $\frac{13}{25}$ of the 12,247,000 college students in the United States were females. How many were females?

52. ▦ In a recent year $\frac{12}{25}$ of the 12,247,000 college students in the United States were males. How many were males?

53. A car travels 561 miles on $18\frac{7}{10}$ gallons of gasoline. How many miles per gallon does it get?

54. How many boxes of powder, each containing $\frac{2}{3}$ oz, can be filled with 150 oz of powder?

55. Jolaré Interiors reimbursed an interior designer $22\frac{1}{2}$¢ a mile for consulting work. Reimbursement last month was $99. How many miles were driven?

56. ▦ In a recent year the United States Government allowed $20\frac{1}{2}$¢ a mile for business use of an automobile. A taxpayer deducted $922.50. How many miles were driven?

57. Mei Liao paid $18.00 for steak that cost $2\frac{1}{4}$ a pound. How many pounds were purchased?

58. One state pays $\frac{1}{50}$ of lottery proceeds to education. How much were lottery proceeds if $20,000 was paid to education?

✓ **SKILL MAINTENANCE**

Multiply.

59. 478×67

60. 6785×459

Convert to fractional notation.

61. $45\frac{16}{37}$

62. $671\frac{3}{8}$

1.5

Addition and Subtraction Using Fractional Notation

⚀ LEAST COMMON MULTIPLES

The number 12 is a *multiple* of 4 because it can be written as a product of 4 and another nonzero *number*:

$$12 = 4 \cdot 3.$$

The number 72 is a **common multiple** of 12 and 18 because it is a multiple of both 12 and 18. The number 36 is the **least common multiple**, or **LCM**, of 12 and 18 because it is the smallest nonzero number that is a multiple of both.

> The *least common multiple*, or LCM, of two nonzero whole numbers is the smallest number that is a multiple of both.

The following is an efficient method for finding LCMs.

> **To find the LCM of a set of numbers:**
>
> **a)** Check to see if the largest number is a multiple of the other numbers. If so, it is the LCM.
>
> **b)** If (a) is not so, compute multiples of the larger number until a number is obtained that is a multiple of the others. That number will be the LCM.

Example 1 Find the LCM: 8 and 10.

Solution

a) Is 10 a multiple of 8? No, so 10 is not the LCM.

b) Compute multiples of 10 until a multiple of 8 is obtained:

$2 \cdot 10 = 20,$ not a multiple of 8;
$3 \cdot 10 = 30,$ not a multiple of 8;
$4 \cdot 10 = 40,$ 40 is a multiple of 8.

The LCM is 40.

DO EXERCISE 1.

⚁ LEAST COMMON DENOMINATORS

> The *least common denominator*, **LCD**, is the LCM of the denominators.

Example 2 Find the LCD: $\dfrac{3}{5}$ and $\dfrac{1}{8}$.

Solution The denominators are 5 and 8.

a) Is 8 a multiple of 5? No, so 8 is not the LCM.

b) Compute multiples of 8 until a multiple of 5 is obtained:

$2 \cdot 8 = 16,$ not a multiple of 5;
$3 \cdot 8 = 24,$ not a multiple of 5;
$4 \cdot 8 = 32,$ not a multiple of 5;
$5 \cdot 8 = 40,$ 40 is a multiple of 5.

The LCD is 40.

Find the LCM.

1. 12 and 15

ANSWER ON PAGE A-2

Find the LCD.

2. $\dfrac{5}{6}$ and $\dfrac{4}{7}$

Find the LCD.

3. $\dfrac{1}{3}, \dfrac{4}{5},$ and $\dfrac{11}{15}$

Add and simplify.

4. $\dfrac{3}{12} + \dfrac{5}{12}$

Add and simplify.

5. $18\dfrac{3}{6} + 7\dfrac{5}{6}$

When two numbers have no common factor greater than 1, their **LCM** is the product of the numbers.

DO EXERCISE 2.

Example 3 Find the LCD: $\dfrac{1}{10}, \dfrac{3}{100},$ and $\dfrac{77}{1000}$.

Solution The denominators are 10, 100, and 1000.

Is 1000 a multiple of 10 and a multiple of 100? Yes, so it is the LCD. The LCD is 1000.

DO EXERCISE 3.

••• ADDING

To add, using fractional notation, when there is a common denominator (the same denominator):

a) Add the numerators.
b) Put the sum over the common denominator.
c) Simplify, if possible.

Example 4 Add and simplify: $\dfrac{3}{16} + \dfrac{5}{16}$.

Solution

$$\frac{3}{16} + \frac{5}{16} = \frac{3+5}{16} = \frac{8}{16} = \frac{1}{2}$$

DO EXERCISE 4.

With mixed numerals, we add the fractions first and then the whole numbers.

Example 5 Add and simplify: $9\dfrac{5}{8} + 14\dfrac{7}{8}$.

Solution

$$\begin{array}{r} 9\dfrac{5}{8} \\ + 14\dfrac{7}{8} \\ \hline 23\dfrac{12}{8} \end{array} = 23\frac{3}{2} = 23 + \frac{3}{2} = 23 + 1\frac{1}{2} = 24\frac{1}{2}$$

Add the fractions.
Add the whole numbers.

DO EXERCISE 5.

To add, using fractional notation, when denominators are different:

a) Determine the LCD.
b) Multiply by 1 so that each fraction has the LCD.
c) Add as with common denominators.
d) Simplify, if possible.

Example 6 Add and simplify: $\dfrac{3}{4} + \dfrac{5}{6}$.

Solution The LCD is 12.

$$\frac{3}{4} + \frac{5}{6} = \frac{3}{4} \cdot \boxed{\frac{3}{3}} + \frac{5}{6} \cdot \boxed{\frac{2}{2}}$$

Think: $4 \times ? = 12$. The answer is 3, so we multiply by $\frac{3}{3}$.

Think: $6 \times ? = 12$. The answer is 2, so we multiply by $\frac{2}{2}$.

$$= \frac{9}{12} + \frac{10}{12} = \frac{19}{12} = 1\frac{7}{12}$$

DO EXERCISE 6.

Example 7 Add and simplify: $11\dfrac{5}{6} + 4\dfrac{7}{8}$.

Solution The LCD is 24.

$$11\frac{5}{6} = 11 + \frac{5}{6} = 11 + \boxed{\frac{5}{6} \cdot \frac{4}{4}} = 11 + \frac{20}{24}$$

$$+ \; 4\frac{7}{8} = \;\; 4 + \frac{7}{8} = \;\; 4 + \boxed{\frac{7}{8} \cdot \frac{3}{3}} = \;\; 4 + \frac{21}{24}$$

$$15 + \frac{41}{24} = 15 + 1\frac{17}{24} = 16\frac{17}{24}$$

DO EXERCISE 7.

⠒ SUBTRACTING

To subtract, using fractional notation, when there is a common denominator:

a) **Subtract the numerators.**

b) **Put the difference over the common denominator.**

c) **Simplify, if possible.**

Example 8 Subtract: $\dfrac{3}{5} - \dfrac{1}{5}$.

Solution

a) Subtract the numerators:

$$\frac{3}{5} - \frac{1}{5} = \frac{3 - 1}{5} = \frac{2}{5}.$$

b) Put the difference over the common denominator.

DO EXERCISES 8 AND 9.

Example 9 Subtract and simplify: $13\dfrac{7}{8} - 9\dfrac{3}{8}$.

Solution

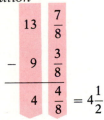

$$\begin{array}{r} 13\frac{7}{8} \\ -\; 9\frac{3}{8} \\ \hline 4\frac{4}{8} \end{array} = 4\frac{1}{2}$$

Subtract the fractions.
Subtract the whole numbers.

DO EXERCISE 10.

Add and simplify.

6. $\dfrac{5}{6} + \dfrac{1}{8}$

Add and simplify.

7. $10\dfrac{1}{8} + 10\dfrac{7}{12}$

Subtract and simplify.

8. $\dfrac{10}{12} - \dfrac{2}{12}$

9. $\dfrac{11}{6} - \dfrac{7}{6}$

Subtract and simplify.

10. $19\dfrac{5}{6} - 11\dfrac{1}{6}$

ANSWERS ON PAGE A-2

Subtract and simplify.

11. $\dfrac{8}{9} - \dfrac{5}{7}$

Subtract and simplify.

12. $11\dfrac{1}{8} - 4\dfrac{5}{12}$

Subtract and simplify.

13. $10 - 7\dfrac{5}{8}$

> **To subtract, using fractional notation, when denominators are different:**
>
> a) **Determine the LCD.**
> b) **Multiply by 1 so each fraction has the LCD.**
> c) **Subtract as with common denominators.**
> d) **Simplify, if possible.**

Example 10 Subtract and simplify: $\dfrac{5}{6} - \dfrac{5}{8}$.

Solution The LCD is 24.

$$\frac{5}{6} - \frac{5}{8} = \frac{5}{6} \cdot \frac{4}{4} - \frac{5}{8} \cdot \frac{3}{3} = \frac{20}{24} - \frac{15}{24} = \frac{5}{24}$$

DO EXERCISE 11.

Example 11 Subtract and simplify: $8\dfrac{1}{3} - 2\dfrac{4}{5}$.

Solution The LCD is 15.

$$8\frac{1}{3} = 8 + \frac{1}{3} = 8 + \frac{1}{3} \cdot \frac{5}{5} = 8 + \frac{5}{15} = 7 + \frac{20}{15}$$

$$-2\frac{4}{5} = 2 + \frac{4}{5} = 2 + \frac{4}{5} \cdot \frac{3}{3} = 2 + \frac{12}{15} = 2 + \frac{12}{15}$$

$$5 + \frac{8}{15} = 5\frac{8}{15}$$

In this problem we could not subtract until we borrowed:

$$8 + \frac{5}{15} = 7 + 1 + \frac{5}{15} = 7 + \frac{15}{15} + \frac{5}{15} = 7 + \frac{20}{15}.$$

DO EXERCISE 12.

Example 12 Subtract and simplify: $13 - 1\dfrac{3}{4}$.

Solution

$$13 \quad = 12\frac{4}{4} \qquad 13 = 12 + 1 = 12 + \frac{4}{4} = 12\frac{4}{4}$$

$$- 1\frac{3}{4} = \quad 1\frac{3}{4}$$

$$11\frac{1}{4}$$

DO EXERCISE 13.

Example 13 On a recent day the stock of IBM opened at $126\frac{7}{8}$ per share and gained $1\frac{3}{4}$. What was the closing price?

Solution

$$\begin{array}{c} \text{Closing} \\ \text{price} \end{array} = \begin{array}{c} \text{Value at} \\ \text{opening} \end{array} + \begin{array}{c} \text{Amount} \\ \text{of gain} \end{array}$$

$$= \$126\frac{7}{8} + \$1\frac{3}{4}$$

The LCD is 8. We add as follows:

$$126\frac{7}{8} = 126 + \frac{7}{8} \qquad = 126 + \frac{7}{8}$$

$$+ \quad 1\frac{3}{4} = \quad 1 + \boxed{\frac{3}{4} \cdot \frac{2}{2}} = \quad 1 + \frac{6}{8}$$

$$127 + \frac{13}{8} = 127 + 1\frac{5}{8} = 128\frac{5}{8}$$

The closing price was $128\frac{5}{8}$.

DO EXERCISE 14.

Example 14 On two business days a salesperson drove $144\frac{9}{10}$ miles and $87\frac{1}{4}$ miles. What was the total distance driven?

Solution We translate.

$$\left(\begin{array}{c}\text{Distance driven} \\ \text{first day}\end{array}\right) + \left(\begin{array}{c}\text{Distance driven} \\ \text{second day}\end{array}\right) = \left(\begin{array}{c}\text{Total distance} \\ \text{driven}\end{array}\right)$$

$$144\frac{9}{10} \qquad + \qquad 87\frac{1}{4} \qquad =$$

The sentence tells us what to do. We add.

The LCM is 20.

$$144\frac{9}{10} = \quad 144\boxed{\frac{9}{10} \cdot \frac{2}{2}} = \quad 144\frac{18}{20}$$

$$+ \; 87\frac{1}{4} = + \; 87\boxed{\frac{1}{4} \cdot \frac{5}{5}} = + \; 87\frac{5}{20}$$

$$231\frac{23}{20} = 232\frac{3}{20}$$

The total distance driven was $232\frac{3}{20}$ miles.

DO EXERCISE 15.

14. On a recent day the stock of Delta Airlines opened at $45\frac{1}{4}$ and gained $2\frac{7}{8}$. What was the closing price?

15. Hershel's Fabrics sold two pieces of material $6\frac{1}{4}$ yd and $10\frac{5}{6}$ yd long. What was the total length of the material?

ANSWERS ON PAGE A-2

16. On a recent day the stock of TWA opened at $20 per share and dropped $1\frac{1}{8}$. What was the closing price?

17. There are $20\frac{1}{8}$ gallons of water in a barrel. $5\frac{3}{4}$ gallons are poured out and $8\frac{3}{8}$ gallons are poured back in. How many gallons of water are there in the barrel?

ANSWERS ON PAGE A-2

Example 15 On a recent day the stock of IBM opened at $127\frac{1}{4}$ per share and dropped $1\frac{5}{8}$. What was the closing price?

Solution

$$\begin{array}{c}\text{Closing} \\ \text{price}\end{array} = \begin{array}{c}\text{Value at} \\ \text{opening}\end{array} - \begin{array}{c}\text{Amount of} \\ \text{drop}\end{array}$$

$$= \$127\frac{1}{4} - \$1\frac{5}{8}$$

The LCD is 8. We subtract as follows:

$$127\frac{1}{4} = 127 + \boxed{\frac{1}{4} \cdot \frac{2}{2}} = 127 + \frac{2}{8} = 126 + \frac{10}{8}$$

$$- \quad 1\frac{5}{8} = \quad 1 + \frac{5}{8} \quad = \quad 1 + \frac{5}{8} = \quad 1 + \frac{5}{8}$$

$$\overline{\qquad\qquad 125 + \frac{5}{8} \; = 125\frac{5}{8}}$$

The closing price was $125\frac{5}{8}$.

DO EXERCISE 16.

Example 16 One morning the stock of LTD Corporation opened at a price of $100\frac{3}{8}$ per share. By noon the price had risen $4\frac{7}{8}$. At the end of the day it had fallen $10\frac{3}{4}$ from the price at noon. What was the closing price?

Solution We first draw a picture or at least visualize the situation.

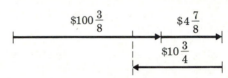

This is a two-step problem.

a) We first add $4\frac{7}{8}$ to $100\frac{3}{8}$ to find the price of the stock at noon.

$$\begin{array}{r} 100\dfrac{3}{8} \\[2mm] + \quad 4\dfrac{7}{8} \\[1mm] \hline 104\dfrac{10}{8} = 105\dfrac{1}{4} \end{array}$$

b) Next we subtract $10\frac{3}{4}$ from $105\frac{1}{4}$ to find the price of the stock at closing.

$$\begin{array}{r} 105\dfrac{1}{4} = 104\dfrac{5}{4} \\[2mm] - \quad 10\dfrac{3}{4} = \quad 10\dfrac{3}{4} \\[1mm] \hline 94\dfrac{2}{4} = 94\dfrac{1}{2} \end{array}$$

The stock closed at $94\frac{1}{2}$.

DO EXERCISE 17.

Chapter 1   **Whole Numbers, Fractions, and Decimals**

EXERCISE SET 1.5

• Find the LCM.

1. 7 and 9   **2.** 4 and 11   **3.** 3 and 15   **4.** 6 and 18

5. 18 and 24   **6.** 12 and 16   **7.** 35 and 45   **8.** 24 and 36

• • Find the LCD.

9. $\dfrac{2}{3}$ and $\dfrac{5}{12}$ **10.** $\dfrac{4}{5}$ and $\dfrac{7}{10}$ **11.** $\dfrac{3}{4}$ and $\dfrac{5}{6}$ **12.** $\dfrac{5}{6}$ and $\dfrac{7}{9}$

13. $\dfrac{3}{8}$ and $\dfrac{7}{16}$ **14.** $\dfrac{3}{4}$ and $\dfrac{1}{20}$ **15.** $\dfrac{1}{2}, \dfrac{3}{4},$ and $\dfrac{7}{8}$ **16.** $\dfrac{3}{4}, \dfrac{2}{5},$ and $\dfrac{1}{20}$

• • • Add and simplify.

17. $\dfrac{1}{6} + \dfrac{1}{9}$ **18.** $\dfrac{1}{12} + \dfrac{1}{8}$ **19.** $\dfrac{4}{5} + \dfrac{7}{10}$ **20.** $\dfrac{1}{18} + \dfrac{2}{3}$

21. $4\dfrac{3}{8} + 6\dfrac{5}{12} + 1\dfrac{5}{6}$ **22.** $5\dfrac{1}{6} + 3\dfrac{2}{9}$ **23.** $8\dfrac{4}{5} + 6\dfrac{1}{10} + 4\dfrac{1}{2}$ **24.** $7\dfrac{1}{2} + 11\dfrac{3}{10}$

ANSWERS

1. _____
2. _____
3. _____
4. _____
5. _____
6. _____
7. _____
8. _____
9. _____
10. _____
11. _____
12. _____
13. _____
14. _____
15. _____
16. _____
17. _____
18. _____
19. _____
20. _____
21. _____
22. _____
23. _____
24. _____

⦂ Subtract and simplify.

25. $\dfrac{5}{12} - \dfrac{3}{8}$ **26.** $\dfrac{7}{12} - \dfrac{2}{9}$ **27.** $\dfrac{3}{4} - \dfrac{3}{20}$ **28.** $\dfrac{2}{3} - \dfrac{1}{18}$

29. $7 - 1\dfrac{1}{4}$ **30.** $8 - 3\dfrac{1}{8}$ **31.** $15\dfrac{1}{8} - \dfrac{3}{4}$ **32.** $20\dfrac{1}{4} - \dfrac{5}{6}$

⦂ Solve.

33. On a recent day the stock of Pepsi opened at \$$59\frac{7}{8}$ per share and gained \$$1\frac{1}{2}$. What was the closing price?

34. On a recent day the stock of RCA opened at \$$42\frac{1}{2}$ and gained \$$1\frac{5}{8}$. What was the closing price?

35. A glazier used $4\frac{2}{3}$ lb, $8\frac{4}{5}$ lb, and 10 lb of glazing compound. How much compound was used?

36. A painter used $10\frac{3}{4}$, $12\frac{5}{8}$, and 14 gallons of paint. How much paint was used?

37. On a recent day the stock of General Mills opened at \$$57\frac{1}{8}$ and dropped \$$1\frac{1}{2}$. What was the closing price?

38. On a recent day the stock of General Motors opened at \$67 and dropped \$$1\frac{3}{8}$. What was the closing price?

39. The standard pencil is $7\frac{7}{16}$ inches long. The eraser is $\frac{7}{8}$ inches. How much of the pencil is wood?

40. A corporation is owned by three people. One owns $\frac{1}{2}$ and the second owns $\frac{3}{8}$. What fraction does the third own?

41. A worker knows it will take $12\frac{1}{2}$ hr to complete a job. The first day $3\frac{1}{4}$ hr are spent on the job and the second day $5\frac{2}{3}$ hr are spent. How much time will it take to finish the job?

42. A worker knows it will take $16\frac{2}{3}$ hr to complete a job. The first day $8\frac{1}{2}$ hr are spent on the job and the second day $5\frac{3}{4}$ hr are spent. How much time will it take to finish the job?

✓ **SKILL MAINTENANCE**

43. In a recent year $\frac{29}{50}$ of the 12,247,000 college students in the United States were under 25 years of age. How many were under 25?

44. ▦ In a recent year $\frac{21}{50}$ of the 12,247,000 college students in the United States were 25 or older. How many were 25 or older?

Chapter 1 **Whole Numbers, Fractions, and Decimals**

1.6

Adding and Subtracting Using Decimals

In this section we use **decimal notation.** For example, instead of using fractional notation for $\frac{7}{8}$ we use decimal notation and write 0.875.

■ DECIMAL NOTATION AND WORD NAMES

The cost of a stereo system is

$1768.95.

This is *decimal notation.* The following place-value chart gives the meaning of decimals.

Thousands	Hundreds	Tens	Ones	Tenths	Hundredths	Thousandths	Ten-Thousandths
1000	100	10	1	$\frac{1}{10}$	$\frac{1}{100}$	$\frac{1}{1000}$	$\frac{1}{10,000}$
1	7	6	8	9	5		

Example 1 Write a word name for 1768.95.

Solution One thousand, seven hundred sixty-eight and ninety-five hundredths

DO EXERCISES 1–3.

Example 2 Write a word name for $1768.95, as on a check.

Solution One thousand, seven hundred sixty-eight and $\frac{95}{100}$ dollars

DO EXERCISES 4 AND 5.

Write a word name.

1. 18.49

2. 0.645

3. 12.0005

Write a word name as on a check.

4. $18.49

5. $2346.76

ANSWERS ON PAGE A-2

• • ☐ **CONVERTING FROM DECIMAL TO FRACTIONAL NOTATION**

Decimals are defined in terms of fractions—for example,

$$0.1 = \frac{1}{10}, \qquad 0.6875 = \frac{6875}{10,000}, \qquad 53.47 = \frac{5347}{100}.$$

From these examples we obtain the following procedure.

To convert from decimal to fractional notation:	
a) Count the number of decimal places.	4.98 **2 places**
b) Move the decimal point that many places to the right.	4.98, Move **2 places**
c) Write the answer over a denominator with the same number of zeros.	$\dfrac{498}{100}$ **2 zeros**

Example 3 Convert to fractional notation: 0.876. Do not simplify.

Solution

$$0.876 \qquad 0.876. \qquad 0.876 = \frac{876}{1000}$$

3 places

Example 4 Convert to fractional notation: 1.5018. Do not simplify.

Solution

$$1.5018 \qquad 1.5018. \qquad 1.5018 = \frac{15,018}{10,000}$$

DO EXERCISES 6–8.

Example 5 Convert to a mixed numeral: 9.73.

Solution

$$9.73 = \frac{973}{100} = 9\frac{73}{100}$$

DO EXERCISES 9 AND 10.

• • • ☐ **FROM FRACTIONAL TO DECIMAL NOTATION**

We reverse the procedure we used before.

To convert from fractional to decimal notation:	
a) Count the number of zeros.	$\dfrac{8679}{1000}$ **3 zeros**
b) Move the decimal point that number of places to the left. Leave off the denominator.	8.679, Move **3 places**

Example 6 Convert to decimal notation: $\dfrac{123,067}{10,000}$.

Solution

$$\frac{123,067}{10,000} \qquad 12.3067. \qquad \frac{123,067}{10,000} = 12.3067$$

4 zeros

DO EXERCISES 11–13.

Example 7 Convert to decimal notation: $14\frac{3}{10}$.

Solution We first convert to fractional notation, and then proceed as before.

$$14\frac{3}{10} = \frac{143}{10} = 14.3$$

DO EXERCISES 14–17.

:: ADDITION

Adding with decimal notation is similar to adding whole numbers. We add the thousandths, and then the hundredths, carrying if necessary. Then we go on to the tenths, then the ones, and so on. To keep place values straight, line up the decimal points in a vertical column.

Example 8 Add: $74 + 26.46 + 0.998$.

Solution

a)
```
    7 4 .
    2 6 . 4 6
  +  0 . 9 9 8
```
Line up the decimal points in a vertical column. If there is a whole number such as 74, write in the decimal point.

b)
```
    7 4 .
    2 6.4 6
  +  0.9 9 8
            8
```
Add thousandths.

c)
```
         1
    7 4 .
    2 6.4 6
  +  0.9 9 8
          5 8
```
Add hundredths. Write 5 in the hundredths place and carry 1 above the tenths column.

d)
```
       1  1
    7 4 .
    2 6.4 6
  +  0.9 9 8
       .4 5 8
```
Add tenths. Write 4 in the tenths place and carry 1 above the ones column. Write a decimal point in the answer below the others.

e)
```
     1 1  1
    7 4 .
    2 6.4 6
  +  0.9 9 8
     1 .4 5 8
```
Add ones. Write 1 in the ones place and carry 1 above the tens column.

f)
```
      1 1 1
       7 4 .
      2 6.4 6
  +      0.9 9 8
    1 0 1.4 5 8
```
Add tens.

You may put extra zeros to the right of any decimal point so there are the same number of decimal places, but this is not necessary. The preceding problem would look like this:

```
    7 4.0 0 0
    2 6.4 6 0
  +  0.9 9 8
    1 0 1.4 5 8
```

DO EXERCISES 18 AND 19.

Convert to decimal notation.

14. $14\frac{57}{100}$

15. $22\frac{7}{100}$

16. $3\frac{19}{1000}$

17. $7\frac{6783}{10,000}$

Add.

18. $69 + 1.785 + 213.67$

19. $17.95 + 14.68 + 236$

ANSWERS ON PAGE A-2

Subtract.

20. 29.35 − 1.674

21. 92.375 − 27.692

Subtract.

22. 100 − 0.41

23. 240 − 0.117

⠿ **SUBTRACTION**

Subtracting with decimal notation is similar to subtracting whole numbers. We subtract the thousandths, borrowing if necessary. Then we go on to the hundredths, the tenths, and so on. To keep place values straight, we line up the decimal points.

Example 9 Subtract: 76.14 − 18.953.

Solution

a)
$$\begin{array}{r} 76.140 \\ -18.953 \\ \hline \end{array}$$
Line up the decimal places. We put an extra zero to the right of the decimal point in 76.14 to get the same number of decimal places.

b)
$$\begin{array}{r} 76.1\overset{3\ 10}{4\ \cancel{0}} \\ -18.953 \\ \hline 7 \end{array}$$
Borrow 1 hundredth. Then subtract thousandths.

c)
$$\begin{array}{r} 76.\overset{0\ \ 13}{\cancel{1}\ \cancel{4}\ \overset{10}{\cancel{0}}} \\ -18.953 \\ \hline 87 \end{array}$$
Borrow 1 tenth. Then subtract hundredths.

d)
$$\begin{array}{r} 7\overset{5\ \ 0\ \ 3\ \ 10}{6.\cancel{1}\ \cancel{4}\ \cancel{0}} \\ +18.953 \\ \hline .187 \end{array}$$
Borrow 1 one. Then subtract tenths. Write a decimal point in the answer below the others.

e)
$$\begin{array}{r} \overset{15}{7}\overset{5\ \ 0\ \ 3\ \ 10}{6.\cancel{1}\ \cancel{4}\ \cancel{0}} \\ -18.953 \\ \hline 7.187 \end{array}$$
Borrow 1 ten. Then subtract ones.

f)
$$\begin{array}{r} \overset{15}{7}\overset{5\ \ 0\ \ 3\ \ 10}{6.\cancel{1}\ \cancel{4}\ \cancel{0}} \\ -18.953 \\ \hline 57.187 \end{array}$$
Subtract tens.

DO EXERCISES 20 AND 21.

Example 10 Subtract: 200 − 0.68.

Solution

$$\begin{array}{r} \overset{1\ \ 9\ \ 9\ \ 9\ \ 10}{\cancel{2}\ 0\ 0.0\ 0} \\ -\ \ \ \ \ 0.6\ 8 \\ \hline 1\ 9\ 9.3\ 2 \end{array}$$

DO EXERCISES 22 AND 23.

Let us convert from dollars to cents and cents to dollars.

> $1 = 100¢;
>
> $1¢ = \$\dfrac{1}{100} = \$0.01$

Example 11 Convert to cents: $17.98.

Solution

$$\$17.98 = \$17\frac{98}{100} = \$\frac{1798}{100} = 1798¢$$

We can convert to cents by moving the decimal point two places to the right.

DO EXERCISES 24 AND 25.

Example 12 Convert to dollars: 32¢.

Solution

$$32¢ = \$\frac{32}{100} = \$0.32$$

We can convert to dollars by moving the decimal point two places to the left.

DO EXERCISES 26 AND 27.

Example 13 When making a deposit in a savings account one might have some currency, some coins, and some checks. Find the **net deposit** in the following figure.

TELLER'S STAMP	MAXIMUM INTEREST TIME DEPOSIT	AFNB	20—1 / 740

ACCOUNT NUMBER

| 0 6 0 | – | 2 3 | – | 4 5 6 6 | – | 7 |
| 15 17 | | 5 | | 14 | | 32 |

Date *Aug 9, 1987* 27

Items are received for deposit subject to applicable rules of bank.

CURRENCY	$236	00
COIN	8	19
CHECKS	952	84
LIST	948	67
SINGLY		

CREDIT THE ACCOUNT OF:

Connie Consumer
NAME (PLEASE PRINT)

3010 Spring Ave
ADDRESS

TOTAL		
LESS CASH RECEIVED BY:		
Connie Consumer SIGNATURE	0	00
NET DEPOSIT	18	26

FORM 2271 (Rev 6/76)

Convert to cents.

24. $76.95

25. $0.14

Convert to dollars.

26. 95¢

27. 795¢

ANSWERS ON PAGE A-2

28. Find the net deposit below.

CURRENCY	785	00
COIN	2	49
CHECKS	679	43
	98	29
	822	97
TOTAL		
LESS CASH	0	00
NET DEPOSIT		

29. Find the net deposit below.

CASH LIST CHECKS SINGLY	805	97
	766	66
	438	89
TOTAL FROM OTHER SIDE	220	03
TOTAL		
LESS CASH RECEIVED	300	00
NET DEPOSIT		

ANSWERS ON PAGE A-2

Solution We add the currency, the coins, and the checks as follows:

$$\begin{array}{r} {\scriptstyle 1\;2\;1\;2} \\ 2\;3\;6.0\;0 \\ 8.1\;9 \\ 9\;5\;2.8\;4 \\ +\;\;9\;4\;8.6\;7 \\ \hline 2\;1\;4\;5.7\;0 \end{array}$$

The net deposit is \$2145.70.

DO EXERCISE 28.

Example 14 It can happen that one deposits several checks, gets some cash, and leaves the rest in a checking account. Find the net deposit in the following figure.

Solution We first add the amounts on the checks:

$$\begin{array}{r} {\scriptstyle 1\;1\;2\;1\;1} \\ 1\;2\;7\;8.9\;5 \\ 3\;4\;7.6\;8 \\ +\;\;7\;6\;9.0\;6 \\ \hline 2\;3\;9\;5.6\;9 \end{array}$$ This is TOTAL above.

Then we subtract the amount of cash received.

$$\begin{array}{r} {\scriptstyle 1\;\;13} \\ 2\;3\;9\;5.6\;9 \\ -\;\;\;4\;0\;0.0\;0 \\ \hline 1\;9\;9\;5.6\;9 \end{array}$$

The net deposit is \$1995.69.

DO EXERCISE 29.

Chapter 1   **Whole Numbers, Fractions, and Decimals**

· Write a word name.

1. 34.891   **2.** 12.345   **3.** 0.0903   **4.** 0.4013

Write a word name, as on a check.

5. $326.48   **6.** $125.99   **7.** $0.67   **8.** $3.25

· · Convert to fractional notation. Do not simplify.

9. 4.9   **10.** 1.3   **11.** 0.59   **12.** 0.81

13. 2.0007   **14.** 4.0008   **15.** 7889.8   **16.** 1122.3

Convert to a mixed numeral. Do not simplify.

17. 18.46   **18.** 89.95   **19.** 4.013   **20.** 1.058

21. 234.5   **22.** 456.8   **23.** 5.4111   **24.** 12.6788

· · · Convert to decimal notation.

25. $\dfrac{1}{10}$ **26.** $\dfrac{1}{100}$ **27.** $\dfrac{1}{10,000}$ **28.** $\dfrac{1}{1000}$

29. $\dfrac{3079}{10}$ **30.** $\dfrac{1796}{10}$ **31.** ▦ $\dfrac{9999}{1000}$ **32.** $\dfrac{17}{1000}$

33. $\dfrac{39}{10,000}$ **34.** $\dfrac{4578}{10,000}$ **35.** $\dfrac{1}{100,000}$ **36.** $\dfrac{94}{100,000}$

37. $6\dfrac{14}{1000}$ **38.** $9\dfrac{342}{1000}$ **39.** ▦ $126\dfrac{8}{10}$ **40.** $2345\dfrac{1}{10}$

· · Add.

41. $\begin{array}{r} 4\,1\,5.7\,8 \\ +\ \ 2\,9.1\,6 \\ \hline \end{array}$

42. $\begin{array}{r} 7\,0\,8.9\,9 \\ +\ \ 7\,5.4\,8 \\ \hline \end{array}$

43. ▦ $\begin{array}{r} 2\,3\,4.0\,0\,0 \\ +1\,5\,6.6\,1\,7 \\ \hline \end{array}$

44. $\begin{array}{r} 1\,3\,4\,5.1\,2 \\ +\ \ 5\,6\,6.9\,8 \\ \hline \end{array}$

45. $85 + 67.95 + 2.774$

46. ▦ $119 + 43.74 + 18.876$

47. $17.95 + 16.99 + 28.85$

48. $14.59 + 16.79 + 19.95$

ANSWERS

1. _____
2. _____
3. _____
4. _____
5. _____
6. _____
7. _____
8. _____
9. _____
10. _____
11. _____
12. _____
13. _____
14. _____
15. _____
16. _____
17. _____
18. _____
19. _____
20. _____
21. _____
22. _____
23. _____
24. _____
25. _____
26. _____
27. _____
28. _____
29. _____
30. _____
31. _____
32. _____
33. _____
34. _____
35. _____
36. _____
37. _____
38. _____
39. _____
40. _____
41. _____
42. _____
43. _____
44. _____
45. _____
46. _____
47. _____
48. _____

Subtract.

49.
$$\begin{array}{r} 7\,8.1\,1 \\ -\,4\,5.8\,7\,6 \\ \hline \end{array}$$

50.
$$\begin{array}{r} 1\,4.0\,8 \\ -\,\ \ 9.1\,9\,9 \\ \hline \end{array}$$

51.
$$\begin{array}{r} 3\,8.7\,0\,0 \\ -\,1\,1.8\,6\,5 \\ \hline \end{array}$$

52.
$$\begin{array}{r} 3\,0\,0.0\,0\,0 \\ -\,\ \ \ 2\,4.6\,7\,7 \\ \hline \end{array}$$

53. $57.86 - 9.95$ **54.** $2.6 - 1.08$ **55.** $3 - 1.0807$ **56.** $5 - 3.4051$

Solve.

Convert to cents.

57. $89.95   **58.** $78.34   **59.** $0.45   **60.** $0.13

Convert to dollars.

61. 95¢   **62.** 11¢   **63.** 179¢   **64.** 284¢

Find the net deposit.

65.

CASH	1348	95
LIST CHECKS SINGLY	943	68
	1204	95
	995	64
TOTAL FROM OTHER SIDE		
TOTAL		
LESS CASH RECEIVED	650	00
NET DEPOSIT		

66.

		Dollars	Cents
CURRENCY			
COIN			
CHECKS List singly • Be sure each item is endorsed		125,678	95
		86,435	34
		78,881	24
		34,685	93
		46,784	66
TOTAL			
LESS CASH RETURNED		28,060	88
NET DEPOSIT			

67. The odometer on a car read 39,105.7 before a 489.6-mile trip. What did it read at the end of the trip?

68. The odometer on a car read 18,458.9 before a 575.8-mile trip. What did it read at the end of the trip?

69. The odometer on a car read 22,389.4 before a trip and 23,412.0 at the end. How many miles were driven?

70. The odometer on a car read 58,412.3 before a trip and 61,500.7 at the end. How many miles were driven?

71. Normal body temperature is 37°C. Butter melts at 30.6°C. How much lower is this than normal body temperature?

72. One year a business paid the following salaries. What was the total of the salaries paid?

$62,459.78, $57,577.98, $23,400.00, $22,999.99, $19,680.44, $19,742.66

✓ SKILL MAINTENANCE

Multiply. Simplify, if possible.

73. $4\frac{1}{3} \cdot 7\frac{1}{5}$

74. $4\frac{2}{3} \cdot 1\frac{1}{5}$

Divide. Simplify, if possible.

75. $\dfrac{9}{5} \div \dfrac{8}{10}$

76. $32 \div 3\frac{1}{5}$

1.7

Multiplication and Division Using Decimals

O B J E C T I V E S

After finishing Section 1.7, you should be able to:

• Multiply using decimal notation.

•• Divide using decimal notation.

••• Solve problems involving multiplication and division using decimal notation.

• MULTIPLICATION

Look at this product.

$$5.14 \times 0.8 = \frac{514}{100} \times \frac{8}{10} = \frac{514 \times 8}{100 \times 10} = \frac{4112}{1000} = 4.112$$

2 places   1 place   3 places

We can also do this by multiplying the whole numbers 8 and 514 and determining the position of the decimal point.

> **To multiply using decimal notation:**
>
> a) Ignore the decimal points and multiply as whole numbers.
> b) Place the decimal point in the result of (a) by adding the number of decimal places in the numbers.

Example 1 Multiply: 5.14×0.8.

Solution

a) Ignore the decimal points and multiply as whole numbers.

$$\begin{array}{r} \overset{13}{5.1\,4} \\ \times 0.8 \\ \hline 4\,1\,1\,2 \end{array}$$

b) Place the decimal point in the result of (a) by adding the number of places in the numbers.

$$\begin{array}{r} 5.1\,4 \\ \times 0.8 \\ \hline 4.1\,1\,2 \end{array}$$ ⊞ 2 decimal places / 1 decimal place

3 decimal places

DO EXERCISES 1 AND 2.

Example 2 Multiply: 0.927×0.18.

Solution

a)
$$\begin{array}{r} 0.9\,2\,7 \\ \times 0.1\,8 \\ \hline 7\,4\,1\,6 \\ 9\,2\,7\,0 \\ \hline 0.1\,6\,6\,8\,6 \end{array}$$

b) ⊞ 3 decimal places / 2 decimal places

5 decimal places

DO EXERCISE 3.

Multiply.

1. $\begin{array}{r} 6.5\,2 \\ \times 0.9 \end{array}$

2. $\begin{array}{r} 6.5\,2 \\ \times 0.0\,9 \end{array}$

Multiply.

3. $\begin{array}{r} 5\,6.7\,6 \\ \times 0.9\,0\,8 \end{array}$

ANSWERS ON PAGE A-2

• • DIVISION

Division of Decimals by Whole Numbers

Note that $37.6 \div 8 = 4.7$ because $37.6 = 8 \times 4.7$. If we write this as

```
        4.7
    8 )3 7.6
      3 2
        5 6
        5 6
          0
```

we see how the following method can be used to divide by a whole number.

> **To divide by a whole number:**
>
> a) **Place the decimal point in the quotient directly above the decimal point in the dividend.**
> b) **Divide as though whole numbers.**

Example 3 Divide: $216.75 \div 25$.

Solution

a)
```
                .
    2 5 )2 1 6 . 7 5
```

b)
```
              8  6 7
    2 5 )2 1 6 . 7 5
        2 0 0
          1 6   7
          1 5   0
            1   7 5
            1   7 5
                  0
```

DO EXERCISES 4 AND 5.

It is sometimes helpful to write extra zeros to the right of the decimal point. The answer is not changed. Remember that the decimal point for a whole number, though not normally written, is to the right of the number.

Example 4 Divide: $54 \div 8$.

Solution

a)
```
            .
    8 )5 4 .
```

b)
```
          6.7 5
    8 )5 4.0 0
      4 8
        6 0
        5 6
          4 0
          4 0
            0
```

Extra zeros are written to the right of the decimal point as needed.

DO EXERCISES 6 AND 7.

Chapter 1   Whole Numbers, Fractions, and Decimals

Divisors That Are Not Whole Numbers

To divide when the divisor is not a whole number:

a) Move the decimal point in the divisor as many places to the right as it takes to make it a whole number. Move the decimal point in the dividend the same number of places to the right.

b) Divide as though whole numbers, adding zeros if necessary.

Example 5 Divide: $83.79 \div 0.098$.

Solution

a)

$$0.0\,9\,8\,\overset{\displaystyle .}{)\,8\,3.7\,9\,0.}$$

b)

$$
\begin{array}{r}
8\,5\,5. \\
0.0\,9\,8\,)\overline{8\,3.7\,9\,0.} \\
7\,8\,4 \\
\hline
5\,3\,9 \\
4\,9\,0 \\
\hline
4\,9\,0 \\
4\,9\,0 \\
\hline
0
\end{array}
$$

DO EXERCISES 8 AND 9.

Repeating Decimals

Some decimals repeat.

Example 6 Convert to decimal notation: $\dfrac{7}{12}$.

Solution

$$
\begin{array}{r}
0.5\,8\,3\,3 \\
1\,2\,)\overline{7.0\,0\,0\,0} \\
6\,0 \\
\hline
1\,0\,0 \\
9\,6 \\
\hline
4\,0 \\
3\,6 \\
\hline
4\,0 \\
3\,6 \\
\hline
4
\end{array}
$$

We have 4 repeating as a remainder, so the digits will repeat in the quotient. Therefore,

$$\frac{7}{12} = 0.583333\ldots$$

Instead of the dots, we often put a bar over the repeating part. Thus,

$$\frac{7}{12} = 0.583\bar{3} \quad \text{or} \quad 0.58\bar{3}.$$

DO EXERCISES 10 AND 11.

Divide.

8. $0.0\,2\,4\,)\overline{2\,0.5\,4\,4}$

Divide.

9. $4.6\,)\overline{3.9\,1}$

Convert to decimal notation.

10. $\dfrac{2}{3}$

11. $\dfrac{84}{11}$

ANSWERS ON PAGE A-2

---

12. At Davis Rent-a-Car the cost of an intermediate-size car is $24.95 plus 29¢ a mile. What is the cost, in dollars, of driving 320 miles?

13. Find the gas mileage.

First odometer reading:
22,587.2
Second odometer reading:
23,000.0
Number of gallons at the last fill:
12.9

ANSWERS ON PAGE A-2

Example 7 At Peso Rent-a-Car the daily cost of an intermediate-size car is $29.95 plus 28¢ a mile. What is the cost, in dollars, of driving 240 miles in one day?

Solution

$$\text{Cost} = \text{Basic Charge} + \text{Cost per mile} \times \text{Number of miles}$$
$$= \quad \$29.95 \quad + \quad \$0.28 \quad \times \quad 240$$

We do the multiplication first. We multiply as follows:

$$
\begin{array}{r}
2\ 4\ 0 \\
\times\ \ 0.2\ 8 \\
\hline
1\ 9\ 2\ 0 \\
4\ 8\ 0\ 0 \\
\hline
6\ 7.2\ 0 \\
\end{array}
$$

We then add on the basic charge, $29.95:

$$
\begin{array}{r}
6\ 7.2\ 0 \\
+2\ 9.9\ 5 \\
\hline
9\ 7.1\ 5 \\
\end{array}
$$

The cost is $97.15.

DO EXERCISE 12.

Example 8 *Computing gas mileage.* Get the gas tank filled and write down the mileage on the odometer, say, 19,560.7. The next time the tank is filled write down the mileage, say, 19,938.1. From the gasoline pump find the number of gallons it takes to fill the tank, say, 18.5. Then subtract the odometer readings and divide by the number of gallons on the second fill. Find the gasoline mileage.

Solution

$$\text{Gasoline mileage} = \frac{\text{Difference in the odometer readings}}{\text{Number of gallons at the last fill}}$$
$$= \frac{19{,}938.1 - 19{,}560.7}{18.5}$$

We subtract:

$$
\begin{array}{r}
{}^{8}\ {}^{13}\ {}^{7}\ {}^{11} \\
1\ 9{,}9\ 3\ 8.1 \\
-1\ 9{,}5\ 6\ 0.7 \\
\hline
3\ 7\ 7.4 \\
\end{array}
$$

We then divide the answer by 18.5:

$$
\begin{array}{r}
2\ 0.4 \\
1\ 8.5.\ \overline{)3\ 7\ 7.4.0} \\
3\ 7\ 0 \\
\hline
7\ 4\ 0 \\
7\ 4\ 0 \\
\hline
0 \\
\end{array}
$$

The mileage is 20.4 miles per gallon.

DO EXERCISE 13.

Chapter 1   Whole Numbers, Fractions, and Decimals

• Multiply.

1. 6.2 3
× 1.6

2. 5.4 4
× 3.2

3. 5 6 7 8
×0.0 6 8

4. 1 2 4 5
×0.1 0 7

5. 1 7.9 5
× 1 0

6. 1 7.9 5
× 1 0 0

7. 1 8.9 4
× 0.0 1

8. 1 8.9 4
× 0.1

9. 1 4.7
×1.0 4

10. 0.3 4 2
× 1 0.6

11. ▥ 2 1.9 7
× 2 4

12. 3 6.6 7
× 5 3

13. 0.4 5 7
× 3.0 8

14. 0.0 0 2 4
× 0.0 1 5

15. 3.6 4 2
× 0.9 9

16. 2 8 7.4
× 1.0 8

• • Divide.

17. 7 2) 1 6 5.6

18. 5.2) 4 4.2

19. 8.5) 4 4.2

20. 7.8) 7 2.5 4

21. ▥ 9.9) 0.2 2 7 7

22. 1 0 0) 9 5

23. 0.6 4) 1 2

24. 1.6) 7 5

25. 1.0 5) 6 9 3

Convert to decimal notation.

26. $\dfrac{5}{6}$

27. $\dfrac{13}{11}$

28. ▥ $\dfrac{4}{11}$

ANSWERS

1. _____
2. _____
3. _____
4. _____
5. _____
6. _____
7. _____
8. _____
9. _____
10. _____
11. _____
12. _____
13. _____
14. _____
15. _____
16. _____
17. _____
18. _____
19. _____
20. _____
21. _____
22. _____
23. _____
24. _____
25. _____
26. _____
27. _____
28. _____

ANSWERS

29. _____

30. _____

31. _____

32. _____

33. _____

34. _____

35. _____

36. _____

37. _____

38. _____

39. _____

40. _____

41. _____

42. _____

••• Solve.

29. At Murtz Rent-a-Car the daily cost of an intermediate-size car is $34.95 plus 38¢ a mile. What is the cost, in dollars, of driving 290 miles in one day?

30. At Nudgit Rent-a-Car the daily cost of a compact car is $33.95 plus 30¢ a mile. What is the cost, in dollars, of driving 345 miles in one day?

31. A tax deduction of 21¢ per mile is allowed for mileage driven while on business. What deduction, in dollars, is allowed for 478 miles?

32. A print shop charges 6¢ per page for copies. What is the cost of 750 copies?

33. A computer information network charges $.16 per minute. The network was used for 6.75 minutes. What was the charge?

34. A college student works at a fast food restaurant for 22.5 hours one week. The pay is $3.16 per hour. How much was earned?

35. A farmer was paid $1188.98 for corn which sold for $2.21 a bushel. How many bushels were sold?

36. ▦ A farmer was paid $4520.88 for soybeans which sold for $5.04 a bushel. How many bushels were sold?

Find the gas mileage.

37. ▦ First odometer reading: 34,095.6
Second odometer reading: 34,836.6
Number of gallons at the last fill: 28.5

38. First odometer reading: 18,456.2
Second odometer reading: 19,317.5
Number of gallons at the last fill: 29.7

✓ **SKILL MAINTENANCE**

Subtract.

39. $5618 - 4739$

Multiply.

40. 409×37

Convert to fractional notation.

41. $13\frac{5}{8}$

42. $5\frac{7}{8}$

1.8

Rounding

| • | **ROUNDING** |

Calculators and computers have made estimating increasingly important in checking the reasonableness of results. We usually estimate by **rounding** the numbers.

To round to a certain place:

a) **Locate the digit in that place.**

b) **Then consider the digit to its right.**

c) **If the digit to the right is 5 or higher, round up; If the digit to the right is less than 5, round down.**

Example 1 Round 3872.2459 to the nearest tenth.

Solution

a) Locate the digit in the tenths place.

   3 8 7 2 . 2 4 5 9
           ↑

b) Then consider the next digit to the right.

   3 8 7 2 . 2 4 5 9
             ↑

c) Since that digit is less than 5, round down.

   3 8 7 2 . 2 ←— This is the answer.

Note that 3872.3 is *not* a correct answer to Example 1. It is incorrect to round from the ten-thousandths place over as follows:

   3872.246,   3872.25,   3872.3

DO EXERCISES 1–6.

Example 2 Round 3872.2459 to the nearest thousandth, hundredth, tenth, one, ten, hundred, and thousand.

Solution

Thousandth:	3872.246
Hundredth:	3872.25
Tenth:	3872.2
One:	3872
Ten:	3870
Hundred:	3900
Thousand:	4000

DO EXERCISES 7–15.

We sometimes use the symbol $\approx$, meaning "is approximately equal to." Thus,

   $46.124 \approx 46.1$

Round to the nearest tenth.

1. 2.76   **2.** 13.85

3. 7.009

Round to the nearest hundredth.

4. 7.834   **5.** 34.675

6. 0.025

Round to the nearest thousandth.

7. 0.9434   **8.** 8.0038

9. 43.1119   **10.** 37.4005

Round 7459.3549 to the nearest

11. thousandth

12. hundredth

13. tenth

14. one

15. ten
(*Caution:* "Tens" are not "tenths.")

ANSWERS ON PAGE A-2

16. Find the gas mileage. Round to the nearest tenth of a mile per gallon.

First odometer reading:
  39,401.2
Second odometer reading:
  39,622.0
Number of gallons at the last fill:
  12.6

17. In a recent quarter NIB Corporation with 3,400,000 shares of stock outstanding had $1,181,500 earnings. Find the earnings per share to the nearest cent.

ANSWERS ON PAGE A-2

• • SOLVING PROBLEMS

When decimals repeat in problems, we usually round. To do that we carry the division out one place beyond the place to which we are to round, and then round back.

Example 3 Find the gas mileage. Round to the nearest tenth of a mile per gallon.

First odometer reading: 42,689.3
Second odometer reading: 42,886.7
Number of gallons at the last fill: 15.6

Solution

$$\text{Gasoline mileage} = \frac{\text{Difference in the odometer readings}}{\text{Number of gallons at the last fill}}$$

$$= \frac{42,886.7 - 42,689.3}{15.6}$$

$$= \frac{197.4}{15.6}$$

We divide and round as follows:

```
             1 2.6 5
    15.6.)1 9 7.4.0 0
          1 5 6
          ─────
            4 1 4
            3 1 2
          ─────
            1 0 2 0
              9 3 6
            ─────
                8 4 0
                7 8 0
              ─────
                  6 0
```

We stop the division at the hundredths place and round. The gas mileage is about 12.7 miles per gallon.

DO EXERCISE 16.

Example 4 In a recent quarter Fremont Enterprises with 1,200,000 shares of stock outstanding had $315,000 earnings. Find the earnings per share to the nearest cent.

Solution

$$\text{Earnings per share} = \frac{\text{Earnings}}{\text{Shares outstanding}}$$

$$= \frac{315,000}{1,200,000}$$

We divide and round as follows:

```
                     .2 6 2
    1,2 0 0,0 0 0)3 1 5,0 0 0.0 0 0
                  2 4 0 0 0 0 0
                  ─────────────
                    7 5 0 0 0 0 0
                    7 2 0 0 0 0 0
                  ─────────────
                      3 0 0 0 0 0 0
                      2 4 0 0 0 0 0
                    ─────────────
                        6 0 0 0 0 0
```

We stop the division at the thousandths place and round. The answer is about $.26.

DO EXERCISE 17.

Round to the nearest hundredth, tenth, one, ten, and hundred.

1. 745.06534   **2.** 317.18565   **3.** 6780.50568   **4.** 840.15493

Round to the nearest cent and to the nearest dollar (nearest one).

5. $17.988   **6.** $20.492   **7.** $346.075   **8.** $4.718

Round to the nearest dollar.

9. $16.95   **10.** $17.50   **11.** $189.50   **12.** $567.24

Divide and round to the nearest ten-thousandth, thousandth, hundredth, tenth, and one.

13. $\dfrac{1000}{81}$ **14.** $\dfrac{23}{17}$

Solve. Find the gas mileage. Round to the nearest tenth of a mile per gallon.

15. First odometer reading: 16,322.9
Second odometer reading: 16,606.7
Number of gallons at the last fill: 8.9

16. First odometer reading: 54,113.5
Second odometer reading: 54,432.1
Number of gallons at the last fill: 11.6

17. Rodney Hoon earned $44 working 9 hours. What was his hourly wage? Round to the nearest cent.

18. One week Cheri Bistricky earned $197.32 working 40 hours. What was the hourly wage? Round to the nearest cent.

19. A dozen softballs cost $72.95. What was the cost per ball? Round to the nearest cent.

20. A dozen sweatshirts cost $89.98. What was the cost per shirt? Round to the nearest cent.

21. Ghasson Chorieiri paid $33,000 for a 2.8-acre lot. What was the cost per acre? Round to the nearest dollar.

22. Yolanda Dabney paid $44,000 for a 3.7-acre lot. What was the cost per acre? Round to the nearest dollar.

ANSWERS

1. _____

2. _____

3. _____

4. _____

5. _____

6. _____

7. _____

8. _____

9. _____

10. _____

11. _____

12. _____

13. _____

14. _____

15. _____

16. _____

17. _____

18. _____

19. _____

20. _____

21. _____

22. _____

ANSWERS

23. _____

24. _____

25. _____

26. _____

27. _____

28. _____

29. _____

23. On a recent day a processing plant produced 3744 pounds of chicken. Chickens weigh about 4.5 pounds when processed. How many chickens were processed?

24. ▦ In a recent year the population of Mexico was 78,900,000. Its land area is 764,000 square miles. What was its population per square mile (round to the ones position)?

25. In baseball the percent (Pct) won (in decimal form) is found by dividing the number of games won by the total number of games played. Complete the Pct column (round to the nearest thousandth) for this recent table.

AMERICAN LEAGUE
EASTERN DIVISION

	W.	L.	Pct.	G.B.
Toronto	95	55	.633	—
New York	88	62	.587	7
Baltimore	79	70		16½
Detroit	79	72	.523	16½
Boston	75	76	.497	20½
Milwaukee	66	84	.440	29
Cleveland	54	99		42½

WESTERN DIVISION

	W.	L.	Pct.	G.B.
California	85	66	.563	—
Kansas City	84	66		½
Chicago	78	72	.520	6½
Oakland	74	77	.490	11
Seattle	71	80		14
Minnesota	69	82	.457	16
Texas	57	93	.380	27½

26. In a recent year Bolt, Beranek and Newman had earnings of $5,929,000 with 7,861,997 shares of stock outstanding. Find the earnings per share to the nearest cent.

27. ▦ In a recent year Magic Chef had earnings of $53,564,000 with 9,651,000 shares of stock outstanding. Find the earnings per share to the nearest cent.

✔ **SKILL MAINTENANCE**

28. It takes 1.8 pounds of feed to produce a pound of chicken. How many pounds of feed would be needed to produce 8338.5 pounds of chicken?

29. A newstand collected $123.20 for 352 copies of a newspaper. What was the cost for each paper?

1.9

Exponents and Order of Operations

• EXPONENTIAL NOTATION

Exponents provide a shorter way of writing products. For example,

$\underbrace{5 \times 5 \times 5 \times 5}_{4}$ is shortened to 5^4 —— Exponent
—— Base

We read 5^4 as "five to the fourth power," 4^2 as "four squared," and 7^3 as "seven cubed." 5^4 is an example of **exponential notation.**

Example 1 Write exponential notation: $10 \cdot 10 \cdot 10 \cdot 10 \cdot 10 \cdot 10$.

Solution

$$10 \cdot 10 \cdot 10 \cdot 10 \cdot 10 \cdot 10 = 10^6$$

DO EXERCISES 1–3.

• • EVALUATING EXPONENTIAL EXPRESSIONS

Example 2 Evaluate: 3^4.

Solution

$$3^4 = 3 \times 3 \times 3 \times 3 = 81$$

DO EXERCISES 4–6.

One as an Exponent

Note the following. We divide by 8 each time.

$$8 \cdot 8 \cdot 8 = 8^3 = 512$$
$$8 \cdot 8 = 8^2 = 64$$
$$8 = 8^? = 8$$

If the pattern were to continue, we would have

$$8 = 8^1$$

We define 8^1 to be 8. In general,

We define $a^1 = a$.

Example 3 Evaluate: 37^1.

Solution

$$37^1 = 37$$

DO EXERCISES 7–9.

Zero as an Exponent

Note the following. We divide by 5 each time.

$$5 \cdot 5 = 5^2 = 25$$
$$5 = 5^1 = 5$$
$$1 = 5^? = 1$$

If the pattern were to continue, we would have

$$1 = 5^0$$

We define 5^0 to be 1. In general,

We define $a^0 = 1$, for any nonzero number a.

OBJECTIVES

After finishing Section 1.9, you should be able to:

• Write exponential notation for a product.

• • Evaluate exponential expressions.

• • • Simplify expressions using the rules for order of operations.

Write exponential notation.

1. $5 \cdot 5 \cdot 5$

2. $5 \cdot 5 \cdot 5 \cdot 5 \cdot 5$

3. 1.08×1.08

Evaluate.

4. 10^4

5. 8^3

6. $(1.1)^3$

Evaluate.

7. 5^1

8. 43^1

9. $(5.8)^1$

ANSWERS ON PAGE A-3

Evaluate.

10. 8^0

11. $(1.07)^0$

Simplify.

12. $23 \cdot 82 - 43$

13. $104 \div 4 + 57$

Simplify.

14. $5^3 + 26 \cdot 71 - (16 + 25 \cdot 3)$

15. $4^3 + 10 \cdot 20 + 8^2 - 23$

16. ▥ $2000 \times (3 + 1.14)^2$

ANSWERS ON PAGE A-3

Example 4 Evaluate: 42^0.

Solution

$$42^0 = 1$$

DO EXERCISES 10 AND 11.

••• SIMPLIFYING EXPRESSIONS

Suppose we have a calculation with several operations, parentheses, or exponents.* For example,

$$34 \cdot 56 - 17.$$

How do we find an answer? Do we subtract 17 from 56 and then multiply by 34, or do we multiply 34 by 56 and then subtract? In the first case the answer is 1326. In the second case the answer is 1887. To deal with these questions we have to make some agreement regarding the order in which we perform operations. These rules are as follows:

> **To carry out a calculation:**
>
> **a)** First, carry out operations inside parentheses.
> **b)** Second, evaluate exponential expressions.
> **c)** Third, do all multiplications and divisions in order, from left to right.
> **d)** Fourth, do all additions and subtractions in order, from left to right.

Example 5 Simplify: $34 \cdot 56 - 17$.

Solution There are no parentheses or exponential expressions, so we start with the third step.

$$34 \cdot 56 - 17 = 1904 - 17 \qquad \text{Do all multiplications in order, from left to right.}$$
$$= 1887 \qquad \text{Do all additions and subtractions in order, from from left to right.}$$

DO EXERCISES 12 AND 13.

Example 6 Simplify: $2^4 + 51 \cdot 4 - (37 + 23 \cdot 2)$.

Solution

$$2^4 + 51 \cdot 4 - (37 + 23 \cdot 2)$$
$$= 2^4 + 51 \cdot 4 - (37 + 46) \qquad \text{Carry out operations inside parentheses. To do this we first multiply 23 by 2.}$$
$$= 2^4 + 51 \cdot 4 - 83 \qquad \text{Complete the addition inside parentheses.}$$
$$= 16 + 51 \cdot 4 - 83 \qquad \text{Evaluate exponential expressions.}$$
$$= 16 + 204 - 83 \qquad \text{Do all multiplications.}$$
$$= 220 - 83 \qquad \text{Do all additions and subtractions in order, from left to right.}$$
$$= 137$$

DO EXERCISES 14–16.

---

* Be careful when using a calculator to do problems involving several operations. For example, computing $2 + 3 \cdot 5$ in the order of appearance of symbols is 25 on some calculators and 17 on others. The correct answer is 17.

● Write exponential notation.

1. $3 \times 3 \times 3 \times 3$ **2.** $2 \times 2 \times 2 \times 2 \times 2$ **3.** $10 \cdot 10 \cdot 10 \cdot 10 \cdot 10$

4. $10 \times 10 \times 10 \times 10$ **5.** $1 \cdot 1 \cdot 1 \cdot 1 \cdot 1 \cdot 1 \cdot 1 \cdot 1$ **6.** $16 \cdot 16$

●● Evaluate.

7. 5^2 **8.** 7^3 **9.** 9^5 **10.** ▦ 12^4 **11.** 10^2

12. 1^5 **13.** 1^4 **14.** $(1.8)^2$ **15.** $(2.3)^2$ **16.** $(0.1)^3$

17. $(0.2)^3$ **18.** $(14.8)^2$ **19.** $(20.4)^2$ **20.** $\left(\dfrac{4}{5}\right)^2$ **21.** $\left(\dfrac{3}{8}\right)^2$

22. $8 \times (9.2)^2$ **23.** ▦ $1000 \times (1.07)^4$

24. $20 \times (0.01)^2$ **25.** ▦ $1000 \times (1.08)^3$

26. 5^1 **27.** 4^1 **28.** 27^1 **29.** 15^1

30. 5^0 **31.** 6^0 **32.** 10^0 **33.** 14^0

34. 54^0 **35.** 43^0 **36.** $(22.7)^0$ **37.** $\left(\dfrac{11}{12}\right)^0$

ANSWERS

1. _____
2. _____
3. _____
4. _____
5. _____
6. _____
7. _____
8. _____
9. _____
10. _____
11. _____
12. _____
13. _____
14. _____
15. _____
16. _____
17. _____
18. _____
19. _____
20. _____
21. _____
22. _____
23. _____
24. _____
25. _____
26. _____
27. _____
28. _____
29. _____
30. _____
31. _____
32. _____
33. _____
34. _____
35. _____
36. _____
37. _____

••• Simplify. Use a calculator whenever you wish.

38. $16 \cdot 24 + 50$ **39.** $23 + 18 \cdot 20$ **40.** $15 \cdot 24 - 10 \cdot 20$

41. $23 \cdot 17 + 14 \cdot 50$ **42.** $28 \cdot (15 + 35)$ **43.** $28 \cdot 15 + 28 \cdot 35$

44. $40 - 3^2 - 2^3$ **45.** $275 \div 25 + 256 \div 16$ **46.** $324 \div 20 - 225 \div 25$

47. $23 \times 51 + 4 \times 16.3 - (3 \times 14 + 2 \times 15)$

48. $4 \times 16.8 + 5 \times 23.2 + 36 \times 41.9 + 72 \times 9.8 - 32 \times 50$

49. $200 \cdot 5 - 15 \cdot 4 - 20 \cdot 3 + 500 \cdot 2 + 16 \cdot 16$

50. $4 \cdot (18 + 32 + 16 + 23 + 14 + 78 - 90)$

✓ SKILL MAINTENANCE

Add.

51. $16\frac{1}{4} + 35\frac{3}{10}$ **52.** $24\frac{3}{5} + 16\frac{1}{10}$

Subtract.

53. $20\frac{3}{10} - 11\frac{1}{2}$ **54.** $18\frac{1}{10} - 7\frac{4}{5}$

Chapter 1   **Whole Numbers, Fractions, and Decimals**

NAME: _____

CLASS/SECTION: _____ DATE: _____

If you miss an item, review the indicated section and objective.

Add.

[1.1, **• •**] **1.** $\begin{array}{r} 9\ 8\ 7\ 6 \\ +3\ 0\ 9\ 8 \\ \hline \end{array}$

Subtract.

[1.1, **• • •**] **2.** $\begin{array}{r} 8\ 4\ 7\ 2 \\ -4\ 3\ 6\ 1 \\ \hline \end{array}$

[1.1, **• •/• •**] **3.** Lax Industries pays salaries of \$23,876, \$42,598, and \$37,285. How much is paid in all?

Multiply.

[1.2, **•**] **4.** $\begin{array}{r} 4\ 5\ 6 \\ \times\quad\ \ 8 \\ \hline \end{array}$

Divide.

[1.2, **• •**] **5.** $5\ 6\ \overline{)1\ 1{,}7\ 0\ 4}$

[1.2, **• • •**] **6.** Lisa Cooper pays off a \$5820 loan in 12 equal payments. How much is each payment?

[1.3, **• •**] **7.** Convert to fractional notation: $5\frac{2}{3}$.

[1.3, **• •**] **8.** Convert to a mixed numeral: $\frac{53}{12}$.

Multiply and simplify.

[1.4, **•**] **9.** $\frac{5}{12} \cdot \frac{3}{10}$

Divide and simplify.

[1.4, **• •**] **10.** $20\frac{2}{3} \div 5\frac{1}{6}$

[1.4, **• • •**] **11.** Ellen Cyr purchases 100 shares of CBS stock at \$111$\frac{1}{8}$ per share. What is the total amount invested?

[1.4, **• • •**] **12.** Rib roast contains $2\frac{1}{2}$ servings per pound. How many pounds does a hotel need for 400 servings?

Add and simplify.

[1.5, **• • •**] **13.** $6\frac{3}{4} + 7\frac{5}{6}$

Subtract and simplify.

[1.5, **• •/• •**] **14.** $\frac{5}{6} - \frac{3}{4}$

ANSWERS

1. _____

2. _____

3. _____

4. _____

5. _____

6. _____

7. _____

8. _____

9. _____

10. _____

11. _____

12. _____

13. _____

14. _____

[1.5, ⚄] **15.** Recently the stock of General Foods opened at $89\frac{5}{8}$ per share. By noon the price had risen $17\frac{7}{8}$. At the end of the day it had fallen $8\frac{3}{8}$ from the price at noon. What was the closing price?

[1.6, ⚁] **16.** Convert to fractional notation (do not simplify): 6.78.

[1.6, ⚂] **17.** Convert to decimal notation: $\dfrac{1895}{100}$.

Add.

[1.6, ⚃] **18.** $6.04 + 78 + 1.9898$

Subtract.

[1.6, ⚄] **19.** $20.4 - 11.058$

[1.6, ⚅] **20.** Find the net deposit.

CASH	1274	39
LIST CHECKS SINGLY	865	79
	403	52
	816	95
TOTAL FROM OTHER SIDE		
TOTAL		
LESS CASH RECEIVED	350	00
NET DEPOSIT		

Multiply.

[1.7, ⚀] **21.**

$$\begin{array}{r} 17.95 \\ \times\quad 24 \\ \hline \end{array}$$

Divide.

[1.7, ⚁] **22.** $2.8\,\overline{)155.68}$

[1.7, ⚂] **23.** A fashion model earns $1500 per hour. How much would be earned in 5.5 hours?

[1.8, ⚀] **24.** Round to the nearest tenth: 34.067.

[1.8, ⚁] **25.** Find the gas mileage. Round to the nearest tenth of a mile per gallon.

First odometer reading: 8095.4
Second odometer reading: 8259.8
Number of gallons at last fill: 10.8

[1.9, ⚁] **26.** Evaluate: $(1.06)^2$.

[1.9, ⚂] **27.** Simplify: $42 \cdot 18 + 3^4 - 24 \div 3 + 10^2$.

Chapter 1   **Whole Numbers, Fractions, and Decimals**

2

RATIO AND PERCENT

MARY ANNE BUTTERS

**CARRER: ADVERTISING/
MARKETING** This is Mary Anne
Butters. Formerly a race car driver
(as seen in the pictures on the wall
to the right), she is now President of an
advertising firm, The Meridian
Marketing Group, Inc. To Mary Anne,
the advertising business is truly a
three-way marriage of mathematics,
language, and art.

The notion of percent permeates Mary Anne's work. For example, her firm recently conducted an advertising campaign to increase the ratings of a radio station. Before the campaign, the station held a 1.8% share of the audience. This meant that 1.8% of those listening to the radio were listening to the station. After the campaign, the station held an 11.8% share.

Many other applications of percent relate to Mary Anne's work. Suppose there are three pizza restaurants, A, B, and C, in an area. The average person, wanting to buy a pizza, has a percentage "mind set" about where to buy a pizza. Perhaps there is a 60% chance of going to A, a 10% chance of going to B, and a 30% chance of going to C. Restaurant B might be willing to spend $20,000 in advertising dollars to change their "mind set" percentage to 40%. When they go to a firm such as Mary Anne's, the usual fee paid to the firm for the advertising campaign is 15% of the $20,000, or $3000.

Mary Anne was a political science major in college, and took lots of mathematics and English. She worked as a newspaper reporter for 10 years. It is a fairly normal progression to move from journalism to advertising. People who are successful in her work can make anywhere from $35,000 to $150,000 per year.

This chapter on Ratio and Percent is quite important to most individuals in their daily activities.

2.1

Ratio and Proportion

After finishing Section 2.1, you should be able to:

| · | Write fractional notation for ratios.
| ·· | Solve proportions.
| ··· | Give the ratio of two different kinds of measures as a rate.
| ·· (over two) | Solve problems involving ratios and proportions.

In this chapter we consider two concepts, **ratio** and **percent**. These concepts are basic to most of the rest of the book.

· RATIO

When we say that one number is twice as large as another, the *ratio* of the first number to the second is 2 to 1. We can show this by fractional notation

$$\frac{2}{1}, \quad \text{or by the notation } 2:1$$

Some pairs of numbers whose ratio is $\frac{2}{1}$ are: 20 and 10, 32 and 16, and 8 and 4.

DO EXERCISE 1.

Example 1 Write fractional notation for the ratio 0.4 to 54.

Solution

$$\frac{0.4}{54}$$

Example 2 Write fractional notation for the ratio 5 to 6.

Solution

$$\frac{5}{6}$$

DO EXERCISES 2–5.

Example 3 A family earning $21,400 per year will spend about $3210 for car expenses. What is the ratio of car expenses to yearly income?

Solution

$$\frac{3210}{21,400}$$

DO EXERCISES 6 AND 7.

·· PROPORTION

When two pairs of numbers—say 3, 2 and 6, 4—have the same ratio, we say they are **proportional**. The equation

$$\frac{3}{2} = \frac{6}{4}$$

states that 3, 2 and 6, 4 are proportional. Such an equation is called a **proportion**. A *proportion* states that two ratios are the same. We sometimes read

$$\frac{3}{2} = \frac{6}{4}$$

as "3 is to 2 as 6 is to 4."

1. Find three other pairs of numbers whose ratio is $\frac{2}{1}$. (Answers may vary.)

Write fractional notation for each ratio.

2. 3 to 2

3. 7 to 11

4. 0.189 to 3.4

5. 9 to 3

6. A family earning $22,800 per year will spend about $5928 for food. What is the ratio of food expenses to yearly income?

7. A pitcher gives up 4 earned runs in $7\frac{2}{3}$ innings of pitching. What is the ratio of earned runs to the number of innings pitched?

ANSWERS ON PAGE A-3

We can solve proportions by cross multiplying.

Example 4 Solve: $\dfrac{x}{8} = \dfrac{6}{4}$.

Solution To solve we cross multiply.

$$\dfrac{x}{8} \diagup\!\!\!\!\!\diagdown \dfrac{6}{4}$$

$4x = 8(6)$ Cross multiplying.

$x = 12$ Dividing both sides by 4.

DO EXERCISE 8.

Example 5 Solve: $\dfrac{3}{x} = \dfrac{6}{4}$.

Solution

$$\dfrac{3}{x} \diagup\!\!\!\!\!\diagdown \dfrac{6}{4}$$

$6x = 3(4)$ Cross multiplying.

$x = 2$ Dividing both sides by 6.

DO EXERCISE 9.

••• RATES

When a ratio is used to compare two different kinds of measures, we call it a ***rate***. Suppose a car is driven 200 kilometers in 4 hours. The ratio

$$\dfrac{200 \text{ km}}{4 \text{ hr}}, \quad \text{or} \quad 50 \dfrac{\text{km}}{\text{hr}}, \quad \text{or} \quad 50 \text{ kilometers per hour} \qquad \text{(Recall that ``per'' means ``for each.'')}$$

is the rate traveled in kilometers per hour. A ratio of distance traveled to time is also called *speed*.

Example 6 A cook buys 10 pounds of potatoes for 95¢. What is the rate in cents per pound?

Solution

$$\dfrac{95¢}{10 \text{ lb}}, \quad \text{or} \quad 9.5 \dfrac{¢}{\text{lb}}.$$

Example 7 Maya Lartius earned $3690 for working 3 months one summer. What was her rate of pay?

Solution Maya's rate of pay is the ratio of money earned per time worked, or

$$\dfrac{\$3690}{3 \text{ mo}} = \$1230 \text{ per month}.$$

DO EXERCISES 10–15.

Solve.

8. $\dfrac{x}{63} = \dfrac{2}{9}$

Solve.

9. $\dfrac{2}{3} = \dfrac{6}{x}$

What is the rate, or speed, in kilometers per hour?

10. 45 km, 9 hr

11. 120 km, 10 hr

12. 3 km, 10 hr

What is the rate, or speed, in meters per second?

13. 2200 m, 2 sec

14. 52 m, 13 sec

15. 232 m, 16 sec

ANSWERS ON PAGE A-3

---

16. A bonus of $31,500 is to be allocated to three employees in the ratio 4:2:1. What is the amount each employee receives?

17. Two individuals bought a lottery ticket. The first put in $3 and the second, $2. They won. The second received $400,000. Assuming the winnings are shared in proportion to what each put in, what did the first receive?

ANSWERS ON PAGE A-3

⚅ PROBLEM SOLVING

Sometimes ratios involve more than two quantities.

Example 8 A will specifies an estate of $364,000 be allocated in the ratio 8:5:1 to the spouse, daughter, and son. What is the amount each survivor receives?

Solution The estate is to be divided into $8 + 5 + 1$, or 14 parts. Each part has the value

$$\$364,000 \div 14 = \$26,000$$

Amount received by spouse: $8 \times \$26,000 = \$208,000$

daughter: $5 \times \$26,000 = \$130,000$

son: $1 \times \$26,000 = \$26,000$

DO EXERCISE 16.

Proportions have applications in many fields such as business, chemistry, biology, health sciences, and home economics; as well as to areas of daily life.

Example 9 Two entrepreneurs invested $1500 and $2700 in a computer company. Profits are to be shared in ratio to their investments. The second received $18,000 in profits. What should the first receive?

Solution Suppose x is the amount the first receives. We translate to a proportion.

$$\text{Profit first} \longrightarrow \frac{x}{18,000} = \frac{1500}{2700} \longleftarrow \text{Investment first}$$
$$\text{Profit second} \longrightarrow \qquad\qquad \longleftarrow \text{Investment second}$$

$$2700x = 18,000(1500) \qquad \text{Cross multiplying.}$$
$$x = 10,000 \qquad \text{Dividing both sides by 2700.}$$

The first should receive $10,000.

DO EXERCISE 17.

Chapter 2   Ratio and Percent

EXERCISE SET 2.1

⬚·   Write fractional notation for each of the following ratios.

1. 4 to 5   **2.** 178 to 572   **3.** 0.4 to 12   **4.** 0.078 to 3.456

5. In a bread recipe, there are 2 cups of milk to 12 cups of flour. What is the ratio of cups of milk to cups of flour?

6. There are 2 women to 1 man enrolled in Coed College. What is the ratio of the number of women enrolled to the number of men?

⬚··   Solve.

7. $\dfrac{18}{4} = \dfrac{x}{10}$ **8.** $\dfrac{x}{45} = \dfrac{20}{25}$ **9.** $\dfrac{x}{8} = \dfrac{9}{6}$ **10.** $\dfrac{8}{10} = \dfrac{n}{5}$

11. $\dfrac{t}{12} = \dfrac{5}{6}$ **12.** $\dfrac{12}{4} = \dfrac{x}{3}$ **13.** $\dfrac{2}{5} = \dfrac{8}{n}$ **14.** $\dfrac{10}{6} = \dfrac{5}{x}$

15. $\dfrac{n}{15} = \dfrac{10}{30}$ **16.** $\dfrac{2}{24} = \dfrac{x}{36}$ **17.** $\dfrac{16}{12} = \dfrac{24}{x}$ **18.** $\dfrac{7}{11} = \dfrac{2}{x}$

19. $\dfrac{6}{11} = \dfrac{12}{x}$ **20.** $\dfrac{8}{9} = \dfrac{32}{n}$ **21.** $\dfrac{20}{7} = \dfrac{80}{x}$ **22.** $\dfrac{5}{x} = \dfrac{4}{10}$

23. $\dfrac{12}{9} = \dfrac{x}{7}$ **24.** $\dfrac{x}{20} = \dfrac{16}{15}$ **25.** $\dfrac{x}{13} = \dfrac{2}{9}$ **26.** $\dfrac{1.2}{4} = \dfrac{x}{9}$

⬚···   In Exercises 27–30, find the rates as ratios of distance to time.

27. 120 kilometers, 3 hours   **28.** 18 kilometers, 9 hours

29. 440 meters, 40 seconds   **30.** 200 miles, 25 seconds

31. A car is driven 500 kilometers in 20 hours. What is the rate in kilometers per hour? in hours per kilometer?

32. Leo Mincks eats 3 hamburgers in 15 minutes. What is the rate in hamburgers per minute? in minutes per hamburger?

33. To water a lawn adequately it takes 623 gallons of water for every 1000 square feet. What is the rate in gallons per square foot?

34. An 8-lb shankless ham contains 36 servings of meat. What is the rate in servings per pound?

ANSWERS

1. _____
2. _____
3. _____
4. _____
5. _____
6. _____
7. _____
8. _____
9. _____
10. _____
11. _____
12. _____
13. _____
14. _____
15. _____
16. _____
17. _____
18. _____
19. _____
20. _____
21. _____
22. _____
23. _____
24. _____
25. _____
26. _____
27. _____
28. _____
29. _____
30. _____
31. _____
32. _____
33. _____
34. _____

⁘ Solve.

35. Three state universities are to share $2,625,000 in the ratio 8:5:2. How much does each receive?

36. The assets of a business are divided among the three owners in the ratio 7:4:2. Assets were $845,000. How much does each receive?

37. A car travels 320 miles on 24 gallons of gasoline. How far does it travel on 10 gallons?

38. ▤ A car travels 168 miles on 13 gallons of gasoline. How much gasoline would it take to travel 252 miles?

39. A quality-control inspector checks 100 transistor radios and finds 7 defective. At this rate, how many would be defective in a daily production of 360 radios?

40. A quality-control inspector checks 100 blouses and finds defects in 8 of them. At this rate, how many blouses would be defective out of the 3000 the company makes in a week?

41. On a map $\frac{1}{4}$ inch represents 50 actual miles. If two cities are $3\frac{1}{4}$ inches apart on the map, how far apart are they actually?

42. In a bread recipe, the ratio of flour to milk is $\frac{4}{3}$. If 5 milliliters of flour are used, how many milliliters of milk are used?

43. ▤ It is known that 5 people produce 13 kilograms of garbage in one day. Birmingham, Alabama, has 300,000 people. How many kilograms of garbage are produced in Birmingham in one day?

44. ▤ It is known that 5 people produce 13 kilograms of garbage in one day. San Diego, California, has 700,000 people. How many kilograms of garbage are produced in San Diego in one day?

✔ **SKILL MAINTENANCE**

Divide.

45. $\frac{9}{5} \div \frac{8}{10}$

46. $\frac{5}{12} \div \frac{25}{36}$

47. $32 \div 3\frac{1}{5}$

48. $45 \div 2\frac{1}{4}$

Evaluate.

49. 8^0

50. 6^1

51. $(28.3)^1$

52. $(33.4)^0$

Chapter 2   Ratio and Percent

2.2

Percent

On the average, a family will spend 26% of its income for food. What does this mean? It means that out of every $100 earned, $26 will be spent for food. Thus, 26% is a ratio of 26 to 100.

⚀ PERCENT

The following is the definition of percent.

> $n\%$ means $\dfrac{n}{100}$ or $n \times \dfrac{1}{100}$ or $n \times 0.01$.

Example 1 Write three kinds of notation for 78%.

Solution

a) $78\% = \dfrac{78}{100}$ A ratio of 78 to 100.

b) $78\% = 78 \times \dfrac{1}{100}$ Replacing % by $\times \dfrac{1}{100}$.

c) $78\% = 78 \times 0.01$ Replacing % by $\times 0.01$.

Example 2 Write three kinds of notation for 67.8%.

Solution

a) $67.8\% = \dfrac{67.8}{100}$ A ratio of 67.8 to 100.

b) $67.8\% = 67.8 \times \dfrac{1}{100}$ Replacing % by $\times \dfrac{1}{100}$.

c) $67.8\% = 67.8 \times 0.01$ Replacing % by $\times 0.01$.

DO EXERCISES 1–3.

⚁ CONVERTING FROM PERCENT TO DECIMAL NOTATION

Consider 78%.

$78\% = 78 \times 0.01$ Replacing % by $\times 0.01$ since we are converting to decimal notation.

$= 0.78$

We can convert from percent to decimal notation by moving the decimal point two places to the left.

> **To convert from percent to decimal notation,**   **36.5%**
>
> **a)** drop the percent symbol, and   **36.5**
> **b)** move the decimal point two places to the left.   **0.36.5**   **Move 2 places.**

Example 3 The population growth rate of Europe is 1.1%. Find decimal notation for 1.1%.

Solution

a) Drop the percent symbol.   1.1

b) Move the decimal point two places to the left.   0.01.1

$1.1\% = 0.011$

DO EXERCISES 4–6.

After finishing Section 2.2, you should be able to:

⚀ **Write three kinds of notation for a percent.**

⚁ **Convert from percent to decimal notation.**

⚂ **Convert from decimal to percent notation.**

⚃ **Convert from fractional to percent notation.**

⚄ **Convert from percent to fractional notation.**

⚅ **Solve certain problems involving percent.**

Write three kinds of notation.

1. 90%

2. 3.4%

3. 100%

Find decimal notation.

4. 34%

5. 78.9%

6. One year the rate of inflation was 12.08%. Find decimal notation for 12.08%.

ANSWERS ON PAGE A-3

Find percent notation.

7. 0.24

8. 3.47

9. 1

10. Muscles make up 0.4 of a person's body. Find percent notation for 0.4.

Find percent notation.

11. $\frac{1}{4}$

12. $\frac{7}{8}$

••• **CONVERTING FROM DECIMAL TO PERCENT NOTATION**

Consider 0.38.

$0.38 = 38 \times 0.01$ We factor out 0.01.

$ = 38\%$ Using the definition of percent, replacing $\times 0.01$ by %.

We can convert from decimal to percent notation by moving the decimal point two places to the right.

To convert from decimal to percent notation,	0.675
a) move the decimal point two places to the right and	0.67.5 Move 2 places.
b) write a % symbol.	67.5%

Example 4 Television sets are on 0.25 of the time. Find percent notation for 0.25.

Solution

a) Move the decimal point two places to the right.   0.25.

b) Write a % symbol.   25%

$0.25 = 25\%$

DO EXERCISES 7–10.

:: CONVERTING FROM FRACTIONAL TO PERCENT NOTATION

To convert from fractional to percent notation,	$\frac{3}{5}$
a) find decimal notation by division, and	$\begin{array}{r} 0.6 \\ 5\overline{)3.0} \\ \underline{3\ 0} \\ 0 \end{array}$
b) convert the answer to percent notation.	$0.6 = 0.60 = 60\%$

Example 5 Find percent notation for $\frac{3}{8}$.

Solution

a) Find decimal notation by division.

$\begin{array}{r} 0.3\ 7\ 5 \\ 8\overline{)3.0\ 0\ 0} \\ \underline{2\ 4} \\ 6\ 0 \\ \underline{5\ 6} \\ 4\ 0 \\ \underline{4\ 0} \\ 0 \end{array}$

b) Convert the answer to percent notation.

0.37.5

$\frac{3}{8} = 37.5\%$ or $37\frac{1}{2}\%$

DO EXERCISES 11 AND 12.

In some cases division is not the easiest way to convert. The following are some optional ways this might be done.

Example 6 Find percent notation for $\frac{69}{100}$.

Solution We use the definition of percent.

$$\frac{69}{100} = 69\%$$

Example 7 Find percent notation for $\frac{17}{20}$.

Solution We multiply by 1 to get 100 in the denominator.

$$\frac{17}{20} \cdot \frac{5}{5} = \frac{85}{100} = 85\%$$

DO EXERCISES 13 AND 14.

⠒ CONVERTING FROM PERCENT TO FRACTIONAL NOTATION

To convert from percent to fractional notation,	30%
a) use the definition of percent, and	$\frac{30}{100}$
b) simplify, if possible.	$\frac{3}{10}$

Example 8 Find fractional notation for 75%.

Solution

$$75\% = \frac{75}{100} \qquad \text{Definition of percent.}$$

$$= \frac{3}{4} \cdot \frac{25}{25} \left.\begin{array}{c} \\ \\ \end{array}\right\}$$

$$= \frac{3}{4} \qquad \text{Simplifying.}$$

Example 9 Find fractional notation for $16\frac{2}{3}\%$.

Solution

$$16\frac{2}{3}\% = \frac{50}{3}\% \qquad \text{Converting from the mixed numeral to fractional notation.}$$

$$= \frac{50}{3} \times \frac{1}{100} \qquad \text{Definition of percent.}$$

$$= \frac{50}{300} \qquad \text{Multiplying.}$$

$$= \frac{1}{6} \cdot \frac{50}{50} \left.\begin{array}{c} \\ \\ \end{array}\right\}$$

$$= \frac{1}{6} \qquad \text{Simplifying.}$$

DO EXERCISES 15–17.

Find percent notation.

13. $\frac{57}{100}$

14. $\frac{19}{25}$

Find fractional notation.

15. 60%

16. 3.25%

17. $66\frac{2}{3}\%$

ANSWERS ON PAGE A-3

Complete this table.

18.

Fractional notation	$\frac{1}{5}$		
Decimal notation		$0.83\overline{3}$	
Percent notation			$37\frac{1}{2}\%$

Translate to an equation. Do not solve.

19. 12% of 50 is what?

20. What is 40% of $60?

21. $45 is 20% of what?

22. 120% of what is 60?

23. 16 is what percent of 40?

24. What percent of $9600 is $7104?

25. Solve Exercise 20.

ANSWERS ON PAGE A-3

The table on the inside front cover contains decimal, fractional, and percent equivalents that are used so often you should memorize them. For example, $\frac{1}{3} = 0.3\overline{3}$, so we say that the *decimal equivalent* of $\frac{1}{3}$ is $0.3\overline{3}$, or that $0.3\overline{3}$ has the *fractional equivalent* $\frac{1}{3}$. Memorize the table.

DO EXERCISE 18.

▦ PROBLEM SOLVING

To solve problems involving percents, it is helpful to first translate to equations. Then solve the equation.

Example 10 Translate: 23% of 5 is what?

Solution $23\% \times 5 = a$

> **"Of"** translates to "**×**."
> **"What"** translates to some letter.
> **"Is"** translates to "**=**."

Example 11 Translate: 3 is 10% of what?

Solution $3 = 10\% \times b$ Any letter can be used.

Example 12 Translate: What percent of 50 is 7?

Solution n % $\times 50 = 7$

DO EXERCISES 19–24.

Example 13 What is 11% of 49?

Solution Translate: $a = 11\% \times 49$.

This tells us what to do. We convert 11% to decimal notation and multiply.

$$\begin{array}{r} 4\,9 \\ \times 0.1\,1 \\ \hline 4\,9 \\ 4\,9\,0 \\ \hline 5.3\,9 \end{array} \qquad 11\% = 0.11$$

5.39 is 11% of 49.

A way of checking answers is by estimating as follows:

$$11\% \times 49 \approx 10\% \times 50 = 0.10 \times 50$$
$$= 5$$

Since 5 is close to 5.39, our answer is reasonable.

DO EXERCISE 25.

Example 14 120% of $42 is what?

Solution Translate: $120\% \times 42 = a$.

This tells us what to do.

$$
\begin{array}{r}
4\,2 \\
\times\ \ 1.2 \\
\hline
8\,4 \\
4\,2\,0 \\
\hline
5\,0.4
\end{array}
\qquad 120\% = 1.20 = 1.2
$$

120% of $42 is $50.40.

DO EXERCISE 26.

Example 15 5% of what is 20?

Solution Translate: $5\% \times b = 20$.

To find the number we first divide by 5%.

$b = 20 \div 5\%$ We divide on both sides by 5%.

This tells us what to do. We convert 5% to decimal notation and divide.

$$
\begin{array}{r}
4\,0\,0. \\
0.0\,5_\wedge \overline{)\,2\,0\,0.0\,0_\wedge} \\
2\,0\,0\,0 \\
\hline
0
\end{array}
\qquad 5\% = 0.05
$$

5% of 400 is 20.

DO EXERCISE 27.

Example 16 $3 is 16% of what?

Solution Translate: $3 = 16\% \times b$.

To find the number we first divide by 16%.

$3 \div 16\% = b$.   We divide on both sides by 16%.

This tells us what to do. We convert 16% to decimal notation and divide.

$$
\begin{array}{r}
1\,8.7\,5 \\
0.1\,6_\wedge \overline{)\,3.0\,0_\wedge 0\,0} \\
1\,6 \\
\hline
1\,4\,0 \\
1\,2\,8 \\
\hline
1\,2\,0 \\
1\,1\,2 \\
\hline
8\,0 \\
8\,0 \\
\hline
0
\end{array}
$$

$3 is 16% of $18.75.

DO EXERCISE 28.

Solve

26. 64% of $55 is what?

Solve.

27. 20% of what is 45?

Solve.

28. $60 is 120% of what?

ANSWERS ON PAGE A-3

Solve.

29. 16 is what percent of 40?

Solve.

30. What percent of $84 is $10.50?

Example 17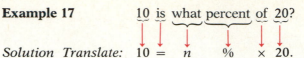

Solution Translate: $10 = n$ % $\times$ 20.

Next we use the definition of percent.

$10 = n \times 0.01 \times 20$

$10 = n \times 0.2$

To find the number we first divide by 0.2.

$10 \div 0.2 = n$ We divide on both sides by 0.2.

This tells us what to do. We divide.

$$0.2_\wedge \overline{)\begin{array}{r} 5\ 0. \\ 1\ 0.0_\wedge \\ \underline{1\ 0\ 0} \\ 0 \end{array}}$$

10 is **50%** of 20.

Strictly speaking, the answer to this problem is 50, but we will consider either 50 or 50% correct.

DO EXERCISE 29.

Example 18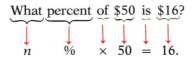

Solution Translate: n % $\times$ 50 = 16.

Next, we use the definition of percent.

$n \times 0.01 \times 50 = 16$

$n \times 0.5 = 16$

To find the number we first divide by 0.5.

$n = 16 \div 0.5$ We divide on both sides by 0.5.

This tells us what to do. We divide.

$$0.5_\wedge \overline{)\begin{array}{r} 3\ 2. \\ 1\ 6.0_\wedge \\ \underline{1\ 5} \\ 1\ 0 \\ \underline{1\ 0} \\ 0 \end{array}}$$

32% of $50 is $16.

DO EXERCISE 30.

Write three kinds of notation.

1. 80%   **2.** 43.8%   **3.** 12.5%   **4.** 120%

Find decimal notation.

5. 18%   **6.** 0.7%   **7.** 78.9%   **8.** 56.2%

9. 1%   **10.** 100%   **11.** 425%   **12.** 163%

Convert to percent notation.

13. 0.78   **14.** 0.93   **15.** 1.015   **16.** 2.003

17. 0.562   **18.** 0.995   **19.** 0.8   **20.** 0.9

Convert to percent notation.

21. $\dfrac{19}{100}$ **22.** $\dfrac{6}{100}$ **23.** $\dfrac{3}{2}$ **24.** $\dfrac{3}{4}$

25. $\dfrac{1}{8}$ **26.** $\dfrac{3}{8}$ **27.** $\dfrac{3}{5}$ **28.** $\dfrac{4}{5}$

29. ▦ $\dfrac{63}{999}$ (nearest tenth of a percent)   **30.** $\dfrac{7}{6}$

31. ▦ $\dfrac{82}{369}$ (nearest tenth of a percent)   **32.** $\dfrac{10}{3}$

33. ▦ $\dfrac{511}{489}$ (nearest tenth of a percent)   **34.** $\dfrac{27}{25}$

35. $\dfrac{23}{40}$ **36.** $\dfrac{37}{50}$

Convert to fractional notation.

37. 60%   **38.** 70%   **39.** 12.5%   **40.** 37.5%

41. $83\dfrac{1}{3}\%$ **42.** $58\dfrac{1}{3}\%$ **43.** 136%   **44.** 148%

45. The United States uses 35% of the world's energy. Find fractional notation for 35%.

46. The United States has 6% of the world's population. Find fractional notation for 6%.

ANSWERS
1.
2.
3.
4.
5.
6.
7.
8.
9.
10.
11.
12.
13.
14.
15.
16.
17.
18.
19.
20.
21.
22.
23.
24.
25.
26.
27.
28.
29.
30.
31.
32.
33.
34.
35.
36.
37.
38.
39.
40.
41.
42.
43.
44.
45.
46.

Translate to an equation. Do not solve.

47. What is 41% of 89?

48. 87% of 41 is what?

49. 89 is what percent of 100?

50. What percent of 25 is 8?

51. 13 is 25% of what?

52. 3.2% of what is 20?

Solve.

53. What is 120% of 75?

54. What is 7.75% of $10,880?

55. 150% of 30 is what?

56. 100% of 13 is what?

57. $12 is what percent of $50?

58. 50,951.775 is what percent of 78,995?

59. What percent of $300 is $150?

60. What percent of $50 is $40?

61. 56.32 is 64% of what?

62. 34.32 is 44% of what?

63. 70% of what is 14?

64. 70% of what is 35?

✓ **SKILL MAINTENANCE**

65. On a map $\frac{1}{4}$ inch represents 60 actual miles. If two cities are $3\frac{1}{4}$ inches apart on the map, how far apart are they actually?

66. milk is $\frac{4}{3}$. If 10 milliliters of flour are used, how many milliliters of milk are used?

2.3

More Problem Solving

◦ PERCENT PROBLEMS

Applied problems involving percent are not always stated in a manner that is easily translated to a number sentence. In such cases it is helpful to restate the problem before translating. Sometimes it helps to draw a picture.

Example 1 The average family spends 26% of its income for food. A family earned $22,500 one year. How much was spent for food?

Solution We first draw a picture.

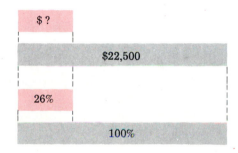

Solve using an equation.

    Restate: 26% of $22,500 is what?

    Translate: 26% × $22,500 = *p*

Next we use the definition of percent.

    0.26 × $22,500 = *p*

This sentence tells us what to do. We multiply 22,500 by 0.26.

```
       2 2,5 0 0
  ×        0.2 6
    1 3 5 0 0 0
    4 5 0 0 0 0
    5 8 5 0.0 0
```

The family spent $5850 for food.

DO EXERCISE 1.

1. The average family spends 15% of its income for car expenses. A family earned $26,000 one year. How much was spent for car expenses?

ANSWER ON PAGE A-3

2. The sales tax rate in Vermont is 4%. On the purchase of a calculator the sales tax was $3.52. How much was the purchase price?

TEXAS TI-58

Incredibly versatile calculator that's fully PROGRAMMABLE to perform an amazing number of functions. For the serious student or pro.

$?

ANSWER ON PAGE A-3

Example 2 The sales tax rate in Arizona is 5%. On the purchase of a sofa the sales tax is $32. How much was the sofa before the sales tax (the purchase price)?

Solution We first draw a picture.

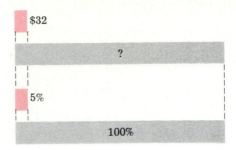

Solve using an equation.

Restate: 5% of what is $32?

Translate: 5% × b = 32

Next we use the definition of percent.

$$0.05 \times b = 32$$

Then we solve for b by dividing on both sides by 0.05.

$$b = 32 \div 0.05$$

To find b we divide.

$$
\begin{array}{r}
6\,4\,0. \\
0.0\,5\,\overline{)\,3\,2.0\,0} \\
\underline{3\,0} \\
2\,0 \\
\underline{2\,0} \\
0
\end{array}
$$

The purchase price was $640.

DO EXERCISE 2.

Example 3 One year Narayan Shankar earns $24,000 and gets a $1200 raise. What percent of the year's salary was the raise?

Solution We first draw a picture.

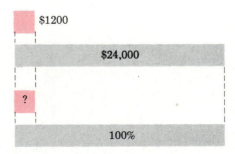

Chapter 2   Ratio and Percent

Solve using an equation.

Restate: $1200 is what percent of $24,000?

Translate: $1200 = r\% \times 24{,}000$

Next we use the definition of percent.

$1200 = r \times 0.01 \times 24{,}000$

$1200 = r \times 240$

Then we solve for r by dividing on both sides by 240.

$1200 \div 240 = r$

To find r we carry out the division.

$$
\begin{array}{r}
5 \\
240\overline{)1\,2\,0\,0} \\
1\,2\,0\,0 \\
\hline
0
\end{array}
$$

The raise was 5%.

DO EXERCISE 3.

:: PROBLEMS INVOLVING PERCENT INCREASE OR DECREASE

Percent is often used to state increases or decreases. Suppose the population of a town has *increased* 70%. This means the increase was 70% of the former population. The population of a town is 2340 and it increases 70%. The increase is 70% of 2340, or 1638. The new population is 2340 + 1638, or 3978. This is shown below.

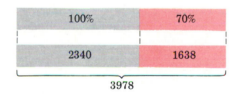

What does it mean when we say that the price of Swiss cheese has decreased 8%? If the price was $1.00 a pound and it went down to $0.92 a pound, the decrease is $0.08, which is 8% of the original price. This is shown below.

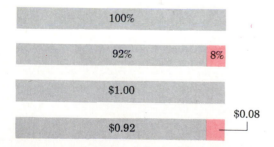

> **To find a percent of increase or decrease, find the amount of increase or decrease and then determine what percent this is of the original amount.**

3. One year Beth Persels has $12,000 in a savings account. The bank adds $1680 in interest to her account at the end of the year. What is the percent of interest earned on the account this year?

ANSWER ON PAGE A-3

Solve.

4. The price of an automobile increased from $5800 to $6322. What was the percent of increase?

Example 4 The price of milk increased from 40¢ per liter to 45¢ per liter. What was the percent of increase?

Solution We first draw a picture.

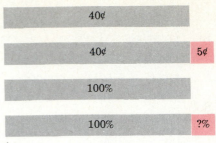

a) First, find the increase by subtracting.

$$
\begin{array}{r l}
4\ 5 & \text{New price} \\
-4\ 0 & \text{Original price} \\
\hline
5 & \text{Increase}
\end{array}
$$

b) The increase is 5¢. Now we ask:

5 is what percent of 40 (the original price)?

(A common error is to use 45 instead of 40, the original amount.)

Solve using a number sentence.

5 is what percent of 40?

$$5 = n \quad \% \quad \times 40$$

Next we use the definition of percent.

$$5 = n \times 0.01 \times 40$$

$$5 = n \times 0.4$$

To find the number we first divide by 0.4.

$$5 \div 0.4 = n \qquad \text{We divide on both sides by 0.4.}$$

This tells us what to do. We divide.

$$
\begin{array}{r}
1\ 2.5 \\
0.4\,\overline{)\,5.0} \\
4 \\
\hline
1\ 0 \\
8 \\
\hline
2\ 0 \\
2\ 0 \\
\hline
0
\end{array}
$$

The percent of increase was 12.5%.

DO EXERCISE 4.

Example 5 By proper furnace maintenance a family that pays a monthly fuel bill of $88.00 can reduce it to $80.20. What is the percent of decrease? Round to the nearest tenth of a percent.

Solution We first draw a picture.

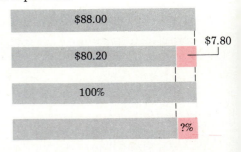

ANSWER ON PAGE A-3

Chapter 2   Ratio and Percent

a) First, find the decrease.

```
  8 8.0 0     Original bill
− 8 0.2 0     New bill
    7.8 0     Decrease
```

b) The decrease is $7.80. Now we ask:

7.80 is what percent of 88.00 (the original bill)?
(A common error is to use $80.20 instead of $88.00, the original amount.)

Solve using a number sentence.

7.80 is what percent of 88.00?

$$7.80 = n \quad \% \quad \times 88.00$$

Next we use the definition of percent.

$$7.8 = n \times 0.01 \times 88$$

$$7.8 = n \times 0.88$$

To find the number we first divide by 0.88.

$$7.8 \div 0.88 = n \qquad \text{We divide on both sides by 0.88.}$$

This tells us what to do. We divide as follows;

```
            8.8 6
0.8 8 ) 7.8 0 0 0
        7.0 4
          7 6 0
          7 0 4
            5 6 0
            5 2 8
              3 2
```

We carry the division out to the hundredth place so the percent can be rounded to the nearest tenth. The percent of decrease is 8.9%.

DO EXERCISE 5.

Example 6 Nancy Luebbese earns $19,400 one year and gets a 6% raise the next. What is her new salary?

Solution We first draw a picture.

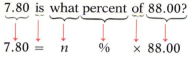

$19,400	$?
100%	6%

a) First, find the increase. We ask: What is 6% of $19,400?

Solve using a number sentence.

What is 6% of 19,400?

$$a = 6\% \times 19,400$$

This tells us what to do. We convert 6% to decimal notation and multiply.

```
    1 9,4 0 0
×       0.0 6      6% = 0.06
  1 1 6 4.0 0
```

The increase is $1164.

DO EXERCISE 6.

b) The new salary is

$$\$19,400 + \$1164 = \$20,564.$$

Example 7 One year the pilots of Pan American Airlines surprised the business world by taking an 11% decrease in salary. The former salary was $55,000. What was the new salary?

Solution We first draw a picture.

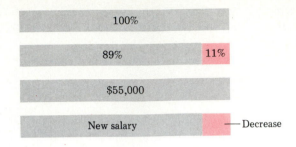

a) First, find the decrease. We ask:

What is 11% of $55,000?

Solve using an equation.

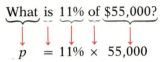

$$p = 11\% \times 55{,}000$$

This tells us what to do. We convert 11% to decimal notation and multiply.

$$
\begin{array}{r}
5\,5{,}0\,0\,0 \\
\times \quad\quad 0.1\,1 \\
\hline
5\,5\,0\,0\,0 \\
5\,5\,0\,0\,0\,0 \\
\hline
6\,0\,5\,0.0\,0
\end{array}
$$

The decrease is $6050.

b) The new salary is found by subtracting the decrease from the former salary:

New salary = $55,000 − $6050 = $48,950

DO EXERCISE 7.

• Solve.

ANSWERS

1. Longman Corporation has a profit of $24,000 one year. It must pay 20% of this in federal taxes. How much is the federal tax?

2. ▦ General Dollar Corporation has a profit of $28,567.98 one year. It must pay federal taxes of 20% on the first $25,000 and 22% on the amount that exceeds $25,000. How much is the federal tax? Round to the nearest cent.

1. _____

2. _____

3. The sales tax rate in Arkansas is 4%. On the purchase of a refrigerator the sales tax is $14.70. How much is the purchase price?

4. The sales tax rate in Pennsylvania is 6%. On the purchase of a suit the sales tax is $10.80. How much is the purchase price?

3. _____

4. _____

5. On a business math test Michael Kelley gets 7 out of 8 questions correct. What percent were correct?

6. Brad Holland makes 40 calls to customers. Of these calls, 13 result in sales of a product. What percent were sales?

5. _____

7. Natalie Kanzmeier, quality-control inspector, examines 100 stereos and finds 8 defective. What percent were defective? What percent were nondefective? At this rate, how many would be defective in a lot of 7500?

8. Che-Wai Lau, quality-control inspector, examines 100 blouses and finds 9 defective. What percent were defective? What percent were nondefective? At this rate, how many would be defective in a lot of 8400?

6. _____

7. _____

9. ▦ A study has revealed that 67% of all people who attend movies are in the 12–29 age group. A theater contained 1200 people for a showing of *The Business of Ghost Busting*. How many were in the 12–29 age group?

10. A study has revealed that most televisions are in use 25% of the time. Of the 8760 hours in a year, for how many would a television be in use?

8. _____

9. _____

10. _____

11. In a medical study it was determined that if 800 people kiss someone else who has a cold, only 56 will actually catch the cold. What percent is this?

12. Deming, New Mexico, claims to have the purest drinking water in the world. It is 99.9% pure. If you had 240 liters of water from Deming, how much of it, in liters, would be pure?

13. In a survey of 5860 consumers 35% indicated that they would most like to vacation in the mountains. How many wanted to vacation in the mountains?

14. ▦ In a survey of 5860 consumers 30% indicated that they would most like to vacation at the beach. How many wanted to vacation at the beach?

• • Solve.

15. The balance in Greg Packard's savings account increased from $400 to $436. What was the percent of increase?

16. The population of Culver City increased from 8400 to 8820. What was the percent of increase?

17. Brett Maxwell earns $32,500 one year and gets an 8% raise in salary. What is his new salary?

18. ▦ In one year, the national debt increased from $746,945,000,000 to $747,828,000,000. What was the percent of increase? Round to the nearest hundredth of a percent.

19. A study has shown that a family that uses only cold water in its washing machine can reduce a monthly fuel bill of $86.00 to $82.56. What is the percent of decrease?

20. A study has shown that a family that maintains its furnace properly can reduce a monthly fuel bill of $110 to $99. What is the percent of decrease?

21. ▦ The original value of a car was $6856.95. During the first year its value decreased 29.47%. What was its new value? Round to the nearest cent.

22. The price of a TV was increased from $500 to $520. What was the percent of increase?

23. The price of a TV was decreased from $520 to $500. What was the percent of decrease? Round to the nearest tenth of a percent.

✓ **SKILL MAINTENANCE**

24. $3\,8\,\overline{)\,3\,4,2\,0\,0}$

25. $6\,1\,\overline{)\,1\,8,3\,0\,0}$

26. $23 + 18 \cdot 20$

27. $15 \cdot 24 - 10 \cdot 20$

NAME: _____

CLASS/SECTION: _____ DATE: _____

ANSWERS

[2.1, ⚀] **1.** Current assets for Shano Corporation are $2,500,000 and current liabilities are $1,250,000. What is the ratio of current assets to current liabilities?

1. _____

[2.1, ⚁] **2.** Solve: $\dfrac{x}{8} = \dfrac{7}{25}$.

2. _____

[2.1, ⚂] **3.** A car is driven 390 miles on 15 gallons of gasohol. Find the rate as a ratio of miles to gallons.

3. _____

[2.1, ⚃] **4.** If 4 cans of peaches cost $2.04, what is the cost of 11 cans?

4. _____

[2.2, ⚁] **5.** Convert to decimal notation: 87.4%.

5. _____

[2.2, ⚂] **6.** Convert to percent notation: 0.31.

6. _____

[2.2, ⚃] **7.** Convert to percent notation: $\dfrac{19}{20}$.

7. _____

[2.2, ⚄] **8.** Convert to fractional notation: 9.5%.

8. _____

[2.2, ⚅] Solve.

    9. What is 16% of 97?

9. _____

    10. 97% of what is $1455?

10. _____

11. $980 is what percent of $1250?

. [2.3, •] Solve.

12. The sales tax rate in Maryland is 5%. On the purchase of a suit the sales tax is $6.60. How much was the purchase price?

13. One month a family spent 67% of their income for loan payments. Their income was $1100. How much was spent for loan payments?

[2.3, ••] Solve.

14. Maureen Ogle earns $17,300 one year and gets a 5.7% raise the following year. What is her new salary?

15. The price of a calculator was increased from $25 to $27. What was the percent of increase?

16. The price of a calculator was decreased from $27 to $25. What was the percent of decrease? Round to the nearest tenth of a percent.

17. During a sale the price of a bottle of shampoo was decreased 50%. The original, or marked, price was $1.99. What was the sale price? Round to the nearest dollar.

3

INTEREST

CAREER: REALTOR This is Patty Sanchez Wignall. Patty is a realtor, and sells houses on a commission basis.

PATTY SANCHEZ WIGNALL

An understanding of all mathematics is very important to Patty's work. However, it is particularly helpful for a realtor to understand interest, as interest rates directly affect the real estate market. If interest rates are low, monthly payments on a mortgage are less than when interest rates are high. People can buy more expensive houses and make the same mortgage payments each month. This makes people more eager to buy houses, which increases Patty's sales and her earnings. Eventually, the price of houses will rise so that the low monthly mortgage payments return to the level they were at with the higher interest rates. Higher housing prices mean that Patty will make more money on each sale.

Patty is a top-notch realtor. Every time Patty closes a sale, she earns a percentage of the sale price instead of earning a salary. Realtors like Patty can have a wide range of salaries, from $0 to $100,000 or more per year, depending on their effort and success. She is a good listener, and can determine her clients' likes and dislikes. She is willing to spend the time and effort needed to help her clients, and is a person of high integrity who inspires trust. Patty continues to study finance, mathematics and related subjects to improve herself. Her hobbies include golfing, water polo, fishing, dancing, knitting, and water skiing.

3.1

After finishing Section 3.1, you should be able to:

·	**Find the interest earned.**
··	**Solve for the rate in interest problems.**
···	**Find the principal in interest problems.**
::	**Find the interest in any payment.**
::·	**Determine the amount paid back.**

Simple Interest

Knowing about interest is important. For example, a knowledge of interest will help you to invest wisely and to borrow advantageously. Simply stated, **interest** is money paid for the use of money. When you have money in a bank you are paid for the use of your money. Likewise, when you borrow money you must pay for its use. Several types of interest will be studied in this chapter.

| · | **FINDING SIMPLE INTEREST** |

> **ENERGY SAVINGS BANK OF BRENTON LOANS**
>
> Insulate your home. Borrow $200 today at 14% Pay back $228 in 1 year.

At Energy Savings Bank you borrow $200 for one year. The amount borrowed ($200) is called the **principal**. The **interest rate** is 14%. This means that in addition to the principal you pay back 14% of the principal, which is

14% of $200,   or   0.14 × $200,   or $28.

This $28 is simple interest. Interest paid on only the principal for the entire time is **simple interest.** If you had borrowed the money for $\frac{1}{4}$ of the year, you would pay

$0.14 \times \$200 \times \frac{1}{4}$,   or $7.00 in interest.

This leads us to the following *simple-interest* formula.

> A formula for *simple interest* is
>
> $$I = P \times R \times T,$$
>
> where **I** is the interest, **P** is the principal (the amount borrowed or invested), **R** is the interest rate, and **T** is the time, in years or fractional parts of a year, that the principal is borrowed or invested.

Unless otherwise indicated the interest rate is an annual or yearly rate.

Example 1 The Polito family borrows $400 on their CNA life insurance policy at 8% simple interest for $1\frac{1}{2}$ years. How much interest must be paid?

Solution Substituting 400 for P, 0.08 for R, and 1.5 for T, we get

$$I = P \times R \times T$$
$$= 400 \times 0.08 \times 1.5$$
$$= 48.$$

An interest charge of $48 must be paid.

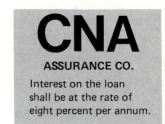

CNA ASSURANCE CO.

Interest on the loan shall be at the rate of eight percent per annum.

DO EXERCISE 1.

1. $800 is borrowed for two years at 15% simple interest. How much interest must be paid?

ANSWER ON PAGE A-4

Example 2 What is the simple interest earned on $250 for three months at 8%?

Solution Substituting 250 for P, 0.08 for R, and $\frac{3}{12}$ for T, we get

$$I = P \times R \times T$$

$$= 250 \times 0.08 \times \frac{3}{12} \qquad \text{3 months is } \frac{3}{12} \text{ year}$$

$$= 5$$

Interest earned is $5.00.

DO EXERCISE 2.

▪ ▪   FINDING THE INTEREST RATE

We know that $I = P \times R \times T$. If we want a formula for R, we can divide both sides of $I = P \times R \times T$ by $P \times T$, and we get

$$R = \frac{I}{P \times T}.$$

As a memory device you might remember $\boxed{R} = \dfrac{I}{P \times T}$ from the diagram

Example 3 A $5000 savings certificate earned $1200 in simple interest in two years. What was the rate?

Solution Substitute 5000 for P, 2 for T, and 1200 for I, and solve for R.

$$R = \frac{I}{P \times T}$$

$$R = \frac{1200}{5000 \times 2}$$

$$R = \frac{1200}{10,000} \qquad \text{Dividing by 10,000 to get } R$$

$$R = 0.12$$

The rate of interest was 12%.

DO EXERCISE 3.

▪ ▪ ▪   FIND THE PRINCIPAL

We know that $I = P \times R \times T$. If we want a formula for P, we divide both sides of $I = P \times R \times T$ by $R \times T$, and we get

$$P = \frac{I}{R \times T}.$$

As a memory device you might remember $\boxed{P} = \dfrac{I}{R \times T}$ from the diagram

---

2. The River Creek Credit Union pays 4% simple interest on checking account average balances. What is the interest on a $300 average balance for 1 month?

3. The simple interest for one month on a $4000 loan was $50. What was the rate?

ANSWERS ON PAGE A-4

4. Short-term student loans are available from the government at 5%. Jamie Scheveer repaid a loan with one payment at the end of three months. The interest charge was $2.25. How much was borrowed?

5. The balance on a mobile home mortgage was $9348.62 one month and $9298.73 the next. A payment of $125 was made. How much interest was paid?

6. $500 is put in a bank paying 11% simple interest. How much is in the account after three years?

ANSWERS ON PAGE A-4

Example 4 Last month on a 11% home mortgage loan the interest was $436.87. What was the amount owed at the beginning of last month?

Solution Substitute 0.11 for R, $\frac{1}{12}$ for T, and 436.87 for I, and solve for P.

$$P = \frac{I}{R \times T}$$

$$P = \frac{436.87}{0.11 \times 1/12}$$

$P = 47{,}658.55$ Rounded to nearest cent as throughout this chapter.

The amount owed at the beginning of last month was $47,658.55.

DO EXERCISE 4.

:: INTEREST IN A PAYMENT

Interest you pay is deductible when you file your Federal Income Tax Return. It is helpful to know how much of each payment is interest.

Example 5 A mortgage balance was $46,434.29 one month and $46,193.56 the following month. A payment of $450 was made. How much of the $450 was interest?

Solution

a) Find the principal payment:

Principal payment $= \$46{,}434.29 - \$46{,}193.56$

$$= \$240.73.$$

b) Find the interest:

Interest $=$ Total payment $-$ Principal payment

$$= \$450 - \$240.73$$

$$= \$209.27.$$

DO EXERCISE 5.

:: AMOUNT PAID BACK

Consumers want to know the amount owed or in savings after a period of time. For example, when $200 is borrowed at 14% for one year the amount owed is $200 + $28 or $228. This leads us to the following formula:

> **$A = P + I$**
>
> where **A** is the amount owed or in savings, **P** is the principal, and **I** is the interest.

Example 6 Tracy Staley borrows $800 at 15% simple interest for two years. How much is owed after two years?

Solution

a) Find the interest. We substitute 800 for P, 0.15 for R, and 2 for T in

$$I = P \times R \times T$$

$$= 800 \times 0.15 \times 2$$

$$= 240.$$

The interest is $240.

b) Find the amount owed. We substitute 800 for P and 240 for I in

$$A = P + I$$

$$= 800 + 240$$

$$= 1040.$$

The amount owed is $1040.

DO EXERCISE 6.

⟐ Find the simple interest.

	Principal	Interest Rate	Time
1.	$500	13%	1 year
2. ▦	$2234	$15\frac{1}{2}$%	$1\frac{1}{4}$ year
3.	$1700	15%	2 years
4.	$800	14%	$\frac{1}{2}$ year

5. A student loan for $1500 at 5% was repaid by Don Tuma in one payment at the end of three years. How much interest was due at that time?

6. ▦ A $2837 loan at $13\frac{3}{4}$% was repaid by Marilyn Stout at the end of 16 months. How much interest was due at that time?

7. A revolving charge account had a balance of $450 last month. The interest rate is 18% a year on the unpaid balance. How much interest was charged for the month?

8. A bank card account had a balance of $300 last month. If the interest rate was 15% a year on the unpaid balance, how much interest was due for the month?

⟐⟐ Find the rate.

	Principal	Interest	Time
9.	$900	$153	1 year
10.	$1800	$252	1 year
11. ▦	$6345	$606.74	9 months
12.	$1600	$288	$1\frac{1}{2}$ years

13. The interest on a $2500 loan for $2\frac{1}{2}$ years was $687.50. What was the rate?

14. The interest on a $300 loan for two years was $84. What was the rate?

⟐⟐⟐ Find the principal.

	Interest	Interest Rate	Time
15.	$1260	18%	1 year
16.	$750	15%	1 year
17.	$133	14%	$\frac{1}{2}$ year
18. ▦	$183.98	$15\frac{1}{4}$%	3 months

19. The interest payment on a mobile home loan last month was $71.25 at 13%. How much was owed at the beginning of the month?

20. Interest on a 14% car loan last month was $33.75. How much was owed at the beginning of the month?

ANSWERS

1. _____
2. _____
3. _____
4. _____
5. _____
6. _____
7. _____
8. _____
9. _____
10. _____
11. _____
12. _____
13. _____
14. _____
15. _____
16. _____
17. _____
18. _____
19. _____
20. _____

21. At the end of six months a bank pays you $90 interest on your 12% savings certificate. How much was the principal?

22. At the end of two years, $36 in interest was paid on an 18% loan. How much had been borrowed?

⠿ Find the interest in each payment.

	Payment	Old Balance	New Balance
23.	$450	$32,465.29	$32,183.31
24. 🖩	$625	$60,834.15	$60,561.23
25.	$586	$53,982.83	$53,719.26
26.	$941	$80,625.47	$80,139.62

27. 🖩 Last month Cheryl owed $7426.18 on her car. After this month's $236.14 payment the balance is $7318.82. How much of the payment was interest?

28. Last month Mark owed $638.62 on his stereo. After this month's $75.27 payment the balance is $588.53. How much of the payment was interest?

⠿ Find the amount owed at the stated time.

	Principal	Interest Rate	Time
29.	$1400	15%	1 year
30. 🖩	$2738	$12\frac{1}{4}$%	$1\frac{1}{4}$ year
31.	$800	13%	$\frac{1}{2}$ year
32.	$3500	16%	$1\frac{1}{2}$ years

33. Noele Shahan borrows $1250 at 14% for three years. How much will she owe after three years?

34. 🖩 Brad Vinchattle invests $2500 in a savings certificate paying $9\frac{3}{4}$% interest. How much is in his account after nine months?

✓ **SKILL MAINTENANCE**

Add.

35. $\frac{3}{8} + \frac{5}{6}$

36. $\frac{2}{9} + \frac{7}{12}$

Evaluate.

37. $16 \cdot 24 + 50$

38. $23 \times 51 + 4 \times 16.3 - (3 \times 14 + 2 \times 15)$

3.2

Simple Interest Computation Methods

• BANKER'S 360-DAY METHOD

The *banker's 360-day method* is often used to compute simple interest when you borrow money from a bank or brokerage firm. This method is also used in international and domestic business. The method assumes that

a) a year has 360 days, and

b) the exact number of days from one day to another is used.

You pay more interest on your loan with this method.

Example 1 Brian Drilling borrowed $389 at 13% for 90 days to buy a Whirlpool range. How much interest did he pay?

Limited Edition!

30" Whirlpool Range
with continuous cleaning oven.

• Continuous Cleaning oven • Automatic MEALTIMER† clock • "Infinite"-heat, push-to-turn controls • Removable oven door • Lift-up SPILLGUARD† cook top †Tmk.

Model RDE350P

$389

IT'S THE BEST RANGE VALUE OF THE YEAR!

Solution Substituting 389 for P, 0.13 for R, and $\frac{90}{360}$ for T, we get

$$I = P \times R \times T$$

$$= 389 \times 0.13 \times \frac{90}{360}$$

$$= 12.64.$$

An interest charge of $12.64 was paid.

DO EXERCISE 1.

A table may be used to find the time in days, as shown in Example 2.

Example 2 Deborah Foss borrowed $700 at 15% on April 17 and repaid it on September 5. How much interest was paid?

Solution

a) Find the number of days from April 17 through September 5. (See Table 3.1.)

Number of days = 248 − 107 or 141

After finishing Section 3.2, you should be able to:

• Compute interest, using the banker's 360-day method.

•• Compute interest using the exact interest method.

••• Compute interest using a 360-day year and approximate time.

:: Compute interest using a 365-day year and approximate time.

1. Chin Chore borrowed $389 at 13% for 130 days to buy a Whirlpool range. How much interest was paid?

ANSWER ON PAGE A-4

2. Randet Jensen borrowed $450 at 12% on June 26 and repaid it on October 7. How much interest was paid?

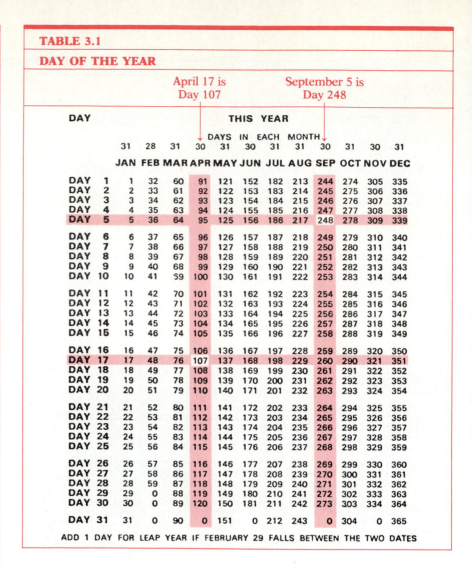

TABLE 3.1

DAY OF THE YEAR

April 17 is Day 107

September 5 is Day 248

DAY	THIS YEAR											
	DAYS IN EACH MONTH											
	31	28	31	30	31	30	31	31	30	31	30	31
	JAN	FEB	MAR	APR	MAY	JUN	JUL	AUG	SEP	OCT	NOV	DEC
DAY 1	1	32	60	91	121	152	182	213	244	274	305	335
DAY 2	2	33	61	92	122	153	183	214	245	275	306	336
DAY 3	3	34	62	93	123	154	184	215	246	276	307	337
DAY 4	4	35	63	94	124	155	185	216	247	277	308	338
DAY 5	5	36	64	95	125	156	186	217	248	278	309	339
DAY 6	6	37	65	96	126	157	187	218	249	279	310	340
DAY 7	7	38	66	97	127	158	188	219	250	280	311	341
DAY 8	8	39	67	98	128	159	189	220	251	281	312	342
DAY 9	9	40	68	99	129	160	190	221	252	282	313	343
DAY 10	10	41	69	100	130	161	191	222	253	283	314	344
DAY 11	11	42	70	101	131	162	192	223	254	284	315	345
DAY 12	12	43	71	102	132	163	193	224	255	285	316	346
DAY 13	13	44	72	103	133	164	194	225	256	286	317	347
DAY 14	14	45	73	104	134	165	195	226	257	287	318	348
DAY 15	15	46	74	105	135	166	196	227	258	288	319	349
DAY 16	16	47	75	106	136	167	197	228	259	289	320	350
DAY 17	17	48	76	107	137	168	198	229	260	290	321	351
DAY 18	18	49	77	108	138	169	199	230	261	291	322	352
DAY 19	19	50	78	109	139	170	200	231	262	292	323	353
DAY 20	20	51	79	110	140	171	201	232	263	293	324	354
DAY 21	21	52	80	111	141	172	202	233	264	294	325	355
DAY 22	22	53	81	112	142	173	203	234	265	295	326	356
DAY 23	23	54	82	113	143	174	204	235	266	296	327	357
DAY 24	24	55	83	114	144	175	205	236	267	297	328	358
DAY 25	25	56	84	115	145	176	206	237	268	298	329	359
DAY 26	26	57	85	116	146	177	207	238	269	299	330	360
DAY 27	27	58	86	117	147	178	208	239	270	300	331	361
DAY 28	28	59	87	118	148	179	209	240	271	301	332	362
DAY 29	29	0	88	119	149	180	210	241	272	302	333	363
DAY 30	30	0	89	120	150	181	211	242	273	303	334	364
DAY 31	31	0	90	0	151	0	212	243	0	304	0	365

ADD 1 DAY FOR LEAP YEAR IF FEBRUARY 29 FALLS BETWEEN THE TWO DATES

b) Find the interest. Substituting 700 for P, 0.15 for R, and $\frac{141}{360}$ for T, we get

$$I = P \times R \times T$$

$$= 700 \times 0.15 \times \frac{141}{360}$$

$$= 41.13.$$

An interest charge of $41.13 was paid.

DO EXERCISE 2.

Time in days may be found without the use of a table, as shown in Example 3.

Example 3 Dorci Land borrowed $590 at 11% on May 23 and repaid it on July 17. How much interest was paid?

ANSWER ON PAGE A-4

Solution

a) Find the number of days from May 23 through July 17.

8 days left in May (don't count the first day, May 23)
30 days in June
17 days in July (count the last day)
‾‾‾‾‾
55 days

Remember:
"30 days hath September, April, June, and November. All the rest have 31 except February (when not a leap year) which has 28."

b) Find the interest. Substituting 590 for P, 0.11 for R, and $\frac{55}{360}$ for T, we get

$$I = P \times R \times T$$

$$= 590 \times 0.11 \times \frac{55}{360} = 9.92.$$

An interest charge of $9.92 was paid.

DO EXERCISE 3.

●● EXACT INTEREST METHOD

The United States government and many states compute simple interest using the **exact (*accurate*) *interest method*.** The method assumes that

a) a year has 365 days, and   **b)** the exact number of days is used.

Example 4 Andrew Renk borrowed $249.95 at 11% for 67 days to buy a Hitachi SR703 receiver. How much interest was paid?

40 WATTS PLUS!
Hitachi SR703
40 watts RMS per channel into 8 ohms from 20-20,000 Hz 0.3% total harmonic distortion
Reg. $399.95
While They Last!
$249⁹⁵ Each
Complete with Foto & Stereo's Exclusive 5-Year Parts and Labor Limited Warranty.
From The Company That Brought You Class "G" Circuitry.
All Hitachi Receivers In Stock Similarly Reduced!!
If You Can't Take A Bargain, Don't Shop At.....
THE FOTO & STEREO SHOP
317 Main   Ames   232-8050

Solution Substituting 249.95 for P, 0.11 for R, and $\frac{67}{365}$ for T, we get

$$I = P \times R \times T$$

$$= 249.95 \times 0.11 \times \frac{67}{365}$$

$$= 5.05.$$

An interest charge of $5.05 was paid.

DO EXERCISE 4.

Note: If 360 days had been used in place of one year, the interest charge would have been 249.95 × 0.11 × $\frac{67}{360}$, or $5.12. The banks would make *more* money. This is probably why consumer protection laws were enacted.

3. Sey Chye Ooi borrowed $650 at 11% on April 25 and repaid it on June 11. How much interest was paid?

4. Lisa Sears borrowed $249.95 at 14% for 100 days to buy a Hitachi receiver. How much interest was paid?

ANSWERS ON PAGE A-4

5. Dan Swift borrowed $850 on April 21 at 12% and repaid it July 5. How much interest was due?

••• 360-DAY, APPROXIMATE TIME INTEREST

This method uses (1) a 360-day year, and (2) approximate time based on 30-day months to compute simple interest. It is used in computing interest in monthly real estate payments and installment purchases.

Example 5 Find the interest on $400 borrowed on June 26 at 15% and repaid on October 17.

Solution

a) Find the number of days based on 30-day months.

	Month	Day	
October 17	$\overset{9}{\cancel{10}}$	$\overset{47}{\cancel{17}}$	(change to 9 months, 47 days)
June 26	6	26	
Subtracting, we get	3	21	

Total days = 111 (3 months of 30 days and 21 days)

b) Find the interest. Substituting 400 for P, 0.15 for R, and $\frac{111}{360}$ for T, we get

$$I = P \times R \times T$$

$$= 400 \times 0.15 \times \frac{111}{360} = 18.50.$$

The interest was $18.50.

DO EXERCISE 5.

6. Find the interest due on $600 borrowed April 27 at 15% and repaid August 21.

•• 365-DAY, APPROXIMATE TIME INTEREST

This method uses (1) a 365-day year, and (2) approximate time based on 30-day months to compute simple interest.

Example 6 Sara Sueppel borrowed $500 at 14% on May 24 and repaid it on September 11. How much interest was due?

Solution

a) Find the number of days based on 30-day months.

	Month	Day
September 11	$\overset{8}{\cancel{9}}$	$\overset{41}{\cancel{11}}$
May 24	5	24
Subtracting, we get	3	17

Total days = 107 (3 months of 30 days and 17 days)

b) Find the interest. Substituting 500 for P, 0.14 for R, and $\frac{107}{365}$ for T, we get

$$I = P \times R \times T$$

$$= 500 \times 0.14 \times \frac{107}{365}$$

$$= 20.52.$$

The interest was $20.52.

DO EXERCISE 6.

ANSWERS ON PAGE A-4

• Find the interest using the 360-day method.

	Principal	Interest Rate	Time (Days)
1.	$500	12%	30
2.	$1000	9%	30
3.	$1200	18%	120
4. ▦	$3000	16%	150

Solve using the 360-day method.

5. Find the interest due on an $800, 12% loan for 400 days.

6. Find the interest due on a $650, 14% loan for 580 days.

7. Lori Swotek took out a $500, 9% loan on September 5 and repaid it on January 12. Find the interest.

8. ▦ Sonya Wassom took out a $700, 14% loan on October 11 and repaid it on February 12. Find the interest.

• • Find the interest using the *exact* interest method.

	Principal	Interest Rate	Time (Days)
9.	$600	14%	90
10.	$800	5%	70
11. ▦	$2240	13%	112
12.	$1780	10%	231

Solve using the *exact* interest method.

13. Find the interest on a $1250, 13% loan for 150 days.

14. Find the interest on a $1600, 17% loan for 190 days.

15. Farshid Oskidari took out a $500 loan at 12% for 100 days. Find the interest.

16. Julianne Marley took out a $1000 loan at 10% for 90 days. Find the interest.

ANSWERS

1. _____
2. _____
3. _____
4. _____
5. _____
6. _____
7. _____
8. _____
9. _____
10. _____
11. _____
12. _____
13. _____
14. _____
15. _____
16. _____

••• Use a 360-day year and approximate time to find the interest on the following loans.

17. $1250 borrowed January 17 at 11% and repaid March 5

18. ▦ $1800 borrowed February 26 at 12% and repaid August 25

19. $2600 borrowed June 18 at 14% and repaid December 9

20. $2300 borrowed July 7 at 12% and repaid October 28

21. $650,000 borrowed September 7 at $14\frac{1}{4}$% and repaid December 6

22. $450,000 borrowed August 12 at $12\frac{1}{2}$% and repaid February 7

∷ Find the 365-day, approximate time interest on a $479.99 video cassette recorder loan using the rates and dates which follow.

Magnavox 8-Hour VHS Video Cassette Recorder

479⁹⁹

Features electronic quartz digital clock, soft touch function controls, remote pause still, automatic fine tuning, more.

	Rate	Borrowed	Repaid
23.	19%	June 3	October 17
24.	21%	June 3	August 12
25.	13%	June 3	September 15
26.	15%	June 3	November 23

Use a 365-day year and approximate time to find the interest on the following loans.

27. ▦ $350,000 borrowed June 6 at $10\frac{1}{2}$% and repaid November 5

28. ▦ $750,000 borrowed July 9 at 12.75% and repaid January 5

✔ **SKILL MAINTENANCE**

Round each to the nearest hundredth.

29. 4.451811

30. 5480.175

Evaluate.

31. 2^4

32. $(1.02)^2$

Simple Interest Tables

• 360-DAY SIMPLE INTEREST TABLES

In this section we find simple interest using tables. Examples 1 and 2 show how to use the 360-day simple interest table on p. T-2 in the appendix. Part of that table (Table 3.2) is shown below.

TABLE 3.2

SIMPLE INTEREST ON $100, 360 DAY BASIS

DAY	11.50 % INTEREST	DAY	11.75 % INTEREST	DAY	12.00 % INTEREST	DAY	12.25 % INTEREST
1	0.031944	1	0.032639	1	0.033333	1	0.034028
2	0.063889	2	0.065278	2	0.066667	2	0.068056
3	0.095833	3	0.097917	3	0.100000	3	0.102083
4	0.127778	4	0.130556	4	0.133333	4	0.136111
5	0.159722	5	0.163194	5	0.166667	5	0.170139
6	0.191667	6	0.195833	6	0.200000	6	0.204167
7	0.223611	7	0.228472	7	0.233333	7	0.238194
8	0.255556	8	0.261111	8	0.266667	8	0.272222
9	0.287500	9	0.293750	9	0.300000	9	0.306250
10	0.319444	10	0.326389	10	0.333333	10	0.340278
11	0.351389	11	0.359028	11	0.366667	11	0.374306
12	0.383333	12	0.391667	12	0.400000	12	0.408333
13	0.415278	13	0.424306	13	0.433333	13	0.442361
14	0.447222	14	0.456944	14	0.466667	14	0.476389
15	0.479167	15	0.489583	15	0.500000	15	0.510417
16	0.511111	16	0.522222	16	0.533333	16	0.544444
17	0.543056	17	0.554861	17	0.566667	17	0.578472
18	0.575000	18	0.587500	18	0.600000	18	0.612500
19	0.606944	19	0.620139	19	0.633333	19	0.646528
20	0.638889	20	0.652778	20	0.666667	20	0.680556

Example 1 Asisie Struchens borrowed $320 at 11.5% for 20 days to pay college expenses. How much interest was paid?

Solution

a) Find the interest on $100 in Table 3.2.

The 20-day row and the 11.5% column meet at 0.638889. Thus, the interest on $100 at 11.5% for 20 days is $0.638889.

b) Find the interest on $1.00 for 20 days at 11.5%.

Move the decimal point in $0.638889 two places to the left:

.00.638889

c) Find the interest on $320.

The interest on $1.00 is $0.00638889, so the interest on $320 is $2.04 (320 × $0.00638889).

DO EXERCISE 1.

1. Nico Kotsopoulos borrowed $450 at 12% for 9 days to pay college expenses. How much interest was paid?

ANSWER ON PAGE A-4

2. Lisa Logeman borrowed $299 at 11.75% for 95 days to purchase an upright freezer. How much interest was paid?

Freeze your food bargains and save ... with this Whirlpool 12 cu. ft. power-saving upright freezer.
Convenient super-storage door, built-in juice can rack. Fast-freeze shelves with cold coils. Power-saving heater control switch. Million Magnet® door. Defrost drain.

$299

See the complete selection of money saving freezers ...

Example 2 Lance Cotton borrowed $299 at 11.75% for 67 days to purchase an upright freezer. How much interest was paid?

Solution Find the interest on $100 from Table 2 (p. T-2).

a) The interest on $100 at 11.75% for

60 days is	1.958333
7 days is	0.228472
Interest on $100 for 67 days is	2.186805

b) Find the interest on $1.00 for 67 days at 11.75%.

Move the decimal point in 2.186805 two places to the left:

0.02186805

The interest on $1.00 for 67 days at 11.75% is $0.02186805.

c) Find the interest on $299.

The interest on $1.00 is $0.02186805, so the interest on $299 is $6.54 (299 × $0.02186805).

DO EXERCISE 2.

●● 365-DAY SIMPLE INTEREST TABLES

Examples 3 and 4 show how to use the 365-day simple interest table on p. T-3 in the appendix. Part of that table (Table 3.3) appears on the top of the next page.

ANSWER ON PAGE A-4

TABLE 3.3

SIMPLE INTEREST ON $100, 365 DAY BASIS

DAY	11.50 % INTEREST	DAY	11.75 % INTEREST	DAY	12.00 % INTEREST	DAY	12.25 % INTEREST
1	0.031507	1	0.032192	1	0.032877	1	0.033562
2	0.063014	2	0.064384	2	0.065753	2	0.067123
3	0.094521	3	0.096575	3	0.098630	3	0.100685
4	0.126027	4	0.128767	4	0.131507	4	0.134247
5	0.157534	5	0.160959	5	0.164384	5	0.167808
6	0.189041	6	0.193151	6	0.197260	6	0.201370
7	0.220548	7	0.225342	7	0.230137	7	0.234932
8	0.252055	8	0.257534	8	0.263014	8	0.268493
9	0.283562	9	0.289726	9	0.295890	9	0.302055
10	0.315068	10	0.321918	10	0.328767	10	0.335616
11	0.346575	11	0.354110	11	0.361644	11	0.369178
12	0.378082	12	0.386301	12	0.394521	12	0.402740
13	0.409589	13	0.418493	13	0.427397	13	0.436301
14	0.441096	14	0.450685	14	0.460274	14	0.469863
15	0.472603	15	0.482877	15	0.493151	15	0.503425
16	0.504110	16	0.515068	16	0.526027	16	0.536986
17	0.535616	17	0.547260	17	0.558904	17	0.570548
18	0.567123	18	0.579452	18	0.591781	18	0.604110
19	0.598630	19	0.611644	19	0.624658	19	0.637671
20	0.630137	20	0.643836	20	0.657534	20	0.671233

Example 3 Tim Smith borrowed $320 at 11.5% for 20 days to pay college expenses. How much interest was paid?

Solution

a) Find the interest on $100 in Table 3.3.

   The 20-day row and the 11.5% column meet at 0.630137. Thus, the interest on $100 at 11.5% for 20 days is $0.630137.

b) Find the interest on $1.00 for 20 days at 11.5%.

   Move the decimal point in $0.630137 two places to the left:

   .00.630137

c) Find the interest on $320.

   The interest on $1.00 is $0.00630137, so the interest on $320 is $2.02 (320 × $0.00630137).

DO EXERCISE 3.

3. Hai-Yeu Lee borrowed $450 at 12% for 9 days to pay college expenses. How much interest was paid?

ANSWER ON PAGE A-4

4. A $679 loan for the trip to Hawaii was paid for in 275 days at 11.75%. What was the interest?

Example 4 A $679 loan for a trip to Hawaii was paid for in 335 days at 11.75%. What was the interest?

Solution

a) Find the interest on $100 from Table 3 (p. T-3).

The interest on $100 at 11.75% for

330 days is   10.623288
  5 days is   0.160959

The interest on $100 for

335 days is   10.784247   Adding

b) Find the interest on $1.00 for 335 days at 11.75%.

Move the decimal point in 10.784247 two places to the left:

.10.784247

The interest on $1.00 at 11.75% for 335 days is $0.10784247.

c) Find the interest on $679.

The interest on $1.00 is $0.10784247, so the interest on $679 is $73.23 (679 × $0.10784247).

DO EXERCISE 4.

ANSWER ON PAGE A-4

Find the interest using the 360-day table (Table 2, p. T-2).

	Principal	Rate	Days
1.	$5000	12.25%	360
2.	$3600	12.25%	150
3.	$4200	12.75%	210
4. ▦	$3900	12.75%	240
5.	$4800	11.75%	330
6.	$2900	11.50%	300
7.	$4700	12%	322
8.	$3200	12%	186
9.	$2700	12.50%	123
10.	$5500	12.50%	151

Use the 360-day table (Table 2, p. T-2).

11. Kathryn Ozakyol borrowed $847.75 at 12% for 150 days to buy a used car. How much interest did she pay?

12. Debra Oxenreider borrowed $1530 at 12% for 180 days to buy a computer. How much interest did she pay?

13. ▦ Mike Neighbor borrowed $499.99 at 12.75% for 93 days to buy a video camera. How much interest did he pay?

14. ▦ Julie Mayer borrowed $725 at 12.75% for 187 days to buy a set of encyclopedias. How much interest did she pay?

ANSWERS

1. _____

2. _____

3. _____

4. _____

5. _____

6. _____

7. _____

8. _____

9. _____

10. _____

11. _____

12. _____

13. _____

14. _____

•• Find the interest using the 365-day table (Table 3, p. T-3). Notice interest is less than in the comparable exercises 1–10.

	Principal	Rate	Days
15.	$5000	12.25%	360
16.	$3600	12.25%	150
17.	$4200	12.75%	210
18. ▦	$3900	12.75%	240
19.	$4800	11.75%	330
20.	$2900	11.50%	300
21.	$4700	12%	322
22.	$3200	12%	186
23.	$2700	12.50%	123
24.	$5500	12.50%	151

Use the 365-day table (Table 3, p. T-3).

25. A $249 loan for a color television was paid for in 60 days at 12.50%. What was the interest?

26. ▦ A $2795 loan for a prebuilt garage was paid for in 180 days at 12.25%. What was the interest?

27. A $240 loan for a ceiling fan was paid for in 124 days at 11.75%. What was the interest?

28. ▦ A $5069 loan for a dining room set was paid for in 247 days at 12.75%. What was the interest?

✓ SKILL MAINTENANCE

29. On January 8, 1986 the Dow Jones Industrial Average fell from 1565.71 to 1526.61. What was the percent decrease to the nearest tenth?

30. On October 28, 1929 the Dow Jones Industrial Average fell from 298.97 to 260.64. What was the percent decrease to the nearest tenth?

Chapter 3   Interest

3.4

Compound Interest

SOLVING COMPOUND INTEREST PROBLEMS

Most forms of savings earn compound interest. **Compound interest** is interest paid on (1) principal, and (2) previously earned interest. Interest is usually compounded continuously, daily, monthly, quarterly, semi-annually, or annually. The more often interest is compounded, the more interest your money earns.

Example 1 Jerome McCann invests $400 at 7% compounded quarterly in the General Motors Credit Union for six months. How much interest is earned?

Solution

a) Find the interest for the first quarter. Substituting 400 for P, 0.07 for R, and $\frac{3}{12}$ for T, we get

$$I = P \times R \times T$$

$$= 400 \times 0.07 \times \frac{3}{12}$$

$$= 7$$

Interest earned during the first quarter is $7.00. Thus, the amount in savings is now $400 + $7 = $407.

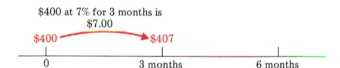

$400 at 7% for 3 months is $7.00
$400 → $407
0   3 months   6 months

b) Going into the second quarter the principal is $407. Find the interest for the second quarter. Substituting 407 for P, 0.07 for R, and $\frac{3}{12}$ for T, we get

$$I = P \times R \times T$$

$$= 407 \times 0.07 \times \frac{3}{12}$$

$$= 7.12.$$

Interest earned during the second quarter is $7.12. Thus, the total amount of interest earned is $14.12 ($7 + $7.12).

$407 at 7% for 3 months is $7.12
$400 $407 → $414.12
0   3 months   6 months

Simple interest earned would have been $14. The extra $0.12 is interest earned on interest.

DO EXERCISE 1.

OBJECTIVES

After finishing Section 3.4, you should be able to:

- Solve compound interest problems without a formula.
- Use a formula to solve compound interest problems.
- Solve compound interest problems using a table.
- Use a table to solve daily compound interest problems.
- Use a table to solve continuous compound interest problems (optional).

1. A savings and loan institution pays 8% compounded quarterly. How much interest would $800 earn in six months?

ANSWER ON PAGE A-4

2. Use the formula to find the interest earned on $800 at 6% compounded quarterly for six months.

3. Lu Bry invests $10,000 for three years at 8% compounded quarterly. Use the formula to find the amount and interest.

•• A COMPOUND INTEREST FORMULA

Now we use a formula to solve compound interest problems.

> For compound interest, principal **P** grows to the amount **A** given by
>
> $$A = P \times (1 + i)^n$$
>
> where **P** is the principal, **i** is the rate **per compounding period, n is the total number of compounding periods, and A is the amount after n compounding periods.**

Example 2 Milton Moyer invests $400 at 7% compounded quarterly in the General Motors Credit Union for six months. Use the formula to find the amount and interest.

Solution Substituting 400 for P, $\dfrac{0.07}{4}$ for i, and 2 for n, we get

$$A = P \times (1 + i)^n$$

Remember: The order of operations is multiplication and division first from left to right and then addition and subtraction, start with parenthesis.

$$= 400 \times \left(1 + \frac{0.07}{4}\right)^2$$
$$= 400 \times (1 + 0.0175)^2$$
$$= 400 \times (1.0175)^2$$
$$= 400 \times 1.0353062$$
$$= 414.12.$$

The amount after six months is $414.12. Hence, the interest is $14.12 ($414.12 − $400).

This agrees with the answer for Example 1.

DO EXERCISE 2.

Example 3 Mary Oberhaus invests $2000 for three years at 12% compounded quarterly. Use the formula to find the amount and interest.

Solution Substituting 2000 for P, $\dfrac{0.12}{4}$ for i, and 12 for n (3 years × 4 compounding periods each year), we get

$$A = P \times (1 + i)^n$$
$$= 2000 \times \left(1 + \frac{0.12}{4}\right)^{12}$$
$$= 2000 \times (1.03)^{12}$$
$$= 2000 \times 1.425760887$$

We find this power by multiplying or by using a calculator.

$$= 2851.52 \quad \text{Rounding}$$

The amount after 3 years is $2851.52. Hence, the interest is $851.52 ($2851.52 − $2000).

DO EXERCISE 3.

Chapter 3   Interest

⬤⬤⬤ COMPOUND INTEREST USING TABLES

Tables are often used to calculate compound interest. Appendix Table 4 (p. T-4) contains compound interest for various rates and time periods. Part of that table (Table 3.4) is shown below.

TABLE 3.4

COMPOUND INTEREST*
(AMOUNT WHEN $1.00 IS COMPOUNDED)

Period	Interest Rate Each Period					
	$1\frac{1}{4}$%	$1\frac{1}{2}$%	$1\frac{3}{4}$%	2%	$2\frac{1}{2}$%	3%
1	1.012500	1.017500	1.015000	1.020000	1.025000	1.030000
2	1.025156	1.030225	1.035306	1.040400	1.050625	1.060900
3	1.037970	1.045678	1.053424	1.061208	1.076891	1.092727
4	1.050945	1.061363	1.071859	1.082432	1.103813	1.125509
5	1.064082	1.077283	1.090617	1.104081	1.131308	1.159274
6	1.077383	1.093442	1.109703	1.126163	1.159693	1.194052
7	1.090850	1.109844	1.129123	1.148686	1.188685	1.229874
8	1.104486	1.126492	1.148883	1.171660	1.218402	1.266770
9	1.118292	1.143389	1.168988	1.195093	1.248862	1.304773
10	1.132271	1.160540	1.189445	1.218995	1.280084	1.343916

* The entries in this table are the amounts when $P = \$1.00$ is substituted in the compound interest formula $A = P \times (1 + i)^n$.

Example 4 How much interest is earned on $400 for six months at 7% compounded quarterly?

Solution

a) In Table 3.4, find the $1\frac{3}{4}$% column (7% ÷ 4, because the interest is compounded quarterly).

b) Find 2 in the column headed Period (interest is compounded two times in six months).

c) The row containing 2 and the column for $1\frac{3}{4}$% meet at 1.035306. So $1.00 grows to $1.035306 at 7% after 6 months.

d) And $400 will grow to 400 × $1.035306 = $414.12 at 7% after 6 months.

e) The interest is $14.12 ($414.12 − $400).

Note that this answer agrees with the answer for Example 1, page 103.

DO EXERCISE 4.

4. Find the interest on $1500 for two years at 10% compounded quarterly.

ANSWER ON PAGE A-4

5. Find the amount after four years if $250 is invested at 16% compounded semiannually.

6. Find the amount after 5 years if $800 is invested at 8% compounded annually.

ANSWERS ON PAGE A-4

Example 5 Find the amount after 10 years if $2000 is invested at 12% compounded semiannually.

Solution

a) In Table 4 (p. T-4) find the 6% column (12% ÷ 2, because the interest is compounded twice yearly).

b) Find 20 in the column headed Period (the interest is compounded 20 times in 10 years).

c) The row containing 20 and the 6% column meet at 3.207135. So $1.00 grows to $3.207135 at 12% after 10 years.

d) And $2000 will grow to 2000 × $3.207135 = $6414.27 at 12% after 10 years.

DO EXERCISE 5.

Example 6 Find the amount after 10 years if $2000 is invested at 8% compounded annually.

Solution

a) In Table 4 (p. T-4) find the 8% column (8% ÷ 1, because the interest is compounded annually).

b) Find 10 in the column headed Period (the interest is compounded 10 times in 10 years).

c) The row containing 10 and the 8% column meet at 2.158925. So $1.00 grows to $2.158925 at 8% after 10 years.

d) And $2000 will grow to 2000 × $2.158925 = $4317.85 at 8% after 10 years.

DO EXERCISE 6.

Chapter 3   Interest

⠿ DAILY COMPOUND INTEREST

Inter-State Federal Savings compounds interest daily on a 365-day basis. Example 7 shows how to use Table 5 (page T-6) to find interest compounded daily.

Example 7 Mark Novotny invests $950 for 104 days at Inter-State Federal Savings. How much interest did he earn?

Solution

a) Find the interest on $100 for 104 days.

From Table 5 we see that the interest is $1.507026.

b) Determine the interest on $950.

Since 950 is 9.5 × 100, the interest on $950 is $14.32 (9.5 × $1.507026).

DO EXERCISE 7.

7. Erin Renty invests $600 at Inter-State Federal Savings for 307 days. How much interest did she earn?

ANSWER ON PAGE A-4

8. Becky McNeal invests $765 at New York Bank for Savings for 321 days. How much interest did she earn?

The New York Bank for Savings compounds interest daily on a 360-day basis. Examples 8 and 9 show how to use the 360-day tables to find interest compounded daily.

Example 8 Lisa Nyse invests $950 at New York Bank for Savings for 104 days. How much interest did she earn?

Solution

a) Find the interest on $100 for 104 days.

From Table 6 (p. T-7) we see that the interest is $1.528114.

b) Determine the interest on $950.

Since 950 is 9.5 × 100, the interest on $950 is $14.52 (9.5 × $1.528114).

DO EXERCISE 8.

9. Kristine Kelly invests $42,000 for 165 days at a bank paying 5% compounded daily. How much interest is earned?

Example 9 Suk Lee invests $12,362 for 178 days at a bank paying 5% compounded daily. How much interest is earned?

Solution

a) From Table 7 (p. T-8) we see that $1.00 becomes $1.025028 after 178 days.

b) Thus, $12,362 grows to $12,671.40 ($12,362 × 1.025028).

The interest earned is $309.40 ($12,671.40 − $12,362).

DO EXERCISE 9.

⠿ CONTINUOUS COMPOUND INTEREST (OPTIONAL)

At some banks interest is compounded continuously (continuously accumulating). Example 10 shows how to use the 360-day table (Table 8, p. T-8) to find interest compounded continuously.

10. If $42,000 is invested for 165 days at a bank paying 5% compounded continuously, how much interest is earned?

Example 10 If $12,362 is invested for 178 days at a bank paying 5% compounded continuously, how much interest is earned?

Solution

a) From Table 8 we see that $1.00 becomes $1.025030 after 178 days.

b) Thus, $12,362 grows to $12,671.42 (12,362 × $1.025030).

The interest earned is $309.42 ($12,671.42 − $12,362).

Note that continuous compounding (Example 10) results in slightly more interest ($0.02) than daily compounding (Example 9). Unless very large amounts of money are invested the interest difference is very little.

DO EXERCISE 10.

ANSWERS ON PAGE A-4

● Find the compound interest without a formula.

	Principal	Rate	Compounded	Time
1.	$600	10%	Quarterly	2 quarters
2.	$900	8%	Quarterly	2 quarters
3.	$1400	14%	Semiannually	6 months
4.	$500	6%	Semiannually	6 months
5.	$1600	7%	Annually	2 years
6.	$1100	8%	Annually	2 years

1. _____

2. _____

3. _____

4. _____

5. _____

6. _____

7. National Thrift pays 8% compounded quarterly. How much interest would be earned on $1000 for six months?

8. AllSavers Bank pays 6% compounded semiannually. How much interest would be earned on $700 for one year?

7. _____

●● Use a formula to find the compound interest.

	Principal	Rate	Compounded	Time
9.	$1000	12%	Monthly	5 months
10.	$1500	12%	Semiannually	6 months

8. _____

9. _____

11. Pasadena Savings pays 8% compounded quarterly. Find the amount and interest on $1000 after three quarters.

12. Thorp Investments pay 10% compounded semiannually. Find the amount and interest on $2500 after one year.

10. _____

11. _____

Use the y^x or similar key and the compound interest formula to find interest. Assume a 365-day year and daily compounding.

13. $10,000 at 12% for 180 days.

14. $5000 at 9% for 270 days.

12. _____

13. _____

14. _____

••• Use Table 4 (p. T-4) to find the interest.

	Principal	Rate	Compounded	Time
15.	$700	10%	Quarterly	9 months
16.	$600	16%	Semiannually	18 months
17.	$1000	18%	Monthly	2 years
18.	$5000	8%	Annually	1 year

19. Cara Bredeson bought a $5000 bank certificate paying 12% compounded semiannually. How much money did she obtain upon cashing in the certificate two years later?

20. Bill Dryers bought a $5000 bank certificate paying 14% compounded semiannually. How much money did he obtain upon cashing in the certificate three years later?

⠒

21. Junus Hanitio had $400 in a checking account which paid 5.25% interest compounded daily. Use Table 5 (p. T-6) to find the interest for 30 days.

22. Karoline Jeon had $700 in a checking account which paid 5.25% interest compounded daily. Use Table 5 (p. T-6) to find the interest for 28 days.

23. Pacific Brokerage pays 5.25% interest compounded daily on all balances to $2000. Use Table 6 (p. T-7) to find the interest on a $1200 balance for 25 days.

24. The Sunset Credit Union pays 5% interest compounded daily on all share draft account balances. Use Table 7 (p. T-8) to find the interest on a $425 balance for 30 days.

⠪

25. First Banks Passbook Savings Account pays 5% interest compounded continuously. Use Table 8 (p. T-8) to find the interest on $800 for 50 days.

26. Seattle Savings Passbook Savings Account pays 5% interest compounded continuously. Use Table 8 (p. T-8) to find the interest on $690 for 60 days.

✓ **SKILL MAINTENANCE**

27. In a bread recipe, there are 2 cups of milk to 12 cups of flour. What is the ratio of cups of milk to cups of flour?

28. A car travels 800 kilometers in 3 days. At this rate, how far would it travel in 15 days?

3.5

Nominal and Effective Interest Rates

After finishing Section 3.5, you should be able to:

- • Find the effective interest rate.
- • • Select the most favorable interest rate.

• EFFECTIVE INTEREST RATE

Financial institutions often compound interest several times each year. This has the effect of increasing the **nominal (published) rate of interest.** This increased rate of interest is called the **effective interest rate.** Suppose you invested $1000 at 8%, compounded annually for one year. At the end of one year you will have $1000(1 + 0.08)^1$, or $1080. If interest is compounded quarterly, you will have $1000(1 + 0.08/4)^4$, or $1082.43. The amount obtained from quarterly compounding is the same as if you had invested $1000 at 8.243%, compounded annually. That is, 8.243% is the effective interest rate corresponding to the nominal rate of 8%.

1. What is the effective rate on four-year certificates offered by Postal Thrift at $8\frac{1}{2}\%$ compounded quarterly?

> **To find the effective rate,**
>
> a) use the compound interest formula to compute the compound amount **A** for **P = $1.00,**
>
> b) compute the interest earned for **P = $1.00,** and
>
> c) change the answer to a percent.

Example 1 At Postal Thrift the nominal rate on passbook accounts is 6% compounded quarterly. What is the effective rate?

POSTAL THRIFT OFFERS

4 YEARS	2 YEARS	180 DAYS	PASSBOOK
8½%	7½%	6¾%	6%
Interest compounded to maturity yields	Interest compounded to maturity yields	Interest compounded to maturity yields	Interest compounded quarterly yields
	7.71%	6.92%	

This announcement is neither an offer to sell nor a solicitation of an offer to buy these securities. The offer is made only by the Prospectus and only to Iowa residents. You may obtain a Prospectus at any of 18 Iowa Postal Thrift locations.

Solution

a) Compute the compound amount *A*.

Substitute 1 for *P*, $\dfrac{0.06}{4}$ for *i*, and 4 for *n* in

$$A = P \times (1 + i)^n$$
$$= 1 \times \left(1 + \frac{0.06}{4}\right)^4$$
$$= 1 \times (1 + 0.015)^4$$
$$= 1 \times (1.015)^4$$
$$= 1.06136 \qquad \text{We find this power by multiplying, using a calculator or Table 4.}$$

b) Compute the interest for *P* = $1.00.

Interest = Amount − Principal
$$= 1.06136 − 1 = 0.06136$$

c) Change to a percent, $0.06136 = 6.14\%$. The effective rate is 6.14%.

DO EXERCISE 1.

ANSWER ON PAGE A-4

▪ ▪ COMPARING INTEREST RATES

The effective rate allows consumers to compare and decide which interest rates are most favorable.

Example 2 One bank offers $5\frac{1}{4}$% compounded quarterly on their passbook accounts. Another offers $5\frac{1}{2}$% compounded semiannually. At which bank would you earn more interest?

Solution

a) For the $5\frac{1}{4}$% rate, we substitute 1 for P, $\dfrac{0.0525}{4}$ for i, and 4 for n in

$$A = P \times (1 + i)^n$$
$$= 1 \times \left(1 + \frac{0.0525}{4}\right)^4$$
$$= 1.0535$$

The interest is $1.0535 - 1 = 0.0535$.

The effective rate is 5.35%.

b) For the $5\frac{1}{2}$% rate, we substitute 1 for P, $\dfrac{0.055}{2}$ for i, and 2 for n in

$$A = P \times (1 + i)^n$$
$$= 1 \times \left(1 + \frac{0.055}{2}\right)^2$$
$$= 1.05575$$

The interest is $1.05575 - 1 = 0.05575$.

The effective rate is 5.58%.

Thus, more interest is earned at the bank that offers $5\frac{1}{2}$% compounded semiannually.

DO EXERCISE 2.

ANSWER ON PAGE A-4

• Find the effective interest rate.

	Nominal Rate	Compounded
1.	5%	Quarterly
2.	7%	Quarterly
3.	8%	Quarterly
4.	10%	Annually
5.	12%	Quarterly
6.	14%	Quarterly
7.	5%	Semiannually
8.	7%	Semiannually
9.	8%	Annually
10.	10%	Semiannually
11.	12%	Semiannually
12.	14%	Semiannually

At Nevada Federal Savings and Loan interest is compounded daily. Use a 365-day year and the y^x or similar key to find the effective interest rate.

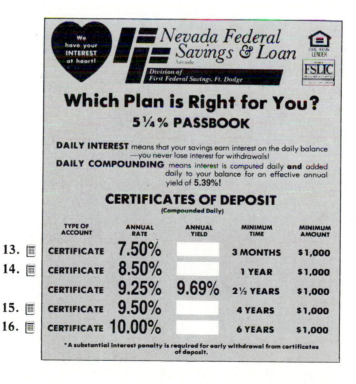

ANSWERS

1. _____
2. _____
3. _____
4. _____
5. _____
6. _____
7. _____
8. _____
9. _____
10. _____
11. _____
12. _____
13. _____
14. _____
15. _____
16. _____

ANSWERS

17. _____

18. _____

19. _____

20. _____

21. _____

22. _____

23. _____

24. _____

25. _____

26. _____

27. _____

28. _____

29. _____

30. _____

17. At Postal Thrift, where interest is compounded quarterly, 180-day certificates pay a nominal rate of $6\frac{3}{4}\%$. What is the effective rate?

18. ▦ At Postal Thrift, where interest is compounded quarterly, 2-year certificates pay a nominal rate of $7\frac{1}{2}\%$. What is the effective rate?

• • Tell which earns more interest.

19. 9% compounded monthly or $9\frac{1}{4}\%$ compounded quarterly.

20. $7\frac{1}{4}\%$ compounded monthly or $7\frac{1}{2}\%$ compounded quarterly.

21. $10\frac{1}{4}\%$ compounded monthly or $10\frac{1}{2}\%$ compounded quarterly.

22. 12% compounded monthly or $12\frac{1}{4}\%$ compounded quarterly.

23. 14% compounded monthly or $14\frac{1}{2}\%$ compounded semiannually.

24. ▦ 11% compounded monthly or $11\frac{1}{4}\%$ compounded semiannually.

25. Delaware Federal Bank offers 9% compounded monthly. Another bank offers $9\frac{1}{2}\%$ compounded semiannually. At which bank would you earn more interest?

26. Hawkeye Savings offers $10\frac{1}{4}\%$ compounded monthly. Another bank offers $10\frac{1}{2}\%$ compounded semiannually. At which bank would you earn more interest?

✓ SKILL MAINTENANCE

Solve.

27. $\dfrac{t}{0.16} = \dfrac{0.15}{0.40}$

28. $\dfrac{x}{11} = \dfrac{7.1}{2}$

29. A 12-lb boneless rib roast contains 30 servings of meat. What is the rate in servings per pound?

30. A car is driven 200 kilometers on 40 liters of gasoline. What is the rate in kilometers per liter?

3.6

Present Value

• FINDING THE PRESENT VALUE

A consumer wants $7500 four years from now to help purchase an automobile. How much must be invested now at 12% compounded semiannually so that $7500 will be available in four years? This type of problem is called a *present value* problem. Table 9 (p. T-9), contains present values for various rates and time periods. Part of that table (Table 3.5) is shown below.

TABLE 3.5

PRESENT VALUE OF $1.00

| Period | Interest Rate Each Period | | | | | |
	$3\frac{1}{2}$%	4%	5%	6%	7%	8%
1	.966183	.961538	.952380	.943396	.934579	.925925
2	.933510	.924556	.907029	.889996	.873438	.857338
3	.901942	.888996	.863837	.839619	.816297	.793832
4	.871442	.854804	.822702	.792093	.762895	.735029
5	.841973	.821927	.783526	.747258	.712986	.680583
6	.813500	.790314	.746215	.704960	.666342	.630169
7	.785990	.759917	.710681	.665057	.622749	.583490
8	.759411	.730690	.676839	.627412	.582009	.540268
9	.733731	.702586	.644608	.591898	.543933	.500248
10	.708918	.675564	.613913	.558394	.508349	.463193

Example 1 Find the present value of $7500 needed in four years at 12% compounded semiannually.

Solution

a) In Table 3.5, find the 6% column (12% ÷ 2, because the interest is compounded semiannually).

b) Find 8 in the column headed Period (interest is compounded 8 times in 4 years).

c) The row containing 8 and the column for 6% meet at 0.627412. The present value of $1.00 at 12% compounded semiannually for 4 years is $0.627412.

d) Find the present value of $7500 at 12% compounded semiannually for 4 years.

Present value of $7500 = Present value of $1.00 × 7500

$$= \$0.627412 \times 7500$$

$$= \$4705.59$$

Therefore, $4705.59 invested now at 12% compounded semiannually will grow to $7500 in four years.

DO EXERCISE 1.

After finishing Section 3.6, you should be able to:

- • **Find the present value using a table.**
- •• **Find the present value without a table.**

1. Find the present value of $6300 needed in three years at 10% compounded semiannually.

ANSWER ON PAGE A-4

2. Find the present value of $12,000 needed in 5 years at 10% compounded quarterly.

3. Find the present value of $8000 needed in 5 years at 8% compounded quarterly.

In the context of Example 1, $7500 is called the *future value* of $4705.59 compounded semiannually at 12%.

Example 2 Find the present value of $20,000 needed in 10 years at 14% compounded quarterly.

Solution

a) In Table 9 (p. T-9) find the $3\frac{1}{2}$% column (14% ÷ 4, because the interest is compounded quarterly).

b) Find 40 in the column headed Period (interest is compounded 40 times in 10 years).

c) The row containing 40 and the column for $3\frac{1}{2}$% meet at 0.252572. The present value of $1.00 at 14% compounded quarterly for 10 years is $0.252572.

d) Find the present value of $20,000 at 14% compounded quarterly for 10 years.

$$\text{Present value of } \$20,000 = \text{Present value of } \$1.00 \times 20,000$$
$$= \$0.252572 \times 20,000$$
$$= \$5051.44$$

Therefore, $5051.44 invested now at 14% compounded quarterly will grow to $20,000 in 10 years.

DO EXERCISE 2.

● ● FINDING THE PRESENT VALUE WITHOUT USING A TABLE

The present value can be found without a table.

> **To find the present value,**
>
> **a)** compute $(1 + i)^n$, where i is the interest rate per compounding period and n is the total number of compounding periods,
> **b)** compute the reciprocal of the number found in a), and
> **c)** multiply by the amount you eventually want available, the future value.

Example 3 Find the present value of $20,000 needed in 10 years at 14% compounded quarterly.

Solution

a) Compute $(1 + i)^n$.

Substitute $\dfrac{0.14}{4}$ for i and 40 for n in

$$(1 + i)^n = \left(1 + \frac{0.14}{4}\right)^{40}$$
$$= (1.035)^{40}$$
$$= 3.9592597 \quad \text{Use a calculator.}$$

b) The reciprocal of 3.9592597 is
0.252572   Use a calculator.

c) Multiply by 20,000: $0.252572 × 20,000 = $5051.44.

As expected this answer agrees with the answer for Example 2.

DO EXERCISE 3.

• Find the present value using Table 9 (p. T-9).

	Amount Needed (Future Value)	When Needed	Rate	Compounded
1.	$7000	3 years	12%	Quarterly
2.	$7000	3 years	12%	Semiannually
3.	$10,000	3 years	10%	Quarterly
4.	$10,000	3 years	18%	Monthly
5.	$20,000	4 years	12%	Semiannually
6. ▦	$20,000	4 years	21%	Monthly
7.	$3000	2 years	16%	Quarterly
8.	$3000	2 years	15%	Monthly

9. Find the present value of $8760 needed in five years at 12% compounded semiannually.

10. ▦ Find the present value of $4590 needed in four years at 16% compounded semiannually.

11. Find the present value of $6780 needed in fourteen years at 8% compounded annually.

12. Find the present value of $9870 needed in nine years at 7% compounded annually.

ANSWERS

1. _____

2. _____

3. _____

4. _____

5. _____

6. _____

7. _____

8. _____

9. _____

10. _____

11. _____

12. _____

•• Find the present value without a table.

13. Find the present value of $1500 needed in five years at 10% compounded quarterly.

14. ▦ Find the present value of $5680 needed in seven years at 12% compounded quarterly.

15. Joe Wicks has $3470.92 in an account that has been paying 11% compounded semiannually for six years. What must he have put into the account six years ago assuming no deposits were made in the interim?

16. Sally Strawn has $9465.82 in an account that has been paying 12% compounded quarterly for five years. What must she have put into the account five years ago assuming no deposits were made in the interim?

17. ▦ Gwang Joo Jeon wants to have $5000 for a trip to Hawaii in five years. How much must be invested now at 10% compounded semiannually so the trip will be possible?

18. The Knutson's need $10,000 for a trip to Hawaii in five years. How much must be invested now at 12% compounded quarterly so the trip will be possible?

✓ **SKILL MAINTENANCE**

Write fractional notation for each of the following ratios.

19. 4 to 5

20. 178 to 572

21. The present world population growth rate is 2.1% per year. Find decimal notation for 2.1%.

22. An electric bill was $149.77 for 1762 kWh of electricity. What was the price per kWh?

Chapter 3   Interest

If you miss an item, review the indicated section and objective.

ANSWERS

[3.1, •] **1.** A $5000 certificate of deposit pays 9% simple interest. How much interest is earned in 18 months?

1. _____

[3.1, • •] **2.** A $10,000 certificate of deposit earned $1600 in simple interest in two years. What was the rate?

2. _____

[3.1, • • •] **3.** Alfredo Ziyold paid $600 interest last month on a 12% mortgage. What was the amount owed at the beginning of last month?

3. _____

[3.1, •••] **4.** Lisa Watson borrowed $1000 from her insurance policy at 5%. In two years the loan was repaid. How much was repaid?

4. _____

[3.2, •] **5.** Kermit Smith borrowed $850 at 14% on March 24 and repaid it July 1. Use the 360-day method to find how much interest was paid.

5. _____

[3.2, • •] **6.** Paul Pomykala borrowed $575 at 11% on May 13 and repaid it September 5. Use the exact interest method to find how much interest was paid.

6. _____

[3.2, ::] **7.** Elizabeth Ragusa borrowed $785 at 15% on March 20 and repaid it on June 7. Use 365-day and approximate time to find the interest.

7. _____

[3.3, • •] **8.** A $3500 loan for a Jacuzzi was paid for in 182 days at 11.50%. Use Table 3 (p. T-3) to find the interest.

8. _____

[3.4, •] **9.** Amy Nigg invests $700 at 8% compounded quarterly in the City Employees Credit Union for six months. Find the interest without using a formula or table.

9. _____

[3.4, • •] **10.** Scott Oakes invests $1000 at 9% compounded semiannually in a thrift certificate for two years. Find the interest with the use of a formula.

10. _____

[3.4, • •] **11.** Dale Mechler invests $2500 at 10% compounded semiannually in a certificate of deposit. Find the amount after two years with the use of a formula.

11. _____

[3.4, •••] **12.** Thriftway Financial pays 18% compounded monthly. Use Table 4 (p. T-4) to find the amount after three years on a $10,000 investment.

12. _____

13. _____

14. _____

15. _____

16. _____

17. _____

18. _____

[3.4, ⁚⁚] **13.** The New Haven Savings Bank compounds interest daily on a 360-day basis. Find the interest on $575 at 5.25% for 30 days using **Table 6 (p. T-7).**

[3.4, ⁚•⁚] **14.** The Garden State Credit Union compounds interest continuously on share draft accounts. Find the interest on $380 at 5% for 30 days using **Table 8 (p. T-8).**

[3.5, •] **15.** The Hawkeye State Credit Union compounds interest quarterly and pays 8% interest on savings accounts with balances to $2000. What is the effective rate?

[3.5, ••] **16.** One bank offers $10\frac{1}{4}$% compounded semiannually on certificates of deposit. Another offers 10% compounded quarterly. Which earns more interest?

[3.6, •] **17.** Kimberly Jansen wants to have $40,000 as a balloon mortgage payment in 5 years. How much must be invested now at 14% compounded quarterly so the payment may be paid? Use **Table 9 (p. T-9).**

[3.6, ••] **18.** Joyce Klodt, an entrepreneur wants to have $20,000 for a franchise in 3 years. How much must be invested now at 9% compounded semiannually so the franchise may be purchased? Do not use a table.

4

CHECKING, SAVINGS, AND MONEY MARKET ACCOUNTS

CAREER: DATA PROCESSING   This is Barbara Dickerson. Barbara is a data processor.

BARBARA DICKERSON

Data Processors work with computers and do many different kinds of jobs. Barbara is a bookkeeper, and uses a computer to prepare ledger accounts which record cash disbursements. She also uses a computer to prepare financial statements in conjunction with an accountant. Barbara studied business math in school. An important benefit of this has been that she is better able to communicate with accountants, her employer and other employees using the language of the business world. People who are successful in the type of work Barbara does make $16,000–$19,000 per year.

After finishing Section 4.1, you should be able to:

- Fill out a check for $17.95 written to Chuck's Records.
- Endorse a check.
- Identify information on a check.
- Identify the payee and the amount a bank will pay.
- Find the new balance.
- Find the net deposit.

---

1. Fill out a check for $17.95 written to Chuck's Records.

Paying by Check

The nature of financial transactions has changed in recent years. For example, mortgage payments and transfers from checking to savings may be done automatically each month. Interest rates for loans and savings fluctuate because government regulations are now less restrictive.

In this chapter we discuss checking, savings, and money market accounts.

■ HOW TO WRITE A CHECK

Businesses and consumers use checks to pay bills and receive checks in payment for goods and services. The bank on which the check is written then pays the amount written on the check.

Example 1 Fill out a check for $29.35 written to Electronic Supply.

Solution

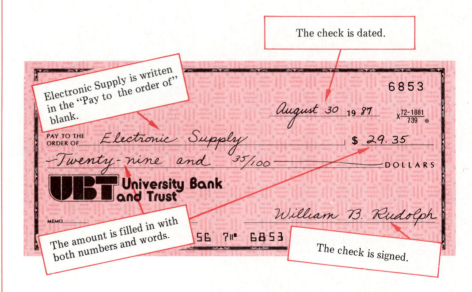

The check is dated.

Electronic Supply is written in the "Pay to the order of" blank.

The amount is filled in with both numbers and words.

The check is signed.

DO EXERCISE 1.

HOW TO ENDORSE A CHECK

The recipient of a check may either cash, deposit, or transfer the check. An endorsement on the back of the check will tell the bank what to do.

Example 2 A check written to Clyde Williams is endorsed. Show some possible endorsements.

Solution

1.

The bank pays the amount written on the check.

2.

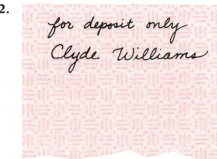

The bank deposits the amount written on the check into Clyde William's account.

3.

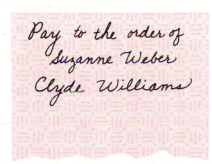

The bank pays Suzanne Weber the amount written on the check.

DO EXERCISE 2.

THE INFORMATION ON A CHECK

Besides the typical information on a check there are several numbers that help a clearinghouse to sort and route checks. The canceled check on the next page illustrates these numbers.

2. You endorse a check written to you Show the endorsements.

a) The bank pays the amount written on the check.

b) The bank deposits the amount written on the check into your account.

c) The bank pays Joe Banks the amount written on the check.

ANSWERS ON PAGE A-4–A-5

3. Identify the account number and the amount of the check.

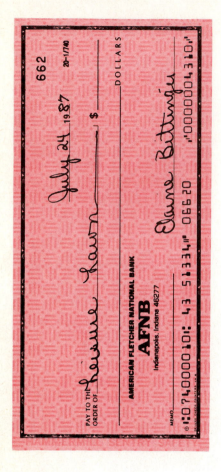

ANSWERS ON PAGE A-5

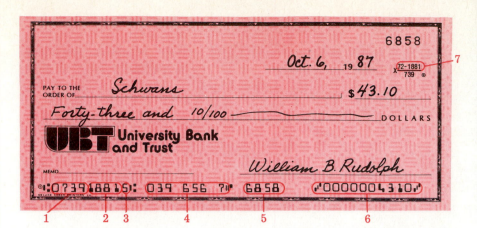

1 This is a Federal Reserve routing symbol, which identifies geographic areas. The first two digits (07) designate one of the Federal Reserve districts numbered 01–12; the third digit (3), the Federal Reserve Bank that serves the area; and the fourth digit (9), the state within the particular Federal Reserve district.

2 This number identifies the bank (1881).

3 This digit (5) enables computers to reconstruct an illegible digit among the other eight digits and to detect and reject misreads.

4 This number identifies the particular account in the bank (039 656 7).

5 This number (6858) is the check number. The number will not appear when the person who makes out the check must number each check (as in Example 3).

6 This shows the amount of the check ($43.10). Computers often read the decimal point incorrectly, so it is omitted.

7 This is the American Bankers Association transit number. Banks want depositors to use this number (72-1881) to identify checks on deposit slips. Digits to the left of the hyphen (72) identify the large city or state in which the bank is located, whereas the digit(s) to the right (1881) identify the bank.

Example 3 Identify the account number and the amount of the check.

Solution

a) Identify the account number. The account number is 0273 562.

b) Identify the amount of the check. The amount of the check is $48.40.

DO EXERCISE 3.

Chapter 4   **Checking, Savings, and Money Market Accounts**

∷ PAYEE AND CHECK AMOUNT

Check-writing pointers are given by a bank when an account is opened.

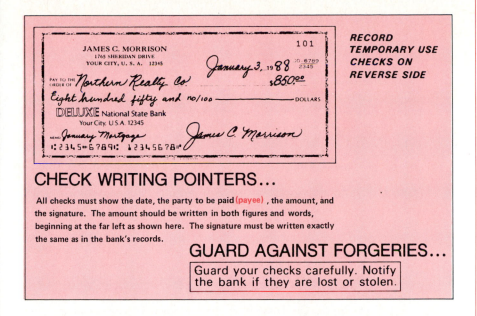

RECORD TEMPORARY USE CHECKS ON REVERSE SIDE

CHECK WRITING POINTERS...

All checks must show the date, the party to be paid (payee), the amount, and the signature. The amount should be written in both figures and words, beginning at the far left as shown here. The signature must be written exactly the same as in the bank's records.

GUARD AGAINST FORGERIES...

Guard your checks carefully. Notify the bank if they are lost or stolen.

When there is a discrepancy between the amounts written in figures and in words, federal law requires the amount given in words be paid.

Example 4 Identify the **payee** and the amount that the bank will pay.

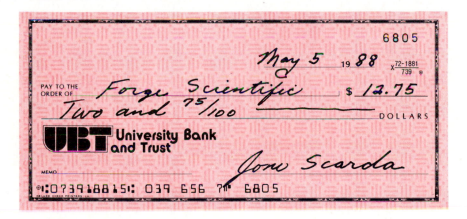

Solution

a) Identify the payee.

   The payee is Forge Scientific.

b) Identify the amount that the bank will pay.

   The bank will pay the amount given in words, which is "Two and 75/100 dollars ($2.75)."

DO EXERCISE 4.

4. Identify the payee and the amount that the bank will pay.

ANSWERS ON PAGE A-5

ANSWER ON PAGE A-5

5. Find the new balance.

CHECK NO	DATE	CHECKS ISSUED TO OR DESCRIPTION OF DEPOSIT	(–) AMOUNT OF CHECK	√ T	CHECK FEE (IF ANY)	(+) AMOUNT OF DEPOSIT	BALANCE
							872 24
181	5/3	Peterson's	47 93				824 31
182	5/7	Tricia's Bootery	96 14				

FINDING THE NEW BALANCE

A **check record book** often attached to a checkbook is used to record information on checks written and deposits made.

CHECK NO	DATE	CHECKS ISSUED TO OR DESCRIPTION OF DEPOSIT	(–) AMOUNT OF CHECK	√ T	CHECK FEE (IF ANY)	(+) AMOUNT OF DEPOSIT	BALANCE
							598 47
435	9/9/87	Nelson Electric	45 62				552 85
436	9/12/87	Fox Haven	156 50				396 35
437	9/15/87	Harlan Grocery	28 70				367 65
	9/18/87	Deposit				112 40	480 05
438	9/20/87	S & H Builders	52 80				427 25

Subtract to find the new balance after a check has been written.

New balance = Previous balance – Check amount

Example 5 Find the new balance of the following checking account.

CHECK NO	DATE	CHECKS ISSUED TO OR DESCRIPTION OF DEPOSIT	(–) AMOUNT OF CHECK	√ T	CHECK FEE (IF ANY)	(+) AMOUNT OF DEPOSIT	BALANCE
							392 70
822	5/6/87	Follette Repairs	14 60				378 10
823	5/7/87	Hope's Linens	26 49				351 61
824	5/8/87	Toni's Lamps	78 62				

Solution

$$\text{New balance} = \text{Previous balance} - \text{Check amount}$$
$$= \quad \$351.61 \quad - \quad 78.62$$
$$= \quad \$272.99$$

The new balance is $272.99.

DO EXERCISE 5.

Add to find the new balance after a deposit has been made.

New balance = Previous balance + Deposit

Example 6 Find the new balance.

CHECK NO	DATE	CHECKS ISSUED TO OR DESCRIPTION OF DEPOSIT	(-) AMOUNT OF CHECK	√ T	(-) CHECK FEE (IF ANY)	(+) AMOUNT OF DEPOSIT	BALANCE
		PLEASE BE SURE TO **DEDUCT** ANY PER CHECK CHARGES OR SERVICE CHARGES THAT MAY APPLY TO YOUR ACCOUNT					682 98
154	2/1/88	World Craft	147 89				535 09
155	2/3/88	Kral Cosmetics	21 80				513 29
	2/5/88	Deposit				89 50	

Solution

New balance = Previous balance + Deposit
= $513.29 + $89.50
= $602.79

The new balance is $602.79.

DO EXERCISE 6.

SUGGESTION

Shop around for a checking account. Shop for the lowest service charges. Some are free if you forfeit receiving canceled checks; some are free if you maintain a specified balance in a savings or checking account; some have a Direct Deposit Plan through which your paycheck is deposited directly in your account by your employer; and some financial institutions offer free checking and pay interest on your balance.

6. Find the new balance.

CHECK NO	DATE	CHECKS ISSUED TO OR DESCRIPTION OF DEPOSIT	(-) AMOUNT OF CHECK	√ T	(-) CHECK FEE (IF ANY)	(+) AMOUNT OF DEPOSIT	BALANCE
		PLEASE BE SURE TO **DEDUCT** ANY PER CHECK CHARGES OR SERVICE CHARGES THAT MAY APPLY TO YOUR ACCOUNT					324 17
201	6/4	Gleason's	93 27				230 90
202	6/5	National Hea Co	58 27				172 63
		Deposit				103 37	

ANSWER ON PAGE A-5

7. Find the net deposit.

CASH	CURRENCY	157	—
	COIN	24	82
LIST CHECKS SINGLY			
2 - 23		893	61
27 - 8		381	14
113 - 6		1973	21
TOTAL FROM OTHER SIDE		—	—
TOTAL			
LESS CASH RECEIVED		328	75
NET DEPOSIT			

8. Find the net deposit.

CASH	CURRENCY	87	00
	COIN	14	96
LIST CHECKS SINGLY			
4 - 85		97	29
TOTAL FROM OTHER SIDE		103	07
TOTAL			
LESS CASH RECEIVED		20	65
NET DEPOSIT			

ANSWERS ON PAGE A-5

▦ THE DEPOSIT SLIP

Money (currency, coins, and checks) is put in a checking account using a **deposit slip.** The checks deposited are listed on the deposit slip by transit number (see p. 124).

Example 7 Find the net deposit.

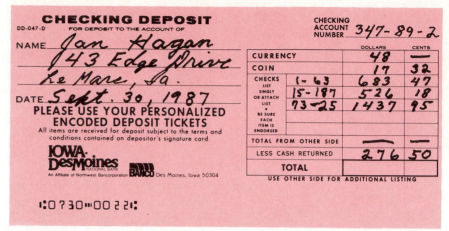

Solution

a) Add the currency, coins, and checks.

Sum = $48.00 + $17.32 + $683.47 + $526.18 + $1437.95

= $2712.92

b) Subtract the cash returned.

Net deposit = $2712.92 − $276.50

= $2436.42

The net deposit is $2436.42.

DO EXERCISE 7.

Example 8 Find the net deposit.

CASH	CURRENCY	94	00
	COIN	15	42
LIST CHECKS SINGLY			
1 - 76		478	16
23 - 42		932	05
TOTAL FROM OTHER SIDE		1039	47
TOTAL			
LESS CASH RECEIVED		215	80
NET DEPOSIT			

Solution

a) Add the currency, coins, checks, and the total from other side.

Sum = $94.00 + $15.42 + $478.16 + $932.05 + $1039.47

= $2559.10

b) Subtract the cash returned.

Net deposit = $2559.10 − $215.80

= $2343.30

The net deposit is $2343.30.

DO EXERCISE 8.

Chapter 4   Checking, Savings, and Money Market Accounts

• Fill out each check as indicated. Put in today's date and sign your name.

1. To Ferber's for $29.99.

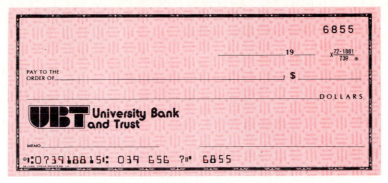

2. To Maude's Restaurant for $34.62.

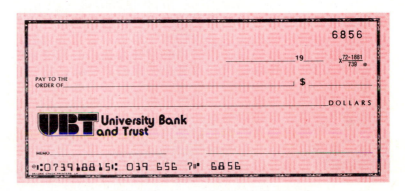

3. To Jay Haus for $19.25.

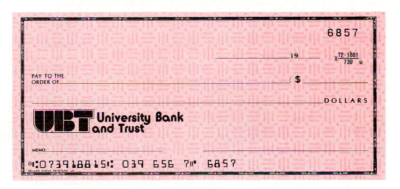

4. To Stephanie Burns for $16.85.

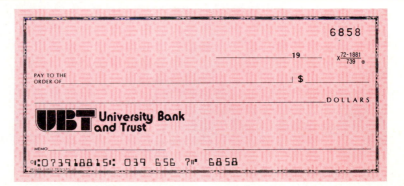

 Endorse a check for these situations.

5.

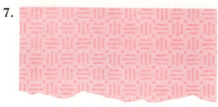

The bank pays you the amount written on the check.

6.

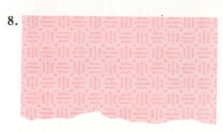

The bank deposits the amount written on the check into your account.

7.

The bank pays Jim Felbo the amount written on the check drawn from your account.

8.

The bank pays Academic Information Company the amount written on the check drawn from your account.

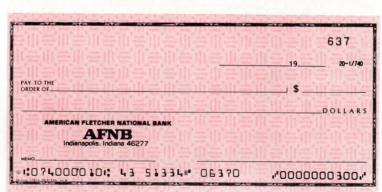 Identify the account number and the amount of the check.

9. _____

10. _____

9.

290

56-103/442

_____ 19 ___

PAY TO THE
ORDER OF _____ $ _____

_____ DOLLARS

THE **HOCKING VALLEY BANK**
OF ATHENS COMPANY • ATHENS, OHIO

MEMO _____

⑆044201030⑆ 40 041 8⑈ 0290 ⑈000000075 0⑈

10.

637

20-1/740

_____ 19 ___

PAY TO THE
ORDER OF _____ $ _____

_____ DOLLARS

AMERICAN FLETCHER NATIONAL BANK
AFNB
Indianapolis, Indiana 46277

MEMO _____

⑆074000010⑆ 43 51334⑈ 06370 ⑈000000030 0⑈

Chapter 4 Checking, Savings, and Money Market Accounts

Identify the payee and the amount that the bank will pay.

11.

	6807
	19____ X$\frac{72-1881}{739}$ ®
PAY TO THE ORDER OF _____	$ _____
_____	DOLLARS

UBT University Bank and Trust

MEMO _____

⑆073918815⑆ 039 656 7⑈ 6807

11. _____

12.

	6808
	19____ X$\frac{72-1881}{739}$ ®
PAY TO THE ORDER OF _____	$ _____
_____	DOLLARS

UBT University Bank and Trust

MEMO _____

⑆073918815⑆ 039 656 7⑈ 6808

12. _____

Find the new balance.

13.

PLEASE BE SURE TO **DEDUCT** ANY PER CHECK CHARGES OR SERVICE CHARGES THAT MAY APPLY TO YOUR ACCOUNT

CHECK NO	DATE	CHECKS ISSUED TO OR DESCRIPTION OF DEPOSIT	(−) AMOUNT OF CHECK		√ T	(−) CHECK FEE (IF ANY)	(+) AMOUNT OF DEPOSIT	BALANCE	
								731	19
432	12/3	Buss Wilbur	57	16				674	03
433	12/5	Pyle Photo	48	11				625	92
434	12/6	Lester's	95	16					

13. _____

14. 🖩

PLEASE BE SURE TO **DEDUCT** ANY PER CHECK CHARGES OR SERVICE CHARGES THAT MAY APPLY TO YOUR ACCOUNT

CHECK NO	DATE	CHECKS ISSUED TO OR DESCRIPTION OF DEPOSIT	(−) AMOUNT OF CHECK		√ T	(−) CHECK FEE (IF ANY)	(+) AMOUNT OF DEPOSIT	BALANCE	
								557	15
511	11/2	Central Roofing	68	14				489	01
512	11/3	Cooper Excavating	37	91				451	10
513	11/8	Sigler Printing	104	07					

14. _____

15. 🖩

PLEASE BE SURE TO **DEDUCT** ANY PER CHECK CHARGES OR SERVICE CHARGES THAT MAY APPLY TO YOUR ACCOUNT

CHECK NO	DATE	CHECKS ISSUED TO OR DESCRIPTION OF DEPOSIT	(−) AMOUNT OF CHECK		√ T	(−) CHECK FEE (IF ANY)	(+) AMOUNT OF DEPOSIT	BALANCE	
								718	45
718	9/3	Harris TV	87	19				631	26
719	9/7	Unitog Rentals	62	17				569	09
	9/20	Deposit					381	14	

15. _____

16.

PLEASE BE SURE TO **DEDUCT** ANY PER CHECK CHARGES OR SERVICE CHARGES THAT MAY APPLY TO YOUR ACCOUNT

CHECK NO.	DATE	CHECKS ISSUED TO OR DESCRIPTION OF DEPOSIT	(-) AMOUNT OF CHECK	√T	(-) CHECK FEE (IF ANY)	(+) AMOUNT OF DEPOSIT	BALANCE
							365 42
261	1/5	Ralph Kennedy	15 68				349 74
262	1/8	McDonald Mann	37 16				312 58
	1/12	Deposit				114 15	

▦ Complete the check record.

PLEASE BE SURE TO **DEDUCT** ANY PER CHECK CHARGES OR SERVICE CHARGES THAT MAY APPLY TO YOUR ACCOUNT

CHECK NO	DATE	CHECKS ISSUED TO OR DESCRIPTION OF DEPOSIT	(-) AMOUNT OF CHECK	√T	(-) CHECK FEE (IF ANY)	(+) AMOUNT OF DEPOSIT	BALANCE
							682 17
17. 611	8/7	Drury Well	47 18				
18.	8/11	Deposit					796 33
19. 612	8/14	Sorenson Boutique					682 86
20.	8/17	Deposit				58 14	

∷∷ Find the net deposit.

21.

CASH	CURRENCY	314	—
	COIN	16	38
LIST CHECKS SINGLY	1-188	462	20
	72-16	132	50
TOTAL FROM OTHER SIDE		—	—
TOTAL			
LESS CASH RECEIVED		—	—
NET DEPOSIT			

22.

CASH	CURRENCY	217	—
	COIN	31	15
LIST CHECKS SINGLY	2-14	314	17
	27-8	416	32
TOTAL FROM OTHER SIDE		—	—
TOTAL			
LESS CASH RECEIVED		—	—
NET DEPOSIT			

23.

CASH	CURRENCY	321	—
	COIN	14	27
LIST CHECKS SINGLY	7-21	468	31
	93-121	548	56
TOTAL FROM OTHER SIDE		—	—
TOTAL			
LESS CASH RECEIVED		410	25
NET DEPOSIT			

▦ Complete the deposit slips.

24.

CASH	CURRENCY		
	COIN	14	38
LIST CHECKS SINGLY	1-53	891	62
	14-3	763	35
	162-5	1324	17
TOTAL FROM OTHER SIDE		—	—
25. TOTAL			
LESS CASH RECEIVED		368	25
NET DEPOSIT		2838	27

26.

CASH	CURRENCY	415	—
	COIN		
LIST CHECKS SINGLY	1-27	368	41
	42-63	489	15
	37-29	1622	19
TOTAL FROM OTHER SIDE			
TOTAL			
27. LESS CASH RECEIVED		523	25
NET DEPOSIT		2527	87

28.

CASH	CURRENCY	128	—
	COIN	46	02
LIST CHECKS SINGLY	5-68	1468	15
	41-17	724	31
	3-162	608	17
TOTAL FROM OTHER SIDE		—	—
TOTAL			
LESS CASH RECEIVED		320	50
NET DEPOSIT			

 **SKILL MAINTENANCE**

29. Pasadena Savings pays 8% compounded quarterly. Find the amount and interest on $1000 after three quarters.

30. Brenda Egan placed $10,000 in a money market certificate paying 6% compounded quarterly. How much money did she obtain upon cashing in the certificate three years later?

Chapter 4   **Checking, Savings, and Money Market Accounts**

4.2

Reconciling a Bank Statement With a Check Record

• BANK STATEMENT BALANCES

At regular intervals banks send depositors **bank statements** together with the canceled checks for the account. The depositor then uses these and the check record to see whether there are any errors.

BEGINNING BALANCE	TOTAL CHECKS PAID	NO.	TOTAL DEPOSIT AMOUNT	NO.	SER. CHG.	BALANCE THIS STATEMENT
590.88	451.13	12	579.69	3	.00	719.44

CHECKS AND OTHER CHARGES		DEPOSITS AND OTHER CREDITS	DATE	BALANCE
7.00			07/24	583.88
		459.69	07/31	1,043.57
10.00			08/02	1,033.57
233.00			08/03	800.57
50.00		20.00	08/15	770.57
35.00			08/16	735.57
		100.00	08/17	835.57
8.50			08/18	827.07
4.00	4.90		08/21	
10.00	20.49			
27.80	40.44			719.44

Observe that:

1. To get each new balance figure, we add any deposits to the previous balance and then subtract checks paid.
2. The beginning balance ($590.88 in the preceding example) and ending balance ($719.44) are given.
3. The total checks paid ($451.13) and total deposit ($579.69) amounts are given.
4. The dates of each transaction are given.

Example 1 Pat Darcy's bank statement shows that the balance on 8/3 was $800.57. Verify that the balance on 8/15 was $770.57.

Solution

New balance = Previous balance + Deposits − Checks

$$= \quad \$800.57 \quad + \ 20.00 \ - \$50.00$$

$$= \quad \$770.57$$

The balance on 8/15 was $770.57.

DO EXERCISE 1.

After finishing Section 4.2, you should be able to:

| • | Verify bank statement balances. |
| •• | Reconcile a bank statement with a check record. |

1. Pat Darcy's bank statement balance on 7/24 was $583.88. Verify that the balance on 8/2 was $1033.57.

ANSWER ON PAGE A-5

2. Find the statement balance.

Beginning balance	$425.59
Deposits	378.21
Checks paid	287.75
Service charge	1.57

To find the statement balance,

1. **find the sum of the beginning balance and deposits, and then**
2. **subtract the checks paid and the service charge (the amount that banks charge for check processing and record keeping).**

Example 2 Verify that Pat Darcy's statement balance in the figure on the preceding page is $719.44.

Solution

a) Find the sum of the beginning balance and deposits.

Sum = $590.88 + $579.69

   = $1170.57

b) Subtract the checks paid and the service charge.

Statement balance = Sum − Checks paid − Service charge

   = $1170.57 − $451.13 − $0

   = $719.44

The statement balance is $719.44

DO EXERCISE 2.

•• RECONCILING

The process of comparing the bank statement with the check record is called **reconciling.**

Example 3 Reconcile the bank statement with the check record.

Solution

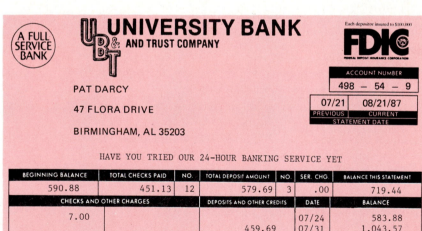

BEGINNING BALANCE	TOTAL CHECKS PAID	NO.	TOTAL DEPOSIT AMOUNT	NO.	SER. CHG	BALANCE THIS STATEMENT
590.88	451.13	12	579.69	3	.00	719.44

CHECKS AND OTHER CHARGES		DEPOSITS AND OTHER CREDITS	DATE	BALANCE
7.00			07/24	583.88
		459.69	07/31	1,043.57
10.00			08/02	1,033.57
233.00			08/03	800.57
50.00		20.00	08/15	770.57
35.00			08/16	735.57
		100.00	08/17	835.57
8.50			08/18	827.07
4.00	4.90		08/21	
10.00	20.49			
27.80	40.44			719.44

UNIVERSITY BANK AND TRUST COMPANY

PAT DARCY
47 FLORA DRIVE
BIRMINGHAM, AL 35203

ACCOUNT NUMBER 498 – 54 – 9

07/21 PREVIOUS   08/21/87 CURRENT
STATEMENT DATE

HAVE YOU TRIED OUR 24-HOUR BANKING SERVICE YET

ANSWER ON PAGE A-5

CHECK NO	DATE	CHECKS ISSUED TO OR DESCRIPTION OF DEPOSIT	(−) AMOUNT OF CHECK	√ T	(−) CHECK FEE (IF ANY)	(+) AMOUNT OF DEPOSIT	BALANCE	
		PLEASE BE SURE TO DEDUCT ANY PER CHECK CHARGES OR SERVICE CHARGES THAT MAY APPLY TO YOUR ACCOUNT					767	73
432	8/16	Bach Sales	23 56				744	17
433	8/19	Rogers TV	20 49	√			723	68
	8/19	Deposit				75 —	798	68
434	8/19	T Galaxy Athel	27 80	√			770	88
435	8/29	Electronic Supply	48 21				722	67

A ✓ in this column shows that the bank has paid the check.

3. Reconcile. Draw a form as in Example 3.

Check record balance	$516.84
Checks outstanding	62.17
	45.82
Deposits not recorded	167.98
Service charges	0.
Bank statement balance	456.85

A typical bank-supplied reconciliation form is used. Under ① list the checks not yet paid by the bank. Deposits not yet credited on the statement are placed under ②.

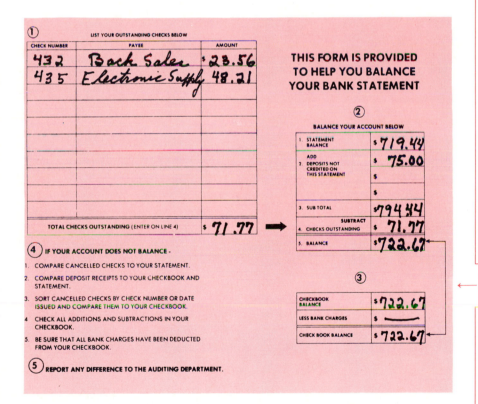

These are equal, which shows that the bank statement and check record agree

ANSWERS ON PAGE A-5

DO EXERCISE 3.

Whenever there is a service charge, subtract it from the checkbook balance when reconciling.

Example 4 Reconcile.

Check record balance	$739.54
Checks outstanding	32.48
Deposits not recorded	312.78
Service charges	2.50
Bank statement balance	456.74

Solution

a) Find the adjusted statement balance.

$$\underset{\text{balance}}{\text{Adjusted statement}} = \underset{\text{balance}}{\text{Statement}} + \underset{\text{recorded}}{\text{Deposits not}} - \underset{\text{outstanding}}{\text{Checks}}$$

$$= \$456.74 + \$312.78 - \$32.48$$

$$= \$737.04$$

b) Find the adjusted check record balance.

$$\text{Adjusted check balance} = \text{Check record balance} - \text{Service charges}$$

$$= \$739.54 - \$2.50$$

$$= \$737.04$$

The adjusted statement balance and adjusted check record balance are equal, so the statement and check record are reconciled.

DO EXERCISE 4.

Chapter 4   Checking, Savings, and Money Market Accounts

• Find the balance

	DATE	CHECKS AND OTHER DEBITS		DEPOSITS	BALANCE
	07/28	10.00			51.40
	07/30	8.00			43.40
1.	07/31	4.00		533.14	5.
	08/03	2.00	8.17		
		202.40			359.97
	08/04	9.79	10.00		
		25.00	32.51		282.67
	08/05	6.50	12.62		
		15.00	15.74		
2.		19.09			
	08/06	2.04	8.00		
		10.00			193.68
	08/10	4.25	25.00		164.43
	08/11	18.15	20.00		126.28
	08/12	3.00			123.28
	08/13	10.25			113.03
	08/14	10.00			103.03
3.	08/17	1.03	10.00	247.69	
	08/18	2.06			337.63
	08/19	15.00	18.22		
		20.00	100.00		184.41
	08/20	31.38			153.03
	08/24	5.22	24.00		
4.		43.40			

Fill in the bank statement where indicated.

	DATE	DESCRIPTION CHECKS/DEBITS		DEPOSITS/CREDITS	BALANCE
5. ▦	08/25	20.65	30.00		288.58
	08/29	10.00			258.58
	08/30	7.00			251.58
	08/31	20.00		635.45	867.03
	09/01	233.00			634.03
	09/02	10.00	39.51		
		50.00			534.52
6. ▦	09/06	25.00			
				136.25	681.93
	09/07	30.00	30.00		621.93
	09/08	42.96	231.14		347.83
7. ▦	09/12	8.10			
		20.00	30.00		269.88
	09/13			425.81	695.69
	09/14	6.00	6.45		
		10.00	15.00		
		18.29			639.95
	09/15	9.00	15.00		615.95
	09/19	20.00	20.00		
8. ▦		40.00			

Find the statement balance

9.

BALANCE LAST STATEMENT	CHECKS AND DEBITS		DEPOSITS		SERVICE CHARGE	BALANCE THIS STATEMENT
	NO.	AMOUNT	NO.	AMOUNT		
491.51	24	678.16	1	250.00	1.95	

10.

BALANCE LAST STATEMENT	CHECKS AND DEBITS		DEPOSITS		SERVICE CHARGE	BALANCE THIS STATEMENT
	NO.	AMOUNT	NO.	AMOUNT		
32.57	34	903.94	1	1,040.29	2.45	

11.

BALANCE LAST STATEMENT	CHECKS AND DEBITS		DEPOSITS		SERVICE CHARGE	BALANCE THIS STATEMENT
	NO.	AMOUNT	NO.	AMOUNT		
138.75	42	882.63	1	962.01	2.60	

12.

BALANCE LAST STATEMENT	CHECKS AND DEBITS		DEPOSITS		SERVICE CHARGE	BALANCE THIS STATEMENT
	NO.	AMOUNT	NO.	AMOUNT		
61.40	40	806.91	2	780.83	2.75	

•• Reconcile. Draw a form as in Example 3.

	Check Record Balance	Checks Outstanding	Deposits not Recorded	Services Charges	Bank Statement Balance
13.	$340.81	$125.63 $462.13	$525.48	0	$403.09
14.	$424.47	$189.01	0	0	$613.48
15. ▦	$765.92	$51.23 $79.96	$159.17	$0.72	$737.22
16.	$329.02	$91.15	0	$1.55	$418.62
17. ▦	$1091.66	$42.63 $115.95	$426.83	0	$823.41
18.	$1162.85	$215.85 $463.21	$325.50 $463.75	$2.35	$1050.31
19.	$1194.22	$321.90	$527.80	$1.75	$986.57
20. ▦	$1331.43	0	$648.26	0	$683.17

✓ **SKILL MAINTENANCE**

21. In a recent survey of 1346 high school student leaders, 50% said the Republican Party best expressed their political views. How many expressed this viewpoint?

22. A recent study showed retail sales rose to $120.23 billion from $117.04 billion the previous month. How many dollars was the increase?

21. _____

22. _____

4.3

Other Financial Transactions

▪ SAVINGS

Financial institutions such as banks and savings and loans provide many services. Among the services are:

Savings and Checking Accounts	**Payroll Deposit**
Certificates of Deposit (CD's)	**Direct Deposit of Government**
Retirement Accounts	**Checks**
Loans	**Automatic Teller Machines**
Notary Services	**(24-hour banking)**
Safety Deposit Boxes	

Transmatic Service (automatic transfer between accounts and payment of certain bills)

Interest computation methods vary. Examples 1 and 2 show that it is important to understand how your financial institution computes interest.

Example 1 Network Savings and Loan pays 8% interest compounded quarterly on the total amount in accounts having more than $2500. How much interest is earned on $3000 in one year?

Solution We substitute $3000 for P, 0.02 for i, and 4 for n in

$$A = P \times (1 + i)^n$$
$$= \$3000 \times (1 + 0.02)^4$$
$$= \$3247.30 \qquad \text{Use a calculator if you have one.}$$

The interest is $247.30 ($3247.30 − $3000).

DO EXERCISE 1.

Example 2 Adelphi Savings and Loan pays 8% interest compounded quarterly on all amounts over $2500 and 6% compounded quarterly on the balance. How much interest is earned on $3000 in one year?

Solution

a) We substitute $500 ($3000 − $2500) for P, 0.02 for i, and 4 for n in

$$A = P \times (1 + i)^n$$
$$= \$500 \times (1 + 0.02)^4 \qquad \text{Use a calculator if you have one.}$$
$$= \$541.22$$

The interest on $500 is $41.22 ($541.22 − $500).

b) We substitute $2500 for P, 0.015 for i, and 4 for n in

$$A = P \times (1 + i)^n$$
$$= \$2500 \times (1 + 0.015)^4 \qquad \text{Use a calculator if you have one.}$$
$$= \$2653.41$$

The interest on $2500 is $153.41 ($2653.41 − $2500). From (a) and (b) we see that the total interest is

$$\$41.22 + \$153.41 \quad \text{or} \quad \$194.63$$

DO EXERCISE 2.

1. Birmingham Federal pays 9% interest compounded quarterly on the total amount in accounts having more than $2500. How much interest is earned on $4000 in one year?

2. Forest City Savings and Loan pays 11% interest compounded quarterly on all amounts over $2500 and 5% compounded quarterly on the balance. How much interest is earned on $4000 in one year?

ANSWERS ON PAGE A-10

State the seven-day annualized yield for each fund.

3. American Liquid Trust Fund.

4. Capital Preservation Fund.

5. Cash Reserve Management Fund.

6. An investor had $10,000 in the American Liquid Trust Fund seven days ago. How much is in the fund now if the past seven-day annualized yield was 9.98%?

ANSWERS ON PAGE A-10

• • MONEY MARKET MUTUAL FUNDS

Money Market Mutual Funds are investment companies which pool investors' money to purchase large denomination (usually no less than $100,000) savings instruments. Interest rates are compounded daily and fluctuate. Investors have immediate access to their invested funds through check writing (usually $500 minimum), wiring of funds, or phone redemption, and there is no penalty for withdrawing money at any time. An initial investment of at least $1000 is often required with subsequent deposits of at least $100. The following table shows information on money market funds on a recent day.

		Days	Yield	Chg.
Money	Market:			
AAA US	Gvt	21	7.58	+ .01
AARP US	Gvt f	51	9.79	+ .36
AetnaMMkt	ab	40	10.37	— .08
AlexBrownCash		30	10.50	— .35
AllianceCapRes f		33	9.64	— .29
AllianceGovtRes f		36	8.40	....
AmerGentMoney		26	10.53	— .40
AmerGenResrv b		36	10.82	+ .29
AmerLiquidTrust		30	9.98	— .31
AmNatl	a	34	10.70	— .24
BabsonMoneyMkt		33	10.66	— .30
BirrWilson		23	9.87	— .95
BostonCoCash		38	10.66	— .33
CapitalCashMgt		25	9.41	— .13
CapitalPreservFd		31	8.26	— .47
CapitPreserv II		3	8.26	+1.31
CardinalGvtSec		10	15.03	+5.15
CarnegieCvtSecur		17	8.65	+ .70
CashEquivlntMMkt		36	11.45	— .26
CashEquivlntPort		30	9.20	+1.04
CashMgmtTrAm b		19	10.05	+ .05
CashResrvMgmt bf		30	10.16	— .35
CentennialMMTr		30	10.25	+ .02
ChanclrGvt	b	40	8.93	— .28
Chanc . TaxFr	e	90	6.44	+ .09
ColonialMMkt	a	23	9.66	— .25
ColumbDivIncm bf		23	9.89	— .33
CompositeCashMgmt		28	10.27	—1.16
CurrentInterest		34	10.54	— .29
DBL MM	Portfolio	36	11.25	— .21
DBL GvtSec		44	9.04	+ .21
DailyCashAccum		26	10.00	— .10
DailyCashGovt		27	7.45	— .04
DailyIncomeFd		30	10.40	+ .07

Money Market Daily Cash Accum	Days	Yield	Chg.
	26	10.00	—.10
1	**2**	**3**	**4**

1 The name of the money market fund. In this case it is the Daily Cash Accumulation Fund.

2 The average maturity in days for the savings instruments in the fund. In this case it is 26 days.

3 The previous seven-day annualized yield. In this case, 10.00%.

4 The change in yield from that of seven days ago. In this case the yield decreased by 0.10% over what it was seven days ago.

DO EXERCISES 3–5.

Example 3 Comfort Equirube had $10,000 in the Daily Cash Accumulation Fund seven days ago. How much is in the fund now if the past seven-day annualized yield was 10.00%?

Solution We substitute $10,000 for P, 0.10 for R, and $\frac{7}{365}$ for T in

$$I = P \times R \times T$$

$$= \$10,000 \times 0.10 \times \frac{7}{365}$$

$$= \$19.18$$

The amount now is $10,000 + $19.18, or $10,019.18.

DO EXERCISE 6.

• Solve.

1. Clive Bank pays 9% interest compounded semiannually on the total amount in accounts having more than $2500. How much interest is earned on $5000 in one year?

2. ▦ Jackson Savings and Loan pays 10% compounded semiannually on the total amount in accounts having more than $2500. How much interest is earned on $5000 in one year?

3. Trenton Bank pays 10% interest compounded semiannually on all amounts over $2500 and 8% compounded semiannually on the balance. How much interest is earned on $5000 in one year?

4. ▦ Laramie Savings and Loan pays 8% compounded semiannually on all amounts over $2500 and 6% compounded semiannually on the balance. How much interest is earned on $5000 in one year?

5. ▦ Pittsburgh National Bank pays 11% interest compounded quarterly on the total amount in accounts having more than $2500. When the balance falls below $2500, the bank pays 6% compounded quarterly. How much interest is earned in one year on $3000 for nine months and $1500 for three months?

6. Faribault National Savings pays 10% interest compounded semiannually on the total amount in accounts having more than $2500. When the balance falls below $2500, the bank pays 6% compounded semiannually. How much interest is earned in one year on $4500 for six months and $2000 for six months?

ANSWERS

1. _____

2. _____

3. _____

4. _____

5. _____

6. _____

• • Use the table to find the seven-day annualized yield.

7. Merrill Lynch Government Fund.

8. Municipal Cash Reserves.

9. Mutual of Omaha Money Market Fund.

10. Phoenix Chase Fund.

ManagedCashAcct	b	41	10.12 — .30
MassCashMgmt	b	41	11.32 — .27
McDonald		33	10.04 — .22
MerrLynchGovt bf		43	9.22 — .84
MerrLynchInst bf		37	9.72 —1.11
MidwIncTrGvt		30	9.34 — .12
MidwIncTrCsh		31	10.39 — .61
MoneyMktInstr		35	10.26 — .26
MoneyMktMgmt	f	35	10.54 — .50
MoneyMktTrust		34	10.91 — .25
MonMartAssets		27	10.94 — .33
MorganKeegDly	f	32	10.12 — .23
MunicipalCashRsv	e	83	6.66 — .04
MunicipalTempInv	e	47	5.91 — .14
MutualOmahaMMkt		31	9.08 — .15
NEL CashMgmt		32	11.01 — .36
NatlCashReserve	a	38	10.57 — .32
NatLiqResv		37	11.25 — .20
NuveenTax	e	61	6.27 + .04
OffermanMMkt		22	9.16 —2.29
OppenMoneyMkt		31	10.32 — .22
PaineWebbCashFd	f	29	10.55 — .13
PaMoneyFd		32	9.24 — .40
ParkCsh		29	10.17 — .34
PhoenixChase		26	10.17 — .22
PlimoneyFund		29	9.57 + .09
PutnamDailyDiv	b	40	11.19 — .34
ReserveFund		40	11.01 — .32
ReserveFd	Gvt	30	9.03 + .42

$15,000 was placed in each of the funds below seven days ago.
How much is in each fund now? Use the table.

11. Massachussetts Cash Management Fund.

12. ▤ Money Market Management Fund.

13. Money Market Assets Fund.

14. ▤ National Cash Reserve Fund.

15. Paine Webber Cash Fund.

16. Plimoney Fund.

✔ SKILL MAINTENANCE

17. What is 5% of $300?

18. What is 3% of $45?

19. 2.1% of 50 is what?

20. $33\frac{1}{3}$% of 240 is what?
(*Hint:* $33\frac{1}{3}$% $= \frac{1}{3}$.)

Chapter 4 **Checking, Savings, and Money Market Accounts**

If you miss an item, review the indicated section and objective.

[4.1, •] **1.** Fill out a check for $87.65 written to Foster's Clothing.

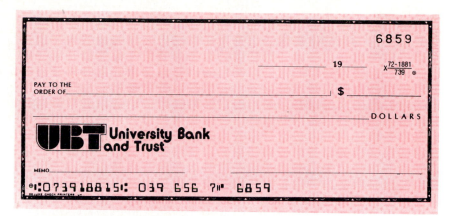

[4.1, ••] **2.** Endorse a check for these situations.

a)

The bank pays you the amount written on the check.

b)

The bank deposits the amount written on the check into your account.

c)

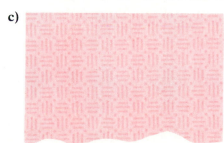

The bank pays Kleeber's the amount written on the check.

3. _____

[4.1, ●●●] **3.** Identify the account number and the amount of this check.

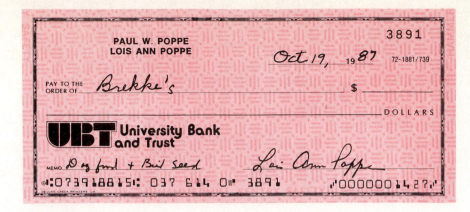

[4.1, ⚁] **4.** Identify the payee and the amount that the bank will pay.

4. _____

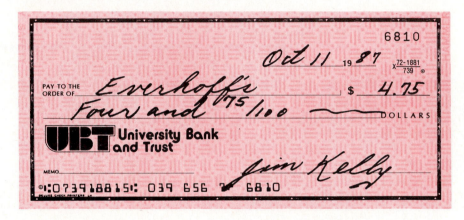

[4.1, ⚂] **5.** Find the new balance.

CHECK NO.	DATE	CHECKS ISSUED TO OR DESCRIPTION OF DEPOSIT	(−) AMOUNT OF CHECK	√ T	(−) CHECK FEE (IF ANY)	(+) AMOUNT OF DEPOSIT	BALANCE
		PLEASE BE SURE TO **DEDUCT** ANY PER CHECK CHARGES OR SERVICE CHARGES THAT MAY APPLY TO YOUR ACCOUNT					
							463 51
620	9/15	Lambert's Colore	29 98				

5. _____

[4.1, ⚃] **6.** Find the net deposit.

CASH	CURRENCY	216	—
	COIN	1	86
LIST CHECKS SINGLY			
4-19		423	71
12-7		119	29
TOTAL FROM OTHER SIDE		—	
TOTAL			
LESS CASH RECEIVED		75	—
NET DEPOSIT			

6. _____

[4.2, •] Find the balance.

7.

BALANCE LAST STATEMENT	NO.	CHECKS AND DEBITS AMOUNT	NO	DEPOSITS AMOUNT	SERVICE CHARGE	BALANCE THIS STATEMENT
370.88	48	1,350.01	1	1,091.40	2.65	

DATE	CHECKS AND OTHER DEBITS		DEPOSITS	BALANCE
10/27	15.00			355.88
10/28	10.00			345.88
8. 10/30	15.20		1,091.40	
11/02	1.54	4.12		
9.	202.40			

[4.2, ••] **10.** Reconcile on the form.

Check record balance	$760.25
Checks outstanding	56.28, 14.96
Deposits not recorded	418.32
Service charges	0
Bank statement balance	413.17

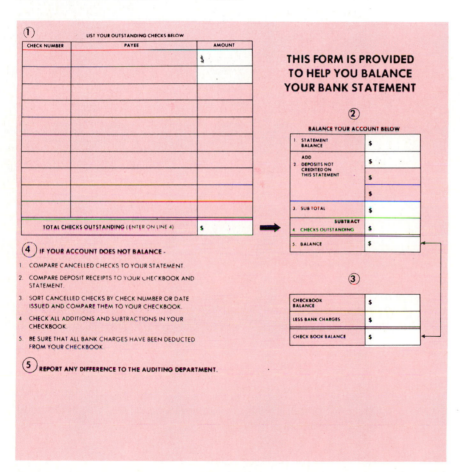

[4.2, • •] **11.** Reconcile on the form.

Check record balance	$454.23
Checks outstanding	85.96
Deposits not recorded	49.24
Service charges	3.45
Bank statement balance	487.50

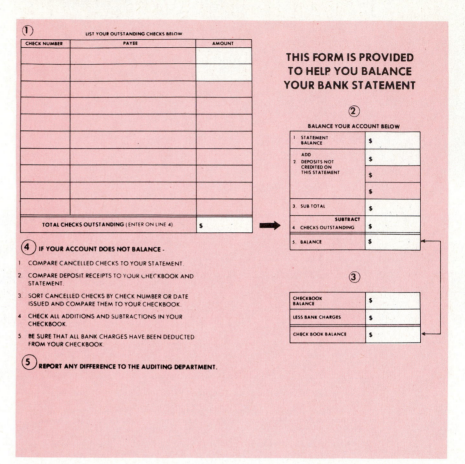

[4.3, •] **12.** Corning Federal pays 10% interest compounded quarterly on the total amount in accounts having more than $2500. How much interest is earned on $3500 in one year?

[4.3, •] **13.** American Federal pays 9% interest compounded quarterly on all amounts over $2500 and 6% compounded quarterly on the balance. How much interest is earned on $4000 in one year?

[4.3, • •] **14.** Chong Hong had $5000 in the Cash Equivalent Money Market Fund seven days ago. How much is in the fund now if the past seven-day annualized yield was 11.45%?

5

LOANS AND ANNUITIES

CAREER: LOAN OFFICER   This is
James R. Bayless.

JAMES R. BAYLESS

Jim is partially paralyzed as a result of a stroke. With the help of vocational re-
habilitation, Jim took several business and pyschology courses and is now a loan
officer for the Small Business Administration. This is a federal agency which grants
loans to existing or start-up small businesses either directly through the government, or indirectly by guaranteeing loans from other financial institutions.

Jim's job is to evaluate loan applications and decide whether or not loans
should be granted to the applicants. As a direct loan can be as much as $150,000
and a guaranteed loan can be as much as $500,000, there is a great deal of
responsibility involved. When making his evaluation Jim takes into account many
factors such as industry averages for the type of business seeking the loan and
the credit rating of the owner of the business.

People who work for the government in a job such as Jim's are paid according to their "GS rating." One might begin with a GS-7 and make about
$17,000 per year, and through promotion and service advance to a GS-12, making
about $40,000.

Jim has many qualities which make for success. He is friendly and likes people.
He also is a "stick-to-it" person who perseveres until a job is finished. His hobbies
include visiting friends, eating out and watching golf tournaments.

5.1

After finishing Section 5.1, you should be able to:

- • Calculate interest due on a note.
- •• Determine the due date of a note.
- ••• Find the discount and proceeds of a note.

1. Find the interest Sara Stokes must pay at the end of six months on a $1000 12% interest-bearing note.

Notes and Discounts

From time to time individuals and businesses need a *loan* (to borrow money). Likewise regular savings is encouraged. Questions such as how payments are credited and the amount in savings after a time period arise. These topics will be studied in this chapter.

• INTEREST DUE ON A NOTE

Lenders often require borrowers to sign a note (**promissory note**) at the time a loan is made. By signing the note, the borrower promises to pay to the lender the amount borrowed plus a charge for the use of the money. Notes may be **interest bearing** (as in Example 1) or **noninterest bearing** (as in Example 2).

Example 1 Find the interest Chris A. Hanson must pay at the end of six months on this 13% interest-bearing note.

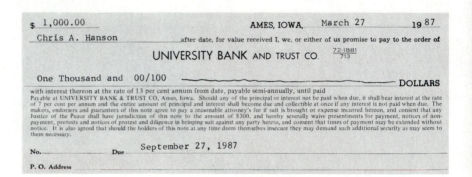

Solution

Find the interest due at the end of six months.
Substituting 1000 for P, 0.13 for R, and $\frac{6}{12}$ for T, we get

$$I = P \times R \times T$$

$$= 1000 \times 0.13 \times \frac{6}{12}$$

$$= 65.$$

The interest·due is $65.

DO EXERCISE 1.

⬤⬤ DUE DATE

For noninterest-bearing notes a charge (discount) is deducted at the time the loan is made. The amount on the face of the note is then due at maturity.

Example 2 Find the due date for Jo Phillips on this 90-day noninterest-bearing note.

Solution The note is for 90 days, and 90 days from May 15 is

May 15–31	16 days
June 1–30	30 days
July 1–31	31 days
August 1–13	13 days
Total	90 days

Thus, the note is due August 13.

DO EXERCISE 2.

⬤⬤⬤ DISCOUNT AND PROCEEDS

As mentioned, a lender may deduct a loan charge (***discount***) at the time a loan is obtained. This discount is often considered interest paid in advance.

> **A formula for finding the discount is**
>
> $$D = M \times R \times T,$$
>
> where D = the discount, M = the amount due at maturity, R = the discount rate, and T = the time.

The amount the borrower receives is the ***proceeds.***

> **A formula for finding the proceeds is**
>
> $$P = M - D,$$
>
> where P = the proceeds, M = the amount due at maturity, and D = the discount.

2. Find the due date for Carlos Lopez on a 135-day noninterest-bearing note taken out May 21.

3. A three-year noninterest-bearing note for $6000 was presented to a bank that uses an 11% discount rate by Felicity Kendall. Find the discount and proceeds.

ANSWERS ON PAGE A-11

4. A 90-day noninterest-bearing note for $600 dated July 7 was converted to cash by Fargo Products at a bank at which the discount rate is 12% on August 12. Find the discount and proceeds.

ANSWER ON PAGE A-11

Example 3 A $2295 two-year non-interest-bearing note for money to purchase a two-car garage was presented to a bank that uses a 14% discount rate by Joel Gray. Find the discount and proceeds.

Solution

a) Find the discount. Substituting 2295 for M, 0.14 for R, and 2 for T, we get

$D = M \times R \times T$

$= 2295 \times 0.14 \times 2$

$= 642.60.$ The amount of money the bank charges for the loan.

The discount is $642.60.

b) Find the proceeds. Substituting 2295 for M and 642.60 for D, we get

$P = M - D$

$= 2295 - 642.60$

$= 1652.40.$ The amount received by the borrower.

The proceeds are $1652.40.

DO EXERCISE 3.

Sometimes a businessperson is given a note and converts the note to cash at a bank before its maturity date. For example, a person may purchase an item from Lee Company. The person gives Lee Company a promissory note for the amount of the item. Lee Company then converts the note to cash at a bank. Example 4 shows the process and assumes a 365-day year.

Example 4 A three-month noninterest-bearing note for $500 dated March 24 was converted to cash by Kern Electric at a bank at which the discount rate is 13% on May 19. Find the discount and proceeds.

Solution

a) Find the number of days from the date that the note was converted to cash to the maturity date.

From Table 1 (p. T-1) we find that the number of days between June 24 (maturity date) and May 19 is $175 - 139$, or 36.

b) Find the discount. Substituting 500 for M, 0.13 for R, and $\frac{36}{365}$ for T, we get

$D = 500 \times 0.13 \times \dfrac{36}{365}$

$= 6.41.$

The discount is $6.41.

c) Find the proceeds. Substituting 500 for M and 6.41 for D, we get

$P = 500 - 6.41$

$= 493.59.$

The proceeds are $493.59.

DO EXERCISE 4.

The notes in Examples 3 and 4 are noninterest-bearing notes. Example 5 illustrates the process if the note is interest bearing.

Example 5 A four-month 15% note dated March 28 for $500 was sold to a bank on June 5 by Coe Enterprises where it was discounted at 10%. What were the proceeds of the note?

Solution

a) Find the amount due at maturity. Substituting 500 for P, 0.15 for R, and $\frac{4}{12}$ for T, we get

$$I = P \times R \times T$$

$$= 500 \times 0.15 \times \frac{4}{12}$$

$$= 25.$$

The amount due at maturity is $525 ($500 + $25).

b) Find the number of days that the bank held the note.

From Table 1 (p. T-1) we find that the number of days from July 28 (maturity date) to June 5 is $209 - 156$, or 53.

c) Find the discount. Substituting 525 for M, 0.10 for R, and $\frac{53}{365}$ for T, we get

$$D = 525 \times 0.10 \times \frac{53}{365}$$

$$= 7.62.$$

d) Find the proceeds. Substituting 525 for M and 7.62 for D, we get

$$P = 525 - 7.62$$

$$= 517.38.$$

The proceeds are $517.38.

DO EXERCISE 5.

5. A three-month 12% note dated August 7 for $700 was sold to a bank on October 4 by General Products where it was discounted at 10%. What were the proceeds of the note?

ANSWER ON PAGE A-11

6. Jill Kegley needs $7500. How much must be borrowed at 13% discount if the loan is to be repaid in seven months? Round the divisor to three decimal places before dividing.

Cy Erb (see advertisement) needs $5000. If this money is borrowed under the discount method, then more than $5000 must be borrowed.

$$\text{Amount borrowed} = \frac{\text{Amount needed}}{1 - (\text{Rate} \times \text{Time})}$$

Example 6 Cy Erb (see the advertisement) wants $5000. How much must be borrowed at 11% discount if the loan is to be repaid in nine months?

Solution Substituting 5000 for the amount needed, 0.11 for the rate, and $\frac{9}{12}$ for the time, in

$$\text{Amount borrowed} = \frac{\text{Amount needed}}{1 - (\text{Rate} \times \text{Time})}$$

we get

$$\text{Amount borrowed} = \frac{5000}{1 - \left(0.11 \times \frac{9}{12}\right)}$$

$$= 5449.59.$$

Thus, Cy must borrow $5449.59 but receives only $5000.

DO EXERCISE 6.

EXERCISE SET **5.1**

• Solve.

1. Find the interest Kwan Choi must pay at the end of eight months on an 11% note for $450.

2. Find the interest Darren Hamre must pay at the end of three months on a 10% note for $568.

3. ▦ Find the interest Kathy Kennedy must pay on a $648.75 note at the end of 195 days if the rate is $11\frac{1}{2}$%. (Assume a 360-day year.)

4. Find the interest Victoria Manning must pay at the end of two years on a 14% note for $780.

5. Find the interest Paul Matter must pay at the end of three years on a 12% note for $1500.

6. ▦ Find the interest Alice Pollard must pay on a $4562.45 note at the end of 155 days if the rate is $10\frac{3}{4}$%. (Assume a 365-day year.)

7. Find the interest Kelby Spann must pay at the end of two years on a 13% note for $825.

8. Find the interest Wen-Bih Tseng must pay at the end of seven months on a 15% note for $2000.

•• Solve.

9. Find the due date on a 90-day noninterest-bearing note to Dorothy Ubbelohde dated July 5.

10. Find the due date on a 90-day noninterest-bearing note to George Reyher dated May 2.

11. Find the due date on a 190-day noninterest-bearing note to Lance Nehring dated August 4.

12. Find the due date on a 270-day noninterest-bearing note to Anita Myers dated June 3.

13. Find the due date on a 180-day noninterest-bearing note to Eleanor Murray dated June 2.

14. Find the due date on a 100-day noninterest-bearing note to Mark Brandt dated March 1.

••• Find the discount and proceeds.

15. A $3500 two-year note to Donna Drefke with a discount rate of 11%

16. ▦ A five-month $15\frac{1}{2}$% note to Jeff Bredeson dated May 28 for $768.67 and converted to cash on August 24 at a discount rate of $12\frac{1}{4}$% (assume a 360-day year)

17. ▦ A seven-month 11.75% note to Karen Breinig dated May 14 for $4503.25 and converted to cash on September 11 at a discount rate of 11.35% (assume a 365-day year)

18. A $1400 note to Peter Drew for 150 days with a discount rate of 13% (assume a 360-day year)

19. A four-month note to Barbara Huth dated April 7 for $750 that was converted to cash at a discount rate of 9% on May 15 (assume a 365-day year)

20. An $8700 three-year note to Cindy Juchems with a discount rate of 12%

ANSWERS

1. _____
2. _____
3. _____
4. _____
5. _____
6. _____
7. _____
8. _____
9. _____
10. _____
11. _____
12. _____
13. _____
14. _____
15. _____
16. _____
17. _____
18. _____
19. _____
20. _____

21. A $450 note to Dave Larue for 120 days with a discount rate of 10% (assume a 360-day year)

22. A six-month note to Susan Larson dated June 3 for $850 that was converted to cash at a discount rate of 8% on August 21 (assume a 365-day year)

23. A three-month 8% note to Todd Minnihan dated May 5 for $875 and converted to cash on July 6 at a discount rate of 6% (assume a 365-day year)

24. A six-month 11% note to Linda Richardson dated August 14 for $1450 and converted to cash on November 23 at a discount rate of 9% (assume a 365-day year)

Find the amount borrowed at 12% discount if:

25. $4000 is needed for one year.

26. $3500 is needed for one year.

27. $3600 is needed for two years.

28. ⊞ $1500 is needed for two years.

29. $2500 is needed for 90 days (assume a 360-day year).

30. $4200 is needed for 120 days (assume a 360-day year).

31. $6250 is needed for 100 days (assume a 365-day year). Round divisor to three decimal places before dividing.

32. $5340 is needed for 150 days (assume a 365-day year). Round divisor to three decimal places before dividing.

33. ⊞ How much must be borrowed by Mary Schott at $13\frac{1}{4}\%$ discount if $4568 is needed for 132 days? (Assume a 360-day year.) Round divisor to three decimal places before dividing.

34. ⊞ How much must be borrowed by Mickey Stolp at $12\frac{3}{4}\%$ discount if $6285 is needed for 135 days? (Assume a 365-day year.) Round divisor to three decimal places before dividing.

✓ SKILL MAINTENANCE

35. At Washington National the nominal rate on Thrift Savings Accounts is 8% compounded quarterly. What is the effective rate?

36. Bankers Trust offers 7% compounded quarterly on their savings accounts while Peoples Bank offers $7\frac{1}{4}\%$ compounded semiannually. At which bank would you earn more interest?

5.2

Partial Payment of Notes

• THE UNITED STATES RULE

A borrower will often make several payments on a note before it is due. The **United States Rule** is one method used to apply partial payments toward the principal of a note. It is the method accepted in most states. Lending institutions may use either a 365- or 360-day year. Examples 1 and 2 illustrate the process, on the basis of a 360-day year.

Example 1 Elmer Ratzloff borrowed $2500 on February 2, 1986, for two years at 12%. The following payments were made: $450 on August 15, 1986; $675 on March 5, 1987; and $900 on October 12, 1987. How much was due on February 2, 1988? How much was the total interest?

Solution Steps (a) through (d) show how the first payment was applied toward paying off the loan.

a) Find the number of days from February 2 through August 15, 1986.

From Table 1 (p. T-1) we find there were 194 days.

b) Find the interest due on August 15, 1986. Substituting 2500 for P, 0.12 for R, and $\frac{194}{360}$ for T, we get

$$I = P \times R \times T$$

$$= 2500 \times 0.12 \times \frac{194}{360}$$

$$= 161.67.$$

c) Find the principal payment.

$$\text{Principal payment} = \text{Payment} - \text{Interest}$$
$$= 450 - 161.67$$
$$= 288.33$$

d) $\text{New balance} = \text{Old balance} - \text{Principal payment}$
$$= 2500 - 288.33$$
$$= 2211.67$$

Steps (e) through (h) show how the second payment was applied toward paying off the loan.

e) Find the number of days from August 15, 1986, through March 5, 1987.

From Table 1 (p. T-1), we find there were 202 days (March 5 = 64 + 365 = 429, and August 15 = 227; and 429 − 227 = 202 days).

f) Find the interest due on March 5, 1987. Substituting 2211.67 for P, 0.12 for R, and $\frac{202}{360}$ for T, we get

$$I = P \times R \times T$$

$$= 2211.67 \times 0.12 \times \frac{202}{360}$$

$$= 148.92.$$

g) Find the principal payment. $\text{Principal payment} = \text{Payment} - \text{Interest}$
$$= 675 - 148.92$$
$$= 526.08$$

After finishing Section 5.2, you should be able to:

• Use the United States Rule to apply partial payments to a note.

•• Use the Merchant's Rule to apply partial payments to a note.

h) Find the new balance.

New balance = Old balance − Principal payment
$$= 2211.67 - 526.08$$
$$= 1685.59$$

The procedure for the third and fourth payments is similar. Remember that for the third payment the principal is $1685.59, and for the fourth payment it is $909.76. The following table summarizes the results.

Payment Number	Payment Date	Amount	Days	Interest to Payment Date	Principal Payment	Balance Owed After Payment
	February 2, 1986					$2500.00
1	August 15, 1986	$450.00	194	$161.67	$288.33	$2211.67
2	March 5, 1987	$675.00	202	$148.92	$526.08	$1685.59
3	October 12, 1987	$900.00	221	$124.17	$775.83	$909.76
4	February 2, 1988	$944.03	113	$34.27	$909.76	0

The amount due on February 2, 1988, is $909.76 + $34.27, or $944.03. The total interest was $161.67 + $148.92 + $124.17 + $34.27 or $469.03.

DO EXERCISE 1.

Example 2 shows the process when some payments are smaller than the interest due. When this is the case, the payment is held until future payments added to it are greater than the interest due. To illustrate, in Example 2, the second payment (for $200) is smaller than the interest due ($308.25). Consequently, the principal payment of $674.19 ($200 + $900 − $308.25 − $117.56) is not made until the time of the next payment.

Example 2 You borrow $3000 on May 11, 1985, for two years at 12%. The following payments are to be made: $400 on November 4, 1985; $200 on October 3, 1986, and $900 on February 7, 1987. How much is due on May 11, 1987?

Solution The computations are similar to those used in Example 1. Steps (a) through (d) show how the first payment is applied to paying off the loan.

a) Find the number of days from May 11 through November 4, 1985.

From Table 1 (p. T-1), we find that there are 177 days.

b) Find the interest due on November 4, 1985. Substituting 3000 for P, 0.12 for R, and $\frac{177}{360}$ for T, we get

$$I = P \times R \times T$$
$$= 3000 \times 0.12 \times \frac{177}{360}$$
$$= 177.$$

c) Find the principal payment. Principal payment = Payment − Interest
$$= 400 - 177$$
$$= 223$$

Chapter 5   **Loans and Annuities**

d) Find the new balance.

New balance = Old balance − Principal payment

$$= 3000 - 223$$
$$= 2777$$

A similar procedure is used to show how payments 2, 3, and 4 are applied toward paying off the loan.

The following table summarizes the results.

Payment Number	Payment Date	Amount	Days	Interest to Payment Date	Principal Payment	Balance Owed After Payment
	May 11, 1985					$3000.00
1	November 4, 1985	$400.00	177	$177.00	$223.00	$2777.00
2	October 3, 1986	$200.00	333	$308.25	0	$2777.00
3	February 7, 1987	$900.00	127	$117.56	$674.19	$2102.81
4	May 11, 1987	$2168.00	93	$65.19	$2102.81	0

The amount due on May 11, 1987, is

$2102.81 + $65.19,   or $2168.00.

DO EXERCISE 2.

The following example is based on a 365-day year.

Example 3 Anne Caruso borrowed $3200 on April 15, 1985, for two years at 15%. The following payments were made: $500 on July 2, 1985; $300 on December 14, 1985; and $200 on March 23, 1986. How much was due on April 15, 1987?

Solution The following table shows how each payment was applied to paying off the loan.

Payment Number	Payment Date	Amount	Days	Interest to Payment Date	Principal Payment	Balance Owed After Payment
	April 15, 1985					$3200.00
1	July 2, 1985	$500.00	78	$102.58	$397.42	$2802.58
2	December 14, 1985	$300.00	165	$190.04	$109.96	$2692.62
3	March 23, 1986	$200.00	99	$109.55	$90.45	$2602.17
4	April 15, 1987	$3017.09	388	$414.92	$2602.17	0

The amount due on April 15, 1987, is

$2602.17 + $414.92,   or $3017.09.

DO EXERCISE 3.

2. Larry Lee borrows $2800 on March 1, 1985, for two years at 14%. The following payments were made: $100 on November 5, 1985; $700 on January 2, 1986; and $1500 on September 29, 1986. How much is due on March 1, 1987 (assume a 360-day year)?

3. Jeri Lees borrowed $4500 on January 12, 1986, for two years at 13%. The following payments were made: $800 on March 15, 1986; $1000 on October 1, 1986; and $1800 on April 2, 1987. How much was due on January 12, 1988 (assume a 365-day year)?

ANSWERS ON PAGE A-11

● ● THE MERCHANT'S RULE

Lenders sometimes apply partial payments on a note using the **Merchant's Rule.** The process involves:

1. Calculating interest and adding it to the amount borrowed, and
2. Finding interest on each payment from the payment date to the note due date. Then the sum of interest and payment is subtracted from the balance due.

Example 4 illustrates this process based on a 360-day year. The same example was used to illustrate how partial payments are applied using the United States Rule (Example 1).

Example 4 Joe Tice borrowed $2500 on February 2, 1986, for two years at 12%. The following payments were made: $450 on August 15, 1986; $675 on March 5, 1987; and $900 on October 12, 1987. How much was due on February 2, 1988? What was the total interest paid?

Solution

a) Find the interest on the amount borrowed. Substituting 2500 for P, 0.12 for R, and 2 for T, we get

$I = P \times R \times T$

$= 2500 \times 0.12 \times 2$

$= 600.$

The interest is $600.00.

b) Add the interest to the amount borrowed.

Total amount = Interest + Amount borrowed

$= \$600 + \$2500$

$= \$3100$

c) Find the number of days from August 15, 1986, through February 2, 1988.

Using the methods discussed in Section 3.2, we find that the number of days was 536.

d) Find the interest on the first payment from the payment date to the note due date.

$I = P \times R \times T$

$= 450 \times 0.12 \times \dfrac{536}{360}$

$= 80.40$

e) Add payment and interest.

Payment + Interest $= 450 + 80.40$

$= 530.40$

f) Find the new balance.

New Balance = Total amount $-$ (Payment + Interest)

$= 3100 - 530.40$

$= 2569.60$

Similarly, steps (g) through (j) illustrate how the second payment was applied toward paying off the loan.

g) Find the number of days from March 5, 1987, through February 2, 1988.

Using the methods discussed in Section 3.2, we find that the number of days is 334.

h) Find the interest on the second payment from the payment date through the note due date.

$I = P \times R \times T$

$= 675 \times 0.12 \times \dfrac{334}{360}$

$= 75.15$

i) Add payment and interest.

Payment + Interest = 675 + 75.15

= 750.15

j) Find the new balance.

New balance = 2569.60 − 750.15

= 1819.45

The following table shows similar information for all payments.

Payment Number	Payment Date	Amount	Days to Due Date	Interest on Payment to Due Date	Payment + Interest	New Balance
	February 2, 1986					$3100.00
1	August 15, 1986	$450.00	536	$80.40	$530.40	$2569.60
2	March 5, 1987	$675.00	334	$75.15	$750.15	$1819.45
3	October 12, 1987	$900.00	113	$33.90	$933.90	$885.55
4	February 2, 1988	$885.55				0

The amount due on February 2, 1988, is $885.55.

Total interest = $600 − ($80.40 + $75.15 + $33.90)

= $410.55

Note that the final payment ($885.55) and the total interest paid ($410.55) using the Merchant's Rule are each less than the final payment ($944.03) and the total interest paid ($469.03) using the United States Rule. Using the Merchant's Rule results in lower interest and a smaller final payment than using the United States Rule.

DO EXERCISE 4.

4. Nancy Farmer borrowed $2000 on March 5, 1987, for one year at 11%. The following payments were made: $350 on July 17; $560 on October 25; and $450 on January 3, 1988. How much was due on March 5, 1988 (assume a 360-day year and remember 1988 is a leap year)?

ANSWER ON PAGE A-11

5. Sue Feche borrowed $4500 on January 12, 1986 for two years at 13%. The following payments were made: $800 on March 15, 1986; $1000 on October 1, 1986; and $1800 on April 2, 1987. How much was due on January 12, 1988 (assume a 365-day year)?

ANSWER ON PAGE A-11

Example 5 shows how payments are applied using a 365-day year.

Example 5 Lu Garrison borrowed $3200 on April 15, 1985, for two years at 15%. The following payments were made: $500 on July 2, 1985; $300 on December 14, 1985; and $200 on March 23, 1986. How much was due on April 15, 1987?

Solution The following table shows how each payment was applied to the principal.

Payment Number	Payment Date	Amount	Days to Due Date	Interest on Payment to Due Date	Payment + Interest	New Balance
	April 15, 1985					$4160
1	July 2, 1985	$500.00	652	$133.97	$633.97	$3526.03
2	December 14, 1985	$300.00	487	$60.04	$360.04	$3165.99
3	March 23, 1986	$200.00	388	$31.89	$231.89	$2934.10
4	April 15, 1987	$2934.10				0

The amount due on April 15, 1987, is $2934.10.

DO EXERCISE 5.

- • Use the United States Rule when applying partial payments.

Complete the table for a $5000 two-year loan made July 2, 1985, at 14% (assume a 360-day year).

Payment Number	Payment Date	Amount	Days	Interest to Payment Date	Principal Payment	Balance Owed After Payment
	July 2, 1985					$5000.00
1. 1	December 1, 1985	$450.00				
2. 2	October 5, 1986	$240.00				
3. 3	January 12, 1987	$960.00				
4. 4	July 2, 1987					

5. ▦ Jan Seitz borrows $5000 on March 1, 1988, for two years at 14%. The following payments are made: $600 on June 2, 1988; $350 on February 7, 1989; and $1500 on October 13, 1989. How much is due on March 1, 1990 (assume a 360-day year)?

6. Sam Shaw borrows $6000 on June 3, 1986, for two years at 15%. The following payments are made: $700 on October 3, 1988; $200 on April 7, 1989; and $2500 on February 1, 1990. How much is due on June 3, 1990 (assume a 360-day year)?

Complete the table for a $4000 one-year loan made May 1, 1988, at 11% (assume a 365-day year).

Payment Number	Payment Date	Amount	Days	Interest to Payment Date	Principal Payment	Balance Owed After Payment
	May 1, 1988					$4000.00
7. 1	August 2, 1988	$100.00				
8. 2	November 30, 1988	$700.00				
9. 3	February 4, 1989	$50.00				
10. 4	May 1, 1989					

11. ▦ Upon graduation on May 31, 1988, Jamie Simpson borrowed $9000 for two years at 11%. The following payments were made: $400 on December 5, 1988, and $6000 on August 1, 1989. How much was due on May 31, 1990 (assume a 365-day year)?

12. Estin Enterprises borrowed $7500 on July 7, 1988, for two years at 12%. The following payments were made: $300 on February 10, 1989, and $5000 on May 3, 1990. How much was due on July 7, 1990 (assume a 365-day year)?

5. _____

6. _____

11. _____

12. _____

•• Use the Merchant's Rule when applying partial payments.

Complete the table for a $5000 two-year loan made July 2, 1985, at 14% (assume a 360-day year).

	Payment Number	Payment Date	Amount	Days to Due Date	Interest on Payment to Due Date	Payment + Interest	New Balance
13.		July 2, 1985					
14.	1	December 1, 1985	$450.00				
15.	2	October 5, 1986	$240.00				
16.	3	January 12, 1987	$960.00				
17.	4	July 2, 1987					

18. Daryl Springle borrows $4500 on March 5, 1986, for one year at 15%. The following payments are made: $600 on October 13; $1500 on February 3, 1987; and $700 on February 26, 1987. How much is due on March 5, 1987 (assume a 360-day year)?

19. ▦ Joan Lunden borrows $3200 on April 11, 1986, for one year at 11%. The following payments are made: $1000 on July 5; $950 on November 3; and $700 on February 12, 1987. How much is due on April 11, 1987 (assume a 360-day year)?

Complete the table for a $4000 11% loan made May 1, 1988, payable over one year (assume a 365-day year).

	Payment Number	Payment Date	Amount	Days to Due Date	Interest on Payment to Due Date	Payment + Interest	New Balance
20.		May 1, 1988					
21.	1	August 2, 1988	$100.00				
22.	2	November 30, 1988	$700.00				
23.	3	February 4, 1989	$50.00				
24.	4	May 1, 1989					

25. ▦ Upon graduation on May 31, 1988, Tonya James borrowed $9000 for two years at 11%. The following payments were made: $400 on December 5, 1988, and $6000 on August 1, 1989. How much was due on May 31, 1990 (assume a 365-day year)?

26. Elko Enterprises borrowed $7500 on July 7, 1988, for two years at 12%. The following payments were made: $300 on February 10, 1989, and $5000 on May 3, 1990. How much was due on July 7, 1990 (assume a 365-day year)?

✓ **SKILL MAINTENANCE**

Divide. Simplify, if possible.

27. $\dfrac{3}{5} \div \dfrac{3}{4}$

28. $\dfrac{6}{7} \div \dfrac{3}{5}$

29. $\dfrac{9}{8} \div \dfrac{1}{3}$

30. $\dfrac{10}{9} \div \dfrac{1}{2}$

5.3

Annuities

Equal payments over time are **annuities.** Examples include equal deposits into savings over a period of time or periodic payments from an insurance company after retirement.

• ORDINARY ANNUITIES

An annuity in which payments are made at the end of a time period is an **ordinary annuity.** The following figure shows an ordinary annuity situation where $1.00 is deposited at the end of each of three years in an account paying 12% interest compounded annually. The solid line represents the interest earning period.

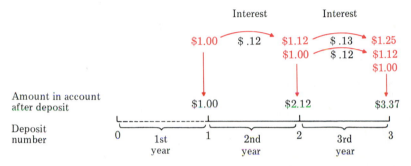

Note that after three yearly $1.00 deposits earning 12% compounded annually the total amount in the account is $3.37. The first $1.00 deposit earns $0.25 interest in two years, the second $1.00 deposit earns $0.12 in one year, and the third $1.00 deposit earns no interest although it is included in the total amount.

An ordinary annuity table may also be used to find how much will be in the account after three payments. Part of the ordinary annuity table (Table 10, p. T-11) appears at right.

	$S_{\overline{n}|i}$ Amount of Annuity	
n	Rate 11%	Rate 12%
1	1.00000000	1.00000000
2	2.11000000	2.12000000
3	3.34210000	3.37440000
4	4.70973100	4.77932800
5	6.22780141	6.35284736
6	7.91285957	8.11518904
7	9.78327412	10.08901173
8	11.85943427	12.29969314
9	14.16397204	14.77565631
10	16.72200896	17.54873507

$S_{\overline{n}|i}$ is the amount accumulated after n $1.00 payments at i% interest for each payment period. In this problem we want to find $S_{3|12}$.

Read down the n column to 3 and across that row to the 12% column. The answer is $3.37 (rounded) as before.

DO EXERCISES 1–3.

O B J E C T I V E S

After finishing Section 5.3, you should be able to:

•	**Find the accumulated amount in an ordinary annuity.**
• •	**Find the accumulated amount in an annuity due.**
• • •	**Find the accumulated amount in an IRA account.**
::	**Find the accumulated amount in a Keogh account.**

Find the amount accumulated after n $1.00 payments at 12% interest for each payment period. The n value is

1. 5

2. 6

3. 9

ANSWERS ON PAGE A-11

For regular deposits of $P the total accumulation A is

$$A = P \times S_{\overline{n}|i}$$

Example 1 At the end of every quarter you deposit $500 into your credit union account, which pays 12% compounded quarterly. How much is in your account after the 40th payment?

Solution We find $S_{\overline{40}|3}$, $3\% = 12\% \div 4$

Read down the n column of Table 10 (p. T-11) to 40 and across that row to the 3% column.

$$S_{\overline{40}|3} = 75.40125973$$

We substitute $500 for P and 75.40125973 for $S_{\overline{40}|3}$ in

$$A = P \times S_{\overline{40}|3}$$
$$= \$500 \times 75.40125973$$
$$= \$37,700.63.$$

The accumulated amount is $37,700.63. Note that a total of $20,000 was deposited. The rest, $17,700.63, is interest.

DO EXERCISE 4.

•• ANNUITIES DUE

An annuity in which payments are made at the beginning of a time period is an **annuity due.** The following figure shows an annuity due situation where $1.00 is deposited at the beginning of each of three years in an account paying 12% interest compounded annually. The solid line represents the interest earning period.

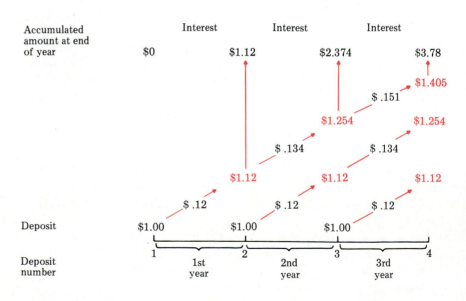

Note that at the end of the year in which the third $1.00 deposit was made the accumulated amount was $3.78. The first $1.00 deposit grows to $1.12 after one year, $1.254 after two years, and $1.405 after three years. Similarly the other two $1.00 deposits grow to $1.254 and $1.12. The total amount does not include any deposit made at the beginning of the fourth year.

Even though this is an annuity due situation, an ordinary annuity table (Table 10, p. T-11) may be used to find the accumulated amount at the end of the third year. To do this:

We add 1 to n.

n is 3 so $n + 1$ is 4

We find $S_{\overline{4}|12}$.

$S_{\overline{4}|12} = 4.77932800$

We subtract 1 and round.

$4.77932800 - 1 = 3.78$

The answer is $3.78 (rounded) as before.

Notice 4.77932800 is the accumulated amount immediately after the fourth deposit. When we subtract 1 (the fourth deposit) we get the amount immediately before the fourth deposit, that is, the amount at the end of three years.

DO EXERCISES 5–7.

For regular deposits of P in an annuity due situation the total accumulation A is

$$A = P \times (S_{\overline{n+1}|i} - 1)$$

Example 2 You deposit $500 at the beginning of every quarter into your credit union account, which pays 12% compounded quarterly. How much is in your account at the end of the 40th quarter, that is, immediately before the 41st payment?

Solution We add 1 to n.

n is 40 so $n + 1$ is 41

We find $S_{\overline{41}|3}$. $3\% = 12\% \div 4$ Use Table 10, p. T-11.

$S_{\overline{41}|3} = 78.66329753$

We subtract 1 and round.

$78.66329753 - 1 = 77.6633$

We find A by substituting $500 for P and 77.6633 for $(S_{\overline{n+1}|i} - 1)$ in

$A = P \times (S_{\overline{n+1}|i} - 1)$

$= \$500 \times 77.6633$

$= \$38,831.65.$

The accumulated amount is $38,831.65.

DO EXERCISE 8.

Find the accumulated amount at the end of the nth year where $1.00 deposits are made at the beginning of each year in an account paying 12% compounded yearly. The n value is

5. 5

6. 6

7. 9

8. Mark Pabst deposits $700 at the beginning of every quarter into his credit union account, which pays 11% compounded quarterly. How much is in his account at the end of the 30th quarter?

ANSWERS ON PAGE A-11

Calculate the decrease in federal income tax for a $2000 IRA deposit for those in the

9. 30% tax bracket.

10. 50% tax bracket.

11. 47% tax bracket.

Calculate the total amount paid to the federal government for early withdrawal of $50,000 from an IRA for someone in the

12. 50% tax bracket.

13. 35% tax bracket.

14. 45% tax bracket.

ANSWERS ON PAGE A-11

Many individuals regularly invest some of their current income on a tax deferred basis in **Individual Retirement Accounts** and **Keogh Plans.** Because taxes are not paid on this money, such plans exemplify what are called **tax shelters.** The tax is due when this money and the earnings from it are paid (usually during retirement).

••• INDIVIDUAL RETIREMENT ACCOUNTS*

An Individual Retirement Account (IRA) is an example of an annuity. A deposit made into an IRA may be deducted from gross income, thereby reducing current federal income tax. For example, a $2000 IRA deposit will decrease current federal income taxes $800 for those in the 40% tax bracket. (40% of $2000 is $800).

DO EXERCISES 9–11.

In effect no current federal income taxes are paid on IRA deposits (nor the income earned on the deposits) until the money is withdrawn after age $59\frac{1}{2}$. Then the money is taxed at ordinary income tax rates. If money is withdrawn prior to age $59\frac{1}{2}$, the total amount withdrawn is taxed in the year in which it is received, and there is also a 10% penalty. For example, if you withdraw $20,000 from your IRA account at age 50 and are in the 40% tax bracket, you pay the federal government

$8000	Tax (40% of $20,000)
$2000	Penalty (10% of $20,000)
$10,000	Total paid to the federal government.

DO EXERCISES 12–14.

The Dreyfus IRA is one example of an IRA.

The Dreyfus IRA

IRAs are now for everyone—and Dreyfus does it all for you!

How Dreyfus can help you take full advantage of the new, liberalized tax law provisions on Individual Retirement Accounts:

It is now possible for you to open an IRA of your own, even though you may be covered under tax-qualified plans (including Keogh plans), government plans or certain annuities.

An IRA is a hedge against inflation.

Accumulating money for your future is a serious business. More and more, the responsibility of providing for the future is in your own hands.

The IRA provides a way for you to save in a tax-favored environment. What is equally important is where to invest these dollars for maximum growth and protection from inflation.

The maximum annual IRA contribution has been raised to $2,000. An IRA is tax deductible and its earnings are tax deferred. The tax savings are substantial: $2,000 put into an IRA is completely free of Federal tax. If a husband and wife both work and each contributes $2,000, the joint deduction from taxable income is $4,000.

If your spouse is not employed, a separate IRA may still be opened and between the two plans you may contribute and deduct 100% of income up to $2,250.

The compounding of interest, dividends or gains tax deferred in an IRA plan can really add up. Even if you only put in small amounts now, the amount you can accumulate over time, because of compounding, becomes very significant. For example, if your overall average return is 12%, your money will double in 6 years. If the overall return is higher your money grows even faster. Here's what you would accumulate toward retirement at only 12% after various periods of time, compounded annually:

$2,000 a year in an IRA Plan Hypothethical 12% Return	
After	Amount in Plan
5 years	$ 14,230
10	39,309
15	83,506
20	161,397
25	298,668
30	540,585
40	1,718,284

Note: If both you and your spouse work, each may open an IRA providing up to $4,000 annual deduction. After 20 years, earning 12%, you and your spouse could have a total nest egg of $322,794.94. And this can be done, even if you or your spouse works part-time.

If you work part-time, you can contribute the $2,000 maximum.

This example is calculated on a fixed interest rate compounded annually and assumes no fluctuation in the value of the principal. While no return is guaranteed, the 12% rate was chosen for illustrative purposes.

* Proposed tax laws may change some information in this section.

Let's see how you may become a millionaire after 40 years by investing in the Dreyfus IRA.

Example 3 How much is the accumulated amount in the Dreyfus IRA at the end of the 40th year if $2000 is invested at the beginning of each year at 12% compounded annually?

Solution This is an annuity due situation as payments are at the beginning of each year (not clear from the ad).

We add 1 to n.

n is 40 so $n + 1$ is 41

We find $S_{\overline{41}|12}$.

$S_{\overline{41}|12} = 860.14239079$ (Table 10, p. T-11)

We subtract 1 and round.

$860.14239079 - 1 = 859.142$

We find A by substituting $2000 for P and 859.142 for $(S_{\overline{(n+1)}|i} - 1)$ in

$A = P \times (S_{\overline{(n+1)}|i} - 1)$

$ = \$2000 \times 859.142$

$ = \$1,718,284.$

At the end of 40 years your accumulated amount is $1,718,284.

DO EXERCISE 15.

Amounts contributed regularly at the end of a year (ordinary annuity) will result in a smaller accumulated amount. Financial institutions use annuity due situations when advertising IRAs because the results look better.

15. How much is the accumulated amount in the Dreyfus IRA at the end of the 30th year if $2000 is invested at the beginning of each year at 12% compounded annually?

ANSWER ON PAGE A-11

State the maximum amount you may contribute annually to your Keogh Plan if you are self-employed and have earned income of

16. $80,000

17. $60,000

18. $120,000

How much will a $12,000 deposit in a Keogh Plan reduce current federal income taxes for a person in the

19. 48% tax bracket?

20. 50% tax bracket?

21. 30% tax bracket?

22. How much is the accumulated amount in a Keogh Plan after the 30th annual end-of-year payment of $4000 into a 11% compounded annually account?

ANSWERS ON PAGE A-11

KEOGH PLAN*

Self-employed individuals are eligible to contribute the lesser of $30,000 or 25% of annual earned income on a tax deferred basis into a Keogh Plan for retirement. For example, if your income from self-employment is $56,000, you may contribute $14,000 (25% of $56,000) on a tax deferred basis into a Keogh Plan for retirement.

DO EXERCISES 16–18.

As with an IRA a deposit in a Keogh Plan may be deducted from gross income, thereby reducing current federal income taxes. For example, a $14,000 Keogh Plan deposit will decrease federal income taxes $5600 for those in the 40% tax bracket (40% of $14,000 is $5600).

DO EXERCISES 19–21.

At retirement, periodic payments from a Keogh Plan are taxed as ordinary income. However, a participant may select a lump-sum withdrawal which is subject to a 10-year income averaging method.

Example 4 How much is the accumulated amount in Sara Ott's Keogh Plan after the 20th annual end-of-year payment of $6000 into her 12% compounded annually account?

Solution This is an ordinary annuity situation as payments are made at the end of the year.

We find $S_{\overline{20}|12}$.

$$S_{\overline{20}|12} = 72.05244244$$

We substitute $6000 for P and 72.05244244 for $S_{\overline{20}|12}$ in

$$A = P \times S_{\overline{20}|12}$$
$$= \$6000 \times 72.05244244$$
$$= \$432,314.65.$$

The accumulated amount is $432,314.65.

DO EXERCISE 22.

---

* Proposed tax laws may change some information in this section.

Use Table 10 (p. T-11) for this exercise set.

| • Find the accumulated amount immediately after the last payment. Assume each payment occurs at the end of a period.

	Amount of Each Payment	Payment and Compounding Period	Rate	Number of Payments
1.	$1.00	Annually	14%	10
2.	$1.00	Annually	7%	25
3.	$100	Semiannually	6%	20
4.	$100	Semiannually	14%	50
5.	$50	Monthly	12%	48
6.	$125	Monthly	12%	30

7. Your parents loan you $120 at the end of each of the 48 months you attend college. The interest rate is 12% compounded monthly. How much do you owe them immediately after the 48th payment?

8. Your parents loan you $75 at the end of each of the 48 months you attend college. The interest rate is 12% compounded monthly. How much do you owe them immediately after the 48th payment?

| •• Find the accumulated amount at the end of the last payment period. Assume each payment occurs at the beginning of the period.

	Amount of Each Payment	Payment and Compounding Period	Rate	Number of Payments
9.	$100	Semiannually	14%	20
10.	$100	Semiannually	$5\frac{1}{2}$%	40
11.	$200	Annually	14%	10
12.	$200	Annually	7%	20
13.	$125	Monthly	12%	30
14.	$125	Monthly	15%	30

15. David Mortimer deposits $1200 at the beginning of every six months in his savings account, which pays 14% compounded semiannually. How much is in his account at the end of 10 years?

16. Lisa Mracek deposits $900 at the beginning of every six months in her savings account, which pays 6% compounded semiannually. How much is in her account at the end of 15 years?

ANSWERS

1. _____
2. _____
3. _____
4. _____
5. _____
6. _____
7. _____
8. _____
9. _____
10. _____
11. _____
12. _____
13. _____
14. _____
15. _____
16. _____

ANSWERS

17. _____

18. _____

19. _____

20. _____

21. _____

22. _____

23. _____

24. _____

25. _____

26. _____

27. _____

28. _____

29. _____

30. _____

31. _____

32. _____

33. _____

34. _____

••• Use Table 10 (p. T-11) for these exercises.

For each find the equity (accumulated amount) immediately before your 65th birthday. Assume deposits are made on the day you reach each age and the interest rate is 12% compounded annually. Round to the nearest dollar.

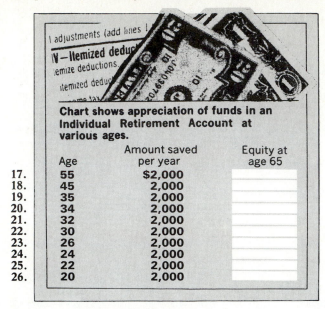

Chart shows appreciation of funds in an Individual Retirement Account at various ages.

	Age	Amount saved per year	Equity at age 65
17.	55	$2,000	
18.	45	2,000	
19.	35	2,000	
20.	34	2,000	
21.	32	2,000	
22.	30	2,000	
23.	26	2,000	
24.	24	2,000	
25.	22	2,000	
26.	20	2,000	

27. What is the accumulated amount in an IRA immediately after the 30th payment if $1300 is invested at the end of each year at 7% compounded annually?

28. What is the accumulated amount in an IRA immediately after the 25th payment if $1400 is invested at the end of each year at 11% compounded annually?

29. Joe Schmidt deposited $15,000 at the end of each of five successive years into a Keogh Plan paying 14% compounded annually. What is the accumulated amount immediately after the fifth payment?

30. Monica Lange deposited $8,000 at the end of each of five successive years into a Keogh Plan paying 7% compounded annually. What is the accumulated amount immediately after the fifth payment?

31. You deposit $500 at the end of each month into a Keogh Plan paying 12% compounded monthly. What is the accumulated amount immediately after the 36th payment?

32. You deposit $200 at the end of each month into a Keogh Plan paying 12% compounded monthly. What is the accumulated amount immediately after the 36th payment?

✔ **SKILL MAINTENANCE**

Complete the deposit slips.

33.

CASH	CURRENCY	458	00
	COIN	3	67
LIST CHECKS SINGLY			
TOTAL FROM OTHER SIDE		42	76
TOTAL		504	43
LESS CASH RECEIVED		35	50
NET DEPOSIT			

34.

CASH	CURRENCY	675	00
	COIN	12	58
LIST CHECKS SINGLY			
16-37		85	47
TOTAL FROM OTHER SIDE			
TOTAL		773	05
LESS CASH RECEIVED			
NET DEPOSIT		727	30

5.4

Present Value of an Annuity

Suppose we want to know how much we must invest now at 12% compounded annually so that a certain amount will be paid to us for each of the next five years with no money left over after the 5th payment. This is a present value of an annuity problem. The ***present value of an annuity*** is the sum of the present value of each of the payments. Present value of annuity problems will be studied in this section.

O B J E C T I V E S

After finishing Section 5.4, you should be able to:

| • | **Solve present value of ordinary annuity problems.** |
| • • | **Solve present value of annuity due problems.** |

• PRESENT VALUE OF AN ORDINARY ANNUITY

The present value of an ordinary annuity situation arises when a certain amount invested now results in equal payments at the end of a series of equal time periods. The following figure shows the present value of an ordinary annuity situation where a certain amount invested now at 12% compounded annually results in $1.00 payments at the end of the first and second years with no money left over after the second payment.

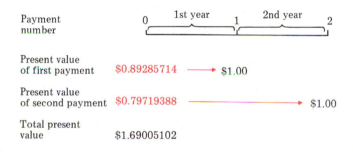

From the figure we see that

$0.79719388 grows to $1.00 at the end of two years.

This follows when we substitute $1.00 for A, 0.12 for i, and 2 for n in

$$A = P(1 + i)^n \qquad \text{Compound Interest Formula}$$
$$\$1.00 = P(1 + 0.12)^2$$
$$\$1.00 = P(1.12)^2$$
$$\$1.00 = P(1.2544)$$
$$0.79719388 = P \qquad \text{Dividing on both sides by 1.2544}$$

Likewise $0.89285714 grows to $1.00 at the end of one year. To find the total investment now we add

$$
\begin{array}{r}
0.79719388 \\
0.89285714 \\
\hline
1.69005102
\end{array}
$$

An investment of a little over $1.69 now at 12% compounded annually will permit annual payments of $1.00 each for the next two years.

A present value of an ordinary annuity table (Table 11, p. T-12) may also be used to solve this problem. Part of that table is shown below.

	$A_{\overline{n}|i}$ Present Value of Annuity	
n	Rate 11%	Rate 12%
1	0.90090090	0.89285714
2	1.71252333	1.69005102
3	2.44371472	2.40183127
4	3.10244569	3.03734935
5	3.69589702	3.60477620
6	4.23053785	4.11140732
7	4.71219626	4.56375654
8	5.14612276	4.96763977
9	5.53704753	5.32824979
10	5.88923201	5.65022303
11	6.20651533	5.93769913
12	6.49235615	6.19437423

$A_{\overline{n}|i}$ is the amount that must be invested now at $i\%$ per payment period so n $1.00 payments (withdrawals) are possible.

Example 1 How much money must be invested now at 12% compounded annually so that $1.00 may be withdrawn at the end of each of the next two years with no money left over after the second payment?

Solution In this problem we find $A_{\overline{2}|12}$.

a) Find the 12% column.

b) Find 2 in the n column.

c) The row containing 2 and the 12% column meet at 1.69005102.

The answer is $1.69005102 as before.

DO EXERCISES 1–3.

For regular withdrawals of P, the total amount A that must be invested now is

$$A = P \times A_{\overline{n}|i}$$

Example 2 You need $5000 at the end of each of the next four years. To do this, how much must be invested now at 12% compounded annually?

Solution We find $A_{\overline{4}|12}$.

$$A_{\overline{4}|12} = 3.03734935$$

We find A by substituting $5000 for P and 3.03734935 for $A_{\overline{4}|12}$ in

$$A = P \times A_{\overline{4}|12}$$
$$= \$5000 \times 3.03734935$$
$$= \$15,186.75.$$

If $15,186.75 is invested now at 12% compounded annually, we may withdraw $5000 for each of the next four years.

DO EXERCISE 4.

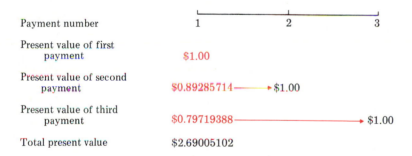

●● PRESENT VALUE OF AN ANNUITY DUE

For present value of annuity due situations, equal withdrawals start immediately and continue at the beginning of each subsequent time period. The following figure shows a present value of an annuity due situation where a certain amount invested now at 12% compounded annually results in $1.00 payments now and at the beginning of each of the next two years with no money left over after the third payment.

Payment number	1	2	3
Present value of first payment	$1.00		
Present value of second payment	$0.89285714 ⟶ $1.00		
Present value of third payment	$0.79719388 ⟶ $1.00		
Total present value	$2.69005102		

An investment now of a little over $2.69 at 12% compounded annually will permit an immediate $1.00 withdrawal as well as $1.00 withdrawals at the beginning of each of the next two years. Even though this is a present value of an annuity due situation, the present value of an ordinary annuity table (Table 11, p. T-12) may be used to solve it. To do this

We subtract 1 from n. n is 3 so $n - 1$ is 2.
We find $A_{\overline{2}|12}$. $A_{\overline{2}|12} = 1.69005102$.
We add 1. $1.69005102 + 1 = 2.69005102$.

The answer is $2.69005102 as before.

DO EXERCISES 5–7.

4. Cheri Steon needs $3000 at the end of each of the next five years. To do this how much must be invested now at 12% compounded annually?

How much must be invested now at 12% compounded annually to receive n $1.00 payments starting today? The value of n is

5. 5

6. 7

7. 10

ANSWERS ON PAGE A-11

8. How much must Jon Stolee invest today at 12% compounded monthly to meet his next 12 monthly $230 car payments, the first of which is due now?

In present value of annuity due situations where equal withdrawals of $P start immediately, the amount A that must be invested now is

$$A = P \times (A_{\overline{n-1}|i} + 1)$$

Example 3 You will travel overseas for the next year. How much should you now invest at 12% compounded monthly to meet your next twelve $620 monthly house payments, where the first payment is due today?

Solution We subtract 1 from n. n is 12 so $n - 1$ is 11.

Find $A_{\overline{11}|1}$.   1% = 12% ÷ 12

$A_{\overline{11}|1} = 10.36762825$ Table 11, p. T-12

Add 1 to $A_{\overline{11}|1}$.   10.36762825 + 1 = 11.36762825

To find A we substitute $620 for P and 11.36762825 for $(A_{\overline{n-1}|i} + 1)$ in

$A = P \times (A_{\overline{n-1}|i} + 1)$

    = $620 × 11.36762825

    = $7047.93.

If $7047.93 is invested today, your next twelve $620 house payments can be made.

DO EXERCISE 8.

ANSWERS ON PAGE A-11

Chapter 5   Loans and Annuities

Use Table 11 (p. T-12) for these exercises.

• Solve.

ANSWERS

1. When you retire you plan to buy an annuity which pays you $14,000 at the end of each of 10 years. How much should you pay for the annuity if interest is 11% compounded annually?

2. When you retire you plan to buy an annuity which pays you $9000 at the end of each of 15 years. How much should you pay for the annuity if interest is 11% compounded annually?

3. Wendy Sargent is the winner in a sweepstakes that pays $20,000 at the end of each of the next 10 years. Contest rules require the sponsor to deposit the money now. How much does the sponsor need to deposit now at 12% compounded annually?

4. You are the winner in a sweepstakes that pays you $15,000 at the end of each of the next 20 years. Contest rules require the sponsor to deposit the money now. How much does the sponsor need to deposit now at 11% compounded annually?

5. The highway commission buys some of your land. For tax purposes you want $7000 payments at the end of each of the next five years. How much should the highway commission deposit now at 7% compounded annually to meet this obligation?

6. The highway commission buys some of your land. For tax purposes you want $10,000 payments at the end of each of the next four years. How much should the highway commission deposit now at 12% compounded annually to meet this obligation?

7. Ed Sarobel must pay a neighbor $175 at the end of each of the next 12 months. How much should Ed deposit now at 12% compounded monthly to meet this obligation?

8. Ruth Skjeie must pay a neighbor $500 at the end of each of the next 20 months. How much should Ruth deposit now at 12% compounded monthly to meet this obligation?

9. Santo's Cars tells you the monthly payments for a Rolls-Royce car are $2593.88 for 48 months at 12% compounded monthly. How much does the Roll's Royce cost? Round to the nearest dollar.

10. Santo's Cars tells you the monthly payments for a Rolls-Royce car are $2093.54 for 48 months at 12% compounded monthly. How much does the Rolls-Royce cost? Round to the nearest dollar.

'83 Rolls-Royce Corniche Convertible. Silver sand over nutmeg. 1 owner. Bought new for '84. Balance of factory warranty until 4/87.

Rolls-Royce Corniche Convertible. Ivory with tan top and int. 1 yr. unlimited mileage warranty.

11. Your property taxes are $635 semiannually. How much should you invest now at 12% compounded semiannually to pay the next two installments?

12. Susan Thomson's property taxes are $430 semiannually. How much should Susan invest now at 12% compounded semiannually to pay the next two installments?

1. _____
2. _____
3. _____
4. _____
5. _____
6. _____
7. _____
8. _____
9. _____
10. _____
11. _____
12. _____

•• Solve.

How much must Cynthia Senne invest now at the given rate to make these withdrawals beginning immediately?

	Each Withdrawal	Number of Withdrawals	Withdrawal and Rate Period	Rate
13.	$8000	5	Annually	12%
14.	$5000	4	Annually	14%
15.	$3000	20	Semiannually	14%
16.	$1200	25	Semiannually	14%
17.	$1500	20	Quarterly	11%
18.	$1800	24	Quarterly	12%
19.	$700	36	Monthly	12%
20.	$950	24	Monthly	12%

21. Your parents plan to give you $5000 at the start of each of the next four years for college expenses. How much must they invest today at 14% compounded annually so payments may start immediately?

22. Your parents plan to give you $3000 at the start of each of the next four years for college expenses. How much must they invest today at 12% compounded annually so payments may start immediately?

23. Your estimated federal income taxes are $3500 each quarter to be paid at the beginning of each of the next four quarters starting with the first payment now. How much must you invest today at 11% compounded quarterly to meet this obligation?

24. Melinda Sally's estimated federal income taxes are $900 each quarter to be paid at the beginning of each of the next four quarters starting with the first payment now. How much must she invest today at 12% compounded quarterly to meet this obligation?

25. You are on a budget balancing account with the utility company so that each monthly bill is $110. How much must you invest today at 12% compounded monthly to meet this obligation for the next 12 months, where the first payment is due today?

26. Tim Rusk is on a budget balancing account with the utility company so that each monthly bill is $90. How much must he invest today at 12% compounded monthly to meet this obligation for the next 12 months, where the first payment is due today?

27. Starting immediately, an insurance company must pay $200 at the beginning of each of the next 48 months to a claimant on disability. How much should the insurance company invest today at 12% compounded monthly to meet this obligation?

28. Starting immediately, Merrill Insurance Company must pay $300 at the beginning of each of the next 36 months to a claimant on disability. How much should Merrill Insurance Company invest today at 12% compounded monthly to meet this obligation?

✓ SKILL MAINTENANCE

29. Faribault Thrift pays 12% compounded quarterly. Find the amount and interest on $1000 after three quarters.

30. Brenton Savings pays 8% compounded semiannually. How much interest would be earned on $900 for one year?

NAME: _____

CLASS/SECTION: _____ DATE: _____

If you miss an item, review the indicated section and objective.

ANSWERS

[5.1, •] **1.** Find the interest due at the end of nine months on a 14% $750 note.

1. _____

[5.1, • •] **2.** Find the due date on a 120-day noninterest-bearing note dated May 7.

2. _____

[5.1, • • •] **3.** A six-month note to Alice Ludley for $4200 was discounted at 11%. What were the discount and proceeds?

3. _____

[5.2, •] **4.** Use the United States Rule to find the amount due at maturity on a 12%, three-month, $2000 note dated May 21, if partial payments of $450 and $370 were made on July 28 and August 2, respectively. (Assume a 365-day year.)

4. _____

[5.2, • •] **5.** Use the Merchant's Rule to find the amount due at maturity on a 12%, three-month, $2000 note dated May 21, if partial payments of $450 and $370 were made on July 28 and August 2, respectively. (Assume a 365-day year.)

5. _____

Use Table 10 (p. T-11) for 6–9.

[5.3, •] **6.** Janice Kelly deposits $150 at the end of every month into her savings account which pays 12% compounded monthly. How much is in her account after the 48th payment?

6. _____

[5.3, ●●] **7.** Julie Lewis deposits $120 at the beginning of each month in a savings account paying 12% compounded monthly. How much is in her account at the end of the 18th month?

[5.3, ●●●] **8.** How much is the accumulated amount in Alana Moss's IRA at the end of the 40th year if $2000 is invested at the beginning of each year at 11% compounded annually?

[5.3, ⦂⦂] **9.** How much is the accumulated amount in a Keogh Plan after the 15th annual end-of-year payment of $2500 into a 7% compounded annually account?

Use Table 11 (p. T-12) for 10–12.

[5.4, ●] **10.** You plan to give your parents $3500 at the end of each of the next four years. To do this how much must be invested now at 12% compounded annually?

[5.4, ●] **11.** Letcher's Snowmobiles tells you the monthly payments for a snowmobile are only $98.23 at the end of each of the next 36 months at 12% compounded monthly. How much does the snowmobile cost? Round to the nearest dollar.

[5.4, ●●] **12.** Your parents plan to give you $8000 at the start of each of the next five years for your new business. How much must they invest today at 14% compounded annually so payments may start immediately?

6

INSTALLMENT AND CONSUMER CREDIT

CAREER: BUSINESS CONSULTANT
This is Henry Taylor. Henry took a Business Math course while studying for a BS degree in Business Education at Indiana Central University. He also received an MA in Economics.

HENRY M. TAYLOR

Henry is presently Executive Director of the Indianapolis Business Development Foundation, a not-for-profit organization. The purpose of this organization is to help new minority enterprises get started and to assist them in their development, as well as to help existing minority firms grow. Some of these firms together now gross over $80 million annually.

In Henry's role as a business consultant, he must frequently decide whether a business is capable of paying off a loan. He also advises businesses regarding the advisability of granting credit to potential customers. Of the other subjects covered in this book, ratio and percent, interest and statistics are also relevant to Henry's work. For example, the ratio of a company's assets to liabilities may be used in financial planning and loan decisions. People who are successful in Henry's type of work usually earn from $30,000 to $80,000 annually.

Henry's hobbies include gardening, music, and art.

After finishing Section 6.1, you should be able to:

- **⊙** **Determine finance charges.**
- **⊙ ⊙** **Use a table to find the APR.**
- **⊙ ⊙ ⊙** **Calculate APR using a formula.**

1. Diego borrowed $4000 for 36 months from University Bank. His monthly payment will be $129.53. Find the finance charge.

ANSWER ON PAGE A-12

The Annual Percentage Rate (APR)

Intelligent buying requires not only an awareness of product quality but also a good knowledge of borrowing costs. In this chapter we study consumer financing of purchases so you will have the necessary information for intelligent buying.

⊙ FINANCE CHARGE

The federal Truth-in-Lending Law requires all lenders to state

1. the finance charge, and
2. the **annual percentage rate** (**APR**).

Consumers use this information to tell how much loans actually cost.

Example 1 Cecile borrowed $2000 from University Bank to buy a car. Her monthly payment will be $92.52 for 24 months. Find the finance charge.

Solution

$$\frac{\text{Finance}}{\text{charge}} = \frac{\text{Number}}{\text{of payments}} \times \frac{\text{Monthly}}{\text{payment}} - \frac{\text{Amount}}{\text{of loan}}$$

$$= (24 \times \$92.52) - \$2000$$

$$= \$2220.48 - \$2000 = \$220.48$$

The finance charge was $220.48.

DO EXERCISE 1.

⊙ ⊙ FINDING THE ANNUAL PERCENTAGE RATE

The *APR* is the effective interest rate paid when you borrow money.

Let's consider two loans, Loan A and Loan B.

Loan A Jane Richardson borrowed $100 for one year. At the end of one year she repaid Twin Cities Bank $114 in a single payment.

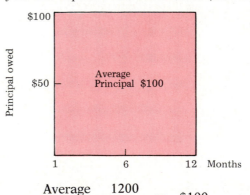

Start of Month	Principal Owed
1	$100
2	$100
3	$100
4	$100
5	$100
6	$100
7	$100
8	$100
9	$100
10	$100
11	$100
12	$100
Sum	**$1200**

$$\frac{\text{Average}}{\text{principal}} = \frac{1200}{12} \quad \text{or} \quad \$100$$

$14.00 interest was paid at the end of one year. To find the rate (APR) substitute 100 for *P*, 1 for *T*, and 14 for *I*.

$$I = P \times R \times T$$

$$14 = 100 \times R \times 1$$

$$R = \frac{14}{100} = 0.14 \qquad \text{The interest rate (APR) is 14\%.}$$

Loan B Stuart Wills borrowed $100 for one year from Twin Cities Bank. He repaid the loan in 12 monthly payments of $9.50.

Start of Month	Principal Owed	Payment Amount	Applied Toward Principal	Applied Toward Interest
1	$100.00	$9.50	$7.42	$2.08
2	$92.58	$9.50	$7.58	$1.92
3	$85.00	$9.50	$7.74	$1.76
4	$77.26	$9.50	$7.90	$1.60
5	$69.36	$9.50	$8.06	$1.44
6	$61.30	$9.50	$8.23	$1.27
7	$53.07	$9.50	$8.40	$1.10
8	$44.67	$9.50	$8.57	$0.93
9	$36.10	$9.50	$8.75	$0.75
10	$27.35	$9.50	$8.93	$0.57
11	$18.42	$9.50	$9.12	$0.38
12	$9.30	$9.50	$9.30	$0.20
Sum	$674.41	$114.00	$100.00	$14.00

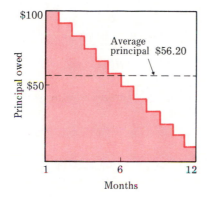

$$\frac{\text{Average}}{\text{principal}} = \frac{\$674.41}{12} \quad \text{or} \quad \$56.20$$

To find the rate (APR) substitute 56.20 for P, 1 for T, and 14 for I.

$$I = P \times R \times T$$
$$14 = 56.20 \times R \times 1$$
$$\frac{14}{56.20} = R$$
$$0.2491 = R$$

The interest rate (APR) is 24.91%.

The interest paid on both loans was $14. However, the effective interest rate was different. Jane had the use of the entire $100 for a whole year. Stuart had the use of the entire $100 for the first month only. Thereafter, he had the use of less than $100 until finally during the last month he had the use of only $9.30.

Note that the entries in the interest column in the preceding table are the result of multiplying the monthly interest rate 2.076% (24.91% ÷ 12) by the principal owed at the beginning of the month. In this chapter you will be able to find the APR (24.91% for Loan B) by using tables or a formula.

2. Find the APR for the $4000 University Bank auto loan payable over 36 months. Use Table 12, p. T-13–T-19.

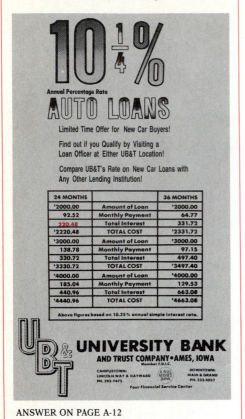

ANSWER ON PAGE A-12

The APR is based on the average principal.

$$\text{Average principal} = \frac{\text{Sum of amount owed each month}}{\text{Total number of payments}}$$

For Loan A the average principal was $100, and the APR was 14%. For Loan B the average principal was $56.20, and the APR was 24.91%.

Table 12 (p. T-13–T-19) contains APR values. Part of that table also appears as Table 6.1.

Example 2 Lee McCue borrowed $2000 from University Bank to buy a Hyundai motor car. The loan is to be repaid over 24 months. Find the APR.

Solution

a) Find the finance charge per $100 of the amount borrowed. From the ad we see the total interest is $220.48.

Total interest ⟶ $\dfrac{220.48}{2000} = \dfrac{x}{100}$ ⟵ Interest on $100

Amount borrowed ⟶ ⟵ $100

$2000x = 100(220.48)$ Cross multiplying.

$x = 11.024$ Dividing both sides by 2000.

b) Find 24 in the column headed Number of Payments in Table 6.1 and read across the row until the value nearest 11.024 is found (11.02 in this example).

c) The rate at the top of the column containing 11.02 is 10.25%. The APR is thus 10.25%.

DO EXERCISE 2.

TABLE 6.1

ANNUAL PERCENTAGE RATE TABLE FOR MONTHLY PAYMENT PLANS

| NUMBER OF PAYMENTS | ANNUAL PERCENTAGE RATE | | | | | | | | | | | | | | | |
	10.00%	10.25%	10.50%	10.75%	11.00%	11.25%	11.50%	11.75%	12.00%	12.25%	12.50%	12.75%	13.00%	13.25%	13.50%	13.75%
	(FINANCE CHARGE PER $100 OF AMOUNT FINANCED)															
1	0.83	0.85	0.87	0.90	0.92	0.94	0.96	0.98	1.00	1.02	1.04	1.06	1.08	1.10	1.12	1.15
2	1.25	1.28	1.31	1.35	1.38	1.41	1.44	1.47	1.50	1.53	1.57	1.60	1.63	1.66	1.69	1.72
3	1.67	1.71	1.76	1.80	1.84	1.88	1.92	1.96	2.01	2.05	2.09	2.13	2.17	2.22	2.26	2.30
4	2.09	2.14	2.20	2.25	2.30	2.35	2.41	2.46	2.51	2.57	2.62	2.67	2.72	2.78	2.83	2.88
5	2.51	2.58	2.64	2.70	2.77	2.83	2.89	2.96	3.02	3.08	3.15	3.21	3.27	3.34	3.40	3.46
6	2.94	3.01	3.08	3.16	3.23	3.31	3.38	3.45	3.53	3.60	3.68	3.75	3.83	3.90	3.97	4.05
7	3.36	3.45	3.53	3.62	3.70	3.78	3.87	3.95	4.04	4.12	4.21	4.29	4.38	4.47	4.55	4.64
8	3.79	3.88	3.98	4.07	4.17	4.26	4.36	4.46	4.55	4.65	4.74	4.84	4.94	5.03	5.13	5.22
9	4.21	4.32	4.43	4.53	4.64	4.75	4.85	4.96	5.07	5.17	5.28	5.39	5.49	5.60	5.71	5.82
10	4.64	4.76	4.88	4.99	5.11	5.23	5.35	5.46	5.58	5.70	5.82	5.94	6.05	6.17	6.29	6.41
11	5.07	5.20	5.33	5.45	5.58	5.71	5.84	5.97	6.10	6.23	6.36	6.49	6.62	6.75	6.88	7.01
12	5.50	5.64	5.78	5.92	6.06	6.20	6.34	6.48	6.62	6.76	6.90	7.04	7.18	7.32	7.46	7.60
13	5.93	6.08	6.23	6.38	6.53	6.68	6.84	6.99	7.14	7.29	7.44	7.59	7.75	7.90	8.05	8.20
14	6.36	6.52	6.69	6.85	7.01	7.17	7.34	7.50	7.66	7.82	7.99	8.15	8.31	8.48	8.64	8.81
15	6.80	6.97	7.14	7.32	7.49	7.66	7.84	8.01	8.19	8.36	8.53	8.71	8.88	9.06	9.23	9.41
16	7.23	7.41	7.60	7.78	7.97	8.15	8.34	8.53	8.71	8.90	9.08	9.27	9.46	9.64	9.83	10.02
17	7.67	7.86	8.06	8.25	8.45	8.65	8.84	9.04	9.24	9.44	9.63	9.83	10.03	10.23	10.43	10.63
18	8.10	8.31	8.52	8.73	8.93	9.14	9.35	9.56	9.77	9.98	10.19	10.40	10.61	10.82	11.03	11.24
19	8.54	8.76	8.98	9.20	9.42	9.64	9.86	10.08	10.30	10.52	10.74	10.96	11.18	11.41	11.63	11.85
20	8.98	9.21	9.44	9.67	9.90	10.13	10.37	10.60	10.83	11.06	11.30	11.53	11.76	12.00	12.23	12.46
21	9.42	9.66	9.90	10.15	10.39	10.63	10.88	11.12	11.36	11.61	11.85	12.10	12.34	12.59	12.84	13.08
22	9.86	10.12	10.37	10.62	10.88	11.13	11.39	11.64	11.90	12.16	12.41	12.67	12.93	13.19	13.44	13.70
23	10.30	10.57	10.84	11.10	11.37	11.63	11.90	12.17	12.44	12.71	12.97	13.24	13.51	13.78	14.05	14.32
24	10.75	11.02	11.30	11.58	11.86	12.14	12.42	12.70	12.98	13.26	13.54	13.82	14.10	14.38	14.66	14.95
25	11.19	11.48	11.77	12.06	12.35	12.64	12.93	13.22	13.52	13.81	14.10	14.40	14.69	14.98	15.28	15.57

Example 3 Find the APR Lana Knox must pay for the Buick loan.

Solution

a) Find the amount financed.

$$\underset{\substack{\text{Cash}\\\text{price}}}{\$3348} - \underset{\substack{\text{Down}\\\text{payment}}}{\$348} = \underset{\substack{\text{Amount}\\\text{financed}}}{\$3000}$$

b) Find the total of all payments.

$$\$87.68 \times 42 = \$3682.56$$

c) Find the finance charge.

$$\$3682.56 - \$3000 = \$682.56$$

d) Find the finance charge per $100.

$$\frac{682.56}{3000} = \frac{x}{100}$$

$3000x = 100(682.56)$ Cross multiplying.

$x = 22.752$ Dividing both sides by 3000.

e) Find 42 in the column headed Number of Payments in Table 12, p. T-13–T-19 and read across the row until the value nearest 22.752 is found (22.96 in this example).

f) The rate at the top of the column containing 22.96 is 12%. The APR Lana must pay is 12%.

Note that the ad gives the APR as 11.90%. The Federal Reserve System requires the estimated APR to be within $\frac{1}{8}$% of the actual APR, so 12% would meet that requirement.

DO EXERCISE 3.

Intermediate values may be obtained from a table by interpolation. The process is explained in Example 4.

Example 4 Use interpolation to show that the APR for financing the Buick is 11.90%.

Solution

a) From Example 3, we know that the finance charge per 100 is 22.752.

b) In the row containing 42 in Table 12, p. T-13–T-19, we find that 22.752 is between 22.45 and 22.96.

c) The rate for the column containing 22.45 is 11.75%, and for 22.96 it is 12.00%.

d) This is represented by

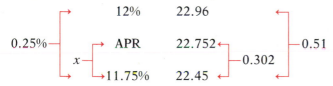

e) The APR = 11.75% + x% and

$$\frac{x}{0.25} = \frac{0.302}{0.51}$$

$0.51x = (0.25)(0.302)$ Cross multiplying.

$x = 0.15$ Dividing both sides by 0.51.

The APR is 11.90% (11.75% + 0.15%).

DO EXERCISE 4.

3. After a down payment an auto is financed for $3342.80 at $89.27 per month for 48 months. Find the APR.

4. Use interpolation to find the APR of the following.

ANSWERS ON PAGE A-12

5. Use the formula to estimate the APR for the Pinto.

●●● A FORMULA FOR ESTIMATING THE ANNUAL PERCENTAGE RATE

A good estimate of the APR* is given by

$$APR = \frac{72I}{3P(n + 1) + I(n - 1)},$$

where I = the interest (finance charge), P = the principal, and n = the number of monthly payments.

Example 5 Estimate the APR on a loan to Rodrigo Ibanez-Meier to buy the Monarch.

Solution The loan is for $3530 − $500 or $3030.

a) Find, I, P, and n.

$I = 36(100.63) − 3030$

$\quad = 3622.68 − 3030$

$\quad = 592.68$

$P = 3030$

$n = 36$

b) Substituting 592.68 for I, 3030 for P, and 36 for n, we get

$$APR = \frac{72(592.68)}{3(3030)(37) + (592.68)(35)}$$

$$= 0.1195.$$

The APR is about 11.95%.

Note that the actual APR is 11.99%. The formula is more complicated than others frequently used, but it provides greater accuracy as required by the Federal Reserve System when the Truth-in-Lending Law was updated.

DO EXERCISE 5.

---

* Constantine D. Kazarinoff showed this formula is a better approximation than the often used.

$$APR = \frac{24I}{P(n + 1)} \quad \text{or} \quad APR = \frac{24I}{(P + I)(n + 1)}.$$

ANSWER ON PAGE A-12

• Find the finance charge for each of 1–4.

We can give you the approval you want in just a matter of days — even on very large amounts.

Amount Financed	Monthly Payment	Number of Payments
$ 5,000	$108.04	84
$10,000	$186.67	120
$15,000	$280.00	120
$25,000	$466.67	120

1.
2.
3.
4. 🖩

HOW DO YOU APPLY?
Just phone. When you see for yourself how fast we say "yes, you'll wonder why you waited so long! Call today!

CREDITHRIFT
OF AMERICA
We've got your loan

•• Use Table 12 (p. T-13–T-19) to find the APR to the nearest $\frac{1}{4}$%.

5. **HAMMOND ORGAN**
WITH EXCLUSIVE ELECTRONIC FEATURES! ALL IT TAKES IS TWO FINGERS FOR INSTANT FUN AND MUSICAL ACCOMPLISHMENT. COME IN TODAY, SEE HOW EASY IT IS TO PLAY!
$1999 Cash Price (Not Including Sales Tax)
$56.62 Monthly Payment
48 MONTHS

6. 🖩 **KIMBALL PIANO**
A PIANO CREATED TO SATISFY YOUR HIGH STANDARDS FOR MUSICAL SOUND WITH RICH, RESONANT TONE, QUALITY AND SUPERIOR HAND-CRAFTED STYLING. THIS IS A PIANO THAT WILL PROVIDE MAXIMUM MUSICAL PLEASURE.
$999 Cash Price (Not Including Sales Tax)
$36.06 Monthly Payment
36 MONTHS

7. **NEW KIMBALL Grand PIANO**
$2999 Cash Price (Not Including Sales Tax)
$71.64 Monthly Payment
60 MONTHS

8. **USED ORGAN**
$599 Cash Price (Not Including Sales Tax)
$29.95 Monthly Payment
24 MONTHS

9.
COUGAR $5416
2-dr., silver metallic, automatic trans., power and air conditioning. List price $5873; $416 down payment. Finance $5,000 at $134.22 per month for 48 months.

10. 🖩
SUBARU

ONLY
**$104**^{85} per/mo
with qualified credit, $4393 cash, or $343 down, 48 mo.

ANSWERS	
1.	
2.	
3.	
4.	
5.	
6.	
7.	
8.	
9.	
10.	

11.

CUTLASS SUPREME
AT-PS-AC
Vinyl Roof
$58.72 Mo.
$1687 Cash
$500 Down 24 mo. APR
Deferred price $1909.28

12.

MUSTANG II
Coupe
Vinyl Roof
$103.63 Mo.
$3100 Cash
$500 Down 30 mo. APR
Deferred price $3608.90

 Use the formula to estimate the APR to the hundredths position in Exercises 13–22.

	Amount Borrowed	Monthly Payment	Number of Payments
13.	$3000	$155	24
14.	$4600	$230	24
15.	$6000	$155	48
16.	$7500	$195	48
17.	$4200	$1125	4
18.	$1700	$460	4

19.

VW BEETLE
Low Miles
Like New
$80.19 Mo.
$2495
$500 Down 30 mo.

20.

MALIBU CLASSIC
$121.94 PER MO.
Malibu Classic, Stk. No. 4196, 6 cyl., power steering, air, automatic. Sale price $5170 with $570 down. Finance $4600 for 48 months.

21.

CUTLASS
SUPREME
AT-PS-AC
NICE CAR
$85.24 Mo.
$2973 Cash
$500 down, 36 mo. APR
Deferred Price $3563.64

22.

MERCURY
4-DR
AT-PS-AC
LIKE NEW
$62.22 Mo.
$2268 Cash
$500 down, 36 mo.

23. Use the formula to find the amount Ali Ibrahim borrowed if the APR is 26%, the number of monthly payments is 24, and the interest is $430.

24. Use the formula to find the amount Lisa Gukeisen borrowed if the APR is 19%, the number of monthly payments is 36, and the interest is $940.

✓ SKILL MAINTENANCE

25. Faragut Savings pays 8% compounded quarterly on certificates of deposit. What is the effective interest rate?

26. Palo Alto Commercial Bank pays 9% compounded semiannually on certificates of deposit. What is the effective interest rate?

6.2

Finding the Payment Amount

O B J E C T I V E S

After finishing Section 6.2, you should be able to:

▪ Calculate monthly payments.

▪▪ Find the amount of each payment which is applied to interest and principal.

When considering a purchase, a consumer often wants to know the monthly payments and how much of each payment is for principal and how much is for interest. This information enables the consumer to determine whether the purchase is affordable. In this section we study these topics.

▪ MONTHLY PAYMENTS

Example 1 Find the monthly payment for Kathleen Duggan on a $3000 Industrial Investment Company loan payable over 60 months.

1. Find the monthly payment for Sandra Burke on a $7500 Industrial Investment Company loan payable for 36 months.

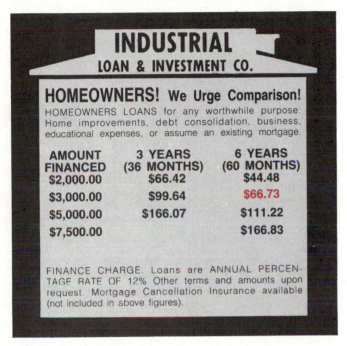

INDUSTRIAL
LOAN & INVESTMENT CO.

HOMEOWNERS! We Urge Comparison!
HOMEOWNERS LOANS for any worthwhile purpose: Home improvements, debt consolidation, business, educational expenses, or assume an existing mortgage.

AMOUNT FINANCED	3 YEARS (36 MONTHS)	6 YEARS (60 MONTHS)
$2,000.00	$66.42	$44.48
$3,000.00	$99.64	$66.73
$5,000.00	$166.07	$111.22
$7,500.00		$166.83

FINANCE CHARGE. Loans are ANNUAL PERCENTAGE RATE OF 12% Other terms and amounts upon request. Mortgage Cancellation Insurance available (not included in above figures).

Solution

a) Find the finance charge per $100.

Read down the column headed Number of Payments in Table 12 (p. T-13–T-19) to 60 and across that row to the 12% column.

The finance charge per $100 is $33.47.

b) A proportion gives the finance charge for the loan:

$$\frac{33.47}{100} = \frac{x}{3000}$$

$100x = 3000(33.47)$ Cross multiplying.

$x = 1004.10$ Dividing both sides by 100.

The finance charge is $1004.10.

c) Find the total to be paid.

$1004.10 + $3000 = $4004.10

d) Kathleen's monthly payment is $66.73, or $4004.10 ÷ 60.

DO EXERCISE 1.

ANSWER ON PAGE A-12

2. An 11.25% home mortgage loan of $65,000 was taken out for 26 years. What were the monthly payments? Use Table 12, p. T-13–T-19.

3. An 11.00% home mortgage loan of $65,000 was taken out for 25 years. What were the monthly payments? Use Table 13, p. T-13–T-19.

ANSWERS ON PAGE A-12

CITIZEN SMITH   **By Dave Gerard**

"He hates me. I've got a house mortgage at 6¼ per cent which still has ten years to go!"

The interest rate for a mortgage and the price of homes have varied considerably in recent years. Loans extending over a long time period in which all payments are equal are called ***amortized loans.*** Real estate, automobile, and other large loans are often amortized loans.

Example 2 An 11.5% home mortgage loan of $50,000 is taken out by Pamela Jess for 30 years (360 months). What are the finance charge and the monthly payment?

Solution

a) Find the finance charge per $100.

Read down the column headed Number of Payments in Table 12 (p. T-13–T-19) to 360 and across that row to the 11.5% column.

The finance charge per $100 is $256.50.

b) A proportion gives the finance charge for the loan:

$$\frac{\$256.50}{100} = \frac{x}{50,000}$$

$$100x = 256.50(50,000) \quad \text{Cross multiplying.}$$

$$x = \$128,250 \quad \text{Dividing both sides by 100.}$$

The finance charge is $128,250.

c) Find the total amount to be paid.

$$\$128,250 + \$50,000 = \$178,250$$

d) Pamela's monthly payment is $495.15, or $178,250 ÷ 360.

Note that the finance charge is over twice the amount of the loan.

DO EXERCISE 2.

Amortization tables exist, from which the payments may be found directly. Table 13 (p. T-20–T-23) is an amortization table. Part of that table is shown in Table 6.2.

Example 3 Suppose you took out an 11.5% home mortgage loan of $50,000 for 30 years. What were the monthly payments?

Solution Read down the column headed Amount in Table 6.2 to 50,000 and across that row to the 30-year column. The monthly payment is $495.15.

DO EXERCISE 3.

     Chapter 6   **Installment and Consumer Credit**

TABLE 6.2

MONTHLY PAYMENT REQUIRED TO AMORTIZE A LOAN   **11.500%**

TERM AMOUNT	15 Years	16 Years	17 Years	18 Years	19 Years	20 Years	21 Years	22 Years	23 Years	24 Years	25 Years	30 Years	35 Years	40 Years
	:	:	:	:	:	:	:	:	:	:	:	:	:	:
46000	537.37	524.94	514.33	505.22	497.37	490.56	484.65	479.50	474.99	471.05	467.58	455.54	449.01	445.41
47000	549.05	536.35	525.51	516.20	508.18	501.23	495.19	489.92	485.32	481.29	477.75	465.44	458.78	455.10
48000	560.74	547.76	536.69	527.19	518.99	511.89	505.72	500.34	495.64	491.53	487.91	475.34	468.54	464.78
49000	572.42	559.18	547.87	538.17	529.80	522.56	516.26	510.77	505.97	501.77	498.07	485.25	478.30	474.46
50000	584.10	570.59	559.05	549.15	540.61	533.22	526.79	521.19	516.30	512.01	508.24	495.15	488.06	484.15
55000	642.51	627.65	614.96	604.07	594.67	586.54	579.47	573.31	567.92	563.21	559.06	544.67	536.86	532.56
60000	700.92	684.70	670.86	658.98	648.74	639.86	632.15	625.43	619.55	614.41	609.89	594.18	585.67	580.97
65000	759.33	741.76	726.77	713.90	702.80	693.18	684.83	677.55	671.18	665.61	660.71	643.69	634.47	629.39
70000	817.74	798.82	782.67	768.81	756.86	746.51	737.51	729.67	722.81	716.81	711.53	693.21	683.28	677.80
75000	876.15	855.88	638.58	823.73	810.92	799.83	790.19	781.79	774.44	768.01	762.36	742.72	732.09	726.22

Example 4 A 10.75% home mortgage loan of $62,500 was taken out by Mark Gullett for 35 years (420 months). What were the monthly payments and the finance charge?

Solution

a) Find the monthly payment.

From Table 13 (p. T-20–T-23) we find that the monthly payment for

$60,000 is $550.51
$ 2,000 is $ 18.36
$ 500 is $ 4.59

So for $62,500 Mark's monthly payment is $573.46 (adding).

b) Find the finance charge.

Finance charge = Total amount paid − Amount borrowed

$$= (\$573.46 \times 420) - \$62,500$$
$$= \$178,353.20$$

DO EXERCISE 4.

▪▪ **INTEREST AND PRINCIPAL PAYMENTS**

Lending institutions can provide a borrower with an amortization schedule on request. The schedule shows how much of each payment is interest and how much is principal. In addition, the interest rate, loan amount, and balance of the loan are given. Part of an amortization schedule, based on a 360-day year and 30-day month, is shown below.

SCHEDULE OF DIRECT REDUCTION LOAN

BANK A COUNT
RUDOLPH, WI 54475
715-435-3131

CUSTOMER NAME KELIN ABBOTT   LOAN NUMBER 6375

| CUSTOMER NUMBER 721881 | ORDER NUMBER 732801 | $ PAYMENT 687 25 | RATE 13 500 % | $ LOAN 60 000 00 |

PAYMENT NUMBER	INTEREST	PAYMENT ON DUE DATE—PAID TO	PRINCIPAL	TOTAL PAYMENT	BALANCE OF LOAN	DATE PAID
1	675 00	1-1-87	12 25	687 25	59 987 75	
2	674 86	2-1-87	12 39	687 25	59 975 36	
3	674 72	3-1-87	12 53	687 25	59 962 83	
4	674 58	4-1-87	12 67	687 25	59 950 16	
5	674 44	5-1-87	12 81	687 25	59 937 35	
6	674 30	6-1-87	12 95	687 25	59 924 40	
7	674 15	7-1-87	13 10	687 25	59 911 30	
8	674 00	8-1-87	13 25	687 25	59 898 05	
9	673 85	9-1-87	13 40	687 25	59 884 65	
10	673 70	10-1-87	13 55	687 25	59 871 10	
11	673 55	11-1-87	13 70	687 25	59 857 40	
12	673 40	12-1-87	13 85	687 25	59 843 55	

4. A 10.75% home mortgage loan of of $52,350 was taken out by Teri Jones for 25 years. What were the monthly payments and the finance charge? Use Table 13, p. T-20–T-23.

ANSWER ON PAGE A-12

5. How much of payment 8 is interest? How much is principal? What is the new balance?

6. The amount owed by Susan Pond on a 10.5% loan is $59,828.60. How much of the $548.85 monthly payment is interest? How much is principal? What is the new balance? Assume a 360-day year and 30-day month.

Example 5 How much of payment 6 for Kelin Abbott in the figure on p. 189 is interest? How much is principal? What is the new balance?

Solution

a) Find the amount of interest.

Read down the payment column to 6 and across to the column headed Interest.

The interest is $674.30.

b) Find the amount of principal.

Read down the payment column to 6 and across to the column headed Principal.

The principal is $12.95.

c) Find the new balance.

Read down the payment column to 6 and across to the column headed Balance of Loan.

The new balance is $59,924.40.

DO EXERCISE 5.

A borrower can find how much of each payment is interest and how much is principal without the use of an amortization schedule. Example 6 illustrates the process for payment 6.

Example 6 The amount owed by Kelin Abbott on a 13.5% loan is $59,937.35. How much of the $687.25 monthly payment is interest? How much is principal? What is the new balance? Assume a 360-day year and 30-day month.

Solution

a) Find the interest. Substituting $59,937.35 for P, 0.135 for R, and $\frac{30}{360}$ for T, we get

$$I = P \times R \times T$$

$$= \$59,937.35 \times 0.135 \times \frac{30}{360}$$

$$= \$674.30.$$

The interest is $674.30.

b) Find the amount of principal.

$$
\begin{aligned}
\text{Amount of principal} &= \text{Total payment} - \text{Interest} \\
&= \quad \$687.25 \quad - \$674.30 \\
&= \quad \$12.95
\end{aligned}
$$

The amount of principal is $12.95.

c) Find the new balance.

$$
\begin{aligned}
\text{New balance} &= \text{Previous balance} - \text{Principal payment} \\
&= \quad \$59.937.35 \quad - \quad \$12.95 \\
&= \quad \$59,924.40
\end{aligned}
$$

The new balance is $59,924.40.

DO EXERCISE 6.

You are having difficulty deciding which car to buy. Use Table 12 (p. T-13–T-19) to find the monthly payments.

1.

VOLKWAGEN
Four Speed, BEETLE
$20.00 DOWN
PER MONTH
24 Months, Cash Price, $802.18, Time
Sale Price, Interest Rate, 26.00%
CALL 553-6900 For Credit OK
SUNSET AUTOS
With Qualified Credit

2.

MARQUIS
COUPE
AT-PS-AC
Double Sharp

Mo.

$3468 Cash

$500 down, 36 mo. APR 12.00%
Deferred Price

3.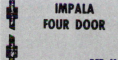

VEGA
HATCHBACK, Automatic.
$20.00 DOWN
PER MONTH
24 Months, Cash Price, $802.18, Time
Sale Price, Interest Rate, 26.25%
CALL 553-6900 For Credit Approval
SUNSET AUTOS
5115 CENTER ST.
With Qualified Credit

4.

PONTIAC
GRAND VILLE SEDAN, All
Power, Factory Air,.
$20.00 DOWN
PER MONTH
24 Months, Cash Price,
$887.68, Time Sale, Price,
Interest Rate, 24.5%
CREDIT OK BY PHONE, 553-
6900
SUNSET AUTOS
5115 CENTER
With Qualified Credit

5.

IMPALA
FOUR DOOR

PER MO.

Stk. no. 4174, V8, cruise, tilt,
air conditioned. Sale Price
$5367 with $567 down. Fi-
nance $4800 for 48 months.
Deferred price
APR 12%.

6.

MAVERICK
4 Door Sedan
AT-PS-PB-AC

Mo.

$3450 Cash

$500 down, 36 mo. APR 12.00%
Deferred price

7.

LTD
PER MO.
OR $5224

Dk. blue metallic with paint
stripes, bumper guards &
much more. Other colors at
this price & many more with
all the options. 4 door, V-8,
automatic transmission, factory air conditioning, power
steering, power brakes, tinted
glass, white wall radials,
remote control mirrors, Finance 48 monthly payments
of   per mo. with only
$500 down at 11% APR. &
Deferred payment price

8.

OLDS
VISTA CRUISER WAGON
$10.00 DOWN
PER MONTH
24 Months, Cash Price,
$507.85, Time Sale Price,
Interest Rate, 28%
Credit OK BY Phone, 553-6900
SUNSET AUTOS
5115 CENTER
With Qualified Credit

1. _____

2. _____

3. _____

4. _____

5. _____

6. _____

7. _____

8. _____

Use Table 13 (p. T-20–T-23) to find the monthly payments in Exercises 9–11.

9. On a 20-year 11.25% loan for $80,000.　　**10.** On a 25-year 11% loan for $55,000.

11. On a 30-year 11.5% loan for $93,000 to buy the Montego home.

THE MONTEGO
The Montego offers 1306 sq. ft. of finished living area with 3 full sized bedrooms and 1¾ baths, formal dining room and an eat-in kitchen with breakfast bar

•• Use the following amortization schedule to answer Exercises 12–13.

		SCHEDULE OF DIRECT REDUCTION LOAN					1965 BANK A COUNT FORM NO. 78
BANK A COUNT ® RUDOLPH, WI 54475 715-435-3131	CUSTOMER NAME **KELIN ABBOTT**					LOAN NUMBER **6375**	
721881 CUSTOMER NUMBER	**732801** ORDER NUMBER	$	**687 25** PAYMENT	**13 500 %** RATE	$	**60 000 00** LOAN	
PAYMENT		PAYMENT ON			TOTAL PAYMENT	BALANCE OF LOAN	DATE PAID
NUMBER	INTEREST	DUE DATE—PAID TO	PRINCIPAL				
46	666 98	10-1-90	20 27		687 25	59 267 19	
47	666 76	11-1-90	20 49		687 25	59 246 70	
48	666 53	12-1-90	20 72		687 25	59 225 98	

12. How much of payment 47 is interest? How much is principal? What is the new balance?

13. How much of payment 48 is interest? How much is principal? What is the new balance?

14. ▤ The amount owed by Donna Lea on a 10.5% loan is $57,710.02. How much of the $548.85 monthly payment is interest? How much is principal? What is the new balance? (Assume a 360-day year and 30-day month.)

15. ▤ The amount owed by Ivan Hanthorn on a 10.5% loan is $57,253.45. How much of the $548.85 monthly payment is interest? How much is principal? What is the new balance? (Assume a 360-day year and 30-day month.)

✓ **SKILL MAINTENANCE**

Find.

16. $\dfrac{6}{78} \times \$60$

17. $\dfrac{45}{406} \times \$153$

18. What is 120% of 75?

19. What is 65% of 480?

6.3

More on Interest

In this section we study how interest is computed on several different types of loans and the interest refund on early payment of a loan.

O B J E C T I V E S

After finishing Section 6.3, you should be able to:

- Compute add-on interest.
- Find the APR for add-on interest.
- Compute installment plan interest.
- Determine the interest refund.
- Calculate the final payment.

▪ ADD-ON INTEREST

At the time of purchase, interest is often added on to the amount borrowed. For example, $600 borrowed at 15% add-on for 12 months means that 15% of $600 (or $90) is added on to the $600 borrowed as interest, and $690 must be repaid. Interest computed in this manner is called *add-on interest*.

Example 1 Laura Seborg used a 9% add-on loan for 36 months to purchase a $933 seven-piece bedroom suite. How much interest was charged?

COMPLETE 7-PC. GROUPS
INCLUDE MATTRESS & BOXSPRING
TRIPLE DRESSER
MIRROR • CHEST
HEADBOARD • FRAME
933.00

Solution Substituting 933 for P, 0.09 for R, and 3 for T, we get

$$I = P \times R \times T$$
$$= 933 \times 0.09 \times 3 = 251.91$$

The interest charged was $251.91.

DO EXERCISE 1.

On this type of loan the interest is added on to the amount borrowed and then the monthly payments are computed.

Example 2 Find Laura's monthly payments for the 9% add-on loan for the bedroom suite.

Solution

a) Find the amount borrowed plus interest.

Amount borrowed + interest = $933 + $251.91 = $1184.91

b) Find the monthly payment.

Monthly payment = $1184.91 ÷ 36 = $32.91

DO EXERCISE 2.

▪▪ THE APR FOR ADD-ON INTEREST

Since the amount borrowed by Laura was paid back over 36 months, she did not have the use of it for the entire time. As a result, the APR is greater than the add-on interest rate.

1. Compute the interest if a loan to purchase the $933 seven-piece bedroom suite is at an 11% add-on rate for 36 months.

2. Find the monthly payment for an 11% add-on loan for 36 months for the $933 bedroom suite.

ANSWERS ON PAGE A-12

3. Find the APR for an 11% add-on loan for 36 months for the $933 bedroom suite. Give your answer to the nearest 0.25%. Use Table 12, p. T-13–T-19

ANSWER ON PAGE A-12

Example 3 Compute the APR for a 9% add-on loan for the $933 bedroom suite.

Solution

a) Find the finance charge per $100 of the amount borrowed.

$$\frac{251.91}{933} = \frac{x}{100}$$

$$x = 27$$

b) Find 36 in the column headed Number of Payments in Table 6.3 and read across the row until the value nearest 27 is found (27.01 in this example).

c) The rate at the top of the column containing 27.01 is 16.25%. The APR is 16.25%.

DO EXERCISE 3.

TABLE 6.3

ANNUAL PERCENTAGE RATE TABLE FOR MONTHLY PAYMENT PLANS

NUMBER OF PAYMENTS	14.00%	14.25%	14.50%	14.75%	15.00%	15.25%	15.50%	15.75%	16.00%	16.25%	16.50%	16.75%	17.00%	17.25%	17.50%	17.75%
						(FINANCE CHARGE PER $100 OF AMOUNT FINANCED)										
1	1.17	1.19	1.21	1.23	1.25	1.27	1.29	1.31	1.33	1.35	1.37	1.40	1.42	1.44	1.46	1.48
2	1.75	1.78	1.82	1.85	1.88	1.91	1.94	1.97	2.00	2.04	2.07	2.10	2.13	2.16	2.19	2.22
3	2.34	2.38	2.43	2.47	2.51	2.55	2.59	2.64	2.68	2.72	2.76	2.80	2.85	2.89	2.93	2.97
4	2.93	2.99	3.04	3.09	3.14	3.20	3.25	3.30	3.36	3.41	3.46	3.51	3.57	3.62	3.67	3.73
5	3.53	3.59	3.65	3.72	3.78	3.84	3.91	3.97	4.04	4.10	4.16	4.23	4.29	4.35	4.42	4.48
6	4.12	4.20	4.27	4.35	4.42	4.49	4.57	4.64	4.72	4.79	4.87	4.94	5.02	5.09	5.17	5.24
7	4.72	4.81	4.89	4.98	5.06	5.15	5.23	5.32	5.40	5.49	5.58	5.66	5.75	5.83	5.92	6.00
8	5.32	5.42	5.51	5.61	5.71	5.80	5.90	6.00	6.09	6.19	6.29	6.38	6.48	6.58	6.67	6.77
9	5.92	6.03	6.14	6.25	6.35	6.46	6.57	6.68	6.78	6.89	7.00	7.11	7.22	7.32	7.43	7.54
10	6.53	6.65	6.77	6.88	7.00	7.12	7.24	7.36	7.48	7.60	7.72	7.84	7.96	8.08	8.19	8.31
11	7.14	7.27	7.40	7.53	7.66	7.79	7.92	8.05	8.18	8.31	8.44	8.57	8.70	8.83	8.96	9.09
12	7.74	7.89	8.03	8.17	8.31	8.45	8.59	8.74	8.88	9.02	9.16	9.30	9.45	9.59	9.73	9.87
13	8.36	8.51	8.66	8.81	8.97	9.12	9.27	9.43	9.58	9.73	9.89	10.04	10.20	10.35	10.50	10.66
14	8.97	9.13	9.30	9.46	9.63	9.79	9.96	10.12	10.29	10.45	10.62	10.78	10.95	11.11	11.28	11.45
15	9.59	9.76	9.94	10.11	10.29	10.47	10.64	10.82	11.00	11.17	11.35	11.53	11.71	11.88	12.06	12.24
16	10.20	10.39	10.58	10.77	10.95	11.14	11.33	11.52	11.71	11.90	12.09	12.28	12.46	12.65	12.84	13.03
17	10.82	11.02	11.22	11.42	11.62	11.82	12.02	12.22	12.42	12.62	12.83	13.03	13.23	13.43	13.63	13.83
18	11.45	11.66	11.87	12.08	12.29	12.50	12.72	12.93	13.14	13.35	13.57	13.78	13.99	14.21	14.42	14.64
19	12.07	12.30	12.52	12.74	12.97	13.19	13.41	13.64	13.86	14.09	14.31	14.54	14.76	14.99	15.22	15.44
20	12.70	12.93	13.17	13.41	13.64	13.88	14.11	14.35	14.59	14.82	15.06	15.30	15.54	15.77	16.01	16.25
21	13.33	13.58	13.82	14.07	14.32	14.57	14.82	15.06	15.31	15.56	15.81	16.06	16.31	16.56	16.81	17.07
22	13.96	14.22	14.48	14.74	15.00	15.26	15.52	15.78	16.04	16.30	16.57	16.83	17.09	17.36	17.62	17.88
23	14.59	14.87	15.14	15.41	15.68	15.96	16.23	16.50	16.78	17.05	17.32	17.60	17.88	18.15	18.43	18.70
24	15.23	15.51	15.80	16.08	16.37	16.65	16.94	17.22	17.51	17.80	18.09	18.37	18.66	18.95	19.24	19.53
25	15.87	16.17	16.46	16.76	17.06	17.35	17.65	17.95	18.25	18.55	18.85	19.15	19.45	19.75	20.05	20.36
26	16.51	16.82	17.13	17.44	17.75	18.06	18.37	18.68	18.99	19.30	19.62	19.93	20.24	20.56	20.87	21.19
27	17.15	17.47	17.80	18.12	18.44	18.76	19.09	19.41	19.74	20.06	20.39	20.71	21.04	21.37	21.69	22.02
28	17.80	18.13	18.47	18.80	19.14	19.47	19.81	20.15	20.48	20.82	21.16	21.50	21.84	22.18	22.52	22.86
29	18.45	18.79	19.14	19.49	19.83	20.18	20.53	20.88	21.23	21.58	21.94	22.29	22.64	22.99	23.35	23.70
30	19.10	19.45	19.81	20.17	20.54	20.90	21.26	21.62	21.99	22.35	22.72	23.08	23.45	23.81	24.18	24.55
31	19.75	20.12	20.49	20.87	21.24	21.61	21.99	22.37	22.74	23.12	23.50	23.88	24.26	24.64	25.02	25.40
32	20.40	20.79	21.17	21.56	21.95	22.33	22.72	23.11	23.50	23.89	24.28	24.68	25.07	25.46	25.86	26.25
33	21.06	21.46	21.85	22.25	22.65	23.06	23.46	23.86	24.26	24.67	25.07	25.48	25.88	26.29	26.70	27.11
34	21.72	22.13	22.54	22.95	23.37	23.78	24.19	24.61	25.03	25.44	25.86	26.28	26.70	27.12	27.54	27.97
35	22.38	22.80	23.23	23.65	24.08	24.51	24.94	25.36	25.79	26.23	26.66	27.09	27.52	27.96	28.39	28.83
36	23.04	23.48	23.92	24.35	24.80	25.24	25.68	26.12	26.57	27.01	27.46	27.90	28.35	28.80	29.25	29.70
37	23.70	24.16	24.61	25.06	25.51	25.97	26.42	26.88	27.34	27.80	28.26	28.72	29.18	29.64	30.10	30.57
38	24.37	24.84	25.30	25.77	26.24	26.70	27.17	27.64	28.11	28.59	29.06	29.53	30.01	30.49	30.96	31.44
39	25.04	25.52	26.00	26.48	26.96	27.44	27.92	28.41	28.89	29.38	29.87	30.36	30.85	31.34	31.83	32.32
40	25.71	26.20	26.70	27.19	27.69	28.18	28.68	29.18	29.68	30.18	30.68	31.18	31.68	32.19	32.69	33.20
41	26.39	26.89	27.40	27.91	28.41	28.92	29.44	29.95	30.46	30.97	31.49	32.01	32.52	33.04	33.56	34.08
42	27.06	27.58	28.10	28.62	29.15	29.67	30.19	30.72	31.25	31.78	32.31	32.84	33.37	33.90	34.44	34.97
43	27.74	28.27	28.81	29.34	29.88	30.42	30.96	31.50	32.04	32.58	33.13	33.67	34.22	34.76	35.31	35.86
44	28.42	28.97	29.52	30.07	30.62	31.17	31.72	32.28	32.83	33.39	33.95	34.51	35.07	35.63	36.19	36.76
45	29.11	29.67	30.23	30.79	31.36	31.92	32.49	33.06	33.63	34.20	34.77	35.35	35.92	36.50	37.08	37.66

⚫⚫⚫ INSTALLMENT PLAN INTEREST

Buying on an ***installment plan*** means paying for goods and services over a period of time. Expensive items such as major appliances, televisions, and stereo equipment, and even medical bills are sometimes paid for using the installment plan.

CITIZEN SMITH   **By Dave Gerard**

1977, The Register and Tribune Syndicate

"We could break up your bill into installments — pay one every four hours!"

Example 4 Pamela Low purchased a $695 stereo for $50 down and $57 a month for 12 months. What was the finance charge?

Solution

a) Find the amount of the loan.

Amount of loan = Purchase price − Down payment

$$= 695 - 50$$
$$= 645$$

b) Find the total amount paid.

Total amount paid (excluding down payment) = Number of payments × Amount of each payment

$$= 12 \times 57$$
$$= 684$$

c) Find the finance charge.

Finance charge = Total amount paid − Amount of loan

$$= 684 - 645$$
$$= 39$$

The finance charge was $39.

DO EXERCISE 4.

4. Susan Kesler's $870 medical bill was paid for with $50 down and $75 a month for 12 months. What was the finance charge?

ANSWER ON PAGE A-12

Example 5 Jim Mose paid for a $450 television in three monthly installments of $150 plus $1\frac{1}{2}\%$ each month on the unpaid balance. What was the finance charge?

Solution

a) Find the finance charge for each month.

Month	Unpaid balance	Finance charge
1	$450	$450 × 0.015, or $6.75
2	$300	$300 × 0.015, or $4.50
3	$150	$150 × 0.015, or $2.25

b) Find the total finance charge.

$$\text{Total finance charge} = \text{Sum of monthly finance charges}$$
$$= \$6.75 + \$4.50 + \$2.25$$
$$= \$13.50$$

The total finance charge was $13.50.

DO EXERCISE 5.

A formula for finding the finance charge on installment loans is

$$I = \frac{n(n+1)}{2}(P)(i)$$

where I = the finance charge, n = the number of payments, P = the monthly payment, and i = the interest rate charged on the unpaid balance.

---

6. Jim Laska paid for a $445 freezer in five monthly installments of $89 plus 2% each month on the unpaid balance. What was the finance charge?

The following example, identical to Example 5, uses this formula to compute the finance charge.

Example 6 Kathy Jurgens paid for a $450 television in three monthly installments of $150 plus $1\frac{1}{2}\%$ each month on the unpaid balance. What was the finance charge?

Solution Substituting 3 for n, 150 for P, and 0.015 for i in

$$I = \frac{n(n+1)}{2}(P)(i)$$

we get

$$I = \frac{3(3+1)}{2}(150)(0.015)$$
$$= 13.50.$$

The finance charge was $13.50.

DO EXERCISE 6.

∷ INTEREST REFUND

Consumers may wish to pay off an installment loan early. They may then get an interest refund.

> **To find the refund,**
>
> a) **add 1 through the number of payments,**
> b) **add 1 through the number of payments remaining,**
> c) **divide the sum in b) by the sum in a), and then multiply by the total interest.**

Example 7 Deb Knonar was paying for a loan for a stereo system in 12 equal monthly payments of $63. The total amount of interest was $190. At the end of 9 months the loan was paid in full. How much was the interest refund?

Solution

a) The number of payments is 12, so we add*

$$1 + 2 + \cdots + 12 = \frac{12 \times 13}{2}.$$

The answer is 78.

b) There were 3 payments remaining, so we add

$$1 + 2 + 3 = \frac{3 \times 4}{2}.$$

The answer is 6.

c) We divide 6 by 78 and then multiply by $190.

$$\left(\frac{6}{78}\right)(\$190) = \$14.62$$

The interest refund was $14.62.

DO EXERCISE 7.

Notice in part a) that a year is divided into 78 increments. In effect, $\frac{12}{78}$ of the interest is paid the first month, $\frac{11}{78}$ the second month, and so forth to $\frac{1}{78}$ the last month. This makes sense because more interest should be paid the first month as more money is owed the first month. As noted a year is divided into 78 parts so the method is named the **Rule of 78.**

---

* A quick way to find the sum of the numbers 1 through n is to use the formula

$$1 + 2 + 3 + \cdots + n = \frac{n \times (n + 1)}{2};$$

thus

$$1 + 2 + 3 + \cdots + 12 = \frac{12 \times 13}{2} = 78.$$

7. Mary Gemhart's loan for a home computer is being repaid in 12 equal monthly payments of $113. The total amount of interest is $137. At the end of 8 months the loan is paid in full. How much is the interest refund?

ANSWER ON PAGE A-12

8. A 26-month installment loan with $90 payments and an interest charge of $214 was paid in full by Wendell Boelye at the end of 20 months. How much was the final payment?

ANSWER ON PAGE A-12

⠿ **FINAL PAYMENT**

Example 8 A 28-month installment loan with $80 payments and an interest charge of $153 was paid in full by Marabeth Cooney at the end of 19 months. How much was the final payment?

Solution

a) The number of payments is 28, so we add

$$1 + 2 + \cdots + 28 = \frac{28 \times 29}{2}$$
$$= 406.$$

b) There are $28 - 19$, or 9 payments remaining, so we add

$$1 + 2 + \cdots + 9 = \frac{9 \times 10}{2}$$
$$= 45.$$

c) We divide 45 by 406 and then multiply by $153.

$$\left(\frac{45}{406}\right)(\$153) = \$16.96$$

The interest refund is $16.96.

Now we find the final payment.

Final payment = (Number of payments left × Payments) − Refund
$$= (9 \times \$80) - \$16.96$$
$$= \$703.04$$

The final payment is $703.04.

DO EXERCISE 8.

Chapter 6   **Installment and Consumer Credit**

EXERCISE SET **6.3**

• | •• Complete. Use Table 12 (p. T-13–T-19) and give answer to the nearest $\frac{1}{4}$%.

	Amount of Loan	Add-on-Rate	Interest	Monthly Payment	Payments	APR
1.	$500	$6\frac{1}{2}$%			24	
2.	$399	8%			18	
3.	$950		$242.25		36	
4.	$700		$140.00		24	
5.	$1200			$34.00	48	
6.	$1000			$50.83	24	
7.		$6\frac{1}{2}$%	$58.50		24	
8.		$7\frac{1}{2}$%	$390.00		48	
9.			$120.00	$24.00	30	
10.			$101.20	$16.70	36	

••• Find the finance charge on each of these purchases for your new home.

11. A $379 freezer is purchased for $75 down and $28 a month for twelve months.

12. A $285 dishwasher is purchased for $25 down and $47 a month for six months.

13. ▦ A $320 washer is purchased for $45 down and $42 a month for seven months.

14. A $700 riding mower is purchased for $80 down and $55 a month for twelve months.

15. A $595 amplifier is paid for in seven monthly installments of $85 plus 2% each month on the unpaid balance.

16. ▦ A $430 range is paid for in five monthly payments of $86 plus $2\frac{1}{2}$% each month on the unpaid balance.

17. A $492 color television is paid for in six monthly installments of $82 plus 3% each month on the unpaid balance.

18. An $1104 video cassette recorder is paid for in six monthly installments of $184 plus $1\frac{1}{2}$% each month on the unpaid balance.

19. ▦ A $511.92 microwave oven is paid for in twelve equal monthly payments plus $1\frac{3}{4}$% each month on the unpaid balance. Find the finance charge.

20. ▦ A $317.10 chord organ is paid for in six equal monthly payments plus $1\frac{1}{4}$% each month on the unpaid balance. Find the finance charge.

ANSWERS

11. _____

12. _____

13. _____

14. _____

15. _____

16. _____

17. _____

18. _____

19. _____

20. _____

Find the interest refund in Exercises 21–24.

21. Tony Lucatorto's loan is being repaid in five equal monthly payments of $80 each. The total amount of interest is $43. At the end of the third month the loan is paid in full.

22. Natasha Thomas's loan is being repaid in seven equal monthly payments of $125 each. The total amount of interest is $95. At the end of the second month the loan is paid in full.

23. ▦ Lisa Vinchattle's 30-month installment loan with $140 monthly payments and an interest charge of $230 was paid in full at the end of 23 months.

24. Colleen White's 18-month installment loan with $106 monthly payments and an interest charge of $270 was paid in full at the end of 15 months.

Determine the final payment in Exercises 25–32.

25. For the loan in 21.

26. For the loan in 22.

27. ▦ For the loan in 23.

28. For the loan in 24.

29. 24 monthly payments of $90.55, interest of $288.77, and paid in full at the end of 19 months

30. ▦ 48 monthly payments of $90.55, interest of $486.33, and paid in full at the end of 36 months

31. 36 monthly payments of $125.34, interest of $356.94, and paid in full at the end of 23 months

32. 30 monthly payments of $125.33, interest of $304.56, and paid in full at the end of 21 months

✓ SKILL MAINTENANCE

33. You deposit $300 at the end of every quarter into your savings account, which pays 11% compounded quarterly. How much is in your account after the 36th payment?

34. Charlotte Wilkinson deposits $500 at the end of every quarter into her savings account, which pays 5% compounded quarterly. How much is in her account after the 16th payment?

6.4

Charge Cards

Credit cards have become very much a part of our daily lives. We charge purchases, receive monthly statements, and make payments regularly. In this section we study this form of credit.

• REVOLVING CREDIT

A charge account in which amounts for new purchases are added to existing amounts owed is a **revolving credit plan.** A monthly statement for a J. R. Nickel revolving credit plan appears below. The method for computing finance charges appears in the lower left corner of the statement.

Example 1 Find the finance charge for the J. R. Nickel statement.

Solution The finance charge is $1\frac{1}{2}\%$ per month (for amounts up to $500) of the average daily balance.

Finance charge $= 0.015 \times 108.69 = 1.63$

The finance charge is $1.63.

DO EXERCISE 1.

For average daily balances in excess of $500 the finance charge is $1\frac{1}{4}\%$ of the excess and $1\frac{1}{2}\%$ of $500.

Example 2 Find the finance charge for a J. R. Nickel statement in which the average daily balance was $823.75.

Solution

a) Find the finance charge on the amount over $500.

The amount over $500 is $323.75 ($823.75 − $500), so

Finance charge $= 0.0125 \times 323.75 = 4.05.$
(amount over $500)

b) Find the finance charge on $500.

Finance charge $= 0.015 \times 500 = 7.50$
(on $500)

c) Find the total finance charge.

Total finance charge $= 4.05 + 7.50 = 11.55$

The total finance charge was $11.55.

DO EXERCISE 2.

OBJECTIVES

After finishing Section 6.4, you should be able to:

• Determine the finance charge, new balance, and minimum payment for revolving credit plans.

•• Calculate the costs for bank card use.

1. The average daily balance on a J. R. Nickel statement was $435.97. What was the finance charge?

2. Find the finance charge on a J. R. Nickel statement in which the average daily balance was $698.67.

ANSWERS ON PAGE A-12

3. Find the new balance for a J. R. Nickel statement in which the previous balance was $246.89, purchases totaled $54.67, the finance charge was $2.38, and the payment was $45.

4. Find the minimum payment for a J. R. Nickel statement having a new balance of $385.67.

ANSWERS ON PAGE A-12

The following example shows the computation needed to find the new balance.

Example 3 Find the new balance for the J. R. Nickel statement on the preceding page.

Solution

$$\text{New balance} = \frac{\text{Previous}}{\text{balance}} + \text{Purchases} + \frac{\text{Finance}}{\text{charge}} - \text{Payment}$$
$$= 199.28 + 22.70 + 1.63 - 100.00$$
$$= 123.61$$

The new balance is $123.61.

DO EXERCISE 3.

The following table shows the minimum payment for J. R. Nickel charge accounts.

New Balance (less insurance premiums)	Minimum Payment
11.00 or less	Balance
11.01–200	$10
200.01–250	15
250.01–300	20
300.01–350	25
350.01–400	30
400.01–450	35
450.01–500	40
Over $500	1/10 of Balance

Example 4 Find the minimum payment for the J. R. Nickel statement on p. 201.

Solution Because the new balance is $123.61, the minimum payment is $10.00.

DO EXERCISE 4.

●● BANK CARDS

Bank cards have made credit purchases readily available. MasterCard and Visa are two examples of widely used bank cards.

These cards may be used to purchase goods and services in both the United States and foreign countries. For this service the banks usually charge both the business (about 3% of the purchase amount) and the purchaser (presently 12% to 22% APR) a finance charge. In addition, an annual fee may be charged to the cardholder. The fee may vary but is typically about $18.00.

Example 5 MasterCard purchases by patrons of City Graphics amounted to $4000. How much did City Graphics pay MasterCard?

Solution The amount paid by City Graphics is 3% of the amount of the purchases, so

Amount paid = 0.03 × 4000

= 120.

City Graphics paid MasterCard $120.

DO EXERCISE 5.

Here is a typical MasterCard statement.

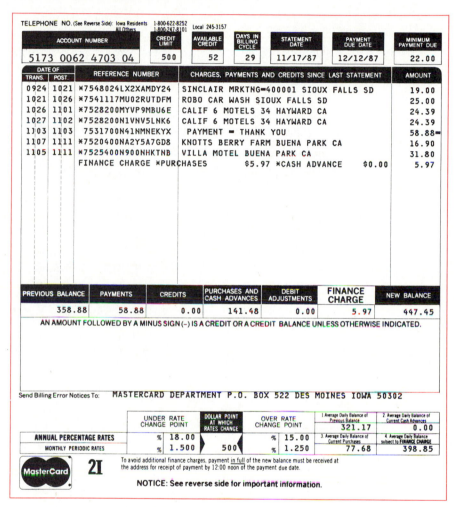

We will find the new balance.

Example 6 Find the new balance.

Solution

$$\frac{\text{New}}{\text{balance}} = \frac{\text{Previous}}{\text{balance}} + \frac{\text{Purchases and}}{\text{cash advances}} + \frac{\text{Finance}}{\text{charges}} - \text{Payments}$$

$$= \$358.88 + \$141.48 + \$5.97 - \$58.88$$

$$= \$447.45$$

The new balance is $447.45.

DO EXERCISE 6.

5. MasterCard purchases amounted to $8000 for a business. How much did the business pay to MasterCard?

ANSWER ON PAGE A-12

Next we find the finance charge.

Example 7 Determine the finance charge.

Solution

a) Find the average daily balance of the previous balance (Box 1 lower right on MasterCard statement).

The previous balance

10/19–11/2   There are 29 days in the billing cycle and 10/19 is 29 days before 11/17.

14 days at $343.85 ($358.88 − $15.03*) $4813.90

11/3–11/17

15 days at $300 ($358.88 − $58.88**) $4500.00

Daily balance (Previous balance) $9313.90

$$\text{Average daily balance (Previous balance)} = \frac{\$9313.90}{29}$$

$$= \$321.17$$

b) Find the average daily balance of current cash advances (Box 2).

There was no money borrowed, so 0 is in Box 2.

c) Find the average daily balance of current purchases (Box 3).

Charge	Posted	Days through 11/17	Amount	Amount × Days
Sinclair	10/21	28	$19.00	$532.00
Robo	10/26	23	25.00	575.00
Motel	11/1	17	24.39	414.63
Motel	11/2	16	24.39	390.24
Knotts	11/11	7	16.90	118.30
Villa Motel	11/11	7	31.80	222.60

Daily balance (Current purchases) $2252.77

$$\text{Average daily balance (Current purchases)} = \frac{\$2252.77}{29}$$

$$= \$77.68$$

d) Find the finance charge.

Add entries in Boxes 1, 2, and 3.

$321.17 + 0 + $77.68 = $398.85

Multiply by 1.5% (For amounts less than $500).

Finance charge = 0.015 × $398.85

$$= \$5.97$$

The finance charge was $5.97.

DO EXERCISE 7.

The computations for Visa are similar.

---

* The previous month's finance charge was $15.03 and no interest is charged on interest.

** When the payment ($58.88) arrives the finance charge ($15.03) is paid first and then the remainder ($43.85) is applied. The result is $358.88 − $15.03 = $343.85 and then $343.85 − $43.85 = $300.

1. Fill in the finance charge, new balance, and minimum payment where indicated.

2. _____

Sears Charge   Sears, Roebuck and Co.

You may pay by mail or at any Sears Store. If you pay by mail, please send only the top portion of your statement with your payment.
If you pay at any Sears Store, please bring the entire statement with you. Your payment will be credited as of the date received if you use the enclosed self-addressed envelope. Payment made in any other manner will be processed promptly but could result in up to a 5 day delay in crediting your account. **PLEASE MAKE ADDRESS CHANGE OR CORRECTIONS IN ADDRESS AREA BELOW.**

If state of residence changes, your account will be transferred, as required, for servicing.

Thank You for Shopping at Sears
Amount Due

3 47601 57893 4

Francis T. Hoyt
321 Edge Rd.
Sumner, IA 50103

OFFICE USE ONLY

$ _____
AMOUNT PAID

347601578934

MAIL ANY BILLING ERROR NOTICE TO Sears Credit Department at address shown below. Direct other inquiries to nearest Sears store.

Mo.	Day	Reference	TRANSACTION DESCRIPTION See reverse for detailed description of department numbers indicated below.	CHARGES	PAYMENTS & CREDITS
**	FINANCE	CHARGE**ON AVG DAILY BAL OF $346.85			
1103	5314	PAYMENT			50.00
1108	DRO2	HOUSEWARES 11		10.28	
1115	DRO6	AUTOMOTIVE ACCESSORIES 28		36.96	

PLEASE MENTION THIS ACCOUNT NUMBER WHEN ORDERING OR WRITING.	BILLING DATE	PREVIOUS BALANCE	NEW BALANCE	MINIMUM PAYMENT
3 47601 57893 4	Nov 21, 1987	$ 376.28	$	$

If the _FINANCE CHARGE_ exceeds 50¢, the _ANNUAL PERCENTAGE RATE_ is 18% on the first $500 of the AVERAGE DAILY BALANCE and 15% on that part of the AVERAGE DAILY BALANCE in excess of $500. The AVERAGE DAILY BALANCE excludes any purchases added during the monthly billing period and any unpaid _FINANCE CHARGE._

To avoid a _FINANCE CHARGE_ next month, pay this amount within 30 days from Billing Date.

If you prefer to pay in installments, pay this amount or more within **30** days from Billing Date. The sooner you pay and the more you pay, the smaller your _FINANCE CHARGE._

14351-161 7/1/78   **NOTICE: SEE REVERSE SIDE FOR IMPORTANT INFORMATION.**

If your highest "New Balance" is:	Your Minimum Payment will be:	If your highest "New Balance" is:	Your Minimum Payment will be:	If your highest "New Balance" is:	Your Minimum Payment will be:
$ .01 to $ 8.00	Balance	$240.01 to $260.00	$13.00	$440.01 to $470.00	$19.00
8.01 to 160.00	$ 8.00	260.01 to 290.00	14.00	470.01 to 500.00	20.00
160.01 to 180.00	9.00	290.01 to 340.00	15.00	Over $500.00 . . 1/25th of Highest	
180.01 to 200.00	10.00	340.01 to 380.00	16.00	Account Balance rounded to	
200.01 to 220.00	11.00	380.01 to 410.00	17.00	next higher whole dollar amount	
220.01 to 240.00	12.00	410.01 to 440.00	18.00		

3. _____

2. Find the finance charge for a Sears statement having an average daily balance of $645.

3. Find the new balance for a Sears statement in which the previous balance was $436, the purchases totaled $32, the payment was $50, and the finance charge was $6.35.

4. Find the minimum payment for a Sears statement having a new balance of $476.85.

4. _____

5. Fill in where indicated.

There was no finance charge the previous month.

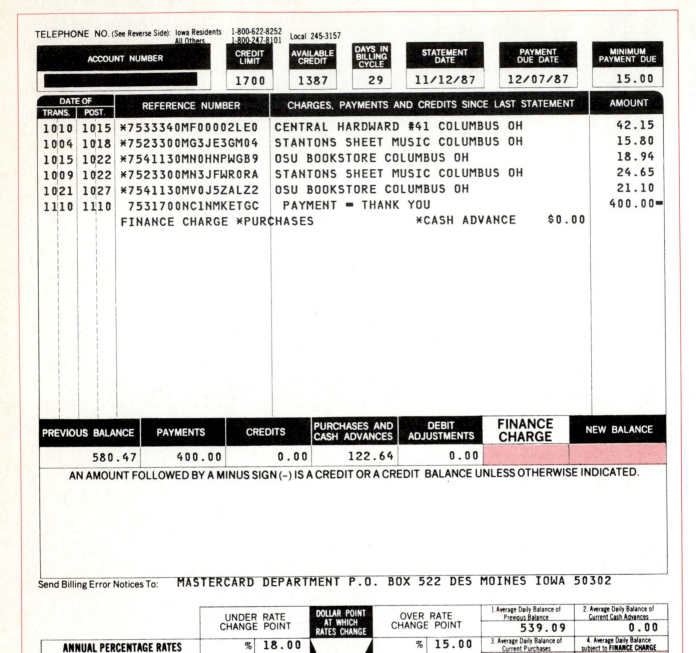

TELEPHONE NO. (See Reverse Side): Iowa Residents 1-800-622-8252 / All Others 1-800-247-8101 Local 245-3157					

ACCOUNT NUMBER	CREDIT LIMIT	AVAILABLE CREDIT	DAYS IN BILLING CYCLE	STATEMENT DATE	PAYMENT DUE DATE	MINIMUM PAYMENT DUE
	1700	1387	29	11/12/87	12/07/87	15.00

DATE OF TRANS.	POST.	REFERENCE NUMBER	CHARGES, PAYMENTS AND CREDITS SINCE LAST STATEMENT	AMOUNT
1010	1015	*7533340MF00002LE0	CENTRAL HARDWARE #41 COLUMBUS OH	42.15
1004	1018	*7523300MG3JE3GM04	STANTONS SHEET MUSIC COLUMBUS OH	15.80
1015	1022	*7541130MN0HNPWGB9	OSU BOOKSTORE COLUMBUS OH	18.94
1009	1022	*7523300MN3JFWR0RA	STANTONS SHEET MUSIC COLUMBUS OH	24.65
1021	1027	*7541130MV0J5ZALZ2	OSU BOOKSTORE COLUMBUS OH	21.10
1110	1110	7531700NC1NMKETGC	PAYMENT – THANK YOU	400.00–
		FINANCE CHARGE *PURCHASES	*CASH ADVANCE $0.00	

PREVIOUS BALANCE	PAYMENTS	CREDITS	PURCHASES AND CASH ADVANCES	DEBIT ADJUSTMENTS	FINANCE CHARGE	NEW BALANCE
580.47	400.00	0.00	122.64	0.00		

AN AMOUNT FOLLOWED BY A MINUS SIGN (–) IS A CREDIT OR A CREDIT BALANCE UNLESS OTHERWISE INDICATED.

Send Billing Error Notices To: MASTERCARD DEPARTMENT P.O. BOX 522 DES MOINES IOWA 50302

	UNDER RATE CHANGE POINT	DOLLAR POINT AT WHICH RATES CHANGE	OVER RATE CHANGE POINT	1. Average Daily Balance of Previous Balance	2. Average Daily Balance of Current Cash Advances
				539.09	0.00
ANNUAL PERCENTAGE RATES	% 18.00		% 15.00	3. Average Daily Balance of Current Purchases	4. Average Daily Balance subject to FINANCE CHARGE
MONTHLY PERIODIC RATES	% 1.500	500	% 1.250		

MasterCard 2I

To avoid additional finance charges, payment in full of the new balance must be received at the address for receipt of payment by 12:00 noon of the payment due date.

NOTICE: See reverse side for important information.

6. Fill in where indicated. The previous finance charge was $3.69.

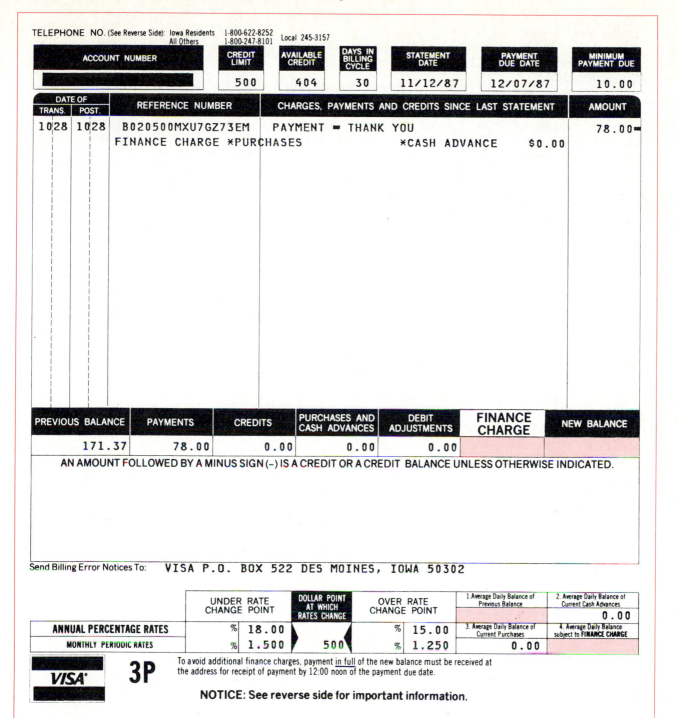

TELEPHONE NO. (See Reverse Side): Iowa Residents 1-800-622-8252 All Others 1-800-247-8101 Local 245-3157						
ACCOUNT NUMBER	CREDIT LIMIT	AVAILABLE CREDIT	DAYS IN BILLING CYCLE	STATEMENT DATE	PAYMENT DUE DATE	MINIMUM PAYMENT DUE
▮▮▮▮▮▮	500	404	30	11/12/87	12/07/87	10.00

DATE OF TRANS.	POST.	REFERENCE NUMBER	CHARGES, PAYMENTS AND CREDITS SINCE LAST STATEMENT	AMOUNT
10 28	10 28	B020500MXU7GZ73EM	PAYMENT - THANK YOU	78.00-
		FINANCE CHARGE *PURCHASES *CASH ADVANCE $0.00		

PREVIOUS BALANCE	PAYMENTS	CREDITS	PURCHASES AND CASH ADVANCES	DEBIT ADJUSTMENTS	FINANCE CHARGE	NEW BALANCE
171.37	78.00	0.00	0.00	0.00		

AN AMOUNT FOLLOWED BY A MINUS SIGN (–) IS A CREDIT OR A CREDIT BALANCE UNLESS OTHERWISE INDICATED.

Send Billing Error Notices To: **VISA P.O. BOX 522 DES MOINES, IOWA 50302**

	UNDER RATE CHANGE POINT	DOLLAR POINT AT WHICH RATES CHANGE	OVER RATE CHANGE POINT	1. Average Daily Balance of Previous Balance	2. Average Daily Balance of Current Cash Advances
ANNUAL PERCENTAGE RATES	% 18.00		% 15.00	3. Average Daily Balance of Current Purchases	0.00
MONTHLY PERIODIC RATES	% 1.500	500	% 1.250	0.00	4. Average Daily Balance subject to **FINANCE CHARGE**

VISA®   **3P**   To avoid additional finance charges, payment in full of the new balance must be received at the address for receipt of payment by 12:00 noon of the payment due date.

NOTICE: See reverse side for important information.

7. ▦ Fill in where indicated. The previous finance charge was $14.98.

| TELEPHONE NO. (See Reverse Side): Iowa Residents 1-800-622-8252 | | | | | | |
| All Others 1-800-247-8101 Local 245-3157 | | | | | | |

ACCOUNT NUMBER	CREDIT LIMIT	AVAILABLE CREDIT	DAYS IN BILLING CYCLE	STATEMENT DATE	PAYMENT DUE DATE	MINIMUM PAYMENT DUE
▮▮▮▮▮▮▮▮▮	600	74	30	11/10/87	12/05/87	26.00

DATE OF TRANS.	POST.	REFERENCE NUMBER	CHARGES, PAYMENTS AND CREDITS SINCE LAST STATEMENT	AMOUNT
1019	1020	*7531700MM1EP7MGDV	TARGET #171 BILLINGS BILLINGS MT	33.24
1025	1025	7531700MV1N3M9P53	PAYMENT — THANK YOU	52.00—
		FINANCE CHARGE *PURCHASES	*CASH ADVANCE $0.00	

PREVIOUS BALANCE	PAYMENTS	CREDITS	PURCHASES AND CASH ADVANCES	DEBIT ADJUSTMENTS	FINANCE CHARGE	NEW BALANCE
536.24	52.00	0.00	33.24	0.00		

AN AMOUNT FOLLOWED BY A MINUS SIGN (–) IS A CREDIT OR A CREDIT BALANCE UNLESS OTHERWISE INDICATED.

Send Billing Error Notices To: **MASTERCARD DEPARTMENT P.O. BOX 522 DES MOINES IOWA 50302**

	UNDER RATE CHANGE POINT	DOLLAR POINT AT WHICH RATES CHANGE	OVER RATE CHANGE POINT	1. Average Daily Balance of Previous Balance	2. Average Daily Balance of Current Cash Advances
					0.00
ANNUAL PERCENTAGE RATES	% 18.00		% 15.00	3. Average Daily Balance of Current Cash Advances	4. Average Daily Balance subject to FINANCE CHARGE
MONTHLY PERIODIC RATES	% 1.500	500	% 1.250		

MasterCard **2I** To avoid additional finance charges, payment in full of the new balance must be received at the address for receipt of payment by 12:00 noon of the payment due date.

NOTICE: See reverse side for important information.

NAME: _____

CLASS/SECTION: _____ DATE: _____

If you miss an item, review the indicated section and objective.

[6.1, •] **1.** A consumer borrowed $3500 to buy a Jacuzzi. Her monthly payments were $123.50 for 36 months. Find the finance charge.

1. _____

[6.1, ••] **2.** Find the APR (to the nearest 0.25%) on a $4000 auto loan payable over 36 months with payments of $135 (Table 12).

2. _____

[6.1, •••] **3.** Use the APR formula to estimate the APR for a $3600 loan payable over 24 months with payments of $170.

3. _____

[6.2, •] **4.** Find the monthly payments on a $5600 loan payment over 48 months at an APR of $11\frac{1}{4}\%$ (Table 12).

[6.2, ••] **5.** Use the following amortization schedule to find how much of payment 91 is interest, how much is principal, and what the new balance is.

4. _____

		SCHEDULE OF DIRECT REDUCTION LOAN				*1965 BANK A COUNT FORM NO. 28
BANK **A COUNT** ® RUDOLPH, WI 54475 715-435-3131	CUSTOMER NAME **KELIN ABBOTT**				LOAN NUMBER **6375**	
721881 CUSTOMER NUMBER	**732801** ORDER NUMBER	$ **687 25** PAYMENT	**13 500 %** RATE	$ **60 000 00** LOAN		

PAYMENT		PAYMENT ON			TOTAL PAYMENT	BALANCE OF LOAN	DATE PAID
	NUMBER	INTEREST	DUE DATE—PAID TO	PRINCIPAL			
	90	654 10	6-1-94	33 15	687 25	58 108 65	
	91	653 72	7-1-94	33 53	687 25	58 075 12	
	92	653 35	8-1-94	33 90	687 25	58 041 22	
	93	652 96	9-1-94	34 29	687 25	58 006 93	

5. _____

[6.3, •] **6.** An 11% add-on loan for $5200 over 24 months was used to buy furniture. How much interest was charged?

6. _____

[6.3, ••] **7.** Find the APR (to the nearest 0.25%) for an $1800 7% add-on loan payable over 24 months (Table 12).

7. _____

[6.3, •••] **8.** An $845 stereo is purchased for $75 down and $68 a month for 12 months. What is the finance charge?

8. _____

[6.3, ⁞⁞] **9.** A 12-month installment loan with $95 payments and an interest charge of $68 was paid in full at the end of eight months. How much was the interest refund?

9. _____

[6.3, ⁞•⁞] **10.** Find the final payment in Exercise 9.

10. _____

[6.4, •] **11.** Find the finance charge for a J. R. Nickel statement in which the average daily balance is $764.96.

11. _____

[6.4, ] **12.** Complete where indicated. The previous finance charge was $2.85.

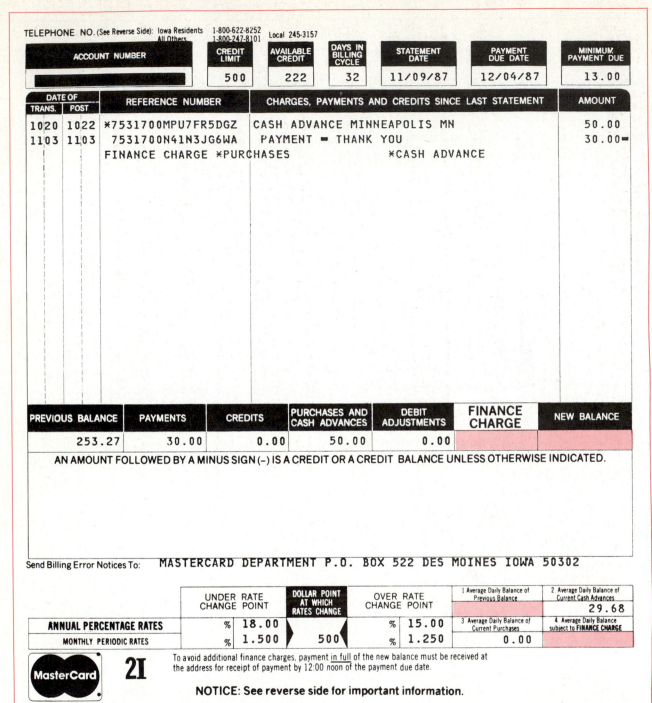

TELEPHONE NO. (See Reverse Side):	Iowa Residents 1-800-622-8252 All Others 1-800-247-8101	Local 245-3157					
ACCOUNT NUMBER		**CREDIT LIMIT**	**AVAILABLE CREDIT**	**DAYS IN BILLING CYCLE**	**STATEMENT DATE**	**PAYMENT DUE DATE**	**MINIMUM PAYMENT DUE**
		500	222	32	11/09/87	12/04/87	13.00

DATE OF TRANS.	POST	REFERENCE NUMBER	CHARGES, PAYMENTS AND CREDITS SINCE LAST STATEMENT	AMOUNT
1020	1022	*7531700MPU7FR5DGZ	CASH ADVANCE MINNEAPOLIS MN	50.00
1103	1103	7531700N41N3JG6WA	PAYMENT — THANK YOU	30.00—
		FINANCE CHARGE *PURCHASES	*CASH ADVANCE	

PREVIOUS BALANCE	PAYMENTS	CREDITS	PURCHASES AND CASH ADVANCES	DEBIT ADJUSTMENTS	**FINANCE CHARGE**	NEW BALANCE
253.27	30.00	0.00	50.00	0.00		

AN AMOUNT FOLLOWED BY A MINUS SIGN (–) IS A CREDIT OR A CREDIT BALANCE UNLESS OTHERWISE INDICATED.

Send Billing Error Notices To: **MASTERCARD DEPARTMENT P.O. BOX 522 DES MOINES IOWA 50302**

		UNDER RATE CHANGE POINT	DOLLAR POINT AT WHICH RATES CHANGE	OVER RATE CHANGE POINT	1 Average Daily Balance of Previous Balance	2 Average Daily Balance of Current Cash Advances
ANNUAL PERCENTAGE RATES	%	18.00		% 15.00		29.68
MONTHLY PERIODIC RATES	%	1.500	500	% 1.250	3 Average Daily Balance of Current Purchases	4 Average Daily Balance subject to FINANCE CHARGE
					0.00	

MasterCard **2I**

To avoid additional finance charges, payment in full of the new balance must be received at the address for receipt of payment by 12:00 noon of the payment due date.

NOTICE: See reverse side for important information.

ANSWERS

13. _____

14. _____

 **SKILL MAINTENANCE**

13. How much is the accumulated amount in Hector Freells IRA at the end of the 30th year if $1300 is invested at the beginning of each year at 7% compounded annually?

14. How much is the accumulated amount in Samatha Jones's IRA at the end of the 25th year if $1400 is invested at the beginning of each year at 14% compounded annually?

7

STOCKS
AND BONDS

CAREER: STOCKBROKER/FINANCIAL CONSULTANT   This is Clarence W. Schnicke. He is a very successful stockbroker and Financial Consultant for Shearson/American Express. Clarence enjoys mathematics and finds that on a day-to-day basis all of Chapters 1–13 and 15 are necessary to his work.

CLARENCE W. SCHNICKE

Usual salaries for people in his field are from $25,000 to $65,000, with a few people over $100,000. These salaries come after being registered at state and national levels and a period of about five years to build up clientele.

Clarence received a BS in Zoology from Wheaton College, but near the end of his studies counselors discovered an aptitude for business. He took several business courses while at Wheaton and went on to study stocks, bonds, and other financial subjects at the University of Chicago.

A Financial Consultant's job is to help others achieve financial security or benefits. A consultant must develop confidence between the client and himself. A detailed interview with the client is necessary to determine their personal financial needs. Both consultant and client must realize that there are pitfalls in investing which must be avoided, if possible. No action should ever be taken on the impulse of the moment. The consultant must understand the client's financial standing. For example, does the client have a will? Does the client have sufficient insurance? Is the client a salaried worker? Has the client built up an estate? The answers to all these questions help the Consultant meet the needs of the client.

The Financial Consultant should be cordial and outgoing. The consultant must keep abreast of economic trends and maintain the confidentiality of each client and all of that client's business.

Clarence's hobbies are travel, gardening, and musical activities.

7.1

Stocks and Commissions

When you own a share of stock in a corporation, you own part of the company. A stock exchange is like a supermarket in which stocks are bought and sold. The following table shows some quotations for a recent day on the New York Stock Exchange.

52 Weeks High	Low	Stock	Div.	Yld %	P-E Ratio	Sales 100s	High	low	Close	Net Chg.		52 Weeks High	Low	Stock	Div.	Yld %	P-E Ratio	Sales 100s	High	low	Close	Net Chg.
39½	19	Bard	.56	1.5	14	452	38½	38	38⅛	– ⅛		36¼	25⅛	CnsFrt	1.10	3.1	12	178	35¾	35	35⅜	– ⅜
25	19¼	BarnGp	.80	3.5	16	12	22⅝	22⅝	22⅝	+ ⅛		47⅞	38⅜	CnsNG	2.32	5.5	9	1321	42⅛	41⅞	42	.....
41⅝	25¾	Barnet	s1.04	2.7	11	412	38⅜	38	38¼	+ ¼		8⅞	4⅛	ConsPw	...	...	...	970	7½	7⅜	7½	...
28⅞	16⅞	BaryWr	.60	3.1	15	59	19⅜	19	19⅛	+ ⅛		31½	18½	CnP	pfA4.16	15.	..	z200	28	28	28	– 1
13⅜	6¼	BASIX	.12b	1.4	12	104	8⅞	8⅝	8⅞	.....		33⅜	19¼	CnP	pfB4.50	14.	..	z210	31½	30¼	31½	+ 1¼
35⅝	24¼	Bausch	.78	2.6	14	391	30⅝	30⅛	30¼	– ⅛		54⅞	32¼	CnP	pfD7.45	14.	..	z280	53	52	52	.....
16⅞	11¾	BaxtTr	.37	2.8	56	11580	13⅜	12⅝	13⅜	+ ⅝		56	32½	CnP	pfE7.72	14.	..	z30	53½	53½	53½	+ ½
27½	20⅜	BayFin	.20	.8	..	41	24½	24	24¼	+ ¼		56	33	CnP	pfG7.76	15.	..	z100	53½	53½	53½	+ 1¼

Here is how we read a typical listing:

52 Weeks High	Low	Stock	Div.	Yld %	P-E Ratio	Sales 100s	High	Low	Close	Net Chg.
$41\frac{5}{8}$	$25\frac{3}{4}$	Barnet	s1.04	2.7	11	412	$38\frac{3}{8}$	38	$38\frac{1}{4}$	$+\frac{1}{4}$

1. 2. 3. 4. 5. 6. 7. 8. 9. 10. 11.

1. The highest price per share of the stock during the preceding 52 weeks.

2. The lowest price of the stock during the preceding 52 weeks.

3. The abbreviated name of the corporation. In this case, it is Barnett Banks of Florida.

4. The yearly dividend per share that the company is paying. In this case, it is $1.04 per share. The s means there was a stock split or dividend of 25% or more in the last 52 weeks.

5. The yield per share. We will explain this later.

6. The price-earnings ratio. We will explain this later. Both the yield and price-earnings ratio are indicators of the quality of the stock, but there are other indicators.

7. The sales in 100s on that day. In this case, 41,200 shares were sold.

8. The highest selling price per share of the stock that day. In this case, it was $38\frac{3}{8}$, or $38.375 per share.

9. The lowest selling price per share of the stock that day. In this case, it was $38 per share.

10. The selling price per share for the last sale of the day (the closing price). In this case, it was $38\frac{1}{4}$, or $38.25 per share.

11. The difference between the closing price on this day and the closing price the day before. In this case, it is $+\$\frac{1}{4}$, or $+$0.25 per share.

- **BUYING STOCKS**

Suppose you see a listing such as the preceding one for Barnett and decide to buy 100 shares. What should you have to pay? From the listing you can get only an idea of the cost. On the actual day that you tell your broker to buy the stock, a representative goes to a person dealing in Barnett stock and makes a bid, say $38\frac{1}{4}$. If it is accepted, you pay $100 \times \$38\frac{1}{4}$ *plus* commission. However, the bid may not be accepted. Whatever is finally agreed on is the ***selling price.***

Commission rates depend on the brokerage firm. To approximate commission, assume that

Value of purchase = Number of shares × Price per share

Price per Share	Commission
Less than or equal to $47 per share	2% of the value of the purchase
More than $47 per share	$0.85 × the number of shares

Example 1 Find the total cost of purchasing 100 shares.

Solution

Stock	Selling price
Barnett	$38\frac{3}{8}$

a) Find the value of the purchase.

Value = Number of shares × Price per share

$\quad = 100 \times \$38\frac{3}{8}$

$\quad = 100 \times \$38.375 = \$3837.50$

b) Find the commission.

Commission = 2% of the value   Because the price per share is less than $47.

$\quad = 0.02 \times \$3837.50$

$\quad = \$76.75$

c) Add the value and the commission. This is the total cost.

Total cost = Value + Commission

$\quad = \$3837.50 + \$76.75$

$\quad = \$3914.25$

DO EXERCISE 1.

Example 2 Find the total cost of purchasing 200 shares.

Stock	Selling price
IBM	$297\frac{1}{2}$

Solution

a) Find the value of the purchase.

Value = Number of shares × Price per share

$\quad = 200 \times \$297\frac{1}{2}$

$\quad = 200 \times \$297.50 = \$59,500$

b) Find the commision.

Commission = $0.85 × Number of shares   Because the price per share is more than $47.

$\quad = \$0.85 \times 200$

$\quad = \$170$

c) Find the total cost.

Total cost = Value + Commission

$\quad = \$59,500 + \$170$

$\quad = \$59,670$

DO EXERCISE 2.

---

1. Find the total cost of purchasing 100 shares.

Stock	Selling price
GTE	$28\frac{5}{8}$

2. Find the total cost of purchasing 300 shares.

Stock	Selling price
IndiM	$109\frac{1}{4}$

ANSWERS ON PAGE A-12

3. Find the total return on the sale of 100 shares.

Stock	Selling price
GTE	$28\frac{5}{8}$

4. Find the total return on the sale of 300 shares.

Stock	Selling price
IndiM	$109\frac{1}{4}$

ANSWERS ON PAGE A-12

●● SELLING STOCKS

Suppose you own 100 shares of Barnett stock and want to sell them. If the selling price is $38\frac{1}{8}$, your *return* is $100 \times \$38\frac{1}{8}$ *minus* the commission. Note that a commission is paid by the buyer on the purchase of stock and also by the seller on the sale of stock. Commission is computed as before.

Example 3 Find the total return on the sale of 100 shares.

Stock	Selling price
Barnett	$38\frac{1}{8}$

Solution

a) Find the value of the sale.

Value = Number of shares × Price per share
$$= 100 \times \$38\tfrac{1}{8} = 100 \times \$38.125 = \$3812.50$$

b) Find the commission.

Commission = 2% of the value   *Because the price per share is less than $47.*
$$= 0.02 \times \$3812.50$$
$$= \$76.25$$

c) Subtract the commission from the value. This is the total return.

Total return = Value − Commission
$$= \$3812.50 - \$76.25 = \$3736.25$$

DO EXERCISE 3.

Example 4 Find the total return on the sale of 200 shares.

Stock	Selling price
IBM	$297\frac{1}{2}$

Solution

a) Find the value of the purchase.

Value = Number of shares × Price per share
$$= 200 \times \$297\tfrac{1}{2} = 200 \times \$297.50 = \$59,500$$

b) Find the commission.

Commission = $0.85 × Number of shares   *Because the price per share is more than $47.*
$$= \$0.85 \times 200$$
$$= \$170$$

c) Find the total return.

Total return = Value − Commission
$$= \$59,500 - \$170 = \$59,330$$

DO EXERCISE 4.

Stocks sold in multiples of 100 are called **round lots.** These would be lots such as 100 shares, 400 shares, and 3000 shares. Other sales are called **odd lots,** such as 97 shares, 142 shares, and so on. Usually the method of computing commission that we discussed in this section can be used, but in some cases commission per share for odd lots is higher—$\frac{1}{8}$ to $\frac{1}{2}$ of a dollar.

Chapter 7   Stocks and Bonds

• Find the total cost of purchasing 100 shares in Exercises 1–4.

Stock	Selling price
1. GMot	$68\frac{3}{4}$
2. Beverly	$33\frac{1}{2}$
3. GPU	$15\frac{3}{4}$
4. GnRefr	$7\frac{7}{8}$

Find the total cost of purchasing 200 shares in Exercises 5–8.

Stock	Selling price
5. IngerR	$58\frac{1}{2}$
6. ▦ Gillette	$66\frac{1}{2}$
7. AHome	$59\frac{1}{4}$
8. ▦ UAL	$48\frac{3}{4}$

9. ▦ Find the total cost of purchasing 6000 shares.

Stock	Selling price
ATT	$21\frac{7}{8}$

ANSWERS

1. _____

2. _____

3. _____

4. _____

5. _____

6. _____

7. _____

8. _____

9. _____

•• Find the total return on the sale of 100 shares in Exercises 10–13.

Stock	Selling price
10. Chrysler	$41\frac{1}{4}$
11. ▦ ColGas	37
12. CnDt	$17\frac{5}{8}$
13. McDnld	$69\frac{7}{8}$

Find the total return on the sale of 500 shares in Exercises 14–17.

Stock	Selling price
14. ▦ Pndrosa	$15\frac{1}{8}$
15. Pueblo	$14\frac{1}{4}$
16. TexInst	$90\frac{1}{4}$
17. Telex	$48\frac{1}{4}$

18. ▦ Find the total return on the sale of 8000 shares.

Stock	Selling price
Exxon	$53\frac{1}{2}$

 SKILL MAINTENANCE

Divide.

19. $11\frac{1}{4} \div 2\frac{1}{2}$ 　　　　　　　　**20.** $10\frac{1}{3} \div 3\frac{2}{5}$

21. 20 is 50% of what? 　　　　　**22.** 45 is 20% of what?

7.2

Stocks: Yield and Price-Earnings Ratio

⚬ YIELD

Suppose a company has earnings of $500,000 in one year. They may elect to pay part of this, say, $300,000, to their stockholders. If there are 10,000 shares of stock, they would pay $30 per share in what are called **dividends.** It is helpful to know what percent the yearly dividend is of the price per share. This percent is called the **yield.**

$$\text{Yield} = \frac{\text{Yearly dividend}}{\text{Price per share}}$$

Example 1 Find the yield.

Stock	Dividend	Price per share
Goodyr	$1.30	$16\frac{7}{8}$

Solution

$$\begin{aligned}
\text{Yield} &= \frac{\text{Yearly dividend}}{\text{Price per share}} \\
&= \frac{\$1.30}{\$16\frac{7}{8}} \\
&= \frac{\$1.30}{\$16.875} \\
&\approx 0.077 \qquad \text{Divide and round to the nearest thousandth.} \\
&= 7.7\% \qquad \text{Convert to percent.}
\end{aligned}$$

The yield is 7.7%.

DO EXERCISES 1 AND 2.

To interpret yield, compare it with what you might get in a savings account, say, 7%. Thus, the yield in Example 1 is good, but a yield of 1.9% might not be too profitable. This is not the only consideration, however. Remember the capital gain. The yield on a stock might be low, but it still may have gained considerably in value.

⚬⚬ PRICE-EARNINGS RATIO

If a company has earnings of $500,000 in one year, and there are 10,000 shares of stock, the earnings per share is $50. Note that this is not dividends per share. A company may not elect to pay any dividends, but the earnings per share can still be considered. The **price-earnings ratio,** *P/E*, is the price per share of the stock divided by the earnings per share.

O B J E C T I V E S

After finishing Section 7.2, you should be able to:

⚬ Find the yield of a stock.

⚬⚬ Find the price-earnings ratio of a stock.

Find the yield.

1. *Stock:* GTE
   Dividend: $2.24
   Price per share: $28\frac{5}{8}$

2. *Stock:* IndiM
   Dividend: $12
   Price per share: $109\frac{1}{4}$

ANSWERS ON PAGE A-12

Find the price-earnings ratio.

3. *Stock:* K mart

Price per share: $29

Earnings per share: $2.50

Example 2 Find the price-earnings ratio.

Stock	Price per share	Earnings per share
IBM	$297\dfrac{3}{4}$	$18.61

Solution

$$\dfrac{P}{E} = \dfrac{\text{Price per share}}{\text{Earnings per share}}$$

$$= \dfrac{\$297\frac{3}{4}}{\$18.61}$$

$$= \dfrac{\$297.75}{\$18.61}$$

$$\approx 16.0 \qquad \text{Divide and round to the nearest tenth.}$$

DO EXERCISES 3 AND 4.

To interpret price-earnings ratio, we might think of 6 as low and 20 as high. Generally speaking, the lower the price-earnings ratio, the better. Again, there are other things to consider. A low price-earnings ratio sometimes indicates a time to buy. In Example 2, we might think that the price-earnings ratio of 16 for IBM is poor, but this has been a stock with lots of growth potential. On the other hand, a low price-earnings ratio might indicate faulty management. A stock with increasing price will have an increasing price-earnings ratio, but if you bought the stock before the price started increasing, you would be quite pleased that the price-earnings ratio is getting larger. In conclusion, we can say that all indicators of the quality of a stock are relative. Learn as much as you can before making a sale or purchase of stock.

4. *Stock:* Mobil

Price per share: $60\dfrac{1}{8}$

Earnings per share: $9.40.

ANSWERS ON PAGE A-12

Chapter 7   Stocks and Bonds

Find the yield in Exercises 1–7.

Stock	Dividend	Price per share
1. GMot	$5	$$65\frac{3}{4}$$
2. Brl Nth	$7.28	$$65\frac{1}{2}$$
3. CBS	$2.40	$$53\frac{5}{8}$$
4. ▦ AriP	$9.50	$$112\frac{7}{8}$$
5. ▦ PacGE	$2.16	$$23\frac{7}{8}$$
6. NCR	$1	$$55\frac{3}{8}$$
7. GAF	$0.60	$$13\frac{1}{2}$$

ANSWERS

1. _____

2. _____

3. _____

4. _____

5. _____

6. _____

7. _____

•• Find the price-earnings ratio in Exercises 8–14.

Stock	Price per share	Earnings per share
8. McDnld	$53	$3.53
9. BakrInt	30\frac{5}{8}$	$2.36
10. ▦ MMM	59\frac{3}{8}$	$3.96
11. ContAir	13\frac{3}{4}$	$1.96
12. duPont	116\frac{1}{4}$	$12.92
13. ▦ ARA	40\frac{1}{8}$	$4.00
14. MGM	38\frac{7}{8}$	$3.00

✓ **SKILL MAINTENANCE**

Find the interest using the 360-day, approximate time method.

	Principal	Rate	Borrowed	Repaid
15.	$1400	9%	March 6	June 5
16. ▦	$900	12%	May 12	August 8
17.	$2500	13%	April 23	November 24
18.	$1900	7%	June 21	December 14

8. _____

9. _____

10. _____

11. _____

12. _____

13. _____

14. _____

15. _____

16. _____

17. _____

18. _____

7.3

Bonds and Commissions

OBJECTIVES

After finishing Section 7.3, you should be able to:

- • **Find the total cost of a bond purchase.**
- •• **Find the current yield of a bond.**
- ••• **Find the yield on purchase price.**

Some corporations sell ***bonds,*** which are a way of borrowing money from the general public. The owner of a bond has somewhat more security than the owner of stock in a corporation. If you are a bondholder, you are a creditor and as such have priority in getting your money if the corporation goes bankrupt. You also get a fixed amount of interest on your investment as opposed to stock dividends, which a corporation can decide to change. The price of a bond is affected, as with stocks, by supply and demand. The following table shows some quotations from a recent day on the New York Exchange.

Bonds	Cur Yld	Vol	High	Low	Close	Net Chg
CnNG 4⅜90	5.3	5	82⅞	82⅞	82⅞	.....
CnNG 5s87	6.1	2	82	82	82	.....
CnNG 4⅜90	5.6	5	78	78	78	−1⅛
CnNG 8⅝99	9.0	5	96	96	96	.....
CnNG 8⅜96	8.9	25	94	94	94	− ⅞
CnPw 5⅞96	8.6	5	68½	68½	68½	.....
CnPw 7½01	9.6	5	78¼	78¼	78¼	+ ⅛
CnPw 11⅜94	10.	5	109¼	109¼	109¼	+1¼
CnPw 11¼90	11.	38	105½	105½	105½	.....
CnPw 9¾87	9.6	13	101½	101⅜	101½	+ ⅛
CnPw 11½00	11.	3	109	109	109	−1
CnPw 9s06	9.5	4	94⅞	94⅞	94⅞	.....
CtlAir 3½92	cv	2	60½	60½	60½	+ ½
Ct IC 7.55s89	7.5	6	100⅜	100⅜	100⅜	+ ⅝
Ct IC 8½89	8.6	5	98½	98½	98½	− ⅛
CtlIllR 7⅝01	8.9	5	85¾	85¾	85¾	+ ⅛
CtlOil 4½91	5.8	11	77	76½	77	+1¼
CtlOil 7½99	8.7	10	86⅝	86⅝	86⅝	−1⅞
CoopL 7½91	cv	13	109	107	107	−2

Bonds	Cur Yld	Vol	High	Low	Close	Net Chg
IntTT 8⅝00	cv	15	122	121¼	121¼	−2
IpcoH 5¼89	cv	1	73¾	73¾	73¾	− ¼
Itel 9⅝98	11.	232	88¼	88	88¼	+ ¼
K mart 6s99	cv	35	93	93	93	− ½
Kellog 8⅝89	8.7	2	99⅜	99⅜	99⅜	− ⅝
KerrMc 8s87	8.4	25	95¾	95¾	95¾	−1¼
Kirsch 6s95	cv	50	93⅛	93⅛	93⅛	− ⅞
LigGp 7.6s97	8.7	8	87⅜	87¼	87¼	− ½
Litton 3½87	cv	8	68¼	68¼	68¼	+1⅛
Lockh 4¼92	cv	20	58½	58	58	− ¾
Loew 6⅞93	9.3	144	74¾	73¾	74	− ¼
LonSl 5⅛93	cv	32	83	83	83	.....
Lorilld 6⅝93	8.5	9	78⅛	78⅛	78⅛	.....
LouN 7⅜93	8.9	10	83	83	83	−1⅜
LuckSt 6¾00	cv	77	116	115½	115½	− ¾
MGIC 5s93	cv	66	63⅞	63	63	−1
MGIC 8⅜88	9.0	19	93½	93	93	− ½
MckF 9⅝90	9.6	6	100	100	100	+1
MckF 9¾91	9.8	7	99⅞	99¾	99¾	− ⅛

A bond listing differs from a stock listing. Here is how we read a bond listing:

Bonds	Cur Yld	Vol	High	Low	Close	Net Chg
Kellog $8\frac{5}{8}$89	8.7	2	$99\frac{3}{8}$	$99\frac{3}{8}$	$99\frac{3}{8}$	$-\frac{5}{8}$
1. 2.	3.	4.	5.	6.	7.	8.

1. The name of the company.
2. The $8\frac{5}{8}$ is the interest rate paid per year. The basic value of a bond is usually \$1000. This is also called ***par value.*** In one year, interest of $8\frac{5}{8}\% \times \$1000$, or \$86.25, is paid on the bond. The 89 is an abbreviation for 1989, the year in which the bond ***matures*** (is paid off). If the listing had said $8\frac{5}{8}$s89, it would mean that interest is paid semiannually.
3. The current yield. We will explain this later.
4. The volume is the number of bonds sold that day, in thousands. In this case, it is 2000.
5.
6. The high and low for the day, but this is not given in dollars. It is a percentage of \$1000. Thus, if the selling price is $99\frac{3}{8}$, it means that the bond sold for $99\frac{3}{8}\% \times \$1000$, or \$993.75. Thus, a bond that sells for 102, or \$1020, is more in demand than this one.
7. The closing price, which is the selling price for the last sale of the day.
8. The difference between the closing price on this day and the closing price on the previous day. For this bond, it is $-\frac{5}{8}$. The minus sign means that this is lower than the price the day before.

1. Find the total cost of purchasing three bonds.

Bond	Selling price
CnPw $5\frac{7}{8}96$	$68\frac{1}{2}$

2. Find the total cost of purchasing 18 bonds.

Bond	Selling price
McyCr $9\frac{1}{4}90$	$100\frac{1}{8}$

ANSWERS ON PAGE A-12

● BUYING BONDS

Suppose you see the preceding listing and decide that you want to buy some *Kellog* bonds; the selling price is $99\frac{3}{8}$. Each bond you buy costs $99\frac{3}{8}\% \times \$1000$ *plus* commission. Again, commission rates vary with the brokerage firm. Here is a method of computing approximate commission.

Number of bonds	Commission
1–3	$25
4 or more	$7.50 × Number of bonds

Example 1 Find the total cost of purchasing two bonds.

Bond	Selling price
Kellog $8\frac{5}{8}89$	$99\frac{3}{8}$

Solution

a) Find the value.

Value = Number of bonds × Selling price
$$= 2 \times 99\tfrac{3}{8}\% \times \$1000$$
$$= 2 \times \$993.75 = \$1987.50$$

b) Find the commission.

Commission = $25   Since there are only two bonds purchased.

c) Add the value and the commission.

Total cost = Value + Commission
$$= \$1987.50 + \$25 = \$2012.50$$

DO EXERCISE 1.

Example 2 Find the total cost of purchasing 15 bonds.

Bond	Selling price
CrdF $10\frac{1}{8}91$	$101\frac{7}{8}$

Solution

a) Find the value of the purchase.

Value = Number of bonds × Selling price
$$= 15 \times 101\tfrac{7}{8}\% \times \$1000$$
$$= 15 \times \$1018.75 = \$15{,}281.25$$

b) Find the commission.

Commission = $7.50 × Number of bonds   Because more than four are bought.
$$= \$112.50$$

c) Find the total cost.

Total cost = Value + Commission
$$= 15{,}281.25 + \$112.50 = \$15{,}393.75$$

DO EXERCISE 2.

Chapter 7   Stocks and Bonds

CURRENT YIELD

A person who is considering buying a bond may be interested in the ***current yield.*** This figure allows the buyer to compare present bank interest rates with those available by purchasing a bond.

$$\text{Current yield} = \frac{\text{Annual interest}}{\text{Current market price}}$$

Example 3 Find the current yield for Kellog.

Solution

a) As noted earlier the interest is $86.25.

b) The current market price is $993.75 as noted earlier.

c) Compute the current yield.

$$\text{Current yield} = \frac{\$86.25}{\$993.75}$$
$$\approx 0.0868, \text{ or } 8.7\%$$

DO EXERCISE 3.

3. Find the current yield for Public Service of New Hampshire.

Bonds	Cur Yld	Vol	High	Low	Close	Net Chg.
PSNH 15s03	15.	42	99⅞	99	99⅞	+ ⅞

ANSWER ON PAGE A-12

ANSWER ON PAGE A-12

4. You bought a $1000 9% bond at $650. The commission paid was $25. What is the yield on purchase price?

••• YIELD ON PURCHASE PRICE

Investors who already own bonds are interested in *yield on purchase price.* For example, they might ask themselves whether the yield on purchase price is more or less favorable than other possible investments.

$$\text{Yield on purchase price} = \frac{\text{Annual interest}}{\text{Total cost}}$$

Example 4 You bought a $1000 8% bond at $700. The commission paid was $25. What is the yield on purchase price?

Solution

a) The interest is $80 (8% × $1000).

b) The total cost was $700 + $25, or $725.

c) Yield on purchase price $= \dfrac{\$80}{\$725}$

$$\approx 0.11, \text{ or } 11\%$$

DO EXERCISE 4.

• Find the total cost of purchasing two bonds in Exercises 1–4.

	Bond	Selling price
1.	ATT $8\frac{3}{4}$00	$99\frac{5}{8}$
2.	Arco 8.70s91	$99\frac{3}{4}$
3.	OcciP 11s92	$106\frac{1}{4}$
4.	▦ TWA 11s89	$102\frac{7}{8}$

1. _____

2. _____

3. _____

4. _____

Find the total cost of purchasing ten bonds in Exercises 5–10.

	Bond	Selling price
5.	Woolw 9s99	97
6.	Xerox 6s95	87
7.	▦ UAL 8s03	$146\frac{1}{8}$
8.	PorG $9\frac{7}{8}$s88	$103\frac{1}{8}$
9.	Sears 8s06	$91\frac{3}{4}$
10.	▦ MGM 10s94	$95\frac{5}{8}$

5. _____

6. _____

7. _____

8. _____

9. _____

10. _____

ANSWERS

11. ______

12. ______

13. ______

14. ______

15. ______

16. ______

17. ______

18. ______

19. ______

20. ______

21. ______

22. ______

23. ______

24. ______

25. ______

26. ______

•• Find the current yield to the nearest tenth of a percent. The current market price is the closing price.

	Bonds	Cur Yld	Vol	High	Low	Close	Net Chg.
11.	AMR 10¼06	☐	43	87	86¼	86¼	− ¾
	ANR 8⅝93	9.5	20	90⅝	90⅝	90⅝	− 1
	Advst 9s08	cv	37	85	85	85	.....
	Aerflx 9⅜05	cv	54	115½	115¼	115½	− ½
12.	AlaBn 9¼99t	☐	10	99⅞	99⅞	99⅞	.....
	AlaP 9s2000	11.	53	84⅜	83¾	84⅛	− ⅛
	AlaP 8½s01	11.	23	80	79¾	80	− ¼
	AlaP 8⅞s03	11.	15	82	82	82	+ ⅜
13.	AlaP 9¾s04	☐	8	88½	88½	88½	+ 1
	AlaP 10⅞05	11.	27	97	96⅝	97	+ 1
	AlaP 8⅞06	11.	1	80¾	80¾	80¾	+ ¾
	AlaP 9¼07	11.	30	83⅝	83½	83⅝	+ ⅝
	AlaP 9½08	11.	13	86⅝	85	86⅝	+ 3⅜
	AlaP 9⅝08	11.	13	86⅜	85½	86⅜	+ ⅞
14.	AlaP 15¼10	☐	92	110⅞	110¼	110⅞	.....
	AlaP 17⅜11	15.	70	117¼	116	116	− ½
	AlaP 18¼89	17.	82	111¼	110⅜	110⅜	.....
	AlskA 9s03	cv	30	120	120	120	.....
15.	AlskH 16¼94	☐	16	107⅞	106½	107⅞	.....
	AlskH 16¼99	14.	52	113½	112⅝	113	+ 1¼
16.	AlskH 18⅜01	☐	180	113⅞	113	113	− ⅛
	AlskH 15¼92	14.	5	108	108	108	.....

••• Find the yield on purchase price to the nearest tenth of a percent in Exercises 17–22.

	Bond	*Total cost*
17.	Woolw 9s99	$970
18.	Xerox 6s95	$875
19.	UAL 8s03	$685
20.	▦ PorG $9\frac{7}{8}$s88	$760
21.	Sears 8s06	$1065
22.	MGM 10s94	$1125

✓ SKILL MAINTENANCE

Find the date.

23. 90 days from June 4.

24. 130 days from August 14.

Subtract.

25. 2171.25 − 565.35

26. 2439.70 − 731.36

If you miss an item, review the indicated section and objective.

[7.1, •] Find the total cost of purchasing 100 shares.

Stock	Selling price
1. Comsat	$42\frac{1}{8}$
2. EsKod	$56\frac{1}{4}$

1. _____

2. _____

[7.1, ••] Find the total return on the sale of 100 shares.

Stock	Selling price
3. Comsat	$42\frac{1}{8}$
4. EsKod	$56\frac{1}{4}$

3. _____

4. _____

[7.2, •] Find the yield.

Stock	Dividend	Price per share
5. EsKod	$1.72	$56\frac{1}{4}$

5. _____

[7.2, ••] Find the price-earnings ratio.

Stock	Price per share	Earnings per share
6. EsKod	$\$56\frac{1}{4}$	$4.33

6. _____

[7.3, •] Find the total cost of purchasing three bonds.

Bond	Selling price
7. GnEl $6\frac{1}{4}89$	$97\frac{7}{8}$

7. _____

Find the total cost of purchasing 14 bonds.

Bond	Selling price
8. PAA $10\frac{1}{2}01$	$121\frac{1}{2}$

8. _____

[7.3, ••] Find the current yield.

Bond	Market price
9. GnEl $6\frac{1}{4}89$	$97\frac{7}{8}$

9. _____

Find the current yield.

Bond	Market price
10. PAA $10\frac{1}{2}01$	$121\frac{1}{2}$

10. _____

[7.3, •••] Find the yield on purchase price.

Bond	Total cost
11. DaytH $9\frac{3}{4}95$	$890

11. _____

| **12.** CapHd $12\frac{3}{4}06$ | $940 |

12. _____

Chapter 7   Stocks and Bonds

8

INSURANCE

CAREER: LIFE INSURANCE AGENT
Barton L. Kaufman, a Life Insurance Agent, is the President and Chief Executive Officer of the Kaufman Financial Corporation. Bart took a course such as this while preparing for a BS degree in Life Insurance at Indiana University. He also has a Law degree from the same university, and has earned the title, CLU, Chartered Life Underwriter. A CLU has taken specialized training in life insurance.

BARTON L. KAUFMAN

Should you be considering a career in life insurance, keep in mind that you do not have to have this amount of preparation. Bart is at the top of his profession both in terms of educational preparation and performance. In most states, one can sell life insurance upon passing a state test, but it is advisable to have additional study such as becoming a Chartered Life Underwriter.

Clearly, of all the material in this book, the mathematics in this chapter is the most relevant to Bart's work. An understanding of Ratio and Percent is also important.

There are many qualities, apart from mathematical knowledge, which are necessary in order to be an excellent life insurance agent. The most important is the ability to work on your own. You must be a self-starter. You should like people and be able to help them overcome a natural resistance towards buying life insurance. The range of salaries in this field is wide. Some life insurance agents make $20,000 to $25,000. Others make $50,000 to $100,000. People who are highly successful in the field can earn over $1,000,000 per year.

After finishing Section 8.1, you should be able to:

- **•** **Compute a business owner's fire insurance premiums.**
- **• •** **Find the amount of a loss a homeowner's insurer will pay.**
- **• • •** **Determine the premium for homeowner's insurance.**

1. Trembly Enterprises is in a fire resistive building which would cost $75,000 to replace. What is the annual fire insurance premium for the building?

2. The contents in a frame building would cost $20,000 to replace. What is the annual fire insurance premium on the contents?

ANSWERS ON PAGE A-13

8.1

Business and Homeowner's Insurance

Prudent planning for financial investments protects you against future financial hardship. In much the same way, insurance protects you and your family against financial loss due to accidents, sickness, liability, death, and other unexpected occurrences. We discuss insurance coverage and its cost in this chapter.

• BUSINESS OWNER'S FIRE INSURANCE

Business owners pay far less for fire insurance when their businesses are in fire-resistant buildings. Three types of construction are:

1. *Frame:* Exterior walls are predominantly wood or stucco or other combustible materials, and the floors and roof are wood or steel frame.
2. *Incombustible:* Exterior walls, floors, and roof are constructed of—and supported by—metal, asbestos, gypsum, or other noncombustible materials.
3. *Fire-resistive:* Walls are of reinforced concrete or structural steel encased in masonry or concrete materials with fire-proofed floors and roof decks and their supports.

The following table lists the annual fire insurance **premiums** (payment for coverage) for each $100 of building-and-contents replacement cost.

	Frame	Incombustible	Fire-resistive
Building	$0.68	$0.29	$0.06
Contents	$2.32	$1.97	$0.96

Example 1 Eck Engineering is in a frame building which would cost $75,000 to replace. What is the annual fire insurance premium for the building?

Solution

$$\text{Total premium} = \frac{\text{Premium}}{\text{per } \$100} \times \frac{\text{Replacement cost}}{\text{(in hundreds)}}$$

$$= \$0.68 \times 750 \quad \text{There are 750 hundreds in 75,000.}$$

$$= \$510$$

The total premium is $510.

DO EXERCISE 1.

Example 2 The contents in a fire-resistive building would cost $20,000 to replace. What is the annual fire insurance premium on the contents?

Solution

$$\text{Total premium} = \frac{\text{Premium}}{\text{per } \$100} \times \frac{\text{Replacement cost}}{\text{(in hundreds)}}$$

$$= \$0.96 \times 200 \quad \text{There are 200 hundreds in 20,000.}$$

$$= \$192$$

The total premium is $192.

DO EXERCISE 2.

Other types of insurance businessowners might consider include income loss from temporary business interruption and liability. Coverage and premiums vary greatly.

 HOMEOWNER'S INSURANCE

Homeowners can purchase fire insurance providing protection against

Fire

Lightning

Damage due to extinguishing fire

or one of three types of homeowner's policies.

Each type provides the coverage shown for the preceding policy as well as the protection indicated in the figure. For example, the broad type provides protection against the perils listed as well as the protection provided by the basic and fire policies. In addition, all three homeowner's policies provide:

Comprehensive personal liability

Medical payments (other than to insureds)

Physical damage to property of others

All costs of defending suits (whether you are liable or not)

Additional living expense when home is not habitable

The Basic policy

Glass breakage

Windstorm, Hail

Explosion

Vehicles (non-owned)

Riot and civil commotion

Damage to trees, shrubs and lawns

Smoke

Theft, on or off premises

Vandalism and malicious mischief

Aircraft

The Broad policy covers these additional perils.

Vehicles (owned)

Collapse of building

Artificially generated electrical current

Freezing of plumbing system

Falling objects

Tearing or bulging of water heating appliances

Weight of ice and snow

Water escape from plumbing, heating, air conditioning or appliances

The "All-Risk" Special policy adds these coverages for your home plus many others not specifically excluded.

Moisture damage* caused by malfunction of thermostat

Building damage*

Water damage*

Paint spill*

Scorched surface*

Siding damaged* by missiles

Damage by* wild animal

Falling objects* within dwelling

Chemical spill*

Chipping of sink*

*Building coverage only.

3. A broad-form homeowner's policy for $65,000 is taken out on the Barb's home that would cost $70,000 to replace. A fire destroys the home. How much is paid by the insurance company?

4. A broad-form homeowner's policy for $45,000 is taken out on the Kyle's home whose replacement cost is $56,000. A fire does $10,000 damage to the house. How much does the insurance company pay?

ANSWERS ON PAGE A-13

The amount of coverage for complete loss of dwelling is the insurance amount carried or the replacement cost of the home, whichever is smaller.

Example 3 A broad-form homeowner's policy for $80,000 is taken out on a home that would cost $90,000 to replace. A tornado destroys the home. How much is paid by the insurance company?

Solution The insurance company pays the amount of insurance carried ($80,000).

DO EXERCISE 3.

Full coverage is provided for partial loss of dwelling whenever the amount of insurance carried is 80% or more of the dwelling's **replacement cost.** The replacement cost is the present value of the house less the value of the land and basement.

Inflation riders keyed to the Composite Construction Cost Index of the U.S. Department of Commerce keep the 80% or more coverage current as property values increase.

Example 4 An all-risk homeowner's policy for $52,000 is taken out on the Keel's home whose replacement cost is $60,000. A nonowned automobile does $5000 damage to the house. How much does the insurance company pay?

Solution

a) Find out if the insurance coverage is at least 80%.

$$\text{Replacement cost feature} = 80\% \times \$60,000$$
$$= 0.80 \times \$60,000$$
$$= \$48,000$$

The insurance coverage ($52,000) is greater than 80%.

b) Find the amount that the insurance company pays.

The insurance company pays the total loss ($5000), because the insurance carried ($52,000) is more than the minimum 80% coverage ($48,000).

DO EXERCISE 4.

Full coverage is not provided for the partial loss of a dwelling whenever the insurance carried is less than 80% of the replacement cost. This **co-insurance** means the insurer and policyowner both pay certain amounts when a loss occurs.

Example 5 An all-risk homeowner's policy for $30,000 is taken out on the Barbetta's home that would cost $50,000 to replace. Water damage to the home from an open window during a storm is $6000. How much is paid by the insurance company?

Solution

a) Find 80% of $50,000.

$$\text{Replacement cost feature} = 80\% \times \$50,000$$
$$= 0.80 \times \$50,000$$
$$= \$40,000$$

The amount of insurance carried ($30,000) is *not* 80% of the replacement cost ($40,000), so not all of the loss is covered by the insurance company.

Chapter 8   Insurance

b) Find the amount that the insurance company pays.

$$\text{Amount insurance pays} = \frac{\text{Insurance carried}}{80\% \text{ of replacement cost}} \times \text{Loss}$$

$$= \frac{30{,}000}{40{,}000} \times \$6{,}000$$

$$= \$4{,}500$$

The insurance company pays $4,500.

Note that the loss was coinsured, as the company pays $4500 and the policyowner pays $1500.

DO EXERCISE 5.

Homeowner's policies also provide coverage on the contents (up to 50% of dwelling coverage) and living expenses (up to 20% of dwelling coverage) should the house become uninhabitable because of a covered loss.

Example 6 An all-risk homeowner's policy for $56,000 is taken out on the Smith's house. How much coverage is provided for contents and living expenses?

Solution

a) Find the coverage for contents.

$$\text{Coverage for contents} = 50\% \times \text{Dwelling coverage}$$

$$= 0.50 \times \$56{,}000$$

$$= \$28{,}000$$

Contents loss is covered up to $28,000.

b) Find the coverage for living expenses.

$$\text{Coverage for living expenses} = 20\% \times \text{Dwelling coverage}$$

$$= 0.20 \times \$56{,}000$$

$$= \$11{,}200$$

The family in Example 6 would have as much as $11,200 to live on after their house was damaged or destroyed.

DO EXERCISE 6.

The 80% feature applies only to the dwelling and not to the contents or living expenses.

SUGGESTION

The 80% feature is calculated on the replacement cost, *not* the present value of the house. For example, a house with a present value of $65,000 may have a replacement cost of $50,000 since the replacement cost would not include the value of land or an unfinished basement. The 80% feature on $65,000 indicates that at least $52,000, or 80% of $65,000, of insurance must be purchased on the house. However, only $40,000, or 80% of $50,000, of insurance need be purchased to qualify for the 80% feature. The consumer can save on premium dollars by insuring only on the replacement cost and *not* the present value.

Contents on which there is a loss are first evaluated on the basis of replacement cost and then depreciated according to industry guidelines. Industry guidelines for depreciation appear in Table 14 (p. T-24). Most insurance companies use straight-line depreciation (see p. 312) to determine reimbursement for loss.

5. A basic-form homeowner's policy for $45,000 is taken out on the Lyle's home that would cost $85,000 to replace. Lightning damage is $10,000. How much is paid by the insurance company?

6. A basic-form homeowner's policy for $48,000 is taken out on the Cary's house. How much coverage is provided for contents and living expenses?

ANSWERS ON PAGE A-13

7. An all-risk homeowner's policy for $42,000 is taken out on the Rust's house. A refrigerator purchased 3 years ago at a cost of $600 was destroyed in a tornado. The comparable refrigerator today costs $800. How much of the loss will the insurance company pay? Assume a 10 year refrigerator life.

Example 7 A basic-form homeowner's policy for $58,000 is taken out on the Ott's house. A stereo purchased for $500 four years ago was stolen. The comparable model costs $700 today. How much of the loss will the insurance company pay?

Solution

a) Find the coverage on the contents.

Coverage on contents = 50% × Dwelling coverage
$$= 0.50 \times \$58,000$$
$$= \$29,000$$

Losses up to $29,000 are covered.

b) Find straight-line depreciation on the comparable model.

From Table 14 (p. T-24), we see that depreciation is 7–10 years. Suppose the stereo is a good model and therefore would last 10 years.

Depreciation for four years = Depreciation for one year × 4
$$= (700 \div 10) \times 4$$
$$= 70 \times 4$$
$$= 280$$

The depreciation is $280.

c) Find the amount after depreciation (the trade-in value).

Amount after depreciation = Comparable model cost − Depreciation
$$= 700 - 280$$
$$= 420$$

The insurance company will pay $420 since this amount does not exceed the maximum coverage.

DO EXERCISE 7.

Some insurers do not depreciate contents, that is, the full replacement cost is paid. This coverage is available to consumers whose homes have fire extinguishers, smoke alarms, and deadbolt locks and which were built since 1955.

••• THE COST OF HOMEOWNER'S INSURANCE

The cost of homeowner's insurance depends on several factors. Among them are the type of construction (frame, masonry, or other), roof type (composition or wood shingles), distance from fire station, type of fire department (volunteer or professional), and location (for example, windstorm damage is more likely in certain sections of the country than others).

Table 15 (p. T-25) lists the annual premiums (costs) for one home insurer. Part of that table appears as Table 8.1. Form 1 is the basic policy; Form 2, the broad-form policy; and Form 3, the all-risk policy.

Example 8 Find the annual premium for a $36,000 Form 2, $100 all-peril deductible homeowner's policy on the Fisk's frame house in Zone 1, Protection Class 2.

TABLE 8.1

Zone I
Protection Class: 1-4   **Annual Premiums**

	$50 All-Peril Deductible						$100 All-Peril Deductible					
	Masonry or Mas. Veneer			Frame			Masonry or Mas. Veneer			Frame		
	Form			Form			Form			Form		
Amount	1	2	3	1	2	3	1	2	3	1	2	3
$ 5,000	41	47	48	41	48	49	37	43	44	37	44	45
7,000	43	49	50	43	49	51	39	45	46	39	45	46
⋮	⋮	⋮	⋮	⋮	⋮	⋮	⋮	⋮	⋮	⋮	⋮	⋮
32,000	94	105	107	94	107	108	85	95	97	85	97	98
33,000	97	109	111	97	111	112	88	99	101	88	101	102
34,000	101	113	115	101	115	117	92	103	105	92	105	106
35,000	104	116	118	104	118	119	95	105	107	95	107	108
36,000	107	120	122	107	122	123	97	109	111	97	111	112
37,000	111	124	126	111	126	128	101	113	115	101	115	116
38,000	114	128	130	114	130	131	104	116	118	104	118	119
39,000	118	132	134	118	134	136	107	120	122	107	122	124
40,000	122	136	138	122	138	140	111	124	125	111	125	127
42,000	129	144	146	129	146	148	117	131	133	117	133	135

Solution In Table 8.1 read down the amount column to $36,000 and across to the column headed $100 all-peril deductible, frame, Form 2. The annual premium is $111.

DO EXERCISE 8.

The premium for a homeowner's policy falling between two table entries can be found by **interpolation.** For example, if the amount of insurance needed is halfway between two entries, the premium charged is halfway between the corresponding premiums.

Example 9 Find the annual premium for a $41,000 Form 3, $50 all-peril deductible homeowner's policy on the Lopez's masonry house in Zone 1, Protection Class 3.

Solution

a) Find the premium for the entries between which $41,000 falls.

From Table 8.1 we see that the premium for $40,000 is $138 and for $42,000 is $146.

b) Find the premium for $41,000.

Since $41,000 is halfway between the two entries, the premium will be halfway between the corresponding entries:

$$\text{Premium} = \frac{138 + 146}{2}$$

$$= 142.$$

The annual premium for the $41,000 policy is $142.

DO EXERCISE 9.

8. Using Table 8.1, find the annual premium for a $40,000 Form 3, $100 all-peril deductible homeowner's policy on the Zin-Faire's frame house in Zone 1, Protection Class 4.

9. Find the annual premium for an $41,000 Form 2, $100 all-peril deductible homeowner's policy on the Lee's frame house in Zone 1, Protection Class 2.

ANSWERS ON PAGE A-13

10. Find the annual premium for a $230,000 Form 2, $100 all-peril deductible homeowner's policy on a frame house in Zone 1, Protection Class 3.

The premium for a homeowner's policy with coverage greater than $200,000 can be found by adding the appropriate $10,000-premium increments to the premium for $200,000.

Example 10 Find the annual premium for a $240,000 Form 3, $50 all-peril deductible homeowner's policy on the Penney-Crocker's masonry veneer house in Zone 1, Protection Class 2.

Solution

a) Find the premium for $200,000.

From Table 15 (p. T-25) we see that the premium is $1042.

b) Find the premium for each $10,000 increment.

From Table 15 (p. T-25) we find that the premium for each $10,000 increment is $54.

c) Find the premium for four $10,000 increments.

$$\text{Premium for four increments} = 4 \times \text{Premium for one increment}$$
$$= 4 \times 54$$
$$= 216$$

The premium for the additional $40,000 is $216.

d) Find the total premium.

$$\text{Total premium} = \text{Premium for } \$200,000 + \text{Premium for increment}$$
$$= 1042 + 216$$
$$= 1258$$

The total premium is $1258.

DO EXERCISE 10.

ANSWERS ON PAGE A-13

ANSWERS

• Find the business owner's fire insurance premiums in Exercises 1–6. Use the table on p. 230.

1. Peacock Tree Service is in a frame building which would cost $125,000 to replace. What is the annual fire insurance premium for the building?

2. Brice Computer, Incorporated, is in an incombustible building that would cost $125,000 to replace. What is the annual fire insurance premium for the building?

3. ▦ Hetzler Construction is in a fire-resistive building that would cost $250,000 to replace. What is the annual fire insurance premium for the building?

4. Jones Brothers Concrete is in an incombustible building that would cost $250,000 to replace. What is the annual fire insurance premium for the building?

5. Armstrong Company is in a frame building that would cost $90,000 to replace. What is the annual fire insurance premium for the building?

6. Randy's Carpets is in a fire-resistive building that would cost $90,000 to replace. What is the annual fire insurance premium for the building?

• • Solve.

7. Fire destroys the Alvarez home which has a $45,000 broad-form homeowner's policy on it. The replacement cost of the home is $80,000. How much does the insurance company pay?

8. An airplane destroys the Reed home which has a $52,000 basic-form homeowner's policy on it. The replacement cost of the home is $58,000. How much does the insurance company pay?

9. An all-risk policy for $35,000 is taken out on the Ruppert's house with a replacement cost of $43,000. A chemical spill does $5000 in damage to the floors. How much does the insurance company pay?

10. ▦ A broad-form policy for $62,000 is taken out on the Norem's house with a replacement cost of $77,500. Part of the house collapses, causing $8000 damage. How much does the insurance company pay?

11. A basic-form policy for $30,000 is taken out on the Nabrotzky's house with a replacement cost of $55,000. A nonowned vehicle does $6000 in damage to the house. How much does the insurance company pay?

12. A broad-form policy for $75,000 is taken out on the Talbot's house with a replacement cost of $100,000. A falling tree limb does $1500 in damage to the house. How much does the insurance company pay?

13. A basic-form policy for $37,000 is taken out on the Szopinski's house. How much coverage is provided for contents and living expenses?

14. An all-risk policy for $49,000 is taken out on the Sturm's house. How much coverage is provided for contents and living expenses?

1.
2.
3.
4.
5.
6.
7.
8.
9.
10.
11.
12.
13.
14.

ANSWERS

15. _____

16. _____

17. _____

18. _____

19. _____

20. _____

21. _____

22. _____

23. _____

24. _____

25. _____

26. _____

27. _____

28. _____

29. _____

30. _____

15. A broad-form policy for $80,000 is taken out on the Swan's house. A bicycle purchased three years ago for $600 was stolen. The cost to replace it today is $800. How much of the loss will the insurance company pay? Assume the bike would last 10 years.

••• Solve. Use Table 15 (p. T-25).

17. An insurance agent determines that Eric Nikkel needs $90,000 protection for a masonry home in Protection Class 3, Zone 1. What is the annual homeowner's premium for a Form 2, $100 all-peril deductible policy?

16. A basic-form policy for $43,000 is taken out on the Munro's house. A furnace purchased two years ago for $2800 was ruined by an explosion. The cost to replace it today is $3500. How much of the loss will the insurance company pay? Use Table 14 (p. T-24).

18. An insurance agent determines that Chui Kon needs $48,000 protection for a frame home in Protection Class 4, Zone 1. What is the annual homeowner's premium for a Form 3, $100 all-peril deductible policy?

Find the annual premium in Exercises 19–28.

	Amount of Insurance	Deductible	Construction Type	Form	Zone	Class
19.	$24,000	$50	Frame	2	1	4
20.	$32,000	$50	Frame	2	1	4
21.	$37,000	$100	Masonry	3	1	2
22.	$44,000	$100	Masonry	3	1	2
23.	$70,000	$50	Masonry veneer	1	1	3
24.	$90,000	$50	Masonry veneer	1	1	3
25.	$65,000	$100	Frame	2	1	1
26.	$55,000	$100	Frame	2	1	1
27.	$220,000	$100	Masonry	3	1	4
28.	$230,000	$100	Masonry	3	1	4

✓ **SKILL MAINTENANCE**

Use the amortization schedule to answer 29 and 30.

NUMBER	INTEREST	DUE DATE-PAID TO	PRINCIPAL	TOTAL PAYMENT	BALANCE OF LOAN
1	525 00	7-1-89	23 85	548 85	59 976 15

29. How much of payment 1 is interest?

30. How much of payment 1 is principal?

8.2

Automobile Insurance

Drivers can purchase automobile insurance, which protects them and others driving their automobile against loss. Table 8.2 lists coverage descriptions.

• AMOUNT OF THE LOSS PAYABLE

Example 1 A motorist has 100,000/300,000 bodily injury liability coverage. What is the maximum coverage when two or more people are injured in an accident?

Solution The second limit (300,000) is the maximum coverage when two or more people are injured in one accident. The insurance company will pay up to $300,000 for bodily injuries.

DO EXERCISE 1.

TABLE 8.2

COVERAGE DESCRIPTIONS

1. Bodily Injury and Property Damage Liability

Pays damages for which you are liable arising from injuries or death, or from damage to property of others. Includes defense of suits and bail bonds. Pays up to the first limit for any one person and up to the second limit for two or more people injured or killed. Pays up to the limit shown for damage to property of others.

A minimum of $50,000/$100,000 Bodily Injury and $25,000 Property Damage is suggested due to today's high claim cost. In fact even higher limits are needed in many cases.

2. Uninsured Motorists

Protects you and occupants of your car for personal injuries if caused by an uninsured motorist or unknown hit-and run driver.

You must carry Bodily Injury and Property Damage to obtain this coverage.

3. Comprehensive

Pays loss by fire, theft, accidental damage, and glass damage, less any deductible. CB ratios and tape decks are not covered. Coverage is available at extra cost. *Usually required if car is financed.*

Collision

Pays for damage to your car, less your deductible, for collision with another object or upset. *Usually required if car is financed.*

4. Towing and Labor

Pays towing and labor repair costs at place of disablement up to $50 ($25 in Texas).

5. Personal Injury Protection (PIP)—(No Fault) Medical Payments

Must carry Bodily Injury and Property Damage to buy these coverages. Many states offer Personal Injury Protection, a form of "No Fault" coverage in place of or with Medical Payments coverage.

Medical Payments coverage is available in other states.

Pays medical and/or funeral expenses for each family member and other passengers in your car who are injured or killed. Pays up to limits shown except when other insurance policies pay all or part of such expenses.

After finishing Section 8.2, you should be able to:

- • Determine the loss payable by the insurer and the policyowner.
- •• Figure the cost of automobile insurance.

---

1. A motorist has 50,000/100,000 bodily injury liability coverage. What is the maximum coverage when two or more people are injured in an accident?

ANSWER ON PAGE A-13

---

2. A motorist with 25,000/50,000/ 10,000 coverage does $12,435 damage to a Lincoln. How much does the motorist pay?

3. Cindy Legg who has 10,000/20,000 uninsured-motorist coverage is injured by a hit-and-run driver and has medical expenses of $13,632. How much does the motorist pay?

4. A car worth $3500 is stolen from Bill Schultz who has $250 deductible comprehensive coverage. How much does the insurance company pay?

ANSWERS ON PAGE A-13

Example 2 A motorist with 50,000/100,000/25,000 (sometimes abbreviated 50/100/25) coverage does $25,678 damage to a house. How much does the motorist pay?

Solution

a) Find the maximum property damage coverage.

The maximum property damage coverage is the third limit ($25,000).

b) Find the amount that the motorist pays.

Amount motorist pays = Total damage − Amount insurance pays

$$= 25,678 - 25,000$$
$$= 678$$

The motorist pays $678.

DO EXERCISE 2.

Uninsured motorist coverage is often 10,000/20,000, which means that, if hit by an uninsured motorist, the motorist and occupants are protected for personal injuries up to $10,000 for one person and up to $20,000 for each occurrence.

Many insurers have underinsured motorist coverage available. For example, while driving you are involved in an accident for which the other driver is liable. That driver has inadequate insurance. If you have underinsured coverage your company will pay an amount up to the specified limits to you. However, you must hire your own lawyer and sue your own company to recover any damages.

Example 3 Curtis Houge, who has 10,000/20,000 uninsured motorist coverage, is injured by a hit-and-run driver and has medical expenses of $11,560. How much does Curtis pay?

Solution

a) Find the maximum coverage.

The maximum coverage for one person is $10,000.

b) Find the amount that Curtis pays.

Amount Curtis pays = Total damage − Amount insurance pays

$$= 11,560 - 10,000$$
$$= 1560$$

Curtis pays $1560.

DO EXERCISE 3.

Example 4 A rock breaks the car windshield of Elaine Borz who has $50 deductible comprehensive coverage. How much does the insurance company pay of the $175 needed to replace the windshield?

Solution Find the amount that the insurance companys pays.

Amount insurance pays = Amount of damage − Deductible

$$= 175 - 50$$
$$= 125$$

The insurance company pays $125.

DO EXERCISE 4.

Collision coverage pays up to the value of the automobile less the deductible. After the policyowner pays the deductible the company pays the smaller of either the repair cost or the automobile's value.

Example 5 Sue Horn, who has $250 deductible collision coverage and a car worth $1400, has an accident that requires $2000 in repairs. How much does the insurance company pay?

Solution The car's value is $1400. The insurance company will pay $1150, or $1400 − $250.

DO EXERCISE 5.

SUGGESTION

Don't file collision claims that are just over your deductible. Otherwise the insurance company may raise your premium. Pay the expense yourself.

Towing and labor coverage does not pay for parts or gasoline that may be required in case of a breakdown.

Example 6 A motorist with towing and labor coverage up to $25 is charged $22 by the mechanic who repairs the car. The $22 includes a $15 service fee, $4 for parts, and $3 for gasoline. How much does the insurance pay?

Solution Find the amount that the insurance company pays.

$$\text{Amount insurance pays} = \text{Total charge} - \begin{array}{c}\text{Amount for}\\\text{gasoline and parts}\end{array}$$
$$= 22 - (4 + 3)$$
$$= 15$$

The insurance company pays $15.

DO EXERCISE 6.

A passenger riding with you at the time of an accident can be reimbursed for medical expenses under the medical-payments coverage.

Example 7 A motorist with medical-payments coverage to a maximum of $5000 for each person is involved in an accident that injures one passenger. The passenger has $6235 in medical expenses. How much does the passenger pay?

Solution Find the amount that the passenger pays.

$$\text{Amount passenger pays} = \text{Amount of expenses} - \begin{array}{c}\text{Amount}\\\text{insurance pays}\end{array}$$
$$= 6235 - 5000$$
$$= 1235$$

The passenger pays $1235.

DO EXERCISE 7.

5. Sam Shepherd, who has $100 deductible collision coverage and a car worth $2650, has an accident that requires $700 in repairs. How much does the insurance company pay?

6. A motorist with towing and labor coverage up to $25 is charged $35 by the mechanic who repairs the car. The $35 includes a $10 towing fee, $11 for service, and $14 for parts. How much does the insurance company pay?

7. A motorist with medical-payments coverage to a maximum of $2500 for each person is involved in an accident that injures one passenger. The passenger has $4368 in medical expenses. How much does the passenger pay?

ANSWERS ON PAGE A-13

8. Alan Johans, a single male, age 18, with a medium-size 1987 car, selects the following coverage:

Liability	100/300/50
Medical	25,000
Comprehensive	ACV
Collision	100 deductible
Uninsured motorist	25/50

Find his premium for six months.

●● THE COST OF AUTOMOBILE INSURANCE

The cost of automobile insurance depends on several factors. Among them are the kind of car, the location and use of the car, and the age, sex, driving record, and marital status of the driver. A basic premium table and a rating factor table, Tables 16 and 17 (p. T-26) for one insurer are used in Example 8.

Example 8 Lynette Thomas, a single female, age 18, with a medium-size 1987 car, selects the following coverage:

Liability	100/300/50
Medical	25,000
Comprehensive	Actual cash value (ACV)
Collision	100 deductible
Uninsured motorist	25/50

Find her premium for six months.

Solution Find the basic premium and rating factor for each coverage from Tables 16 and 17 (p. T-26).

	Basic Premium	Rating Factor	Premium
Liability	28.80	1.95	28.80×1.95 or 56.16
Medical	6.60	1.95	6.60×1.95 or 12.87
Comprehensive	27.40	1.95	27.40×1.95 or 53.43
Collision	46.80	1.95	46.80×1.95 or 91.26
Uninsured motorist	2.30	1.00	2.30×1.00 or 2.30
TOTAL			216.02 (adding)

The premium for six months is $216.02.

DO EXERCISE 8.

Note that uninsured motorist coverage is the only coverage in which the rating factor is not used (in effect, it is 1.00). The motorist who drives carelessly and gets tickets or is involved in an accident in which the insurance company pays over $100 can expect to pay even higher premiums. For example, an accident in which the insurance company pays over $100 may result in at least a 10% premium increase during each of the following three to five years.

SUGGESTION

You will want to get bids from several reputable car insurers, using a form like the one below, before deciding which company to choose.

Coverage	Limits	Six-month rate
Bodily injury	100/300	———
Property damage	50	———
Medical	5000	———
Comprehensive	ACV	———
Collision	100 deductible	———
Uninsured motorist	10/20	———

ANSWER ON PAGE A-13

Alison Johnston has the coverages and limits shown below.

```
             COVERAGES/LIMITS/PREMIUM
AB BODILY INJ/PROP DAMAGE
   100,000/300,000/25,000
C MEDICAL PAYMENTS  5,000
D  COMPREHENSIVE (ACV)
G 100 DEDUCT COLLISION
U UNINSURED MOTOR VEHICLE
   10,000/20,000
H EMERGENCY ROAD SERVICE
```

• Find the amounts (a) that Alison pays and (b) that the insurance company pays for each loss in Exercises 1–10.

1. A bodily injury suit by one person, in which the award by the jury was $106,250.

2. A bodily injury suit by three people in which the award by the jury was $432,000.

3. Property damage of $238 to a telephone pole.

4. Property damage of $21,628 to a building.

5. Medical payments of $8679 to one injured passenger.

6. Medical payments of $4568 to one injured passenger and of $6782 to another.

7. Theft of an automobile valued at $5675.

8. Windstorm damage of $567 to an automobile.

9. Repair work of $3546 (for accident-caused damage) to Alison's car, valued at $6580.

10. Repair work of $2587 (for accident-caused damage) to Alison's car, valued at $1785.

Dennis Lange has the coverage and limits shown below.

```
             COVERAGES/LIMITS/PREMIUM
AB BODILY INJ/PROP DAMAGE
   300,000/500,000/50,000
C MEDICAL PAYMENTS  5,000
D  COMPREHENSIVE (ACV)
G 500 DEDUCT COLLISION
U UNINSURED MOTOR VEHICLE
   10,000/20,000
H EMERGENCY ROAD SERVICE
```

Find the amounts (a) Dennis pays and (b) the insurance company pays for each loss in Exercises 11–20.

11. A bodily injury suit by one person in which the award by the jury was $275,000.

12. A bodily injury suit by two people in which the award by the jury was $615,000.

ANSWERS

1. _____

2. _____

3. _____

4. _____

5. _____

6. _____

7. _____

8. _____

9. _____

10. _____

11. _____

12. _____

13. Property damage of $52,000 to an expensive sport car.

14. Property damage of $635 to a fire hydrant.

15. Medical payments of $4200 to one injured passenger.

16. Medical payments of $1287 to one injured passenger and $7300 to another.

17. Repair of windshield damage of $317.

18. Theft of an automobile valued at $9254.

19. Repair work of $780 (for accident-caused damage) to Dennis's car, valued at $9490.

20. Repair work of $4342 (for accident-caused damage) to Dennis's car, valued at $3500.

One insurance company had to pay jury awards for policyholders with the following coverages.

Total Award by Jury	Policyholder's Coverage	Number of Injured Persons
$325,876.50	250,000/500,000	3
$172,564.75	50,000/100,000	1
$567,892.25	100,000/300,000	2
$467,985.50	200,000/400,000	1

21. ▦ What is the total amount that the insurance company paid?

22. ▦ What is the total amount that the policyholders paid?

• •   Use Tables 16 and 17 (p. T-26) to find the six-month premiums for these medium-size cars. All have actual cash value comprehensive and $100 deductible collision coverage.

	Sex	Age	Miles/Week Work	Marital Status	Car Year	Liability	Medical	Uninsured Motorist
23.	M	26	50	S	1986	50/100/10	5,000	25/50
24.	M	26	50	M	1986	50/100/10	5,000	25/50
25.	F	22	70	S	1987	25/50/10	5,000	100/300
26.	F	19	0	S	1987	100/300/50	5,000	10/20
27.	M	24	0	S	1985	100/300/50	25,000	25/50
28.	F	24	0	S	1985	100/300/50	25,000	25/50
29.	M	18	0	S	1984	25/50/10	5,000	10/20
30.	F	18	0	S	1984	25/50/10	5,000	10/20
31.	M	27	120	M	1987	50/100/10	25,000	100/300
32.	F	27	120	M	1987	50/100/10	25,000	100/300

✓ SKILL MAINTENANCE

33. A corporation has a profit of $18,500 one year. It must pay 20% of this in federal taxes. How much is the federal tax?

34. A baseball player gets 11 hits in 40 at bats. What percent are hits?

Chapter 8   Insurance

8.3

Life Insurance

Life insurance provides financial protection in the event of the insured's death. The two most common types of policies are known as **term** and **permanent** insurance. Their features appear in Table 8.3.

After finishing Section 8.3, you should be able to:

- • Find the amount of coverage after a certain number of years.
- •• Determine the cash value of an insurance policy.
- ••• Find extended term coverage.
- ⦂⦂ Determine reduced paid up coverage.
- ⦂⦂ Calculate the cost of life insurance.

TABLE 8.3

Basic Type	Features	Comments
Term	Provides benefits only when the insured dies within a specified period. If the specified period may be extended without new medical evidence, the policy is *renewable.* If the policy can be exchanged for permanent insurance without new medical evidence, the policy is *convertible.* If the amount of insurance remains constant, the policy is known as *level term,* whereas if the amount of insurance becomes less according to some type of schedule, the policy may be known as *decreasing, declining,* or *diminishing term.*	The most common term policies are the one-year renewable and convertible policy, the five-year renewable and convertible policy, and various durations of decreasing term insurance, with the most popular being 15, 20, or 25 years. The premium for level term insurance is constant only until renewal, whereas the premium for decreasing term insurance remains level as the face amount of the policy becomes less.
Permanent	Provides benefits without regard to the date when the insured dies. This type of insurance may also be known as *ordinary life, whole life,* or *cash value insurance.* The premium remains level and payable until the insured's death. The policy develops a subsidiary account within the contract that is known as *cash value.*	If the premium paying period is designed to be less than the insured's lifetime, the policy is known as a *limited pay policy.* A common type of this contract is a 20 payment life or a life paid up at 65 contract. If the insurance benefit payable to the insured at a specified date while he or she is living is equal to that which would have been paid if he or she had died, the policy is known as an *endowment.*

Universal Life, a recent life insurance product, accounts for over 10% of sales. As with whole life your premium buys protection and savings. However, the savings earn a much higher rate of interest than with whole life. Taxes on the earnings are deferred. Moreover, the policyholder can adjust the premium size so that more is placed in savings.

• AMOUNT OF COVERAGE

A decreasing term policy is often purchased to pay off a home mortgage at the insured's death. The death benefit and mortgage balance decrease each year. The year the insured dies is important in determining exactly how large a death benefit the insurance company will pay. Table 8.4 (next page) lists the coverage for each year in a 15-year decreasing term policy.

ANSWER ON PAGE A-13

1. Barb Cain has a $35,000 15-year decreasing term policy and dies during the ninth policy year. How much does the insurance company pay?

Example 1 William Brock has a $25,000 15-year decreasing term policy and dies during the fifth policy year. How much will the insurance company pay?

TABLE 8.4					
Schedule of Insurance					
The Amount payable per $1,000 of Initial Face Amount will be determined at the corresponding Policy Year at death. Policy Year 1 begins on the Date of Issue, Policy Year 2 begins one year after the Date of Issue, etc.					
Policy Year	Amount per $1000 of Initial Face Amount	Policy Year	Amount per $1000 of Initial Face Amount	Policy Year	Amount per $1000 of Initial Face Amount
1	$1000	6	$761	11	$438
2	958	7	704	12	361
3	913	8	643	13	278
4	865	9	579	14	191
5	815	10	511	15	99

Solution

a) Find the amount payable per $1000.

Read down to 5 in the policy year column of Table 8.4 and across to the column headed Amount per $1000 of Initial Face Amount. The amount payable for each $1000 is $815.

b) Since the initial policy was issued for $25,000, the total amount payable will be

Amount payable per $1000 × Number of thousands = $815 × 25

= $20,375.

The amount paid by the insurance company was $20,375.

DO EXERCISE 1.

●● CASH VALUE

Permanent insurance has a cash value, which permits the insured to borrow against the policy. If the insured elects to do so, he or she will be charged an interest rate that has been specified in the policy. Frequently this interest rate is lower than the interest rates charged for personal loans by commercial lenders. The major disadvantage of borrowing from one's policy is that upon death the amount of the loan that may remain unpaid is deducted from the face amount of coverage and the result is a death benefit lower than the one specified in the policy. A second disadvantage of borrowing from one's insurance is that, if the loan becomes large, the loan interest required may equal or even exceed the premium charged. Table 19 (p. T-27) lists the cash values for insurance policies. Part of that table appears as Table 8.5 (p. 248).

Example 2 After a $10,000 permanent insurance policy that was issued at age 22 has been in force for 12 years, Charles Calhoun, the insured, wants to borrow on the policy. How much is available?

Solution

a) Determine the amount available to be borrowed per $1000 of insurance.

Locate the box headed Age 22 At Issue on Table 8.5 and read down to 12 in the column headed Years in Force with all Due Premiums Paid. Read across to the column headed Guaranteed Cash or Loan Value. The amount per $1000 is $148.00.

b) Since the policy was issued for $10,000, the total amount available is

$$\text{Amount available per } \$1000 \times \text{Number of thousands} = \$148.00 \times 10$$
$$= \$1480.$$

The amount available to be borrowed is $1480.

DO EXERCISE 2.

••• EXTENDED TERM COVERAGE

Permanent insurance offers other options upon surrender of the policy in addition to surrendering the policy for cash. An insured may elect to exchange the policy for extended term insurance, which provides the original amount of insurance to be kept in force without any additional premium payments for a limited time. Table 8.5 (p. 248) lists the benefits.

Example 3 Joe Barta purchased a $15,000 permanent insurance policy at age 24. After he has paid premiums for 14 years, what will his extended term insurance option be?

Solution Determine the period of time that the insurance company will continue the policy on the extended term basis.

Locate the box headed Age 24 at Issue on Table 8.5 and read down to 14 in the column headed Years in Force with all Due Premiums Paid. Read across to the column headed Extended Term Insurance. The extended term insurance option is 22 years, 234 days. If the insured wishes to cease paying premiums, the insurance company will keep the policy in force on an extended term insurance basis for the next 22 years, 234 days; however, if Joe dies after that time period the insurance company is under no further obligation.

DO EXERCISE 3.

•• REDUCED PAID UP COVERAGE

Another option that permanent insurance offers upon surrender of the policy in addition to either surrendering the policy for cash or accepting extended term insurance is that of reduced paid up insurance. This provision permits the insured to keep the policy in force until death without any further premium payments on a reduced face amount basis. Whereas the extended term insurance option keeps the policy going without further premium payments for a certain specified period for the full face amount, the reduced paid up insurance option keeps the policy going indefinitely without further premium payments but for a lesser amount. Table 8.5 (p. 248) lists the benefits.

2. Theresa Barron, who has a $26,000 permanent insurance policy, wants to know its cash value after 15 years. The insured was 24 when she bought the policy. What is the policy's cash value?

3. Art Barton purchased a $15,000 permanent insurance policy at age 23. After he has paid premiums for 19 years, what will his extended term insurance option be?

ANSWERS ON PAGE A-13

TABLE 8.5

Guaranteed Cash or Loan Value, Reduced Paid-up Insurance, Extended Term Insurance
Applicable to a Policy without Either Paid-up Additions or Dividend Accumulations and without Indebtedness
Values at end of years other than those shown will be quoted on request.

Years In Force with all Due Premiums Paid	Age 20 — Guaran-teed Cash or Loan Value	Age 20 — Reduced Paid-up Insurance	Age 20 — Ext. Term Yrs.	Age 20 — Ext. Term Days	Age 21 — Guaran-teed Cash or Loan Value	Age 21 — Reduced Paid-up Insurance	Age 21 — Ext. Term Yrs.	Age 21 — Ext. Term Days	Age 22 — Guaran-teed Cash or Loan Value	Age 22 — Reduced Paid-up Insurance	Age 22 — Ext. Term Yrs.	Age 22 — Ext. Term Days	Age 23 — Guaran-teed Cash or Loan Value	Age 23 — Reduced Paid-up Insurance	Age 23 — Ext. Term Yrs.	Age 23 — Ext. Term Days	Age 24 — Guaran-teed Cash or Loan Value	Age 24 — Reduced Paid-up Insurance	Age 24 — Ext. Term Yrs.	Age 24 — Ext. Term Days
1/2	–	–	0	60	–	–	0	60	–	–	0	60	–	–	0	60	–	–	0	60
1	–	–	0	60	–	–	0	60	–	–	0	60	–	–	0	60	–	–	0	60
2	$1	$3	0	141	$1	$3	0	136	$1	$3	0	131	$1	$3	0	126	$1	$3	0	122
3	12	33	4	139	13	35	4	205	13	34	4	140	14	36	4	189	15	38	4	228
4	25	67	8	180	26	68	8	166	27	70	8	143	29	73	8	209	30	74	8	166
5	39	102	12	60	40	103	11	336	42	106	11	330	44	109	11	309	45	109	11	195
6	53	136	15	41	55	138	14	335	56	138	14	176	59	143	14	164	61	145	14	66
7	67	169	17	164	69	170	17	36	71	172	16	266	74	175	16	188	76	177	16	40
8	81	200	19	113	84	203	19	2	87	206	18	243	90	209	18	113	92	209	17	287
9	96	232	20	344	99	234	20	186	102	237	20	23	105	239	19	217	109	243	19	90
10	111	263	22	86	114	265	21	258	118	269	21	107	122	272	20	314	125	274	20	107
11	125	290	23	49	129	294	22	238	133	297	22	57	137	300	21	235	141	303	21	44
12	139	316	23	305	143	319	23	104	148	324	22	303	152	326	22	93	157	330	21	280
13	154	344	24	175	158	346	23	318	163	350	23	127	168	353	22	297	173	357	22	98
14	169	370	24	356	173	371	24	114	178	374	23	269	184	380	23	87	189	383	22	234
15	184	395	25	124	189	398	24	264	194	400	24	37	200	405	23	201	205	407	22	333
16	198	417	25	187	203	419	24	313	209	423	24	101	215	427	23	251	221	431	23	33
17	212	437	25	219	218	441	24	363	224	445	24	137	230	448	23	274	236	451	23	44
18	226	457	25	226	232	461	24	358	238	464	24	121	245	469	23	273	252	473	23	57
19	240	477	25	209	247	481	24	357	254	486	24	135	260	488	23	251	267	492	23	26
20	255	497	25	198	262	501	24	335	269	505	24	103	276	509	23	234	283	512	23	0
to Age 60	566	788	19	131	562	783	19	67	557	776	18	352	552	769	18	278	546	761	18	188
to Age 65	642	837	17	78	638	831	17	14	634	826	16	320	629	820	16	248	625	815	16	191

(Column note: "For each $1,000 of Face Amount" applies to the Guaranteed Cash or Loan Value and Reduced Paid-up Insurance columns.)

---

4. Cheryl Bara purchased a $30,000 permanent insurance policy at age 24. How much reduced paid-up insurance will she have in 16 years if she wishes to stop paying her premiums at that time?

ANSWER ON PAGE A-13

Example 4 Lynne Barthlomew has a $40,000 permanent insurance policy, which she bought at age 20. She wants to know how much the policy will be for on a reduced paid-up basis at age 60.

Solution

a) To determine the amount of the reduced paid up insurance, locate the box headed Age 20 at Issue on Table 8.5 and read down to Age 60 in the column headed Years in Force with all Due Premiums Paid. Read across to the column headed Reduced Paid-Up Insurance. The amount of insurance that will be in force on a Reduced Paid-Up basis at age 60 for the duration of Lynne's life would be $788 per $1000.

b) Since the policy was issued for $40,000, the total amount of reduced paid up insurance is

Amount per $1000 × Number of thousands = $788 × 40 = $31,520.

DO EXERCISE 4.

⠿ THE COST OF LIFE INSURANCE

Life insurance companies levy charges known as premiums to the insured. Premiums are based on several variables, including the age and sex of the insured (women are considered as having a life expectancy that is three years longer than men), the type of insurance applied for, the amount of insurance requested, and the addition of any optional features known as *riders*. The equal rights issue is changing the costs and benefits of life insurance.

Chapter 8   Insurance

Example 5 David Barth, age 25, wishes to buy a $10,000 permanent insurance policy. How much is the premium?

Solution

a) Find the premium payable for $1000 for a male, age 25.

Read down to age 25 on Table 8.6 and across to Life-M. The amount payable for each $1000 is $13.46.

b) Since the initial policy is to be issued for $10,000, the total amount payable will be

Amount payable per $1000 × Number of thousands = $13.46 × 10
$$= \$134.60.$$

The amount charged by the insurance company is $134.60.

DO EXERCISE 5.

Many life insurance companies offer the insured the option of adding an **accidental death benefit** to the basic policy. This feature, which is also known as **double indemnity**, will customarily double the face amount of the policy in the event that the insured's death results from an accident.

Example 6 Richard Freed, a 20-year-old male, wishes to purchase a $15,000 policy with double indemnity. How much is his premium?

Solution

a) Find the premium payable for $1000 for a male, age 20.

Read down to age 20 on Table 8.6 and across to Life-M. The amount payable for each $1000 is $11.72.

b) Since the initial policy is to be issued with the accidental death benefit, or double indemnity, we must add in the charge for this rider. Read down to Age 20 Male on Table 8.6 and across to the column headed A.D.B. The charge for the accidental death benefit is $0.91 per $1000.

c) The charge for the basic policy is, therefore, $11.72 + $0.91 = $12.63 per $1000. Since the initial policy is to be issued for $15,000, to find the cost of the policy we multiply:

Base rate × Number of thousands = $12.63 × 15 = $189.45

The premium is thus $189.45.

DO EXERCISE 6.

TABLE 8.6

ORDINARY LIFE (PER $1000)

| Age At Issue | ANNUAL PREMIUMS | | | | | Years To Pay Up W/Divs. | Total Mo. Inc. At 65 | | Interest Adj. Cost Index | |
	Life-M	Life-F	Non-Smokers	W.P.	A.D.B.		Male	Female	10 Yrs.	20 Yrs.
0	$ 7.77	$ 7.58		$ .20	$ .64	24	$15.24	$14.04	$ 3.46	$ 2.01
⋮	⋮	⋮	⋮	⋮	⋮	⋮	⋮	⋮	⋮	⋮
16	10.61	10.29		.28	.94	25	10.50	9.66	3.07	1.89
17	10.87	10.53		.29	.94	25	10.23	9.42	3.16	1.89
18	11.15	10.79		.30	.94	25	10.00	9.21	3.19	1.92
19	11.43	11.04		.31	.93	25	9.75	8.98	3.22	1.95
20	11.72	11.29	$ 11.42	.32	.91	25	9.51	8.76	3.25	1.96
21	12.04	11.58	11.72	.33	.90	25	9.31	8.57	3.23	2.00
22	12.37	11.88	12.02	.34	.89	25	9.09	8.37	3.30	2.02
23	12.72	12.20	12.35	.35	.88	25	8.88	8.17	3.31	2.06
24	13.08	12.53	12.68	.37	.87	25	8.67	7.98	3.41	2.11
25	13.46	12.87	13.03	.38	.88	25	8.46	7.79	3.45	2.18
26	13.91	13.28	13.46	.40	.88	25	8.29	7.63	3.54	2.25
27	14.38	13.70	13.92	.41	.88	25	8.11	7.46	3.56	2.38
28	14.88	14.15	14.40	.43	.89	25	7.93	7.30	3.70	2.47
29	15.39	14.61	14.89	.45	.90	25	7.75	7.13	3.85	2.64
30	15.93	15.10	15.42	.48	.91	25	7.57	6.97	3.95	2.77

5. Connie Franey, a 30-year-old female, wishes to buy a $20,000 permanent insurance policy. How much is the premium?

6. Felicity Kendall, age 20, wishes to purchase a $25,000 policy with double indemnity. How much is her premium?

ANSWERS ON PAGE A-13

7. Karen Flinn, age 20, wishes to purchase a $30,000 policy with a waiver of premium benefit. How much is her premium?

8. It is determined that an insurance premium is $300.45 per year, but the insured wants to pay monthly. (a) What is the monthly premium? (b) What is the total paid for the year?

ANSWERS ON PAGE A-13

The *disability waiver of premium* benefit is another rider that can be added to a policy. This rider waives all premiums in the event that the insured is totally disabled for a period of at least six months.

Example 7 Larry Francis, a 19-year-old male, wishes to purchase an $18,000 policy with a waiver of premium benefit. How much is the premium?

Solution

a) Find the premium payable for $1000 for a male, age 19.

Read down to age 19 on Table 8.6 and across to Life-M. The amount payable for each $1000 is $11.43.

b) Since the initial policy is to be issued with the waiver of premium benefit, we must add in the charge for this rider. Read down to age 19 on Table 8.6 and across to the column headed W.P. The charge for the waiver of premium rider is $0.31 per $1000. The charge for the basic policy is, therefore, $11.43 plus $0.31 = $11.74 per $1000. Since the initial policy is to be issued for $18,000, to find the cost of the policy, we multiply:

Base rate × Number of thousands = $11.74 × 18 = $211.32

The premium is thus $211.32.

DO EXERCISE 7.

Frequently, insurance premiums are paid on an other-than-annual basis. One of the most popular methods of paying premiums in recent years has been the automatic bank draft method. The insurance company automatically withdraws the amount of the premium from the insured's bank on a monthly basis.

Premiums that are paid more frequently than annually are increased. The reasons include the greater expense of collection, the loss of interest on the policyholder's money, and a greater tendency toward lapse. Typical charges for premium methods other than annual are shown below.

Semiannual	51.000%
Quarterly	26.000%
Automatic bank draft	8.417%
Regular monthly	8.833%

Example 8 It is determined that an insurance premium is $317.16 per year, but the insured wants to pay quarterly. (a) What is the quarterly premium? (b) What is the total paid for the year?

Solution

a) According to the list above, for a quarterly payment, we take 26% of the annual premium, which is $317.16.

26% × $317.16 = 0.26 × $317.16 = $82.46

b) Total paid = Amount each quarter × Number of payments
= $82.46 × 4 = $329.84

Note that the actual amount paid for the year is $329.84 − $317.16, or $12.68 more by paying in four payments rather than by paying the entire $317.16 at the beginning of the year.

DO EXERCISE 8.

Chapter 8   Insurance

For these exercises use Tables 18, 19, and 20 (pp. T-26, T-27, and T-28).

• Find the amount payable.

1. Denise Woods, who is insured with an $80,000 15-year decreasing term policy, dies during the twelfth policy year.

2. Raf Wyns, who is insured with a $125,000 15-year decreasing term policy, dies during the second policy year.

3. ▥ Issac Yalda-Mooshabad, who is insured with a $40,000 15-year decreasing term policy, dies during the tenth policy year.

4. Carolyn Terrill, who is insured with a $50,000 15-year decreasing term policy, dies during the fourth policy year.

5. ▥ Ahamad Khan, who is insured with a $235,000 15-year decreasing term policy, dies during the twelfth policy year. How much does the insurance company pay?

• • Solve.

6. After a $50,000 permanent insurance policy that was issued at age 20 had been in force for 17 years, Pam Upchurch, the insured, wanted to borrow on the policy. How much was available?

7. ▥ After a $40,000 permanent insurance policy that was issued at age 21 had been in force for 11 years, Saki Tume, the insured, wanted to borrow on the policy. How much was available?

8. After a $20,000 permanent insurance policy that was issued at age 27 had been in force for nine years, Dawn Trenary, the insured, wanted to borrow on the policy. How much was available?

9. ▥ After a $35,000 permanent insurance policy that was issued at age 25 had been in force for four years, Dod Schimph, the insured, wanted to borrow on the policy. How much was available?

• • • Solve.

10. Diane Seiler stops premium payments after 20 years on a $40,000 permanent policy bought at age 24. How long will the insurance policy be continued under the extended term option?

11. Chung Wong stops premium payments after 18 years on a $60,000 permanent policy bought at age 28. How long will the insurance policy be continued under the extended term option?

12. Garold Parks, the insured, has a $25,000 permanent insurance policy bought at age 28 on which premiums have been paid for 18 years. Premium payments are stopped. How long will the insurance company continue coverage under the extended term insurance option?

13. Ruth Percival, the insured, has a $40,000 permanent insurance policy bought at age 20 on which premiums have been paid for 10 years. Premium payments are stopped. How long will the insurance company continue coverage under the extended term insurance option?

ANSWERS

1. _____

2. _____

3. _____

4. _____

5. _____

6. _____

7. _____

8. _____

9. _____

10. _____

11. _____

12. _____

13. _____

:: Solve.

14. Brian Pence bought a $40,000 permanent policy at age 23. What will be the reduced paid-up value at 60?

15. Patricia Pendola bought a $70,000 permanent policy at age 26. What will be the reduced paid-up value at 65?

16. Carla Olsson bought a $35,000 permanent insurance policy at age 27. How much will the policy be for on a reduced paid-up basis at age 65?

17. Enor Peniston bought a $40,000 permanent insurance policy at age 24. How much will the policy be for on a reduced paid-up basis at age 60?

18. ▦ Sonia Kirkendale has a $110,000 permanent policy bought at age 28. Find the cash value after 19 years; the extended term coverage after 15 years; and the reduced paid-up value at age 65.

:·: Determine the cost.

19. Joyce Pepper, a 21-year-old female, wishes to buy a $35,000 permanent insurance policy. How much is the premium?

20. Paul McDernott, a 21-year-old male, wishes to buy a $35,000 permanent insurance policy. How much is the premium?

21. Laura McCall, a female, age 24, wishes to purchase a $30,000 policy with double indemnity. How much is the premium?

22. Grant McIntosh, a male, age 24, wishes to purchase a $30,000 policy with double indemnity. How much is the premium?

23. ▦ Suzanne Kelly, a female, age 23, wishes to purchase a $25,000 policy with a waiver of premium benefit. How much is the premium?

24. We Ne, a male, age 23, wishes to purchase a $25,000 policy with a waiver of premium benefit. How much is the premium?

25. It is determined that an insurance premium is $458.68 per year, but the insured wants to pay quarterly. What is the quarterly premium? What is the total paid for the year?

26. It is determined that an insurance premium is $679.54 per year, but the insured wants to pay quarterly. What is the quarterly premium? What is the total paid for the year?

27. ▦ Find the automatic bank draft monthly premium for a $56,000 permanent insurance policy with double indemnity and waiver of premium riders purchased by Katy Flick, a 31-year-old female.

28. ▦ Find the quarterly premium for a $47,000 permanent insurance policy with double indemnity and waiver of premium riders purchased by a 27-year-old male.

✓ SKILL MAINTENANCE

29. Of the 8760 hours in a year most TV sets are on 2190 hours. What percent is this?

30. The value of a car decreased 30% one year. Its value the year before was $5600. What was its new value?

Chapter 8   Insurance

If you miss an item, review the indicated section and objective.

[8.1, • •] **1.** An all-risk homeowner's policy for $60,000 is taken out on the Coe's home whose replacement cost is $80,000. A water heater breaks doing $5000 damage. How much is paid by the insurance company?

1. _____

2. A basic-form homeowner's policy for $70,000 is taken out on the Aman's house. A stereo bought two years ago was stolen. The comparable stereo today costs $2400 while the one stolen cost $1600. It was expected to last eight years. How much does the insurance pay? Use Table 14 (p. T-24).

2. _____

[8.1, • • •] **3.** Find the annual premium for a $60,000 Form 3, $50 all-peril deductible homeowner's policy on the Sampson's masonry house in Zone 1, Protection Class 3. Use Table 15 (p. T-25).

3. _____

[8.2, •] **4.** A motorist with 75,000/150,000/25,000 coverage does $28,500 damage to a building. How much does the motorist pay?

4. _____

5. A motorist with 100,000/300,000/50,000 coverage loses a lawsuit brought by an injured person for $142,000. How much does the insurance company pay?

5. _____

6. A motorist with medical-payments coverage up to $5000 for each person is involved in an accident that injures one passenger. The passenger has $7450 in medical expenses. How much does the passenger pay?

6. _____

[8.2, • •] **7.** Zal Frisk, a single male, age 17, with a medium-size 1987 car, selects 100/300/50 liability, 5000 medical, ACV comprehensive, $100 deductible collision, and 10/20 uninsured-motorist coverage. Find the six-month premium. Use Tables 16 and 17 (p. T-26).

7. _____

[8.3, •] **8.** Curt Farms has a $45,000 15-year decreasing term policy and dies during the fifth policy year. How much will the insurance company pay? Use Table 18 (p. T-26).

8. _____

Use Table 19 (T-27) for Exercises 9–11.

[8.3, ••] **9.** After a $35,000 permanent insurance policy that was issued at age 23 had been in force for 14 years, the insured wanted to borrow on the policy. How much was available?

9. _____

[8.3, •••] **10.** Leslie Nicoll purchased a $30,000 permanent policy at age 27. After she has paid premiums for 11 years, what will her extended term insurance be?

10. _____

[8.2, ⁞⁞] **11.** George Pary has a $50,000 permanent insurance policy bought at age 26. How much will the policy be for on a reduced paid-up basis at age 65?

11. _____

Use Table 20 (p. T-28) for Exercises 12–14.

[8.3, ⁞•⁞] **12.** Sammie Spear, a female, age 24, wishes to buy a $80,000 permanent insurance policy. What is the premium?

12. _____

13. Elena Nott, a 22-year old female, wishes to purchase a $40,000 policy with double indemnity. How much is the premium?

13. _____

14. Joe Falbo, a 25-year old male, wishes to purchase a $30,000 policy with a waiver of premium benefit. How much is the premium?

14. _____

9

TAXES

ELIZABETH McCORD

CAREER: PERSONAL TRUST ADMINISTRATOR This is Elizabeth McCord. Liz is a personal trust administrator for a large financial institution in Chicago. The path she has traveled to her present position is impressive. She first received a Bachelor's Degree in French, but then took a three-month course of study in a Lawyer's Assistant (Paralegal) Program at Roosevelt University, specializing in estates, trusts, and wills. After completion of this program, she obtained a position in a law firm. From there she went to her present employer, where she first worked as an income tax preparer and analyst. She was promoted in the company, first as an administrative assistant, then to a supervisor, and finally to her present position as Trust Officer.

A trust is a fund of money which serves many purposes. For example, one can put a block of money away for a child. The income from the money is then taxed in a different way, which saves taxes. The money and/or its income can be used for the child's education or other expenses. Through a will, a trust can also be set up on a person's death. A trust officer, such as Liz, then helps make decisions about the appropriate use of the money in the trust. Thus business mathematics comes into play quite often. For example, what percentage of interest is the fund making? By what percent will an expense deplete the fund? Will an expense deplete the fund so much that future financial needs, for which the fund was set up, cannot be met?

People in Liz's kind of work can make between $20,000 and $30,000 per year. Liz is an organized, inquisitive person who enjoys woking with people.

9.1

Sales Tax

Taxes provide money for governmental services. Our taxes are used for social programs, research, defense, education, police, fire protection, and many other services. In this chapter we study sales and property taxes. Federal income taxes will be studied in Chapter 14.

• FINDING THE SALES TAX

State and local governments often tax goods and services. The taxes (expressed as percentages) are **sales taxes.** Rates vary among states. The *sales tax* is a percentage added on to the purchase price.

Various methods are used to compute sales tax. For example, some states use the **major fraction rule.** For this method any fraction of a cent less than $\frac{1}{2}$ is disregarded, whereas for fractions greater than or equal to $\frac{1}{2}$, another penny is added.

Example 1 Find the sales tax on one furnace filter in a 3% sales tax state. Use the major fraction rule.

1. Find the sales tax on a 78¢ purchase in a 5% sales tax state. Use the major fraction rule.

Solution The filter costs 69¢ so the sales tax is

$$3\% \times 69¢ = 2.07¢.$$

The sales tax is 2¢.

DO EXERCISE 1.

Several states do not use the major fraction rule. Table 9.1 lists several of them together with their method of computation.

2. Find the sales tax on a 47¢ purchase made in Pennsylvania.

TABLE 9.1

State	Rate	1¢	2¢	3¢	4¢	5¢
Iowa	4%	13–37	38–62	63–87		
Georgia	3%	11–35	36–66	67–1.00*		
Pennsylvania	6%	11–17	18–34	35–50	51–67	68–84†

* Any fraction is treated as a cent on larger amounts. For example, the sales tax on $23.42 is 70.26¢, which is treated as 71¢.
† Use the major fraction rule for any larger amount.

Example 2 Find the sales tax if the 69¢ furnace filter is bought in Georgia.

Solution From Table 9.1 we see that any purchase from 67¢ to $1.00 in Georgia has a 3¢ sales tax.

Thus, the Georgia sales tax on the 69¢ furnace filter is 3¢.

DO EXERCISE 2.

ANSWERS ON PAGE A-13

Many states that do not use the major fraction rule for small amounts do use it for larger purchases.

Example 3 Find the sales tax on the $28.95 battery in a 4% sales tax state. Use the major fraction rule.

Firestone
BATTERIES

Firestone
MOTOR KING

**for tractors, trucks
cars and implements**
AS LOW AS $**28**⁹⁵ 12 volt
MK22F, MK24, MK24F
EXCHANGE PRICE

Solution The price is $28.95 and

$$4\% \times \$28.95 = \$1.158.$$

Thus, the sales tax is $1.16.

DO EXERCISE 3.

To find the total cost the sales tax and the price of the article are added.

Example 4 Find the total cost for a $28.95 battery in a 4% sales tax state. Use the major fraction rule.

Solution

a) Find the sales tax.

From Example 3 we know that the sales tax is $1.16.

b) Find the total cost.

$$\text{Total cost} = \text{Price} + \text{Sales tax}$$
$$= \$28.95 + \$1.16$$
$$= \$30.11$$

The total cost is $30.11.

DO EXERCISE 4.

3. Find the sales tax on a $567.25 freezer in a 5% sales tax state. Use the major fraction rule.

4. Find the total cost of a $10,120 automobile in a 5% sales tax state. Use the major fraction rule.

ANSWERS ON PAGE A-13

5. Joyce's Circuits had receipts of $7689, which include a 4% sales tax. How much were sales?

•• ☐ **SALES**

Business people collect the sales tax and send it to the government periodically. Often only the total amount of each sale is recorded, so the amount of sales tax due the government must be determined at the time that the tax is sent.

Example 5 Sally's Ceramics had receipts of $4317, which include a 3% sales tax. How much were sales? How much were taxes?

Solution Let x be the sales. Then

$$100\% \text{ of sales} + 3\% \text{ of sales is } 4317$$

$$1.00 \cdot x + 0.03 \cdot x = 4317$$
$$1.03x = 4317$$
$$x = 4191.26. \qquad \text{Dividing both sides by 1.03.}$$

Thus, sales were $4191.26.

$$\text{Sales tax} = \text{Receipts} - \text{Sales}$$
$$= 4317 \quad - 4191.26$$
$$= 125.74$$

Taxes were $125.74.

DO EXERCISE 5.

ANSWER ON PAGE A-13

• Find the sales tax. Use Table 9.1 when necessary.

1. An $0.86 purchase in a state having a 4% sales tax. Use the major fraction rule.

2. A $0.76 purchase in Nevada with a 5.75% sales tax. Use the major fraction rule.

3. A $1.14 purchase in Iowa.

4. An $0.82 purchase in Pennsylvania.

5. A $0.72 purchase in Georgia.

6. A $0.72 purchase in Iowa.

7. A $149.95 purchase in West Virginia with a 5% sales tax. Use the major fraction rule.

8. A $645.49 lawn tractor in Nebraska with a $3\frac{1}{2}$% sales tax. Use the major fraction rule.

9. Find the total cost of an $1879 motorcycle in Washington with a $6\frac{1}{2}$% sales tax. Use the major fraction rule.

10. Find the total cost of a $12,425 automobile in Utah with a $4\frac{1}{2}$% sales tax. Use the major fraction rule.

Find the sales tax on these items purchased in Georgia.

11.
JON BOAT, 14′, deck, swival seat, carpeting, Balko trailer, 15 hp electric start Johnson, 12 hours $1,650. 864-2798 after 5

12.
35′ PARK MODEL Travel Trailer, Roll out awnings, air, many extras. Must sell this week, $8500. Can be seen at Kennedy Park.

ANSWERS

1. _____

2. _____

3. _____

4. _____

5. _____

6. _____

7. _____

8. _____

9. _____

10. _____

11. _____

12. _____

13. _____

14. _____

15. _____

16. _____

17. _____

18. _____

19. _____

20. _____

21. _____

22. _____

23. _____

24. _____

25. _____

26. _____

13.

A 16' x 32'
Swimming Pool $8400 INSTALLED

- Steel Walls
- 3' Concrete Deck
- Diving Board & Ladder
- Deluxe Filtration System with Heater
- Maint. Kit & Chemicals

10 YEARS EXPERIENCE
"Quality For Less"
PETERSON POOLS

14.

$2988
SONY MODEL ICF-700
AM/FM, AC/DC
Portable Radio AC Adaptor Included

• • Solve.

15. Ken's Service has $6789 in receipts, which include a 5% sales tax. How much were sales?

16. Central Roofing has $9875 in receipts, which include a 6% sales tax. How much were sales?

17. Paragon Waste Incorporated has $9802 in receipts, which include a 4% sales tax. How much were sales?

18. Avator Productions has $7690 in receipts, which include a 6% sales tax. How much were sales?

19. Tasler Lumber has $3780 in receipts, which include a 4% sales tax. How much was the sales tax?

20. A business has $7540 in receipts, which include a 5% sales tax. How much was the sales tax?

▦ Complete. Use the major fraction rule.

	Purchase	Price	Rate	Sales Tax	Total Cost
21.	Scanner	$289.95	4%		
22.	Chain saw		5%		$68.24
23.	Radial saw			$6.90	$236.89
24.	Cutlass	$3894.75		$233.69	

✔ **SKILL MAINTENANCE**

Find the interest using the 365-day, approximate time method.

	Principal	Rate	Borrowed	Repaid
25.	$850	13%	February 12	May 7
26.	$1875	9%	March 26	September 4

9.2

Property Tax

• ASSESSED VALUE

Local governments tax real estate and personal property to pay for schools and other governmental services. These taxes are **property taxes** and vary nationwide. Property taxes are based on the **assessed value** (determined by a tax assessor) of the property.

Example 1 The current market value of the Riva's home is $65,000, and the assessment rate is 27%. Find the assessed value.

Solution

$$\text{Assessed value} = 27\% \times \$65,000$$
$$= 0.27 \times \$65,000$$
$$= \$17,550$$

The assessed value is $17,550.

DO EXERCISE 1.

•• TAX RATE

The tax rate (**levy**) is determined by dividing the amount of money needed (stated in the budget) by the total assessed value of property (the sum of all property assessments) within the governmental boundaries.

$$\text{Tax rate} = \frac{\text{Money needed}}{\text{Total assessed value}}$$

Example 2 The Belmar School District needs $635,747 in property tax revenue and has property assessed at $42,091,402 within its boundaries. What is the tax rate?

Solution Substitute 635,747 for money needed and 42,091,402 for total assessed value in

$$\text{Tax rate} = \frac{\text{Money needed}}{\text{Total assessed value}}$$
$$= \frac{635,747}{42,091,402}$$
$$= 0.015104.$$

The tax rate is 1.5104%, or 1.5104¢ per dollar; thus,

$$\$1.5104 \text{ per } \$100 \left(\frac{1.5104}{\$1} \cdot \frac{100}{100} = \frac{151.04¢}{\$100} = \frac{\$1.5104}{\$100} \right)$$

or $15.104 per $1000 (often expressed as 15.104 mills, where a **mill** is one-thousandth of a dollar).

DO EXERCISE 2.

After finishing Section 9.2, you should be able to:

- • Determine assessed value.
- •• Compute the tax rate.
- ••• Determine the tax.

1. The current market value of Duane Duit's home is $52,000. Find the assessed value if the assessment rate is 43%.

2. The town of Rippey needs $342,000 from property taxes and has property assessed at $27,454,103 within its boundaries. What is the tax rate in mills?

ANSWERS ON PAGE A-13

3. Find the tax for city expenses on Sam Stahl's home assessed at $47,000 where the tax rate is 2.364 mills.

●●● **AMOUNT OF TAX**

The tax rate is used to find the tax on each property within the boundaries of the governmental body.

Tax = Assessed value × Tax rate

Example 3 Find the tax for schools on Fran Simpson's home assessed at $62,000 where the tax rate is 17.445 mills.

Solution Substitute 62,000 for assessed value and 0.017445 for tax rate in

Tax = Assessed value × Tax rate

$= 62{,}000 \times 0.017445$

$= 1081.59.$

The tax is $1081.59.

DO EXERCISE 3.

Solve.

1. The current market value of the Klein's home is $53,875. Find the assessed value if the assessment rate is 58%.

2. The current market value of Yi Wan's home is $98,000. Find the assessed value if the assessment rate is 40%.

3. ▦ The current market value of Roger Lamp's home is $67,500. Find the assessed value if the assessment rate is 55%.

4. The current market value of Debra Kruse's home is $85,000. Find the assessed value if the assessment rate is 60%.

5. The assessment rate is 64% of the current market value. Find the assessed value of the Larsen's home with market value $58,500.

6. ▦ The assessment rate is 72% of the current market value. Find the assessed value of the Landis's home with market value $87,600.

Solve.

7. Brevart County needs $346,780 from property taxes and has $83,567,765 of assessed property within its boundaries. What is the tax rate (in mills)?

8. Stark Township needs $1,250,000 from property taxes and has $215,654,900 of assessed property within its boundaries. What is the tax rate (in mills)?

9. Story County needs $560,870 from property taxes and has $45,789,000 of assessed property within its boundaries. What is the tax rate (as a percentage)?

10. ▦ The Elko School District needs $867,905 from property taxes and has $93,684,500 of assessed property within its boundaries. What is the tax rate (as a percentage)?

ANSWERS

1. _____

2. _____

3. _____

4. _____

5. _____

6. _____

7. _____

8. _____

9. _____

10. _____

ANSWERS

11. _____

12. _____

13. _____

14. _____

15. _____

16. _____

17. _____

18. _____

19. _____

• • • Solve.

11. Find the tax for county roads on the Wang's home assessed at $43,000 where the tax rate is 1.6035%.

12. Find the tax for county roads on the Swift's home assessed at $57,800 where the tax rate is 2.0168%.

13. Find the tax for county operations on Sara Goode's home assessed at $68,000 where the tax rate is 9.0345 mills.

14. ▦ Find the tax for schools on Hung Vu's home assessed at $59,000 where the tax rate is 17.035 mills.

▦ Complete the table for Frieda Hedrick's home assessed at $46,387.

Taxing Body	Rate in Mills	Amount
15. County	6.6258	
16. Water district		$18.85
17. School		$699.87
18. Township	0.3255	

✓ **SKILL MAINTENANCE**

19. After a $50,000 permanent insurance policy that was issued at age 24 has been in force for 15 years, Sally Rand the insured wants to borrow on the policy. How much is available? Use Table 19, p. T-27.

If you miss an item, review the indicated section and objective.

ANSWERS

[9.1, •] **1.** Find the sales tax on the $29.88 clock radio in a 5% sales tax state. Use the major fraction rule.

1. _____

[9.1, ••] **2.** The Ark Pet Shop had receipts of $9862, which include a 4% sales tax. How much were sales?

2. _____

3. The Bairnco Company had receipts of $12,494, which include a 5% sales tax. How much were taxes?

3. _____

4. _____

5. _____

6. _____

[9.2, •] **4.** The current market value of the Warland's home is $112,500, and the assessment rate is 31%. Find the assessed value.

[9.2, ••] **5.** Lake Mills School District needs $982,460 in property tax revenue and has property assessed at $92,872,450 within its boundaries. What is the tax rate in mills?

[9.2, •••] **6.** Find the tax for schools on Janet Roby's home assessed at $87,000 where the tax rate is 14.324 mills.

10

FINANCIAL STATE-MENTS

CAREER: BUSINESS ADMINISTRATION This is Ray Carucci. Ray is the Executive Director of the Memorial Clinic in Indianapolis, which is a multi-specialty medical group with satellite offices throughout Indiana. As Executive Director, Ray is directly responsible for the financial management and smooth operation of the clinic, which employs forty physicians.

RAY CARUCCI

All the material in this book is relevant to Ray's job, but this chapter on financial statements is the most important. People who are successful in this field, as Ray is, can expect to make a salary between $60,000–$70,000 per year.

Ray has an interesting background. He took Business Math at Florida Southern College where he was studying for a BS degree in Business Administration. Upon graduation he served in the U.S. Army, where he held many key positions in the areas of personnel administration and management. In one such position he was directly responsible for establishing the first School of Administration of Saudi Arabia. While in college, Ray acted as Assistant General Manager of the Lakeland Pilots, a minor league baseball team in the Florida State League.

Ray's hobbies include watching all kinds of sports and playing tennis.

After finishing Section 10.1, you should be able to:

- $\bullet$ **Compute gross profit.**
- $\bullet$ $\bullet$ **Determine net income.**

1. Minn's Suppliers bought hardware for $8765 and sold it for $12,645. There were no adjustments or returns. What was the gross profit?

2. Redeker's Furnishings sold furniture costing $6785 for $9875. Returns were $987. How much was the gross profit?

ANSWERS ON PAGE A-13

Profit and Loss

Owners, managers, and investors want to know whether a business is making a profit or incurring a loss. A financial picture of a business is often obtained by looking at income statements and balance sheets. These topics will be studied in this chapter.

$\bullet$ GROSS PROFIT

A retailer can calculate **gross profit** (or loss) by subtracting the cost of goods sold from the **net sales** (revenue brought in by the sale of the goods less returns and adjustments).

> **Gross profit = Net sales − Cost**

Example 1 Ryan's Clothing bought clothes for $2567 and sold them for $4589. There were no adjustments or returns. What was the gross profit?

Solution Find the gross profit.

$$\text{Gross profit} = \text{Net sales} - \text{Cost}$$
$$= \$4589 - \$2567$$
$$= \$2022$$

Ryan's gross profit was $2022.

DO EXERCISE 1.

For a retailer, **revenue** is income from sales. Consumers sometimes return unsatisfactory items. As mentioned above, when computing gross profit these sales returns are subtracted from revenue (sales) to get *net sales.*

> **Net sales = Revenue − Returns**

Example 2 Durlam's sold clothing costing $4525 for $6895. Returns were $345. How much was the gross profit?

Solution

a) Find the net sales.

$$\text{Net sales} = \text{Revenue} - \text{Returns}$$
$$= \$6895 - \$345$$
$$= \$6550$$

b) Find the gross profit.

$$\text{Gross profit} = \text{Net sales} - \text{Cost}$$
$$= \$6550 - \$4525$$
$$= \$2025$$

The gross profit was $2025.

DO EXERCISE 2.

• • NET INCOME

Net income, sometimes called **net profit**, is the final amount remaining after all deductions. Retailers incur certain expenses such as rent, utilities, labor, and some miscellaneous expenses in doing business. The net income is found by subtracting the sum of these expenses from the gross profit.

> **Net income = Gross profit − Expenses**

Example 3 Lyon Company had a gross profit of $4589. Expenses were $135 for utilities, $250 for rent, and $165 for miscellaneous items. What was the net income?

Solution

a) Find the sum of the expenses.

$$\text{Sum of expenses} = \$135 + \$250 + \$165$$
$$= \$550$$

b) Find the net income.

$$\text{Net income} = \text{Gross profit} - \text{Expenses}$$
$$= \$4589 - \$550$$
$$= \$4039$$

The net income was $4039.

DO EXERCISE 3.

For a service business, the net income is found by subtracting the expenses from the revenue (amount earned).

> **Net income = Revenue − Expenses**

Example 4 Sylvia's repair shop earned $1875 one month and had $325 in expenses. What was the net income?

Solution Find the net income.

$$\text{Net income} = \text{Revenue} - \text{Expenses}$$
$$= \$1875 - \$325$$
$$= \$1550$$

The net income was $1550.

DO EXERCISE 4.

3. Suzanne's Tanning had a gross profit of $7895. Expenses were $348 for utilities, $785 for rent, and $1395 for labor. What was the net income?

4. Ron's automobile repair shop earned $3567 one month and had $1475 in expenses. What was the net income?

ANSWERS ON PAGE A-13

5. Mason's Clothiers earned $6578 from sales, paid $4360 for the goods sold, and had expenses of $2564. There were no adjustments or returns. What was the net income (loss)?

The net income (loss) can be calculated in several steps. Example 5 illustrates the procedure.

Example 5 Halverson's Electronics earned $7825 from sales, paid $4985 for the goods sold, and had expenses of $3200. What was the net income (loss)? There were no adjustments or returns.

Solution

a) Find the gross profit.

Gross profit = Net sales − Cost

$$= \$7825 - \$4985$$
$$= \$2840$$

b) Net income = Gross profit − Expenses

$$= \$2840 - \$3200$$
$$= -\$360 \qquad \text{Subtract } \$2840 \text{ from } \$3200 \text{ and put a minus sign in front of the answer to show a loss.}$$

The loss was $360.

DO EXERCISE 5.

Parentheses or angle brackets are used to indicate that an amount is a loss rather than a profit. In Example 5 the loss of $360 is written ($360), or ⟨$360⟩.

ANSWER ON PAGE A-13

• Solve.

1. Sidney's Fabrics bought yard goods for $3642 and sold them for $4875. There were no adjustments or returns. What was the gross profit?

2. The Varsity Club bought fruit for $1468 and sold it for $3125. There were no adjustments or returns. What was the gross profit?

3. ▦ Lamplighters sold lighting fixtures costing $1568 for $2379. Returns were $142. How much was the gross profit?

4. Bill's Cookery sold cookery costing $2275 for $3865. Returns were $567. How much was the gross profit?

5. Earl May's bought $4378 of plants and supplies and sold them for $6582. How much was the gross profit?

6. Electronic Supply Company bought $10,635 of merchandise and sold it for $14,379. How much was the gross profit?

7. Ken's appliance store sold goods that cost $4390 for $6807. What was the gross profit?

8. Laura's sold products that cost $1560 for $2300. What was the gross profit?

•• Solve.

9. Joanne's flower shop had a gross profit of $2568. Its expenses were $876 for utilities, $500 for rent, and $235 for miscellaneous items. What was the net income?

10. ▦ Rachel's sporting goods store had a gross profit of $7685. Its expenses were $1385 for labor, $876 for rent, and $567 for miscellaneous items. What was the net income?

11. Computerland had a gross profit of $12,336. Its expenses were $2865 for personnel, $537 for rent, and $321 for miscellaneous items. What was the net income?

12. ▦ Simpson's automobile repair shop had a gross profit of $7654. Its expenses were $3895 for labor, $390 for utilities, and $123 for miscellaneous items. What was the net income?

ANSWERS

1. _____

2. _____

3. _____

4. _____

5. _____

6. _____

7. _____

8. _____

9. _____

10. _____

11. _____

12. _____

13. _____

14. _____

15. _____

16. _____

17. _____

18. _____

19. _____

20. _____

13. C and K Plumbing earned $2895 one month and had $643 in expenses. What was the net income?

14. Cecile's Electric earned $2645 one month and had $458 in expenses. What was the net income?

15. Janelle's Sportswear earned $4798 from sales, paid $2375 for the goods sold, and had expenses of $568. What was the net income (loss)?

16. Hershel's Parts earned $6789 from sales, paid $3568 for the goods sold, and had expenses of $4389. What was the net income (loss)?

▦ Find the gross profit and net income (loss).

17. Net sales $8925.68
    Cost of goods $3679.87
    Expenses $5699.87

18. Net sales $7896.58
    Cost of goods $2564.94
    Expenses $1567.98

✓ SKILL MAINTENANCE

19. Katy Polasky earns $18,940 one year and gets an 8% raise the next. What is her new salary?

20. John Nolan who is on a diet goes from a weight of 125 lb to a weight of 110 lb. What is the percentage decrease?

10.2

Income Statements

Profit and loss figures are displayed on **income statements** (sometimes called earnings reports or profit and loss statements). The statement shows how much the business made or lost and is quite useful. For example, we may examine sales, profits, and expenses for comparable periods (monthly, quarterly, and annually).

• ENTRIES ON THE INCOME STATEMENT

Income statements are not all exactly alike, but most are similar. An income statement for Axtel Company appears below.

AXTEL COMPANY
FARMINGTON, VIRGINIA

	Income Statement	1987	1986
1	Net sales	140,000	105,000
	Cost of sales and operating expenses		
2	Cost of goods sold	102,000	80,000
3	Depreciation	5,000	2,000
4	Selling and administrating expenses	24,000	19,000
5	Operating profit	9,000	4,000
6	Other income		
	Dividends and interest	4,000	1,500
7	Total income	13,000	5,500
8	Less bond interest	3,500	3,500
9	Income before federal tax	9,500	2,000
10	Federal tax	1,400	300
11	Net profit for year	8,100	1,700

Net Sales The primary revenue source is always listed first on the income statement. For Axtel Company, a manufacturer, it is net sales, whereas for a utility company it would be operating revenues. A comparison of net sales shows Axtel had more sales in 1987 than 1986.

1	**Net sales**	140,000	105,000

Cost of Sales and Operating Expenses For a manufacturer like Axtel Company this includes all costs incurred from the raw materials to the finished product. Included are raw materials, labor, overhead expenses, and depreciation.

Cost of Goods Sold The largest item (listed first) under cost of sales and operating expenses is cost of goods sold.

2	**Cost of goods sold**	102,000	80,000

Depreciation Depreciation (see Chapter 12) is an expense because it represents a decline in the useful life of an asset (such as machinery) due to wear and tear.

| 3 | Depreciation | 5,000 | 2,000 |

Selling and Administrating Expenses This item includes salaries and commissions for salespeople, travel, entertainment, advertising, and executives' salaries.

| 4 | Selling and administrating expenses | 24,000 | 19,000 |

We subtract all previous expenses from net sales to get operating profit.

| 5 | Operating profit | 9,000 | 4,000 |

DO EXERCISES 1–2.

Other Income Companies may invest in stocks and bonds. Interest and dividends obtained are considered other income.

| 6 | Other income
Dividends and interest | 4,000 | 1,500 |

We add operating profit and other income to get total income.

| 7 | Total income | 13,000 | 5,500 |

DO EXERCISES 3–4.

Bond Interest This item is a fixed expense as it must be paid each year. Axtel Company's bonds pay 10% interest on $35,000 so the interest expense is $3,500.

| 8 | Less bond interest | 3,500 | 3,500 |

We subtract bond interest from total income to get income before federal income tax.

| 9 | Income before federal tax | 9,500 | 2,000 |

DO EXERCISES 5–6.

Federal Income Tax The federal income tax on companies with no more than $25,000 income before tax is 15%. The 1987 federal income tax for Axtel Company is 15% of $9500, or $1400 (rounded).

| 10 | Federal tax | 1,400 | 300 |

DO EXERCISE 7.

Net Profit This item is obtained when all expenses have been subtracted from all income. For Axtel Company, after we subtract federal tax from income before tax we get net profit.

| 11 | Net profit for year | 8,100 | 1,700 |

DO EXERCISES 8–9.

•• ANALYZING THE INCOME STATEMENT

Comparisons are useful for investors. One example is the ***operating margin of profit.*** For Axtel Company, 1987 sales were $140,000 and operating profit $9,000, so the

$$\text{Operating margin of profit} = \frac{\text{Operating profit}}{\text{Net sales}}$$

$$= \frac{9,000}{140,000}$$

$$= 6.4\%.$$

This figure shows that after operating expenses, 6.4¢ of every $1 of sales was still available to the company. Similarly, in 1986

$$\text{Operating margin of profit} = \frac{4,000}{105,000}$$

$$= 3.8\%.$$

Comparing these figures indicates that Axtel Company is becoming more profitable. This increased profitability might be attributable to more efficient operating procedures, new product lines, or an increased customer base.

5. Verify the income before federal tax for 1986.

6. Verify the income before federal tax for 1987.

7. Verify the federal tax for 1986.

8. Verify the net profit for 1986.

9. Verify the net profit for 1987.

ANSWERS ON PAGE A-13

10. Calculate the 1986 net profit ratio for Axtel Company.

11. In 1987, federal tax was what percentage of net sales for Axtel Company?

12. For 1987 find to the nearest tenth the percentage increase (decrease) in selling and administrating expenses from 1986 for Axtel Company.

Another useful comparison is the **net profit ratio.** For Axtel Company in 1987, sales were $140,000 and net profit $8,100, so the

$$\text{Net profit ratio} = \frac{\text{Net profit}}{\text{Net sales}}$$

$$= \frac{8,100}{140,000}$$

$$= 5.8\%.$$

In 1987, for every $1 in sales, 5.8¢ went to the company.

DO EXERCISE 10.

A comparison of these figures from year to year and with similar figures from other companies in the same product line will enable us to better evaluate profit progress.

Another analysis technique (called **vertical analysis**) tells us how each sales dollar was spent. We find the percentage of net sales for each entry on the income statement. For example, in 1987 the cost of goods sold was $72.9\% \left(\frac{102,000}{140,000}\right)$ of net sales for Axtel Company.

DO EXERCISE 11.

An income statement may not supply figures for two years as we have done. However, these figures permit use of **horizontal analysis** to study a company's finances. Horizontal analysis is a method used to compare figures for two or more time intervals and helps us to spot trends. It enables us to ask such questions as: What is the gain (loss) in sales, expenses, or profit from year to year? The method involves finding the percentage increase (decrease) for each item on the income statement. For example, to find the percentage gain in net sales from 1986 to 1987, we find

a) the net sales gain

Sales gain = 140,000 − 105,000

= 35,000

and then

b) divide by the 1986 sales.

$$\frac{35,000}{105,000} = .33, \text{ or } 33\%$$

The sales increase from 1986 to 1987 was 33%.

The figure in the denominator is always taken from the earlier time period.

DO EXERCISE 12.

Vertical and horizontal analysis are applicable to the balance sheet, which will be discussed in the next section.

1. Complete where indicated.

TRAUX COMPANY
MARBLEBORO, MASSACHUSETTS

Income Statement	1987	1986
Net sales	250,000	210,000
Cost of sales and operating expenses		
Cost of goods sold	187,000	163,000
Depreciation	9,000	6,000
Selling and administrating expenses	43,000	38,000
Operating profit		
Other income		
Dividends and interest	12,000	8,000
Total income		
Less bond interest	6,000	6,000
Income before federal tax		
Federal tax	2,550	750
Net profit for year		

2. Fill in the boxes.

MICROELECTRONICS
SUNNYVALE, CALIFORNIA

Income Statement	1987	Percent of Net Sales
Net sales	530,000	
Cost of sales and operating expenses		
Cost of goods sold	260,000	
Depreciation	25,000	
Selling and administrating expenses	80,000	
Operating profit	165,000	
Other income		
Dividends and interest	20,000	
Total income	185,000	
Less bond interest	42,000	
Income before federal tax	143,000	
Federal tax	25,000	
Net profit for year	118,000	

3. Fill in the boxes with the percentage increase (decrease).

HUSKY TOOLS PORTSMOUTH, MAINE			
Income Statement	Percent Change	1987	1986
Net sales		370,000	315,000
Cost of sales and operating expenses			
Cost of goods sold		230,000	160,000
Depreciation		10,000	10,000
Selling and administrating expenses		50,000	45,000
Operating profit		80,000	100,000
Other income			
Dividends and interest		30,000	5,000
Total income		110,000	105,000
Less bond interest		20,000	20,000
Income before federal tax		90,000	85,000
Federal tax		16,000	14,000
Net profit for year		74,000	71,000

4. Find the operating margin of profit for the indicated year for the following.

	1987	1986
Traux Company		
Microelectronics		no
Husky Tools		

5. Find the net profit ratio for the indicated year for the following.

	1987	1986
Traux Company		
Microelectronics		no
Husky Tools		

✓ SKILL MAINTENANCE

6. Lauren Oats invested $3000 in an account paying 8% compounded quarterly. How much will be in her account at the end of one year?

7. How much should Philip Coy invest now in an account paying 10% compounded quarterly so he will have $5000 in one year?

6. _____

7. _____

10.3

Balance Sheets

Balance sheets provide a financial picture of a company at a particular time. On a balance sheet assets are generally on the left, whereas liabilities and owners equity are on the right. However, sometimes these components appear at the top and bottom, respectively, of the balance sheet.

After finishing Section 10.3, you should be able to:
- • Find entries on a balance sheet.
- • • Analyze the balance sheet.

• ENTRIES ON THE BALANCE SHEET

Balance sheets aren't all exactly alike but most are similar. The left side of a balance sheet for the Axtel Company appears below.

AXTEL COMPANY
FARMINGTON, VIRGINIA

Balance Sheet—December 31, 1987

	Assets	1987	1986
	Current Assets		
1	Cash	7,000	5,200
2	Marketable securities at cost		
	(1987—$15,000, 1986—$12,000)	13,000	9,800
3	Accounts receivable		
	(1987—$2000, 1986—$1500)	28,000	20,000
4	Inventories	41,000	43,000
5	Total current assets	89,000	78,000
6	Fixed Assets		
	Land	6,000	6,000
	Buildings	48,000	45,000
	Machinery	14,000	11,000
	Office equipment	2,000	1,500
		70,000	63,500
7	Less accumulated depreciation	14,000	11,500
8	Net fixed assets	56,000	52,000
9	Prepayments and deferred charges	2,000	1,000
10	Intangibles	1,000	1,000
11	Total assets	148,000	132,000

Current Assets Included in current assets are cash and other assets which will be converted to cash within a year.

Cash Cash means bills, silver, and bank deposits.

1	Cash	7,000	5,200

Marketable Securities Examples of marketable securities include treasury bills, certificates of deposit, and commercial paper. These securities are readily convertible to cash. Listed values are at cost with current values in parentheses.

2	Marketable securities at cost		
	(1987—$15,000, 1986—$12,000)	13,000	9,800

1. Verify the total current assets on December 31, 1986.

2. Verify the total current assets on December 31, 1987.

3. Verify the total fixed assets on December 31, 1986.

4. Verify the total fixed assets on December 31, 1987.

5. Verify net fixed assets on December 31, 1986.

6. Verify net fixed assets on December 31, 1987.

ANSWERS ON PAGE A-14

Accounts Receivable This item is for goods already shipped to customers, the payment for which has not yet been received. The figure represents the receivable amount after an allowance for bad debts of $2000 in 1987 and $1500 in 1986.

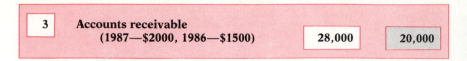

| 3 | Accounts receivable (1987—$2000, 1986—$1500) | 28,000 | 20,000 |

Inventories Inventory valuation (see Chapter 11) assigns a value to the materials on hand.

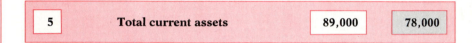

| 4 | Inventories | 41,000 | 43,000 |

We add to get total current assets.

| 5 | Total current assets | 89,000 | 78,000 |

DO EXERCISES 1–2.

Fixed Assets These assets are not generally sold and are used in the manufacturing process. Included are land, property, machinery, and equipment.

6	Fixed Assets		
	Land	6,000	6,000
	Buildings	48,000	45,000
	Machinery	14,000	11,000
	Office equipment	2,000	1,500

We add to get total fixed assets 70,000 and 63,500.

DO EXERCISES 3–4.

Depreciation This item represents a decline in useful life of an asset (excluding land) due to wear and tear. Depreciation is discussed in Chapter 12.

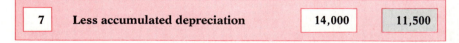

| 7 | Less accumulated depreciation | 14,000 | 11,500 |

We subtract accumulated depreciation from the total of fixed assets to get net fixed assets.

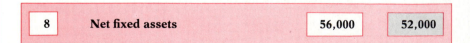

| 8 | Net fixed assets | 56,000 | 52,000 |

DO EXERCISES 5-6.

Chapter 10   Financial Statements

Prepayments and Deferred Charges

Prepayments occur when charges are paid in advance. For example, insurance premiums and leasing arrangements are sometimes paid for several years in advance. These benefits have not yet been used and therefore are assets. Likewise, expenditures for activities like research and development have benefits that extend over several years and are assets. They are called deferred charges.

9	Prepayments and deferred charges	2,000	1,000

Intangibles This type of asset has no physical existence but does have value. For example, the exclusive privilege of a microcomputer manufacturer to market its products in the schools of a state would be an intangible.

10	Intangibles	1,000	1,000

We add all of the assets to get total assets.

11	Total assets	148,000	132,000

DO EXERCISES 7–8.

The right side of the balance sheet for Axtel Company appears below.

7. Verify the total assets on December 31, 1986.

8. Verify the total assets on December 31, 1987.

AXTEL COMPANY FARMINGTON, VIRGINIA		
Liabilities	**1987**	**1986**
Current liabilities		
12 Accounts payable	25,000	21,000
13 Notes payable	8,000	9,000
14 Accrued expenses payable	6,700	2,000
15 Federal income tax payable	1,300	1,000
16 Total current liabilities	41,000	33,000
Long-term liabilities		
17 Bonds: 10% interest due 1998	35,000	35,000
18 Total liabilities	76,000	68,000
Stockholders' Equity		
Capital stock		
19 Common stock, $10 par value each, 3300 shares	33,000	33,000
20 Capital surplus	9,000	9,000
21 Accumulated retained earnings	30,000	22,000
22 Total stockholders' equity	72,000	64,000
23 Total liabilities and stockholders' equity	148,000	132,000

ANSWERS ON PAGE A-14

9. Verify the total current liabilities on December 31, 1986.

10. Verify the total current liabilities on December 31, 1987.

ANSWERS ON PAGE A-14

Current Liabilities Included in this item are debts payable during the coming year.

Accounts Payable This item includes the amount payable to creditors from whom the company purchased goods.

12	Accounts payable	25,000	21,000

Notes Payable Money owed to a financial institution or other lender is included in this item. A note signed by a company official is given to the lender.

13	Notes payable	8,000	9,000

Accrued Expenses Payable This item represents the amount the company owes to its employees, for interest, and for legal services as well as similar items.

14	Accrued expenses payable	6,700	2,000

Federal Income Tax Payable This is similar to items listed under accrued expenses but listed separately because of its importance.

15	Federal income tax payable	1,300	1,000

We add all amounts under current liabilities to get total current liabilities.

16	Total current liabilities	41,000	33,000

DO EXERCISES 9–10.

Long-Term Liabilities Liabilities due in more than a year from the date on the balance sheet are in this category.

Bonds These are long-term securities on which the company pays interest regularly (see Chapter 7). Axtel Company issued $35,000 in bonds due in 1998 on which 10% interest is paid.

17	Bonds: 10% interest due in 1998	35,000	35,000

We add current and long-term liabilities to get total liabilities.

18	Total liabilities	76,000	68,000

DO EXERCISES 11–12.

Capital Stock This item represents ownership of Axtel Company. Each shareholder owns a certain proportionate amount of the company.

Common Stock Common stock and its features are discussed in Chapter 7.

19	Common stock, $10 par value each 3300 shares	33,000	33,000

Capital Surplus This item is the amount over the par value that stockholders paid. For example, suppose stockholders of Axtel Company paid a total of $42,000 for 3300 shares of $10 par value common stock. The $42,000 of stockholders' equity is then allocated to capital stock and capital surplus.

20	Capital surplus	9,000	9,000

Accumulated Retained Earnings Suppose that during its first year Axtel Company has $10,000 of profit and pays out $6,600 in stock dividends. At the end of the first year, accumulated retained earnings are $3,400 ($10,000 − $6,600), as the company had no accumulated earnings prior to the start of business. On December 31, 1987, accumulated retained earnings (sometimes called earned surplus) were $30,000.

21	Accumulated retained earnings	30,000	22,000

We add the amount in the above three items to get total stockholders' equity.

22	Total stockholders' equity	72,000	64,000

DO EXERCISES 13–14.

11. Verify the total liability on December 31, 1986.

12. Verify the total liability on December 31, 1987.

13. Verify the total stockholders' equity on December 31, 1986.

14. Verify the total stockholders' equity on December 31, 1987.

ANSWERS ON PAGE A-14

15. Verify the total liabilities and stockholders' equity on December 31, 1986.

16. Verify the total liabilities and stockholders' equity on December 31, 1987.

For Ajax Company find

17. Current ratio.

For Ajax Company find

18. Quick assets ratio.

To obtain the total liabilities and stockholders' equity we add the amounts for these items.

23	Total liabilities and stockholders' equity	148,000	132,000

DO EXERCISES 15–16.

Note that total assets equal total liabilities and stockholders' equity, hence the name "balance sheet."

ANALYZING THE BALANCE SHEET

Balance sheet figures provide opportunities to evaluate a company. For example, working capital is needed for business expansion and new opportunities. **Working capital** is the difference between total current assets and current liabilities. For Axtel Company

$$\text{Working capital} = \text{Current assets} - \text{Current liabilities}$$
$$= \$89,000 - \$41,000$$
$$= \$48,000.$$

An investor may ask whether this is an adequate amount of working capital for Axtel Company. The **current ratio** helps answer this question. It is the ratio of current assets to current liabilities. For Axtel Company

$$\text{Current ratio} = \frac{\text{Current assets}}{\text{Current liabilities}}$$
$$= \frac{\$89,000}{\$41,000} = \frac{2.2}{1}, \quad 2.2 \text{ to } 1.$$

This means that for each $2.20 of current assets there is $1.00 of current liabilities. Many investors feel the current ratio should be at least 2 to 1. However, the current ratio is just one of several tests that aid the decision making process.

DO EXERCISE 17.

Often investors use the **quick assets ratio** (sometimes called the **acid test ratio**), which eliminates inventories as they are not necessarily quickly convertible to cash.

$$\text{Quick assets ratio} = \frac{\text{Current assets} - \text{Inventories}}{\text{Current liabilities}}$$
$$= \frac{\$89,000 - \$41,000}{\$41,000}$$
$$= \frac{1.2}{1}, \quad \text{or} \quad 1.2 \text{ to } 1.$$

Investors find a quick assets ratio of 1 to 1 acceptable, because a company then has the ability to quickly meet its obligations.

DO EXERCISE 18.

☐ • **1.** Fill in the boxes.

MARLAX INDUSTRIES
McALLEN, TEXAS

Balance Sheet—December 31, 1987

Assets	1987
Current Assets	
Cash	25,000
Marketable securities at cost ($19,000)	15,000
Accounts receivable ($1500)	32,000
Inventories	48,000
Total current assets	
Fixed Assets	
Land	12,000
Buildings	80,000
Machinery	42,000
Office equipment	8,000
Less accumulated depreciation	16,000
Net fixed assets	
Prepayments and deferred charges	3,000
Intangibles	2,000
Total assets	

2. Fill in the boxes.

MARLAX INDUSTRIES	
Liabilities	**1987**
Current liabilities	
Accounts payable	15,000
Notes payable	20,000
Accrued expenses payable	5,000
Federal income tax payable	3,000
Total current liabilities	
Long-term liabilities	
Bonds: 12% interest due 2004	25,000
Total liabilities	
Stockholders' Equity	
Capital stock	
Common stock, $5 par value each, 12,000 shares	60,000
Capital surplus	45,000
Accumulated retained earnings	78,000
Total stockholders' equity	
Total liabilities and stockholders' equity	

For Marlax Industries find the

3. Working capital.

4. Current ratio.

5. Quick assets ratio.

✓ **SKILL MAINTENANCE**

6. You deposit $2000 at the beginning of each year in your Individual Retirement Account which pays 7% compounded annually. How much is in your account at the end of 20 years?

7. You deposit $2000 at the end of each year in your Individual Retirement Account which pays 7% compounded annually. How much is in your account immediately after the 20th payment?

If you miss an item, review the indicated section and objective.

[10.1, •]   **1.** Hudson's bought appliances for $12,686 and sold them for $17,499. There were no adjustments or returns. What was the gross profit?

[10.1, • •]   **2.** Maui Dive had a gross profit of $5789. Expenses were $135 for utilities, $425 for rent, and $768 for labor. What was the net income?

[10.2, • • •]   **3.** Complete where indicated.

HARBISON WALKER
PITTSBURGH, PENNSYLVANIA

Income Statement	1987	Percent of Net Sales
Net sales	205,000	
Cost of sales and operating expenses		
Cost of goods sold	110,000	
Depreciation	18,000	
Selling and administrating expenses	37,000	
Operating profit		
Other income		
Dividends and interest	5,000	
Total income		
Less bond interest	15,000	
Income before federal tax		
Federal tax	4,600	
Net profit for year		

1. _____

2. _____

[10.2, • •]   **4.** Complete where indicated.

	TELEX INDUSTRIES TULSA, OKLAHOMA		
Income Statement	Percent Change	1987	1986
Net sales		315,000	280,000
Cost of sales and operating expenses			
Cost of goods sold		170,000	155,000
Depreciation		30,000	25,000
Selling and administrating expenses		80,000	70,000
Operating profit		35,000	30,000
Other income			
Dividends and interest		15,000	12,000
Total income		50,000	42,000
Less bond interest		10,000	10,000
Income before federal tax		40,000	32,000
Federal tax		6,400	5,000
Net profit for year		33,600	27,000

5. _____

[10.2, • •]   **5.** Find the 1987 margin of profit for Telex Industries.

6. Find the 1987 net profit ratio for Telex Industries.

6. _____

7. Complete as indicated.

ARMSTRONG COMPANY
ELY, NEVADA

Balance Sheet—December 31, 1987

Assets	1987
Current Assets	
Cash	12,000
Marketable securities at cost ($35,000)	26,000
Accounts receivable ($3200)	51,000
Inventories	63,000
Total current assets	
Fixed Assets	
Land	21,000
Buildings	93,000
Machinery	49,000
Office equipment	8,000
Less accumulated depreciation	18,000
Net fixed assets	
Prepayments and deferred charges	27,000
Intangibles	4,000
Total assets	

[10.3, •]   **8.** Complete as indicated.

ARMSTRONG COMPANY	
Liabilities	**1987**
Current liabilities	
Accounts payable	34,000
Notes payable	13,000
Accrued expenses payable	46,000
Federal income tax payable	11,000
Total current liabilities	
Long-term liabilities	
Bonds: 11% interest due 2005	60,000
Total liabilities	
Stockholders' Equity	
Capital stock	
Common stock, $5 par value each, 25,000 shares	125,000
Capital surplus	28,000
Accumulated retained earnings	19,000
Total stockholders' equity	
Total liabilities and stockholders' equity	

[10.3, • •]   For Armstrong Company find the

    9. Working capital.

    10. Current ratio.

    11. Quick assets ratio.

11

PURCHASING AND INVENTORY

CAREER: MANAGEMENT   This is Dixie Chavis Theodorou. She is an American Indian, born of the Lumbee Tribe in North Carolina. She is now the President of Dixie Painting Co., Inc., which specializes in industrial painting and sandblasting.

DIXIE CHAVIS THEODOROU

Dixie was a housewife for a number of years, but, thanks to the encouragement of her husband, became president of her own company. What would Dixie like to say to math students today? Her answer is, "Stay in school and take all the math you can get. You will be surprised at the many ways you will need it, even around the household."

How is math used in the painting business? The most critical part of the business is the ability to estimate cost. One needs to figure the number of square feet to be covered. Usually one gallon of paint will cover anywhere from 200 to 450 square feet. Once the cost of paint is figured one must add supplies, the number of work-hours required for the job, and overhead costs such as office space and equipment. Once the estimate is determined, an increase of from 20% to 40% is built in for profit.

What qualities make Dixie a success? She is patient and not afraid to ask questions. If she does not know the answer to a question, she is quite willing to make a trip to the library or call other people for information. She continues to educate herself, taking courses in blueprint reading, paint estimating, and mathematics.

11.1

1. The list price of a microcomputer is $1530, and the net price is $1117. What is the trade discount?

2. The list price of a stereo is $349.98. Taschetti, a manufacturer, gives a 35% discount to all retailers. What is the trade discount?

Discount and Price

To stay in business, a retailer must pay expenses and make a profit. To do this, a retailer sells merchandise for more than was paid for it. In this chapter we discuss (a) the difference between what a retailer pays for merchandise and what it is sold for and (b) inventory methods.

• TRADE DISCOUNT

Merchandise is sold to retailers by manufacturers and wholesalers at a lower price than the consumer pays. This **trade discount** helps retailers to make a profit.

> **Trade discount =   List price   —   Net price**
>
>   Manufacturer's   Retailer pays
>   catalog price

Example 1 The list price of a color television is $409.98, and the net price is $325.50. What is the trade discount?

Solution

$$\text{Trade discount} = \text{List price} - \text{Net price}$$
$$= \$409.98 - \$325.50$$
$$= \$84.48$$

The trade discount is $84.48.

DO EXERCISE 1.

It is common practice for manufacturers to quote a trade discount as a percentage of the list price.

> **Trade discount = Discount rate × List price**

Example 2 The list price of a radio is $24.99. Electronic Imports gives a 30% discount to all retailers. What is the trade discount?

Solution

$$\text{Trade discount} = \text{Discount rate} \times \text{List price}$$
$$= \quad 30\% \quad \times \quad \$24.99$$
$$= \quad 0.30 \quad \times \quad \$24.99$$
$$= \quad \$7.50$$

The trade discount is $7.50.

DO EXERCISE 2.

Retailers can find the net price when the list price and trade discount are known.

> **Net price = List price − Trade discount**

Example 3 Hasur Manufacturing gives a 28% discount on a refrigerator with a list price of $468.99. What is the net price?

Solution

a) Find the trade discount.

$$\text{Trade discount} = 28\% \times \$468.99$$
$$= 0.28 \times \$468.99$$
$$= \$131.32$$

b) Find the net price.

$$\text{Net price} = \text{List price} - \text{Trade discount}$$
$$= \$468.99 - \$131.32$$
$$= \$337.67$$

The net price is $337.67.

DO EXERCISE 3.

3. Troy Bilt gives a 20% discount on a rototiller with a list price of $645. What is the net price?

•• DISCOUNT RATE

Suppose a manufacturer's net price is $10.50 for a calculator with a list price of $16.99. The trade discount is $6.49. What percentage of the list price is the trade discount? To find out we translate as follows.

What percentage of the list price is the trade discount?

$$x \quad \cdot \quad \$16.99 \quad = \quad \$6.49$$

To find the missing number, we divide:

$$x = \frac{\$6.49}{\$16.99}$$

$$x = 0.38 = 38\%$$

We can formalize this as follows:

> **To find the discount rate,**
>
> 1. **find the trade discount;**
> 2. **divide the trade discount by the list price; and**
> 3. **convert to a percent.**

4. Casablanca Manufacturing's net price is $98.95 for a fan with a list price of $122.99. What is the discount rate to the nearest percent?

Example 4 Casio's net price is $10.50 for a calculator with a list price of $16.99. What is the discount rate?

Solution

1. $\text{Trade discount} = \$16.99 - \$10.50$ Find the trade discount.

$$= \$6.49$$

2. $\text{Discount rate} = \dfrac{\$6.49}{\$16.99}$ Divide by the list price.

$$= 0.38$$

3. $\qquad\qquad\quad = 38\%$ Convert to a percent.

The discount rate is 38%.

DO EXERCISE 4.

ANSWERS ON PAGE A-14

5. Redi-Vac sets the net price of a vacuum sweeper at $59.30 and offers a 21% discount. What is the list price?

A manufacturer may want to find the list price for merchandise when the net price and discount rate are known.

To find the list price,

1. **write the discount rate in decimal notation,**
2. **subtract from 1.00, and**
3. **divide the net price by the answer found in step 2.**

Example 5 Jolaré Industries sets the net price of a range at $295.50 and offers a 40% discount. What is the list price?

Solution

1. The discount in decimal notation is 0.40.
2. Subtract 0.40 from 1.00:

   $1.00 - 0.40 = 0.60$
3. Divide $295.50 by 0.60:

   $$\frac{\$295.50}{0.60} = \$492.50$$

The list price is $492.50.

DO EXERCISE 5.

• Solve.

1. The list price of a lamp is $121.99; the net price, $87.50. What is the trade discount?

2. The list price of a vase is $14.95; the net price, $9.25. What is the trade discount?

3. The list price of a car is $7847. La Porte Cars gives a 20% discount to all dealers. What is the trade discount?

4. The list price of a dishwasher is $249.99. Secot gives a 25% discount to all retailers. What is the trade discount?

Find the trade discount.

5.

TWIN SIZE
MATRESS
AND BOX
$109⁹⁵

Net Price $74.95

6.

FULL SIZE
MATTRESS
AND BOX
$119⁹⁵

Net Price $79.95

7. BRAND NEW CHROME FRAME STENO POSTURE CHAIR.............. **69.95**

Discount 45%

8. BRAND NEW WALNUT GRAIN 62x18 MATCHING CREDENZA... **189.95**

Discount 40%

9. Hanarhan Manufacturing gives a 30% discount on a couch with a list price of $899.98. What is the net price?

10. Kitchen Rite gives a 40% discount on all kitchen appliances. The list price of a disposal is $159.99. What is the net price?

Find the net price. The list price and discount are given.

11.

JAYMAR
GOLF SLACKS
18⁹⁵

Discount 27%

12.

MEN'S
GOLF SHOES
Foot Joy & Etonic
39⁹⁵

Discount 35%

• • Solve.

13. Independent Publisher's net price is $13.20 for a book with a list price of $16.50. What is the discount rate?

14. Heirloom's net price is $4.95 for a clock with a list price of $7.50. What is the discount rate?

ANSWERS

1. _____

2. _____

3. _____

4. _____

5. _____

6. _____

7. _____

8. _____

9. _____

10. _____

11. _____

12. _____

13. _____

14. _____

What is the discount rate to the nearest percent? The list and net prices are given.

15.

OLYMPUS
XA1

The 35mm
you don't have to set

$69⁹⁵

Net Price $41.97

16.

NIKON EM

9 PIECE 3 LENS
OUTFIT (with FLASH)

- Totally automatic
- Super lightweight
- Nikon quality at a low price

- EM body
- 50mm 1.8 Nikon lens
- 135 aux. tele. lens
- 28mm aux. wide angle
- Electronic flash
- Lens cap
- Body cap
- Color film
- Lens tissue

179⁹⁵

Net Price $71.98

17. White Manufacturing sets the net price of a freezer at $287.45 and offers a 30% discount. What is the list price?

18. First Furniture Company sets the net price of an end table at $47.75 and offers a 28% discount. What is the list price?

19.  Terrayaki Computers sets the net price of a computer at $398 and offers a 32% discount. What is the list price?

20. Jolan Industries sets the net price of a large screen television at $1850 and offers a 25% discount. What is the list price?

✓ **SKILL MAINTENANCE**

21. In a recent month, 30.7% of the 863,713 new cars sold in the United States were imports. How many were imports?

22. Between April and August of a recent year, 3655 complaints were filed against United States airlines. Lost, damaged, or delayed baggage accounted for 31% of these complaints. How many complaints were about lost, damaged, or delayed baggage?

11.2

More Trade and Cash Discounts

⚬ SEVERAL DISCOUNTS

Manufacturers may give additional discounts (sometimes called **chain** or **series discounts**) to move their products quickly. Example 1 illustrates the process.

Example 1 Amfes, a shoe manufacturer, offers a trade discount of 5% in addition to a previously offered discount of 20%. Find the net price for a pair of shoes that lists for $36.95.

Solution

a) Apply the first discount to the list price.

Discount = 20% × $36.95
= 0.20 × $36.95 = $7.39

b) Find the net price after the first discount.

Net price = $36.95 − $7.39 = $29.56

c) Apply the second discount to this price.

Discount = 5% × $29.56
= 0.05 × $29.56 = $1.48

d) Find the net price after the second discount.

Net price = $29.56 − $1.48 = $28.08

The net price is $28.08.

DO EXERCISE 1.

Example 2 illustrates another method for solving this problem called the **method of complements.** It involves finding the *complement* of each percent (the percent which when added to the given percent results in 100%).

Example 2 Amfes, a shoe manufacturer, offers a trade discount of 5% in addition to a previously offered discount of 20%. Find the net price for a pair of shoes that lists for $36.95.

Solution

a) Subtract each percent from 100%.

100% − 20% = 80% = 0.80

100% − 5% = 95% = 0.95

b) Find the net price.

Net price = 0.80 × 0.95 × $36.95
= 28.08

The net price is $28.08.

DO EXERCISE 2.

1. Lurlee, a dress manufacturer, offers a trade discount of 7% in addition to a previously offered discount of 32%. Find the net price for a dress that lists for $62.49.

2. Lurlee, a dress manufacturer, offers a trade discount of 7% in addition to a previously offered discount of 32%. Using the method of complements, find the net price for a dress that lists for $62.49.

ANSWERS ON PAGE A-14

3. Find the single discount rate for a 10% discount followed by a 20% discount.

4. Find the single discount rate and trade discount on a hydraulic lift with a list price of $9875 and successive discounts of 15%, 7%, and 11%.

ANSWERS ON PAGE A-14

▪ ▪ SINGLE RATE EQUIVALENT OF SEVERAL RATES

Several discount rates may be changed to a single rate.

> **To change several discount rates to a single rate,**
> 1. **subtract each discount rate from 100% and convert to a decimal;**
> 2. **multiply and convert back to a percent; and**
> 3. **subtract from 100%.**

Example 3 Find the single discount rate for a 10% discount followed by a 30% discount.

Solution

1. $100\% - 10\% = 90\% = 0.90$ Subtract from 100% and convert to
   $100\% - 30\% = 70\% = 0.70$ a decimal.

2. $0.90 \times 0.70 = 0.63 = 63\%$ Multiply and convert back to a percent.

3. $100\% - 63\% = 37\%$ Subtract from 100%.

The single discount rate is 37%.

DO EXERCISE 3.

Example 4 Find the single discount rate and trade discount on a lawn tractor with a list price of $2985 and successive discounts of 10%, 8%, and 12%.

Solution

a) Find the single discount rate.

1. $100\% - 10\% = 90\% = 0.90$
   $100\% - 8\% = 92\% = 0.92$ Subtract from 100% and convert to a decimal.
   $100\% - 12\% = 88\% = 0.88$

2. $0.90 \times 0.92 \times 0.88 = 0.729 = 72.9\%$ Multiply and convert back to a percent.

3. $100\% - 72.9\% = 27.1\%$ Subtract from 100%.

The single discount rate is 27.1%.

b) Find the trade discount.

Trade discount $= 27.1\% \times \$2985 = 0.271 \times \$2985 = \$808.94$

The trade discount is $808.94.

DO EXERCISE 4.

▪ ▪ ▪ COMPARING RATES

Finding the single discount rate can be helpful for comparison when retailers make purchases.

Example 5 One manufacturer offers a sofa at discounts of 10% and 30%, whereas another manufacturer offers a comparable sofa for the same list price at discounts of 25% and 15%. Which is the better buy?

Solution

a) Find the single discount for the first manufacturer.

1. $100\% - 10\% = 90\% = 0.90$ Subtract from 100% and convert to a decimal.
   $100\% - 30\% = 70\% = 0.70$

2. $0.90 \times 0.70 = 0.63 = 63\%$ Multiply and convert back to a percent.

3. $100\% - 63\% = 37\%$ Subtract from 100%.

The single discount rate for the first manufacturer is 37%.

b) Find the single discount rate for the second manufacturer.

   1. $100\% - 25\% = 75\% = 0.75$ Subtract from 100% and convert to a decimal.
       $100\% - 15\% = 85\% = 0.85$

   2. $0.75 \times 0.85 = 0.63\frac{3}{4} = 63\frac{3}{4}\%$ Multiply and convert back to a percent.

   3. $100\% - 63\frac{3}{4}\% = 36\frac{1}{4}\%$ Subtract from 100%.

The single discount rate for the second manufacturer is $36\frac{1}{4}\%$.

c) The larger discount, and therefore the better buy, is obtained from the first manufacturer.

DO EXERCISE 5.

⠿ CASH DISCOUNTS

Manufacturers and wholesalers often give a discount for early payment. The cash discount is subtracted after trade discount(s) but before transportation charges are added.

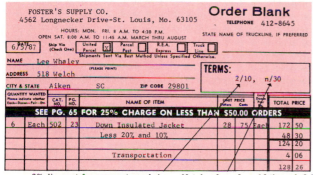

2% discount for payments made by June 15 (10 days from invoice date).   Net due from June 16 through July 5 (thereafter, interest may be charged).

Example 6 Lee Whaley pays the invoice on June 8. How much does he pay?

Solution

a) Find the amount paid excluding transportation charges. The 2% discount applies because payment was made before June 15.

Discount $= 2\% \times \$124.20$

$\qquad = 0.02 \times \$124.20 = \$2.48$

The amount paid (excluding transportation) is $\$124.20 - \$2.48 = \$121.72$.

b) Add transportation charges.

Total paid $= \$121.72 + \$4.06 = \$125.78$

The total paid is $125.78.

DO EXERCISE 6.

---

5. One manufacturer offers a dishwasher at discounts of 12% and 8%, whereas another manufacturer offers a comparable dishwasher for the same list price at discounts of 15% and 5%. Which is the better buy?

6. On the Foster's invoice, suppose that each jacket cost $31.25 and payment is made on June 11. How much is paid?

ANSWERS ON PAGE A-14

7. On the Brook's Tools invoice, suppose each leverage cutter was $21.49 and each expansive bit was $7.85. The goods were received March 20 and the bill was paid March 28. How much was paid?

Table 11.1 lists other notations for cash discount appearing on invoices.

TABLE 11.1	
Terms	**Meaning**
3/10 1/30, n/60	3% discount within 10 days of invoice date, 1% discount from 11th to 30th day, and net from 31st to 60th day.
2/10, E.O.M.	2% discount within 10 days of beginning of next month (E.O.M. means End Of Month).
n/30	Net within 30 days of invoice date.
3/10, n/30, R.O.G.	3% within 10 days of Receipt Of Goods (R.O.G.), net from 11th to 30th day.

Example 7 The goods listed on the Brook's Tools invoice were received on March 25 and the bill was paid on April 2. How much was paid?

Brook's Tools, Inc.
Weirton, WV 26062

Date: March 12, 1987   Invoice No. 807
Ship To: Fremont Bros.
         Millard, NE 68137
Shipped: Yellow Freight   Terms: 4/10, n/30, R.O.G.

Quantity	Description	Unit Price	Amount
40	Leverage Cutters	18.95	758.00
50	Expansive Bit	6.95	347.50
	Subtotal		1105.50
	Less 30% and 10%		409.04
	Balance		696.46
	Freight		29.85
	Total		726.31

Solution

a) Find the amount paid excluding freight charges. The 4% discount applies because payment was made within 10 days of receipt of goods.

Discount = 4% × $696.46

$$= 0.04 \times \$696.46$$

$$= \$27.86$$

Amount paid (excluding freight) = $696.46 − $27.86

$$= \$668.60$$

b) Add the freight charges.

Total paid = $668.60 + $29.85

$$= \$698.45$$

The total paid was $698.45.

DO EXERCISE 7.

ANSWER ON PAGE A-14

• Solve.

1. Minol offers a 5% trade discount in addition to a previously offered discount of 16%. Find the net price of the Minol Camera.

3. Intell offers a 5% trade discount in addition to a previously offered discount of 20%. Find the net price of the Matt Space Armada.

5. Van Huesn offers a trade discount of 8% in addition to a previously offered discount of 15%. Find the net price of a shirt that lists for $13.50.

7. Black offers a trade discount of 32% in addition to a previously offered discount of 9%. Find the net price of a power drill that lists for $54.49.

9. Rexmode offers successive discounts of 8%, 7%, and 10% in June. Find the net price of a lightweight jacket that lists for $27.00.

•• Solve.

11. Find the single discount rate for a 20% discount followed by a 5% discount.

13. ▦ Find the single discount rate to the nearest tenth of a percent for successive discounts of 10%, 4%, and 5%.

2. Cann offers a 10% trade discount in addition to a previously offered discount of 26%. Find the net price of the Cann Camera.

4. Intell offers a 10% trade discount in addition to a previously offered discount of 30%. Find the net price of the Matt Star Strike.

6. Marx offers a trade discount of 10% in addition to a previously offered discount of 6%. Find the net price of a suit that lists for $225.99.

8. Pride Clothes offers a trade discount of 6% in addition to a previously offered discount of 5%. Find the net price of a one-piece sleeper that lists for $4.44.

10. Hunt Manufacturing offers successive discounts of 9%, 5%, and 12% in September. Find the net price of a storage building that lists for $319.99.

12. Find the single discount rate for a 10% discount followed by a 10% discount.

14. Find the single discount rate to the nearest tenth of a percent for successive discounts of 15%, 12%, and 5%.

ANSWERS

1. _____
2. _____
3. _____
4. _____
5. _____
6. _____
7. _____
8. _____
9. _____
10. _____
11. _____
12. _____
13. _____
14. _____

15. Use the single discount rate to find the trade discount on a luggage set with a list price of $275 and discounts of 13% and 5%.

16. ▦ Use the single discount rate to find the trade discount on a stereo with a list price of $525 and discounts of 20% and 7%.

••• Solve.

17. One manufacturer offers a blender at discounts of 15% and 9%, whereas another manufacturer offers a comparable model for the same list price at discounts of 20% and 4%. Which is the better buy?

18. One manufacturer offers a piano at discounts of 25% and 7%, whereas another manufacturer offers a comparable model for the same list price at discounts of 20% and 12%. Which is the better buy?

19. One manufacturer offers a bedroom set at discounts of 20% and 7%, whereas another manufacturer offers a comparable set for the same list price at discounts of 25% and 2%. Which is the better?

20. One manufacturer offers a range at discounts of 23% and 8%, whereas another manufacturer offers a comparable range for the same list price at discounts of 30% and 1%. Which is the better buy?

⠿ Find the retailer's cost.

21. Date received: May 7, 1987; date paid: June 1, 1987.

Balance	$1286
Freight	$ 168
Total	$1454
Date	May 3, 1987
Terms	4/10, 2/30, n/60

22. ▦ Date received: May 9, 1987; date paid: May 14, 1987.

Balance	$2700
Freight	$ 305
Total	$3005
Date	May 5, 1987
Terms	5/10, 1/30, n/60

23. Date received: August 15, 1987; date paid: September 11, 1987.

Balance	$3685
Freight	$ 426
Total	$4111
Date	August 3, 1987
Terms	5/15, E.O.M.

24. Date received: December 4, 1988; date paid: December 19, 1988.

Balance	$4736
Freight	$ 396
Total	$5132
Date	November 30, 1988
Terms	5/10, n/30, R.O.G.

25. ▦ Date received: September 5, 1987; date paid: October 7, 1987.

Balance	$5682
Freight	$ 318
Total	$6000
Date	September 2, 1987
Terms	3/10, E. O. M.

26. Date received: October 1, 1987; date paid: October 9, 1987.

Balance	$8531
Freight	$ 623
Total	$9154
Date	September 28, 1987
Terms	4/10, n/30, R. O. G.

✓ **SKILL MAINTENANCE**

27. How much must you invest now at 8% compounded quarterly to have $16,900 for a new car in four years?

28. How much must you invest now at 8% compounded semiannually to have $16,900 for a new car in four years?

11.3

Inventory

We know

Gross profit = Net sales − Cost of the goods sold

Inventory helps a business to determine the cost of the goods sold, and it will be studied in this section.

• COST OF THE GOODS

Businesses take *inventory* (they count and price their goods) at regular intervals—usually monthly, quarterly, semiannually, or annually. The inventory sheet for Computonics shows how the cost is found.

INVENTORY SHEET

Computonics
Sunnyvale, CA

Date June 30, 1987				2
QUANTITY	DESCRIPTION 1 ✓ PRICE	UNIT	EXTENSIONS
20	Commodore Computers	867.25	ea	$17,345.00
35	Apple Disc Drives	375.00	ea	
500	Floppy Discs	2.50	ea	

1 "Price" is the unit cost to the business.
2 "Extensions" is the price times the quantity.

For example, 20 Commodore computers were purchased at $867.25 each for a total cost of $17,345. That is,

$$\underbrace{\$17{,}345}_{\text{Total cost}} = \underbrace{20}_{\substack{\text{Number of}\\\text{computers}}} \times \underbrace{\$867.25}_{\substack{\text{Cost of each}\\\text{computer}}}$$

Example 1 Find the total cost of the Apple disc drives on the Computonics inventory sheet.

Solution

Total cost = Number of units × Cost of each unit

=   35   × $375

= $13,125

The total cost of 35 disc drives is $13,125.

DO EXERCISE 1.

OBJECTIVES

After finishing Section 11.3, you should be able to:

- ▪ Calculate the cost of goods.
- ▪▪ Find the cost of goods sold.
- ▪▪▪ Evaluate inventory.
- ▪▪▪▪ Find gross profit.

1. Find the total cost of the floppy discs on the Computonics Inventory Sheet.

ANSWER ON PAGE A-14

2. Find the inventory on December 31, 1987, for General Appliance if 25 freezers, which cost $340 each, are in stock in addition to items in Example 2.

When we add the total cost for each product, we obtain the total cost of all items on hand. This sum is the inventory at that time.

Example 2 Find the inventory on December 31, 1987, for General Appliances.

Solution

INVENTORY SHEET

General Appliances
Athens, GA

Date December 31, 1987

QUANTITY	DESCRIPTION	√	PRICE	UNIT	EXTENSIONS
12	Hotpoint Ranges		$410.00	ea	$4920.00
15	Amana Radar Ranges		285.00	ea	4275.00
18	Whirlpool Refrigerators		550.00	ea	9900.00

Adding the total cost for each product, we obtain

$4920 + $4275 + $9900

or

$19,095

The inventory on December 31, 1987, is $19,095.

DO EXERCISE 2.

3. What would the cost of goods sold for Stanford's have been if the ending inventory was $2600?

• • COST OF THE GOODS SOLD

To find the cost of the goods sold, use

Cost of goods sold = Beginning inventory + Purchases − Ending inventory

Example 3 What was the cost of the goods sold for Stanfords?

Solution

STANFORD'S

Beginning inventory	$8000
Purchases	$6500
Ending inventory	$5000

a) Add the beginning inventory and purchases.

$8000 + $6500 = $14,500

b) Subtract the ending inventory.

$14,500 − $5000 = $9500

The cost of the goods sold was $9500.

DO EXERCISE 3.

ANSWERS ON PAGE A-14

••• INVENTORY VALUATION

In practice the same item may be purchased several times in an inventory period at a different cost each time. For example, suppose two identical VHS video recorders were purchased by a retailer at different times. The purchase price for the first was $624 and for the second, $710. One of the units is sold. Which one remains? The method used to take ending inventory answers this question. Ending inventory methods include the *F*irst *I*n, *F*irst *O*ut (*FIFO*); *L*ast *I*n, *F*irst *O*ut (*LIFO*); or weighted average methods. Different inventory valuation methods result in different financial pictures and therefore different tax consequences.

To illustrate, suppose the retailer sold the VHS recorder for $900. If it was the first purchased, the gross profit was $276.

$900	Net sales
624	Cost to retailer
$276	Gross profit

However, if it was the second purchased, the gross profit was $190.

$900	Net sales
710	Cost to retailer
$190	Gross profit

The gross profit in the first case looks much better. However, this more favorable financial picture may result in increased taxes. Example 4 provides a detailed illustration.

Example 4 Roger's Television purchased quantities of the same model television set three times during an inventory period. The first purchase was 32 sets at $335.30 each; the second, 21 sets at $374.80 each; and the third, 25 at $406.75 each. In all, 44 sets were sold (34 sets were in inventory). Evaluate the ending inventory by the FIFO, LIFO, and weighted average methods.

Solution

a) Evaluate using FIFO.

The 34 sets in inventory are the last 25 and 9 from the second purchase.

25 @ $406.75 = $10,168.75
9 @ $374.80 = $ 3,373.20
$13,541.95   Ending inventory value at cost using FIFO

b) Evaluate using LIFO.

The 34 sets in inventory are the first 32 and 2 from the second purchase.

32 @ $335.30 = $10,729.60
2 @ $374.80 = $ 749.60
$11,479.20   Ending inventory value at cost using LIFO

4. Evaluate the ending inventory in Example 4 by the FIFO, LIFO, and weighted average methods if 40 sets were sold (38 sets were in inventory).

c) Evaluate using the weighted average method.

Find the cost of each purchase.

First	32 @ $335.30	= $10,729.60	
Second	21 @ $374.80	= $ 7,870.80	
Third	25 @ $406.75	= $10,168.75	
Total number	78	$28,769.15	Total cost

Find the average cost.

$$\text{Average cost} = \frac{\text{Total cost}}{\text{Total number}}$$

$$= \frac{\$28,769.15}{78}$$

$= \$368.84$ Rounding; see Section 1.8.

$$\begin{array}{c}\text{Ending inventory value} \\ \text{at cost using weighted average}\end{array} = \begin{array}{c}\text{Number of items} \\ \text{in inventory}\end{array} \times \begin{array}{c}\text{Average} \\ \text{cost}\end{array}$$

$$= \quad 34 \quad\quad \$368.84$$

DO EXERCISE 4. $= \$12,540.56$

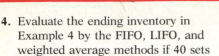 **GROSS PROFIT**

The following example illustrates how to calculate gross profit using each of the three inventory methods.

Example 5 Net sales in Example 4 were $24,935. Find the gross profit using the FIFO, LIFO, and weighted average methods.

Solution

a) Find the gross profit using FIFO.

$$\begin{array}{ccc}\text{Cost of televisions sold} = & \text{Total cost} & - \text{FIFO inventory value}\end{array}$$

$$= \quad \$28,769.15 \quad - \quad \$13,541.95$$
$$\text{(From Example 4c)} \quad \text{(From Example 4a)}$$

$$= \quad \$15,227.20$$

So

$$\begin{array}{l}\text{Gross profit} = \text{Net sales} - \quad \text{Cost} \\ \quad\quad = \$24,935 - \$15,227.20 = \$9707.80\end{array}$$

b) Find the gross profit using LIFO.

$$\text{Cost of televisions sold} = \text{Total cost} - \text{LIFO inventory value}$$
$$= \$28,769.15 - \quad \$11,479.20 \quad = \$17,289.$$

So

$$\begin{array}{l}\text{Gross profit} = \text{Net sales} - \quad \text{Cost} \\ \quad\quad = \$24,935 - \$17,289.95 = \$7645.05\end{array}$$

c) Find the gross profit using weighted averages.

$$\begin{array}{l}\text{Cost of televisions} \\ \text{sold}\end{array} = \text{Total cost} - \begin{array}{l}\text{Weighted average} \\ \text{inventory value}\end{array}$$

$$= \$28,769.15 - \quad \$12,540.56 \quad = \$16,228.59$$

So

$$\begin{array}{l}\text{Gross profit} = \text{Net sales} - \quad \text{Cost} \\ \quad\quad = \$24,935 - \$16,228.59 = \$8706.41\end{array}$$

DO EXERCISE 5

5. Net sales in Example 4 were $27,460. Find the gross profit using the FIFO, LIFO, and weighted average methods.

ANSWERS ON PAGE A-14

• Find the cost of the quantity of each item on the inventory sheet.

ANSWERS

INVENTORY SHEET

The Sharper Image
Baton Rouge, LA

Date May 1, 1987

	QUANTITY	DESCRIPTION	√	PRICE	UNIT
1.	3	Captain's Clock		$140.00	ea
2.	15	Cordless Muraphone		95.25	ea
3.	4	Float to Relax Tank		2750.00	ea
4.	12	Phone Dialer		62.50	ea
5.	5	Biofeedback Earphones		119.75	ea
6.	30	Sanyo Flashlights		18.00	ea
7.	18	Citizen's Travel Clock		32.45	ea
8.	25	Compact Paper Shredder		107.50	ea

INVENTORY SHEET

Eddie Bauer
Denver, CO

Date September 30, 1987

	QUANTITY	DESCRIPTION	√	PRICE	UNIT
9.	16	Ridgeline Parka		$123.00	ea
10.	14	Blizzard Master Vest		87.00	ea
11.	36	Thinsulate Deerskin Gloves		24.25	ea
12.	50	Polypropylene Underwear		15.65	ea
13.	24	Chino Pants		14.75	ea
14.	10	Gore-Tex Down Jacket		122.45	ea
15.	40	Turtleneck Pullovers		11.50	ea
16.	8	Ragg Wool Sweater		21.75	ea

17. Find the inventory on May 1, 1987, for The Sharper Image (from Exercises 1–8).

18. Find the inventory on September 30, 1987, for Eddie Bauer (from Exercises 9–16).

•• Find the cost of the goods sold.

19. **HECKEL'S**

| Beginning Inventory | $9,847 |
| Ending Inventory | $2,347 |

20. **BABE'S**

| Beginning Inventory | $12,809 |
| Ending Inventory | $ 4,957 |

21. **RACHAEL'S**

Beginning Inventory	$46,302
Purchases	$ 7,328
Ending Inventory	$12,694

22. **THE WHIRLWIND**

Beginning Inventory	$43,256
Purchases	$13,507
Ending Inventory	$25,892

1. _____
2. _____
3. _____
4. _____
5. _____
6. _____
7. _____
8. _____
9. _____
10. _____
11. _____
12. _____
13. _____
14. _____
15. _____
16. _____
17. _____
18. _____
19. _____
20. _____
21. _____
22. _____

23. **LACKAWANNA PARTS**

Beginning Inventory	$67,367
Purchases	$18,000
Ending Inventory	$31,794

24. **STONES**

Beginning Inventory	$32,786
Purchases	$ 9,680
Ending Inventory	$17,329

••• Solve.

Luah's Stereo purchased quantities of the same model stereo three times during an inventory period. The first purchase was 37 stereos at $246.80 each; the second, 26 at $264.50 each; and the third, 31 at $294.60 each. In all, 38 stereos were sold (56 stereos were in inventory). Net sales were $11,856. Find the following.

25. ▦ The ending inventory by FIFO.

26. ▦ The ending inventory by LIFO.

27. ▦ The ending inventory by the weighted average method.

Forgione Cameras purchased quantities of the same model camera four times during an inventory period. The first purchase was 7 cameras at $256.30 each; the second, 11 at $263.75 each; the third, 9 at $276.70 each; and the fourth, 8 at $295.40 each. In all, 26 cameras were sold (9 cameras were in inventory). Net sales were $10,918. Find the following.

28. The ending inventory by FIFO.

29. The ending inventory by LIFO.

30. The ending inventory by the weighted average method.

⚃ Find the gross profit.

31. Using FIFO for the stereo purchases (Exercises 25–27).

32. Using LIFO for the stereo purchases (Exercises 25–27).

33. Using the weighted average method for the stereo purchases (Exercises 25–27).

34. Using FIFO for the camera purchases (Exercises 28–30).

35. Using LIFO for the camera purchases (Exercises 28–30).

36. Using the weighted average method for the camera purchases (Exercises 28–30).

✓ **SKILL MAINTENANCE**

37. Financial Services pay 14% compounded semiannually. Find the amount and interest on $2800 after one year.

38. Sheilah Thorn placed $10,000 in a money market certificate paying 6% compounded quarterly. How much money did she obtain upon cashing in the certificate four years later?

If you miss an item, review the indicated section and objective.

[11.1, •] **1.** Find the trade discount for the wine rack.

> **TWELVE BOTTLE WINE RACK**
> **BY RIVERSIDE**
> **Solid antique pine and brass**   **$98**

       Net Price $65

[11.1, ••] **2.** Kacuzzi Products' net price is $1350 for a hot tub with a list price of $1800. What is the discount rate?

[11.2, •] **3.** Tirestone offers discounts of 15%, 10%, and 5% during June. Find the net price of a radial snow tire that lists for $54.99.

[11.2, ••] **4.** Find the single discount rate for a 15% discount followed by a 10% discount.

[11.2, •••] **5.** One manufacturer offers lawn furniture at discounts of 15% and 5%, whereas another manufacturer offers comparable furniture for the same list price at discounts of 10% and 10%. Which is the better buy?

[11.2, ::] **6.** Find the amount paid on the following invoice if the date received was May 18, 1987, and the date paid was May 24, 1987.

Balance	$1457
Freight	$ 149
Total	$1606
Date	May 15, 1987
Terms	3/10, 2/30, n/60

[11.3, •] **7.** Find the inventory on December 31, 1987, for Beane and Company.

INVENTORY SHEET				
Beane and Company Greenville, NC				
Date December 31, 1987				
QUANTITY	DESCRIPTION	√	PRICE	UNIT
15	Moccasins		$ 26.00	ea
20	Corduroy Skirt		31.50	ea
8	Icelandic Jackets		119.75	ea

ANSWERS

1. _____

2. _____

3. _____

4. _____

5. _____

6. _____

7. _____

[11.3, • •] **8.** Find the cost of the goods sold.

FREDRICK'S	
Beginning Inventory	**$25,752**
Purchases	**$ 8,945**
Ending Inventory	**$11,563**

Suzanne's Jewelry purchased quantities of the same digital watch three times during an inventory period. The first purchase was 17 watches at $26.50 each; the second, 10 at $29.75 each; and the third, 16 at $31.80 each. In all, 18 watches were sold (25 watches were in inventory). Net sales were $855.

[11.3, • • •] **9.** Evaluate the ending inventory by FIFO.

[11.3, • • / • •] **10.** Find the gross profit using FIFO.

12

DEPRECIA- TION

CAREER: CERTIFIED PUBLIC ACCOUNTANT This is Daniel Dennis. He is Founder and Managing Partner of Daniel Dennis and Company, a regional Certified Public Accounting firm providing audit, accounting, tax and management advisory services to commercial businesses, government offices and non-profit organizations.

DANIEL DENNIS

An understanding of the different types of depreciation covered in this chapter is crucial to an accountant like Dan. The value of a fixed asset such as a piece of furniture or a company car decreases over the lifetime of the asset, or depreciates. The Federal Government sets standards governing the rate at which depreciation can be accelerated for tax returns.

When preparing tax returns for clients, Dan must work closely with them to develop an understanding of their financial needs. He must also keep himself informed of the latest Government regulations regarding depreciation, which are sometimes changed in an effort to encourage spending and bolster the economy. A thorough understanding of depreciation can help Dan save his clients thousands of dollars in income tax payments.

Dan received a B.S. in Business Administration from the University of Bridgeport and an M.B.A. from the Harvard Business School. After working as a Certified Public Accountant for other companies, he founded Daniel Dennis and Company in 1981. He is a Trustee of the University of Bridgeport and serves on the board of several local financial institutions. Extensive training is required to become a CPA, as you must work for a CPA firm for two to three years, and then pass a rigorous exam. CPA's are highly respected professionally, and earn a yearly salary ranging from $18,000–$24,000 to an unlimited amount.

Although Dan is very busy, he enjoys travelling and playing tennis when he can. He feels that one of the great benefits of his position is access to community service at a high level.

Depreciation: The Straight-Line Method

As defined by the American Institute of Certified Public Accountants, ***depreciation*** is "an accounting principle which aims to distribute the cost of tangible capital assets, less salvage value (if any), over the estimated useful life of the asset in a systematic and rational manner. It is a process of allocation of cost, not of valuation."

Let us try to understand this somewhat complicated definition in terms of an example. A company buys an office machine for $5200 on January 1 of a given year. The machine is expected to last for eight years after which its ***trade-in value***, or ***salvage value***, will be $1100. Over its lifetime it declines in value or *depreciates* $5200 − $1100, or $4100. The decline in value from $5200 to $1100 can occur in many ways, as shown below.

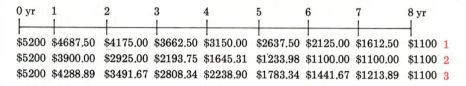

0 yr	1	2	3	4	5	6	7	8 yr	
$5200	$4687.50	$4175.00	$3662.50	$3150.00	$2637.50	$2125.00	$1612.50	$1100	1
$5200	$3900.00	$2925.00	$2193.75	$1645.31	$1233.98	$1100.00	$1100.00	$1100	2
$5200	$4288.89	$3491.67	$2808.34	$2238.90	$1783.34	$1441.67	$1213.89	$1100	3

For financial accounting purposes, there are several frequently used methods to compute depreciation. In the above table, Method ① is called the ***straight-line method***, Method ② the ***double declining-balance method***, and Method ③ the ***sum-of-the-years'-digits method***. We shall consider these and others.

● THE STRAIGHT-LINE METHOD

Suppose, for the machine above, the company figures the decline in value to be the *same* each year, that is, $\frac{1}{8}$ (or 12.5%) of $4100, which is $512.50. After one year the *salvage value*, or simply *value*, is

$5200 − $512.50, or $4687.50.

After two years it is

$4687.50 − $512.50, or $4175.00.

After three years it is

$4175.00 − $512.50, or $3662.50,

and so on.

> For straight-line depreciation,
>
> a) **Total depreciation = Cost − Salvage value.**
>
> b) **Annual depreciation** $= \dfrac{\text{Cost} - \text{Salvage value}}{\text{Expected life}}.$
>
> c) **Rate of depreciation** $= \dfrac{\text{Annual depreciation}}{\text{Total depreciation}}.$

Example 1 For the following item, find the total depreciation, annual depreciation, and rate of depreciation:

    Item: Office machine

    Cost = $5200

    Expected life = 8 years

    Salvage value = $1100

Solution

a) Total depreciation = Cost − Salvage value

$$= \$5200 - \$1100$$
$$= \$4100$$

b) Annual depreciation $= \dfrac{\text{Cost} - \text{Salvage value}}{\text{Expected life}}$

$$= \frac{\$5200 - \$1100}{8}$$
$$= \frac{\$4100}{8}$$
$$= \$512.50$$

c) Rate of depreciation $= \dfrac{\text{Annual depreciation}}{\text{Total depreciation}}$

$$= \frac{\$512.50}{\$4100}$$
$$= 0.125, \text{ or } 12.5\%$$

In many cases salvage values are considered to be $0, but not always.

DO EXERCISE 1.

A depreciation schedule gives a complete list of the values and total depreciation throughout the life of an item.

ANSWERS ON PAGE A-14

2. Prepare a depreciation schedule for the automobile discussed in Margin Exercise 1, using the blank table below. Round answers to the nearest cent.

Year	Rate of depreciation	Annual depreciation	Value	Total depreciation
0				
1				
2				
3				
4				
5				

ANSWERS ON PAGE A-14

Example 2 Prepare a depreciation schedule for the office machine discussed in Example 1.

Solution

Year	Rate of depreciation	Annual depreciation	Value	Total depreciation
0			$5200	
1	$\frac{1}{8}$ or 12.5%	$512.50	4687.50	$ 512.50
2	12.5%	512.50	4175.00	1025.00
3	12.5%	512.50	3662.50	1537.50
4	12.5%	512.50	3150.00	2050.00
5	12.5%	512.50	2637.50	2562.50
6	12.5%	512.50	2125.00	3075.00
7	12.5%	512.50	1612.50	3587.50
8	12.5%	512.50	1100.00	4100.00

1. The rate of depreciation is the same each year.

2. The annual depreciation is the same each year.

3. We find the values by starting with the initial cost, $5200, and successively subtracting $512.50. For example, $5200 − $512.50 = $4687.50. Then. $4687.50 − $512.50 = $4175.00, and so on.

4. We find the total depreciations by starting with $512.50 after the first year and successively adding $512.50. For example, $512.50 + $512.50 = $1025.00. Then $1025.00 + $512.50 = $1537.50, and so on.

DO EXERCISE 2.

Why do we call this *straight-line depreciation?* If we make a graph relating values to time, we see that the values lie in a *straight line.*

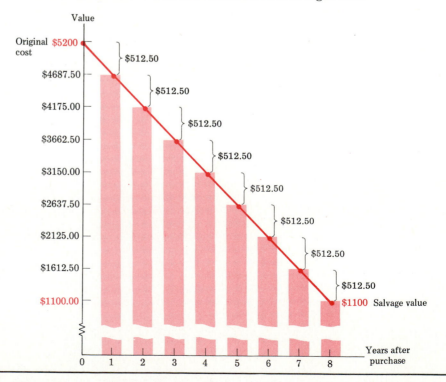

• For each of the following items find (a) the total depreciation, and (b) the annual depreciation.

1. *Item:* Automobile
   Cost = $8000
   Expected life = 4 years
   Salvage value = $2000

2. *Item:* Automobile
   Cost = $12,000
   Expected life = 3 years
   Salvage value = $4800

3. *Item:* Postage machine
   Cost = $450
   Expected life = 8 years
   Salvage value = $0

4. *Item:* Typewriter
   Cost = $2500
   Expected life = 6 years
   Salvage value = $0

5. *Item:* Building
   Cost = $50,000
   Expected life = $33\frac{1}{3}$ years
   Salvage value = $0

6. *Item:* Building
   Cost = $100,000
   Expected life = 40 years
   Salvage value = $0

Prepare a depreciation schedule for the situation in:

7. Exercise 1.

Year	Rate of depreciation	Annual depreciation	Value	Total depreciation
0				
1				
2				
3				
4				

8. Exercise 2.

Year	Rate of depreciation	Annual depreciation	Value	Total depreciation
0				
1				
2				
3				

ANSWERS

1. _____

2. _____

3. _____

4. _____

5. _____

6. _____

11. _____

9. Exercise 3.

Year	Rate of depreciation	Annual depreciation	Value	Total depreciation
0				
1				
2				
3				
4				
5				
6				
7				
8				

12. _____

10. Exercise 4.

Year	Rate of depreciation	Annual depreciation	Value	Total depreciation
0				
1				
2				
3				
4				
5				
6				

13. _____

11. ▥ For the situation in Exercise 5, find the total depreciation, annual depreciation, and values after the first and second years.

12. ▥ For the situation in Exercise 6, find the total depreciation, annual depreciation, and values after the first and second years.

✓ **SKILL MAINTENANCE**

13. Recently, Ducktrap River Fish Farm in Lincolnville, Maine, sold Maine smoked trout for $45 a dozen. Santé Gourmet ordered 14 dozen. How much was the bill?

14. According to a recent survey, 35% of 105 outside directors feel corporations could make better use of their skills. How many feel this way?

14. _____

12.2

Depreciation: The Declining-Balance Method

After finishing Section 12.2, you should be able to:

- Prepare a depreciation schedule using the double declining-balance method.

• DOUBLE DECLINING BALANCE

A company buys a machine for $5200. The machine is expected to last for eight years, after which its salvage value will be $1100. The straight-line rate of depreciation would be $\frac{1}{8}$, or 12.5%. Depreciation can be deducted as a business expense when a business computes its taxes. When a business is starting out it has many expenses and less income and therefore needs all the tax advantages it can get. For this, and other reasons, the Internal Revenue Service has allowed certain assets to be depreciated at a rate that is larger than the straight-line rate, but *no more than twice the straight-line rate.* (Such a rate could be, for example, $1\frac{1}{4}$, $1\frac{1}{2}$, or 2 times the straight-line rate.) Suppose for the above that the rate is $2 \cdot \frac{1}{8}$, or 25%. This is called the *double declining-balance method.* Then the value after one year is

$$\$5200 - (25\% \times \$5200) \qquad \text{We subtract 25\% of the initial value.}$$
$$= \$5200 - (0.25 \times \$5200)$$
$$= \$5200 - \$1300$$
$$= \$3900.$$

After two years it is

$$\$3900 - (0.25 \times \$3900) \qquad \text{We subtract 25\% of the preceding value.}$$
$$= \$3900 - \$975$$
$$= \$2925.$$

After three years it is

$$\$2925 - (0.25 \times \$2925) = \$2925 - \$731.25$$
$$= \$2193.75.$$

After four years it is

$$\$2193.75 - (0.25 \times \$2193.75)$$
$$= \$2193.75 - \$548.44 \qquad \text{Rounded to the nearest cent.}$$
$$= \$1645.31,$$

and so on.

Example 1 Prepare a depreciation schedule for the situation below. Use the double declining-balance method.

Item: Office machine
Cost = $5200
Expected life = 8 years
Salvage value = $1100

1. Prepare a depreciation schedule for the item below. Use the double declining-balance method.

Item: Automobile

Cost = $8700

Expected life = 5 years

Salvage value = $1600

Solution

Year	Rate of depreciation	Annual depreciation	Value	Total depreciation
0			$5200	
1	$\frac{2}{8}$ or 25%	$1300.00	3900.00	$1300
2	25%	975.00	2925.00	2275
3	25%	731.25	2193.75	3006.25
4	25%	548.44	1645.31	3554.69
5	25%	411.33	1233.98	3966.02
6		133.98	1100.00	4100.00
7		0	1100.00	4100.00
8		0	1100.00	4100.00

1. The rate of depreciation is the same each year: twice the straight-line rate.

2. We find the values by starting with the initial cost, $5200, and successively subtracting 0.25 times the value. For example, $5200 − (0.25 × $5200) = $3900. Then, $3900 − (0.25 × $3900) = $2925, and so on.

3. We find the annual depreciations when we multiply each successive value by 0.25. For example, 0.25 × $5200 = $1300, and 0.25 × $3900 = $975.

DO EXERCISE 1.

* Note that

$$\$1233.98 - (0.25 \times \$1233.98) = \$1233.98 - \$308.50$$
$$= \$925.48,$$

but the value cannot drop below the salvage value. Thus, after $1233.98 the next value becomes $1100.00, and the annual depreciation for that year is $1233.98 − $1100.00, or $133.98.

● Prepare a depreciation schedule for each situation. Use the ***double declining-balance method.***

1. *Item:* Automobile—Cost = $8000, Expected life = 4 years, Salvage value = $2000

Year	Rate of depreciation	Annual depreciation	Value	Total depreciation
0				
1				
2				
3				
4				

2. 🖩 *Item:* Automobile—Cost = $12,000, Expected life = 3 years, Salvage value = $4800

Year	Rate of depreciation	Annual depreciation	Value	Total depreciation
0				
1				
2				
3				

3. 🖩 *Item:* Typewriter—Cost = $2500, Expected life = 6 years

Year	Rate of depreciation	Annual depreciation	Value	Total depreciation
0				
1				
2				
3				
4				
5				
6				

4. *Item:* Postage machine—Cost = $450, Expected life = 8 years

Year	Rate of depreciation	Annual depreciation	Value	Total depreciation
0				
1				
2				
3				
4				
5				
6				
7				
8				

5. *Item:* Computer—Cost = $5400, Expected life = 5 years, Salvage value = $1000

Year	Rate of depreciation	Annual depreciation	Value	Total depreciation
0				
1				
2				
3				
4				
5				

For each of the following items, find the annual depreciation, the rate of depreciation, and the values after the first and second years. Use the declining-balance method and a rate that is $1\frac{1}{2}$ times the straight-line rate.

6.  *Item:* Building
Cost = $50,000
Expected life = $33\frac{1}{3}$ years
Salvage value = $0

7. *Item:* Building
Cost = $100,000
Expected life = 40 years
Salvage value = $0

✓ **SKILL MAINTENANCE**

8. The current market value of Keith Smith's home is $86,500. Find the assessed value if the assessment rate is 72%.

9. An $825 refrigerator was purchased in Nevada which has a 5.75% sales tax. Find the sales tax. Use the major fraction rule.

12.3

Depreciation: The Sum-of-the-Years'-Digits Method

• DEPRECIATION FRACTIONS

Another method of depreciation, which allows larger amounts of depreciation in early years and smaller amounts in later years, is the *sum-of-the-years'-digits method*. Each year a different rate (a fraction) of depreciation is used.

Example 1 For the item below, find (a) the depreciation fractions, and (b) the depreciation and values after one year and after two years.

> *Item:* Office machine   Expected life = 8 years
>
> Cost = $5200   Salvage value = $1100

Solution

a) To find the depreciation we first find the sum-of-the-years' digits:

$$8 + 7 + 6 + 5 + 4 + 3 + 2 + 1 = 36:*$$

The number 36 will be the denominator of each fraction. We then find the depreciation fractions (rates) by dividing each number in the sum by 36:

$$\frac{8}{36}, \frac{7}{36}, \frac{6}{36}, \frac{5}{36}, \frac{4}{36}, \frac{3}{36}, \frac{2}{36}, \frac{1}{36}.$$

b) The total depreciation is $5200 − $1100, or $4100. The depreciation the first year is

$$\frac{8}{36} \times \$4100 = \frac{8 \times \$4100}{36} = \frac{\$32,800}{36}$$

$$= \$911.11. \quad \text{Round to the nearest cent.}$$

The value after one year is

$5200 − $911.11,   or $4288.89.

The depreciation the second year is

$$\frac{7}{36} \times \$4100 = \frac{7 \times \$4100}{36} = \frac{\$28,700}{36} = \$797.22.$$

The value after two years is

$4288.89 − $797.22,   or $3491.67.

DO EXERCISE 1.

---

* There is a formula for doing this faster (*n* represents the expected life):

$$n + \cdots + 3 + 2 + 1 = \frac{n \times (n + 1)}{2}$$

We multiply the expected life by one more than the expected life and divide by 2. Thus

$$8 + 7 + 6 + 5 + 4 + 3 + 2 + 1 = \frac{8 \times 9}{2} = \frac{72}{2} = 36.$$

See p. 197 for a further discussion of this formula.

1. For the item below, find (a) the depreciation fractions, and (b) the depreciation and values after one year, two years, and three years.

> *Item:*   Automobile
>
> Cost = $8700
>
> Expected life = 5 years
>
> Salvage value = $1600

ANSWERS ON PAGE A-15

•• SUM-OF-THE-YEARS'-DIGITS METHOD

Example 2 Prepare a depreciation schedule for the situation below. Use the sum-of-the-years'-digits method.

Cost = $5200

Expected life = 8 years

Salvage value = $1100

Solution

Year	Rate of depreciation	Annual depreciation	Value	Total depreciation
0			$5200	
1	$\frac{8}{36}$ or 22.2%	$911.11	4288.89	$ 911.11
2	$\frac{7}{36}$ or 19.4%	797.22	3491.67	1708.33
3	$\frac{6}{36}$ or 16.7%	683.33	2808.34	2391.66
4	$\frac{5}{36}$ or 13.9%	569.44	2238.90	2961.10
5	$\frac{4}{36}$ or 11.1%	455.56	1783.34	3416.66
6	$\frac{3}{36}$ or 8.3%	341.67	1441.67	3758.33
7	$\frac{2}{36}$ or 5.6%	227.78	1213.89	3986.11
8	$\frac{1}{36}$ or 2.8%	113.89	1100.00	4100.00

1. The rate of depreciation gets lower each year.

2. We find the annual depreciations first. To do this we multiply the total depreciation by each fraction. For example, $\frac{8}{36} \times \$4100 = \$911.11$, $\frac{7}{36} \times \$4100 = \$797.22$, and so on.

3. We find the values by subtracting each annual depreciation in succession. For example, $5200 - $911.11 = 4288.89, $4288.89 - $797.22 = 3491.67, and so on.

DO EXERCISE 2.

⊡ For each of the following situations, find the depreciation fractions. Use the sum-of-the-years'-digits method.

1. *Item:* Automobile

Cost = $8000

Expected life = 4 years

Salvage value = $2000

2. *Item:* Automobile

Cost = $12,000

Expected life = 3 years

Salvage value = $4800

1. _____

3. *Item:* Postage machine

Cost = $450

Expected life = 8 years

Salvage value = $0

4. *Item:* Typewriter

Cost = $2500

Expected life = 6 years

Salvage value = $0

⊡⊡ Use the sum-of-the-years'-digits method to prepare a depreciation schedule for the situation in:

5. Exercise 1.

2. _____

Year	Rate of depreciation	Annual depreciation	Value	Total depreciation
0				
1				
2				
3				
4				

6. ▥ Exercise 2.

3. _____

Year	Rate of depreciation	Annual depreciation	Value	Total depreciation
0				
1				
2				
3				

4. _____

9. _____

10. _____

11. _____

12. _____

7. Exercise 3.

Year	Rate of depreciation	Annual depreciation	Value	Total depreciation
0				
1				
2				
3				
4				
5				
6				
7				
8				

8. ▦ Exercise 4.

Year	Rate of depreciation	Annual depreciation	Value	Total depreciation
0				
1				
2				
3				
4				
5				
6				

For each situation, find the depreciation fractions, the annual depreciation, and the values after the first and second years. Use the sum-of-the-years'-digits method.

9. ▦ _Item:_ Building—Cost = $80,000, Expected life = 25 years, Salvage value = $0

10. ▦ _Item:_ Building—Cost = $100,000, Expected life = 40 years, Salvage value = $0

✔ **SKILL MAINTENANCE**

11. During a recent season of the National Football League, Dave Archer of the Altanta Falcons completed 101 of 192 passes. What percentage of passes were completed?

12. In a survey 84% of the 32,000 women with a masters degree in Business Administration earned more than $30,000 annually. How many earned more than $30,000 annually?

Chapter 12   Depreciation

12.4

Depreciation: ACRS and Federal Taxes

How does a company go about choosing a depreciation method? The following comments may be helpful.

Straight-Line Method. This method is the most often used. It allows for consistent yearly depreciation over the life of the asset, and has an advantage over the accelerated methods in that it allows for higher profits (before taxes) in the early years of a business.

Declining Balance Method and Sum-of-the-Years'-Digits Method. These methods are used when management wants a large depreciation expense in the beginning years of an asset's life. The reason for this could be to write off more depreciation on a machine that will be more efficient when it is new. Another reason could be the tax advantage of having a larger expense in the early years of an asset's life, thus less income tax in those early years, when a new business is usually struggling.

● ACRS AND TAX DEPRECIATION

The *1981 Economic Recovery Act* completely changed depreciation write-off as applied to taxes. The **Accelerated Cost Recovery System (ACRS)** has replaced other depreciation methods for those assets placed in service after 1980. ACRS places all depreciable assets in one of four categories:

3-Year Property: autos, light equipment, race horses.
5-Year Property: heavy trucks, most manufacturing equipment.
10-Year Property: certain public utility property as well as manufactured homes, railroad tank cars, certain coal utilization property of public utilities.
15-Year Property: most real estate and certain other utility property.

The Act sets laws regarding percentages to be used to write off the cost recovery (depreciation) of the asset.

It should be noted that ACRS is for tax purposes and the results can differ greatly between ACRS and the other methods discussed. ACRS was "invented" in an attempt to encourage private sector businesses to invest in new assets and therefore help the economy rebound from recession. Examples 1 and 2 will demonstrate the differing results. ACRS is, simply stated, a special write-off method involving declining balance and straight-line depreciation.

At right is a table of the percentages for three- and five-year property. Percentages for ten-year property are given in the exercise set.

Year	3-Year Property	5-Year Property
1	25%	15%
2	38%	22%
3	37%	21%
4	—	21%
5	—	21%

The Act specifies that the salvage value will be $0.

1. Prepare a depreciation schedule for the item listed below. Use ACRS.

Item: Race horse
Cost = $300,000
Expected life = 3 years (by law)

2. Prepare a depreciation schedule. Use ACRS.

Item: Heavy truck
Cost = $200,000
Expected life = 5 years (by law)

ANSWERS ON PAGE A-16

Example 1 Prepare a depreciation schedule for a $10,000 automobile with 3 years expected life. Use ACRS.

Solution

a) First, look for the percentages on the 3-year table.

b) Then, multiply the percentages by the $10,000 cost.

Year 1: 0.25 × $10,000 = $2500
Year 2: 0.38 × $10,000 = $3800
Year 3: 0.37 × $10,000 = $3700
Total cost recovery $10,000

The depreciation schedule is as follows.

Year	Rate of depreciation	Annual depreciation	Value	Total depreciation
0			$10,000	
1	25%	$2500	7,500	$2,500
2	38%	3800	3,700	6,300
3	37%	3700	0	10,000

DO EXERCISE 1.

Example 2 Prepare a depreciation schedule for a $250,000 engine block molding machine with 5 years expected life. Use ACRS.

Solution

a) First, look for the percentages on the 5-year table.

b) Then, multiply the percentages by the $250,000 cost.

Year 1: 0.15 × $250,000 = $37,500
Year 2: 0.22 × $250,000 = $55,000
Year 3: 0.21 × $250,000 = $52,500
Year 4: 0.21 × $250,000 = $52,500
Year 5: 0.21 × $250,000 = $52,500
Total cost recovery $250,000

The depreciation schedule is as follows.

Year	Rate of depreciation	Annual depreciation	Value	Total depreciation
0			$250,000	
1	15%	$37,500	212,500	$ 37,500
2	22%	55,000	157,500	92,500
3	21%	52,500	105,000	145,000
4	21%	52,500	52,500	197,500
5	21%	52,500	0	250,000

DO EXERCISE 2.

The government's search for additional revenue sources may alter the ACRS in the years ahead. Readers should be aware that continuing changes in tax laws make any depreciation system temporary. However, in the event of change, existing depreciation methods would probably be applicable until the date of the change, and property put in service thereafter would be subject to the new depreciation rules.

Prepare a depreciation schedule for each situation. Use ACRS.

1. *Item:*   Automobile

   Cost = $15,000

   Expected life = 3 years (by law)

Year	Rate of depreciation	Annual depreciation	Value	Total depreciation
0				
1				
2				
3				

2. *Item:*   Race horse

   Cost = $280,000

   Expected life = 3 years (by law)

Year	Rate of depreciation	Annual depreciation	Value	Total depreciation
0				
1				
2				
3				

3. *Item:*   Heavy truck

   Cost = $210,000

   Expected life = 5 years (by law)

Year	Rate of depreciation	Annual depreciation	Value	Total depreciation
0				
1				
2				
3				
4				
5				

4. *Item:* Molding machine—Cost: $80,000, Expected life = 5 years (by law)

Year	Rate of depreciation	Annual depreciation	Value	Total depreciation
0				
1				
2				
3				
4				
5				

5. *Item:* Manufactured home

Cost: $130,000

Expected life = 10 years (by law)

PERCENTAGES FOR 10-YEAR PROPERTY

1st year	8%
2nd year	14%
3rd year	12%
4th through 6th year	10%
7th through 10th year	9%

Year	Rate of depreciation	Annual depreciation	Value	Total depreciation
0				
1				
2				
3				
4				
5				
6				
7				
8				
9				
10				

✓ SKILL MAINTENANCE

Computer Electronics purchased the same model computer three times during an inventory period. The first purchase was 20 computers at $99.95 each; the second, 25 at $102.50 each; the third, 15 at $105.80 each. In all, 43 computers were sold. Find.

6. The ending inventory by FIFO   **7.** The ending inventory by LIFO

8. The ending inventory by the weighted average method

ANSWERS

Consider this situation in the following exercises.

Item: Manufacturing equipment

Cost: $8500

Expected life = 5 years

Salvage value = $0

[12.1, •] **1.** Prepare a depreciation schedule. Use the straight-line method.

Year	Rate of depreciation	Annual depreciation	Value	Total depreciation
0				
1				
2				
3				
4				
5				

[12.2, •] **2.** Prepare a depreciation schedule. Use the double declining-balance method.

Year	Rate of depreciation	Annual depreciation	Value	Total depreciation
0				
1				
2				
3				
4				
5				

[12.3, •] **3.** Find the depreciation fractions for the sum-of-the-years'-digits method.

3. _____

[12.3, ••] **4.** Prepare a depreciation schedule. Use the sum-of-the-years'-digits method.

Year	Rate of depreciation	Annual depreciation	Value	Total depreciation
0				
1				
2				
3				
4				
5				

[12.4, •] **5.** Prepare a depreciation schedule. Use ACRS.

Year	Rate of depreciation	Annual depreciation	Value	Total depreciation
0				
1				
2				
3				
4				
5				

13

PRICING

CAREER: MERCHANDISING This is Michael Daryanani. Michael is the manager of a large clothing store, one of many owned by L. Strauss and Co.

MICHAEL DARYANANI

Michael's work is in the field of merchandising. This field entails preparing a product for sale, pricing, cost markup, cost markdown, and sales forecasting. His work as manager also includes preparing work schedules of employees as well as determining sales quotas.

People who work in the sale of clothing usually receive a base salary, but their income can be increased substantially by a bonus system. Each sale they make yields a commission, perhaps 6.8%. If, for a certain period of time, the total commission exceeds the base salary, the employee receives the commission. If the total commission is less than the base salary, the employee receives the base salary. This can result in a strong motivation to work for a higher pay through commission.

Michael's is a living portrait of a self-made man. Business mathematics is very important in his work. His parents are from India, but he was born and raised in Hong Kong. It was there that he began working in clothing sales. He moved to this country and began work as a sales clerk for his present employer. From that position he has been promoted to manager of the firm's largest store. The secret to Michael's success is hard work, and steadfast determination.

Michael's hobbies include bowling and watching tennis, baseball, and football.

After finishing Section 13.1, you should be able to:

•	**Find the markup.**
••	**Determine the retailer's cost.**
•••	**Express markup as a percentage of cost.**
•• ••	**Calculate selling price.**
••• ••	**Find the most a retailer should pay for goods.**

1. Schwank's cost for a digital watch was $48.75. The watch sold for $72.30. What was the markup?

2. Jones Luggage pays $22 for an attaché case and $1.05 in transportation charges. What is Jones's cost?

ANSWERS ON PAGE A-17

Pricing Goods: Cost Price Basis

The pricing of goods and services is important. Prices must be competitive, yet assure the business a profit. In this chapter we study methods of pricing.

• MARKUP

The difference between the selling price and the cost of an article to a retailer is the **markup.**

> **Markup = Selling price − Cost**

Example 1 Cooper Bedding's cost for a mattress was $47.25. The mattress sold for $68.88. What was the markup?

Solution Find the markup.

$$\text{Markup} = \text{Selling price} - \text{Cost}$$
$$= \$68.88 - \$47.25 = \$21.63$$

The markup was $21.63.

DO EXERCISE 1.

SEALY
FIRM QUILTED

$**68**$^88 Twin size each piece

Durable innerspring construction for famous Sealy firmness combined with Sealy's rugged torsion bar foundation. Decorator cover over layers of puffy cushioning. Sensational buy!

•• RETAILER'S COST

Transportation charges are considered part of the retailer's cost.

Example 2 Gulliver's Electronics pays $349.97 for a stereo receiver and $3.74 in transportation charges. What is Gulliver's cost?

Solution Find Gulliver's cost.

$$\text{Gulliver's cost} = \text{Transportation charges} + \text{Cost of article}$$
$$= \$3.74 + \$349.97 = \$353.71$$

Gulliver's cost is $353.71.

DO EXERCISE 2.

••• MARKUP AS A PERCENTAGE OF COST

Sometimes markup is stated as a percentage of cost. Suppose a retailer sells a black and white television that costs $54.75 for $79.95. The markup is $25.20. What percentage of the cost is the markup? To find out we translate:

What percentage of the   cost   is the markup?
$$x \qquad \cdot \qquad \$54.75 = \qquad \$25.20$$

To find the missing number, we divide:

$$x = \frac{\$25.20}{\$54.75} = 0.46 = 46\%.$$

We can formalize this as follows:

To find markup as a percentage of cost,

a) **find the markup;**
b) **divide the markup by the cost; and**
c) **convert to percent notation.**

Example 3 uses this procedure to solve the problem.

Example 3 Kelley's TV sells a television that costs $54.75 for $79.95 What is the percentage markup based on cost?

Solution

a) Markup = Selling price − Cost

$\qquad$ = $79.95 − $54.75 $\qquad$ Find the markup.

$\qquad$ = $25.20

b) $\dfrac{\text{Markup}}{\text{Cost}} = \dfrac{\$25.20}{\$54.75}$ $\qquad$ Divide the markup by the cost.

$\qquad$ = 0.46

c) $\qquad$ = 46% $\qquad$ Convert to percent notation.

The percentage markup based on cost is 46%.

DO EXERCISE 3.

⠿ PRICING

A retailer may apply markup based on cost to set prices. Example 4 illustrates the procedure.

Example 4 Sports Page's cost for a basketball is $10.15. Sports Page wants an 80% markup based on cost. What is the selling price?

Solution

a) Find the markup based on cost.

Markup based on cost = Percentage markup × Cost

$\qquad$ = 80% × $10.15

$\qquad$ = 0.80 × $10.15

$\qquad$ = $8.12

b) Find the selling price.

Selling price = Cost + Markup based on cost

$\qquad$ = $10.15 + $8.12

$\qquad$ = $18.27

The selling price is $18.27.

DO EXERCISE 4.

3. Kelley's TV sells a color television that costs $342 for $520. What is the percentage markup based on cost?

4. Abba's Appliances' cost for an electric griddle is $26.56. Abba's wants a 70% markup based on cost. What is the selling price?

ANSWERS ON PAGE A-17

5. Kazimour's Ties knows that consumers will pay at most $15.00 for a tie and wants a 35% markup based on cost. What is the maximum cost that Kazimour's can pay for the tie?

⠒⠒ RETAILER COST

When buying merchandise a retailer often knows from past experience how much consumers will pay for an item. When the selling price and markup based on cost are known, the retailer can find the maximum cost that he or she can pay for the merchandise.

> **To find the maximum cost for a retailer.**
>
> **a)** add 100% to the percentage markup;
>
> **b)** convert the answer from step (a) to decimal notation; and
>
> **c)** divide the selling price by the answer to step (b).

Example 5 Durlam's Clothing knows that consumers will pay at most $18.00 for a shirt and wants a 40% markup based on cost. What is the maximum cost that Durlam's can pay for the shirt?

Solution

a) $100\% + 40\% = 140\%$ Add 100% to the percentage markup.

b) $140\% = 1.40$ Convert to decimal notation.

c) $\dfrac{\text{Selling price}}{1.40} = \dfrac{\$18.00}{1.40}$ Divide the selling price by 1.40

$$= \$12.86$$

The maximum cost that Durlam's can pay is $12.86.

DO EXERCISE 5.

ANSWER ON PAGE A-17

• Find the markup.

1.

Oldsmobile
Sedan

Tinted glass, bucket seats, body side mouldings, rear defrost, air conditioning, sport mirrors, paint stripe, cruise control, tilt wheel, white wall tires, AM/FM stereo. #22598

$9495

Retailer's cost: $7596

2.

Oldsmobile

Coupe, tinted glass, sport mirrors, paint stripe, power steering, power brakes, super stock wheels, AM/FM stereo, 4 speed, front wheel drive, #22727

$7595

Retailer's cost: $5848

3.

WATERBED
LOWEST PRICE
IN TOWN
COMPLETE

175.00

Retailer's cost: $96

4.

ELECTRIC
BED

$695.00
Lifetime Guar.
Mattress

Retailer's cost: $452

5. Beilby's Appliances cost for an electric blanket was $21.88. It sold for $41.95. What was the markup?

6. Daker's Hardware cost for a rug shampooer was $34.43. It sold for $44.95. What was the markup?

•• Find the retailer's cost.

7. Walton's pays $37.09 for a vacuum cleaner and $2.10 in transportation charges. What is Walton's cost?

8. Shop Mart pays $7.75 for a digital alarm clock and $0.88 in transportation charges. What is Shop Mart's cost?

9. Skeii Pontiac pays $8200 for a Pontiac and transportation charges of $350. What is Skeii Pontiac's cost?

10. Gabus Ford pays $4300 for a Ford and $360 transportation charges. What is Gabus Ford's cost?

••• What is the percentage markup based on cost? Round to the nearest percent.

11.

MAGNAVOX 13" COLOR
TV
WHILE 20
LAST
Model 4038
ONLY 1 PER CUSTOMER
100% Solid-State 13"
Diagonal Portable TV
$199

Retailer's cost: $145

12. 🖩

5 ONLY
PHILCO 19" COLOR
PORTABLE TV

Deluxe Features
No Dealers
$249

Retailer's cost: $180

ANSWERS

1. _____

2. _____

3. _____

4. _____

5. _____

6. _____

7. _____

8. _____

9. _____

10. _____

11. _____

12. _____

13. _____

14. _____

15. _____

16. _____

17. _____

18. _____

19. _____

20. _____

21. _____

22. _____

23. _____

24. _____

25. _____

26. _____

27. _____

28. _____

13.

HOWARD MILLER FLOOR CLOCK
This contemporary floor clock is made of Carpathian olive ash burl and accented with chrome.

$571

Retailer's cost: $385

14.

CONTEMPORARY LOVESEAT
Striped Herculon in colors of gold, beige and brown. Oak wood trim with cane insert at base.

$349

Retailer's cost: $255

⋮ Find the selling price.

15.

MALIBU
Classic 2 Dr. V-8, auto, PS, PB, A/C, Tutone, extra nice.

Dealer's cost: $6780
Markup based on cost: 21%

16.

COUGAR
XR-7, V-8, auto, PS, PB, A/C, vinyl top, cloth seats.

Dealer's cost: $5975
Markup based on cost: 18%

17.

LYNX
4 cyl, 4 speed, PS, Like New.

Dealer's cost: $6490
Markup based on cost: 20%

18.

ZEPHYR
4 door, 6 cyl, auto, PS, PB, A/C, vinyl top.

Dealer's cost: $5200
Markup based on cost: 26%

⋰ Find the most a dealer should pay for these items. The selling price and markup based on cost are given.

19. NEW SHARP VX1184 PRINT & DISPLAY CALCULATOR 109.95

35%

20. BRAND NEW SELF-CORRECT ELEC. PORT. TYPEWRITERS 239.95

27%

21. BRAND NEW SINGLE ELEMENT ELECTRIC TYPEWRITERS 495.00

32%

22. NEW SILVER-REED PRINT & DISPLAY CALCULATOR 69.95

28%

23. Fontaine's Clothing knows that consumers will pay at most $8.00 for a scarf and wants a 35% markup based on cost. What is the maximum cost that Fontaine's can pay for the scarf?

24. Haupt's Sporting Goods knows that consumers will pay at most $14.00 for jogging shorts and wants a 42% markup based on cost. What is the maximum cost that Haupt's can pay for the shorts?

✓ SKILL MAINTENANCE

Subtract.

25. $7825 − $4985

26. $3200 − $2840

Add.

27.
```
  7,000
 13,000
 28,000
+41,000
```

28.
```
  5,200
  9,800
 20,000
+43,000
```

13.2

Pricing Goods: Selling Price Basis

◦ MARKUP AS A PERCENTAGE OF SELLING PRICE

Sometimes markup is stated as a percentage of the selling price. Suppose a retailer sells a microwave oven that costs $180 for $289. The markup is $109. What percentage of the selling price is the markup? To find out, we translate as follows:

What percentage of the selling price is the markup?

$$x \cdot \$289 = \$109$$

To find the missing number, we divide:

$$x = \frac{\$109}{\$289} = 0.377 = 37.7\%$$

We can formalize this as follows:

> **To find markup as a percentage of selling price,**
>
> **a) find the markup;**
>
> **b) divide the markup by the selling price; and**
>
> **c) convert to percent notation.**

Example 1 uses this procedure to solve the problem.

Example 1 Nwokedi's Appliances sells a microwave oven that costs $180 for $289. What is the percentage markup based on selling price (to the nearest percent)?

Solution

a) Markup = Selling price − Cost

$$= \$289 - \$180 \quad \text{Find the markup.}$$

$$= \$109$$

b) $\dfrac{\text{Markup}}{\text{Selling price}} = \dfrac{\$109}{\$289}$ Divide the markup by the selling price.

$$= 0.377$$

$$= 37.7\% \quad \text{Convert to percent notation.}$$

The percentage markup based on the selling price is 38%.

DO EXERCISE 1.

OBJECTIVES

After finishing Section 13.2, you should be able to:

◦ Solve problems involving markup as a percentage of selling price.

◦◦ Find the selling price.

◦◦◦ Calculate dealer cost.

1. Novak's TV sold a color television that cost $342 for $520. What was the percentage markup based on the selling price (to the nearest percent)?

ANSWER ON PAGE A-17

ANSWER ON PAGE A-17

2. The percentage markup based on the selling price of a refrigerator was 30%. The selling price was $580. What was the markup?

Suppose a retailer sells a color television for $579. The markup based on the selling price is 25%. What is the markup; that is, what is 25% of the selling price? To find out, we translate as follows:

What is 25% of the selling price?

$$x = 25\% \cdot \$579$$
$$= 0.25 \cdot \$579$$
$$= \$144.75$$

We can formalize this as follows:

> **To find the markup when the selling price and the percentage markup on the selling price are known,**
>
> **a) convert the percentage markup to decimal notation; and**
>
> **b) multiply this decimal by the selling price.**

Example 2 uses this procedure to solve the problem.

Example 2 The percentage markup based on the selling price of a color television was 25%. The selling price was $579. What was the markup?

23" diagonal measure Color TV

Early American styling in a beautiful Maple woodgrain finish. Features Chromacolor picture tube, Titan chassis with power sentry, color sentry, EVG electronic video guard tuning system, and 1 knob channel selector.

579⁰⁰

Solution

a) $25\% = 0.25$ Convert the percentage markup to a decimal.

b) Markup = $0.25 \times \$579$
            $= \$144.75$ Multiply by the selling price.

The markup based on the selling price was $144.75.

DO EXERCISE 2.

•• SELLING PRICE

A retailer may apply markup based on the selling price to set prices. That is, if the retailer's cost and the percentage markup based on the selling price are known, the selling price may be found.

> **To find the selling price when the cost and the percentage markup based on the selling price are known,**
>
> a) **subtract the percentage markup from 100%;**
> b) **convert the answer from step (a) to decimal notation; and**
> c) **divide the cost by this decimal.**

Example 3 Bates Office Supply's cost for an electric typewriter is $229. Bates wants a 40% markup based on the selling price. What is the selling price?

Solution

a) $100\% - 40\% = 60\%$ Subtract from 100%.

b) $\qquad 60\% = 0.60$ Convert to decimal notation.

c) Selling price $= \dfrac{\$229}{0.60}$ Divide the cost by 0.60.

$\qquad\qquad = \$381.67$

The selling price is $381.67.

DO EXERCISE 3.

3. Nyhus's Artics' cost for a down jacket is $53.90. Nyhus wants a 38% markup based on the selling price. What is the selling price?

ANSWER ON PAGE A-17

4. Swartz's knows that consumers will pay at most $15.00 for a tie and wants a 35% markup based on the selling price. What is the maximum cost that Swartz's can pay for the tie?

••• DEALER COST

When buying merchandise a retailer often knows how much customers will pay for an item. When the selling price and the markup based on the selling price are known, the retailer can determine the maximum cost that he or she can pay for the merchandise.

> **To find the maximum cost for a retailer,**
>
> **a) find the markup; and**
>
> **b) subtract the markup from the selling price.**

Example 4 Obando's Clothes knows that consumers will pay at most $18.00 for a shirt and wants a 40% markup based on the selling price. What is the maximum cost that Obando's may pay for the shirt?

Solution

a) Markup = 40% × Selling price

$\quad\quad\quad\quad = 0.40 \times \$18.00$ Find the markup.

$\quad\quad\quad\quad = \$7.20$

b) Maximum cost = $18.00 − $7.20

$\quad\quad\quad\quad\quad\quad = \$10.80$ Subtract the markup from the selling price.

The maximum cost that Obando's can pay is $10.80.

DO EXERCISE 4.

ANSWER ON PAGE A-17

Chapter 13   Pricing

ANSWERS

● Find the percentage markup to the nearest percent based on selling price. The retailer's cost is below each ad.

1.

LADIES'
ETONIC SKIRTS
18^{95}

$14.97

1. _____

2.

MEN'S
GOLF SHOES
Etonic & Green Joys
19^{95}

$13.96

2. _____

3.

UMBRELLAS
3^{95}

$2.37

3. _____

4.

LADIES'
#7 WOOD
**$14**^{95}

$10.00

4. _____

Round the percent answers to the nearest percent.

5. Han Outfitters sold a pack tent that cost $43.95 for $72.95. What was the percentage markup based on the selling price?

6. ▦ Li Yang-Fan's Supply sold a desk lamp that cost $8.75 for $12.50. What was the percentage markup based on the selling price?

5. _____

7. Suzanne's Furnishings sold a rocking chair that cost $98.00 for $159.00. What was the percentage markup based on the selling price?

8. Li Qi Ming's Scientific sold a telescope that cost $52.75 for $82.50. What was the percentage markup based on the selling price?

6. _____

7. _____

9. ▦ The percentage markup based on the selling price of a slide projector was 40%. The selling price was $122.50. What was the markup?

10. The percentage markup based on the selling price of a camera was 55%. The selling price was $419.95. What was the markup?

8. _____

9. _____

11. The percentage markup based on the selling price of a radio was $33\frac{1}{3}$%. The selling price was $69.95. What was the markup?

12. The percentage markup based on the selling price of a stereo was 27%. The selling price was $369.95. What was the markup?

10. _____

11. _____

12. _____

•• Complete the table.

	Retailer's Cost	Markup Based on Selling Price	Selling Price
13.	$ 27.50	35%	
14.	$112	26%	
15.	$476	19%	
16.	$625	28%	

17. ▣ McBreen Supply's cost for a calculator is $16.00. McBreen's wants a 30% markup based on the selling price. What is the selling price?

18. Rossiter Appliances' cost for a blender is $19.80. Rossiter's wants a 65% markup based on the selling price. What is the selling price?

••• Below each ad is the markup based on selling price. What is the most a dealer should pay for each item?

19.

TRUNDLE
BED. COMP.
$279⁹⁵
VERY STURDY
312 COIL
MATTRESSES

35%

20.

KING
SIZE
$289⁹⁵
MATTRESS &
BOX

40%

21.

HIDEABED
MATTRESS
$49⁹⁵

45%

22.

WATER
BED
SHEETS
$34⁹⁵

42%

23. ▣ Viswanath's Clothing has $600 with which to buy shirts. Consumers will pay $24.49 for each shirt. The markup based on the selling price for each shirt is to be $33\frac{1}{3}$%. How many shirts can be purchased? How much is left over?

24. ▣ White's Formal has $500 with which to buy neckties. Consumers will pay $17.99 for each tie. The markup based on the selling price is to be 29%. How many neckties can be purchased? How much is left over?

✓ SKILL MAINTENANCE

25. Recently, Tri-State Veneer President Barry Martin bought a black walnut tree for $20,000. The tree had 776 board feet of usable wood. What is the cost per board foot?

26. Recently, $134,980,000 and $2,821,000 in construction at military facilities in Alaska and Vermont, respectively, were approved. What is the difference?

13.3

Markdown

• MARKDOWN PROBLEMS

Sometimes businesses have sales. At that time merchandise is marked down. **Markdown** is the difference between the regular price and the sale price.

> **Markdown = Regular price − Sale price**

Example 1 A casting reel regularly priced at $63.29 is on sale for $49.95. What is the markdown?

Reg. Price $63.29 Sale $49⁹⁵

Solution

$$\text{Markdown} = \text{Regular price} - \text{Sale price}$$
$$= \$63.29 - \$49.95$$
$$= \$13.34$$

The markdown is $13.34.

DO EXERCISE 1.

Markdown is sometimes stated as a percent. The markdown is the product of the percentage markdown and the regular price.

> **Markdown = Percentage of markdown × Regular price**

Example 2 In the bookstore advertisement the markdown is 20%. The regular price of a book is $17.50. What is the markdown on the book?

Solution

$$\text{Markdown} = \text{Percent of markdown} \times \text{Regular price}$$
$$= 20\% \times \$17.50$$
$$= 0.20 \times \$17.50$$
$$= \$3.50$$

The markdown is $3.50.

DO EXERCISE 2.

1. A smoke detector regularly priced at $24.99 is on sale for $18.99. What is the markdown?

2. The regular price of a book is $23.00. What is the markdown when the percentage markdown is 20%?

> To give our patrons a good buy on good books, and to reduce our stock we are reducing our prices.
>
> # 20% Off
> ## Every Item
> ## In Our Shop

ANSWERS ON PAGE A-17

3. An automobile is on sale at 15% off the regular price of $6578. What is the sale price?

• • SALE PRICE

Sale price = Regular price − Markdown

To find the sale price,

a)   find the markdown; and

b)   subtract the markdown from the regular price.

Example 3 A suit is on sale at 20% off the regular price of $110. What is the sale price?

20% off our Quad® suit. Sale $88

Reg. $110. A highly versatile four-piece vested suit tailored in polyester double-knit. Classic styling includes a soft shoulder jacket with flapped patch pockets, reversible vest and two pairs of coordinating slacks. Fashion colors in regular, short and long sleeves.

Solution

a)   Markdown = 20% × $110

$\qquad\qquad$ = 0.20 × $110 $\qquad$ **Find the markdown.**

$\qquad\qquad$ = $22

b)   Sale price = $110 − $22 $\qquad$ **Subtract the markdown from the regular price.**

$\qquad\qquad$ = $88

The sale price is $88.

DO EXERCISE 3.

• • • MARKDOWN AS A PERCENTAGE OF REGULAR PRICE

® Stereo Receiver
Reg. 199.95
129⁹⁵

Suppose a retailer sold a stereo receiver regularly priced at $199.95 for $129.95. The markdown was $70.00. What percentage of the regular price was the markdown? To find out, we translate as follows:

What percentage of the regular price is the markdown?

$$x \cdot \$199.95 = \$70.00$$

To find the missing number, we divide:

$$x = \frac{\$70.00}{\$199.95}$$

$$x = 0.35 = 35\%$$

We can formalize this as follows:

> **The percentage markdown on the regular price can be found by**
>
> **a)** **finding the markdown; and**
> **b)** **dividing the markdown by the regular price.**

Example 4 uses this procedure to solve the problem.

Example 4 Find the percentage markdown on the regular price for the stereo receiver.

Solution

a) Markdown = $199.95 − $129.95

= $70   Find the markdown.

b) Percentage markdown = $\dfrac{\$70}{\$199.95}$ Divide by the regular price.

= 0.35

= 35%

The percentage markdown on the regular price is 35%.

DO EXERCISE 4.

⠿ MARKDOWN AS A PERCENTAGE OF SALE PRICE

Suppose a retailer sold a stereo receiver regularly priced at $199.95 for $129.95. The markdown was $70.00. What percentage of the sale price was the markdown? To find out, we translate as follows:

What percentage of the sale price is the markdown?

$$x \cdot \$129.95 = \$70.00$$

To find the missing number, we divide:

$$x = \frac{\$70.00}{\$129.95}$$

$$x = 0.54 = 54\%$$

4. Find the percentage markdown on the regular price for the scanner (to the nearest percent).

UHF/VHF Scanner*
Reg. 169.95 **119**⁹⁵

ANSWER ON PAGE A-17

WASHER

18 lb. capacity Heavy duty,
fabric softener & bleach,
dispenser, 4 wash & rinse
temp., Magic Clean lint filter,
4 wash cycles, 2 speeds.

Reg. $579   **$368**

5. Find the percentage markdown on the sale price for the washer (to the nearest percent).

We can formalize this as follows:

> The percentage markdown on the sale price can be found by
>
> a) finding the markdown; and
> b) dividing the markdown by the sale price.

Example 5 uses this procedure to solve the problem.

® **Stereo Receiver**
Reg. 199.95
129⁹⁵

Example 5 Find the percentage markdown on the sale price for the stereo receiver.

Solution

a)   Markdown = $199.95 − $129.95

= $70   Find the markdown.

b)   Percentage markdown = $\dfrac{\$70}{\$129.95}$ Divide by the sale price.

= 0.54

= 54%

The percentage markdown on the sale price is 54%.

DO EXERCISE 5.

Examples 4 and 5 show that, although the markdown may be the same, it is advantageous for the retailer to advertise percentage markdown based on the sale price rather than on the regular price. A 54% markdown seems larger than a 35% markdown to the consumer.

ANSWER ON PAGE A-17

• Find the markdown.

ANSWERS

1. reg. $189.50 CORNER SOLID OAK ETAGERE BY BUTLER.   **$148**

2. reg. $229.50 COLONIAL SWIVEL ROCKER
   Tufted back with wood trim, adjustable swivel base. Nylon cream color velvet.   **$168**

3. reg. $789.50 SECRETARY DESK BY RIVERSIDE
   For the small space, 26″ wide. Solid oak and oak veneers, lighted top.   **$598**

4. reg. $359.50 SOFA GAME TABLE BY LANE   **$189**
   Flip-top opens to expose backgammon game.

5. Clip & bring this coupon to Sunderland's Home Gallery
   30% OFF
   Mannington JT88® Duracon®
   Never-wax Vinyl Flooring

   Regular price: $456

6. Clip & bring this coupon to Sunderland's Home Gallery
   40% OFF
   Merillat®
   Kitchen Cabinets

   Regular price: $1850

7. **25% OFF**
   ON ALL
   ANDERSEN WINDOWS

   Regular price: $387

8. **50% Off**
   Henri
   Fountains &
   Bird Baths

   Regular price: $26.00

9. A maintenance-free automobile battery regularly priced at $49.99 is on sale for $42.99. What is the markdown?

10. A spa regularly priced at $1695 is on sale for $1495. What is the markdown?

11. ▦ The regular price of patio furniture is $840. The sale price is 25% off the regular price. What is the markdown?

12. The regular price of a tree fern is $6.98. The sale price is 29% off the regular price. What is the markdown?

ANSWERS
1.
2.
3.
4.
5.
6.
7.
8.
9.
10.
11.
12.

⚈⚈ What is the sale price?

35% OFF OF SELECTED BICYCLES

13. Regular price: $460

14. Regular price: $285

15. A 14-piece cookware set is on sale at 30% off the regular price of $147.90. What is the sale price?

16. ▦ A sleeping bag is on sale at 35% off the regular price of $142.95. What is the sale price?

⚈⚈⚈ Find the markdown as a percentage of the regular price. Round to the nearest percent.

17.

DOUGLAS®
POST HOLE DIGGER
REGULAR 15.99   **12⁸⁸**
Wood handle. Perfect tool for putting up fences, mail boxes, clothesline poles and more.

18.
HEDGE TRIMMER
REGULAR 39.99   **29⁸⁸**
Double insulated 13" hedge trimmer. 2.2 amp motor. Three position safety switch. 8118.

19. ▦ The regular price of an egg cooker is $17.90, and the sale price is $13.50. Find the percentage markdown on the regular price.

20. The regular price of a deep-fat fryer is $26.95, and the sale price is $18.75. Find the percentage markdown on the regular price.

⚈⚈ Find the markdown as a percentage of the sale price. Round to the nearest percent.

21.

ATARI®
Personal Computer System   **268.99** Reg. 299.00

22.
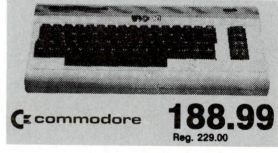

⊑ commodore   **188.99** Reg. 229.00

23. The regular price of a whirlpool bath is $249.95, and the sale price is $199.95. Find the percentage markdown on the sale price.

24. The regular price of a toaster is $22.95, and the sale price is $16.95. Find the percentage markdown on the sale price.

✓ **SKILL MAINTENANCE**

25. Faribault Thrift pays 8% compounded quarterly. Find the amount and interest on $1000 after three quarters.

26. How much should Juan Lopez invest now at 8% compounded quarterly to have $5000 in three years?

NAME:

CLASS/SECTION: DATE:

If you miss an item, review the indicated section and objective.

ANSWERS

[13.1, •]   **1.** Handoyo Electric's cost for the Toshiba is $52. What is the markup?

1. _____

TOSHIBA
KTS-3
FM Stereo and cassette player w/headset
$**69**⁹⁵

2. _____

[13.1, •••]   **2.** For the Toshiba find the percentage markup based on cost (round to the nearest percent).

[13.1, •:•]   **3.** Geomatt's Bike's cost for a bicycle is $87.88. Geomatt's wants a 37% markup based on the cost. What is the selling price?

[13.1, •:•]   **4.** Gerstein's Boutique knows that customers will pay at most $35 for a sweater and wants a 40% markup based on cost. What is the most Gerstein's should pay for the sweater?

3. _____

[13.2, •]   **5.** Schowengerdt Electronics' cost for the Sony is $179.37. Find the percentage markup based on selling price (round to the nearest percent).

SONY.
PORTABLE RECORDER
SL2000
• Slow-fast motion   • Lightweight-9lbs.
• 5 hour beta   • Auto rewind
• Audio dub
$**259**⁹⁵

4. _____

[13.2, •]   **6.** The percentage markup based on the selling price of the sofa was 34%. What was the markup?

5. _____

BROYHILL TRADITIONAL SOFA
Crescent shaped with cinnamon background, blue and rust mini-print. 100% Scotchgard cotton. $**588**

6. _____

ANSWERS

7. _____

8. _____

9. _____

10. _____

11. _____

12. _____

[13.2, ••] **7.** Retz Sport's cost for golf shoes is $6.50. Retz wants a 42% markup based on the selling price. What is the selling price?

[13.2, •••] **8.** Rondeau's Furnishings wants 42% markup based on selling price for the bedroom suite. What is the most Rondeau's should pay?

DIXIE BEDROOM SUITE
Traditional honey pine ... consists of dresser, chest and bookcase headboard and matching two drawer nightstand. **$939**

[13.3, •] **9.** A Baldwin Piano regularly priced at $2695 is on sale for $1347.50. What is the markdown?

PIANOS
	WAS	NOW
Baldwin built piano	2695	$1347.50

[13.3, ••] **10.** A tub enclosure regularly priced at $238 is on sale at 25% off its regular price. What is the sale price?

[13.3, •••] **11.** Find the percentage markdown on the regular price for an oxford cloth shirt (round to the nearest percent).

FAMOUS LABEL CLASSIC BUTTON DOWN
OXFORD CLOTH SHIRTS!
• COTTON-POLY BLENDS!
• WHITE, PASTELS!
• FINE LINE STRIPES!
• RUFFLE NECKS!
19⁹⁰
REG. $24

[13.3, ::] **12.** Find the percentage markdown on the sale price for the mink coat (round to the nearest percent).

Natural Blackglama® mink coats. Originally $5,995. Now $3,995.

14

PAYROLL

CAREER: PAYROLL SUPERVISOR
This is Alma Stanford. Alma is both Payroll Supervisor and Accounts Payable Supervisor for a mutual fund transfer company in Boston.

ALMA STANFORD

Alma works for Mellon Financial Services, a company that handles mutual fund transactions and paperwork for large investment corporations. Mellon uses an independent data processing company, ADP, to print out bi-weekly paychecks for its 270 employees.

As Payroll Supervisor, Alma and several assistants are responsible for collecting time cards, determining the number of regular or over-time hours worked by non-salaried personnel, and inputting the information into a computerized system that is linked to ADP. ADP prints the paychecks after deducting Federal and State taxes and Social Security payments for each employee based on information given to them by Alma when the employee was hired. ADP also provides payroll statements which Alma must reconcile monthly. Someone in Alma's position can earn $18,000 to $25,000 per year.

Alma received a diploma in Accounting from the Burdett School, and is currently studying for a B.S. in Accounting at New Hampshire State College. She also has a Medical Assistant's certificate from ITT Technical Institute, and worked as a medical assistant at the New England Medical Center. Several years ago, she and her husband were the subjects of a documentary on black families returning to the deep South to seek out their roots, which was produced by Thames Television, London. Alma is ambitious and works hard to be successful. She believes that the most important factor in achieving success is determination—"Remember, the only time failure should come before success is in the dictionary. Work hard to make that always be true for you."

14.1

After finishing Section 14.1, you should be able to:

•	**Calculate gross earnings for regular and overtime work.**
••	**Compute straight piecework earnings.**
•••	**Compute differential piecework earnings.**
::	**Compute earnings with piecework overtime.**

1. Find the gross earnings for Ed Ramey who accepts the job of medical records transcriptionist and works 29 hours.

2. Find the gross earnings for Cuong Dai Quach who accepts the interstate job listed below and works a 56-hour week.

ANSWERS ON PAGE A-17

Hourly and Piecework Wages

What you earn may be figured on an hourly, production unit, salary, commission, or other basis. You receive paychecks for your earnings less deductions. These important financial matters will be studied in this chapter.

•	**GROSS EARNINGS**

The amount of money earned before deductions is called **gross earnings**. Working time up to and including 40 hours a week is **regular time**.

Example 1 Find the gross earnings of Adnan Ozakyol who accepts the job shown at right and works 36 hours.

Solution

$$\text{Gross earnings} = \text{Hourly wage} \times \text{Hours worked}$$
$$= \$4.00 \times 36 = \$144.00$$

The gross earnings are $144.00.

DO EXERCISE 1.

The Fair Labor Standards Act requires a company that does business in more than one state to pay employees time and a half for overtime. This means that an employee is paid $1\frac{1}{2}$ times the hourly rate for every hour worked over 40 in one week.

Example 2 Find the gross earnings for Cid Ramirez who accepts the interstate job shown at right and works 50 hours a week.

Solution

a) Find the earnings for regular time.

$$\text{Regular time earnings} = \text{Regular time worked} \times \text{Regular rate}$$
$$= 40 \times \$6.60 = \$264.00$$

b) Find the earnings for overtime.

$$\text{Earnings for overtime} = \text{Overtime hours worked} \times \text{Overtime rate}$$
$$= 10 \times (1.5 \times \$6.60) = \$99.00$$

c) Find the gross earnings.

$$\text{Gross earnings} = \text{Regular earnings} + \text{Overtime earnings}$$
$$= \$264.00 + \$99.00 = \$363.00$$

Cid Ramirez earned $363.00 for the 50 hours worked.

DO EXERCISE 2.

In addition to time-and-a-half pay for Saturdays, double time is often paid for work on Sundays and holidays. Moreover, some employee contracts require that time and a half be paid for hours worked over eight daily, regardless of the number worked each week. The following example illustrates this.

Example 3 Find the gross earnings for Doug Owens who accepts the job shown at right and works six hours on each of Monday, Tuesday, and Wednesday, ten hours on each of Thursday and Friday, five hours Saturday, and four hours Sunday.

PRESERVATION PACKAGER
$5.95 per hour

Solution

a) Find the gross earnings for regular time.

Regular time earnings = Regular time worked × Regular rate

$$= 34 \times \$5.95$$

$$= \$202.30$$

b) Find the gross earnings for time-and-a-half overtime.

$$\text{Earnings for time and a half} = \text{Overtime hours worked} \times \text{Overtime rate}$$

$$= 9 \times (1.5 \times \$5.95)$$

$$= \$80.33$$

c) Find the gross earnings for double time.

Earnings for double time = Hours worked double time × Rate

$$= 4 \times (2 \times \$5.95)$$

$$= \$47.60$$

d) Find the total gross earnings.

Total gross earnings = Regular earnings + Time-and-a-half earnings
+ Double-time earnings

$$= \$202.30 + \$80.33 + \$47.60$$

$$= \$330.23$$

Doug's total gross earnings are $330.23.

DO EXERCISE 3.

Employees are sometimes paid for the number of units they produce. Such a pay plan is called a *piecework plan.* If the employee is paid a fixed amount for each unit, the plan is a *straight piecework plan.*

⬛⬛ STRAIGHT PIECEWORK EARNINGS

A certain minimum amount is guaranteed for workers on the piecework plan. Otherwise when production equipment failed, wages would be lost at no fault of the worker.

Example 4 Heather Ramsdell, a press operator in a brick refractory, is paid $0.07 for each brick produced with $50 guaranteed daily. In one day 816 bricks were produced. How much was earned?

Solution Find the amount earned.

Amount earned = Number produced × Earnings each unit

$$= 816 \times \$0.07$$

$$= \$57.12$$

The amount Heather earned was $57.12 because it was more than the guaranteed amount.

DO EXERCISE 4.

3. Find the gross earnings for Jeri Erwine who accepts the job shown below and works nine hours on each of Monday through Thursday, seven hours on Friday, eight hours on Saturday, and five hours on Sunday.

A/C MECHANIC (RUBBER)
$6.37 per hour

4. Darryl Ramon, a machine assembler is paid $0.04 for each part assembled with $45 guaranteed daily. In one day 1500 parts were assembled. How much was earned?

ANSWERS ON PAGE A-17

5. In Example 5, how much was earned if 223 connections were made?

6. Karen Heuchelin on piecework earns $2.15 for each unit produced and produced 195 units in one 43-hour week. Calculate the gross earnings.

ANSWERS ON PAGE A-17

••• DIFFERENTIAL PIECEWORK EARNINGS

A *differential piecework plan* is used to provide employees with an incentive to produce more units. Under this plan the employee is paid an increased rate per unit as the number of units produced increases.

Example 5 Jacqueline Slaats, a microprocessor assembler, is paid according to the number of soldering connections made. The differential pay scale is shown in the chart at left. How much was earned if 300 soldering connections were made?

Solution

a) Find the rate per connection.

From the chart we see that the rate per connection is $0.15.

b) Find the amount earned.

Amount earned = Rate per connection × Number of connections

= $0.15 × 300

= $45.00

The amount Jacqueline earned was $45.00.

DO EXERCISE 5.

▪▪ OVERTIME PIECEWORK EARNINGS

Piecework plans where employees work in excess of 40 hours weekly also pay overtime wages. In this situation we:

1. Find earnings for piecework completed.
2. Find an equivalent hourly wage.
3. Compute gross earnings for regular and overtime hours.

Example 6 Jo Sindelar on piecework earns $3.80 for each unit produced and produced 125 units in one 44-hour week. Calculate her gross earnings.

Solution We find earnings for piecework completed.

Piecework earnings = Units × Rate per unit

= 125 × $3.80

= $475

Next we find an equivalent hourly rate.

Hourly rate = Amount earned ÷ Hours worked

= $475 ÷ 44

= $10.80

Finally, we calculate gross earnings.

Regular earnings	40 × $10.80	= $432.00
Overtime earnings	4 × $10.80 × 1.5 =	$64.80
Gross earnings		$496.80 Adding

Jo's gross earnings were $496.80.

DO EXERCISE 6.

ANSWERS

⊡ Calculate gross earnings for a regular 40-hour week.

1.
TYPIST-Recept.P/T,6hr/day 10-4 or 11-5 $6/hr, will train on word proc. immed Robin Castler P.O. Box 92911 LA 90009

2.
TEL. SALES   ADV. SPECIALTIES
$8 PER HOUR
or high comm. bonuses. Make orders easily without selling.   AM/PM
Joe   213/466-2198

3.
SECURITY GUARD
Armed security officer needed. Immediate opening for prestigious position at Century Plaza Hotel. $5 hour starting salary and excellent benefits after 90 days. Valid Weapons Permit required. For appt. call Usps
(213) 543-1610 or 543-1619
Equal Opportunity Employer M/F

4.
★ WAREHOUSE ★
TENT INSTALLERS
Must be over 21 with valid Driver's License. On job training. Advancement opportunity. $4.25/hour. Apply in person between 11 a.m. & 2 p.m.
627 Hazel Street, Glendale

5. 🖩
SERVICE PERSON. Install & maintain air conditioners, dishwashers, washer & dryers & refrigerators. 3yrs exper. $6.25/hr. Report in person to Hollywood Job Service, 6725 Santa Monica Bl, LA. Re order #1242463/827261-010. Ad pd by Er

6.
TELEPHONE INV PROD. FULL TIME
★ QUALIFIERS ★
No selling $4/hr. to start, raises bonuses. Prestigious Beverly Hills office. Call Mr. Johnson   213/273-5465

Calculate gross earnings for a person who works a total of 40 hours at regular rate, 7 hours at time-and-a-half rate, and 5 hours at double rate.

7.
SUPERVISOR night psych brd/care facil. 1AM-9AM $4/hr   213/450-1748

8. 🖩
★ SECRETARIES $9.00 ★
STAR TEMPS   213/480-0617

9.
Sign maker $9.30/hr, form sign base, reinforce, install electrical components, make individual letters. Must have knowledge of working metal. 1 yr. exp. as asst. sign maker. Job in Wilmington. Send this ad and resume to Job #91948, P.O. Box 15102, LA 90015 no later than Aug. 21

10.
UPHOLSTERER $8.25/hr. 1 yr as upholsterer or 1 yr in creative design construction. Read blue prints, cut material, fit each individual piece. Job in Sun Valley. Send this ad & resume to Job #91916, PO Box 15102, LA 90015 no later than Aug. 21.

11. 🖩
P/T SWITCHBOARD OPER
Hours 10-4 in busy real estate office. Grand Central area. $6.00/hr. 682-2300 x204

12.
PHYSICIAN-CARDIOLOGIST
BC IM/BE Cardio.   Fee Paid
$30.HR. Part Time-Prvt Pract.
LARKIN MEDICAL
25 W. 43st/off 5/agency   695-2668

1. _____
2. _____
3. _____
4. _____
5. _____
6. _____
7. _____
8. _____
9. _____
10. _____
11. _____
12. _____

∙∙

13. Ladonna Knolte is paid $4.26 for each part assembled with $385 guaranteed weekly. In one week 93 parts were assembled. How much was earned?

14. A hydropump assembly plant pays Keyla Homan $1.57 for each bearing with $425 guaranteed weekly. In one week 280 bearings were placed on motor shafts. How much was earned?

15. ▦ A transmission assembly plant pays David Mottet $3.61 for each differential gear assembled with $535 guaranteed weekly. In one week 127 differential gears were assembled. How much was earned?

16. An engraving firm pays Melanie Richardson $5.05 for each stamping with $362 guaranteed weekly. In one week 65 stampings were made. How much was earned?

∙∙∙ Use the chart at the right to find the amount earned.

Units Produced

17. 22

18. 29

19. 15

20. 33

DIFFERENTIAL PAY SCALE	
Units Produced	**Rate per Unit**
16 or fewer	$17.00
17–19	$17.50
20–25	$18.00
26–35	$18.75
36 or over	$19.75

∙∙ ∙∙ Solve.

21. Michael Lehet on piecework earns $1.37 for each unit produced and produced 367 units in one 45-hour week. Calculate the gross earnings.

22. ▦ Han Soo Han on piecework earns $2.85 for each unit produced and produced 165 units in one 42-hour week. Calculate the gross earnings.

23. ▦ Sheree Fantz produced 231 units in one 48-hour week at $2.10 for each unit. Calculate the gross earnings.

24. Mohammad Fahim produced 416 units in one 46-hour week at $1.35 for each unit. Calculate the gross earnings.

✓ SKILL MAINTENANCE

25. Nearly 99% of the 4.7 million businesses are classified as small to mid-size (fewer than 500 employees at one site). How many businesses are classified as small to mid-size?

26. At the end of a recent month 107.8 million people were employed in the U.S. In the comparable period in the previous year 105.6 million were employed. What is the percentage increase?

14.2

Salary and Commission

Salaried employees' earnings are usually given as weekly, monthly, or annual amounts. For example, a dental nurse who accepts the position shown below would earn at least $1300 salary each month.

> **DENTAL NURSE**
> Exper. only. RDA preferred w/X-Ray cert. & knowledge of expanded duties. Super professionally motivated staff. Salary $1300 + depending on qualifications. Benefits. Call 474-4495

• AMOUNT OF PAY

Pay periods may be weekly, biweekly, semimonthly, or monthly. Example 1 shows how to compute the weekly pay.

Example 1 Find the weekly pay for the dental nurse who earns $1300 a month.

Solution

a) Find the annual salary.

Annual salary = Monthly salary × 12

$\qquad = \$1300 \times 12 = \$15,600$

b) Find the weekly pay.

Weekly pay $= \dfrac{\text{Annual salary}}{52}$

$\qquad = \dfrac{\$15,600}{52} = \$300$

> Reminder:
>
> Weekly $\longrightarrow$ 52 times/yr.
> Biweekly $\longrightarrow$ 26 times/yr.
> Semimonthly $\longrightarrow$ 24 times/yr.
> Monthly $\longrightarrow$ 12 times/yr.

The weekly pay is $300.

DO EXERCISE 1.

Note that weekly earnings cannot be found by dividing the earnings each month by four since there are more than four weeks in a month. Individuals paid biweekly are paid every other week (a total of 26 pay periods each year).

Example 2 Find the biweekly pay for a keypunch operator who accepts the position shown below and earns $950 each month.

> **KEYPUNCH OPERS TO $950**

Solution

a) Find the annual salary.

Annual salary = Monthly salary × 12 = $950 × 12 = $11,400

b) Find the biweekly pay.

Biweekly pay $= \dfrac{\text{Annual salary}}{26} = \dfrac{\$11,400}{26} = \$438.46$

The biweekly pay is $438.46.

DO EXERCISE 2.

1. Find the weekly pay for the bank teller who accepts the position shown below and earns $850 each month.

> **BANK TELLER**
> *$850*
> Position available for a full time commercial & savings teller. 1k yr recent teller exper rea. Must be service oriented well groomed & able to deal professionally with public. Salary to $850 downtown location, full Xbenefits + parking subsidy
> **UNION BAPK 238-7006**
> An Equal Opportunity Employer

2. Find the biweekly pay for an office clerk who accepts the position shown below and earns $800 each month.

> **OFFICE CLERK $800**
> **KEARNY MESA AREA**
> **EMPLOYER PAID FEE**
> Skills needed are 10 key add machine by touch, lite bkkpng.
> **FEE JOBS ALSO**
> El Cajon EMPLOYMENT AGENCY
> 905 W. Main at Richfield   44 6176

ANSWERS ON PAGE A-17

3. Find the semimonthly pay for a computer programmer who accepts the position shown below and earns $30,000 annually.

DATA PROCESSING
COMPUTER PRGRS TO $30,000

4. Find the monthly pay for a food service manager who accepts the position shown below and earns $17,000 annually.

FOOD SERVICER MGR.
Experienced, or qualifications of chief commissaryman, S.D. area. Advancement opportunity, send resume to I.M.I. - 32591N 53rd St. San Diego, Ca. 92105

ANSWERS ON PAGE A-17

An individual who is paid semimonthly (twice each month) has 24 pay periods each year (2 each month × 12 months).

Example 3 Find the semimonthly pay for a claims adjustor trainee who accepts the position shown below and earns $15,000 annually.

CLAIMS
ADJUSTOR
TRAINEE $15,000
4 YEAR DEGREE
Ability to deal with people & customer service personality
EASTRIDGE Personnel Service
4338 54th Street
at El Cajon Blvd
287-8220

Solution Find the semimonthly pay.

$$\text{Semimonthly pay} = \frac{\text{Annual pay}}{24}$$

$$= \frac{\$15,000}{24}$$

$$= \$625$$

The semimonthly pay is $625.

DO EXERCISE 3.

A person paid monthly has 12 pay periods annually.

Example 4 Find the monthly pay for a civil engineer who accepts the position shown below and earns $22,800 annually.

CIVIL ENGINEER
Trainee to $22,800
FEE NEGOTIABLE. Prefer BSE degree tho would consider AA degree in civil engineering. Estimating, drafting or construction exper. helpful.
287-0800   5381 El Cajon Blvd.
THE WESTBROOKE AGENCY

Solution Find the monthly pay.

$$\text{Monthly pay} = \frac{\text{Annual pay}}{12}$$

$$= \frac{\$22,800}{12}$$

$$= \$1900$$

The monthly pay is $1900.

DO EXERCISE 4.

Chapter 14   Payroll

Some employees earn a straight **commission.** This means that the employees are paid a certain amount (usually a percentage) of sales made. The rate (percent) of commission depends on the product being sold, the ease of selling the product, and any additional benefits for the employee. Commissions act as an incentive to salespeople; the more sold, the more money earned.

•• EARNINGS

Example 5 Bob Van Doren, a real estate salesperson, had sales of $1.6 million in a recent year. The commission rate was 7%. How much was earned?

BOB VAN DOREN, 1.6 Million

Solution

Earnings = Sales × Rate
$$= \$1,600,000 \times 0.07$$
$$= \$112,000$$

Bob's earnings were $112,000.

DO EXERCISE 5.

Sometimes a salesperson will earn a salary plus commission.

Example 6 Joyce Lendt accepts the position shown below and earns $250 each week plus a commission of 8% on the clothing sold. Joyce sold $1875 in clothing last week. What were her earnings?

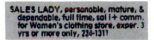

SALES LADY, personable, mature, & dependable, full time, sal l + comm. for Women's clothing store, exper. 3 yrs or more only, 234-1311

Solution

Earnings = Salary + Commission
$$= \$250 + (0.08 \times \$1875)$$
$$= \$250 + \$150$$
$$= \$400$$

Her earnings were $400.00

DO EXERCISE 6.

5. Sharon Hogle, a real estate salesperson had sales of $1 million in a recent year. The commission rate was 7%. How much was earned?

SHARON HOGLE, Million Dollars in sales

6. Tim Simmons earned $200 plus 7% commission on $3000 in sales last week. What were his earnings?

ANSWERS ON PAGE A-17

7. Ghazi Kefel earns 8% commission on personal sales and 3% on sales of employees supervised. Personal sales were $22,000 and employees' sales $74,000. Find Ghazi's earnings.

Sometimes a sales supervisor earns a straight commission on sales plus a commission on sales of those he or she supervises. This additional commission on the earnings of those supervised is called an **override**.

Example 7 Janis Meier sold $65,000 of machinery at 5% commission and was paid a 2% commission on $125,000 sold by the employees supervised. Find Janis's earnings.

Solution

$$\text{Earnings} = (0.05 \times \$65,000) + (0.02 + \$125,000)$$
$$= \$3250 + \$2500$$
$$= \$5750$$

Her earnings were $5750.00.

DO EXERCISE 7.

Some employees are paid a bonus in addition to a salary. The bonus may be paid for additional sales above a certain goal called a **quota**.

Example 8 Perry Kellogg accepted the canvasser position shown below and earned $250 a week plus 5% on orders received in excess of $3000. If $3700 in orders were taken, what were Perry's earnings?

CANVASSERS
$250 week. Salary & Bonuses.
Call Bob Rogers 292-8233

Solution

a) Find the amount in excess of the quota.

Excess = Amount ordered − Quota
= $3700 − $3000
= $700

b) Find the bonus earned.

Bonus earned = Rate × Excess
= 0.05 × $700
= $35

c) Find the total earnings.

Total earnings = Salary + Bonus
= $250 + $35
= $285

Perry's earnings were $285.00.

DO EXERCISE 8.

8. The sports sales position shown below pays $200 a week plus 4% on sales above $1500. If a person who accepts one of the positions sells $2300 in equipment one week, what are the earnings?

MERCHANDISING
SPORTS SALES
EMPLOYMENT OPENINGS
1. ATHLETIC EQUIPMENT
   SALES TRAINEE
   (BASEBALL/BASKETBALL)
2. TENNIS/RACQUETBALL
   EQUIPMENT
   SALES TRAINEE
3. FISHING/CAMPING
   EQUIPMENT
   SALES TRAINEE

To encourage additional sales, an employer sometimes pays a salary and a graduated bonus. The greater the sales, the greater the bonus rate.

ANSWERS ON PAGE A-17

Example 9 Valerie Kepka accepts the position shown to the right and earns $21,000 each year plus a bonus of 1% on sales to $500,000, 2% on sales from $500,000 to $800,000, and 4% on sales over $800,000. Find her earnings if sales were $900,000.

Solution

a) Find the total bonus.

Bonus on first $500,000 = Rate × $500,000

$$= 0.01 \times \$500,000$$

$$= \$5000$$

Bonus on next $300,000 = Rate × $300,000

$$= 0.02 \times \$300,000$$

$$= \$6000$$

Bonus on remaining $100,000 = Rate × $100,000

$$= 0.04 \times \$100,000$$

$$= \$4000$$

Total bonus = $5000 + $6000 + $4000 = $15,000

b) Find the total earnings.

Total earnings = Salary + Total bonus

$$= \$21,000 + \$15,000$$

$$= \$36,000$$

The total amount Valerie earned was $36,000.

DO EXERCISE 9.

Sometimes an employee is paid a ***draw*** against commission. The salesperson is paid an amount based on expected sales. Excess sales earn additional money for the salesperson and earnings are adjusted upward. Likewise, sales not meeting expectations result in the draw being reduced.

Example 10 Albert McLoud who accepts the position shown below is given a $350 weekly draw and earns a 9% commission on sales. If sales were $5000, how much did commission differ from draw?

Solution

a) Find the commission.

SALES large printing & direct mail co. is seeking exper. sales person. Draw + comm. & expenses. Xint opportunities for the right person. Call 222-0535

Commission = Rate × Sales

$$= 0.09 \times \$5000$$

$$= \$450$$

b) Find the difference between commission and draw.

Difference = Commission − Draw

$$= \$450 - \$350$$

$$= \$100$$

Albert earned an additional $100 above draw.

DO EXERCISE 10.

— SALES — $18 to $28,000 a year + bonus, xlnt management future, leads furn., car req'd. 272-4902

9. Brenda Luett earns $600 in monthly salary plus a bonus of 1% on sales up to $12,000, 3% on sales from $12,000 to $20,000, and 5% on sales over $20,000. Find her earnings if sales were $23,000.

10. Michelle Skarbick accepts a position paying $275 a week draw and earns 8% commission on all sales. If sales were $4200, how much did commission differ from draw?

ANSWERS ON PAGE A-17

11. Jill Stevens is given a $620 weekly draw and earns 7% commission on sales. If sales were $7000, how much did commission differ from draw?

12. Diane Wasil earns $290 for a 40-hour week plus a commission of 5% on sales. Last week sales were $4700 and hours worked were 47. How much did Diane earn?

Example 11 Sol Estes is given a $500 weekly draw and earns 8% commission on sales. If sales were $5000, how much did commission differ from draw?

Solution

a) Find the commission.

Commission = Rate × Sales

= 0.08 × $5000

= $400

b) Find the difference between commission and draw.

Difference = Commission − Draw

= $400 − $500

= −$100   Subtract $400 from $500 and put a minus sign in front of the answer.

The minus sign shows that Sol earned $100 less than the draw. He will have to repay this amount.

DO EXERCISE 11.

••• COMMISSION OVERTIME

The Fair Labor Standards Act requires salespeople who work on a commission basis be paid for overtime (salespeople working away from the business location are excluded).

Example 12 Scott Skjoldager earns $325 for a 40-hour workweek plus a commission of 7% on sales. Last week sales were $3288.50 and hours worked were 48. How much did Scott earn?

Solution Find the salary and commission.

Salary	$325.00	
Commission	$230.20	7% of $3288.50
Total	$555.20	

The equivalent hourly wage is

Hourly wage = $555.20 ÷ 40

= $13.88.

Find

Regular earnings	40 × $13.88 = $555.20
Overtime earnings	8 × 1.5 × $13.88 = $166.56
Total earnings	$721.76

Scott earned $721.76.

DO EXERCISE 12.

- • Find monthly and annual pay for people hired for these positions.

1.

JEWELRY

Posit avail. Handmaking all items of jewelry. Highly skilled & specialized training in mounting all kinds of precious stones in platinum & 18kt gold jewelry. Ability in use of jewelry making tools. Ability in the cart of invisible setting. Min 3 yrs exp. & 10 yrs exp. $560/wkly. 40 hrs. Work Mon-Fri, 8:30-5 pm. Call 212-371-8580, 1-5 pm.

2.

RESTAURANT—MANAGER

Coordinates food srvc activs, estimates food & bev costs, purchases supplies, plans menus incl Yugoslav specialties such as: Cevapcici, Raznjici, Djuvec, Tripice. Directs hiring & assignment of personnel. Min 4 yrs exper, college deg reqd, refs. 40 hrs, $400/wk. Apply in person, Aug. 4, 4-6 PM: Nikola Rebraka, Panarella Restaurant, 513 Columbus Ave NYC.

3.

Exchange Coordinator-coord xchange for antique British & American toys. 5 yrs exp. 40 hrs $300/wk, call Ehrlich-Bober & Co.-80 Pine St-NY 212-480-0750

4.

BUYER-To purchase fabrics & raw textiles; using knowledge of materials & salability, to inspect, grade & order materials. Arrange for transportation, or payment & delivery of goods & its return if necessary. Requirements: BA deg or equivalency + 3 yrs exp; work week 35 hrs/wk, 5 days/wk, salary $350/wk. Job order #8852395 DOT code 162.157.038 Contact NYS Employment Service, 25 W. 34 St, Rm 1607, NY NY 10001

Find weekly and semimonthly pay for people hired for these positions.

5.

SECTY—Bilingual to perform secretarial & administration functions for int'l. trade co. loc. in L.A. Receive incoming telephone, sched. appts., dispenses information, prepare corres. & business documentation & oper. typewr., telex & related keyboard & transcribing eqpmt. Knowl. of acctg. principles, type 55 wpm, read, write, speak Chinese, 1 yr. exp. Sal. $1386/mo. Send this ad & your resume to Job #4-1656, P.O. Box 15102, L.A., Ca. 90015 no later than 8/23/82.

6.

SECRETARY—PART TIME

Secy/Recept. for WLA offc. Tues, Wed. & Thurs. 9-5 Good typing skills. Exp. only. $725 per mo. Call Pearl
213/273-1850

7.

WORD PROCESSING SPECIALISTS
$20,000

Exclusive position avail in Int'l Investment firm for a profsl word processor w/exp on any type of system. Work in the Controllers Office of this Park Avenue firm. Some stat typg involved. Call:

MARTY FELIX 962-4020

STANTON AGENCY   189 B'WAY

8.

LIGHTING DESIGN CONSULTANT-Designs and implements lighting for use in institutional displays (primarily for jewelry and art) using advanced color-corrective lighting devices. Supervises quality control of lamps manufactured for contracts, 4 yrs exp required, thorough knowledge of lighting designs, techniques & color coordinated lamps & proven ability to create lighting concepts to meet clients display needs. 40 hr/wk; $40,000/yr. Send resume to Box NT 2035, 810 7th Ave, NYC 10019

- • • Solve.

9. Susan Chicoine sold a home for $87,000 and earned a 7% commission. How much was earned?

10. Aik Chong sold a car for $12,400 and earned a 4% commission. How much was earned?

11. Susan Elefson earns 9% commission on personal sales and 2% on sales of employees supervised. Personal sales were $10,000, and employee sales were $35,000. How much was earned?

12. Brenden Eggers earns 8% commission on personal sales and 3% on sales of employees supervised. Personal sales were $40,000, and employee sales were $94,000. How much was earned?

ANSWERS
1.
2.
3.
4.
5.
6.
7.
8.
9.
10.
11.
12.

13. John Ellingrod earns $150 weekly plus 6% of sales in excess of $4000. Sales were $4700. How much was earned?

14. Stacy Holtz earns $600 in monthly salary plus 5% on sales in excess of $19,000. Sales were $23,000. How much was earned?

15. ▦ Dawn Holmes earns $225 weekly plus a bonus of 1% on sales to $5000, 2% on sales from $5000 to $8000, and 3% on sales over $8000. Sales were $8400. How much was earned?

16. Linda Leydeus is given a $300 draw and earns a 10% commission on sales. If sales were $5200, how much did commission differ from draw?

▰▰▰ Solve.

17. Mark Lewis earns $280 for a 40-hour workweek plus a commission of 20% on sales. Last week sales were $800 and hours worked were 54. How much was earned?

18. ▦ Jill Mindrup earns $240 for a 40-hour workweek plus a commission of 8% on sales. Last week sales were $1700 and hours worked were 50. How much was earned?

19. Martin Mineck earns $210 for a 40-hour workweek plus a commission of 9% on sales. Last week sales were $3400 and hours worked were 46. How much was earned?

20. Spyridon Mentzelopoulos earns $175 for a 40-hour workweek plus a commission of 10% on sales. Last week sales were $1050 and hours worked were 45. How much was earned?

✓ **SKILL MAINTENANCE**

21. Retail sales in a recent quarter were $115.5 billion dollars. In the comparable period the previous year sales were $109 billion dollars. What was the percentage increase to the nearest tenth of a percent?

22. The price of gold recently was $325.80 an ounce. The previous year at the comparable time the price was $342.65 an ounce. What was the percentage decrease to the nearest tenth of a percent?

14.3

Federal Withholding and Social Security Withholding

Employers are required by law to withhold federal income tax from employees' paychecks. Each year an income tax form is filed (see Section 14.5 pp. 337), and the difference between what was withheld and what is owed is determined. Then either a refund check is mailed to the taxpayer or the taxpayer sends the Internal Revenue Service a check for the balance of tax owed. One method used to determine the income tax withheld is the ***percentage method.***

(see Section 14.5 pp. 337)

● THE PERCENTAGE METHOD

Example 1 Sylvia Lange, a married taxpayer, earns $1255 each month and claims three exemptions. How much is withheld for federal income tax?

Solution

a) Find the amount of one exemption from Table 14.1.

The payroll period is monthly, so the amount of one exemption is $86.67.

b) Find the amount of three exemptions.

$$\frac{\text{Amount of}}{\text{3 exemptions}} = \text{Amount of 1 exemption} \times \text{Number of exemptions}$$

$$= \$86.67 \times 3$$

$$= \$260.01$$

c) Subtract the exemption amount from the total wages.

$$\text{Total wages} - \text{Exemption amount} = \$1255 - \$260.01$$

$$= \$994.99$$

d) Use Table 14.2 to find the amount of tax withheld from $994.99.

From the table we see that the tax withheld is $75.00 + 17% of the excess over $833.

Tax withheld = $75.00 + 0.17 × ($994.99 − $833) = $102.54

The tax withheld is $102.54.

DO EXERCISE 1.

O B J E C T I V E S

After finishing Section 14.3, you should be able to:

- ● Determine the amount withheld using the percentage method.
- ● ● Determine the amount withheld using the wage bracket method.
- ● ● ● Compute social security tax for employees.
- ⠿ Compute social security tax for self-employed people.

TABLE 14.1

Percentage Method Income Tax Withholding Table

Payroll Period	One with-holding allowance
Weekly	$20.00
Biweekly	40.00
Semimonthly . . .	43.33
Monthly	86.67
Quarterly	260.00
Semiannually . . .	520.00
Annually	1,040.00
Daily or miscellaneous (each day of the payroll period)	4.00

1. Lute Simpson, a married taxpayer, earns $1627 each month and claims four exemptions. How much is withheld for federal income tax?

TABLE 14.2

If the Payroll Period With Respect to an Employee is Monthly

(a) SINGLE person—including head of household:

If the amount of wages is:	The amount of income tax to be withheld shall be:
Not over $118	.0

Over—	But not over—		of excess over—
$118	—$364	. . .12%	—$118
$364	—$800	. . $29.52 plus 15%	—$364
$800	—$1,267	. . $94.92 plus 19%	—$800
$1,267	—$1,908	. . $183.65 plus 25%	—$1,267
$1,908	—$2,411	. . $343.90 plus 30%	—$1,908
$2,411	—$2,871	. . $494.80 plus 34%	—$2,411
$2,871	. . . . . .	. . $651.20 plus 37%	—$2,871

(b) MARRIED person—

If the amount of wages is:	The amount of income tax to be withheld shall be:
Not over $208	.0

Over—	But not over—		of excess over—
$208	—$833	. . .12%	—$208
$833	—$1,663	. . $75.00 plus 17%	—$833
$1,663	—$2,047	. . $216.10 plus 22%	—$1,663
$2,047	—$2,507	. . $300.58 plus 25%	—$2,047
$2,507	—$2,966	. . $415.58 plus 28%	—$2,507
$2,966	—$3,885	. . $544.10 plus 33%	—$2,966
$3,885	. . . . . .	. . $847.37 plus 37%	—$3,885

ANSWER ON PAGE A-17

2. Lony Grotz, a married taxpayer earns $1430 each month and claims four exemptions. How much is withheld for federal income tax?

●● THE WAGE BRACKET METHOD

Another method used to determine the income tax withheld is the *wage bracket method.* This method is used in Example 2, which is identical to Example 1.

Part of the wage bracket method table (Table 23 on page T-33) is given in Table 14.3.

Example 2 Sylvia Lange, a married taxpayer, earns $1255 each month and claims three exemptions. How much is withheld for federal income tax?

Solution

a) Read down the left column of Table 14.3 (Table 23, p. T-33) until you locate the wage bracket containing 1255.

The location is in the bracket reading ''at least 1240 but less than 1280.''

b) Read across that row to the column headed 3.

The tax withheld is $103.

DO EXERCISE 2.

TABLE 14.3

MARRIED Persons–**MONTHLY** Payroll Period

And the wages are–		And the number of withholding allowances claimed is–										
At least	But less than	0	1	2	3	4	5	6	7	8	9	10
		The amount of income tax to be withheld shall be–										
$0	$212	$0	$0	$0	$0	$0	$0	$0	$0	$0	$0	$0
212	216	1	0	0	0	0	0	0	0	0	0	0
216	220	1	0	0	0	0	0	0	0	0	0	0
220	224	2	0	0	0	0	0	0	0	0	0	0
224	228	2	0	0	0	0	0	0	0	0	0	0
228	232	2	0	0	0	0	0	0	0	0	0	0
232	236	3	0	0	0	0	0	0	0	0	0	0
236	240	3	0	0	0	0	0	0	0	0	0	0
240	248	4	0	0	0	0	0	0	0	0	0	0
248	256	5	0	0	0	0	0	0	0	0	0	0
1,080	1,120	119	105	91	79	67	55	43	32	22	12	3
1,120	1,160	125	111	98	85	73	61	49	37	27	17	7
1,160	1,200	132	118	104	91	78	66	54	42	32	21	12
1,200	1,240	138	124	110	96	84	72	60	48	36	26	16
1,240	1,280	144	131	117	103	90	77	65	53	41	31	20
1,280	1,320	151	137	123	109	95	83	71	59	47	36	25
1,320	1,360	158	143	130	116	102	89	77	64	52	40	30
1,360	1,400	165	150	136	122	108	94	82	70	58	46	35
1,400	1,440	172	157	142	128	115	101	88	76	63	51	40
1,440	1,480	180	164	149	135	121	107	93	81	69	57	45

Do you see that the two withholding tax methods result in approximately the same amount being withheld from pay? The actual tax is determined when the income tax return is filed with the Internal Revenue Service (see Section 14.5).

ANSWER ON PAGE A-17

SOCIAL SECURITY*

The social security tax was established with the passage of the Federal Insurance Contributions Act (FICA) and provides old-age, survivor, disability, and hospitalization insurance for employees.

••• EMPLOYEES TAX

The maximum taxable earnings change as the average wage level changes. Table 14.4 lists the maximum taxable earnings and rates for several years.

TABLE 14.4		
SOCIAL SECURITY RATES FOR EMPLOYEES		
Year	**Maximum Taxable Earnings**	**Rate**
1986	$42,000	7.15%
1987	**	7.15%
1988–89	**	7.51%
1990 and after	**	7.65%

** Not available until late in previous year.

Example 3 José Farrar earned $18,600 in 1986. How much social security tax did José pay?

Solution Since $18,600 does not exceed the maximum taxable earnings ($42,000) for 1986, the entire amount was taxed.

$$\text{Social security tax} = \$18,600 \times 7.15\%$$
$$= \$18,600 \times 0.0715$$
$$= \$1329.90$$

The social security tax paid was $1329.90.

DO EXERCISE 3.

Earnings in excess of the maximum taxable earnings are not subject to the social security tax.

Example 4 Cynthia Schroeder earned $44,500 in 1986. How much did Cynthia pay in social security tax?

Solution The maximum taxable earnings in 1986 were $42,000, so there was no social security tax on $44,500 − $42,000, or $2500.

$$\text{Social security tax} = \$42,000 \times 7.15\%$$
$$= \$3003$$

The social security tax Cynthia paid was $3003.

DO EXERCISE 4.

---

* Information in this section, although current at time of writing, tends to change frequently.

3. Paul Pomykala earns $23,500 in 1988. How much social security tax does he pay? Assume the maximum taxable social security earnings are more than $42,000.

4. Tina Zegers earned $45,000 in 1987. How much social security tax did she pay? Assume that the maximum taxable social security earnings are $42,400.

ANSWERS ON PAGE A-17

Employers are required by law to match their employees' social security contributions. To illustrate, a $2000 employee contribution in 1988 would be matched by a $2000 employer contribution. Therefore the 1988 contribution to the employee's social security account would be $2000 + $2000, or $4000. The social security tax (contributions of employee and employer) is deposited periodically in a local bank and then forwarded to a Federal Reserve Bank (some employers deposit directly in a Federal Reserve Bank). Earnings are then credited to the employee's social security account. Social security taxes are deducted from each paycheck that an employee receives until the maximum taxable earnings are reached.

Example 5 During 1986 Leesa Buck earned $725.80 biweekly. How much was deducted from each paycheck for social security tax?

Solution Find the amount deducted.

$$\text{Amount deducted} = \text{Rate} \times \text{Earnings}$$
$$= 7.15\% \times \$725.80$$
$$= 0.0715 \times \$725.80$$
$$= \$51.89$$

Thus, $51.89 was deducted for social security tax.

DO EXERCISE 5.

⠒ SELF-EMPLOYED PERSONS TAX

Self-employed persons pay a different rate than employees do. However, the amount of maximum taxable earnings is the same as for employees. The rates for self-employed persons are shown in Table 14.5.

TABLE 14.5 SOCIAL SECURITY RATES FOR SELF-EMPLOYED PERSONS	
Year	**Rate**
1986	12.3%*
1987	12.3%*
1988–1989	13.02%*
1990 and after	15.30%

* Effective rate after a tax credit.

Example 6 Mark Kuczak, a self-employed person, earned $47,000 in 1986. How much social security tax was paid?

Solution The amount of maximum taxable earnings in 1986 was $42,000, so there was no social security tax on $47,000 − $42,000, or $5000.

$$\text{Social security tax} = \$42,000 \times 12.3\%$$
$$= \$42,000 \times 0.123$$
$$= \$5166$$

The social security tax was $5166.

DO EXERCISE 6.

• Use the percentage method (Tables 21 and 22 on pp. T-30 and T-31).

1. Leaann Keith, a married taxpayer, earns $1780 each month and claims four exemptions. How much is withheld for federal income tax?

2. Jun-Koo Kang, a single taxpayer, earns $2186 each month and claims three exemptions. How much is withheld for federal income tax?

3. Todd Thorson, a married taxpayer, earns $685 weekly and claims four exemptions. How much is withheld for federal income tax?

4. ▦ Marcia Zanatta, a single taxpayer, earns $775 weekly and claims three exemptions. How much is withheld for federal income tax?

•• Use the wage bracket method (Table 23 on p. T-33).

5. Leaann Keith, a married taxpayer, earns $1780 each month and claims four exemptions. How much is withheld for federal income tax?

6. Jun-Koo Kang, a single taxpayer, earns $2186 each month and claims three exemptions. How much is withheld for federal income tax?

7. Todd Thorson, a married taxpayer, earns $685 weekly and claims four exemptions. How much is withheld for federal income tax?

8. Marcia Zanatta, a single taxpayer, earns $775 weekly and claims three exemptions. How much is withheld for federal income tax?

ANSWERS

1. _____

2. _____

3. _____

4. _____

5. _____

6. _____

7. _____

8. _____

ANSWERS

9. _____

10. _____

11. _____

12. _____

13. _____

14. _____

15. _____

16. _____

17. _____

18. _____

19. _____

20. _____

21. _____

22. _____

Assume the maximum taxable earnings for 1987 and 1988 are $42,400 and $43,800, respectively.

●●● Find the social security tax for these employees.

9. A machinist with $23,780 in 1987 earnings.

10. A drill press operator with $27,900 in 1988 earnings.

11. A college president with $85,000 in 1987 earnings.

12. A chemist with $47,000 in 1988 earnings.

13. ▦ A wholesale manager with $27,200 in 1987 earnings.

14. An accountant with $49,000 in 1988 earnings.

●●● Find the social security tax for these self-employed people.

15. A writer with $56,000 in 1987 earnings.

16. A consultant with $72,000 in 1988 earnings.

17. An automobile body shop owner with $34,000 in 1987 earnings.

18. A painter with $25,700 in 1988 earnings.

19. ▦ A RotoRooter owner with $48,000 in 1988 earnings.

20. A cabinet maker with $31,400 in 1988 earnings.

✓ **SKILL MAINTENANCE**

21. Find the decimal notation for 99.44%.

22. Find the net deposit.

	Dollars	Cents
Cash	2048	95
List Checks Singly	1134	02
	668	94
	775	36
Total From Other Side		
Total		
Less Cash Received	250	00
Net Deposit		

Chapter 14 Payroll

14.4

Payroll

⬛ **NET PAY**

A payroll clerk computes the **net pay** an employee earns as well as gross earnings. Net pay is often called **take-home pay.** It is the amount of money an employee receives after deductions. Deductions include income taxes, social security taxes, insurance (group life, automobile, and medical), contributions, stock purchase plans, and savings. Many companies (especially small ones) calculate payroll manually. A time clock records when an employee starts and finishes work, a weekly time ticket is completed, and a payroll register (journal) is used to record information on each employee.

Example 1 Compute the net pay for Lu Ahman who is married and claims three exemptions.

WEEKLY TIME TICKET

EMPLOYEE'S NAME **Lu Ahman**   NO.   WEEK ENDING **May 16**   19 **87**

JOB NAME OR NO.	KIND OF WORK DONE	S	M	T	W	T	F	S	HRS.	RATE	AMOUNT
36824	Assembly		4	6	3	2	5		20	13.	260.00
47815	Labor		1.5	1	1.5	1.3			5.3	13.	68.90
63219	Labeling		1.8	1	3	4	1		10.8	13.	140.40
58739	Trouble Shooting		0.7		0.5	0.7	2		3.9	13.	50.70
	Total Regular Time		8	8	8	8	8		40	13.	520.00
	Total Overtime										

APPROVED **αℒJ**   DEDUCTIONS: WITHHOLD **68.00** S.D.I. F.I.C.A. **37.18** STATE WH. INS. **34.00**   Total Earnings **520.00**   Total Deductions **139.18**

4K 409 Rediform   Date Paid **5/19/87** Check No. **397**   NET PAY **380.82**

Solution

a) Find the total deductions.

Total deductions = Withholding + Social security + Insurance

= $68 + $37.18 + $34 = $139.18

b) Find the net pay.

Net pay = Total earnings − Total deductions

= $520.00 − $139.18 = $380.82

The net pay was $380.82.

DO EXERCISE 1.

WEEKLY TIME TICKET

EMPLOYEE'S NAME **Lee Fisk**   NO.   WEEK ENDING **July 18**   19 **87**

JOB NAME OR NO.	KIND OF WORK DONE	S	M	T	W	T	F	S	HRS.	RATE	AMOUNT
83516	Inventory		1.3	2	0.6	2.5	1.9		8.3	9.75	80.93
49718	Handling		0.8	1.4		1.4	0.7		4.3	9.75	41.92
63492	Stiching		3.8	2.9	2.5	1.7	2.5		13.4	9.75	130.65
47815	Labor			1.7	0.8	0.9	1.6		5.0	9.75	48.75
36824	Assembly		2.1		4.1	1.5	1.3		9.0	9.75	87.75
	Total Regular Time		8	8	8	8	8		40.0	9.75	390.00
	Total Overtime										

APPROVED **αℒJ**   DEDUCTIONS: WITHHOLD **58.00** S.D.I. F.I.C.A. **27.89** STATE WH. SAVINGS **40.50**   Total Earnings **390.00**   Total Deductions

4K 409 Rediform   Date Paid **7/21/87** Check No. **568**   NET PAY

After finishing Section 14.4, you should be able to:

⬛ Compute net pay.

⬛⬛ Find the total and net wages from a payroll journal.

⬛⬛⬛ Read computer printout for payroll.

1. Compute the net pay for Lee Fisk, who is single and claims two exemptions. The weekly time card is shown on the left below.

ANSWER ON PAGE A-18

2.

Compute the total wages and net wages for the payroll journal if an additional employee is hired and is paid gross wages of $570 and net wages of $391.25.

ANSWERS ON PAGE A-18

A payroll journal (register) is used to record payroll information for each employee. The payroll journal provides the employer with information on total payroll costs and deductions.

Example 2 Compute the total wages and net wages for the payroll journal given at the bottom of this page.

Solution

a) Find the total wages.

$$\text{Total wages} = \text{Sum of wages paid each employee}$$
$$= \$520 + \$580 + \$600 + \$500 + \$530$$
$$= \$2730$$

Total wages were $2730.

b) Find the net wages.

$$\text{Net wages} = \text{Sum of net wages paid each employee}$$
$$= \$380.82 + \$430.53 + \$416.10 + \$355.25 + \$371.10$$
$$= \$1953.80$$

Net wages were $1953.80.

DO EXERCISE 2.

● ● ● **COMPUTERIZED PAYROLL**

Many large companies use computers for payroll and increasingly small businesses are using microcomputers for payroll. This section shows one procedure where the employee completes a time record (see Fig. 14.1), the information is put in computer format by keypunch operators, and the computer processes and prints out payroll information for each employee on a register (see Fig. 14.2). Finally, the employee is paid by check (see Fig. 14.3).

PAYROLL JOURNAL — SHEET NO. 5

WORK WEEK, BEGINS—DAY MONDAY   TIME OF DAY 8 a.m.   DATE OF PAYMENT May 19, 1987

EMPLOYEE'S NAME	EXEMP. FED	EXEMP. STATE	S	M	T	W	T	F	S	TOTAL HOURS	REGULAR RATE OF PAY	AT REGULAR RATE	EXTRA FOR OVERTIME	OTHER WAGES	TOTAL WAGES	F.O.A.B. TAX	FED. WITH-HOLDING TAX	STATE WITH-HOLDING TAX	INS.	CONT	SAV	TOTAL DEDUCTIONS	NET CASH WAGES PAID
LU AHMAN (M)	3			8	8	8	8	8		40	13.00/hr.	520 00			520 00	37 18	68 00		34 00			139 18	380 82
ORPHA GRAP (M)	2			8	8	8	8	8		40	14.50/hr.	580 00			580 00	41 47	88 00		20 00			149 47	430 53
ALPHA HOPE (S)	3			8	8	8	8	8		40	15.00/hr.	600 00			600 00	42 90	111 00				30 00	183 90	416 10
FRAN LYNN (M)	4			8	8	8	8	8		40	12.50/hr.	500 00			500 00	35 25	59 00				50 00	144 75	355 25
FAYVA Z SHUJA (S)	2			8	8	8	8	8		40	13.25/hr.	530 00			530 00	37 90	96 00			25 00		158 90	371 10

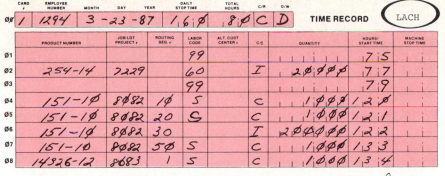

CARD #	EMPLOYEE NUMBER	MONTH	DAY	YEAR	DAILY STOP TIME	TOTAL HOURS	C/R	D/W		
Ø	1294	3	23	87	16.0	8.0	C	D	TIME RECORD	LACH

	PRODUCT NUMBER	JOB LOT PROJECT #	ROUTING SEQ. #	LABOR CODE	ALT. COST CENTER #	C/I	QUANTITY	HOURS/ START TIME	MACHINE STOP TIME
Ø1				99				7.5	
Ø2	254-14	7229	60			I	20000	7.7	
Ø3				99				7.9	
Ø4	151-10	8082	10	5		C	1000	12.0	
Ø5	151-10	8082	20	5		C	1000	12.1	
Ø6	151-10	8082	30			I	200000	12.2	
Ø7	151-10	8082	50	5		C	1000	13.3	
Ø8	14326-12	8083	1	5		C	1000	13.4	

EMPLOYEE NAME J. PAXTON COST CENTER # 707 APPROVED _R.W. Cloud_

	PRODUCT NUMBER	JOB LOT PROJECT #	ROUTING SEQ. #	LABOR CODE	ALT. COST CENTER #	C/I	QUANTITY	HOURS/ START TIME	MACHINE STOP TIME
Ø9	14328-12	8083	1			I	38000	13.5	
10	157-26	8082	1	5		C	1000	13.6	
11	157-26	8082	1			I	18000	13.7	
12				99				13.8	
13									

FIGURE 14.1

Examples 3, 4, and 5 show the procedure for J. T. Paxton (employee number 1294) from the time record to the computer printout of payroll and finally to the paycheck.

Example 3 From Fig. 14.1, determine the hours worked, the quantity of product 254-14 made, and the starting time for employee 1294.

Solution

a) Find the hours worked.

The top boxed row shows that 8 hours were worked.

b) Find the quantity of product 254-14 made.

Row 02 lists 20 as the quantity.

c) Find the starting time.

The starting time is given in row 01 as 7.5. Thus, the starting time is 7:30.

DO EXERCISE 3.

Figure 14.2 lists part of a register that gives payroll information for employee 1294.

3. Find the starting time and quantity for product number 14328-12 in Fig. 14.1.

ANSWERS ON PAGE A-18

Lach CHEMICAL COMPANY
DATE PROCESSED 3/29/87

CURRENT AND YTD EARNINGS REGISTER
BEGIN DATE 3/12/87   END DATE 3/25/87

PAYRO5 PAGE 8
CHECK DATE 3/31/87

*** HOURLY ***

EMP/C/C	REGULAR	PREMIUM	VAC	SICK	P/L	HOL	GONE	VAC LEFT	VAC USED	P/L LEFT	P/L USED	PAY ADJ AMT	CHECK NO.
1294 / 707	68.0		8										
	314.16		36.96					104.0	16.0	49.2	4.0		62282

FIC GROSS	GROSS	FEDERAL	STATE	DISAB	FICA	MEDICAL	STOCK	AUTO	SAVINGS	OTHER	NET	
351.12	351.12	52.26	8.83		21.24						268.79	C/E
2544.23	2544.23	418.20	63.69		153.92	30.48				.62	1877.32	YTD

FIGURE 14.2

4. Find the gross current earnings and amount withheld for federal, state, and social security taxes for employee 1294.

Example 4 Find the regular rate of pay for employee 1294.

Solution

a) Find the regular hours worked.

The regular hours worked are 68.

b) Find the hourly wage.

$$\text{Hourly wage} = \frac{\text{Amount earned for regular hours}}{\text{Regular hours worked}}$$

$$= \frac{314.16}{68}$$

$$= 4.62$$

The hourly wage is $4.62.

DO EXERCISE 4.

The payroll check lists a statement of earnings and the net earnings for J. T. Paxton (employee 1294). It appears in Fig. 14.3.

5. Find the net pay for J. T. Paxton if the gross pay had been $394.36 and the deductions the same as in Example 5.

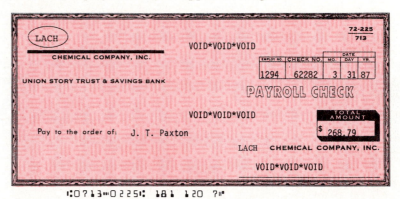

FIGURE 14.3

Example 5 Verify that the net pay is correct for J. T. Paxton.

Solution

$$\text{Net pay} = \text{Gross pay} - \text{Deductions}$$
$$= \$351.12 - (\$52.26 + \$8.83 + \$21.24)$$
$$= \$268.79$$

The net pay is $268.79.

DO EXERCISE 5.

ANSWERS ON PAGE A-18

Chapter 14   Payroll

• Complete weekly time tickets. The number of exemptions claimed and the marital status of each employee are given. Use Table 23 (p. T-33) and Table 14.4 to compute withholding and social security tax.

1. Married with five exemptions

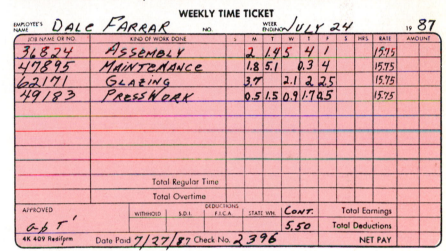

WEEKLY TIME TICKET

EMPLOYEE'S NAME: DANA GARNER   NO.   WEEK ENDING: JULY 24   19 87

JOB NAME OR NO.	KIND OF WORK DONE	S	M	T	W	T	F	S	HRS.	RATE	AMOUNT
36824	ASSEMBLY		3	4	1.7	2	5			13.50	
47895	MAINTENANCE		2.4	1.8	5.4	3.3	0.6			13.50	
18462	TROUBLESHOOTING		0.9	1.1		1.8	1.8			13.50	
49183	PRESS WORK		1.7	1.1	0.9	0.9	0.6			13.50	

Total Regular Time
Total Overtime

APPROVED a b T'

	DEDUCTIONS					Total Earnings
WITHHOLD	S.D.I.	F.I.C.A.	STATE WH.	SAVINGS 18.75		Total Deductions

4K 409 Rediform   Date Paid 7/27/87   Check No. 2395   NET PAY

2. ▦ Single with two exemptions

WEEKLY TIME TICKET

EMPLOYEE'S NAME: DALE FARRAR   NO.   WEEK ENDING: JULY 24   19 87

JOB NAME OR NO.	KIND OF WORK DONE	S	M	T	W	T	F	S	HRS.	RATE	AMOUNT
36824	ASSEMBLY		2	1.4	5	4	1			15.75	
47895	MAINTENANCE		1.8	5.1		0.3	4			15.75	
62171	GLAZING		3.7		2.1	2	2.5			15.75	
49183	PRESSWORK		0.5	1.5	0.9	1.7	2.5			15.75	

Total Regular Time
Total Overtime

APPROVED a b T'

	DEDUCTIONS					Total Earnings
WITHHOLD	S.D.I.	F.I.C.A.	STATE WH.	CONT. 5.50		Total Deductions

4K 409 Rediform   Date Paid 7/27/87   Check No. 2396   NET PAY

3. Married with two exemptions

WEEKLY TIME TICKET

EMPLOYEE'S NAME: STANLEE OTT   NO.   WEEK ENDING: JULY 24   1987

JOB NAME OR NO.	KIND OF WORK DONE	S	M	T	W	T	F	S	HRS.	RATE	AMOUNT
47895	MAINTENANCE		0.5	1.5	2.2	3	2.5			14.50	
18263	WELDING		1.2	3.2	5.1	0.6	3.1			14.50	
18462	TROUBLESHOOTING		5.1	1.7	0.2	0.7	1.6			14.50	
49183	PRESS WORK			1.6	0.4	0.5	0.4			14.50	
62171	GLAZING		1.2		0.1	3.2	0.4			14.50	

Total Regular Time
Total Overtime

APPROVED a b T'

	DEDUCTIONS					Total Earnings
WITHHOLD	S.D.I.	F.I.C.A.	STATE WH.	INS. 20.50		Total Deductions

4K 409 Rediform   Date Paid 7/27/87   Check No. 2397   NET PAY

4. 🖩 Single with one exemption

WEEKLY TIME TICKET

EMPLOYEE'S NAME _TRACEY STOLTZ_   NO. _____   WEEK ENDING _JULY 24_   19 **87**

JOB NAME OR NO.	KIND OF WORK DONE	S	M	T	W	T	F	S	HRS.	RATE	AMOUNT
18263	WELDING		4.6	3.9	6.3	5.4	4.7			12.25	
47895	MAINTENANCE		2.8	2.7		1.8	2.1			12.25	
49183	PRESS WORK		0.6	1.4	1.7	0.8	1.2			12.25	
				Total Regular Time							
				Total Overtime							

APPROVED _apt'_

	DEDUCTIONS					
	WITHHOLD	S.D.I.	F.I.C.A.	STATE WH.		Total Earnings
						Total Deductions

4K 409 Rediform   Date Paid _7/27/87_ Check No. _2398_   NET PAY

•• **5.** 🖩 Complete the payroll journal. Determine the total wages and net wages.

PAYROLL JOURNAL

SHEET NO. _____

WORK WEEK, BEGINS—DAY _MONDAY_   TIME OF DAY _____   DATE OF PAYMENT _JULY 27, 1987_

EMPLOYEE'S NAME (FOR NECESSARY PAYROLL DATA CONCERNING EACH EMPLOYEE REFER TO INSIDE FRONT COVER.)	EXEMPTIONS FED. / STATE	HOURS OF WORK (INCLUDE ALL TIME WHETHER ON PREMISES OR WHERE WORK IS DONE) S M T W T F S TOTAL HOURS	REGULAR RATE OF PAY	AT REGULAR RATE FOR TOTAL HOURS WORKED (1)	EXTRA FOR OVERTIME (1)	OTHER WAGES (ROOM, BOARD, ETC.) (2)	TOTAL WAGES	F.O.A.B. TAX	FED. WITH-HOLDING TAX	STATE WITH-HOLDING TAX	OTHER DEDUCTIONS	TOTAL DEDUCTIONS	NET CASH WAGES PAID
DANA GARNER (M)													
DALE FARRAR (S)													
STANLEE OTT (M)													
TRACEY STOLTZ (S)													

••• For employee 1284, list the

6. Current (C/E) gross earnings   **7.** Federal income tax withheld

8. State income tax withheld   **9.** Social security tax paid

10. Net earnings   **11.** Year-to-date (YTD) net earnings

EMP 1284/	C/C 830	REGULAR 80.0 251.20	PREMIUM 1.3 6.12	VAC	SICK	P/L	HOL	GONE	VAC LEFT	VAC USED	P/L LEFT 6.6	P/L USED	PAY ADJ AMT	CHECK NO. 62280
FIC GROSS 257.32 1216.27	GROSS 257.32 1216.27	FEDERAL 21.90 76.17	STATE 5.98 21.58	DISAB	FICA 15.57 73.59	MEDICAL	STOCK	AUTO	SAVINGS	OTHER			NET 213.87 1044.93	C/E YTD

✔ **SKILL MAINTENANCE**

For Exercises 12 and 13 use Tables 19 and 20.

12. After a $45,000 permanent insurance policy that was issued at age 20 had been in force for 12 years, Sara Forte, the insured, wanted to borrow on the policy. How much was available?

13. Sidney Laws, a 21-year-old male, wishes to buy a $50,000 permanent insurance policy. How much is the premium?

14.5

Federal Income Tax

OBJECTIVES

After finishing Section 14.5, you should be able to:

- • **Prepare Form 1040EZ.**
- • • **Prepare Form 1040A.**

Once a year most Americans must file a federal income tax return. Once you file a return, you are on the Internal Revenue Service mailing list.

FRANK AND ERNEST   by Bob Thaves

HOW DOES THIS SOUND? "...AND IN CONCLUSION, DEAR INTERNAL REVENUE SERVICE, I RESPECTFULLY REQUEST YOU REMOVE ME FROM YOUR MAILING LIST."

Many taxpayers' sources of income and deductions are not complicated. They should consider preparing their own tax returns. In this section we study the preparation of Federal Income Tax Forms 1040EZ and 1040A. A third, Form 1040, will not be studied as it is quite lengthy and may require additional supporting schedules. For example, a taxpayer with rental income, capital gains or losses, or large itemized deductions (medical expenses, contributions, interest expenses, and others) needs to document these items on separate tax forms (supporting schedules).

• FORM 1040EZ

Individuals who meet these conditions may file Form 1040EZ.

You can use Form 1040EZ for:

Single filing status only

Your own personal exemption only

No dependents

Income from:
Wages, salaries, tips
Interest income ($400 or less)
No dividend income
Less than $50,000 in taxable income

Partial charitable contributions deduction

No tax credits

A completed Form 1040EZ appears in Example 1.

Example 1 Complete.

Department of the Treasury — Internal Revenue Service

Form 1040EZ Income Tax Return for Single filers with no dependents (0)

OMB No. 1545-0675

Instructions are on the back of this form.
Tax Table is in the 1040EZ and 1040A Tax Package.

Name and address

Use the IRS mailing label. If you don't have a label, print or type:

Name (first, initial, last)	Social security number
Joyce T. Owens	484-30-5678

Present home address
1418 Fifth Ave

City, town or post office, State, and ZIP code
Chesterland, OH 44026

Presidential Election Campaign Fund
Check this box ☑ if you want $1 of your tax to go to this fund.

Figure your tax

Attach Copy B of Forms W-2 here

1	Wages, salaries, and tips. Attach your W-2 form(s).	1	23,700.—
2	Interest income of $400 or less. If more than $400, you cannot use Form 1040EZ.	2	320.—
3	Add line 1 and line 2. This is your **adjusted gross income**.	3	24,020.—
*④	Allowable part of your charitable contributions. Complete the worksheet on page 18. Do not write more than $25.	4	20.—
5	Subtract line 4 from line 3.	5	24,000.—
6	Amount of your personal exemption.	6	1,000.00
7	Subtract line 6 from line 5. This is your **taxable income**.	7	23,000.—
⑧	Enter your Federal income tax withheld. This is shown on your W-2 form(s).	8	4,800.—
⑨	Use the tax table on pages 26-31 to find the **tax** on your taxable income on line 7.	9	4,690.—

Refund or amount you owe

Attach tax payment here

10	If line 8 is larger than line 9, subtract line 9 from line 8. Enter the amount of your **refund**.	10	110.—
11	If line 9 is larger than line 8, subtract line 8 from line 9. Enter the **amount you owe**. Attach check or money order for the full amount payable to "Internal Revenue Service."	11	

Sign your return

I have read this return. Under penalties of perjury, I declare that to the best of my knowledge and belief, the return is correct and complete.

Your signature   Date

X Joyce T. Owens   April 12, 1987

For **Privacy Act and Paperwork Reduction Act Notice**, see page 34.

* Circled numbers are explained on the next page.

Comments on lines of Form 1040EZ.

④

<table>
<tr><td colspan="2">Use the worksheet below to figure your charitable contributions deduction:</td></tr>
<tr><td>A. Cash contributions</td><td>A. $ 80.00</td></tr>
<tr><td>B. Contributions other than cash</td><td>B. + — 0.—</td></tr>
<tr><td>C. Add lines A and B. Do not write more than $100 ($50 if married filing separately).</td><td>C. = 80.00</td></tr>
<tr><td>D. Multiply the amount on line C by 25% (.25).</td><td>D. x .25</td></tr>
<tr><td>* E. Write your answer here and on line 13 of Form 1040A (or on line 4 of Form 1040EZ).</td><td>E. = $ 20.00</td></tr>
</table>

* Maximum allowable is $25.00.

⑧ Amount withheld this year from earnings.

⑨ First, find the $23,000–$23,050 row in Table 14.6 on p. 380. (This is part of Table 24, p. T-36.) Next, find the column headed ''Single'' and read down the column. The amount where the row and the Single column meet is $4,690. This is the tax.

DO EXERCISE 1 (p. 381)

TABLE 14.6

FEDERAL INCOME TAX TABLE

If 1040A, line 16, OR 1040EZ, line 7 is—		And you are—			
At least	But less than	Single	Married filing jointly	Married filing separately	Head of a household
		Your tax is—			
16,250	16,300	2,674	2,074	3,224	2,515
16,300	16,350	2,688	2,085	3,241	2,527
16,350	16,400	2,701	2,096	3,257	2,538
16,400	16,450	2,715	2,107	3,274	2,550
16,450	16,500	2,728	2,118	3,290	2,561
16,500	16,550	2,742	2,129	3,307	2,573
16,550	16,600	2,755	2,140	3,323	2,584
16,600	16,650	2,769	2,151	3,340	2,596
16,650	16,700	2,782	2,162	3,356	2,607
16,700	16,750	2,796	2,173	3,373	2,619
16,750	16,800	2,809	2,184	3,389	2,630
16,800	16,850	2,823	2,195	3,406	2,642
16,850	16,900	2,836	2,206	3,422	2,653
16,900	16,950	2,850	2,217	3,439	2,665
16,950	17,000	2,863	2,228	3,455	2,676
17,000					
17,000	17,050	2,877	2,239	3,472	2,688
17,050	17,100	2,890	2,250	3,488	2,699
17,100	17,150	2,904	2,261	3,505	2,711
17,150	17,200	2,917	2,272	3,521	2,722
17,200	17,250	2,931	2,283	3,538	2,734
17,250	17,300	2,944	2,294	3,554	2,745
17,300	17,350	2,958	2,305	3,571	2,757
17,350	17,400	2,971	2,316	3,587	2,768
17,400	17,450	2,985	2,327	3,604	2,780
17,450	17,500	2,998	2,338	3,620	2,791
17,500	17,550	3,012	2,349	3,637	2,803
17,550	17,600	3,025	2,360	3,653	2,814
17,600	17,650	3,039	2,371	3,671	2,826
17,650	17,700	3,052	2,382	3,691	2,837
17,700	17,750	3,066	2,393	3,710	2,849
17,750	17,800	3,079	2,404	3,730	2,860
17,800	17,850	3,093	2,415	3,749	2,872
17,850	17,900	3,106	2,426	3,769	2,883
17,900	17,950	3,120	2,437	3,788	2,895
17,950	18,000	3,133	2,448	3,808	2,906
18,000					
18,000	18,050	3,147	2,459	3,827	2,918
18,050	18,100	3,160	2,470	3,847	2,929
18,100	18,150	3,174	2,481	3,866	2,941
18,150	18,200	3,187	2,492	3,886	2,952
18,200	18,250	3,202	2,503	3,905	2,965
18,250	18,300	3,217	2,514	3,925	2,979
18,300	18,350	3,233	2,525	3,944	2,993
18,350	18,400	3,248	2,536	3,964	3,007
18,400	18,450	3,264	2,547	3,983	3,021
18,450	18,500	3,279	2,558	4,003	3,035
18,500	18,550	3,295	2,569	4,022	3,049
18,550	18,600	3,310	2,580	4,042	3,063
18,600	18,650	3,326	2,591	4,061	3,077
18,650	18,700	3,341	2,602	4,081	3,091
18,700	18,750	3,357	2,613	4,100	3,105
18,750	18,800	3,372	2,624	4,120	3,119
18,800	18,850	3,388	2,635	4,139	3,133
18,850	18,900	3,403	2,646	4,159	3,147
18,900	18,950	3,419	2,657	4,178	3,161
18,950	19,000	3,434	2,668	4,198	3,175

If 1040A, line 16, OR 1040EZ, line 7 is—		And you are—			
At least	But less than	Single	Married filing jointly	Married filing separately	Head of a household
		Your tax is—			
19,000					
19,000	19,050	3,450	2,679	4,217	3,189
19,050	19,100	3,465	2,690	4,237	3,203
19,100	19,150	3,481	2,701	4,256	3,217
19,150	19,200	3,496	2,712	4,276	3,231
19,200	19,250	3,512	2,723	4,295	3,245
19,250	19,300	3,527	2,734	4,315	3,259
19,300	19,350	3,543	2,745	4,334	3,273
19,350	19,400	3,558	2,756	4,354	3,287
19,400	19,450	3,574	2,767	4,373	3,301
19,450	19,500	3,589	2,778	4,393	3,315
19,500	19,550	3,605	2,789	4,412	3,329
19,550	19,600	3,620	2,800	4,432	3,343
19,600	19,650	3,636	2,811	4,451	3,357
19,650	19,700	3,651	2,822	4,471	3,371
19,700	19,750	3,667	2,833	4,490	3,385
19,750	19,800	3,682	2,844	4,510	3,399
19,800	19,850	3,698	2,855	4,529	3,413
19,850	19,900	3,713	2,866	4,549	3,427
19,900	19,950	3,729	2,877	4,568	3,441
19,950	20,000	3,744	2,888	4,588	3,455
20,000					
20,000	20,050	3,760	2,899	4,607	3,469
20,050	20,100	3,775	2,910	4,627	3,483
20,100	20,150	3,791	2,921	4,646	3,497
20,150	20,200	3,806	2,932	4,666	3,511
20,200	20,250	3,822	2,943	4,685	3,525
20,250	20,300	3,837	2,956	4,705	3,539
20,300	20,350	3,853	2,968	4,724	3,553
20,350	20,400	3,868	2,981	4,744	3,567
20,400	20,450	3,884	2,993	4,763	3,581
20,450	20,500	3,899	3,006	4,783	3,595
20,500	20,550	3,915	3,018	4,802	3,609
20,550	20,600	3,930	3,031	4,822	3,623
20,600	20,650	3,946	3,043	4,841	3,637
20,650	20,700	3,961	3,056	4,861	3,651
20,700	20,750	3,977	3,068	4,880	3,665
20,750	20,800	3,992	3,081	4,900	3,679
20,800	20,850	4,008	3,093	4,919	3,693
20,850	20,900	4,023	3,106	4,939	3,707
20,900	20,950	4,039	3,118	4,958	3,721
20,950	21,000	4,054	3,131	4,978	3,735
21,000					
21,000	21,050	4,070	3,143	4,997	3,749
21,050	21,100	4,085	3,156	5,017	3,763
21,100	21,150	4,101	3,168	5,036	3,777
21,150	21,200	4,116	3,181	5,056	3,791
21,200	21,250	4,132	3,193	5,075	3,805
21,250	21,300	4,147	3,206	5,095	3,819
21,300	21,350	4,163	3,218	5,114	3,833
21,350	21,400	4,178	3,231	5,134	3,847
21,400	21,450	4,194	3,243	5,153	3,861
21,450	21,500	4,209	3,256	5,173	3,875
21,500	21,550	4,225	3,268	5,192	3,889
21,550	21,600	4,240	3,281	5,212	3,903
21,600	21,650	4,256	3,293	5,231	3,917
21,650	21,700	4,271	3,306	5,251	3,931
21,700	21,750	4,287	3,318	5,270	3,945

If 1040A, line 16, OR 1040EZ, line 7 is—		And you are—			
At least	But less than	Single	Married filing jointly	Married filing separately	Head of a household
		Your tax is—			
21,750	21,800	4,302	3,331	5,290	3,959
21,800	21,850	4,318	3,343	5,309	3,973
21,850	21,900	4,333	3,356	5,329	3,987
21,900	21,950	4,349	3,368	5,348	4,001
21,950	22,000	4,364	3,381	5,368	4,015
22,000					
22,000	22,050	4,380	3,393	5,387	4,029
22,050	22,100	4,395	3,406	5,407	4,043
22,100	22,150	4,411	3,418	5,426	4,057
22,150	22,200	4,426	3,431	5,446	4,071
22,200	22,250	4,442	3,443	5,465	4,085
22,250	22,300	4,457	3,456	5,485	4,099
22,300	22,350	4,473	3,468	5,504	4,113
22,350	22,400	4,488	3,481	5,524	4,127
22,400	22,450	4,504	3,493	5,543	4,141
22,450	22,500	4,519	3,506	5,563	4,155
22,500	22,550	4,535	3,518	5,582	4,169
22,550	22,600	4,550	3,531	5,602	4,183
22,600	22,650	4,566	3,543	5,621	4,197
22,650	22,700	4,581	3,556	5,641	4,211
22,700	22,750	4,597	3,568	5,660	4,225
22,750	22,800	4,612	3,581	5,680	4,239
22,800	22,850	4,628	3,593	5,699	4,253
22,850	22,900	4,643	3,606	5,719	4,267
22,900	22,950	4,659	3,618	5,740	4,281
22,950	23,000	4,674	3,631	5,762	4,295
23,000					
23,000	23,050	4,690	3,643	5,784	4,309
23,050	23,100	4,705	3,656	5,806	4,323
23,100	23,150	4,721	3,668	5,828	4,337
23,150	23,200	4,736	3,681	5,850	4,351
23,200	23,250	4,752	3,693	5,872	4,365
23,250	23,300	4,767	3,706	5,894	4,379
23,300	23,350	4,783	3,718	5,916	4,393
23,350	23,400	4,798	3,731	5,938	4,407
23,400	23,450	4,814	3,743	5,960	4,421
23,450	23,500	4,829	3,756	5,982	4,435
23,500	23,550	4,846	3,768	6,004	4,450
23,550	23,600	4,863	3,781	6,026	4,466
23,600	23,650	4,881	3,793	6,048	4,482
23,650	23,700	4,898	3,806	6,070	4,498
23,700	23,750	4,916	3,818	6,092	4,514
23,750	23,800	4,933	3,831	6,114	4,530
23,800	23,850	4,951	3,843	6,136	4,546
23,850	23,900	4,968	3,856	6,158	4,562
23,900	23,950	4,986	3,868	6,180	4,578
23,950	24,000	5,003	3,881	6,202	4,594
24,000					
24,000	24,050	5,021	3,893	6,224	4,610
24,050	24,100	5,038	3,906	6,246	4,626
24,100	24,150	5,056	3,918	6,268	4,642
24,150	24,200	5,073	3,931	6,290	4,658
24,200	24,250	5,091	3,943	6,312	4,674
24,250	24,300	5,108	3,956	6,334	4,690
24,300	24,350	5,126	3,968	6,356	4,706
24,350	24,400	5,143	3,981	6,378	4,722
24,400	24,450	5,161	3,993	6,400	4,738
24,450	24,500	5,178	4,006	6,422	4,754

1. Provide the necessary information in the white spaces. Cash contributions were $60.00.

Department of the Treasury — Internal Revenue Service

Form 1040EZ Income Tax Return for Single filers with no dependents (0)

OMB No. 1545-0675

Instructions are on the back of this form.
Tax Table is in the 1040EZ and 1040A Tax Package.

Name and address

Use the IRS mailing label. If you don't have a label, print or type:

Name (first, initial, last)
Jerry K. Reid

Social security number
356 13 2684

Present home address
17 Northwestern Ave.

City, town or post office, State, and ZIP code
Burlingame, CA 94010

Presidential Election Campaign Fund

Check this box ☑ if you want $1 of your tax to go to this fund.

Figure your tax

Attach Copy B of Forms W-2 here

1 Wages, salaries, and tips. Attach your W-2 form(s).	1	20,225.00
2 Interest income of $400 or less. If more than $400, you cannot use Form 1040EZ.	2	250.00
3 Add line 1 and line 2. This is your **adjusted gross income.**	3	.
4 Allowable part of your charitable contributions. Complete the worksheet on page 18. Do not write more than $25.	4	.
5 Subtract line 4 from line 3.	5	.
6 Amount of your personal exemption.	6	1,000.00
7 Subtract line 6 from line 5. This is your **taxable income.**	7	.
8 Enter your Federal income tax withheld. This is shown on your W-2 form(s).	8	4,010.00
9 Use the tax table on pages 26-31 to find the **tax** on your taxable income on line 7.	9	.

Refund or amount you owe

Attach tax payment here

10 If line 8 is larger than line 9, subtract line 9 from line 8. Enter the amount of your **refund.**	10	.
11 If line 9 is larger than line 8, subtract line 8 from line 9. Enter the **amount you owe.** Attach check or money order for the full amount payable to "Internal Revenue Service."	11	.

Sign your return

I have read this return. Under penalties of perjury, I declare that to the best of my knowledge and belief, the return is correct and complete.

Your signature   Date

X Jerry K. Reid   April 5, 1987

For **Privacy Act and Paperwork Reduction Act Notice**, see page 34.

:: FORM 1040A

Individuals who meet these conditions may file Form 1040A.

> **You can use Form 1040A for:**
>
> Any of four filing statuses
>
> All exemptions you are entitled to
>
> All qualified dependents
>
> Income from:
> Wages, salaries, tips
> Interest and dividends
> Unemployment compensation
> Less than $50,000 in taxable income
>
> Partial charitable contributions deduction
>
> Deduction for a married couple when both work
>
> Partial credit for political contributions
>
> Earned income credit

Those who file Form 1040A may have any one of four filing statuses. These are:

> **Filing status:**
> Single, married filing joint, married filing separate, or head of household

A completed Form 1040A appears in Example 2.
Comments on lines of Form 1040A.

(11)

Use the following worksheet to figure your deduction:	(a) You	(b) Your Spouse
A. Wages, salaries, tips (from line 6 of Form 1040A).	A. $ 22580 —	$ 1780. —
B. Write amount from column (a) or (b) above, whichever is smaller.		B. $ 1780. —
C. Multiply the amount on line B by 5% (.05).		C. x .05
D. Write your answer here and on line 11 of Form 1040A.		D. $ 89. —

(13) Use same form as (4) on p. 379.

(19a) Use Table 24 (p. T-34–T-38).

DO EXERCISE 2 (p. 384).

Example 2 Complete.

Department of the Treasury—Internal Revenue Service

Form 1040A US Individual Income Tax Return (0)

OMB No. 1545-0085

Step 1
Name and address

Use the IRS mailing label. Otherwise, print or type.

Your first name and initial (if joint return, also give spouse's name and initial)   Last name
Janice M and Jim W Hunter

Your social security no.
167-50-2849

Present home address
416 Edge Road

Spouse's social security no.
261-35-2431

City, town or post office, State, and ZIP code
Lewisburg PA 17837

Your occupation **Merchandiser**
Spouse's occupation **Toolmaker**

Presidential Election Campaign Fund

Do you want $1 to go to this fund? . . . . ☑Yes ☐No
If joint return, does your spouse want $1 to go to this fund? ☑Yes ☐No

Step 2
Filing status
(Check only one)
and Exemptions

Attach Copy B of Forms W-2 here

1 ☐ Single (See if you can use Form 1040EZ.)
2 ☑ Married filing joint return (even if only one had income)
3 ☐ Married filing separate return. Enter spouse's social security no. above and full name here. _____
4 ☐ Head of household (with qualifying person). If the qualifying person is your unmarried child but not your dependent, write this child's name here. _____

Always check the exemption box labeled Yourself. Check other boxes if they apply.

5a ☑ Yourself   ☐ 65 or over   ☐ Blind
  b ☑ Spouse   ☐ 65 or over   ☐ Blind   **Ted**
  c First names of your dependent children who lived with you ____ **Ted** ____

Write number of boxes checked on 5a and b **2**

Write number of children listed on 5c **1**

  d Other dependents:

(1) Name	(2) Relationship	(3) Number of months lived in your home.	(4) Did dependent have income of $1,000 or more?	(5) Did you provide more than one-half of dependent's support?

Write number of other dependents listed on 5d ☐

  e Total number of exemptions claimed . . . .

Add numbers entered in boxes above **3**

Step 3
Adjusted gross income

6 Wages, salaries, tips, etc. *(Attach Forms W-2)* . . . . | 6 | **24360.—**
7 Interest income *(Complete page 2 if over $400 or you have any All-Savers interest)* . . . . | 7 | **170.—**
8a Dividends _____ (Complete page 2 if over $400) 8b Exclusion _____ Subtract line 8b from 8a | 8c |
9a Unemployment compensation (insurance). Total from Form(s) 1099-UC _____
  b Taxable amount, if any, from worksheet on page 16 of Instructions . . . . | 9b |
10 Add lines 6, 7, 8c, and 9b. This is your total income. . . . . | 10 | **24530.—**
⑪ Deduction for a married couple when both work. Complete the worksheet on page 17. . . . | 11 | **89.—**
12 Subtract line 11 from line 10. This is your adjusted gross income. . . . . . | 12 | **24441.—**

Step 4
Taxable income

⑬ Allowable part of your charitable contributions. Complete the worksheet on page 18. . . | 13 | **25.—**
14 Subtract line 13 from line 12 . . . . | 14 | **24416.—**
15 Multiply $1,000 by the total number of exemptions claimed in box 5e . . . . . | 15 | **3000.—**
16 Subtract line 15 from line 14. This is your taxable income. . . . . | 16 | **21416.—**

Step 5
Tax, credits, and payments

Attach check or money order here

17a Partial credit for political contributions. See page 19. . . . . . . ■17a
  b Total Federal income tax withheld, from W-2 form(s). *(If line 6 is more than $32,400, see page 19.)* . . . . 17b **3380 —**

Stop Here and Sign Below if You Want IRS to Figure Your Tax

  c Earned income credit, from worksheet on page 21 . . . . 17c
18 Add lines 17a, b, and c. These are your total credits and payments. . . . . . | 18 | **3380.—**
⑲a Find tax on amount on line 16. Use tax table, pages 26-31. . . . . 19a **3243.—**
  b Advance EIC payment *(from W-2 form(s))* 19b
20 Add lines 19a and 19b. This is your total tax. . . . . | 20 | **3243.—**

Step 6
Refund or amount you owe

21 If line 18 is larger than line 20, subtract line 20 from line 18. Enter the amount to be **refunded to you** . . . . | 21 | **137.—**
22 If line 20 is larger than line 18, subtract line 18 from line 20. Enter the **amount you owe.** Attach payment for full amount payable to "Internal Revenue Service." . . . 22 |

Step 7
Sign your return

I have read this return and any attachments filed with it. Under penalties of perjury, I declare that to the best of my knowledge and belief, the return and attachments are correct and complete.

▶ *Janice Hunter*   **april 1, 1987**   ▶ *Jim W. Hunter*
Your signature   Date   Spouse's signature (If filing jointly, BOTH must sign)

Paid preparer's signature ____ Date ____ Check if self-employed ☐ Preparer's social security no. ____

Firm's name (or yours, if self-employed) ____ E.I. no. ____
Address and Zip code ____

For **Privacy Act and Paperwork Reduction Act Notice,** see page 34.

* Circled numbers are explained on the preceding page.

2. Provide the necessary information in the white spaces. Your wages were $35,520 and your spouse's $1500. Use your name and a fictitious spouse (if not married). Use Table 24 (p. T-34–T-38).

Department of the Treasury — Internal Revenue Service

Form 1040A US Individual Income Tax Return (0)

OMB No. 1545-0085

Step 1
Name and address

Use the IRS mailing label. Otherwise, print or type.

Your first name and initial (if joint return, also give spouse's name and initial)	Last name	Your social security no.
Present home address		Spouse's social security no.
City, town or post office, State, and ZIP code	Your occupation	
	Spouse's occupation	

Presidential Election Campaign Fund

Do you want $1 to go to this fund?...................☐ Yes ☐ No
If joint return, does your spouse want $1 to go to this fund? ☐ Yes ☐ No

Step 2
Filing status
(Check only one)
and Exemptions

1 ☐ Single (See if you can use Form 1040EZ.)
2 ☑ Married filing joint return (even if only one had income)
3 ☐ Married filing separate return. Enter spouse's social security no. above and full name here. _____
4 ☐ Head of household (with qualifying person). If the qualifying person is your unmarried child but not your dependent, write this child's name here. _____

Always check the exemption box labeled Yourself. Check other boxes if they apply.

5a ☑ Yourself ☐ 65 or over ☐ Blind
 b ☑ Spouse ☐ 65 or over ☐ Blind

Write number of boxes checked on 5a and b ☐ **2**

c First names of your dependent children who lived with you _____

Write number of children listed on 5c ☐

Attach Copy B of Forms W-2 here

d Other dependents: (1) Name	(2) Relationship	(3) Number of months lived in your home.	(4) Did dependent have income of $1,000 or more?	(5) Did you provide more than one-half of dependent's support?

Write number of other dependents listed on 5d ☐

e Total number of exemptions claimed ....

Add numbers entered in boxes above ☐ **2**

Step 3
Adjusted gross income

6 Wages, salaries, tips, etc. (Attach Forms W-2)................. 6 **37020 —**
7 Interest income (Complete page 2 if over $400 or you have any All-Savers interest)...... 7 **110 —**
8a Dividends _____ . (Complete page 2 if over $400) 8b Exclusion _____ . Subtract line 8b from 8a 8c
9a Unemployment compensation (insurance). Total from Form(s) 1099-UC
 b Taxable amount, if any, from worksheet on page 16 of Instructions................ 9b
10 Add lines 6, 7, 8c, and 9b. This is your total income. 10
11 Deduction for a married couple when both work. Complete the worksheet on page 17..... 11
12 Subtract line 11 from line 10. This is your adjusted gross income. 12

Step 4
Taxable income

13 Allowable part of your charitable contributions. Complete the worksheet on page 18...... 13 **15 —**
14 Subtract line 13 from line 12................. 14
15 Multiply $1,000 by the total number of exemptions claimed in box 5e.......... 15
16 Subtract line 15 from line 14. This is your taxable income................ 16

Step 5
Tax, credits, and payments

Attach check or money order here

17a Partial credit for political contributions. See page 19........ ■ 17a
 b Total Federal income tax withheld, from W-2 form(s). (If line 6 is more than $32,400, see page 19.)................ 17b **8300 —**

Stop Here and Sign Below if You Want IRS to Figure Your Tax

 c Earned income credit, from worksheet on page 21.......... 17c
18 Add lines 17a, b, and c. These are your total credits and payments........ 18
19a Find tax on amount on line 16. Use tax table, pages 26-31...... 19a
 b Advance EIC payment (from W-2 form(s))............. 19b
20 Add lines 19a and 19b. This is your total tax................ 20

Step 6
Refund or amount you owe

21 If line 18 is larger than line 20, subtract line 20 from line 18. Enter the amount to be **refunded to you**................ 21
22 If line 20 is larger than line 18, subtract line 18 from line 20. Enter the **amount you owe.** Attach payment for full amount payable to "Internal Revenue Service."....... 22

Step 7
Sign your return

I have read this return and any attachments filed with it. Under penalties of perjury, I declare that to the best of my knowledge and belief, the return and attachments are correct and complete.

Your signature	Date	Spouse's signature (If filing jointly, BOTH must sign)
Paid preparer's signature	Date	Check if self-employed ☐	Preparer's social security no.
Firm's name (or yours, if self-employed)		E.I. no.
Address and Zip code		

• Provide the necessary information in the white spaces. Use Table 24 (p. T-34–T-38) and your own own and address.

1.

Department of the Treasury — Internal Revenue Service

Form 1040EZ Income Tax Return for Single filers with no dependents (0)

OMB No. 1545-0675

Instructions are on the back of this form.
Tax Table is in the 1040EZ and 1040A Tax Package.

Name and address

Use the IRS mailing label. If you don't have a label, print or type:

Name (first, initial, last)	Social security number
Present home address	
City, town or post office, State, and ZIP code	

Presidential Election Campaign Fund
Check this box ☐ if you want $1 of your tax to go to this fund.

Figure your tax

Attach Copy B of Forms W-2 here

1	Wages, salaries, and tips. Attach your W-2 form(s).	1	14780.—
2	Interest income of $400 or less. If more than $400, you cannot use Form 1040EZ.	2	70.—
3	Add line 1 and line 2. This is your **adjusted gross income**.	3	.
4	Allowable part of your charitable contributions. Complete the worksheet on page 18. Do not write more than $25.	4	15.—
5	Subtract line 4 from line 3.	5	.
6	Amount of your personal exemption.	6	1,000.00
7	Subtract line 6 from line 5. This is your **taxable income**.	7	.
8	Enter your Federal income tax withheld. This is shown on your W-2 form(s).	8	2340.—
9	Use the tax table on pages 26-31 to find the **tax** on your taxable income on line 7.	9	.

Refund or amount you owe

Attach tax payment here

10	If line 8 is larger than line 9, subtract line 9 from line 8. Enter the amount of your **refund**.	10	.
11	If line 9 is larger than line 8, subtract line 8 from line 9. Enter the **amount you owe**. Attach check or money order for the full amount payable to "Internal Revenue Service."	11	.

Sign your return

I have read this return. Under penalties of perjury, I declare that to the best of my knowledge and belief, the return is correct and complete.

Your signature	Date
X	

2.

Department of the Treasury — Internal Revenue Service

Form 1040EZ Income Tax Return for
Single filers with no dependents (0)

OMB No. 1545-0675

Instructions are on the back of this form.
Tax Table is in the 1040EZ and 1040A Tax Package.

Name and address

Use the IRS mailing label. If you don't have a label, print or type:

Name (first, initial, last)	Social security number
Present home address	
City, town or post office, State, and ZIP code	

Presidential Election Campaign Fund
Check this box ☐ if you want $1 of your tax to go to this fund.

Figure your tax

Attach Copy B of Forms W-2 here

1	Wages, salaries, and tips. Attach your W-2 form(s).	1	27810. —
2	Interest income of $400 or less. If more than $400, you cannot use Form 1040EZ.	2	130. —
3	Add line 1 and line 2. This is your **adjusted gross income.**	3	.
4	Allowable part of your charitable contributions. Complete the worksheet on page 18. Do not write more than $25.	4	15. —
5	Subtract line 4 from line 3.	5	.
6	Amount of your personal exemption.	6	1,000.00
7	Subtract line 6 from line 5. This is your **taxable income.**	7	.
8	Enter your Federal income tax withheld. This is shown on your W-2 form(s).	8	6270. —
9	Use the tax table on pages 26-31 to find the **tax** on your taxable income on line 7.	9	.

Refund or amount you owe

Attach tax payment here

10	If line 8 is larger than line 9, subtract line 9 from line 8. Enter the amount of your **refund.**	10	.
11	If line 9 is larger than line 8, subtract line 8 from line 9. Enter the **amount you owe.** Attach check or money order for the full amount payable to "Internal Revenue Service."	11	.

Sign your return

I have read this return. Under penalties of perjury, I declare that to the best of my knowledge and belief, the return is correct and complete.

Your signature	Date
X	

For **Privacy Act and Paperwork Reduction Act Notice,** see page 34.

Provide the necessary information in the white spaces. Use Table 24 (p. T-34–T-38), your name (and a fictitious spouse when needed).

3.

Department of the Treasury — Internal Revenue Service

Form 1040A US Individual Income Tax Return (0)

OMB No. 1545-0085

Step 1
Name and address

Use the IRS mailing label. Otherwise, print or type.

Your first name and initial (if joint return, also give spouse's name and initial)	Last name	Your social security no.

Present home address | Spouse's social security no.

City, town or post office, State, and ZIP code | Your occupation | Spouse's occupation

Presidential Election Campaign Fund

Do you want $1 to go to this fund? .... ☐ Yes ☐ No
If joint return, does your spouse want $1 to go to this fund? ☐ Yes ☐ No

Step 2
Filing status
(Check only one)
and Exemptions

Attach Copy B of Forms W-2 here

1 ☐ Single (See if you can use Form 1040EZ.)
2 ☑ Married filing joint return (even if only one had income)
3 ☐ Married filing separate return. Enter spouse's social security no. above and full name here. _____
4 ☐ Head of household (with qualifying person). If the qualifying person is your unmarried child but not your dependent, write this child's name here. _____

Always check the exemption box labeled Yourself. Check other boxes if they apply.

5a ☑ Yourself ☐ 65 or over ☐ Blind   Write number of boxes checked on 5a and b **2**
  b ☑ Spouse   ☐ 65 or over ☐ Blind

  c First names of your dependent children who lived with you _____
  JEFF, Jill   Write number of children listed on 5c **2**

  d Other dependents:
  (1) Name | (2) Relationship | (3) Number of months lived in your home | (4) Did dependent have income of $1,000 or more? | (5) Did you provide more than one-half of dependent's support?

  Write number of other dependents listed on 5d ☐

  e Total number of exemptions claimed .... Add numbers entered in boxes above **4**

Step 3
Adjusted gross income

6 Wages, salaries, tips, etc. (Attach Forms W-2) .... 6 **48260.—**
7 Interest income (Complete page 2 if over $400 or you have any All-Savers interest) .... 7 **140.—**
8a Dividends _____ (Complete page 2 if over $400) 8b Exclusion _____ Subtract line 8b from 8a 8c
9a Unemployment compensation (insurance). Total from Form(s) 1099-UC _____
  b Taxable amount, if any, from worksheet on page 16 of Instructions 9b
10 Add lines 6, 7, 8c, and 9b. This is your total income. 10
11 Deduction for a married couple when both work. Complete the worksheet on page 17...... 11 **170.—**
12 Subtract line 11 from line 10. This is your adjusted gross income. 12

Step 4
Taxable income

13 Allowable part of your charitable contributions. Complete the worksheet on page 18... 13 **20.—**
14 Subtract line 13 from line 12.. 14
15 Multiply $1,000 by the total number of exemptions claimed in box 5e........ 15
16 Subtract line 15 from line 14. This is your taxable income. 16

Step 5
Tax, credits, and payments

Attach check or money order here

17a Partial credit for political contributions. See page 19 ...... ■ 17a
  b Total Federal income tax withheld, from W-2 form(s). (If line 6 is more than $32,400, see page 19.) .... 17b **8271.—**

Stop Here and Sign Below if You Want IRS to Figure Your Tax

  c Earned income credit, from worksheet on page 21 .... 17c
18 Add lines 17a, b, and c. These are your total credits and payments. 18
19a Find tax on amount on line 16. Use tax table, pages 26-31..... 19a
  b Advance EIC payment (from W-2 form(s)) 19b
20 Add lines 19a and 19b. This is your total tax. 20

Step 6
Refund or amount you owe

21 If line 18 is larger than line 20, subtract line 20 from line 18. Enter the amount to be **refunded to you** 21
22 If line 20 is larger than line 18, subtract line 18 from line 20. Enter the **amount you owe.** Attach payment for full amount payable to "Internal Revenue Service." 22

Step 7
Sign your return

I have read this return and any attachments filed with it. Under penalties of perjury, I declare that to the best of my knowledge and belief, the return and attachments are correct and complete.

► Your signature | Date | ► Spouse's signature (If filing jointly, BOTH must sign)

Paid preparer's signature | Date | Check if self-employed ☐ | Preparer's social security no.

Firm's name (or yours, if self-employed) | E.I. no.
Address and Zip code

4.

Department of the Treasury — Internal Revenue Service

Form 1040A US Individual Income Tax Return (0)

OMB No. 1545-0085

Step 1
Name and address

Use the IRS mailing label. Otherwise, print or type.

Your first name and initial (if joint return, also give spouse's name and initial) | Last name | Your social security no.

Present home address | Spouse's social security no.

City, town or post office, State, and ZIP code | Your occupation
| Spouse's occupation

Presidential Election Campaign Fund

Do you want $1 to go to this fund?............ ☐ Yes ☐ No
If joint return, does your spouse want $1 to go to this fund? ☐ Yes ☐ No

Step 2
Filing status
(Check only one)
and Exemptions

Attach Copy B of Forms W-2 here

1 ☑ Single (See if you can use Form 1040EZ.)
2 ☐ Married filing joint return (even if only one had income)
3 ☐ Married filing separate return. Enter spouse's social security no. above and full name here. _____
4 ☐ Head of household (with qualifying person). If the qualifying person is your unmarried child but not your dependent, write this child's name here. _____

Always check the exemption box labeled Yourself. Check other boxes if they apply.

5a ☑ Yourself ☐ 65 or over ☐ Blind
b ☐ Spouse ☐ 65 or over ☐ Blind

Write number of boxes checked on 5a and b | **1**

c First names of your dependent children who lived with you _____

Write number of children listed on 5c | ☐

d Other dependents:

(1) Name	(2) Relationship	(3) Number of months lived in your home.	(4) Did dependent have income of $1,000 or more?	(5) Did you provide more than one-half of dependent's support?
ETHEL	MOTHER	12	NO	YES

Write number of other dependents listed on 5d | **1**

e Total number of exemptions claimed ....

Add numbers entered in boxes above | **2**

Step 3
Adjusted gross income

6 Wages, salaries, tips, etc. *(Attach Forms W-2)*................ **6** | *25100* —
7 Interest income *(Complete page 2 if over $400 or you have any All-Savers interest)*...... **7** | *225* —
8a Dividends _____ (Complete page 2 if over $400) **8b** Exclusion _____ Subtract line 8b from 8a | **8c**
9a Unemployment compensation (insurance). Total from Form(s) 1099-UC _____
b Taxable amount, if any, from worksheet on page 16 of Instructions...... **9b**
10 Add lines 6, 7, 8c, and 9b. This is your total income............ **10**
11 Deduction for a married couple when both work. Complete the worksheet on page 17...... **11**
12 Subtract line 11 from line 10. This is your adjusted gross income............ **12**

Step 4
Taxable income

13 Allowable part of your charitable contributions. Complete the worksheet on page 18...... **13** | *10* —
14 Subtract line 13 from line 12............ **14**
15 Multiply $1,000 by the total number of exemptions claimed in box 5e...... **15**
16 Subtract line 15 from line 14. This is your taxable income............ **16**

Step 5
Tax, credits, and payments

Attach check or money order here

17a Partial credit for political contributions. See page 19....... ■ **17a** _____
b Total Federal income tax withheld, from W-2 form(s). *(If line 6 is more than $32,400, see page 19.)*...... **17b** | *4705* —

Stop Here and Sign Below if You Want IRS to Figure Your Tax

c Earned income credit, from worksheet on page 21.......... **17c**
18 Add lines 17a, b, and c. These are your total credits and payments............ **18**
19a Find tax on amount on line 16. Use tax table, pages 26-31...... **19a**
b Advance EIC payment *(from W-2 form(s))*.......... **19b**
20 Add lines 19a and 19b. This is your total tax............ **20**

Step 6
Refund or amount you owe

21 If line 18 is larger than line 20, subtract line 20 from line 18. Enter the amount to be **refunded to you**............ **21**
22 If line 20 is larger than line 18, subtract line 18 from line 20. Enter the **amount you owe.** Attach payment for full amount payable to "Internal Revenue Service."............ **22**

Step 7
Sign your return

I have read this return and any attachments filed with it. Under penalties of perjury, I declare that to the best of my knowledge and belief, the return and attachments are correct and complete.

▶ Your signature | Date | ▶ Spouse's signature (If filing jointly, BOTH must sign)

Paid preparer's signature | Date | Check if self-employed ☐ | Preparer's social security no.

ANSWERS

5. _____

✓ **SKILL MAINTENANCE**

5. You deposit $2000 at the beginning of each of 25 successive years into a retirement account which pays 12% compounded annually. How much is the accumulated amount at the end of the 25th year?

If you miss an item, review the indicated section and objective.

[14.1, •] **1.** Find the gross earnings of John Kendall who accepts the sewing machine operator position and works 35 hours a week.

1. _____

SEWING MACHINE OP Operate semi-automatic short-cycle buttonhole, stitching mach. Position garments, adjust stitch'h cutt'g mechanism. Familiar w/semi-automatic short-cycle machine reqd. 2 yrs exp. $4.50/hr. 35/hrs/wk 924-2262

2. _____

[14.1, ••] **2.** Hartono Harjadi, a machine assembler, is paid $4.65 for each unit assembled. Find the amount Hartono earned in one day if he assembled eight units.

3. _____

[14.1, ::] **3.** Carole Larkin earns $4.10 for each unit produced and produced 105 in one 45-hour week. Calculate her gross earnings.

[14.2, •] **4.** Find the biweekly pay for David Minard whose monthly salary is $1300.

4. _____

[14.2, •] **5.** Find the weekly pay for Paul King, a registered nurse, who earns $1475 a month.

5. _____

[14.2, ••] **6.** Kim Sowards earns a 10% commission on sales made and a 3% commission on supervised employees sales. Sales for Kim were $30,000 and for supervised employees were $98,000. How much was Kim's commission?

6. _____

[14.2, •••] **7.** Mary Tyszkiewicz, a utility salesperson, earns $310 for a 40-hour week plus a commission of 5% on sales. Utility sales last week were $2700 and hours worked 42. How much did she earn?

7. _____

[14.3, •] **8.** Use the percentage method to find the amount of federal income tax withheld weekly from the pay of Ching-Ming Wang, a single taxpayer earning $330 a week and claiming three exemptions. Use Tables 21 and 22, pp. T-30 and T-31.

[14.3, ••] **9.** Use the wage bracket method to find the amount of federal income tax withheld monthly from the pay of Diane Rover, a married taxpayer earning $1420 a month and claiming four exemptions. Use Table 23, p. T-33.

[14.3, •••] **10.** Catherine Lund earned $43,200 in 1986. How much social security tax did Catherine pay if the maximum taxable earnings were $42,000, and the rate was 7.15%?

[14.3, ⋮⋮] **11.** Christopher Juni earned $47,000 in 1986. How much social security tax did Christopher pay if the maximum taxable earnings were $42,000, and the rate was 12.3%?

[14.4, •] **12.** Compute the net pay for Steve Kepley who is married, earns $705 weekly, and claims six exemptions. The only deductions are for federal income tax and social security (7.51%). Use Table 23, p. T-33.

[14.4, •••] For the following payroll data list, find

13. The current gross pay

14. The current social security tax

EMP C/C	REGULAR	PREMIUM	VAC	SICK	P/L	HOL	GONE	VAC LEFT	VAC USED	P/L LEFT	P/L USED	PAY ADJ AMT	CHECK NO.
295 / 701	76.0				4			120.0		25.2	20.0		62283
	385.32				20.28								

FIC GROSS	GROSS	FEDERAL	STATE	DISAB	FICA	MEDICAL	STOCK	AUTO	SAVINGS	OTHER	NET	
405.60	405.60	70.52	13.00		24.54				24.34		273.20	C/E
2805.48	2846.04	447.88	86.72		169.73	59.55			170.79		1911.37	YTD

[14.5, •] **15.** Provide the necessary information in the white spaces. Use your own name and Table 24 (p. T-34–T-38).

Department of the Treasury — Internal Revenue Service

Form 1040EZ Income Tax Return for Single filers with no dependents (0)

OMB No. 1545-0675

Instructions are on the back of this form.
Tax Table is in the 1040EZ and 1040A Tax Package.

Name and address

Use the IRS mailing label. If you don't have a label, print or type:

Name (first, initial, last)	Social security number
Present home address	
City, town or post office, State, and ZIP code	

Presidential Election Campaign Fund
Check this box ☐ if you want $1 of your tax to go to this fund.

Figure your tax

Attach Copy B of Forms W-2 here

1 Wages, salaries, and tips. Attach your W-2 form(s).	1	24820.—
2 Interest income of $400 or less. If more than $400, you cannot use Form 1040EZ.	2	70.—
3 Add line 1 and line 2. This is your **adjusted gross income.**	3	
4 Allowable part of your charitable contributions. Complete the worksheet on page 18. Do not write more than $25.	4	25.—
5 Subtract line 4 from line 3.	5	
6 Amount of your personal exemption.	6	1,000.00
7 Subtract line 6 from line 5. This is your **taxable income.**	7	.
8 Enter your Federal income tax withheld. This is shown on your W-2 form(s).	8	5200.—
9 Use the tax table on pages 26-31 to find the **tax** on your taxable income on line 7.	9	.

Refund or amount you owe

Attach tax payment here

10 If line 8 is larger than line 9, subtract line 9 from line 8. Enter the amount of your **refund.**	10	.
11 If line 9 is larger than line 8, subtract line 8 from line 9. Enter the **amount you owe.** Attach check or money order for the full amount payable to "Internal Revenue Service."	11	.

Sign your return

I have read this return. Under penalties of perjury, I declare that to the best of my knowledge and belief, the return is correct and complete.

Your signature	Date
X	

For **Privacy Act and Paperwork Reduction Act Notice**, see page 34.

[14.5, ●●] **16.** Provide the necessary information in the white spaces. Use your name (and a fictitious spouse if not married) and Table 24 (p. T-34–T-38).

Department of the Treasury — Internal Revenue Service
Form 1040A US Individual Income Tax Return (0)

OMB No. 1545-0085

Step 1
Name and address

Use the IRS mailing label. Otherwise, print or type.

| Your first name and initial (if joint return, also give spouse's name and initial) | Last name | Your social security no. |

Present home address | Spouse's social security no.

City, town or post office, State, and ZIP code | Your occupation

Spouse's occupation

Presidential Election Campaign Fund

Do you want $1 to go to this fund?..................... ☐ Yes ☐ No
If joint return, does your spouse want $1 to go to this fund? ☐ Yes ☐ No

Step 2
Filing status
(Check only one)
and Exemptions

1 ☐ Single (See if you can use Form 1040EZ.)
2 ☑ Married filing joint return (even if only one had income)
3 ☐ Married filing separate return. Enter spouse's social security no. above and full name here. _____
4 ☐ Head of household (with qualifying person). If the qualifying person is your unmarried child but not your dependent, write this child's name here. _____

Always check the exemption box labeled Yourself. Check other boxes if they apply.

5a ☑ Yourself   ☐ 65 or over   ☐ Blind | Write number of boxes checked on 5a and b [2]
 b ☑ Spouse   ☐ 65 or over   ☐ Blind
 c First names of your dependent children who lived with you _____
   SARA | Write number of children listed on 5c [1]

Attach Copy B of Forms W-2 here

d Other dependents:

(1) Name	(2) Relationship	(3) Number of months lived in your home.	(4) Did dependent have income of $1,000 or more?	(5) Did you provide more than one-half of dependent's support?

Write number of other dependents listed on 5d [ ]

 e Total number of exemptions claimed .... | Add numbers entered in boxes above [3]

Step 3
Adjusted gross income

6 Wages, salaries, tips, etc. *(Attach Forms W-2)* .... 6 **27460. —**
7 Interest income *(Complete page 2 if over $400 or you have any All-Savers interest)* ...... 7 **210. —**
8a Dividends _____ . (Complete page 2 if over $400) 8b Exclusion _____ Subtract line 8b from 8a 8c
9a Unemployment compensation (insurance). Total from Form(s) 1099-UC
 b Taxable amount, if any, from worksheet on page 16 of Instructions 9b
10 Add lines 6, 7, 8c, and 9b. This is your total income. 10
11 Deduction for a married couple when both work. Complete the worksheet on page 17..... 11 **112. —**
12 Subtract line 11 from line 10. This is your adjusted gross income........... 12

Step 4
Taxable income

13 Allowable part of your charitable contributions. Complete the worksheet on page 18..... 13 **20. —**
14 Subtract line 13 from line 12 14
15 Multiply $1,000 by the total number of exemptions claimed in box 5e 15
16 Subtract line 15 from line 14. This is your taxable income........... 16

Step 5
Tax, credits, and payments

Attach check or money order here

17a Partial credit for political contributions. See page 19........ ■17a .
 b Total Federal income tax withheld, from W-2 form(s). *(If line 6 is more than $32,400, see page 19.)* .... 17b **3540 —**

Stop Here and Sign Below if You Want IRS to Figure Your Tax

 c Earned income credit, from worksheet on page 21 .... 17c
18 Add lines 17a, b, and c. These are your total credits and payments.......... 18
19a Find tax on amount on line 16. Use tax table, pages 26-31...... 19a .
 b Advance EIC payment *(from W-2 form(s))* 19b
20 Add lines 19a and 19b. This is your total tax............ 20

Step 6
Refund or amount you owe

21 If line 18 is larger than line 20, subtract line 20 from line 18. Enter the amount to be **refunded to you** 21
22 If line 20 is larger than line 18, subtract line 18 from line 20. Enter the **amount you owe.** Attach payment for full amount payable to "Internal Revenue Service." 22

Step 7
Sign your return

I have read this return and any attachments filed with it. Under penalties of perjury, I declare that to the best of my knowledge and belief, the return and attachments are correct and complete.

► Your signature | Date | ► Spouse's signature (If filing jointly, BOTH must sign)

Paid preparer's signature | Date | Check if self-employed ☐ | Preparer's social security no.

Firm's name (or yours, if self-employed) | E.I. no.
Address and Zip code

For **Privacy Act and Paperwork Reduction Act Notice,** see page 34.

Chapter 14   Payroll

Copyright © 1987 by Addison-Wesley Publishing Company, Inc.

PART FOUR
STATISTICS

15

STATISTICS AND GRAPHS

CAREER: DATA PROCESSING/ TELETYPE OPERATOR   This is Toni Venezia. Toni works at a brokerage firm, operating a computer teletype machine that transmits up-to-the-minute stock and bond orders to the stock exchanges in New York City.

TONI VENEZIA

This is an important job as large orders for stocks or bonds can make or lose thousands of dollars in a very short time. To do her job well, Toni must have a knowledge of fractions, ratios, percent, interest, taxes, financial statements, stocks and bonds, and statistics, all of which have been covered in this text. Data Processors usually earn between $14,000 and $20,000.

Toni received a BS degree in Business and Marketing from Indiana University. She has worked in the brokerage business for several years as a sales assistant, cashier, and teletype operator. Toni is dedicated, enjoys working with people, and likes to take on new responsibilities, all of which help her to make a success of anything she does.

Her hobbies include water skiing, tennis, swimming, and aerobic exercise.

O B J E C T I V E S

After finishing Section 15.1, you should be able to:

•	**Determine the mean or average.**
••	**Determine the median.**
•••	**Determine the mode.**

Find the average of each set of numbers.

1. 24, 185, 46

2. 85, 46.8, 105.7, 22.1

3. A student made the following scores on four tests: 78, 81, 82, and 79. What was the average score?

4. One day a car dealer sold five cars for the following amounts: $6800.94 $7680.49, $9834.88, $12,340.90, $7200.00. What was the average amount of each sale? Round to the nearest cent.

ANSWERS ON PAGE A-19

Averages, Medians, and Modes

In this chapter we discuss various ways to organize data into graphs. We also learn to analyze data with measures of central tendency such as averages, medians, and modes.

| • | **AVERAGES** |

Suppose we have a set of data and we wanted to pick one number that is representative, typical, or "central." There are several kinds of such numbers. One is called the **average.**

Suppose a person made the following salaries over a four-week period.

Week 1	$259.70
Week 2	$263.85
Week 3	$284.40
Week 4	$271.93

What is the *average* of the salaries? First, we add the salaries:

$259.70 + $263.85 + $284.40 + $271.93 = $1079.88.

Second, we divide by the number of addends:

$$\frac{\$1079.88}{4} = \$269.97.$$

Note that

$259.70 + $263.85 + $284.40 + $271.93 = $1079.88,

and that

($269.97) + ($269.97) + ($269.97) + ($269.97) = $1079.88.

The number $269.97 is called the average, **arithmetic mean,** or **mean** of the set of salaries.

To find the *average* of a set of numbers,

a) add them; and

b) divide by the number of addends.

Example 1 On a five-day trip a car was driven the following number of kilometers each day: 340, 402, 380, 305, and 314. What was the average number of kilometers per day?

Solution

$$\frac{340 + 402 + 380 + 305 + 314}{5} = \frac{1741}{5} = 348.2$$

The car was driven an average of 348.2 km per day. Thus, if the car had been driven exactly 348.2 km each day, it would have gone exactly the same total distance, 1741 km.

DO EXERCISES 1–4.

Sometimes we know the sum and need only divide.

Example 2 According to EPA estimates in a recent year, a Plymouth Gran Fury was expected to travel 546 miles (highway) on 26 gallons of gasoline. What was the average number of miles per gallons?

Solution

$$\frac{546}{26} = 21$$

The average was 21 miles per gallon.

DO EXERCISE 5.

Example 3 The following are the yearly salaries of the employees of Raggs, Ltd., a clothing store. What is the average salary?

Number	Type	Salary
1	Owner	$22,000
4	Salesperson	19,000
2	Secretary	17,000
1	Custodian	16,000

Solution

a) We first find out how much is paid in salaries:

$1 \cdot \$22,000 = \quad \$22,000$
$4 \cdot \$19,000 = \quad 76,000$
$2 \cdot \$17,000 = \quad 34,000$
$1 \cdot \$16,000 = \quad \underline{16,000}$
$\qquad\qquad\qquad \$148,000 \qquad$ Total salaries paid.

b) Then we divide by the number of people employed:

$$\frac{\$148,000}{8} = \$18,500.$$

The average salary is $18,500.

DO EXERCISE 6.

5. According to EPA estimates in a recent year, an Oldsmobile 88 was expected to travel 660 miles (highway) on 22 gallons of gasoline. What was the average number of miles per gallon?

6. The following are the salaries at the Rollo Motorcycle Shop. What is the average salary?

Number	Type	Salary
1	Owner	$22,000
2	Salesperson	18,500
2	Secretary	16,000
1	Custodian	15,500

ANSWERS ON PAGE A-19

Find the median.

7. 20, 13, 17, 14, 18

8. 18, 18, 18, 18, 18

Find the median.

9. 18, 14, 16, 13, 19, 20

10. 38, 34, 77, 33, 37, 99

11. 7, 6, 7, 5, 8, 9

Find the mode(s).

12. 88, 76, 88, 91, 91, 88, 88, 91, 112

13. 203, 201, 201, 201, 201, 202, 203, 203, 200, 203

ANSWERS ON PAGE A-19

● ● **MEDIANS**

A student makes the following amounts selling magazines:

$79, $82, $83, $77, $85.

Listing the amounts in order, we have

$77, $79, $82, $83, $85.

The middle amount, $82, is called the **median.**

DO EXERCISES 7 AND 8.

If the data set has an odd number of values, there will always be a middle value. If the set of data has an even number of values, there will be two middle values.

If there are two middle values, the median is the number halfway between, that is, the average of the two middle values.

Example 4 Find the median: 34, 33, 35, 36.

Solution

a) Arrange the numbers in order.

33, 34, 35, 36

b) The median is the average of 34 and 35.

33, 34, 35, 36

⌐—————— The median is 34.5. Add 34 and 35 and divide by 2.

DO EXERCISES 9–11.

● ● ● **MODES**

The **mode** of a set of numbers is that number which appears most often.

Example 5 Find the mode: 4, 13, 15, 13, 17, 17, 19, 17.

Solution

a) Arrange the numbers in order.

4, 13, 13, 15, 17, 17, 17, 19

b) The number that appears most often, the mode, is 17.

Sometimes a set of numbers has more than one mode.

Example 6 Find the mode(s): 49, 50, 50, 51, 52, 53, 53, 59.

Solution This set of numbers has two modes: 50 and 53.

DO EXERCISES 12 AND 13.

Find the average, median, and mode of each set of numbers.

1. 18, 17, 25, 25, 25, 22

2. 62, 73, 73, 78, 82

3. 5, 10, 15, 20, 25, 15, 36

4. 32, 27, 25, 13, 13, 4

5. $6.30, $7.70, $9.40, $9.40

6. $23.40, $23.40, $12.60, $42.90

7. 1, 2, 3, 4, 5

8. 9, 9, 9, 9, 9

9. The following prices per pound of hamburger were found at five supermarkets:

$1.59, $1.49, $1.69, $1.79, $1.79.

What was the average price per pound?

10. The following prices per pound of steak were found at five supermarkets:

$3.99, $3.79, $3.89, $3.99, $4.09.

What was the average price per pound?

11. According to EPA estimates in a recent year, a Ford Escort wagon was expected to travel 779 miles (highway) on 19 gallons of gasoline. What was the average number of miles per gallon?

12. According to EPA estimates in a recent year, a Chevrolet Camaro was expected to travel 672 miles (highway) on 21 gallons of gasoline. What was the average number of miles per gallon?

13. The following are the yearly salaries of the employees of Campus Sports Shop. What is the average salary?

Number	Type	Salary
1	Owner	$24,600
5	Salesperson	19,800
3	Secretary	17,400
1	Custodian	16,500

ANSWERS

1. _____

2. _____

3. _____

4. _____

5. _____

6. _____

7. _____

8. _____

9. _____

10. _____

11. _____

12. _____

13. _____

14. The following are the yearly salaries of the employees of Pizza, Unltd. What is the average salary? Round to the nearest cent.

Number	Type	Salary
1	Manager	$18,400
3	Waiters and waitresses	11,200
2	Cooks	11,400
1	Custodian	9,500

15. Joleen Fisk obtained the following scores on five tests:

76, 79, 81, 81, 93.

What was the average? the median? the mode?

16. Mohammad Ghobadi made the following salaries over a four-week period:

$269.70, $273.85, $294.40, $273.85.

What was the average? the median? the mode?

Find the average, median, and mode of each set of numbers.

17. ▦ Price of IBM stock: $141\frac{1}{4}$, $134\frac{1}{8}$, $137\frac{3}{8}$, $135\frac{5}{8}$, $134\frac{1}{8}$, 139, $140\frac{1}{8}$, $137\frac{7}{8}$. (Round to three decimal places.)

18. ▦ Attendances at a recent world series: 56,668, 56,691, 55,992, 55,995, 55,955, 56,407. (Round to the nearest one.)

▦ *Bowling Averages.* Computing a bowling average involves a special kind of rounding. In effect, we never round up. For example, suppose Ted Spitz gets a total of 599 for 3 games. To find the average, we divide 599 by 3 and drop the amount to the right of the decimal point:

$$\frac{599}{3} \approx 199.67 \qquad \text{Ted's average is 199.}$$

In each case find the bowling average.

19. 547 pins in 3 games

20. 4621 pins in 27 games

21. To get a B in math a student must average 80 on five tests. Scores on the first four tests were 80, 74, 81, and 75. What is the lowest score the student can get on the last test and still get a B?

22. To get an A in math a student must average 90 on five tests. Scores on the first four tests were 90, 91, 81, and 92. What is the lowest score the student can get on the last test and still get an A?

✓ **SKILL MAINTENANCE**

23. Paul Bollins knows that consumers will pay at most $4.50 for a meat thermometer and wants a 17% markup based on the selling price. What is the maximum cost that Paul's business can pay for the thermometer?

24. Rick Murphy, a buyer for E-Z Markets, knows that consumers will pay at most $25.50 for a humidifier-vaporizer and wants a 28% markup based on the selling price. What is the maximum cost that Rick Murphy can pay for the humidifier-vaporizer?

15.2

Bar Graphs and Frequency Distributions

• BAR GRAPHS

A bar graph is shown below. Such a graph is convenient for showing comparisons. The bars may be vertical or horizontal.

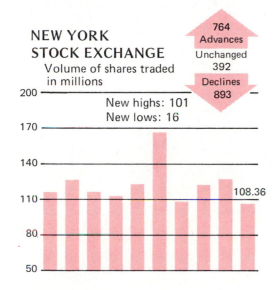

Example 1 Make a bar graph of the data in this table.

Year	Sales of XYZ Pub. Co. (in millions)
1984	$50
1985	55
1986	53
1987	57
1988	62

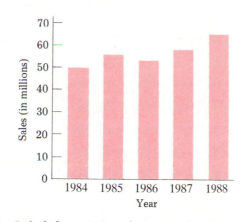

Solution

a) Draw and label a vertical axis. Label the axis in relation to the data.

b) Draw and label a horizontal axis.

c) Draw vertical bars to show the sales each year.

The graph is shown in the right margin. Of course, we start the ''Year'' data with the first year for which we have data (in this case, 1984) instead of with the year 0.

DO EXERCISE 1.

1. Make a bar graph for the data in the table.

Year	Net Income of Luby's Cafeterias, Inc. (in millions)
1981	$ 9.8
1982	11.6
1983	13.9
1984	17.4
1985	19.6

ANSWER ON PAGE A-19

2. Make a bar graph of this frequency distribution.

Salary	Frequency
$32,000	1
$29,000	4
$27,000	2
$26,000	1

ANSWER ON PAGE A-19

• • FREQUENCY DISTRIBUTIONS

When large sets of data are considered, it is sometimes convenient to group the data. For example, suppose we were analyzing the contributions of 266 people to a charity. Rather than make a graph of each of the contributions of the people, we group the data according to how many contributed, say, $50–$99, then how many contributed $100–$199, and so on.

Example 2 Make a bar graph of this frequency distribution.

Contribution	Frequency
Over $2500	2
$1500–$2499	11
$1000–$1499	19
$500–$999	24
$100–$499	20
$0–$99	10

Solution

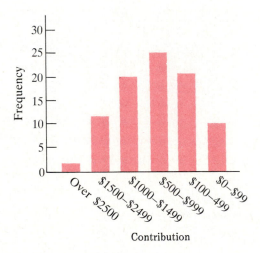

Frequencies are normally located on the vertical axis. The contributions are located on the horizontal axis. The result is six bars, one for each category.

DO EXERCISE 2.

A bar graph in which the rectangles are touching each other is called a histogram.

⊙ Make a bar graph for each of the following.

1.

IMPORTS (USSR TO U.S.)	
Product	**Amount (in millions)**
Light Fuel Oil	$178
Anhydrous ammonia	156
Palladium	60
Urea	52
Crabs	15

2.

Stock	Price Per Share
Texas Intl.	$ $6\frac{1}{8}$
Exxon	$53\frac{1}{4}$
Sears	$36\frac{7}{8}$
Caesar's World	15
American Motors	$2\frac{5}{8}$
General Motors	70

3.

Number of People in a Car Pool	Average Savings Per Person in a Car Pool Driving to Work
2	$427
3	553
4	617
5	654

4.

State	Average Income Per Person
Alaska	$16,820
Washington, D.C.	16,409
New Jersey	14,057
Indiana	10,567
Illinois	12,626
Ohio	11,254

5.

Olympic Winners in Women's 100-Meter Dash	Time (Seconds)
Betty Cuthbert, Australia (1956)	11.5
Wilma Rudolph, United States (1960)	11.0
Wyomia Tyus, United States (1964)	11.4
Wyomia Tyus, United States (1968)	11.0
Renate Stecher, E. Germany (1972)	11.07
Annegret Richter, W. Germany (1976)	11.01

6.

Location	Annual Growth Rate
Western Sahara	10.6%
Mexico	3.5
U.S. Virgin Islands	9.6
Guam	5.0
United States	0.8
U.S.S.R	1.0
World	1.9

● ● Make a bar graph of each frequency distribution.

9. _____

7.

Letter	Frequency of Occurrence for Every 100 Letters of Writing
A	8
E	13
I	7
O	8
U	3

8.

Gasoline Sales in One Day at a Service Station	Frequency
Over $30	1
$25–$29.99	8
$20–$24.99	15
$15–$19.99	20
$10–$14.99	18
$0–$9.99	13

✓ **SKILL MAINTENANCE**

9. Market Securities, Ltd, a brokerage firm, sells 298 shares of a stock for $79,566. What is the value of each share?

10. _____

10. There are 220,522,442 people in the United States. The area of the United States is 3,615,122 square miles. How many people are there per square mile?

Chapter 15   Statistics and Graphs

15.3

Line Graphs and Circle Graphs

LINE GRAPHS

An example of a line graph is shown below. Line graphs are useful for showing comparisons.

After finishing Section 15.3, you should be able to:
- Make a line graph for a set of data.
- Make a circle graph for a set of data.

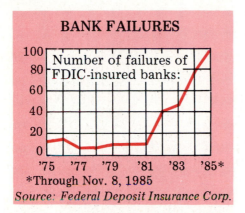

BANK FAILURES

Number of failures of FDIC-insured banks:

*Through Nov. 8, 1985
Source: Federal Deposit Insurance Corp.

Example 1 Make a line graph of this set of data.

Month	Prime Rate (%)
June	10
July	13
August	20
Sept	14

1. Make a line graph for the data in the table below.

Year	Estimated sales (in millions)
1988	$17.0
1990	19.5
1992	17.8
1994	18.1

Solution

a) Draw and label a vertical axis. We label it starting with some number less than or equal to all numbers in the table. In this case we start with 10, and mark units that are multiples of 5%.

b) Draw and label a horizontal axis.

c) We start at each month and move up to its corresponding percentage, and mark a point.

d) Connect each pair of points with a line.

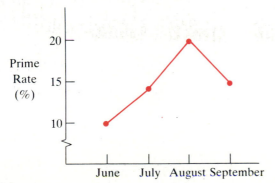

Prime Rate (%)

June   July   August September

DO EXERCISE 1.

ANSWER ON PAGE A-19

●● CIRCLE GRAPHS

Below is a circle graph prepared by the Indiana Gas Company for its customers. It shows how each customer's dollar is spent. Circle graphs are usually used to show percentage parts of a quantity.

How We Spend Each Customer's Dollar On An Annual Basis

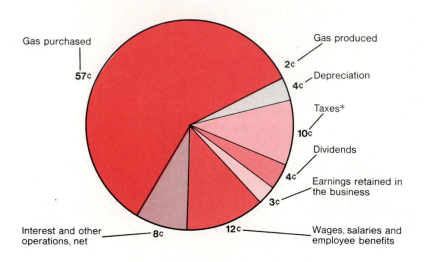

Gas purchased 57¢

Gas produced 2¢

Depreciation 4¢

Taxes* 10¢

Dividends 4¢

Earnings retained in the business 3¢

Wages, salaries and employee benefits 12¢

Interest and other operations, net 8¢

*Does not include sales tax paid by our customers

Example 2 Complete the table and make a circle graph.

Item	Average Monthly Budget Costs for a Family of Four with an Intermediate Income*	Percent	Angle
Food	$ 442		
Housing	427		
Transportation	152		
Clothing	168		
Medical care	183		
Personal care	38		
Other goods and services (reading, recreation, education, etc,.)	94		
Other items such as job expenses, contributions, life insurance, etc.	81		
Total	$1585		

* According to the Bureau of Labor Statistics.

Solution

a) Find what percent each item is of the total, and multiply by 360°, the total number of degrees in a circle.

$\dfrac{442}{1585} \approx 28\%$, $28\% \times 360° = 0.28 \times 360° \approx 101°$

$\dfrac{427}{1585} \approx 27\%$, $27\% \times 360° = 0.27 \times 360° \approx 97°$

$\dfrac{152}{1585} \approx 10\%$, $10\% \times 360° = 0.10 \times 360° \approx 36°$

$\dfrac{168}{1585} \approx 11\%$, $11\% \times 360° = 0.11 \times 360° \approx 40°$

$\dfrac{183}{1585} \approx 12\%$, $12\% \times 360° = 0.12 \times 360° \approx 43°$

$\dfrac{38}{1585} \approx 2\%$, $2\% \times 360° = 0.02 \times 360° \approx 7°$

$\dfrac{94}{1585} \approx 6\%$, $6\% \times 360° = 0.06 \times 360° \approx 22°$

$\dfrac{81}{1585} \approx 5\%$, $5\% \times 360° = 0.05 \times 360° \approx 18°$

Notice that due to rounding the degrees do not add to 360.

2. Complete the table and make a circle graph.

Hair Color	Number of Students	Percent	Angle
Black	11		
Brown	14		
Blonde	4		
Red	3		
Total	32		

b) Draw the circle and a radius.

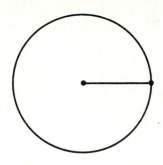

c) Draw angles with measures from the table.

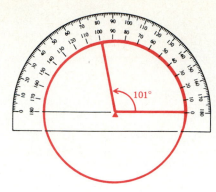

101°

d) Label each part of the circle with the corresponding item and percent.

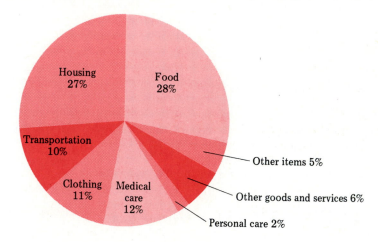

Housing 27%

Food 28%

Transportation 10%

Clothing 11%

Medical care 12%

Other items 5%

Other goods and services 6%

Personal care 2%

DO EXERCISE 2.

ANSWERS ON PAGE A-20

• Make a line graph for each of the following.

1.

Time of Repayment (in Months)	Total Amount Due on a Car Loan of $3000 at 11% Interest (Assuming Monthly Payments)
18	$3268
24	3356
30	3445
36	3536

2.

Year	Estimated U.S. Population (in millions)
1987	242
1989	246
1991	250
1993	255
1995	260
1997	265

3.

Week	Amount Spent for Recreation
1	$10.00
2	14.50
3	8.00
4	16.25
5	12.75

4.

Distance (in Miles)	Cost of 5-min Weekday Direct Dial Phone Call
50	$1.69
100	1.89
150	1.94
200	2.04
250	2.04
300	2.14

Make two graphs together. Use a solid line (—) for men and a dashed line (---) for women.

5.

Height (in Inches)	Desirable Weight for Medium Frame	
	Men	Women
63	133	122
64	136	126
65	139	130
66	143	135
67	147	139
68	152	143

6.

Age	Average Number of Remaining Years of Life	
	Men	Women
50	24	30
55	20	26
60	17	22
65	14	18
70	11	14

Complete each table and make a circle graph.

7.

Deodorant	Number Preferring	Percent	Angle
A	34		
B	26		
C	38		
D	2		
Total	100		

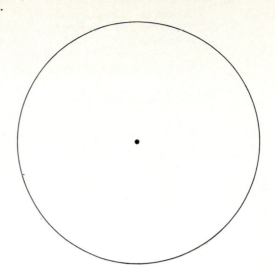

8.

Fast-food Restaurant	Number Preferring	Percent	Angle
A	22		
B	30		
C	12		
D	16		
Total	80		

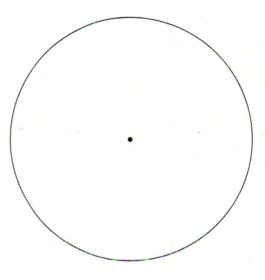

9.

SMALL BUSINESS LOCATIONS
(fewer than 500 people at one site)

Region	Percent	Angle
Pacific	15.3	
West	5.6	
Central	24.6	
South	16.5	
Atlantic	16.1	
Northeast	21.9	

10.

Number of TV Sets in Household	Percent of Homes in U.S. in 1975	Angle
0	3	
1	51	
2 or more	46	

11.

CAR SALES FOR NOVEMBER

Manufacturer	Percent	Angle
General Motors	57.0	
Ford	23.7	
Chrysler	13.3	
Volkswagen	1.2	
American Motors	1.5	
Honda	2.2	
Nissan	1.2	

12.

Sandwich	Percent who Purchased	Angle
Hamburger	42	
Cheeseburger	38	
Fish	10	
Hot dog	10	

13. _____

14. _____

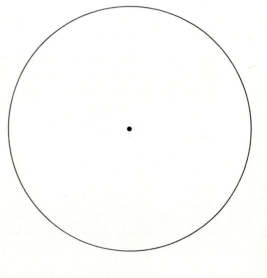

✓ SKILL MAINTENANCE

13. What percent of $289 is $109?

14. What is 25% of $579?

If you miss an item, review the indicated section and objective.

[15.1, •] Find the average, median, and mode of each set of numbers.

[15.1, • •] **1.** 45, 64, 46, 45, 47, 50, 51, 68

[15.1, • • •] **2.** $1.89, $1.79, $2.49, $1.69, $1.80, $1.89

[15.2, •] **3.** Make a bar graph.

Sandwich	Calories
Hamburger	249
Cheeseburger	309
Fish	406
Double hamburger	350

[15.3, •] **4.** Make a line graph

End of Year	Average Cash Value of $10,000 Whole Life Insurance Policy
0	$ 0
5	490
10	1270
15	2000
20	2790

ANSWERS

1. _____

2. _____

[15.3, • •] **5.** Make a circle graph.

Brand of Denim Jeans	Number Purchased	Percent	Angle
A	5		
B	16		
C	10		
D	19		
Total	50		

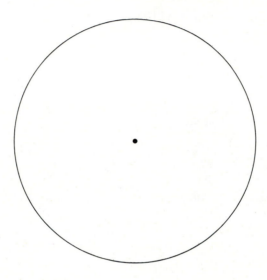

[15.2, • •] **6.** Make a bar graph of this frequency distribution.

Test Scores	Frequency
90–100	8
80–89	10
70–79	20
60–69	5
0–59	2

APPENDIX:

THE METRIC SYSTEM

The Metric System

The **metric system** is used in almost every country in the world. Although there is some resistance to change, it is slowly being used more and more in the United States. Like the U.S. monetary system, the metric system is based on the number 10. Since our numbering system is also based on 10, using the metric system is advantageous.

| • | LENGTH

The basic unit of length is the **meter.** It is just a bit longer than a yard. The other units of length are products of a meter by 10, 100, and 1000, or by fractions of a meter, $\frac{1}{10}$, $\frac{1}{100}$, and $\frac{1}{1000}$.

1 **kilo**meter (km)	= 1000 meters (m)
1 **hecto**meter (hm)	= 100 meters (m)
1 **deka**meter (dam)	= 10 meters (m)
1 **deci**meter (dm)	= $\frac{1}{10}$ meter (m)
1 **centi**meter (cm)	= $\frac{1}{100}$ meter (m)
1 **milli**meter (mm)	= $\frac{1}{1000}$ meter (m)

It will be helpful to memorize the metric prefixes shown in italics on the chart above. Think of *kilo-* for 1000; *centi-* for $\frac{1}{100}$; and so on. These prefixes are used with other metric measures as well as with length.

Converting Metric Lengths

Suppose we want to change 7.84 kilometers to meters. Note the following:

$$7.84 \text{ km} = 7.84 \times 1 \text{ km}$$
$$= 7.84 \times 1000 \text{ m} \qquad 1 \text{ km} = 1000 \text{ m}$$
$$= 7840 \text{ m.}$$

The conversion amounted only to a movement of the decimal point. Think of this in terms of changing 56.9 feet to inches. A multiplication by 12 is necessary and this is much more awkward. Changing from one unit to another in the metric system amounts only to the movement of a decimal point. To see how this works look at the prefix table.

1000	100	10	1	0.1	0.01	0.001
km	hm	dam	m	dm	cm	mm

Each unit in the table is 10 times that to its right and 0.1 times that to its left. Let us see how to use the table when we wish to convert.

Appendix: The Metric System

Example 1 Complete: 5.7 m = _____ cm.

Solution *Think:* To go from "m" to "cm" in the table is a move of 2 places to the right.

| km | hm | dam | m | dm | cm | mm |

2 places

We move the decimal point 2 places to the right.

5.7   5.7̣0.

Thus, 5.7 cm = 570 cm.

Example 2 Complete: 6.91 mm = _____ cm.

Solution *Think:* To go from "mm" to "cm" in the table is a move of 1 place to the left.

| km | hm | dam | m | dm | cm | mm |

1 place

We move the decimal point 1 place to the left.

6.9 1   0.̣6.9 1

Thus, 6.91 mm = 0.691 cm.

DO EXERCISES 1–4.

⠒ CAPACITY

The metric unit of capacity (volume) is the *liter.* A liter is just a bit more than a quart. The liter is defined as follows.

> 1 liter (L) = 1000 cubic centimeters (1000 cm³) = 1000 mL
> = 1 cubic decimeter (1 dm³)
> 1 mL = 0.001 L = 1 cm³

The notation "cc" is also used for cubic centimeter, particularly in medicine. The script letter ℓ is also used for liter. The milliliter (mL) is the most frequently used unit of capacity.

Changing Metric Capacities

We again use a prefix table to convert metric capacities.

1000	100	10	1	0.1	0.01	0.001
kL	hL	daL	L	dL	cL	mL

Complete.

1. 7.106 mm = _____ cm

2. 2.997 km = _____ cm

3. 56.89 mm = _____ dm

4. 7.3 m = _____ cm

ANSWERS ON PAGE A-21

Complete.

5. 0.84 L = _____ mL

6. 7660 mL = _____ L

Example 3 Complete: 8.9 L = _____ mL.

Solution Think: To go from "L" to "mL" in the table is a move of 3 places to the right.

kL   hL   daL   L   dL   cL   mL

3 places

We move the decimal point 3 places to the right.

8.9   8.9 0 0.

Thus, 8.9 L = 8900 mL.

Example 4 Complete: 314 mL = _____ L.

Solution Think: To go from "mL" to "L" in the table is a move of 3 places to the left.

Therefore, we move the decimal point 3 places to the left.

3 1 4.   0.3 1 4.

Thus, 314 mL = 0.314 L.

DO EXERCISES 5 AND 6.

••• MASS

There is a difference between weight and mass even though the words are often used as though they had the same meaning. **Mass** may be measured on a balance scale and always stays the same. **Weight** is related to the gravitational pull on an object and varies with the distance that the object is from the center of the earth. The basic unit of mass is the gram (g), which is the mass of 1 cubic centimeter (1 cm^3 or 1 mL) of water at a temperature of 4° Celsius. A gram is therefore a small unit of mass.

The following table shows metric units of mass. Again, we have the same prefixes and the addition of another—the metric ton, t, which is 1000 kilograms.

1 metric ton (t) = 1000 kilograms (kg)	1 decigram (dg) = $\frac{1}{10}$ g
1 kilogram (kg) = 1000 grams (g)	
1 hectogram (hg) = 100 g	1 centigram (cg) = $\frac{1}{100}$ g
1 dekagram (dag) = 10 g	1 milligram (mg) = $\frac{1}{1000}$ g

Changing Metric Masses

We again use a prefix table to convert metric masses.

1000	100	10	1	0.1	0.01	0.001
kg	hg	dag	g	dg	cg	mg

Appendix: The Metric System

Example 5 Complete: 9 kg = _____ g.

Solution Think: To go from "kg" to "g" in the table is a move of 3 places to the right.

kg   hg   dag   g   dg   cg   mg

3 places

We move the decimal point 3 places to the right.

9.   9.0 0 0.

Thus, 9 kg = 9000 g

Example 6 Complete: 5662 g = _____ kg.

Solution Think: To go from "g" to "kg" in the table is a move of 3 places to the left.

Therefore, we move the decimal point 3 places to the left.

5 6 6 2.   5.6 6 2.

Thus, 5662 g = 5.662 kg.

DO EXERCISES 7–10.

:: TEMPERATURE

The metric temperature scale is called **Celsius** (sometimes **centigrade**). Below we see how Celsius (C) compares with the American measure, **Fahrenheit** (F).

> **1.** **To convert from Celsius to Fahrenheit:**
>
> $$F = \frac{9}{5} \cdot C + 32, \quad \text{or} \quad F = 1.8 \times C + 32.$$
>
> **Multiply by $\frac{9}{5}$, or 1.8, and then add 32.**
>
> **2.** **To convert from Fahrenheit to Celsius:**
>
> $$C = \frac{5}{9} \cdot (F - 32).$$
>
> **Subtract 32 and then multiply by $\frac{5}{9}$.**

Example 7 Convert 37° Celsius (normal body temperature) to Fahrenheit.

Solution

$$F = 1.8 \times 37° + 32° \qquad \text{Substitute 37° into the equation}$$
$$= 66.6° + 32°$$
$$= 98.6°$$

Complete.

7. 8.3 kg = _____ g

8. 209.4 g = _____ kg

9. 2.1 cg = _____ mg

10. 6788 mg = _____ cg

ANSWERS ON PAGE A-21

Convert to Celsius.

11. 25°F (A cold day)

12. 32°F (Water freezes)

Convert to Fahrenheit.

13. 20°C (Room temperature)

14. −22°C (Typical temperature during the day on Mars)

ANSWERS ON PAGE A-21

Example 8 Convert 104°F to Celsius.

Solution

$$C = \frac{5}{9} \cdot (104 - 32) \qquad \text{First subtract 32 from 104°.}$$

$$= \frac{5}{9} \cdot 72 \qquad \text{Then multiply by } \frac{5}{9}.$$

$$= 40°$$

DO EXERCISE 11–14.

Appendix: The Metric System

● Complete.

1. a) 1 km = _____ m
   b) 1 m = _____ km

2. a) 1 dm = _____ m
   b) 1 m = _____ dm

3. a) 1 hm = _____ m
   b) 1 m = _____ hm

4. a) 1 dam = _____ m
   b) 1 m = _____ dam

5. a) 1 mm = _____ m
   b) 1 m = _____ mm

6. a) 1 cm = _____ m
   b) 1 m = _____ cm

7. 7.8 km = _____ m

8. 10 km = _____ m

9. 87 cm = _____ m

10. 0.344 cm = _____ m

11. 7801 m = _____ km

12. 8110 m = _____ km

13. 65.55 m = _____ km

14. 7.999 m = _____ km

15. 7999 m = _____ cm

16. 546 m = _____ cm

17. 788 cm = _____ m

18. 1.08 mm = _____ m

19. 3.11 m = _____ cm

20. 4.22 m = _____ dm

21. 1 mm = _____ cm

22. 1 cm = _____ km

23. 1 km = _____ cm

24. 2 km = _____ cm

25. 4500 mm = _____ cm

26. 8 200 000 m = _____ km

27. 1.3 dam = _____ dm

28. 8 km = _____ hm

29. 0.014 mm = _____ dm

30. 672 dam = _____ km

31. 6.88 m = _____ dam

32. 1.8 m = _____ hm

●● Complete.

33. 1 L = _____ mL = _____ cm³

34. _____ L = 1 mL = _____ cm³

35. 96 L = _____ mL

36. 801 L = _____ mL

37. 69 mL = _____ L

38. 19 mL = _____ L

39. 0.703 mL = _____ L

40. 0.012 mL = _____ L

41. 8.012 L = _____ mL

42. 1.009 L = _____ mL

●●● Complete.

43. 1 kg = _____ g

44. 1 hg = _____ g

45. 1 dag = _____ g

ANSWERS

1. _____
2. _____
3. _____
4. _____
5. _____
6. _____
7. _____
8. _____
9. _____
10. _____
11. _____
12. _____
13. _____
14. _____
15. _____
16. _____
17. _____
18. _____
19. _____
20. _____
21. _____
22. _____
23. _____
24. _____
25. _____
26. _____
27. _____
28. _____
29. _____
30. _____
31. _____
32. _____
33. _____
34. _____
35. _____
36. _____
37. _____
38. _____
39. _____
40. _____
41. _____
42. _____
43. _____
44. _____
45. _____

46. 1 dg = _____ g   **47.** 1 cg = _____ g   **48.** 1 g = _____ mg

49. 1 g = _____ cg   **50.** 1 g = _____ dg   **51.** 25 kg = _____ g

52. 345 kg = _____ g   **53.** 789 g = _____ kg   **54.** 6300 g = _____ kg

55. 0.705 kg = _____ g   **56.** 97 kg = _____ g   **57.** 57 cg = _____ g

58. 0.833 dg = _____ g   **59.** 7890 g = _____ kg   **60.** 6788 g = _____ kg

61. 78 mg = _____ cg   **62.** 89.2 mg = _____ cg   **63.** 0.7 kg = _____ cg

64. 0.01 kg = _____ mg   **65.** 4 hg = _____ kg   **66.** 2 dag = _____ hg

67. 3.4 cg = _____ dag   **68.** 3.2 dg = _____ mg   **69.** 1 t = _____ kg

70. 2 t = _____ kg

:: Convert.

Convert to Fahrenheit. Use the formula $F = \frac{9}{5} \cdot C + 32$, or $1.8 \times C + 32$.

71. 65°C   **72.** 50°C   **73.** 15°C   **74.** 90°C

75. 30.6°C (Butter melts)   **76.** 4.4°C (Ideal temperature for refrigeration of food)

Convert to Celsius. Use the formula $C = \frac{5}{9} \cdot (F - 32)$.

77. 140°F   **78.** 131°F   **79.** 59°F   **80.** 86°F

81. 1832°F (Melting point of gold)   **82.** 98.6°F (Normal body temperature)

TABLES

Table 1   Day of the Year   T–1
Table 2   Simple Interest on $100 (360-day Basis)   T–2
Table 3   Simple Interest on $100 (365-day Basis)   T–3
Table 4   Compound Interest   T–4
Table 5   Daily Compound Interest on $100 (365-day Basis)   T–6
Table 6   Daily Compound Interest on $100 (360-day Basis)   T–7
Table 7   5% Compounded Daily (360-day Basis)   T–8
Table 8   5% Compounded Continuously (360-day Basis)   T–8
Table 9   Present Value   T–9
Table 10   Amount of Annuity $S_{\overline{n}|i}$ T–11
Table 11   Present Value of Annuity $A_{\overline{n}|i}$ T–12
Table 12   Annual Percentage Rate Table for Monthly Payment Plans   T–13
Table 13   Monthly Payment Required to Amortize a Loan   T–20
Table 14   Betterment (Depreciation) Guide   T–24
Table 15   Homeowner's Insurance Rates   T–25
Table 16   Basic Premium for Automobile Insurance (Six Months)   T–26
Table 17   Rating Factors   T–26
Table 18   Life Insurance   T–26
Table 19   Table of Values   T–27
Table 20   Ordinary Life (per $1000)   T–28
Table 21   Percentage Method Income Tax Withholding Table   T–29
Table 22   Tables for Percentage Method of Withholding   T–29
Table 23   Federal Income Tax Withholding Tables   T–30
Table 24   Federal Income Tax Tables   T–34

TABLES

TABLE 1
DAY OF THE YEAR

DAY	THIS YEAR											
	DAYS IN EACH MONTH											
	31	28	31	30	31	30	31	31	30	31	30	31
	JAN	FEB	MAR	APR	MAY	JUN	JUL	AUG	SEP	OCT	NOV	DEC
DAY 1	1	32	60	91	121	152	182	213	244	274	305	335
DAY 2	2	33	61	92	122	153	183	214	245	275	306	336
DAY 3	3	34	62	93	123	154	184	215	246	276	307	337
DAY 4	4	35	63	94	124	155	185	216	247	277	308	338
DAY 5	5	36	64	95	125	156	186	217	248	278	309	339
DAY 6	6	37	65	96	126	157	187	218	249	279	310	340
DAY 7	7	38	66	97	127	158	188	219	250	280	311	341
DAY 8	8	39	67	98	128	159	189	220	251	281	312	342
DAY 9	9	40	68	99	129	160	190	221	252	282	313	343
DAY 10	10	41	69	100	130	161	191	222	253	283	314	344
DAY 11	11	42	70	101	131	162	192	223	254	284	315	345
DAY 12	12	43	71	102	132	163	193	224	255	285	316	346
DAY 13	13	44	72	103	133	164	194	225	256	286	317	347
DAY 14	14	45	73	104	134	165	195	226	257	287	318	348
DAY 15	15	46	74	105	135	166	196	227	258	288	319	349
DAY 16	16	47	75	106	136	167	197	228	259	289	320	350
DAY 17	17	48	76	107	137	168	198	229	260	290	321	351
DAY 18	18	49	77	108	138	169	199	230	261	291	322	352
DAY 19	19	50	78	109	139	170	200	231	262	292	323	353
DAY 20	20	51	79	110	140	171	201	232	263	293	324	354
DAY 21	21	52	80	111	141	172	202	233	264	294	325	355
DAY 22	22	53	81	112	142	173	203	234	265	295	326	356
DAY 23	23	54	82	113	143	174	204	235	266	296	327	357
DAY 24	24	55	83	114	144	175	205	236	267	297	328	358
DAY 25	25	56	84	115	145	176	206	237	268	298	329	359
DAY 26	26	57	85	116	146	177	207	238	269	299	330	360
DAY 27	27	58	86	117	147	178	208	239	270	300	331	361
DAY 28	28	59	87	118	148	179	209	240	271	301	332	362
DAY 29	29	0	88	119	149	180	210	241	272	302	333	363
DAY 30	30	0	89	120	150	181	211	242	273	303	334	364
DAY 31	31	0	90	0	151	0	212	243	0	304	0	365

ADD 1 DAY FOR LEAP YEAR IF FEBRUARY 29 FALLS BETWEEN THE TWO DATES

TABLE 2
SIMPLE INTEREST ON $100 (360-DAY BASIS)

DAY	11.50 % INTEREST	DAY	11.75 % INTEREST	DAY	12.00 % INTEREST	DAY	12.25 % INTEREST	DAY	12.50 % INTEREST	DAY	12.75 % INTEREST
1	0.031944	1	0.032639	1	0.033333	1	0.034028	1	0.034722	1	0.035417
2	0.063889	2	0.065278	2	0.066667	2	0.068056	2	0.069444	2	0.070833
3	0.095833	3	0.097917	3	0.100000	3	0.102083	3	0.104167	3	0.106250
4	0.127778	4	0.130556	4	0.133333	4	0.136111	4	0.138889	4	0.141667
5	0.159722	5	0.163194	5	0.166667	5	0.170139	5	0.173611	5	0.177083
6	0.191667	6	0.195833	6	0.200000	6	0.204167	6	0.208333	6	0.212500
7	0.223611	7	0.228472	7	0.233333	7	0.238194	7	0.243056	7	0.247917
8	0.255556	8	0.261111	8	0.266667	8	0.272222	8	0.277778	8	0.283333
9	0.287500	9	0.293750	9	0.300000	9	0.306250	9	0.312500	9	0.318750
10	0.319444	10	0.326389	10	0.333333	10	0.340278	10	0.347222	10	0.354167
11	0.351389	11	0.359028	11	0.366667	11	0.374306	11	0.381944	11	0.389583
12	0.383333	12	0.391667	12	0.400000	12	0.408333	12	0.416667	12	0.425000
13	0.415278	13	0.424306	13	0.433333	13	0.442361	13	0.451389	13	0.460417
14	0.447222	14	0.456944	14	0.466667	14	0.476389	14	0.486111	14	0.495833
15	0.479167	15	0.489583	15	0.500000	15	0.510417	15	0.520833	15	0.531250
16	0.511111	16	0.522222	16	0.533333	16	0.544444	16	0.555556	16	0.566667
17	0.543056	17	0.554861	17	0.566667	17	0.578472	17	0.590278	17	0.602083
18	0.575000	18	0.587500	18	0.600000	18	0.612500	18	0.625000	18	0.637500
19	0.606944	19	0.620139	19	0.633333	19	0.646528	19	0.659722	19	0.672917
20	0.638889	20	0.652778	20	0.666667	20	0.680556	20	0.694444	20	0.708333
21	0.670833	21	0.685417	21	0.700000	21	0.714583	21	0.729167	21	0.743750
22	0.702778	22	0.718056	22	0.733333	22	0.748611	22	0.763889	22	0.779167
23	0.734722	23	0.750694	23	0.766667	23	0.782639	23	0.798611	23	0.814583
24	0.766667	24	0.783333	24	0.800000	24	0.816667	24	0.833333	24	0.850000
25	0.798611	25	0.815972	25	0.833333	25	0.850694	25	0.868056	25	0.885417
26	0.830556	26	0.848611	26	0.866667	26	0.884722	26	0.902778	26	0.920833
27	0.862500	27	0.881250	27	0.900000	27	0.918750	27	0.937500	27	0.956250
28	0.894444	28	0.913889	28	0.933333	28	0.952778	28	0.972222	28	0.991667
29	0.926389	29	0.946528	29	0.966667	29	0.986806	29	1.006944	29	1.027083
30	0.958333	30	0.979167	30	1.000000	30	1.020833	30	1.041667	30	1.062500
31	0.990278	31	1.011806	31	1.033333	31	1.054861	31	1.076389	31	1.097917
32	1.022222	32	1.044444	32	1.066667	32	1.088889	32	1.111111	32	1.133333
33	1.054167	33	1.077083	33	1.100000	33	1.122917	33	1.145833	33	1.168750
34	1.086111	34	1.109722	34	1.133333	34	1.156944	34	1.180556	34	1.204167
35	1.118056	35	1.142361	35	1.166667	35	1.190972	35	1.215278	35	1.239583
36	1.150000	36	1.175000	36	1.200000	36	1.225000	36	1.250000	36	1.275000
37	1.181944	37	1.207639	37	1.233333	37	1.259028	37	1.284722	37	1.310417
38	1.213889	38	1.240278	38	1.266667	38	1.293056	38	1.319444	38	1.345833
39	1.245833	39	1.272917	39	1.300000	39	1.327083	39	1.354167	39	1.381250
40	1.277778	40	1.305556	40	1.333333	40	1.361111	40	1.388889	40	1.416667
41	1.309722	41	1.338194	41	1.366667	41	1.395139	41	1.423611	41	1.452083
42	1.341667	42	1.370833	42	1.400000	42	1.429167	42	1.458333	42	1.487500
43	1.373611	43	1.403472	43	1.433333	43	1.463194	43	1.493056	43	1.522917
44	1.405556	44	1.436111	44	1.466667	44	1.497222	44	1.527778	44	1.558333
45	1.437500	45	1.468750	45	1.500000	45	1.531250	45	1.562500	45	1.593750
46	1.469444	46	1.501389	46	1.533333	46	1.565278	46	1.597222	46	1.629167
47	1.501389	47	1.534028	47	1.566667	47	1.599306	47	1.631944	47	1.664583
48	1.533333	48	1.566667	48	1.600000	48	1.633333	48	1.666667	48	1.700000
49	1.565278	49	1.599306	49	1.633333	49	1.667361	49	1.701389	49	1.735417
50	1.597222	50	1.631944	50	1.666667	50	1.701389	50	1.736111	50	1.770833
30	0.958333	30	0.979167	30	1.000000	30	1.020833	30	1.041667	30	1.062500
60	1.916667	60	1.958333	60	2.000000	60	2.041667	60	2.083333	60	2.125000
90	2.875000	90	2.937500	90	3.000000	90	3.062500	90	3.125000	90	3.187500
120	3.833333	120	3.916667	120	4.000000	120	4.083333	120	4.166667	120	4.250000
150	4.791667	150	4.895833	150	5.000000	150	5.104167	150	5.208333	150	5.312500
180	5.750000	180	5.875000	180	6.000000	180	6.125000	180	6.250000	180	6.375000
210	6.708333	210	6.854167	210	7.000000	210	7.145833	210	7.291667	210	7.437500
240	7.666667	240	7.833333	240	8.000000	240	8.166667	240	8.333333	240	8.500000
270	8.625000	270	8.812500	270	9.000000	270	9.187500	270	9.375000	270	9.562500
300	9.583333	300	9.791667	300	10.000000	300	10.208333	300	10.416667	300	10.625000
330	10.541667	330	10.770833	330	11.000000	330	11.229167	330	11.458333	330	11.687500
360	11.500000	360	11.750000	360	12.000000	360	12.250000	360	12.500000	360	12.750000
365	11.659722	365	11.913194	365	12.166667	365	12.420139	365	12.673611	365	12.927083
366	11.691667	366	11.945833	366	12.200000	366	12.454167	366	12.708333	366	12.962500

TABLE 3
SIMPLE INTEREST ON $100 (365-DAY BASIS)

DAY	11.50 % INTEREST	DAY	11.75 % INTEREST	DAY	12.00 % INTEREST	DAY	12.25 % INTEREST	DAY	12.50 % INTEREST	DAY	12.75 % INTEREST
1	0.031507	1	0.032192	1	0.032877	1	0.033562	1	0.034247	1	0.034932
2	0.063014	2	0.064384	2	0.065753	2	0.067123	2	0.068493	2	0.069863
3	0.094521	3	0.096575	3	0.098630	3	0.100685	3	0.102740	3	0.104795
4	0.126027	4	0.128767	4	0.131507	4	0.134247	4	0.136986	4	0.139726
5	0.157534	5	0.160959	5	0.164384	5	0.167808	5	0.171233	5	0.174658
6	0.189041	6	0.193151	6	0.197260	6	0.201370	6	0.205479	6	0.209589
7	0.220548	7	0.225342	7	0.230137	7	0.234932	7	0.239726	7	0.244521
8	0.252055	8	0.257534	8	0.263014	8	0.268493	8	0.273973	8	0.279452
9	0.283562	9	0.289726	9	0.295890	9	0.302055	9	0.308219	9	0.314384
10	0.315068	10	0.321918	10	0.328767	10	0.335616	10	0.342466	10	0.349315
11	0.346575	11	0.354110	11	0.361644	11	0.369178	11	0.376712	11	0.384247
12	0.378082	12	0.386301	12	0.394521	12	0.402740	12	0.410959	12	0.419178
13	0.409589	13	0.418493	13	0.427397	13	0.436301	13	0.445205	13	0.454110
14	0.441096	14	0.450685	14	0.460274	14	0.469863	14	0.479452	14	0.489041
15	0.472603	15	0.482877	15	0.493151	15	0.503425	15	0.513699	15	0.523973
16	0.504110	16	0.515068	16	0.526027	16	0.536986	16	0.547945	16	0.558904
17	0.535616	17	0.547260	17	0.558904	17	0.570548	17	0.582192	17	0.593836
18	0.567123	18	0.579452	18	0.591781	18	0.604110	18	0.616438	18	0.628767
19	0.598630	19	0.611644	19	0.624658	19	0.637671	19	0.650685	19	0.663699
20	0.630137	20	0.643836	20	0.657534	20	0.671233	20	0.684932	20	0.698630
21	0.661644	21	0.676027	21	0.690411	21	0.704795	21	0.719178	21	0.733562
22	0.693151	22	0.708219	22	0.723288	22	0.738356	22	0.753425	22	0.768493
23	0.724658	23	0.740411	23	0.756164	23	0.771918	23	0.787671	23	0.803425
24	0.756164	24	0.772603	24	0.789041	24	0.805479	24	0.821918	24	0.838356
25	0.787671	25	0.804795	25	0.821918	25	0.839041	25	0.856164	25	0.873288
26	0.819178	26	0.836986	26	0.854795	26	0.872603	26	0.890411	26	0.908219
27	0.850685	27	0.869178	27	0.887671	27	0.906164	27	0.924658	27	0.943151
28	0.882192	28	0.901370	28	0.920548	28	0.939726	28	0.958904	28	0.978082
29	0.913699	29	0.933562	29	0.953425	29	0.973288	29	0.993151	29	1.013014
30	0.945205	30	0.965753	30	0.986301	30	1.006849	30	1.027397	30	1.047945
31	0.976712	31	0.997945	31	1.019178	31	1.040411	31	1.061644	31	1.082877
32	1.008219	32	1.030137	32	1.052055	32	1.073973	32	1.095890	32	1.117808
33	1.039726	33	1.062329	33	1.084932	33	1.107534	33	1.130137	33	1.152740
34	1.071233	34	1.094521	34	1.117808	34	1.141096	34	1.164384	34	1.187671
35	1.102740	35	1.126712	35	1.150685	35	1.174658	35	1.198630	35	1.222603
36	1.134247	36	1.158904	36	1.183562	36	1.208219	36	1.232877	36	1.257534
37	1.165753	37	1.191096	37	1.216438	37	1.241781	37	1.267123	37	1.292466
38	1.197260	38	1.223288	38	1.249315	38	1.275342	38	1.301370	38	1.327397
39	1.228767	39	1.255479	39	1.282192	39	1.308904	39	1.385616	39	1.362329
40	1.260274	40	1.287671	40	1.315068	40	1.342466	40	1.369863	40	1.397260
41	1.291781	41	1.319863	41	1.347945	41	1.376027	41	1.404110	41	1.432192
42	1.323288	42	1.352055	42	1.380822	42	1.409589	42	1.438356	42	1.467123
43	1.354795	43	1.384247	43	1.413699	43	1.443151	43	1.472603	43	1.502055
44	1.386301	44	1.416438	44	1.446575	44	1.476712	44	1.506849	44	1.536986
45	1.417808	45	1.448630	45	1.479452	45	1.510274	45	1.541096	45	1.571918
46	1.449315	46	1.480822	46	1.512329	46	1.543836	46	1.575342	46	1.606849
47	1.480822	47	1.513014	47	1.545205	47	1.577397	47	1.609589	47	1.641781
48	1.512329	48	1.545205	48	1.578082	48	1.610959	48	1.643836	48	1.676712
49	1.543836	49	1.577397	49	1.610959	49	1.644521	49	1.678082	49	1.711644
50	1.575342	50	1.609589	50	1.643836	50	1.678082	50	1.712329	50	1.746575
30	0.945205	30	0.965753	30	0.986301	30	1.006849	30	1.027397	30	1.047945
60	1.890411	60	1.931507	60	1.972603	60	2.013699	60	2.054795	60	2.095890
90	2.835616	90	2.897260	90	2.958904	90	3.020548	90	3.082192	90	3.143836
120	3.780822	120	3.863014	120	3.945205	120	4.027397	120	4.109589	120	4.191781
150	4.726027	150	4.828767	150	4.931507	150	5.034247	150	5.136986	150	5.239726
180	5.671233	180	5.794521	180	5.917808	180	6.041096	180	6.164384	180	6.287671
210	6.616438	210	6.760274	210	6.904110	210	7.047945	210	7.191781	210	7.335616
240	7.561644	240	7.726027	240	7.890411	240	8.054795	240	8.219178	240	8.383562
270	8.506849	270	8.691781	270	8.876712	270	9.061644	270	9.246575	270	9.431507
300	9.452055	300	9.657534	300	9.863014	300	10.068493	300	10.273973	300	10.479452
330	10.397260	330	10.623288	330	10.849315	330	11.075342	330	11.301370	330	11.527397
360	11.342466	360	11.589041	360	11.835616	360	12.082192	360	12.328767	360	12.575342
365	11.500000	365	11.750000	365	12.000000	365	12.250000	365	12.500000	365	12.750000
366	11.531507	366	11.782192	366	12.032877	366	12.283562	366	12.534247	366	12.784932

TABLE 4
COMPOUND INTEREST (AMOUNT WHEN $1.00 IS COMPOUNDED)

Period	¼%	½%	¾%	1%	1¼%	1½%	1¾%	2%	2½%	3%
1	1.002500	1.005000	1.007500	1.010000	1.012500	1.015000	1.017500	1.020000	1.025000	1.030000
2	1.005006	1.010025	1.015056	1.020100	1.025156	1.030225	1.035306	1.040400	1.050625	1.060900
3	1.007519	1.015075	1.022669	1.030301	1.037971	1.045678	1.053424	1.061208	1.076891	1.092727
4	1.010038	1.020151	1.030339	1.040604	1.050945	1.061364	1.071859	1.082432	1.103813	1.125509
5	1.012563	1.025251	1.038067	1.051010	1.064082	1.077284	1.090617	1.104081	1.131408	1.159274
6	1.015094	1.030378	1.045852	1.061520	1.077383	1.093443	1.109702	1.126162	1.159693	1.194052
7	1.017632	1.035529	1.053696	1.072135	1.090850	1.109845	1.129122	1.148686	1.188686	1.229874
8	1.020176	1.040707	1.061599	1.082857	1.104486	1.126493	1.148882	1.171659	1.218403	1.266770
9	1.022726	1.045911	1.069561	1.093685	1.118292	1.143390	1.168987	1.195093	1.248863	1.304773
10	1.025283	1.051140	1.077583	1.104622	1.132271	1.160541	1.189444	1.218994	1.280085	1.343916
11	1.027846	1.056396	1.085664	1.115668	1.146424	1.177949	1.210260	1.243374	1.312087	1.384234
12	1.030416	1.061678	1.093807	1.126825	1.160755	1.195618	1.231439	1.268242	1.344889	1.425761
13	1.032922	1.066986	1.102010	1.138093	1.175264	1.213552	1.252989	1.293607	1.378511	1.468534
14	1.035574	1.072321	1.110276	1.149474	1.189955	1.231756	1.274917	1.319479	1.412974	1.512590
15	1.038163	1.077683	1.118603	1.160969	1.204829	1.250232	1.297228	1.345868	1.448298	1.557967
16	1.040759	1.083071	1.126992	1.172579	1.219890	1.268986	1.319929	1.372786	1.484506	1.604706
17	1.043361	1.088487	1.135445	1.184304	1.235138	1.288020	1.343028	1.400241	1.521618	1.652848
18	1.045969	1.093929	1.143960	1.196147	1.250577	1.307341	1.366531	1.428246	1.559659	1.702433
19	1.048584	1.099399	1.152540	1.208109	1.266210	1.326951	1.390445	1.456811	1.598650	1.753506
20	1.051205	1.104896	1.161134	1.220190	1.282037	1.346855	1.414778	1.485947	1.638616	1.806111
21	1.053833	1.110420	1.169893	1.232392	1.298063	1.367058	1.439537	1.515666	1.679582	1.860295
22	1.056468	1.115972	1.178667	1.244716	1.314288	1.387564	1.464729	1.545980	1.721571	1.916103
23	1.059109	1.121552	1.187507	1.257163	1.330717	1.408377	1.490361	1.576899	1.764611	1.973586
24	1.061757	1.127160	1.196414	1.269735	1.347351	1.429503	1.516443	1.608437	1.808726	2.032794
25	1.064411	1.132796	1.205387	1.282432	1.364193	1.450945	1.542981	1.640606	1.853944	2.093778
26	1.067072	1.138460	1.214427	1.295256	1.381245	1.472710	1.569983	1.673418	1.900293	2.156591
27	1.069740	1.144152	1.223535	1.308209	1.398511	1.494800	1.597457	1.706886	1.947800	2.221289
28	1.072414	1.149873	1.232712	1.321291	1.415992	1.517222	1.625413	1.741024	1.996495	2.287928
29	1.075096	1.155622	1.241957	1.334504	1.433692	1.539981	1.653858	1.775845	2.046407	2.356565
30	1.077783	1.161400	1.251272	1.347849	1.451613	1.563080	1.682800	1.811362	2.097568	2.427262
31	1.080478	1.167207	1.260656	1.361327	1.469758	1.586526	1.712249	1.847589	2.150007	2.500080
32	1.083179	1.173043	1.270111	1.374941	1.488130	1.610324	1.742213	1.884541	2.203757	2.575083
33	1.085887	1.178908	1.279637	1.388690	1.506732	1.634479	1.772702	1.922231	2.258851	2.652335
34	1.088602	1.184803	1.289234	1.402577	1.525566	1.658996	1.803724	1.960676	2.315322	2.731905
35	1.091323	1.190727	1.298904	1.416603	1.544636	1.683881	1.835290	1.999889	2.373205	2.813862
36	1.094051	1.196681	1.308645	1.430769	1.563944	1.709140	1.867407	2.039887	2.432535	2.898278
37	1.096786	1.202664	1.318460	1.445076	1.583493	1.734777	1.900087	2.080685	2.493349	2.985227
38	1.099528	1.208677	1.328349	1.459527	1.603287	1.760798	1.933338	2.122299	2.555682	2.074783
39	1.102277	1.214721	1.338311	1.474122	1.623328	1.787210	1.967172	2.164745	2.619574	3.167027
40	1.105033	1.220794	1.348349	1.488864	1.643619	1.814018	2.001597	2.208040	2.685064	3.262038
41	1.107796	1.226898	1.358461	1.503752	1.664165	1.841229	2.036625	2.252200	2.752190	3.359899
42	1.110565	1.233033	1.368650	1.518790	1.684967	1.868847	2.072266	2.297244	2.820995	3.460696
43	1.113341	1.239198	1.378915	1.533978	1.706029	1.896880	2.108531	2.343189	2.891520	3.564517
44	1.116125	1.245394	1.389256	1.549318	1.727354	1.925333	2.145430	2.390053	2.963808	3.671452
45	1.118915	1.251621	1.399676	1.564811	1.748946	1.954213	2.182975	2.437854	3.037902	3.781596
46	1.121712	1.257879	1.410173	1.580459	1.770808	1.983526	2.221177	2.486611	3.113851	3.895044
47	1.124517	1.264168	1.420750	1.596263	1.792943	2.013279	2.260048	2.536343	3.191697	4.011895
48	1.127328	1.270489	1.431405	1.612226	1.815355	2.043478	2.299599	2.587070	3.271489	4.132252
49	1.130146	1.270642	1.442141	1.628348	1.818047	2.074130	2.329842	2.638812	3.353277	4.256219
50	1.132072	1.283226	1.452957	1.644632	1.861022	2.105242	2.380789	2.691588	3.437109	4.381906

TABLE 4 (cont.)
COMPOUND INTEREST (AMOUNT WHEN $1.00 IS COMPOUNDED)

Period	3½%	4%	4½%	5%	5½%	6%	6½%	7%	7½%	8%
1	1.035000	1.040000	1.045000	1.050000	1.055000	1.060000	1.065000	1.070000	1.075000	1.080000
2	1.071225	1.081600	1.092025	1.102500	1.113025	1.123600	1.134225	1.144900	1.155625	1.166400
3	1.108718	1.124864	1.141166	1.157625	1.174241	1.191016	1.207950	1.225043	1.242297	1.259712
4	1.147523	1.169859	1.192519	1.215506	1.238825	1.262477	1.286466	1.310796	1.335469	1.360489
5	1.187686	1.216653	1.246182	1.276282	1.306960	1.338226	1.370087	1.402552	1.435629	1.469328
6	1.229225	1.265319	1.302260	1.340096	1.378843	1.418519	1.459142	1.500730	1.543302	1.586874
7	1.272279	1.315932	1.360862	1.407100	1.454679	1.503630	1.553987	1.605781	1.659045	1.713824
8	1.316809	1.368569	1.422101	1.477455	1.534687	1.593848	1.654996	1.718186	1.783478	1.850930
9	1.362897	1.423321	1.486095	1.551328	1.619094	1.689479	1.762570	1.838459	1.917239	1.999005
10	1.410599	1.480244	1.552969	1.628895	1.708144	1.790848	1.877137	1.967151	2.061032	2.158925
11	1.459970	1.539454	1.622853	1.710339	1.802092	1.898299	1.999151	2.104852	2.215609	2.331639
12	1.511069	1.601032	1.695881	1.795856	1.901207	2.012196	2.129096	2.252192	2.381780	2.518170
13	1.563956	1.665073	1.772196	1.885649	2.005774	2.132928	2.267487	2.409845	2.560413	2.719624
14	1.618695	1.731676	1.851945	1.979932	2.116091	2.260904	2.414874	2.578534	2.752444	2.937194
15	1.675349	1.800943	1.935282	2.078928	2.232476	2.396558	2.571841	2.759032	2.958877	3.172169
16	1.733986	1.872981	2.022370	2.182875	2.355263	2.540352	2.739011	2.952164	3.180793	3.425943
17	1.794676	1.947900	2.113377	2.292018	2.484802	2.692773	2.917046	3.158815	3.419353	3.700018
18	1.857489	2.025816	2.208479	2.406619	2.621466	2.854339	3.106654	3.379932	3.675804	3.996019
19	1.922501	2.106849	2.307860	2.526950	2.765647	3.025599	3.308587	3.616527	3.951489	4.315701
20	1.989789	2.191123	2.411714	2.653298	2.917757	3.207135	3.523645	3.869684	4.247851	4.660957
21	2.059431	2.278768	2.520241	2.785963	3.078234	3.399564	3.752682	4.140562	4.566440	5.033834
22	2.131512	2.369919	2.633652	2.925261	3.247537	3.603537	3.996606	4.430402	4.908923	5.436540
23	2.206114	2.464715	2.752166	3.071524	3.426152	3.819750	4.256386	4.740530	5.277092	5.871464
24	2.283328	2.563304	2.876014	3.225100	3.614590	4.048935	4.533051	5.072367	5.672874	6.341181
25	2.363245	2.665836	3.005434	3.386355	3.813392	4.291871	4.827699	5.427433	6.098340	6.848475
26	2.445959	2.772470	3.140679	3.555673	4.023125	4.549383	5.141500	5.807353	6.555715	7.396353
27	2.531567	2.883368	3.282010	3.733456	4.244401	4.822346	5.475697	6.213867	7.047394	7.988061
28	2.620172	2.998703	3.429700	3.920129	4.477843	5.111687	5.831617	6.648838	7.575948	8.627106
29	2.711878	3.118651	3.584037	4.116136	4.724124	5.418388	6.210672	7.114257	8.144144	9.317275
30	2.806794	3.243397	3.745318	4.321942	4.983951	5.743491	6.614366	7.612255	8.754955	10.062657
31	2.905031	3.373133	3.913857	4.538039	5.258068	6.088101	7.044300	8.145113	9.411577	10.867669
32	3.006708	3.508059	4.089981	4.764941	5.547262	6.453387	7.502179	8.715271	10.117445	11.737083
33	3.111942	3.648381	4.274030	5.003188	5.852362	6.840590	7.989821	9.325340	10.876253	12.676049
34	3.220860	3.794316	4.466362	5.253348	6.174242	7.251025	8.509160	9.978113	11.691972	13.690133
35	2.333590	3.946089	4.667348	5.516015	6.513825	7.686087	9.062255	10.676581	12.568870	14.785344
36	3.450266	4.103932	4.877376	5.791816	6.872085	8.147252	9.651301	11.423942	13.511535	15.968171
37	3.571025	4.268090	5.096861	6.081407	7.250050	8.636087	10.278636	12.223618	14.524901	17.245625
38	3.696011	4.438813	5.326219	6.385477	7.648803	9.154252	10.946747	13.079271	15.614268	18.625275
39	3.825372	4.616366	5.565899	6.704751	8.069487	9.703507	11.658286	13.994820	16.785338	20.115297
40	3.959260	4.801020	5.816365	7.039989	8.513309	10.285718	12.416075	14.974457	18.044239	21.724521
41	4.097834	4.993061	6.078101	7.391988	8.981541	10.902861	13.223119	16.022669	19.397557	23.462483
42	4.241258	5.192784	6.351616	7.761587	9.475525	11.557032	14.082622	17.144256	20.852373	25.339481
43	4.389702	5.400495	6.637438	8.149667	9.996679	12.250454	14.997993	18.344354	22.416301	27.366640
44	4.543341	5.616515	6.936123	8.557150	10.546496	12.985482	15.972862	19.628459	24.097524	29.555971
45	4.702358	5.841175	7.248248	8.985008	11.126554	13.764610	17.011098	21.002451	25.904838	31.920449
46	4.866941	6.074822	7.574420	9.434258	11.738514	14.590487	18.116820	22.472622	27.847701	34.474084
47	5.037284	6.317815	7.915269	9.905971	12.384132	15.465916	19.294413	24.045706	29.936278	37.232011
48	5.213589	6.570528	8.271456	10.401269	13.065260	16.393871	20.548550	25.728905	32.181498	40.210572
49	5.396064	6.833349	8.643671	10.921333	13.783849	17.377504	21.884205	27.529929	34.595112	43.427418
50	5.584927	7.106683	9.032636	11.467400	14.541961	18.420154	23.306679	29.457024	37.189745	46.901611

TABLE 5
DAILY COMPOUND INTEREST ON $100 (365-DAY BASIS)

5.25 %
Effective Rate is 5.39%

Description: This table shows the interest on $100 for each day from 1 day to 366 days. Interest is computed on the basis of a 365-day year. Interest is compounded daily.

Example: Interest on $100 at 5.25% for 270 days is $ 3.96. On $10,000 the interest is $ 395.97.

DAY	INTEREST	DAY	INTEREST	DAY	INTEREST	DAY	INTEREST	DAY	INTEREST	DAY	INTEREST
1	0.014384	66	0.953766	131	1.901972	196	2.859084	261	3.825186	326	4.800362
2	0.028769	67	0.968287	132	1.916630	197	2.873879	262	3.840120	327	4.815436
3	0.043157	68	0.982810	133	1.931289	198	2.888676	263	3.855056	328	4.830512
4	0.057547	69	0.997335	134	1.945950	199	2.903475	264	3.869994	329	4.845590
5	0.071938	70	1.011862	135	1.960614	200	2.918276	265	3.884934	330	4.860671
6	0.086332	71	1.026391	136	1.975279	201	2.933080	266	3.899876	331	4.875754
7	0.100728	72	1.040922	137	1.989947	202	2.947885	267	3.914821	332	4.890839
8	0.115126	73	1.055456	138	2.004617	203	2.962693	268	3.929768	333	4.905926
9	0.129527	74	1.069991	139	2.019289	204	2.977502	269	3.944716	334	4.921015
10	0.143929	75	1.084528	140	2.033963	205	2.992314	270	3.959667	335	4.936106
11	0.158333	76	1.099068	141	2.048639	206	3.007128	271	3.974620	336	4.951200
12	0.172739	77	1.113610	142	2.063317	207	3.021944	272	3.989576	337	4.966295
13	0.187148	78	1.128153	143	2.077997	208	3.036763	273	4.004533	338	4.981393
14	0.201558	79	1.142699	144	2.092680	209	3.051583	274	4.019493	339	4.996493
15	0.215971	80	1.157247	145	2.107364	210	3.066405	275	4.034454	340	5.011596
16	0.230385	81	1.171797	146	2.122051	211	3.081230	276	4.049418	341	5.026700
17	0.244802	82	1.186349	147	2.136740	212	3.096057	277	4.064384	342	5.041807
18	0.259221	83	1.200903	148	2.151431	213	3.110886	278	4.079352	343	5.056915
19	0.273642	84	1.215460	149	2.166124	214	3.125717	279	4.094323	344	5.072026
20	0.288065	85	1.230018	150	2.180819	215	3.140550	280	4.109295	345	5.087139
21	0.302490	86	1.244579	151	2.195516	216	3.155385	281	4.124270	346	5.102255
22	0.316917	87	1.259141	152	2.210215	217	3.170223	282	4.139247	347	5.117372
23	0.331346	88	1.273706	153	2.224917	218	3.185062	283	4.154226	348	5.132492
24	0.345777	89	1.288273	154	2.239620	219	3.199904	284	4.169207	349	5.147614
25	0.360210	90	1.302841	155	2.254326	220	3.214748	285	4.184190	350	5.162738
26	0.374646	91	1.317412	156	2.269034	221	3.229594	286	4.199175	351	5.177864
27	0.389083	92	1.331985	157	2.283744	222	3.244442	287	4.214163	352	5.192992
28	0.403523	93	1.346561	158	2.298456	223	3.259292	288	4.229152	353	5.208122
29	0.417964	94	1.361138	159	2.313170	224	3.274144	289	4.244144	354	5.223255
30	0.432408	95	1.375717	160	2.327886	225	3.288999	290	4.259138	355	5.238390
31	0.446854	96	1.390299	161	2.342605	226	3.303855	291	4.274135	356	5.253527
32	0.461302	97	1.404882	162	2.357325	227	3.318714	292	4.289133	357	5.268666
33	0.475752	98	1.419468	163	2.372048	228	3.333575	293	4.304133	358	5.283808
34	0.490204	99	1.434056	164	2.386773	229	3.348438	294	4.319136	359	5.298951
35	0.504658	100	1.448645	165	2.401499	230	3.363303	295	4.334141	360	5.314097
36	0.519114	101	1.463237	166	2.416228	231	3.378171	296	4.349148	361	5.329245
37	0.533572	102	1.477831	167	2.430960	232	3.393040	297	4.364157	362	5.344395
38	0.548032	103	1.492427	168	2.445693	233	3.407912	298	4.379168	363	5.359547
39	0.562495	104	1.507026	169	2.460428	234	3.422785	299	4.394182	364	5.374702
40	0.576959	105	1.521626	170	2.475166	235	3.437661	300	4.409197	365	5.389858
41	0.591426	106	1.536228	171	2.489905	236	3.452539	301	4.424215	366	5.405017
42	0.605894	107	1.550833	172	2.504647	237	3.467420	302	4.439235		
43	0.620365	108	1.565440	173	2.519391	238	3.482302	303	4.454257		
44	0.634838	109	1.580048	174	2.534137	239	3.497186	304	4.469281		
45	0.649313	110	1.594659	175	2.548885	240	3.512073	305	4.484308		
46	0.663790	111	1.609272	176	2.563635	241	3.526962	306	4.499336		
47	0.678269	112	1.623887	177	2.578387	242	3.541852	307	4.514367		
48	0.692750	113	1.638504	178	2.593142	243	3.556745	308	4.529400		
49	0.707233	114	1.653123	179	2.607898	244	3.571641	309	4.544435		
50	0.721718	115	1.667745	180	2.622657	245	3.586538	310	4.559472		
51	0.736206	116	1.682368	181	2.637418	246	3.601437	311	4.574511		
52	0.750695	117	1.696994	182	2.652181	247	3.616339	312	4.589553		
53	0.765187	118	1.711621	183	2.666946	248	3.631243	313	4.604597		
54	0.779680	119	1.726251	184	2.681713	249	3.646148	314	4.619643		
55	0.794176	120	1.740883	185	2.696482	250	3.661056	315	4.634691		
56	0.808674	121	1.755517	186	2.711253	251	3.675967	316	4.649741		
57	0.823174	122	1.770153	187	2.726027	252	3.690879	317	4.664793		
58	0.837676	123	1.784791	188	2.740803	253	3.705793	318	4.679848		
59	0.852180	124	1.799432	189	2.755580	254	3.720710	319	4.694904		
60	0.866686	125	1.814074	190	2.770360	255	3.735629	320	4.709963		
61	0.881194	126	1.828718	191	2.785142	256	3.750550	321	4.725024		
62	0.895704	127	1.843365	192	2.799927	257	3.765473	322	4.740087		
63	0.910217	128	1.858014	193	2.814713	258	3.780398	323	4.755153		
64	0.924731	129	1.872665	194	2.829501	259	3.795325	324	4.770220		
65	0.939248	130	1.887317	195	2.844292	260	3.810255	325	4.785290		

TABLE 6
DAILY COMPOUND INTEREST ON $100 (360-DAY BASIS)

5.25 %

Effective Rate is **5.47%**

Description: This table shows the interest on $100 for each day from 1 day to 366 days. Interest is computed on the basis of a 360-day year. Interest is compounded daily.

Example: Interest on $100 at 5.25% for 270 days is $ 4.02. On $10,000 the interest is $ 401.57.

DAY	INTEREST	DAY	INTEREST	DAY	INTEREST	DAY	INTEREST	DAY	INTEREST	DAY	INTEREST
1	0.014583	66	0.967076	131	1.928640	196	2.899361	261	3.879327	326	4.868626
2	0.029169	67	0.981800	132	1.943505	197	2.914367	262	3.894476	327	4.883919
3	0.043756	68	0.996527	133	1.958371	198	2.929376	263	3.909628	328	4.899215
4	0.058346	69	1.011256	134	1.973240	199	2.944386	264	3.924781	329	4.914513
5	0.072938	70	1.025986	135	1.988111	200	2.959399	265	3.939937	330	4.929813
6	0.087532	71	1.040719	136	2.002985	201	2.974414	266	3.955095	331	4.945115
7	0.102128	72	1.055454	137	2.017860	202	2.989431	267	3.970255	332	4.960420
8	0.116726	73	1.070192	138	2.032738	203	3.004450	268	3.985417	333	4.975726
9	0.131327	74	1.084931	139	2.047617	204	3.019472	269	4.000582	334	4.991035
10	0.145929	75	1.099673	140	2.062499	205	3.034495	270	4.015748	335	5.006346
11	0.160534	76	1.114416	141	2.077383	206	3.049521	271	4.030917	336	5.021660
12	0.175140	77	1.129162	142	2.092270	207	3.064549	272	4.046089	337	5.036976
13	0.189749	78	1.143910	143	2.107158	208	3.079580	273	4.061262	338	5.052293
14	0.204360	79	1.158660	144	2.122049	209	3.094612	274	4.076438	339	5.067614
15	0.218973	80	1.173413	145	2.136942	210	3.109647	275	4.091615	340	5.082936
16	0.233589	81	1.188167	146	2.151837	211	3.124684	276	4.106795	341	5.098261
17	0.248206	82	1.202924	147	2.166734	212	3.139723	277	4.121978	342	5.113587
18	0.262826	83	1.217683	148	2.181633	213	3.154764	278	4.137162	343	5.128916
19	0.277447	84	1.232443	149	2.196535	214	3.169807	279	4.152349	344	5.144248
20	0.292071	85	1.247207	150	2.211438	215	3.184853	280	4.167538	345	5.159581
21	0.306697	86	1.261972	151	2.226344	216	3.199901	281	4.182729	346	5.174917
22	0.321325	87	1.276739	152	2.241252	217	3.214951	282	4.197922	347	5.190255
23	0.335955	88	1.291509	153	2.256162	218	3.230003	283	4.213118	348	5.205595
24	0.350588	89	1.306280	154	2.271075	219	3.245057	284	4.228315	349	5.220938
25	0.365222	90	1.321054	155	2.285989	220	3.260114	285	4.243515	350	5.236282
26	0.379859	91	1.335830	156	2.300906	221	3.275172	286	4.258718	351	5.251629
27	0.394497	92	1.350608	157	2.315825	222	3.290233	287	4.273922	352	5.266979
28	0.409138	93	1.365389	158	2.330746	223	3.305297	288	4.289129	353	5.282330
29	0.423781	94	1.380171	159	2.345669	224	3.320362	289	4.304337	354	5.297684
30	0.438426	95	1.394956	160	2.360594	225	3.335429	290	4.319548	355	5.313040
31	0.453074	96	1.409742	161	2.375522	226	3.350499	291	4.334762	356	5.328398
32	0.467723	97	1.424531	162	2.390452	227	3.365571	292	4.349977	357	5.343758
33	0.482375	98	1.439322	163	2.405384	228	3.380645	293	4.365195	358	5.359121
34	0.497028	99	1.454116	164	2.420318	229	3.395722	294	4.380415	359	5.374486
35	0.511684	100	1.468911	165	2.435254	230	3.410800	295	4.395637	360	5.389853
36	0.526342	101	1.483709	166	2.450193	231	3.425881	296	4.410861	361	5.405222
37	0.541002	102	1.498508	167	2.465133	232	3.440964	297	4.426088	362	5.420594
38	0.555664	103	1.513310	168	2.480076	233	3.456049	298	4.441317	363	5.435968
39	0.570329	104	1.528114	169	2.495021	234	3.471136	299	4.456548	364	5.451344
40	0.584995	105	1.542920	170	2.509968	235	3.486226	300	4.471781	365	5.466722
41	0.599664	106	1.557729	171	2.524918	236	3.501318	301	4.487016	366	5.482103
42	0.614335	107	1.572539	172	2.539869	237	3.516412	302	4.502254		
43	0.629008	108	1.587352	173	2.554823	238	3.531508	303	4.517494		
44	0.643683	109	1.602167	174	2.569779	239	3.546606	304	4.532736		
45	0.658360	110	1.616984	175	2.584737	240	3.561707	305	4.547981		
46	0.673039	111	1.631803	176	2.599697	241	3.576809	306	4.563227		
47	0.687721	112	1.646624	177	2.614660	242	3.591914	307	4.578476		
48	0.702404	113	1.661448	178	2.629624	243	3.607021	308	4.593727		
49	0.717090	114	1.676273	179	2.644591	244	3.622131	309	4.608980		
50	0.731778	115	1.691101	180	2.659560	245	3.637242	310	4.624236		
51	0.746468	116	1.705931	181	2.674531	246	3.652356	311	4.639493		
52	0.761160	117	1.720763	182	2.689505	247	3.667472	312	4.654753		
53	0.775855	118	1.735597	183	2.704480	248	3.682590	313	4.670015		
54	0.790551	119	1.750434	184	2.719458	249	3.697711	314	4.685280		
55	0.805250	120	1.765272	185	2.734438	250	3.712833	315	4.700546		
56	0.819950	121	1.780113	186	2.749420	251	3.727958	316	4.715815		
57	0.834653	122	1.794956	187	2.764404	252	3.743085	317	4.731086		
58	0.849358	123	1.809801	188	2.779391	253	3.758214	318	4.746360		
59	0.864066	124	1.824648	189	2.794379	254	3.773346	319	4.761635		
60	0.878775	125	1.839498	190	2.809370	255	3.788479	320	4.776913		
61	0.893486	126	1.854349	191	2.824363	256	3.803615	321	4.792193		
62	0.908200	127	1.869203	192	2.839358	257	3.818753	322	4.807475		
63	0.922916	128	1.884059	193	2.854356	258	3.833893	323	4.822759		
64	0.937634	129	1.898917	194	2.869355	259	3.849036	324	4.838046		
65	0.952354	130	1.913777	195	2.884357	260	3.864180	325	4.853335		

TABLE 7
5% COMPOUNDED DAILY (360-DAY BASIS)*

Period	Amount of 1	Period	Amount of 1	Period	Amount of 1
1	1.000 138	61	1.008 507	121	1.016 946
2	1.000 277	62	1.008 647	122	1.017 087
3	1.000 416	63	1.008 787	123	1.017 228
4	1.000 555	64	1.008 927	124	1.017 370
5	1.000 694	65	1.009 068	125	1.017 511
6	1.000 833	66	1.009 208	126	1.017 652
7	1.000 972	67	1.009 348	127	1.017 794
8	1.001 111	68	1.009 488	128	1.017 935
9	1.001 250	69	1.009 628	129	1.018 076
10	1.001 389	70	1.009 768	130	1.018 218
11	1.001 528	71	1.009 909	131	1.018 359
12	1.001 667	72	1.010 049	132	1.018 501
13	1.001 807	73	1.010 189	133	1.018 642
14	1.001 946	74	1.010 330	134	1.018 784
15	1.002 085	75	1.010 470	135	1.018 925
16	1.002 224	76	1.010 610	136	1.019 067
17	1.002 363	77	1.010 751	137	1.019 208
18	1.002 502	78	1.010 891	138	1.019 350
19	1.002 642	79	1.011 031	139	1.019 491
20	1.002 781	80	1.011 172	140	1.019 633
21	1.002 920	81	1.011 312	141	1.019 774
22	1.003 060	82	1.011 453	142	1.019 916
23	1.003 199	83	1.011 593	143	1.020 058
24	1.003 338	84	1.011 734	144	1.020 190
25	1.003 478	85	1.011 874	145	1.020 341
26	1.003 617	86	1.012 015	146	1.020 483
27	1.003 756	87	1.012 155	147	1.020 625
28	1.003 896	88	1.012 296	148	1.020 766
29	1.004 035	89	1.012 436	149	1.020 908
30	1.004 175	90	1.012 577	150	1.021 050
31	1.004 314	91	1.012 718	151	1.021 192
32	1.004 454	92	1.012 858	152	1.021 334
33	1.004 593	93	1.012 999	153	1.021 475
34	1.004 733	94	1.013 140	154	1.021 617
35	1.004 872	95	1.013 280	155	1.021 759
36	1.005 012	96	1.013 421	156	1.021 901
37	1.005 151	97	1.013 562	157	1.022 043
38	1.005 291	98	1.013 703	158	1.022 185
39	1.005 430	99	1.013 843	159	1.022 327
40	1.005 570	100	1.013 984	160	1.022 469
41	1.005 710	101	1.014 125	161	1.022 611
42	1.005 849	102	1.014 266	162	1.022 753
43	1.005 989	103	1.014 407	163	1.022 895
44	1.006 129	104	1.014 548	164	1.023 037
45	1.006 269	105	1.014 689	165	1.023 179
46	1.006 408	106	1.014 830	166	1.023 321
47	1.006 548	107	1.014 971	167	1.023 463
48	1.006 688	108	1.015 112	168	1.023 606
49	1.006 828	109	1.015 252	169	1.023 748
50	1.006 968	110	1.015 394	170	1.023 890
51	1.007 107	111	1.015 535	171	1.024 032
52	1.007 247	112	1.015 676	172	1.024 174
53	1.007 387	113	1.015 817	173	1.024 317
54	1.007 527	114	1.015 958	174	1.024 459
55	1.007 667	115	1.016 099	175	1.024 601
56	1.007 807	116	1.016 240	176	1.024 743
57	1.007 947	117	1.016 381	177	1.024 886
58	1.008 087	118	1.016 522	178	1.025 028
59	1.008 227	119	1.016 663	179	1.025 170
60	1.008 367	120	1.016 805	180	1.025 313

TABLE 8
5% COMPOUNDED CONTINUOUSLY (360-DAY BASIS)*

Period	Amount of 1	Period	Amount of 1	Period	Amount of 1
1	1.000 138	61	1.008 508	121	1.016 947
2	1.000 277	62	1.008 648	122	1.017 088
3	1.000 416	63	1.008 788	123	1.017 230
4	1.000 555	64	1.008 928	124	1.017 371
5	1.000 694	65	1.009 068	125	1.017 512
6	1.000 833	66	1.009 208	126	1.017 654
7	1.000 972	67	1.009 348	127	1.017 795
8	1.001 111	68	1.009 489	128	1.017 936
9	1.001 250	69	1.009 629	129	1.018 078
10	1.001 389	70	1.009 769	130	1.018 219
11	1.001 528	71	1.009 909	131	1.018 360
12	1.001 668	72	1.010 050	132	1.018 502
13	1.001 807	73	1.010 190	133	1.018 643
14	1.001 946	74	1.010 330	134	1.018 785
15	1.002 085	75	1.010 471	135	1.018 926
16	1.002 224	76	1.010 611	136	1.019 068
17	1.002 363	77	1.010 751	137	1.019 209
18	1.002 503	78	1.010 892	138	1.019 351
19	1.002 642	79	1.011 032	139	1.019 493
20	1.002 781	80	1.011 173	140	1.019 634
21	1.002 920	81	1.011 313	141	1.019 776
22	1.003 060	82	1.011 453	142	1.019 917
23	1.003 199	83	1.011 594	143	1.020 059
24	1.003 338	84	1.011 734	144	1.020 201
25	1.003 478	85	1.011 875	145	1.020 343
26	1.003 617	86	1.012 016	146	1.020 484
27	1.003 757	87	1.012 156	147	1.020 626
28	1.003 896	88	1.012 297	148	1.020 768
29	1.004 035	89	1.012 437	149	1.020 910
30	1.004 175	90	1.012 578	150	1.021 051
31	1.004 314	91	1.012 719	151	1.021 193
32	1.004 454	92	1.012 859	152	1.021 335
33	1.004 593	93	1.013 000	153	1.021 477
34	1.004 733	94	1.013 141	154	1.021 619
35	1.004 872	95	1.013 281	155	1.021 761
36	1.005 012	96	1.013 422	156	1.021 903
37	1.005 152	97	1.013 563	157	1.022 045
38	1.005 291	98	1.013 704	158	1.022 186
39	1.005 431	99	1.013 844	159	1.022 328
40	1.005 571	100	1.013 985	160	1.022 470
41	1.005 710	101	1.014 126	161	1.022 612
42	1.005 850	102	1.014 267	162	1.022 755
43	1.005 990	103	1.014 408	163	1.022 897
44	1.006 129	104	1.014 549	164	1.023 039
45	1.006 269	105	1.014 690	165	1.023 181
46	1.006 409	106	1.014 831	166	1.023 323
47	1.006 549	107	1.014 972	167	1.023 465
48	1.006 688	108	1.015 113	168	1.023 607
49	1.006 828	109	1.015 254	169	1.023 749
50	1.006 968	110	1.015 395	170	1.023 892
51	1.007 108	111	1.015 536	171	1.024 034
52	1.007 248	112	1.015 677	172	1.024 176
53	1.007 388	113	1.015 818	173	1.024 318
54	1.007 528	114	1.015 959	174	1.024 461
55	1.007 668	115	1.016 100	175	1.024 603
56	1.007 808	116	1.016 241	176	1.024 745
57	1.007 948	117	1.016 382	177	1.024 887
58	1.008 088	118	1.016 523	178	1.025 030
59	1.008 228	119	1.016 665	179	1.025 172
60	1.008 368	120	1.016 806	180	1.025 315

*Courtesy of the Financial Publishing Company of Boston.

TABLE 9
PRESENT VALUE

Period	1¼%	1½%	1¾%	2%	2½%	3%
1	.987654	.985221	.982801	.980392	.975609	.970873
2	.975461	.970661	.965898	.961168	.951814	.942595
3	.963419	.956316	.949285	.942322	.928599	.915141
4	.951525	.942184	.932959	.923845	.905950	.888487
5	.939777	.928260	.916912	.905730	.883854	.862608
6	.928175	.914542	.901142	.887971	.862296	.837484
7	.916716	.901026	.885643	.870560	.841265	.813091
8	.905399	.887711	.870411	.853490	.820746	.789409
9	.894221	.874592	.855441	.836755	.800728	.766416
10	.883181	.861667	.840728	.820348	.781198	.744093
11	.872278	.848933	.826269	.804263	.762144	.722421
12	.861509	.836387	.812057	.788493	.743555	.701379
13	.850873	.824027	.798091	.773032	.725420	.680951
14	.840369	.811849	.784365	.757875	.707727	.661117
15	.829994	.799851	.770875	.743014	.690465	.641861
16	.819747	.788031	.757617	.728445	.673624	.623166
17	.809627	.776385	.744586	.714162	.657195	.605016
18	.799632	.764911	.731780	.700159	.641165	.587394
19	.789760	.753607	.719194	.686430	.625527	.570286
20	.780009	.742470	.706825	.672971	.610270	.553675
21	.770380	.731497	.694668	.659775	.595386	.537549
22	.760869	.720687	.682720	.646839	.580864	.521892
23	.751475	.710037	.670978	.634155	.566697	.506691
24	.742198	.699543	.659438	.621721	.552875	.491933
25	.733035	.689205	.648096	.609530	.539390	.477605
26	.723985	.679020	.636950	.597579	.526234	.463694
27	.715047	.668985	.625995	.585862	.513399	.450189
28	.706219	.659099	.615228	.574374	.500877	.437076
29	.697500	.649358	.604646	.563112	.488661	.424346
30	.688889	.639762	.594247	.552070	.476742	.411986
31	.680385	.630307	.584027	.541245	.465114	.399987
32	.671985	.620992	.573982	.530633	.453770	.388337
33	.663688	.611815	.564110	.520228	.442702	.377026
34	.655495	.602774	.554408	.510028	.431905	.366044
35	.647402	.593866	.544873	.500027	.421371	.355383
36	.639409	.585089	.535501	.490223	.411093	.345032
37	.631516	.576443	.526291	.480610	.401067	.334982
38	.623719	.567924	.517239	.471187	.391284	.325226
39	.616019	.559531	.508343	.461948	.381741	.315753
40	.608414	.551262	.499600	.452890	.372430	.306556
41	.600902	.543115	.491008	.444010	.363346	.297628
42	.593484	.535089	.482563	.435304	.354484	.288959
43	.586157	.527181	.474263	.426768	.345838	.280542
44	.578920	.519390	.466106	.418400	.337403	.272371
45	.571773	.511714	.458090	.410196	.329174	.264438
46	.564714	.504152	.450211	.402153	.321145	.256736
47	.557743	.496702	.442468	.394268	.313312	.249258
48	.550857	.489361	.434858	.386537	.305671	.241998
49	.544056	.482129	.427379	.378958	.298215	.234950
50	.537339	.475004	.420028	.371527	.290942	.228107

TABLE 9 (*cont.*)

Period	3½%	4%	5%	6%	7%	8%
1	.966183	.961538	.952380	.943396	.934579	.925925
2	.933510	.924556	.907029	.889996	.873438	.857338
3	.901942	.888996	.863837	.839619	.816297	.793832
4	.871442	.854804	.822702	.792093	.762895	.735029
5	.841973	.821927	.783526	.747258	.712986	.680583
6	.813500	.790314	.746215	.704960	.666342	.630169
7	.785990	.759917	.710681	.665057	.622749	.583490
8	.759411	.730690	.676839	.627412	.582009	.540268
9	.733731	.702586	.644608	.591898	.543933	.500248
10	.708918	.675564	.613913	.558394	.508349	.463193
11	.684945	.649580	.584679	.526787	.475092	.428882
12	.661783	.624597	.556837	.496969	.444011	.397113
13	.639404	.600574	.530321	.468839	.414964	.367697
14	.617781	.577475	.505067	.442300	.387817	.340461
15	.596890	.555264	.481017	.417265	.362446	.315241
16	.576705	.533908	.458111	.393646	.338734	.291890
17	.557203	.513373	.436296	.371364	.316574	.270268
18	.538361	.493628	.415520	.350343	.295863	.250249
19	.520155	.474642	.395733	.330512	.276508	.231712
20	.502565	.456386	.376889	.311804	.258418	.214548
21	.485570	.438833	.358942	.294155	.241513	.198655
22	.469150	.421955	.341849	.277505	.225713	.183940
23	.453285	.405726	.325571	.261797	.210946	.170315
24	.437957	.390121	.310067	.246978	.197146	.157699
25	.423147	.375116	.295302	.232998	.184249	.146017
26	.408837	.360689	.281240	.219810	.172195	.135201
27	.395012	.346816	.267848	.207367	.160930	.125186
28	.381654	.333477	.255093	.195630	.150402	.115913
29	.368748	.320651	.242946	.184556	.140562	.107327
30	.356278	.308318	.231377	.174110	.131367	.099377
31	.344230	.296460	.220359	.164254	.122773	.092016
32	.332589	.285057	.209866	.154957	.114741	.085200
33	.321342	.274094	.199872	.146186	.107234	.078888
34	.310476	.263552	.190354	.137911	.100219	.073045
35	.299976	.253415	.181290	.130105	.093662	.067634
36	.289832	.243668	.172657	.122740	.087535	.062624
37	.280031	.234296	.164435	.115793	.081808	.057985
38	.270561	.225285	.156605	.109238	.076456	.053690
39	.261412	.216620	.149147	.103055	.071455	.049713
40	.252572	.208289	.142045	.097222	.066780	.046030
41	.244031	.200277	.135281	.091719	.062411	.042621
42	.235779	.192574	.128839	.086527	.058328	.039464
43	.227805	.185168	.122704	.081629	.054512	.036540
44	.220102	.178046	.116861	.077009	.050946	.033834
45	.212659	.171198	.111296	.072650	.047613	.031327
46	.205467	.164613	.105996	.068537	.044498	.029007
47	.198519	.158282	.100949	.064658	.041587	.026858
48	.191806	.152194	.096142	.060998	.038866	.024869
49	.185320	.146341	.091563	.057545	.036324	.023026
50	.179053	.140712	.087203	.054288	.033947	.021321

TABLE 10
AMOUNT OF ANNUITY $S_{\overline{n}|i}$

n	1%	1¼%	2¾%	3%	7%	11%	12%	14%
1	1.00000000	1.00000000	1.00000000	1.00000000	1.00000000	1.00000000	1.00000000	1.00000000
2	2.01000000	2.01250000	2.02750000	2.03000000	2.07000000	2.11000000	2.12000000	2.14000000
3	3.03010000	3.03765625	3.08325625	3.09090000	3.21490000	3.34210000	3.37440000	3.43960000
4	4.06040100	4.07562695	4.16804580	4.18362700	4.43994300	4.70973100	4.77932800	4.92114400
5	5.10100501	5.12657229	5.28266706	5.30913581	5.75073901	6.22780141	6.35284736	6.61010416
6	6.15201506	6.19065444	6.42794040	6.46840988	7.15329074	7.91285957	8.11518904	8.53551874
7	7.21353521	7.26803762	7.60470876	7.66246218	8.65402109	9.78327412	10.08901173	10.73049137
8	8.28567056	8.35888809	8.81383825	8.89233605	10.25980257	11.85943427	12.29969314	13.23276016
9	9.36852727	9.46337420	10.05621880	10.15910613	11.97798875	14.16397204	14.77565631	16.08534658
10	10.46221254	10.58166637	11.33276482	11.46387931	13.81644796	16.72200896	17.54873507	19.33729510
11	11.56683467	11.71393720	12.64441585	12.80779569	15.78359932	19.56142995	20.65458328	23.04451641
12	12.68250301	12.86036142	13.99213729	14.19202956	17.88845127	22.71318724	24.13313327	27.27074871
13	13.80932804	14.02111594	15.37692107	15.61779045	20.14064286	26.21163784	28.02910926	32.08865353
14	14.94742132	15.19637988	16.79978639	17.08632416	22.55048786	30.09491800	32.39260238	37.58106503
15	16.09689554	16.38633463	18.26178052	18.59891389	25.12902201	34.40535898	37.27971466	43.84241413
16	17.25786449	17.59116382	19.76397948	20.15688130	27.88805355	39.18994847	42.75328042	50.98035211
17	18.43044314	18.81105336	21.30748892	21.76158774	30.84021730	44.50084281	48.88367407	59.11760141
18	19.61474757	20.04619153	22.89344487	23.41443537	33.99903251	50.39593551	55.74971496	68.39406560
19	20.81089504	21.29676893	24.52301460	25.11686844	37.37896479	56.93948842	63.43968075	78.96923479
20	22.01900399	22.56297854	26.19739750	26.87037449	40.99549232	64.20283215	72.05244244	91.02492766
21	23.23919403	23.84501577	27.91782593	28.67648572	44.86517678	72.26514368	81.69873554	104.76841753
22	24.47158598	25.14307847	29.68556615	30.53678030	49.00573916	81.21430949	92.50258380	120.43599598
23	25.71630183	26.45736695	31.50191921	32.45288370	53.43614090	91.14788353	104.60289386	138.29703542
24	26.97346485	27.78808403	33.36822199	34.42647022	58.17667076	102.17415072	118.15524112	158.65862038
25	28.24319950	29.13543508	35.28584810	36.45926432	63.24903772	114.41330730	133.33387006	181.87082723
26	29.52563150	30.49962802	37.25620892	38.55304225	68.67647036	127.99877110	150.33393446	208.33274304
27	30.82088781	31.88087337	39.28075467	40.70963352	74.48382328	143.07863592	169.37400660	238.49932707
28	32.12909669	33.27938429	41.36097542	42.93092252	80.69769091	159.81728587	190.69888739	272.88923286
29	33.45038766	34.69537659	43.49840224	45.21885020	87.34652927	178.39718732	214.58275388	312.09372546
30	34.78489153	36.12906880	45.69460831	47.57541571	94.46078632	199.02087793	241.33268434	356.78684702
31	36.13274045	37.58068216	47.95121003	50.00267818	102.07304137	221.91317450	271.29260646	407.73700561
32	37.49406785	39.05044069	50.26986831	52.50275852	110.21815426	247.32362069	304.84771924	465.82018639
33	38.86900853	40.53857120	52.65228969	55.07784128	118.93342506	275.52922230	342.42944555	532.03501249
34	40.25769862	42.04530334	55.10022765	57.73017652	128.25876481	306.83743675	384.52097901	607.51991423
35	41.66027560	43.57086963	57.61548391	60.46208181	138.23687835	341.58955480	431.66349649	693.57270223
36	43.07687836	45.11550550	60.19990972	63.27594427	148.91345984	380.16440582	484.46311607	791.67288054
37	44.50764714	46.67944932	62.85540724	66.17422259	160.33740202	422.98249046	543.59869000	903.50708382
38	45.95272361	48.26294243	65.58393094	69.15944927	172.56102017	470.51056441	609.83053280	1030.99807555
39	47.41225085	49.86622921	68.38748904	72.23423275	185.64029158	523.26672650	684.01019674	1176.33780613
40	48.88637336	51.48955708	71.26814499	75.40125973	199.63511199	581.82606641	767.09142034	1342.02509898
41	50.37523709	53.13317654	74.22801898	78.66329753	214.60956983	646.82693372	860.14239079	1530.90861284
42	51.87898946	54.79734125	77.26928950	82.02319645	230.63223972	718.97789643	964.35947768	1746.23581864
43	53.39777936	56.48230801	80.39419496	85.48389234	247.77649650	799.06546504	1081.08261500	1991.70883325
44	54.93175715	58.18833687	83.60503532	89.04840911	266.12085125	887.96266619	1211.81252880	2271.54806990
45	56.48107472	59.91569108	86.90417379	92.71986139	285.74931084	986.63855947	1358.23003226	2590.56479969
46	58.04588547	61.66463721	90.29403857	96.50145723	306.75176260	1096.16880101	1522.21763613	2954.24387165
47	59.62634432	63.43544518	93.77712463	100.39650095	329.22438598	1217.74736912	1705.88375247	3368.83801368
48	61.22260777	65.22838824	97.35599556	104.40839598	353.27009300	1352.69957973	1911.58980276	3841.47533559
49	62.83483385	67.04374310	101.03328544	108.54064785	378.99899951	1502.49653350	2141.98057909	4380.28188258
50	64.46318218	68.88178989	104.81170079	112.79686729	406.52892947	1668.77115218	2400.01824858	4994.52134614

From Williams, Walter E., and James H. Reed, FUNDAMENTALS OF BUSINESS MATHEMATICS, 2nd. ed. © 1977, 1981 Wm. C. Brown Publishers, Dubuque, Iowa. All Rights Reserved. Reprinted by permission.

TABLE 11
PRESENT VALUE OF ANNUITY $A_{\overline{n}|i}$

n	1%	2¾%	3%	6%	7%	11%	12%	14%
1	0.99009901	0.97323601	0.97087379	0.94339623	0.93457944	0.90090090	0.89285714	0.87719298
2	1.97039506	1.92042434	1.91346970	1.83339267	1.80801817	1.71252333	1.69005102	1.64666051
3	2.94098521	2.84226213	2.82861135	2.67301195	2.62431604	2.44371472	2.40183127	2.32163203
4	3.90196555	3.73942787	3.71709840	3.46510561	3.38721126	3.10244569	3.03734935	2.91371230
5	4.85343124	4.61258186	4.57970719	4.21236379	4.10019744	3.69589702	3.60477620	3.43308097
6	5.79547647	5.46236678	5.41719144	4.91732433	4.76653966	4.23053785	4.11140732	3.88866752
7	6.72819453	6.28940806	6.23028296	5.58238144	5.38928940	4.71219626	4.56375654	4.28830484
8	7.65167775	7.09431441	7.01969219	6.20979381	5.97129851	5.14612276	4.96763977	4.63886389
9	8.56601758	7.87767826	7.78610892	6.80169227	6.51523225	5.53704753	5.32824979	4.94637184
10	9.47130453	8.64007616	8.53020284	7.36008705	7.02358154	5.88923201	5.65022303	5.21611565
11	10.36762825	9.38206926	9.25262411	7.88687458	7.49867434	6.20651533	5.93769913	5.45273302
12	11.25507747	10.10420366	9.95400399	8.38384394	7.94268630	6.49235615	6.19437423	5.66029213
13	12.13374007	10.80701086	10.63495533	8.85268296	8.35765074	6.74987040	6.42354842	5.84236151
14	13.00370304	11.49100814	11.29607314	9.29498393	8.74546799	6.98186523	6.62816823	6.00207150
15	13.86505252	12.15669892	11.93793509	9.71224899	9.10791401	7.19086958	6.81086449	6.14216799
16	14.71787378	12.80457315	12.56110203	10.10589527	9.44664860	7.37916178	6.97398615	6.26505964
17	15.56225127	13.43510769	13.16611847	10.47725969	9.76322299	7.54879440	7.11963049	6.37285933
18	16.39826858	14.04876661	13.75351308	10.82760348	10.05908691	7.70161657	7.24967008	6.46742046
19	17.22600850	14.64600157	14.32379911	11.15811649	10.33559524	7.83929421	7.36577686	6.55036883
20	18.04555297	15.22725213	14.87747486	11.46992122	10.59401425	7.96332812	7.46944362	6.62313055
21	18.85698313	15.79294612	15.41502414	11.76407662	10.83552733	8.07507038	7.56200324	6.68695662
22	19.66037934	16.34349987	15.93691664	12.04158172	11.06124050	8.17573908	7.64464575	6.74294441
23	20.45582113	16.87931861	16.44360839	12.30337898	11.27218738	8.26643160	7.71843370	6.79205650
24	21.24338726	17.40079670	16.93554212	12.55035753	11.46933400	8.34813658	7.78431581	6.83513728
25	22.02315570	17.90831795	17.41314769	12.78335616	11.65358318	8.42174466	7.84313911	6.87292744
26	22.79520366	18.40225592	17.87684242	13.00316619	11.82577867	8.48805826	7.89565992	6.90607670
27	23.55960759	18.88297413	18.32703147	13.21053414	11.98670904	8.54780023	7.94255350	6.93515500
28	24.31644316	19.35082640	18.76410823	13.40616428	12.13711125	8.60162183	7.98442277	6.96066228
29	25.06578530	19.80615708	19.18845459	13.59072102	12.27767407	8.65010976	8.02180604	6.98303709
30	25.80770822	20.24930130	19.60044135	13.76483115	12.40904118	8.69379257	8.05518397	7.00266411
31	26.54228537	20.68058520	20.00042849	13.92908599	12.53181419	8.73314646	8.08498569	7.01988080
32	27.26958947	21.10032623	20.38876553	14.08404339	12.64655532	8.76860042	8.11159436	7.03498316
33	27.98969255	21.50883332	20.76579178	14.23022961	12.75379002	8.80054092	8.13535211	7.04823084
34	28.70266589	21.90640712	21.13183668	14.36814114	12.85400936	8.82931614	8.15656438	7.05985161
35	29.40858009	22.29334026	21.48722007	14.49824636	12.94767230	8.85523977	8.17550391	7.07004528
36	30.10750504	22.66991753	21.83225250	14.62098713	13.03520776	8.87859438	8.19241421	7.07898708
37	30.79950994	23.03641609	22.16723544	14.73678031	13.11701660	8.89963458	8.20751269	7.08683078
38	31.48466330	23.39310568	22.49246159	14.84601916	13.19347345	8.91858971	8.22099347	7.09371121
39	32.16303298	23.74024884	22.80821513	14.94907468	13.26492846	8.93566641	8.23302988	7.09974667
40	32.83468611	24.07810106	23.11477197	15.04629687	13.33170884	8.95105082	8.24377668	7.10504094
41	33.49968922	24.40691101	23.41239997	15.13801592	13.39412041	8.96491065	8.25337204	7.10968504
42	34.15810814	24.72692069	23.70135920	15.22454332	13.45244898	8.97739698	8.26193932	7.11375880
43	34.81000806	25.03836563	23.98190213	15.30617294	13.50696167	8.98864593	8.26958868	7.11733228
44	35.45545352	25.34147507	24.25427392	15.38318202	13.55790810	8.99878011	8.27641846	7.12046692
45	36.09450844	25.63647209	24.51871254	15.45583209	13.60552159	9.00791001	8.28251648	7.12321659
46	36.72723608	25.92357381	24.77544907	15.52436990	13.65002018	9.01613515	8.28796115	7.12562859
47	37.35369909	26.20299154	25.02470783	15.58902821	13.69160764	9.02354518	8.29282245	7.12774438
48	37.97395949	26.47493094	25.26670664	15.65002661	13.73047443	9.03022088	8.29716290	7.12960033
49	38.58807871	26.73959215	25.50165693	15.70757227	13.76679853	9.03623503	8.30103831	7.13122836
50	39.19611753	26.99716998	25.72976401	15.76186064	13.80074629	9.04165318	8.30449849	7.13265646

TABLE 12
ANNUAL PERCENTAGE RATE TABLE FOR MONTHLY PAYMENT PLANS

NUMBER OF PAYMENTS	10.00%	10.25%	10.50%	10.75%	11.00%	11.25%	11.50%	11.75%	12.00%	12.25%	12.50%	12.75%	13.00%	13.25%	13.50%	13.75%
	(FINANCE CHARGE PER $100 OF AMOUNT FINANCED)															
1	0.83	0.85	0.87	0.90	0.92	0.94	0.96	0.98	1.00	1.02	1.04	1.06	1.08	1.10	1.12	1.15
2	1.25	1.28	1.31	1.35	1.38	1.41	1.44	1.47	1.50	1.53	1.57	1.60	1.63	1.66	1.69	1.72
3	1.67	1.71	1.76	1.80	1.84	1.88	1.92	1.96	2.01	2.05	2.09	2.13	2.17	2.22	2.26	2.30
4	2.09	2.14	2.20	2.25	2.30	2.35	2.41	2.46	2.51	2.57	2.62	2.67	2.72	2.78	2.83	2.88
5	2.51	2.58	2.64	2.70	2.77	2.83	2.89	2.96	3.02	3.08	3.15	3.21	3.27	3.34	3.40	3.46
6	2.94	3.01	3.08	3.16	3.23	3.31	3.38	3.45	3.53	3.60	3.68	3.75	3.83	3.90	3.97	4.05
7	3.36	3.45	3.53	3.62	3.70	3.78	3.87	3.95	4.04	4.12	4.21	4.29	4.38	4.47	4.55	4.64
8	3.79	3.88	3.98	4.07	4.17	4.26	4.36	4.46	4.55	4.65	4.74	4.84	4.94	5.03	5.13	5.22
9	4.21	4.32	4.43	4.53	4.64	4.75	4.85	4.96	5.07	5.17	5.28	5.39	5.49	5.60	5.71	5.82
10	4.64	4.76	4.88	4.99	5.11	5.23	5.35	5.46	5.58	5.70	5.82	5.94	6.05	6.17	6.29	6.41
11	5.07	5.20	5.33	5.45	5.58	5.71	5.84	5.97	6.10	6.23	6.36	6.49	6.62	6.75	6.88	7.01
12	5.50	5.64	5.78	5.92	6.06	6.20	6.34	6.48	6.62	6.76	6.90	7.04	7.18	7.32	7.46	7.60
13	5.93	6.08	6.23	6.38	6.53	6.68	6.84	6.99	7.14	7.29	7.44	7.59	7.75	7.90	8.05	8.20
14	6.36	6.52	6.69	6.85	7.01	7.17	7.34	7.50	7.66	7.82	7.99	8.15	8.31	8.48	8.64	8.81
15	6.80	6.97	7.14	7.32	7.49	7.66	7.84	8.01	8.19	8.36	8.53	8.71	8.88	9.06	9.23	9.41
16	7.23	7.41	7.60	7.78	7.97	8.15	8.34	8.53	8.71	8.90	9.08	9.27	9.46	9.64	9.83	10.02
17	7.67	7.86	8.06	8.25	8.45	8.65	8.84	9.04	9.24	9.44	9.63	9.83	10.03	10.23	10.43	10.63
18	8.10	8.31	8.52	8.73	8.93	9.14	9.35	9.56	9.77	9.98	10.19	10.40	10.61	10.82	11.03	11.24
19	8.54	8.76	8.98	9.20	9.42	9.64	9.86	10.08	10.30	10.52	10.74	10.96	11.18	11.41	11.63	11.85
20	8.98	9.21	9.44	9.67	9.90	10.13	10.37	10.60	10.83	11.06	11.30	11.53	11.76	12.00	12.23	12.46
21	9.42	9.66	9.90	10.15	10.39	10.63	10.88	11.12	11.36	11.61	11.85	12.10	12.34	12.59	12.84	13.08
22	9.86	10.12	10.37	10.62	10.88	11.13	11.39	11.64	11.90	12.16	12.41	12.67	12.93	13.19	13.44	13.70
23	10.30	10.57	10.84	11.10	11.37	11.63	11.90	12.17	12.44	12.71	12.97	13.24	13.51	13.78	14.05	14.32
24	10.75	11.02	11.30	11.58	11.86	12.14	12.42	12.70	12.98	13.26	13.54	13.82	14.10	14.38	14.66	14.95
25	11.19	11.48	11.77	12.06	12.35	12.64	12.93	13.22	13.52	13.81	14.10	14.40	14.69	14.98	15.28	15.57
26	11.64	11.94	12.24	12.54	12.85	13.15	13.45	13.75	14.06	14.36	14.67	14.97	15.28	15.59	15.89	16.20
27	12.09	12.40	12.71	13.03	13.34	13.66	13.97	14.29	14.60	14.92	15.24	15.56	15.87	16.19	16.51	16.83
28	12.53	12.86	13.18	13.51	13.84	14.16	14.49	14.82	15.15	15.48	15.81	16.14	16.47	16.80	17.13	17.46
29	12.98	13.32	13.66	14.00	14.33	14.67	15.01	15.35	15.70	16.04	16.38	16.72	17.07	17.41	17.75	18.10
30	13.43	13.78	14.13	14.48	14.83	15.19	15.54	15.89	16.24	16.60	16.95	17.31	17.66	18.02	18.38	18.74
31	13.89	14.25	14.61	14.97	15.33	15.70	16.06	16.43	16.79	17.16	17.53	17.90	18.27	18.63	19.00	19.38
32	14.34	14.71	15.09	15.46	15.84	16.21	16.59	16.97	17.35	17.73	18.11	18.49	18.87	19.25	19.63	20.02
33	14.79	15.18	15.57	15.95	16.34	16.73	17.12	17.51	17.90	18.29	18.69	19.08	19.47	19.87	20.26	20.66
34	15.25	15.65	16.05	16.44	16.85	17.25	17.65	18.05	18.46	18.86	19.27	19.67	20.08	20.49	20.90	21.31
35	15.70	16.11	16.53	16.94	17.35	17.77	18.18	18.60	19.01	19.43	19.85	20.27	20.69	21.11	21.53	21.95
36	16.16	16.58	17.01	17.43	17.86	18.29	18.71	19.14	19.57	20.00	20.43	20.87	21.30	21.73	22.17	22.60
37	16.62	17.06	17.49	17.93	18.37	18.81	19.25	19.69	20.13	20.58	21.02	21.46	21.91	22.36	22.81	23.25
38	17.08	17.53	17.98	18.43	18.88	19.33	19.78	20.24	20.69	21.15	21.61	22.07	22.52	22.99	23.45	23.91
39	17.54	18.00	18.46	18.93	19.39	19.86	20.32	20.79	21.26	21.73	22.20	22.67	23.14	23.61	24.09	24.56
40	18.00	18.48	18.95	19.43	19.90	20.38	20.86	21.34	21.82	22.30	22.79	23.27	23.76	24.25	24.73	25.22
41	18.47	18.95	19.44	19.93	20.42	20.91	21.40	21.89	22.39	22.88	23.38	23.88	24.38	24.88	25.38	25.88
42	18.93	19.43	19.93	20.43	20.93	21.44	21.94	22.45	22.96	23.47	23.98	24.49	25.00	25.51	26.03	26.55
43	19.40	19.91	20.42	20.94	21.45	21.97	22.49	23.01	23.53	24.05	24.57	25.10	25.62	26.15	26.68	27.21
44	19.86	20.39	20.91	21.44	21.97	22.50	23.03	23.57	24.10	24.64	25.17	25.71	26.25	26.79	27.33	27.88
45	20.33	20.87	21.41	21.95	22.49	23.03	23.58	24.12	24.67	25.22	25.77	26.32	26.88	27.43	27.99	28.55
46	20.80	21.35	21.90	22.46	23.01	23.57	24.13	24.69	25.25	25.81	26.37	26.94	27.51	28.08	28.65	29.22
47	21.27	21.83	22.40	22.97	23.53	24.10	24.68	25.25	25.82	26.40	26.98	27.56	28.14	28.72	29.31	29.89
48	21.74	22.32	22.90	23.48	24.06	24.64	25.23	25.81	26.40	26.99	27.58	28.18	28.77	29.37	29.97	30.57
49	22.21	22.80	23.39	23.99	24.58	25.18	25.78	26.38	26.98	27.59	28.19	28.80	29.41	30.02	30.63	31.24
50	22.69	23.29	23.89	24.50	25.11	25.72	26.33	26.95	27.56	28.18	28.80	29.42	30.04	30.67	31.29	31.92
51	23.16	23.78	24.40	25.02	25.64	26.26	26.89	27.52	28.15	28.78	29.41	30.05	30.68	31.32	31.96	32.60
52	23.64	24.27	24.90	25.53	26.17	26.81	27.45	28.09	28.73	29.38	30.02	30.67	31.32	31.98	32.63	33.29
53	24.11	24.76	25.40	26.05	26.70	27.35	28.00	28.66	29.32	29.98	30.64	31.30	31.97	32.63	33.30	33.97
54	24.59	25.25	25.91	26.57	27.23	27.90	28.56	29.23	29.91	30.58	31.25	31.93	32.61	33.29	33.98	34.66
55	25.07	25.74	26.41	27.09	27.77	28.44	29.13	29.81	30.50	31.18	31.87	32.56	33.26	33.95	34.65	35.35
56	25.55	26.23	26.92	27.61	28.30	28.99	29.69	30.39	31.09	31.79	32.49	33.20	33.91	34.62	35.33	36.04
57	26.03	26.73	27.43	28.13	28.84	29.54	30.25	30.97	31.68	32.39	33.11	33.83	34.56	35.28	36.01	36.74
58	26.51	27.23	27.94	28.66	29.37	30.10	30.82	31.55	32.27	33.00	33.74	34.47	35.21	35.95	36.69	37.43
59	27.00	27.72	28.45	29.18	29.91	30.65	31.39	32.13	32.87	33.61	34.36	35.11	35.86	36.62	37.37	38.13
60	27.48	28.22	28.96	29.71	30.45	31.20	31.96	32.71	33.47	34.23	34.99	35.75	36.52	37.29	38.06	38.83

TABLE 12 (*cont.*)

NUMBER OF PAYMENTS	ANNUAL PERCENTAGE RATE															
	14.00%	14.25%	14.50%	14.75%	15.00%	15.25%	15.50%	15.75%	16.00%	16.25%	16.50%	16.75%	17.00%	17.25%	17.50%	17.75%
	(FINANCE CHARGE PER $100 OF AMOUNT FINANCED)															
1	1.17	1.19	1.21	1.23	1.25	1.27	1.29	1.31	1.33	1.35	1.37	1.40	1.42	1.44	1.46	1.48
2	1.75	1.78	1.82	1.85	1.88	1.91	1.94	1.97	2.00	2.04	2.07	2.10	2.13	2.16	2.19	2.22
3	2.34	2.38	2.43	2.47	2.51	2.55	2.59	2.64	2.68	2.72	2.76	2.80	2.85	2.89	2.93	2.97
4	2.93	2.99	3.04	3.09	3.14	3.20	3.25	3.30	3.36	3.41	3.46	3.51	3.57	3.62	3.67	3.73
5	3.53	3.59	3.65	3.72	3.78	3.84	3.91	3.97	4.04	4.10	4.16	4.23	4.29	4.35	4.42	4.48
6	4.12	4.20	4.27	4.35	4.42	4.49	4.57	4.64	4.72	4.79	4.87	4.94	5.02	5.09	5.17	5.24
7	4.72	4.81	4.89	4.98	5.06	5.15	5.23	5.32	5.40	5.49	5.58	5.66	5.75	5.83	5.92	6.00
8	5.32	5.42	5.51	5.61	5.71	5.80	5.90	6.00	6.09	6.19	6.29	6.38	6.48	6.58	6.67	6.77
9	5.92	6.03	6.14	6.25	6.35	6.46	6.57	6.68	6.78	6.89	7.00	7.11	7.22	7.32	7.43	7.54
10	6.53	6.65	6.77	6.88	7.00	7.12	7.24	7.36	7.48	7.60	7.72	7.84	7.96	8.08	8.19	8.31
11	7.14	7.27	7.40	7.53	7.66	7.79	7.92	8.05	8.18	8.31	8.44	8.57	8.70	8.83	8.96	9.09
12	7.74	7.89	8.03	8.17	8.31	8.45	8.59	8.74	8.88	9.02	9.16	9.30	9.45	9.59	9.73	9.87
13	8.36	8.51	8.66	8.81	8.97	9.12	9.27	9.43	9.58	9.73	9.89	10.04	10.20	10.35	10.50	10.66
14	8.97	9.13	9.30	9.46	9.63	9.79	9.96	10.12	10.29	10.45	10.62	10.78	10.95	11.11	11.28	11.45
15	9.59	9.76	9.94	10.11	10.29	10.47	10.64	10.82	11.00	11.17	11.35	11.53	11.71	11.88	12.06	12.24
16	10.20	10.39	10.58	10.77	10.95	11.14	11.33	11.52	11.71	11.90	12.09	12.28	12.46	12.65	12.84	13.03
17	10.82	11.02	11.22	11.42	11.62	11.82	12.02	12.22	12.42	12.62	12.83	13.03	13.23	13.43	13.63	13.83
18	11.45	11.66	11.87	12.08	12.29	12.50	12.72	12.93	13.14	13.35	13.57	13.78	13.99	14.21	14.42	14.64
19	12.07	12.30	12.52	12.74	12.97	13.19	13.41	13.64	13.86	14.09	14.31	14.54	14.76	14.99	15.22	15.44
20	12.70	12.93	13.17	13.41	13.64	13.88	14.11	14.35	14.59	14.82	15.06	15.30	15.54	15.77	16.01	16.25
21	13.33	13.58	13.82	14.07	14.32	14.57	14.82	15.06	15.31	15.56	15.81	16.06	16.31	16.56	16.81	17.07
22	13.96	14.22	14.48	14.74	15.00	15.26	15.52	15.78	16.04	16.30	16.57	16.83	17.09	17.36	17.62	17.88
23	14.59	14.87	15.14	15.41	15.68	15.96	16.23	16.50	16.78	17.05	17.32	17.60	17.88	18.15	18.43	18.70
24	15.23	15.51	15.80	16.08	16.37	16.65	16.94	17.22	17.51	17.80	18.09	18.37	18.66	18.95	19.24	19.53
25	15.87	16.17	16.46	16.76	17.06	17.35	17.65	17.95	18.25	18.55	18.85	19.15	19.45	19.75	20.05	20.36
26	16.51	16.82	17.13	17.44	17.75	18.06	18.37	18.68	18.99	19.30	19.62	19.93	20.24	20.56	20.87	21.19
27	17.15	17.47	17.80	18.12	18.44	18.76	19.09	19.41	19.74	20.06	20.39	20.71	21.04	21.37	21.69	22.02
28	17.80	18.13	18.47	18.80	19.14	19.47	19.81	20.15	20.48	20.82	21.16	21.50	21.84	22.18	22.52	22.86
29	18.45	18.79	19.14	19.49	19.83	20.18	20.53	20.88	21.23	21.58	21.94	22.29	22.64	22.99	23.35	23.70
30	19.10	19.45	19.81	20.17	20.54	20.90	21.26	21.62	21.99	22.35	22.72	23.08	23.45	23.81	24.18	24.55
31	19.75	20.12	20.49	20.87	21.24	21.61	21.99	22.37	22.74	23.12	23.50	23.88	24.26	24.64	25.02	25.40
32	20.40	20.79	21.17	21.56	21.95	22.33	22.72	23.11	23.50	23.89	24.28	24.68	25.07	25.46	25.86	26.25
33	21.06	21.46	21.85	22.25	22.65	23.06	23.46	23.86	24.26	24.67	25.07	25.48	25.88	26.29	26.70	27.11
34	21.72	22.13	22.54	22.95	23.37	23.78	24.19	24.61	25.03	25.44	25.86	26.28	26.70	27.12	27.54	27.97
35	22.38	22.80	23.23	23.65	24.08	24.51	24.94	25.36	25.79	26.23	26.66	27.09	27.52	27.96	28.39	28.83
36	23.04	23.48	23.92	24.35	24.80	25.24	25.68	26.12	26.57	27.01	27.46	27.90	28.35	28.80	29.25	29.70
37	23.70	24.16	24.61	25.06	25.51	25.97	26.42	26.88	27.34	27.80	28.26	28.72	29.18	29.64	30.10	30.57
38	24.37	24.84	25.30	25.77	26.24	26.70	27.17	27.64	28.11	28.59	29.06	29.53	30.01	30.49	30.96	31.44
39	25.04	25.52	26.00	26.48	26.96	27.44	27.92	28.41	28.89	29.38	29.87	30.36	30.85	31.34	31.83	32.32
40	25.71	26.20	26.70	27.19	27.69	28.18	28.68	29.18	29.68	30.18	30.68	31.18	31.68	32.19	32.69	33.20
41	26.39	26.89	27.40	27.91	28.41	28.92	29.44	29.95	30.46	30.97	31.49	32.01	32.52	33.04	33.56	34.08
42	27.06	27.58	28.10	28.62	29.15	29.67	30.19	30.72	31.25	31.78	32.31	32.84	33.37	33.90	34.44	34.97
43	27.74	28.27	28.81	29.34	29.88	30.42	30.96	31.50	32.04	32.58	33.13	33.67	34.22	34.76	35.31	35.86
44	28.42	28.97	29.52	30.07	30.62	31.17	31.72	32.28	32.83	33.39	33.95	34.51	35.07	35.63	36.19	36.76
45	29.11	29.67	30.23	30.79	31.36	31.92	32.49	33.06	33.63	34.20	34.77	35.35	35.92	36.50	37.08	37.66
46	29.79	30.36	30.94	31.52	32.10	32.68	33.26	33.84	34.43	35.01	35.60	36.19	36.78	37.37	37.96	38.56
47	30.48	31.07	31.66	32.25	32.84	33.44	34.03	34.63	35.23	35.83	36.43	37.04	37.64	38.25	38.86	39.46
48	31.17	31.77	32.37	32.98	33.59	34.20	34.81	35.42	36.03	36.65	37.27	37.88	38.50	39.13	39.75	40.37
49	31.86	32.48	33.09	33.71	34.34	34.96	35.59	36.21	36.84	37.47	38.10	38.74	39.37	40.01	40.65	41.29
50	32.55	33.18	33.82	34.45	35.09	35.73	36.37	37.01	37.65	38.30	38.94	39.59	40.24	40.89	41.55	42.20
51	33.25	33.89	34.54	35.19	35.84	36.49	37.15	37.81	38.46	39.12	39.79	40.45	41.11	41.78	42.45	43.12
52	33.95	34.61	35.27	35.93	36.60	37.27	37.94	38.61	39.28	39.96	40.63	41.31	41.99	42.67	43.36	44.04
53	34.65	35.32	36.00	36.68	37.36	38.04	38.72	39.41	40.10	40.79	41.48	42.17	42.87	43.57	44.27	44.97
54	35.35	36.04	36.73	37.42	38.12	38.82	39.52	40.22	40.92	41.63	42.33	43.04	43.75	44.47	45.18	45.90
55	36.05	36.76	37.46	38.17	38.88	39.60	40.31	41.03	41.74	42.47	43.19	43.91	44.64	45.37	46.10	46.83
56	36.76	37.48	38.20	38.92	39.65	40.38	41.11	41.84	42.57	43.31	44.05	44.79	45.53	46.27	47.02	47.77
57	37.47	38.20	38.94	39.68	40.42	41.16	41.91	42.65	43.40	44.15	44.91	45.66	46.42	47.18	47.94	48.71
58	38.18	38.93	39.68	40.43	41.19	41.95	42.71	43.47	44.23	45.00	45.77	46.54	47.32	48.09	48.87	49.65
59	38.89	39.66	40.42	41.19	41.96	42.74	43.51	44.29	45.07	45.85	46.64	47.42	48.21	49.01	49.80	50.60
60	39.61	40.39	41.17	41.95	42.74	43.53	44.32	45.11	45.91	46.71	47.51	48.31	49.12	49.92	50.73	51.55

Tables

TABLE 12 (cont.)

NUMBER OF PAYMENTS	ANNUAL PERCENTAGE RATE															
	18.00%	18.25%	18.50%	18.75%	19.00%	19.25%	19.50%	19.75%	20.00%	20.25%	20.50%	20.75%	21.00%	21.25%	21.50%	21.75%
	(FINANCE CHARGE PER $100 OF AMOUNT FINANCED)															
1	1.50	1.52	1.54	1.56	1.58	1.60	1.62	1.65	1.67	1.69	1.71	1.73	1.75	1.77	1.79	1.81
2	2.26	2.29	2.32	2.35	2.38	2.41	2.44	2.48	2.51	2.54	2.57	2.60	2.63	2.66	2.70	2.73
3	3.01	3.06	3.10	3.14	3.18	3.23	3.27	3.31	3.35	3.39	3.44	3.48	3.52	3.56	3.60	3.65
4	3.78	3.83	3.88	3.94	3.99	4.04	4.10	4.15	4.20	4.25	4.31	4.36	4.41	4.47	4.52	4.57
5	4.54	4.61	4.67	4.74	4.80	4.86	4.93	4.99	5.06	5.12	5.18	5.25	5.31	5.37	5.44	5.50
6	5.32	5.39	5.46	5.54	5.61	5.69	5.76	5.84	5.91	5.99	6.06	6.14	6.21	6.29	6.36	6.44
7	6.09	6.18	6.26	6.35	6.43	6.52	6.60	6.69	6.78	6.86	6.95	7.04	7.12	7.21	7.29	7.38
8	6.87	6.96	7.06	7.16	7.26	7.35	7.45	7.55	7.64	7.74	7.84	7.94	8.03	8.13	8.23	8.33
9	7.65	7.76	7.87	7.97	8.08	8.19	8.30	8.41	8.52	8.63	8.73	8.84	8.95	9.06	9.17	9.28
10	8.43	8.55	8.67	8.79	8.91	9.03	9.15	9.27	9.39	9.51	9.63	9.75	9.88	10.00	10.12	10.24
11	9.22	9.35	9.49	9.62	9.75	9.88	10.01	10.14	10.28	10.41	10.54	10.67	10.80	10.94	11.07	11.20
12	10.02	10.16	10.30	10.44	10.59	10.73	10.87	11.02	11.16	11.31	11.45	11.59	11.74	11.88	12.02	12.17
13	10.81	10.97	11.12	11.28	11.43	11.59	11.74	11.90	12.05	12.21	12.36	12.52	12.67	12.83	12.99	13.14
14	11.61	11.78	11.95	12.11	12.28	12.45	12.61	12.78	12.95	13.11	13.28	13.45	13.62	13.79	13.95	14.12
15	12.42	12.59	12.77	12.95	13.13	13.31	13.49	13.67	13.85	14.03	14.21	14.39	14.57	14.75	14.93	15.11
16	13.22	13.41	13.60	13.80	13.99	14.18	14.37	14.56	14.75	14.94	15.13	15.33	15.52	15.71	15.90	16.10
17	14.04	14.24	14.44	14.64	14.85	15.05	15.25	15.46	15.66	15.86	16.07	16.27	16.48	16.68	16.89	17.09
18	14.85	15.07	15.28	15.49	15.71	15.93	16.14	16.36	16.57	16.79	17.01	17.22	17.44	17.66	17.88	18.09
19	15.67	15.90	16.12	16.35	16.58	16.81	17.03	17.26	17.49	17.72	17.95	18.18	18.41	18.64	18.87	19.10
20	16.49	16.73	16.97	17.21	17.45	17.69	17.93	18.17	18.41	18.66	18.90	19.14	19.38	19.63	19.87	20.11
21	17.32	17.57	17.82	18.07	18.33	18.58	18.83	19.09	19.34	19.60	19.85	20.11	20.36	20.62	20.87	21.13
22	18.15	18.41	18.68	18.94	19.21	19.47	19.74	20.01	20.27	20.54	20.81	21.08	21.34	21.61	21.88	22.15
23	18.98	19.26	19.54	19.81	20.09	20.37	20.65	20.93	21.21	21.49	21.77	22.05	22.33	22.61	22.90	23.18
24	19.82	20.11	20.40	20.69	20.98	21.27	21.56	21.86	22.15	22.44	22.74	23.03	23.33	23.62	23.92	24.21
25	20.66	20.96	21.27	21.57	21.87	22.18	22.48	22.79	23.10	23.40	23.71	24.02	24.32	24.63	24.94	25.25
26	21.50	21.82	22.14	22.45	22.77	23.09	23.41	23.73	24.04	24.36	24.68	25.01	25.33	25.65	25.97	26.29
27	22.35	22.68	23.01	23.34	23.67	24.00	24.33	24.67	25.00	25.33	25.67	26.00	26.34	26.67	27.01	27.34
28	23.20	23.55	23.89	24.23	24.58	24.92	25.27	25.61	25.96	26.30	26.65	27.00	27.35	27.70	28.05	28.40
29	24.06	24.41	24.77	25.13	25.49	25.84	26.20	26.56	26.92	27.28	27.64	28.00	28.37	28.73	29.09	29.46
30	24.92	25.29	25.66	26.03	26.40	26.77	27.14	27.52	27.89	28.26	28.64	29.01	29.39	29.77	30.14	30.52
31	25.78	26.16	26.55	26.93	27.32	27.70	28.09	28.47	28.86	29.25	29.64	30.03	30.42	30.81	31.20	31.59
32	26.65	27.04	27.44	27.84	28.24	28.64	29.04	29.44	29.84	30.24	30.64	31.05	31.45	31.85	32.26	32.67
33	27.52	27.93	28.34	28.75	29.16	29.57	29.99	30.40	30.82	31.23	31.65	32.07	32.49	32.91	33.33	33.75
34	28.39	28.81	29.24	29.66	30.09	30.52	30.95	31.37	31.80	32.23	32.67	33.10	33.53	33.96	34.40	34.83
35	29.27	29.71	30.14	30.58	31.02	31.47	31.91	32.35	32.79	33.24	33.68	34.13	34.58	35.03	35.47	35.92
36	30.15	30.60	31.05	31.51	31.96	32.42	32.87	33.33	33.79	34.25	34.71	35.17	35.63	36.09	36.56	37.02
37	31.03	31.50	31.97	32.43	32.90	33.37	33.84	34.32	34.79	35.26	35.74	36.21	36.69	37.16	37.64	38.12
38	31.92	32.40	32.88	33.37	33.85	34.33	34.82	35.30	35.79	36.28	36.77	37.26	37.75	38.24	38.73	39.23
39	32.81	33.31	33.80	34.30	34.80	35.30	35.80	36.30	36.80	37.30	37.81	38.31	38.82	39.32	39.83	40.34
40	33.71	34.22	34.73	35.24	35.75	36.26	36.78	37.29	37.81	38.33	38.85	39.37	39.89	40.41	40.93	41.46
41	34.61	35.13	35.66	36.18	36.71	37.24	37.77	38.30	38.83	39.36	39.89	40.43	40.96	41.50	42.04	42.58
42	35.51	36.05	36.59	37.13	37.67	38.21	38.76	39.30	39.85	40.40	40.95	41.50	42.05	42.60	43.15	43.71
43	36.42	36.97	37.52	38.08	38.63	39.19	39.75	40.31	40.87	41.44	42.00	42.57	43.13	43.70	44.27	44.84
44	37.33	37.89	38.46	39.03	39.60	40.18	40.75	41.33	41.90	42.48	43.06	43.64	44.22	44.81	45.39	45.98
45	38.24	38.82	39.41	39.99	40.58	41.17	41.75	42.35	42.94	43.53	44.13	44.72	45.32	45.92	46.52	47.12
46	39.16	39.75	40.35	40.95	41.55	42.16	42.76	43.37	43.98	44.58	45.20	45.81	46.42	47.03	47.65	48.27
47	40.08	40.69	41.30	41.92	42.54	43.15	43.77	44.40	45.02	45.64	46.27	46.90	47.53	48.16	48.79	49.42
48	41.00	41.63	42.26	42.89	43.52	44.15	44.79	45.43	46.07	46.71	47.35	47.99	48.64	49.28	49.93	50.58
49	41.93	42.57	43.22	43.86	44.51	45.16	45.81	46.46	47.12	47.77	48.43	49.09	49.75	50.41	51.08	51.74
50	42.86	43.52	44.18	44.84	45.50	46.17	46.83	47.50	48.17	48.84	49.52	50.19	50.87	51.55	52.23	52.91
51	43.79	44.47	45.14	45.82	46.50	47.18	47.86	48.55	49.23	49.92	50.61	51.30	51.99	52.69	53.38	54.08
52	44.73	45.42	46.11	46.80	47.50	48.20	48.89	49.59	50.30	51.00	51.71	52.41	53.12	53.83	54.55	55.26
53	45.67	46.38	47.08	47.79	48.50	49.22	49.93	50.65	51.37	52.09	52.81	53.53	54.26	54.98	55.71	56.44
54	46.62	47.34	48.06	48.79	49.51	50.24	50.97	51.70	52.44	53.17	53.91	54.65	55.39	56.14	56.88	57.63
55	47.57	48.30	49.04	49.78	50.52	51.27	52.02	52.76	53.52	54.27	55.02	55.78	56.54	57.30	58.06	58.82
56	48.52	49.27	50.03	50.78	51.54	52.30	53.06	53.83	54.60	55.37	56.14	56.91	57.68	58.46	59.24	60.02
57	49.47	50.24	51.01	51.79	52.56	53.34	54.12	54.90	55.68	56.47	57.25	58.04	58.84	59.63	60.43	61.22
58	50.43	51.22	52.00	52.79	53.58	54.38	55.17	55.97	56.77	57.57	58.38	59.18	59.99	60.80	61.62	62.43
59	51.39	52.20	53.00	53.80	54.61	55.42	56.23	57.05	57.87	58.68	59.51	60.33	61.15	61.98	62.81	63.64
60	52.36	53.18	54.00	54.82	55.64	56.47	57.30	58.13	58.96	59.80	60.64	61.48	62.32	63.17	64.01	64.86

TABLE 12 (cont.)

NUMBER OF PAYMENTS	ANNUAL PERCENTAGE RATE															
	22.00%	22.25%	22.50%	22.75%	23.00%	23.25%	23.50%	23.75%	24.00%	24.25%	24.50%	24.75%	25.00%	25.25%	25.50%	25.75%
	(FINANCE CHARGE PER $100 OF AMOUNT FINANCED)															
1	1.83	1.85	1.87	1.90	1.92	1.94	1.96	1.98	2.00	2.02	2.04	2.06	2.08	2.10	2.12	2.15
2	2.76	2.79	2.82	2.85	2.88	2.92	2.95	2.98	3.01	3.04	3.07	3.10	3.14	3.17	3.20	3.23
3	3.69	3.73	3.77	3.82	3.86	3.90	3.94	3.98	4.03	4.07	4.11	4.15	4.20	4.24	4.28	4.32
4	4.62	4.68	4.73	4.78	4.84	4.89	4.94	5.00	5.05	5.10	5.16	5.21	5.26	5.32	5.37	5.42
5	5.57	5.63	5.69	5.76	5.82	5.89	5.95	6.02	6.08	6.14	6.21	6.27	6.34	6.40	6.46	6.53
6	6.51	6.59	6.66	6.74	6.81	6.89	6.96	7.04	7.12	7.19	7.27	7.34	7.42	7.49	7.57	7.64
7	7.47	7.55	7.64	7.73	7.81	7.90	7.99	8.07	8.16	8.24	8.33	8.42	8.51	8.59	8.68	8.77
8	8.42	8.52	8.62	8.72	8.82	8.91	9.01	9.11	9.21	9.31	9.40	9.50	9.60	9.70	9.80	9.90
9	9.39	9.50	9.61	9.72	9.83	9.94	10.04	10.15	10.26	10.37	10.48	10.59	10.70	10.81	10.92	11.03
10	10.36	10.48	10.60	10.72	10.84	10.96	11.08	11.21	11.33	11.45	11.57	11.69	11.81	11.93	12.06	12.18
11	11.33	11.47	11.60	11.73	11.86	12.00	12.13	12.26	12.40	12.53	12.66	12.80	12.93	13.06	13.20	13.33
12	12.31	12.46	12.60	12.75	12.89	13.04	13.18	13.33	13.47	13.62	13.76	13.91	14.05	14.20	14.34	14.49
13	13.30	13.46	13.61	13.77	13.93	14.08	14.24	14.40	14.55	14.71	14.87	15.03	15.18	15.34	15.50	15.66
14	14.29	14.46	14.63	14.80	14.97	15.13	15.30	15.47	15.64	15.81	15.98	16.15	16.32	16.49	16.66	16.83
15	15.29	15.47	15.65	15.83	16.01	16.19	16.37	16.56	16.74	16.92	17.10	17.28	17.47	17.65	17.83	18.02
16	16.29	16.48	16.68	16.87	17.06	17.26	17.45	17.65	17.84	18.03	18.23	18.42	18.62	18.81	19.01	19.21
17	17.30	17.50	17.71	17.92	18.12	18.33	18.53	18.74	18.95	19.16	19.36	19.57	19.78	19.99	20.20	20.40
18	18.31	18.53	18.75	18.97	19.19	19.41	19.62	19.84	20.06	20.28	20.50	20.72	20.95	21.17	21.39	21.61
19	19.33	19.56	19.79	20.02	20.26	20.49	20.72	20.95	21.19	21.42	21.65	21.89	22.12	22.35	22.59	22.82
20	20.35	20.60	20.84	21.09	21.33	21.58	21.82	22.07	22.31	22.56	22.81	23.05	23.30	23.55	23.79	24.04
21	21.38	21.64	21.90	22.16	22.41	22.67	22.93	23.19	23.45	23.71	23.97	24.23	24.49	24.75	25.01	25.27
22	22.42	22.69	22.96	23.23	23.50	23.77	24.04	24.32	24.59	24.86	25.13	25.41	25.68	25.96	26.23	26.50
23	23.46	23.74	24.03	24.31	24.60	24.88	25.17	25.45	25.74	26.02	26.31	26.60	26.88	27.17	27.46	27.75
24	24.51	24.80	25.10	25.40	25.70	25.99	26.29	26.59	26.89	27.19	27.49	27.79	28.09	28.39	28.69	29.00
25	25.56	25.87	26.18	26.49	26.80	27.11	27.43	27.74	28.05	28.36	28.68	28.99	29.31	29.62	29.94	30.25
26	26.62	26.94	27.26	27.59	27.91	28.24	28.56	28.89	29.22	29.55	29.87	30.20	30.53	30.86	31.19	31.52
27	27.68	28.02	28.35	28.69	29.03	29.37	29.71	30.05	30.39	30.73	31.07	31.42	31.76	32.10	32.45	32.79
28	28.75	29.10	29.45	29.80	30.15	30.51	30.86	31.22	31.57	31.93	32.28	32.64	33.00	33.35	33.71	34.07
29	29.82	30.19	30.55	30.92	31.28	31.65	32.02	32.39	32.76	33.13	33.50	33.87	34.24	34.61	34.98	35.36
30	30.90	31.28	31.66	32.04	32.42	32.80	33.18	33.57	33.95	34.33	34.72	35.10	35.49	35.88	36.26	36.65
31	31.98	32.38	32.77	33.17	33.56	33.96	34.35	34.75	35.15	35.55	35.95	36.35	36.75	37.15	37.55	37.95
32	33.07	33.48	33.89	34.30	34.71	35.12	35.53	35.94	36.35	36.77	37.18	37.60	38.01	38.43	38.84	39.26
33	34.17	34.59	35.01	35.44	35.86	36.29	36.71	37.14	37.57	37.99	38.42	38.85	39.28	39.71	40.14	40.58
34	35.27	35.71	36.14	36.58	37.02	37.46	37.90	38.34	38.78	39.23	39.67	40.11	40.56	41.01	41.45	41.90
35	36.37	36.83	37.28	37.73	38.18	38.64	39.09	39.55	40.01	40.47	40.92	41.38	41.84	42.31	42.77	43.23
36	37.49	37.95	38.42	38.89	39.35	39.82	40.29	40.77	41.24	41.71	42.19	42.66	43.14	43.61	44.09	44.57
37	38.60	39.08	39.56	40.05	40.53	41.02	41.50	41.99	42.48	42.96	43.45	43.94	44.43	44.93	45.42	45.91
38	39.72	40.22	40.72	41.21	41.71	42.21	42.71	43.22	43.72	44.22	44.73	45.23	45.74	46.25	46.75	47.26
39	40.85	41.36	41.87	42.39	42.90	43.42	43.93	44.45	44.97	45.49	46.01	46.53	47.05	47.57	48.10	48.62
40	41.98	42.51	43.04	43.56	44.09	44.62	45.16	45.69	46.22	46.76	47.29	47.83	48.37	48.91	49.45	49.99
41	43.12	43.66	44.20	44.75	45.29	45.84	46.39	46.94	47.48	48.04	48.59	49.14	49.69	50.25	50.80	51.36
42	44.26	44.82	45.38	45.94	46.50	47.06	47.62	48.19	48.75	49.32	49.89	50.46	51.03	51.60	52.17	52.74
43	45.41	45.98	46.56	47.13	47.71	48.29	48.87	49.45	50.03	50.61	51.19	51.78	52.36	52.95	53.54	54.13
44	46.56	47.15	47.74	48.33	48.93	49.52	50.11	50.71	51.31	51.91	52.51	53.11	53.71	54.31	54.92	55.52
45	47.72	48.33	48.93	49.54	50.15	50.76	51.37	51.98	52.59	53.21	53.82	54.44	55.06	55.68	56.30	56.92
46	48.89	49.51	50.13	50.75	51.37	52.00	52.63	53.26	53.89	54.52	55.15	55.78	56.42	57.05	57.69	58.33
47	50.06	50.69	51.33	51.97	52.61	53.25	53.89	54.54	55.18	55.83	56.48	57.13	57.78	58.44	59.09	59.75
48	51.23	51.88	52.54	53.19	53.85	54.51	55.16	55.83	56.49	57.15	57.82	58.49	59.15	59.82	60.50	61.17
49	52.41	53.08	53.75	54.42	55.09	55.77	56.44	57.12	57.80	58.48	59.16	59.85	60.53	61.22	61.91	62.60
50	53.59	54.28	54.96	55.65	56.34	57.03	57.73	58.42	59.12	59.81	60.51	61.21	61.92	62.62	63.33	64.03
51	54.78	55.48	56.19	56.89	57.60	58.30	59.01	59.73	60.44	61.15	61.87	62.59	63.31	64.03	64.75	65.47
52	55.98	56.69	57.41	58.13	58.86	59.58	60.31	61.04	61.77	62.50	63.23	63.97	64.70	65.44	66.18	66.92
53	57.18	57.91	58.65	59.38	60.12	60.87	61.61	62.35	63.10	63.85	64.60	65.35	66.11	66.86	67.62	68.38
54	58.38	59.13	59.88	60.64	61.40	62.16	62.92	63.68	64.44	65.21	65.98	66.75	67.52	68.29	69.07	69.84
55	59.59	60.36	61.13	61.90	62.67	63.45	64.23	65.01	65.79	66.57	67.36	68.14	68.93	69.72	70.52	71.31
56	60.80	61.59	62.38	63.17	63.96	64.75	65.54	66.34	67.14	67.94	68.74	69.55	70.36	71.16	71.97	72.79
57	62.02	62.83	63.63	64.44	65.25	66.06	66.87	67.68	68.50	69.32	70.14	70.96	71.78	72.61	73.44	74.27
58	63.25	64.07	64.89	65.71	66.54	67.37	68.20	69.03	69.86	70.70	71.54	72.38	73.22	74.06	74.91	75.76
59	64.48	65.32	66.15	67.00	67.84	68.68	69.53	70.38	71.23	72.09	72.94	73.80	74.66	75.52	76.39	77.25
60	65.71	66.57	67.42	68.28	69.14	70.01	70.87	71.74	72.61	73.48	74.35	75.23	76.11	76.99	77.87	78.76

TABLE 12 (cont.)

NUMBER OF PAYMENTS	ANNUAL PERCENTAGE RATE															
	26.00%	26.25%	26.50%	26.75%	27.00%	27.25%	27.50%	27.75%	28.00%	28.25%	28.50%	28.75%	29.00%	29.25%	29.50%	29.75%
	(FINANCE CHARGE PER $100 OF AMOUNT FINANCED)															
1	2.17	2.19	2.21	2.23	2.25	2.27	2.29	2.31	2.33	2.35	2.37	2.40	2.42	2.44	2.46	2.48
2	3.26	3.29	3.32	3.36	3.39	3.42	3.45	3.48	3.51	3.54	3.58	3.61	3.64	3.67	3.70	3.73
3	4.36	4.41	4.45	4.49	4.53	4.58	4.62	4.66	4.70	4.74	4.79	4.83	4.87	4.91	4.96	5.00
4	5.47	5.53	5.58	5.63	5.69	5.74	5.79	5.85	5.90	5.95	6.01	6.06	6.11	6.17	6.22	6.27
5	6.59	6.66	6.72	6.79	6.85	6.91	6.98	7.04	7.11	7.17	7.24	7.30	7.37	7.43	7.49	7.56
6	7.72	7.79	7.87	7.95	8.02	8.10	8.17	8.25	8.32	8.40	8.48	8.55	8.63	8.70	8.78	8.85
7	8.85	8.94	9.03	9.11	9.20	9.29	9.37	9.46	9.55	9.64	9.72	9.81	9.90	9.98	10.07	10.16
8	9.99	10.09	10.19	10.29	10.39	10.49	10.58	10.68	10.78	10.88	10.98	11.08	11.18	11.28	11.38	11.47
9	11.14	11.25	11.36	11.47	11.58	11.69	11.80	11.91	12.03	12.14	12.25	12.36	12.47	12.58	12.69	12.80
10	12.30	12.42	12.54	12.67	12.79	12.91	13.03	13.15	13.28	13.40	13.52	13.64	13.77	13.89	14.01	14.14
11	13.46	13.60	13.73	13.87	14.00	14.13	14.27	14.40	14.54	14.67	14.81	14.94	15.08	15.21	15.35	15.48
12	14.64	14.78	14.93	15.07	15.22	15.37	15.51	15.66	15.81	15.95	16.10	16.25	16.40	16.54	16.69	16.84
13	15.82	15.97	16.13	16.29	16.45	16.61	16.77	16.93	17.09	17.24	17.40	17.56	17.72	17.88	18.04	18.20
14	17.00	17.17	17.35	17.52	17.69	17.86	18.03	18.20	18.37	18.54	18.72	18.89	19.06	19.23	19.41	19.58
15	18.20	18.38	18.57	18.75	18.93	19.12	19.30	19.48	19.67	19.85	20.04	20.22	20.41	20.59	20.78	20.96
16	19.40	19.60	19.79	19.99	20.19	20.38	20.58	20.78	20.97	21.17	21.37	21.57	21.76	21.96	22.16	22.36
17	20.61	20.82	21.03	21.24	21.45	21.66	21.87	22.08	22.29	22.50	22.71	22.92	23.13	23.34	23.55	23.77
18	21.83	22.05	22.27	22.50	22.72	22.94	23.16	23.39	23.61	23.83	24.06	24.28	24.51	24.73	24.96	25.18
19	23.06	23.29	23.53	23.76	24.00	24.23	24.47	24.71	24.94	25.18	25.42	25.65	25.89	26.13	26.37	26.61
20	24.29	24.54	24.79	25.04	25.28	25.53	25.78	26.03	26.28	26.53	26.78	27.04	27.29	27.54	27.79	28.04
21	25.53	25.79	26.05	26.32	26.58	26.84	27.11	27.37	27.63	27.90	28.16	28.43	28.69	28.96	29.22	29.49
22	26.78	27.05	27.33	27.61	27.88	28.16	28.44	28.71	28.99	29.27	29.55	29.82	30.10	30.38	30.66	30.94
23	28.04	28.32	28.61	28.90	29.19	29.48	29.77	30.07	30.36	30.65	30.94	31.23	31.53	31.82	32.11	32.41
24	29.30	29.60	29.90	30.21	30.51	30.82	31.12	31.43	31.73	32.04	32.34	32.65	32.96	33.27	33.57	33.88
25	30.57	30.89	31.20	31.52	31.84	32.16	32.48	32.80	33.12	33.44	33.76	34.08	34.40	34.72	35.04	35.37
26	31.85	32.18	32.51	32.84	33.18	33.51	33.84	34.18	34.51	34.84	35.18	35.51	35.85	36.19	36.52	36.86
27	33.14	33.48	33.83	34.17	34.52	34.87	35.21	35.56	35.91	36.26	36.61	36.96	37.31	37.66	38.01	38.36
28	34.43	34.79	35.15	35.51	35.87	36.23	36.59	36.96	37.32	37.68	38.05	38.41	38.78	39.15	39.51	39.88
29	35.73	36.10	36.48	36.85	37.23	37.61	37.98	38.36	38.74	39.12	39.50	39.88	40.26	40.64	41.02	41.40
30	37.04	37.43	37.82	38.21	38.60	38.99	39.38	39.77	40.17	40.56	40.95	41.35	41.75	42.14	42.54	42.94
31	38.35	38.76	39.16	39.57	39.97	40.38	40.79	41.19	41.60	42.01	42.42	42.83	43.24	43.65	44.06	44.48
32	39.68	40.10	40.52	40.94	41.36	41.78	42.20	42.62	43.05	43.47	43.90	44.32	44.75	45.17	45.60	46.03
33	41.01	41.44	41.88	42.31	42.75	43.19	43.62	44.06	44.50	44.94	45.38	45.82	46.26	46.70	47.15	47.59
34	42.35	42.80	43.25	43.70	44.15	44.60	45.05	45.51	45.96	46.42	46.87	47.33	47.79	48.24	48.70	49.16
35	43.69	44.16	44.62	45.09	45.56	46.02	46.49	46.96	47.43	47.90	48.37	48.85	49.32	49.79	50.27	50.74
36	45.05	45.53	46.01	46.49	46.97	47.45	47.94	48.42	48.91	49.40	49.88	50.37	50.86	51.35	51.84	52.33
37	46.41	46.90	47.40	47.90	48.39	48.89	49.39	49.89	50.40	50.90	51.40	51.91	52.41	52.92	53.42	53.93
38	47.77	48.29	48.80	49.31	49.82	50.34	50.86	51.37	51.89	52.41	52.93	53.45	53.97	54.49	55.02	55.54
39	49.15	49.68	50.20	50.73	51.26	51.79	52.33	52.86	53.39	53.93	54.46	55.00	55.54	56.08	56.62	57.16
40	50.53	51.07	51.62	52.16	52.71	53.26	53.81	54.35	54.90	55.46	56.01	56.56	57.12	57.67	58.23	58.79
41	51.92	52.48	53.04	53.60	54.16	54.73	55.29	55.86	56.42	56.99	57.56	58.13	58.70	59.28	59.85	60.42
42	53.32	53.89	54.47	55.05	55.63	56.21	56.79	57.37	57.95	58.54	59.12	59.71	60.30	60.89	61.48	62.07
43	54.72	55.31	55.90	56.50	57.09	57.69	58.29	58.89	59.49	60.09	60.69	61.30	61.90	62.51	63.11	63.72
44	56.13	56.74	57.35	57.96	58.57	59.19	59.80	60.42	61.03	61.65	62.27	62.89	63.51	64.14	64.76	65.39
45	57.55	58.17	58.80	59.43	60.06	60.69	61.32	61.95	62.59	63.22	63.86	64.50	65.13	65.77	66.42	67.06
46	58.97	59.61	60.26	60.90	61.55	62.20	62.84	63.49	64.15	64.80	65.45	66.11	66.76	67.42	68.08	68.74
47	60.40	61.06	61.72	62.38	63.05	63.71	64.38	65.05	65.71	66.38	67.06	67.73	68.40	69.08	69.75	70.43
48	61.84	62.52	63.20	63.87	64.56	65.24	65.92	66.60	67.29	67.98	68.67	69.36	70.05	70.74	71.44	72.13
49	63.29	63.98	64.68	65.37	66.07	66.77	67.47	68.17	68.87	69.58	70.29	70.99	71.70	72.41	73.13	73.84
50	64.74	65.45	66.16	66.88	67.59	68.31	69.03	69.75	70.47	71.19	71.91	72.64	73.37	74.10	74.83	75.56
51	66.20	66.93	67.66	68.39	69.12	69.86	70.59	71.33	72.07	72.81	73.55	74.29	75.04	75.78	76.53	77.28
52	67.67	68.41	69.16	69.91	70.66	71.41	72.16	72.92	73.67	74.43	75.19	75.95	76.72	77.48	78.25	79.02
53	69.14	69.90	70.67	71.43	72.20	72.97	73.74	74.52	75.29	76.07	76.85	77.62	78.41	79.19	79.97	80.76
54	70.62	71.40	72.18	72.97	73.75	74.54	75.33	76.12	76.91	77.71	78.50	79.30	80.10	80.90	81.71	82.51
55	72.11	72.91	73.71	74.51	75.31	76.12	76.92	77.73	78.55	79.36	80.17	80.99	81.81	82.63	83.45	84.27
56	73.60	74.42	75.24	76.06	76.88	77.70	78.53	79.35	80.18	81.02	81.85	82.68	83.52	84.36	85.20	86.04
57	75.10	75.94	76.77	77.61	78.45	79.29	80.14	80.98	81.83	82.68	83.53	84.39	85.24	86.10	86.96	87.82
58	76.61	77.46	78.32	79.17	80.03	80.89	81.75	82.62	83.48	84.35	85.22	86.10	86.97	87.85	88.72	89.60
59	78.12	78.99	79.87	80.74	81.62	82.50	83.38	84.26	85.15	86.03	86.92	87.81	88.71	89.60	90.50	91.40
60	79.64	80.53	81.42	82.32	83.21	84.11	85.01	85.91	86.81	87.72	88.63	89.54	90.45	91.37	92.28	93.20

TABLE 12 (cont.)

NUMBER OF PAYMENTS	ANNUAL PERCENTAGE RATE															
	6.00%	6.25%	6.50%	6.75%	7.00%	7.25%	7.50%	7.75%	8.00%	8.25%	8.50%	8.75%	9.00%	9.25%	9.50%	9.75%
	(FINANCE CHARGE PER $100 OF AMOUNT FINANCED)															
301	93.66	98.29	102.97	107.70	112.48	117.31	122.18	127.11	132.07	137.09	142.14	147.24	152.37	157.55	162.77	168.02
302	94.02	98.67	103.37	108.13	112.93	117.78	122.67	127.62	132.60	137.64	142.71	147.83	152.99	158.19	163.43	168.71
303	94.39	99.06	103.78	108.55	113.37	118.24	123.16	128.12	133.13	138.19	143.29	148.43	153.61	158.83	164.09	169.39
304	94.76	99.45	104.19	108.98	113.82	118.71	123.65	128.63	133.67	138.74	143.86	149.02	154.23	159.47	164.75	170.07
305	95.12	99.83	104.59	109.41	114.27	119.18	124.14	129.14	134.20	139.29	144.43	149.62	154.84	160.11	165.41	170.76
306	95.49	100.22	105.00	109.83	114.72	119.65	124.63	129.66	134.73	139.85	145.01	150.21	155.46	160.75	166.08	171.44
307	95.86	100.61	105.41	110.26	115.16	120.12	125.12	130.17	135.26	140.40	145.59	150.81	156.08	161.39	166.74	172.13
308	96.23	101.00	105.82	110.69	115.61	120.59	125.61	130.68	135.79	140.96	146.16	151.41	156.70	162.03	167.40	172.81
309	96.60	101.39	106.23	111.12	116.06	121.06	126.10	131.19	136.33	141.51	146.74	152.01	157.32	162.68	168.07	173.50
310	96.97	101.77	106.64	111.55	116.51	121.53	126.59	131.70	136.86	142.07	147.31	152.61	157.94	163.32	168.73	174.19
311	97.34	102.16	107.04	111.98	116.96	122.00	127.08	132.22	137.40	142.62	147.89	153.21	158.56	163.96	169.40	174.88
312	97.71	102.55	107.45	112.41	117.41	122.47	127.57	132.73	137.93	143.18	148.47	153.81	159.19	164.61	170.07	175.57
313	98.08	102.94	107.86	112.84	117.86	122.94	128.07	133.24	138.47	143.73	149.05	154.41	159.81	165.25	170.73	176.26
314	98.45	103.33	108.27	113.27	118.32	123.41	128.56	133.76	139.00	144.29	149.63	155.01	160.43	165.90	171.40	176.95
315	98.82	103.72	108.69	113.70	118.77	123.89	129.05	134.27	139.54	144.85	150.21	155.61	161.05	166.54	172.07	177.64
316	99.19	104.12	109.10	114.13	119.22	124.36	129.55	134.79	140.07	145.41	150.79	156.21	161.68	167.19	172.74	178.33
317	99.56	104.51	109.51	114.56	119.67	124.83	130.04	135.30	140.61	145.97	151.37	156.81	162.30	167.84	173.41	179.02
318	99.93	104.90	109.92	115.00	120.13	125.31	130.54	135.82	141.15	146.53	151.95	157.42	162.93	168.48	174.08	179.71
319	100.31	105.29	110.33	115.43	120.58	125.78	131.03	136.34	141.69	147.09	152.53	158.02	163.56	169.13	174.75	180.40
320	100.68	105.68	110.75	115.86	121.03	126.26	131.53	136.85	142.23	147.65	153.11	158.63	164.18	169.78	175.42	181.10
321	101.05	106.08	111.16	116.30	121.49	126.73	132.03	137.37	142.77	148.21	153.70	159.23	164.81	170.43	176.09	181.79
322	101.42	106.47	111.57	116.73	121.94	127.21	132.52	137.89	143.31	148.77	154.28	159.84	165.44	171.08	176.76	182.49
323	101.80	106.86	111.99	117.16	122.40	127.68	133.02	138.41	143.85	149.33	154.86	160.44	166.06	171.73	177.44	183.18
324	102.17	107.26	112.40	117.60	122.85	128.16	133.52	138.93	144.39	149.89	155.45	161.05	166.69	172.38	178.11	183.88
325	102.55	107.65	112.81	118.03	123.31	128.64	134.02	139.45	144.93	150.46	156.03	161.66	167.32	173.03	178.78	184.57
326	102.92	108.05	113.23	118.47	123.76	129.11	134.51	139.97	145.47	151.02	156.62	162.26	167.95	173.68	179.46	185.27
327	103.29	108.44	113.64	118.90	124.22	129.59	135.01	140.49	146.01	151.58	157.20	162.87	168.58	174.34	180.13	185.97
328	103.67	108.84	114.06	119.34	124.68	130.07	135.51	141.01	146.55	152.15	157.79	163.48	169.21	174.99	180.81	186.67
329	104.04	109.23	114.48	119.78	125.14	130.55	136.01	141.53	147.10	152.71	158.38	164.09	169.84	175.64	181.48	187.37
330	104.42	109.63	114.89	120.21	125.59	131.03	136.51	142.05	147.64	153.28	158.96	164.70	170.48	176.30	182.16	188.07
331	104.80	110.02	115.31	120.65	126.05	131.51	137.01	142.57	148.18	153.84	159.55	165.31	171.11	176.95	182.84	188.77
332	105.17	110.42	115.73	121.09	126.51	131.99	137.51	143.10	148.73	154.41	160.14	165.92	171.74	177.61	183.52	189.47
333	105.55	110.82	116.14	121.53	126.97	132.47	138.02	143.62	149.27	154.98	160.73	166.53	172.37	178.26	184.19	190.17
334	105.93	111.21	116.56	121.97	127.43	132.95	138.52	144.14	149.82	155.54	161.32	167.14	173.01	178.92	184.87	190.87
335	106.30	111.61	116.98	122.40	127.89	133.43	139.02	144.67	150.36	156.11	161.91	167.75	173.64	179.58	185.55	191.57
336	106.68	112.01	117.40	122.84	128.35	133.91	139.52	145.19	150.91	156.68	162.50	168.36	174.28	180.23	186.23	192.27
337	107.06	112.41	117.82	123.28	128.81	134.39	140.03	145.72	151.46	157.25	163.09	168.98	174.91	180.89	186.91	192.98
338	107.44	112.81	118.24	123.72	129.27	134.87	140.53	146.24	152.00	157.82	163.68	169.59	175.55	181.55	187.59	193.68
339	107.82	113.20	118.65	124.16	129.73	135.36	141.04	146.77	152.55	158.39	164.27	170.21	176.18	182.21	188.28	194.38
340	108.20	113.60	119.07	124.60	130.19	135.84	141.54	147.29	153.10	158.96	164.86	170.82	176.82	182.87	188.96	195.09
341	108.57	114.00	119.49	125.05	130.66	136.32	142.04	147.82	153.65	159.53	165.46	171.43	177.46	183.53	189.64	195.79
342	108.95	114.40	119.92	125.49	131.12	136.81	142.55	148.35	154.20	160.10	166.05	172.05	178.10	184.19	190.32	196.50
343	109.33	114.80	120.34	125.93	131.58	137.29	143.06	148.87	154.75	160.67	166.64	172.67	178.73	184.85	191.01	197.21
344	109.71	115.20	120.76	126.37	132.04	137.77	143.56	149.40	155.30	161.24	167.24	173.28	179.37	185.51	191.69	197.91
345	110.09	115.61	121.18	126.81	132.51	138.26	144.07	149.93	155.85	161.82	167.83	173.90	180.01	186.17	192.38	198.62
346	110.48	116.01	121.60	127.26	132.97	138.75	144.58	150.46	156.40	162.39	168.43	174.52	180.65	186.83	193.06	199.33
347	110.86	116.41	122.02	127.70	133.44	139.23	145.08	150.99	156.95	162.96	169.02	175.14	181.29	187.50	193.75	200.04
348	111.24	116.81	122.45	128.14	133.90	139.72	145.59	151.52	157.50	163.54	169.62	175.75	181.93	188.16	194.43	200.75
349	111.62	117.21	122.87	128.59	134.37	140.20	146.10	152.05	158.05	164.11	170.22	176.37	182.58	188.83	195.12	201.46
350	112.00	117.61	123.29	129.03	134.83	140.69	146.61	152.58	158.61	164.68	170.81	176.99	183.22	189.49	195.81	202.17
351	112.38	118.02	123.72	129.48	135.30	141.18	147.12	153.11	159.16	165.26	171.41	177.61	183.86	190.16	196.49	202.88
352	112.77	118.42	124.14	129.92	135.76	141.67	147.63	153.64	159.71	165.83	172.01	178.23	184.50	190.82	197.18	203.59
353	113.15	118.82	124.56	130.37	136.23	142.15	148.14	154.17	160.27	166.41	172.61	178.85	185.15	191.49	197.87	204.30
354	113.53	119.23	124.99	130.81	136.70	142.64	148.65	154.71	160.82	166.99	173.21	179.47	185.79	192.15	198.56	205.01
355	113.92	119.63	125.41	131.26	137.17	143.13	149.16	155.24	161.37	167.56	173.81	180.10	186.43	192.82	199.25	205.72
356	114.30	120.04	125.84	131.71	137.63	143.62	149.67	155.77	161.93	168.14	174.41	180.72	187.08	193.49	199.94	206.44
357	114.68	120.44	126.27	132.15	138.10	144.11	150.18	156.31	162.49	168.72	175.01	181.34	187.73	194.16	200.63	207.15
358	115.07	120.85	126.69	132.60	138.57	144.60	150.69	156.84	163.04	169.30	175.61	181.96	188.37	194.82	201.32	207.87
359	115.45	121.25	127.12	133.05	139.04	145.09	151.20	157.37	163.60	169.88	176.21	182.59	189.02	195.49	202.01	208.58
360	115.84	121.66	127.54	133.50	139.51	145.58	151.72	157.91	164.16	170.46	176.81	183.21	189.66	196.16	202.71	209.30

TABLE 12 (cont.)

NUMBER OF PAYMENTS	ANNUAL PERCENTAGE RATE															
	10.00%	10.25%	10.50%	10.75%	11.00%	11.25%	11.50%	11.75%	12.00%	12.25%	12.50%	12.75%	13.00%	13.25%	13.50%	13.75%
	(FINANCE CHARGE PER $100 OF AMOUNT FINANCED)															
301	173.31	178.64	184.00	189.40	194.83	200.29	205.78	211.30	216.85	222.43	228.04	233.67	239.33	245.01	250.72	256.45
302	174.02	179.37	184.75	190.17	195.62	201.11	206.62	212.17	217.74	223.34	228.97	234.63	240.31	246.01	251.74	257.50
303	174.73	180.10	185.50	190.95	196.42	201.93	207.46	213.03	218.63	224.25	229.91	235.58	241.29	247.02	252.77	258.55
304	175.43	180.83	186.26	191.72	197.22	202.75	208.31	213.90	219.52	225.16	230.84	236.54	242.27	248.02	253.80	259.60
305	176.14	181.56	187.01	192.49	198.01	203.57	209.15	214.76	220.41	226.08	231.77	237.50	243.25	249.03	254.82	260.65
306	176.85	182.29	187.76	193.27	198.81	204.39	209.99	215.63	221.30	226.99	232.71	238.46	244.23	250.03	255.85	261.70
307	177.55	183.02	188.51	194.05	199.61	205.21	210.84	216.50	222.19	227.90	233.65	239.42	245.21	251.04	256.88	262.75
308	178.26	183.75	189.27	194.82	200.41	206.03	211.68	217.37	223.08	228.82	234.58	240.38	246.20	252.04	257.91	263.80
309	178.97	184.48	190.02	195.60	201.21	206.85	212.53	218.23	223.97	229.73	235.52	241.34	247.18	253.05	258.94	264.86
310	179.68	185.21	190.78	196.38	202.01	207.68	213.38	219.10	224.86	230.65	236.46	242.30	248.17	254.06	259.97	265.91
311	180.39	185.95	191.53	197.16	202.81	208.50	214.22	219.97	225.75	231.56	237.40	243.26	249.15	255.07	261.01	266.97
312	181.10	186.68	192.29	197.94	203.62	209.33	215.07	220.85	226.65	232.48	238.34	244.23	250.14	256.08	262.04	268.02
313	181.82	187.41	193.05	198.72	204.42	210.15	215.92	221.72	227.54	233.40	239.28	245.19	251.13	257.09	263.07	269.08
314	182.53	188.15	193.81	199.50	205.22	210.98	216.77	222.59	228.44	234.32	240.22	246.16	252.11	258.10	264.11	270.14
315	183.24	188.89	194.56	200.28	206.03	211.81	217.62	223.46	229.33	235.24	241.17	247.12	253.10	259.11	265.14	271.19
316	183.96	189.62	195.32	201.06	206.83	212.63	218.47	224.34	230.23	236.16	242.11	248.09	254.09	260.12	266.18	272.25
317	184.67	190.36	196.08	201.84	207.64	213.46	219.32	225.21	231.13	237.08	243.05	249.05	255.08	261.13	267.21	273.31
318	185.39	191.10	196.84	202.63	208.44	214.29	220.17	226.09	232.03	238.00	244.00	250.02	256.07	262.15	268.25	274.37
319	186.10	191.83	197.60	203.41	209.25	215.12	221.03	226.96	232.93	238.92	244.94	250.99	257.06	263.16	269.29	275.43
320	186.82	192.57	198.37	204.19	210.06	215.95	221.88	227.84	233.83	239.84	245.89	251.96	258.06	264.18	270.32	276.49
321	187.53	193.31	199.13	204.98	210.86	216.78	222.73	228.71	234.73	240.77	246.83	252.93	259.05	265.19	271.36	277.55
322	188.25	194.05	199.89	205.76	211.67	217.61	223.59	229.59	235.63	241.69	247.78	253.90	260.04	266.21	272.40	278.62
323	188.97	194.79	200.65	206.55	212.48	218.45	224.44	230.47	236.53	242.61	248.73	254.87	261.04	267.23	273.44	279.68
324	189.69	195.53	201.42	207.34	213.29	219.28	225.30	231.35	237.43	243.54	249.68	255.84	262.03	268.24	274.48	280.74
325	190.41	196.28	202.18	208.13	214.10	220.11	226.15	232.23	238.33	244.46	250.62	256.81	263.02	269.26	275.52	281.81
326	191.13	197.02	202.95	208.91	214.91	220.95	227.01	233.11	239.23	245.39	251.57	257.78	264.02	270.28	276.57	282.87
327	191.85	197.76	203.71	209.70	215.72	221.78	227.87	233.99	240.14	246.32	252.52	258.76	265.02	271.30	277.61	283.94
328	192.57	198.51	204.48	210.49	216.54	222.62	228.73	234.87	241.04	247.25	253.47	259.73	266.01	272.32	278.65	285.01
329	193.29	199.25	205.25	211.28	217.35	223.45	229.59	235.75	241.95	248.17	254.43	260.71	267.01	273.34	279.70	286.07
330	194.01	199.99	206.01	212.07	218.16	224.29	230.45	236.64	242.85	249.10	255.38	261.68	268.01	274.36	280.74	287.14
331	194.73	200.74	206.78	212.86	218.98	225.13	231.31	237.52	243.76	250.03	256.33	262.66	269.01	275.39	281.79	288.21
332	195.46	201.49	207.55	213.65	219.79	225.96	232.17	238.40	244.67	250.96	257.28	263.63	270.01	276.41	282.83	289.28
333	196.18	202.23	208.32	214.45	220.61	226.80	233.03	239.29	245.58	251.89	258.24	264.61	271.01	277.43	283.88	290.35
334	196.90	202.98	209.09	215.24	221.42	227.64	233.89	240.17	246.48	252.82	259.19	265.59	272.01	278.46	284.93	291.42
335	197.63	203.73	209.86	216.03	222.24	228.48	234.75	241.06	247.39	253.76	260.15	266.57	273.01	279.48	285.97	292.49
336	198.35	204.47	210.63	216.83	223.06	229.32	235.62	241.94	248.30	254.69	261.10	267.54	274.01	280.50	287.02	293.56
337	199.08	205.22	211.40	217.62	223.87	230.16	236.48	242.83	249.21	255.62	262.06	268.52	275.02	281.53	288.07	294.63
338	199.81	205.97	212.18	218.42	224.69	231.00	237.34	243.72	250.12	256.56	263.02	269.50	276.02	282.56	289.12	295.70
339	200.53	206.72	212.95	219.21	225.51	231.84	238.21	244.61	251.03	257.49	263.97	270.49	277.02	283.58	290.17	296.78
340	201.26	207.47	213.72	220.01	226.33	232.69	239.08	245.50	251.95	258.42	264.93	271.47	278.03	284.61	291.22	297.85
341	201.99	208.22	214.50	220.81	227.15	233.53	239.94	246.38	252.86	259.36	265.89	272.45	279.03	285.64	292.27	298.93
342	202.72	208.98	215.27	221.60	227.97	234.37	240.81	247.27	253.77	260.30	266.85	273.43	280.04	286.67	293.32	300.00
343	203.45	209.73	216.05	222.40	228.79	235.22	241.68	248.16	254.68	261.23	267.81	274.41	281.04	287.70	294.37	301.08
344	204.18	210.48	216.82	223.20	229.61	236.06	242.54	249.06	255.60	262.17	268.77	275.40	282.05	288.73	295.43	302.15
345	204.91	211.23	217.60	224.00	230.44	236.91	243.41	249.95	256.51	263.11	269.73	276.38	283.06	289.76	296.48	303.23
346	205.64	211.99	218.38	224.80	231.26	237.75	244.28	250.84	257.43	264.05	270.69	277.37	284.06	290.79	297.54	304.30
347	206.37	212.74	219.15	225.60	232.08	238.60	245.15	251.73	258.34	264.99	271.65	278.35	285.07	291.82	298.59	305.38
348	207.10	213.50	219.93	226.40	232.91	239.45	246.02	252.63	259.26	265.93	272.62	279.34	286.08	292.85	299.64	306.46
349	207.83	214.25	220.71	227.20	233.73	240.29	246.89	253.52	260.18	266.87	273.58	280.32	287.09	293.88	300.70	307.54
350	208.57	215.01	221.49	228.00	234.56	241.14	247.76	254.41	261.10	267.81	274.54	281.31	288.10	294.92	301.76	308.62
351	209.30	215.76	222.27	228.81	235.38	241.99	248.63	255.31	262.01	268.75	275.51	282.30	289.11	295.95	302.81	309.70
352	210.03	216.52	223.05	229.61	236.21	242.84	249.51	256.20	262.93	269.69	276.47	283.29	290.12	296.99	303.87	310.78
353	210.77	217.28	223.83	230.41	237.03	243.69	250.38	257.10	263.85	270.63	277.44	284.27	291.13	298.02	304.93	311.86
354	211.50	218.04	224.61	231.22	237.86	244.54	251.25	258.00	264.77	271.57	278.41	285.26	292.15	299.06	305.99	312.94
355	212.24	218.80	225.39	232.02	238.69	245.39	252.13	258.89	265.69	272.52	279.37	286.25	293.16	300.09	307.05	314.02
356	212.98	219.55	226.17	232.83	239.52	246.24	253.00	259.79	266.61	273.46	280.34	287.24	294.17	301.13	308.11	315.11
357	213.71	220.31	226.95	233.63	240.35	247.09	253.88	260.69	267.53	274.41	281.31	288.23	295.19	302.16	309.17	316.19
358	214.45	221.07	227.74	234.44	241.18	247.95	254.75	261.59	268.45	275.35	282.27	289.23	296.20	303.20	310.23	317.27
359	215.19	221.84	228.52	235.25	242.01	248.80	255.63	262.49	269.38	276.30	283.24	290.22	297.22	304.24	311.29	318.36
360	215.93	222.60	229.31	236.05	242.84	249.65	256.50	263.39	270.30	277.24	284.21	291.21	298.23	305.28	312.35	319.44

TABLE 13
MONTHLY PAYMENT REQUIRED TO AMORTIZE A LOAN

10.750%

TERM AMOUNT	15 Years	16 Years	17 Years	18 Years	19 Years	20 Years	21 Years	22 Years	23 Years	24 Years	25 Years	30 Years	35 Years	40 Years
5	.06	.06	.06	.06	.06	.06	.06	.05	.05	.05	.05	.05	.05	.05
10	.12	.11	.11	.11	.11	.11	.11	.10	.10	.10	.10	.10	.10	.10
15	.17	.17	.17	.16	.16	.16	.16	.15	.15	.15	.15	.15	.14	.14
25	.29	.28	.27	.27	.26	.26	.26	.25	.25	.25	.25	.24	.23	.23
50	.57	.55	.54	.53	.52	.51	.51	.50	.49	.49	.49	.47	.46	.46
75	.85	.82	.81	.79	.78	.77	.76	.75	.74	.73	.73	.71	.69	.69
100	1.13	1.10	1.07	1.05	1.04	1.02	1.01	.99	.98	.98	.97	.94	.92	.91
200	2.25	2.19	2.14	2.10	2.07	2.04	2.01	1.98	1.96	1.95	1.93	1.87	1.84	1.82
300	3.37	3.28	3.21	3.15	3.10	3.05	3.01	2.97	2.94	2.92	2.89	2.81	2.76	2.73
400	4.49	4.38	4.28	4.20	4.13	4.07	4.01	3.96	3.92	3.89	3.85	3.74	3.68	3.64
500	5.61	5.47	5.35	5.25	5.16	5.08	5.01	4.95	4.90	4.86	4.82	4.67	4.59	4.55
600	6.73	6.56	6.42	6.30	6.19	6.10	6.02	5.94	5.88	5.83	5.78	5.61	5.51	5.46
700	7.85	7.66	7.49	7.35	7.22	7.11	7.02	6.93	6.86	6.80	6.74	6.54	6.43	6.36
800	8.97	8.75	8.56	8.39	8.25	8.13	8.02	7.92	7.84	7.77	7.70	7.47	7.35	7.27
900	10.09	9.84	9.63	9.44	9.28	9.14	9.02	8.91	8.82	8.74	8.66	8.41	8.26	8.18
1000	11.21	10.94	10.70	10.49	10.31	10.16	10.02	9.90	9.80	9.71	9.63	9.34	9.18	9.09
2000	22.42	21.87	21.39	20.98	20.62	20.31	20.04	19.80	19.59	19.41	19.25	18.67	18.36	18.17
3000	33.63	32.80	32.08	31.46	30.93	30.46	30.06	29.70	29.39	29.11	28.87	28.01	27.53	27.26
4000	44.84	43.73	42.77	41.95	41.23	40.61	40.07	39.60	39.18	38.81	38.49	37.34	36.71	36.34
5000	56.05	54.66	53.46	52.43	51.54	50.77	50.09	49.50	48.97	48.51	48.11	46.68	45.88	45.42
6000	67.26	65.59	64.16	62.92	61.85	60.92	60.11	59.39	58.77	58.22	57.73	56.01	55.06	54.51
7000	78.47	76.52	74.85	73.41	72.16	71.07	70.12	69.29	68.56	67.92	67.35	65.35	64.23	63.59
8000	89.68	87.45	85.54	83.89	82.46	81.22	80.14	79.19	78.36	77.62	76.97	74.68	73.41	72.68
9000	100.89	98.38	96.23	94.38	92.77	91.38	90.16	89.09	88.15	87.32	86.59	84.02	82.58	81.76
10000	112.10	109.31	106.92	104.86	103.08	101.53	100.17	98.99	97.94	97.02	96.21	93.35	91.76	90.84
11000	123.31	120.24	117.61	115.35	113.39	111.68	110.19	108.88	107.74	106.73	105.84	102.69	100.93	99.93
12000	134.52	131.17	128.31	125.84	123.69	121.83	120.21	118.78	117.53	116.43	115.46	112.02	110.11	109.01
13000	145.73	142.10	139.00	136.32	134.00	131.98	130.22	128.68	127.32	126.13	125.08	121.36	119.28	118.10
14000	156.94	153.03	149.69	146.81	144.31	142.14	140.24	138.58	137.12	135.83	134.70	130.69	128.46	127.18
15000	168.15	163.97	160.38	157.29	154.62	152.29	150.26	148.48	146.91	145.53	144.32	140.03	137.63	136.26
16000	179.36	174.90	171.07	167.78	164.92	162.44	160.27	158.37	156.71	155.24	153.94	149.36	146.81	145.35
17000	190.57	185.83	181.77	178.26	175.23	172.59	170.29	168.27	166.50	164.94	163.56	158.70	155.98	154.43
18000	201.78	196.76	192.46	188.75	185.54	182.75	180.31	178.17	176.29	174.64	173.18	168.03	165.16	163.52
19000	212.99	207.69	203.15	199.24	195.85	192.90	190.32	188.07	186.09	184.34	182.80	177.37	174.33	172.60
20000	224.19	218.62	213.84	209.72	206.15	203.05	200.34	197.97	195.88	194.04	192.42	186.70	183.51	181.68
21000	235.40	229.55	224.53	220.21	216.46	213.20	210.36	207.87	205.68	203.75	202.04	196.04	192.68	190.77
22000	246.61	240.48	235.22	230.69	226.77	223.36	220.37	217.76	215.47	213.45	211.67	205.37	201.86	199.85
23000	257.82	251.41	245.92	241.18	237.08	233.51	230.39	227.66	225.26	223.15	221.29	214.71	211.03	208.94
24000	269.03	262.34	256.61	251.67	247.38	243.66	240.41	237.56	235.06	232.85	230.91	224.04	220.21	218.02
25000	280.24	273.27	267.30	262.15	257.69	253.81	250.42	247.46	244.85	242.55	240.53	233.38	229.38	227.10
26000	291.45	284.20	277.99	272.64	268.00	263.96	260.44	257.36	254.64	252.26	250.15	242.71	238.56	236.19
27000	302.66	295.13	288.68	283.12	278.31	274.12	270.46	267.25	264.44	261.96	259.77	252.04	247.73	245.27
28000	313.87	306.06	299.37	293.61	288.61	284.27	280.47	277.15	274.23	271.66	269.39	261.38	256.91	254.36
29000	325.08	317.00	310.07	304.09	298.92	294.42	290.49	287.05	284.03	281.36	279.01	270.71	266.08	263.44
30000	336.29	327.93	320.76	314.58	309.23	304.57	300.51	296.95	293.82	291.06	288.63	280.05	275.26	272.52
31000	347.50	338.86	331.45	325.07	319.54	314.73	310.53	306.85	303.61	300.77	298.25	289.38	284.43	281.61
32000	358.71	349.79	342.14	335.55	329.84	324.88	320.54	316.74	313.41	310.47	307.87	298.72	293.61	290.69
33000	369.92	360.72	352.83	346.04	340.15	335.03	330.56	326.64	323.20	320.17	317.50	308.05	302.78	299.78
34000	381.13	371.65	363.53	356.52	350.46	345.18	340.58	336.54	332.99	329.87	327.12	317.39	311.96	308.86
35000	392.34	382.58	374.22	367.01	360.77	355.34	350.59	346.44	342.79	339.57	336.74	326.72	321.13	317.94
36000	403.55	393.51	384.91	377.50	371.07	365.49	360.61	356.34	352.58	349.28	346.36	336.06	330.31	327.03
37000	414.76	404.44	395.60	387.98	381.38	375.64	370.63	366.23	362.38	358.98	355.98	345.39	339.48	336.11
38000	425.97	415.37	406.29	398.47	391.69	385.79	380.64	376.13	372.17	368.68	365.60	354.73	348.66	345.20
39000	437.17	426.30	416.98	408.95	402.00	395.94	390.66	386.03	381.96	378.38	375.22	364.06	357.83	354.28
40000	448.38	437.23	427.68	419.44	412.30	406.10	400.68	395.93	391.76	388.08	384.84	373.40	367.01	363.36
41000	459.59	448.16	438.37	429.92	422.61	416.25	410.69	405.83	401.55	397.79	394.46	382.73	376.18	372.45
42000	470.80	459.09	449.06	440.41	432.92	426.40	420.71	415.73	411.35	407.49	404.08	392.07	385.36	381.53
43000	482.01	470.03	459.75	450.90	443.23	436.55	430.73	425.62	421.14	417.19	413.70	401.40	394.53	390.62
44000	493.22	480.96	470.44	461.38	453.53	446.71	440.74	435.52	430.93	426.89	423.33	410.74	403.71	399.70
45000	504.43	491.89	481.14	471.87	463.84	456.86	450.76	445.42	440.73	436.59	432.95	420.07	412.88	408.78
46000	515.64	502.82	491.83	482.35	474.15	467.01	460.78	455.32	450.52	446.30	442.57	429.41	422.06	417.87
47000	526.85	513.75	502.52	492.84	484.46	477.16	470.79	465.22	460.31	456.00	452.19	438.74	431.23	426.95
48000	538.06	524.68	513.21	503.33	494.76	487.31	480.81	475.11	470.11	465.70	461.81	448.08	440.41	436.04
49000	549.27	535.61	523.90	513.81	505.07	497.47	490.83	485.01	479.90	475.40	471.43	457.41	449.58	445.12
50000	560.48	546.54	534.59	524.30	515.38	507.62	500.84	494.91	489.70	485.10	481.05	466.75	458.76	454.20
55000	616.53	601.19	588.05	576.73	566.92	558.38	550.93	544.40	538.67	533.61	529.16	513.42	504.63	499.62
60000	672.57	655.85	641.51	629.16	618.45	609.14	601.01	593.89	587.63	582.12	577.26	560.09	550.51	545.04
65000	728.62	710.50	694.97	681.59	669.99	659.90	651.10	643.38	636.60	630.63	625.37	606.77	596.38	590.46
70000	784.67	765.15	748.43	734.01	721.53	710.67	701.18	692.87	685.57	679.14	673.47	653.44	642.26	635.88
75000	840.72	819.81	801.89	786.44	773.07	761.43	751.26	742.36	734.54	727.65	721.57	700.12	688.13	681.30
80000	896.76	874.46	855.35	838.87	824.60	812.19	801.35	791.85	783.51	776.16	769.68	746.79	734.01	726.72
85000	952.81	929.11	908.81	891.30	876.14	862.95	851.43	841.34	832.48	824.67	817.78	793.46	779.88	772.14
90000	1008.86	983.77	962.27	943.73	927.68	913.71	901.52	890.83	881.45	873.18	865.89	840.14	825.76	817.56
95000	1064.91	1038.42	1015.72	996.16	979.21	964.47	951.60	940.32	930.42	921.69	913.99	886.81	871.63	862.98
100000	1120.95	1093.07	1069.18	1048.59	1030.75	1015.23	1001.68	989.81	979.39	970.20	962.10	933.49	917.51	908.40

Tables

TABLE 13 (*cont.*)

11.000%

TERM AMOUNT	15 Years	16 Years	17 Years	18 Years	19 Years	20 Years	21 Years	22 Years	23 Years	24 Years	25 Years	30 Years	35 Years	40 Years
5	.06	.06	.06	.06	.06	.06	.06	.06	.05	.05	.05	.05	.05	.05
10	.12	.12	.11	.11	.11	.11	.11	.11	.10	.10	.10	.10	.10	.10
15	.18	.17	.17	.16	.16	.16	.16	.16	.15	.15	.15	.15	.15	.14
25	.29	.28	.28	.27	.27	.26	.26	.26	.25	.25	.25	.24	.24	.24
50	.57	.56	.55	.54	.53	.52	.51	.51	.50	.50	.50	.48	.47	.47
75	.86	.84	.82	.80	.79	.78	.77	.76	.75	.75	.74	.72	.71	.70
100	1.14	1.11	1.09	1.07	1.05	1.04	1.02	1.01	1.00	.99	.99	.96	.94	.93
200	2.28	2.22	2.18	2.14	2.10	2.07	2.04	2.02	2.00	1.98	1.97	1.91	1.88	1.86
300	3.41	3.33	3.26	3.20	3.15	3.10	3.06	3.03	3.00	2.97	2.95	2.86	2.82	2.79
400	4.55	4.44	4.35	4.27	4.19	4.13	4.08	4.03	3.99	3.96	3.93	3.81	3.75	3.72
500	5.69	5.55	5.43	5.33	5.24	5.17	5.10	5.04	4.99	4.95	4.91	4.77	4.69	4.65
600	6.82	6.66	6.52	6.40	6.29	6.20	6.12	6.05	5.99	5.93	5.89	5.72	5.63	5.57
700	7.96	7.77	7.60	7.46	7.34	7.23	7.14	7.06	6.98	6.92	6.87	6.67	6.56	6.50
800	9.10	8.88	8.69	8.53	8.38	8.26	8.16	8.06	7.98	7.91	7.85	7.62	7.50	7.43
900	10.23	9.99	9.77	9.59	9.43	9.29	9.17	9.07	8.98	8.90	8.83	8.58	8.44	8.36
1000	11.37	11.10	10.86	10.66	10.48	10.33	10.19	10.08	9.98	9.89	9.81	9.53	9.37	9.29
2000	22.74	22.19	21.71	21.31	20.95	20.65	20.38	20.15	19.95	19.77	19.61	19.05	18.74	18.57
3000	34.10	33.28	32.57	31.96	31.43	30.97	30.57	30.22	29.92	29.65	29.41	28.57	28.11	27.85
4000	45.47	44.37	43.42	42.61	41.90	41.29	40.76	40.29	39.89	39.53	39.21	38.10	37.48	37.14
5000	56.83	55.46	54.27	53.26	52.38	51.61	50.95	50.37	49.86	49.41	49.01	47.62	46.85	46.42
6000	68.20	66.55	65.13	63.91	62.85	61.94	61.14	60.44	59.83	59.29	58.81	57.14	56.22	55.70
7000	79.57	77.64	75.98	74.56	73.33	72.26	71.33	70.51	69.80	69.17	68.61	66.67	65.59	64.99
8000	90.93	88.73	86.84	85.21	83.80	82.58	81.51	80.58	79.77	79.05	78.41	76.19	74.96	74.27
9000	102.30	99.82	97.69	95.86	94.28	92.90	91.70	90.66	89.74	88.93	88.22	85.71	84.33	83.55
10000	113.66	110.91	108.54	106.51	104.75	103.22	101.89	100.73	99.71	98.81	98.02	95.24	93.70	92.83
11000	125.03	122.00	119.40	117.16	115.23	113.55	112.08	110.80	109.68	108.69	107.82	104.76	103.07	102.12
12000	136.40	133.09	130.25	127.81	125.70	123.87	122.27	120.87	119.65	118.57	117.62	114.28	112.44	111.40
13000	147.76	144.18	141.10	138.46	136.18	134.19	132.46	130.94	129.62	128.45	127.42	123.81	121.81	120.68
14000	159.13	155.27	151.96	149.11	146.65	144.51	142.65	141.02	139.59	138.33	137.22	133.33	131.18	129.97
15000	170.49	166.36	162.81	159.76	157.12	154.83	152.84	151.09	149.56	148.21	147.02	142.85	140.55	139.25
16000	181.86	177.45	173.67	170.41	167.60	165.16	163.02	161.16	159.53	158.09	156.82	152.38	149.92	148.53
17000	193.23	188.54	184.52	181.06	178.07	175.48	173.21	171.23	169.50	167.97	166.62	161.90	159.29	157.82
18000	204.59	199.63	195.37	191.71	188.55	185.80	183.40	181.31	179.47	177.85	176.43	171.42	168.66	167.10
19000	215.96	210.72	206.23	202.36	199.02	196.12	193.59	191.38	189.44	187.73	186.23	180.95	178.03	176.38
20000	227.32	221.81	217.08	213.01	209.50	206.44	203.78	201.45	199.41	197.61	196.03	190.47	187.40	185.66
21000	238.69	232.90	227.93	223.67	219.97	216.76	213.97	211.52	209.38	207.49	205.83	199.99	196.77	194.95
22000	250.06	243.99	238.79	234.32	230.65	227.09	224.16	221.59	219.35	217.37	215.63	209.52	206.14	204.23
23000	261.42	255.08	249.64	244.97	240.92	237.41	234.35	231.67	229.32	227.25	225.43	219.04	215.51	213.51
24000	272.79	266.17	260.50	255.62	251.40	247.73	244.53	241.74	239.29	237.13	235.23	228.56	224.87	222.80
25000	284.15	277.26	271.35	266.27	261.87	258.05	254.72	251.81	249.26	247.01	245.03	238.09	234.24	232.08
26000	295.52	288.35	282.20	276.92	272.35	268.37	264.91	261.88	259.23	256.89	254.83	247.61	243.61	241.36
27000	306.89	299.44	293.06	287.57	282.82	278.70	275.10	271.96	269.20	266.77	264.64	257.13	252.98	250.64
28000	318.25	310.53	303.91	298.22	293.29	289.02	285.29	282.03	279.17	276.65	274.44	266.66	262.35	259.93
29000	329.62	321.62	314.77	308.87	303.77	299.34	295.48	292.10	289.14	286.53	284.24	276.18	271.72	269.21
30000	340.98	332.71	325.62	319.52	314.24	309.66	305.67	302.17	299.11	296.41	294.04	285.70	281.09	278.49
31000	352.35	343.80	336.47	330.17	324.72	319.98	315.85	312.24	309.08	306.29	303.84	295.23	290.46	287.78
32000	363.72	354.89	347.33	340.82	335.19	330.31	326.04	322.32	319.05	316.17	313.64	304.75	299.83	297.06
33000	375.08	365.98	358.18	351.47	345.67	340.63	336.23	332.39	329.02	326.05	323.44	314.27	309.20	306.34
34000	386.45	377.07	369.03	362.12	356.14	350.95	346.42	342.46	338.99	335.93	333.24	323.79	318.57	315.63
35000	397.81	388.16	379.89	372.77	366.62	361.27	356.61	352.53	348.96	345.81	343.04	333.32	327.94	324.91
36000	409.18	399.25	390.74	383.42	377.09	371.59	366.80	362.61	358.93	355.69	352.85	342.84	337.31	334.19
37000	420.55	410.34	401.60	394.07	387.57	381.91	376.99	372.68	368.90	365.57	362.65	352.36	346.68	343.47
38000	431.91	421.43	412.45	404.72	398.04	392.24	387.18	382.75	378.87	375.46	372.45	361.89	356.05	352.76
39000	443.28	432.52	423.30	415.37	408.52	402.56	397.36	392.82	388.84	385.34	382.25	371.41	365.42	362.04
40000	454.64	443.61	434.16	426.02	418.99	412.88	407.55	402.89	398.81	395.22	392.05	380.93	374.79	371.32
41000	466.01	454.70	445.01	436.68	429.47	423.20	417.74	412.97	408.78	405.10	401.85	390.46	384.16	380.61
42000	477.38	465.79	455.86	447.33	439.94	433.52	427.93	423.04	418.75	414.98	411.65	399.98	393.53	389.89
43000	488.74	476.88	466.72	457.98	450.41	443.85	438.12	433.11	428.72	424.86	421.45	409.50	402.90	399.17
44000	500.11	487.97	477.57	468.63	460.89	454.17	448.31	443.18	438.69	434.74	431.25	419.03	412.27	408.45
45000	511.47	499.06	488.43	479.28	471.36	464.49	458.50	453.26	448.66	444.62	441.06	428.55	421.64	417.74
46000	522.84	510.15	499.28	489.93	481.84	474.81	468.69	463.33	458.63	454.50	450.86	438.07	431.01	427.02
47000	534.21	521.24	510.13	500.58	492.31	485.13	478.87	473.40	468.60	464.38	460.66	447.60	440.38	436.30
48000	545.57	532.33	520.99	511.23	502.79	495.46	489.06	483.47	478.57	474.26	470.46	457.12	449.74	445.59
49000	556.94	543.42	531.84	521.88	513.26	505.78	499.25	493.54	488.54	484.14	480.26	466.64	459.11	454.87
50000	568.30	554.51	542.70	532.53	523.74	516.10	509.44	503.62	498.51	494.02	490.06	476.17	468.48	464.15
55000	625.13	609.96	596.96	585.78	576.11	567.71	560.38	553.98	548.36	543.42	539.07	523.78	515.33	510.57
60000	681.96	665.41	651.23	639.03	628.48	619.32	611.33	604.34	598.21	592.82	588.07	571.40	562.18	556.98
65000	738.79	720.86	705.50	692.29	680.86	670.93	662.27	654.70	648.06	642.22	637.08	619.02	609.03	603.40
70000	795.62	776.31	759.77	745.54	733.23	722.54	713.21	705.06	697.91	691.62	686.08	666.63	655.88	649.81
75000	852.45	831.76	814.04	798.79	785.60	774.15	764.16	755.42	747.76	741.02	735.09	714.25	702.72	696.23
80000	909.28	887.21	868.31	852.04	837.98	825.76	815.10	805.78	797.61	790.43	784.10	761.86	749.57	742.64
85000	966.11	942.66	922.58	905.30	890.35	877.37	866.05	856.14	847.46	839.83	833.10	809.48	796.42	789.06
90000	1022.94	998.11	976.85	958.55	942.72	928.97	916.99	906.51	897.31	889.23	882.11	857.10	843.27	835.47
95000	1079.77	1053.56	1031.12	1011.80	995.10	980.58	967.93	956.87	947.16	938.63	931.11	904.71	890.11	881.88
100000	1136.60	1109.01	1085.39	1065.05	1047.47	1032.19	1018.88	1007.23	997.01	988.03	980.12	952.33	936.96	928.30

TABLE 13 (*cont.*)

11.250%

TERM AMOUNT	15 Years	16 Years	17 Years	18 Years	19 Years	20 Years	21 Years	22 Years	23 Years	24 Years	25 Years	30 Years	35 Years	40 Years
5	.06	.06	.06	.06	.06	.06	.06	.06	.06	.06	.05	.05	.05	.05
10	.12	.12	.12	.11	.11	.11	.11	.11	.11	.11	.10	.10	.10	.10
15	.18	.17	.17	.17	.16	.16	.16	.16	.16	.16	.15	.15	.15	.15
25	.29	.29	.28	.28	.27	.27	.26	.26	.26	.26	.25	.25	.24	.24
50	.58	.57	.56	.55	.54	.53	.52	.52	.51	.51	.50	.49	.48	.48
75	.87	.85	.83	.82	.80	.79	.78	.77	.77	.76	.75	.73	.72	.72
100	1.16	1.13	1.11	1.09	1.07	1.05	1.04	1.03	1.02	1.01	1.00	.98	.96	.95
200	2.31	2.26	2.21	2.17	2.13	2.10	2.08	2.05	2.03	2.02	2.00	1.95	1.92	1.90
300	3.46	3.38	3.31	3.25	3.20	3.15	3.11	3.08	3.05	3.02	3.00	2.92	2.87	2.85
400	4.61	4.51	4.41	4.33	4.26	4.20	4.15	4.10	4.06	4.03	4.00	3.89	3.83	3.80
500	5.77	5.63	5.51	5.41	5.33	5.25	5.19	5.13	5.08	5.03	5.00	4.86	4.79	4.75
600	6.92	6.76	6.62	6.49	6.39	6.30	6.22	6.15	6.09	6.04	5.99	5.83	5.74	5.69
700	8.07	7.88	7.72	7.58	7.46	7.35	7.26	7.18	7.11	7.05	6.99	6.80	6.70	6.64
800	9.22	9.01	8.82	8.66	8.52	8.40	8.29	8.20	8.12	8.05	7.99	7.78	7.66	7.59
900	10.38	10.13	9.92	9.74	9.58	9.45	9.33	9.23	9.14	9.06	8.99	8.75	8.61	8.54
1000	11.53	11.26	11.02	10.82	10.65	10.50	10.37	10.25	10.15	10.06	9.99	9.72	9.57	9.49
2000	23.05	22.51	22.04	21.64	21.29	20.99	20.73	20.50	20.30	20.12	19.97	19.43	19.13	18.97
3000	34.58	33.76	33.06	32.45	31.93	31.48	31.09	30.75	30.45	30.18	29.95	29.14	28.70	28.45
4000	46.10	45.01	44.07	43.27	42.58	41.98	41.45	40.99	40.59	40.24	39.93	38.86	38.26	37.94
5000	57.62	56.26	55.09	54.09	53.22	52.47	51.81	51.24	50.74	50.30	49.92	48.57	47.83	47.42
6000	69.15	67.51	66.11	64.90	63.86	62.96	62.18	61.49	60.89	60.36	59.90	58.28	57.39	56.90
7000	80.67	78.76	77.12	75.72	74.51	73.45	72.54	71.74	71.04	70.42	69.88	67.99	66.96	66.38
8000	92.19	90.01	88.14	86.53	85.15	83.95	82.90	81.98	81.18	80.48	79.86	77.71	76.52	75.87
9000	103.72	101.26	99.16	97.35	95.79	94.44	93.26	92.23	91.33	90.54	89.85	87.42	86.09	85.35
10000	115.24	112.51	110.17	108.17	106.43	104.93	103.62	102.48	101.48	100.60	99.83	97.13	95.65	94.83
11000	126.76	123.76	121.19	118.98	117.08	115.42	113.98	112.73	111.63	110.66	109.81	106.84	105.22	104.31
12000	138.29	135.01	132.21	129.80	127.72	125.92	124.35	122.97	121.77	120.72	119.79	116.56	114.78	113.80
13000	149.81	146.26	143.22	140.62	138.36	136.41	134.71	133.22	131.92	130.78	129.78	126.27	124.35	123.28
14000	161.33	157.51	154.24	151.43	149.01	146.90	145.07	143.47	142.07	140.84	139.76	135.98	133.91	132.76
15000	172.86	168.76	165.26	162.25	159.65	157.39	155.43	153.72	152.22	150.90	149.74	145.69	143.48	142.24
16000	184.38	180.01	176.27	173.06	170.29	167.89	165.79	163.96	162.36	160.96	159.72	155.41	153.04	151.73
17000	195.90	191.26	187.29	183.88	180.93	178.38	176.15	174.21	172.51	171.02	169.71	165.12	162.61	161.21
18000	207.43	202.51	198.31	194.70	191.58	188.87	186.52	184.46	182.66	181.08	179.69	174.83	172.17	170.69
19000	218.95	213.76	209.33	205.51	202.22	199.36	196.88	194.71	192.81	191.14	189.67	184.54	181.74	180.17
20000	230.47	225.01	220.34	216.33	212.86	209.86	207.24	204.95	202.95	201.20	199.65	194.26	191.30	189.66
21000	242.00	236.26	231.36	227.15	223.51	220.35	217.60	215.20	213.10	211.26	209.64	203.97	200.87	199.14
22000	253.52	247.51	242.38	237.96	234.15	230.84	227.96	225.45	223.25	221.32	219.62	213.68	210.43	208.62
23000	265.04	258.76	253.39	248.78	244.79	241.33	238.32	235.70	233.40	231.38	229.60	223.40	220.00	218.10
24000	276.57	270.01	264.41	259.59	255.43	251.83	248.69	245.94	243.54	241.44	239.58	233.11	229.56	227.59
25000	288.09	281.26	275.43	270.41	266.08	262.32	259.05	256.19	253.69	251.50	249.56	242.82	239.13	237.07
26000	299.61	292.51	286.44	281.23	276.72	272.81	269.41	266.44	263.84	261.56	259.55	252.53	248.69	246.55
27000	311.14	303.76	297.46	292.04	287.36	283.30	279.77	276.69	273.99	271.61	269.53	262.25	258.26	256.03
28000	322.66	315.01	308.48	302.86	298.01	293.80	290.13	286.93	284.13	281.67	279.51	271.96	267.82	265.52
29000	334.18	326.26	319.49	313.67	308.65	304.29	300.49	297.18	294.28	291.73	289.49	281.67	277.39	275.00
30000	345.71	337.51	330.51	324.49	319.29	314.78	310.86	307.43	304.43	301.79	299.48	291.38	286.95	284.48
31000	357.23	348.77	341.53	335.31	329.93	325.27	321.22	317.68	314.58	311.85	309.46	301.10	296.52	293.96
32000	368.76	360.02	352.54	346.12	340.58	335.77	331.58	327.92	324.72	321.91	319.44	310.81	306.08	303.45
33000	380.28	371.27	363.56	356.94	351.22	346.26	341.94	338.17	334.87	331.97	329.42	320.52	315.65	312.93
34000	391.80	382.52	374.58	367.76	361.86	356.75	352.30	348.42	345.02	342.03	339.41	330.23	325.21	322.41
35000	403.33	393.77	385.60	378.57	372.51	367.24	362.66	358.67	355.16	352.09	349.39	339.95	334.78	331.90
36000	414.85	405.02	396.61	389.39	383.15	377.74	373.03	368.91	365.31	362.15	359.37	349.66	344.34	341.38
37000	426.37	416.27	407.63	400.20	393.79	388.23	383.39	379.16	375.46	372.21	369.35	359.37	353.91	350.86
38000	437.90	427.52	418.65	411.02	404.43	398.72	393.75	389.41	385.61	382.27	379.34	369.08	363.47	360.34
39000	449.42	438.77	429.66	421.84	415.08	409.21	404.11	399.66	395.75	392.33	389.32	378.80	373.04	369.83
40000	460.94	450.02	440.68	432.65	425.72	419.71	414.47	409.90	405.90	402.39	399.30	388.51	382.60	379.31
41000	472.47	461.27	451.70	443.47	436.36	430.20	424.84	420.15	416.05	412.45	409.28	398.22	392.17	388.79
42000	483.99	472.52	462.71	454.29	447.01	440.69	435.20	430.40	426.20	422.51	419.27	407.93	401.73	398.27
43000	495.51	483.77	473.73	465.10	457.65	451.19	445.56	440.65	436.34	432.57	429.25	417.65	411.30	407.76
44000	507.04	495.02	484.75	475.92	468.29	461.68	455.92	450.89	446.49	442.63	439.23	427.36	420.86	417.24
45000	518.56	506.27	495.76	486.73	478.93	472.17	466.28	461.14	456.64	452.69	449.21	437.07	430.43	426.72
46000	530.08	517.52	506.78	497.55	489.58	482.66	476.64	471.39	466.79	462.75	459.20	446.79	439.99	436.20
47000	541.61	528.77	517.80	508.37	500.22	493.16	487.01	481.64	476.93	472.81	469.18	456.50	449.56	445.69
48000	553.13	540.02	528.81	519.18	510.86	503.65	497.37	491.88	487.08	482.87	479.16	466.21	459.12	455.17
49000	564.65	551.27	539.83	530.00	521.51	514.14	507.73	502.13	497.23	492.93	489.14	475.92	468.69	464.65
50000	576.18	562.52	550.85	540.82	532.15	524.63	518.09	512.38	507.38	502.99	499.12	485.64	478.25	474.13
55000	633.79	618.77	605.93	594.90	585.36	577.10	569.90	563.62	558.11	553.28	549.04	534.20	526.08	521.55
60000	691.41	675.02	661.02	648.98	638.58	629.56	621.71	614.85	608.85	603.58	598.95	582.76	573.90	568.96
65000	749.03	731.28	716.10	703.06	691.79	682.02	673.52	666.09	659.59	653.88	648.86	631.32	621.73	616.37
70000	806.65	787.53	771.19	757.14	745.01	734.48	725.32	717.33	710.32	704.18	698.77	679.89	669.55	663.79
75000	864.26	843.78	826.27	811.22	798.22	786.95	777.13	768.56	761.06	754.48	748.68	728.45	717.38	711.20
80000	921.88	900.03	881.35	865.30	851.44	839.41	828.94	819.80	811.80	804.77	798.60	777.01	765.20	758.61
85000	979.50	956.28	936.44	919.38	904.65	891.87	880.75	871.04	862.54	855.07	848.51	825.58	813.02	806.02
90000	1037.12	1012.53	991.52	973.46	957.86	944.34	932.56	922.28	913.27	905.37	898.42	874.14	860.85	853.44
95000	1094.73	1068.79	1046.61	1027.54	1011.08	996.80	984.37	973.51	964.01	955.67	948.33	922.70	908.67	900.85
100000	1152.35	1125.04	1101.69	1081.63	1064.29	1049.26	1036.18	1024.75	1014.75	1005.97	998.24	971.27	956.50	948.26

TABLE 13 (cont.)

11.500%

TERM / AMOUNT	15 Years	16 Years	17 Years	18 Years	19 Years	20 Years	21 Years	22 Years	23 Years	24 Years	25 Years	30 Years	35 Years	40 Years
5	.06	.06	.06	.06	.06	.06	.06	.06	.06	.06	.06	.05	.05	.05
10	.12	.12	.12	.11	.11	.11	.11	.11	.11	.11	.11	.10	.10	.10
15	.18	.18	.17	.17	.17	.16	.16	.16	.16	.16	.16	.15	.15	.15
25	.30	.29	.28	.28	.28	.27	.27	.27	.26	.26	.26	.25	.25	.25
50	.59	.58	.56	.55	.55	.54	.53	.53	.52	.52	.51	.50	.49	.49
75	.88	.86	.84	.83	.82	.80	.79	.78	.78	.77	.77	.75	.74	.73
100	1.17	1.15	1.12	1.10	1.09	1.07	1.06	1.05	1.04	1.03	1.02	1.00	.98	.97
200	2.34	2.29	2.24	2.20	2.17	2.14	2.11	2.09	2.07	2.05	2.04	1.99	1.96	1.94
300	3.51	3.43	3.36	3.30	3.25	3.20	3.17	3.13	3.10	3.08	3.05	2.98	2.93	2.91
400	4.68	4.57	4.48	4.40	4.33	4.27	4.22	4.17	4.14	4.10	4.07	3.97	3.91	3.88
500	5.85	5.71	5.60	5.50	5.41	5.34	5.27	5.22	5.17	5.13	5.09	4.96	4.89	4.85
600	7.01	6.85	6.71	6.59	6.49	6.40	6.33	6.26	6.20	6.15	6.10	5.95	5.86	5.81
700	8.18	7.99	7.83	7.69	7.57	7.47	7.38	7.30	7.23	7.17	7.12	6.94	6.84	6.78
800	9.35	9.15	8.95	8.79	8.65	8.54	8.43	8.34	8.27	8.20	8.14	7.93	7.81	7.75
900	10.52	10.28	10.07	9.89	9.74	9.60	9.49	9.39	9.30	9.22	9.15	8.92	8.79	8.72
1000	11.69	11.42	11.19	10.99	10.82	10.67	10.54	10.43	10.33	10.25	10.17	9.91	9.77	9.69
2000	23.37	22.83	22.37	21.97	21.63	21.33	21.08	20.85	20.66	20.49	20.33	19.81	19.53	19.37
3000	35.05	34.24	33.55	32.95	32.44	32.00	31.61	31.28	30.98	30.73	30.50	29.71	29.29	29.05
4000	46.73	45.65	44.73	43.94	43.25	42.66	42.15	41.70	41.31	40.97	40.66	39.62	39.05	38.74
5000	58.41	57.06	55.91	54.92	54.07	53.33	52.68	52.12	51.63	51.21	50.83	49.52	48.81	48.42
6000	70.10	68.47	67.09	65.90	64.88	63.99	63.22	62.55	61.96	61.45	60.99	59.42	58.57	58.10
7000	81.78	79.89	78.27	76.89	75.69	74.66	73.76	72.97	72.29	71.69	71.16	69.33	68.33	67.78
8000	93.46	91.30	89.45	87.87	86.50	85.32	84.29	83.39	82.61	81.93	81.32	79.23	78.09	77.47
9000	105.14	102.71	100.63	98.85	97.31	95.98	94.83	93.82	92.94	92.17	91.49	89.13	87.85	87.15
10000	116.82	114.12	111.81	109.83	108.13	106.65	105.36	104.24	103.26	102.41	101.65	99.03	97.62	96.83
11000	128.51	125.53	123.00	120.82	118.94	117.31	115.90	114.67	113.59	112.65	111.82	108.94	107.38	106.52
12000	140.19	136.94	134.18	131.80	129.75	127.98	126.43	125.09	123.91	122.89	121.98	118.84	117.14	116.20
13000	151.87	148.36	145.36	142.78	140.56	138.64	136.97	135.51	134.24	133.13	132.15	128.74	126.90	125.88
14000	163.55	159.77	156.54	153.77	151.38	149.31	147.51	145.94	144.57	143.37	142.31	138.65	136.66	135.56
15000	175.23	171.18	167.72	164.75	162.19	159.97	158.04	156.36	154.89	153.61	152.48	148.55	146.42	145.25
16000	186.92	182.59	178.90	175.73	173.00	170.63	168.58	166.78	165.22	163.85	162.64	158.45	156.18	154.93
17000	198.60	194.00	190.08	186.72	183.81	181.30	179.11	177.21	175.54	174.09	172.80	168.35	165.94	164.61
18000	210.28	205.41	201.26	197.70	194.62	191.96	189.65	187.63	185.87	184.33	182.97	178.26	175.70	174.30
19000	221.96	216.83	212.44	208.68	205.44	202.63	200.18	198.06	196.20	194.57	193.13	188.16	185.47	183.98
20000	233.64	228.24	223.62	219.66	216.25	213.29	210.72	208.48	206.52	204.81	203.30	198.06	195.23	193.66
21000	245.32	239.65	234.81	230.65	227.06	223.96	221.26	218.90	216.85	215.05	213.46	207.97	204.99	203.34
22000	257.01	251.06	245.99	241.63	237.87	234.62	231.79	229.33	227.17	225.29	223.63	217.87	214.75	213.03
23000	268.69	262.47	257.17	252.61	248.69	245.28	242.33	239.75	237.50	235.53	233.79	227.77	224.51	222.71
24000	280.37	273.88	268.35	263.60	259.50	255.95	252.86	250.17	247.82	245.77	243.96	237.67	234.27	232.39
25000	292.05	285.30	279.53	274.58	270.31	266.61	263.40	260.60	258.15	256.01	254.12	247.58	244.03	242.08
26000	303.73	296.71	290.71	285.56	281.12	277.28	273.94	271.02	268.48	266.25	264.29	257.48	253.79	251.76
27000	315.42	308.12	301.89	296.54	291.93	287.94	284.47	281.45	278.80	276.49	274.45	267.38	263.55	261.44
28000	327.10	319.53	313.07	307.53	302.75	298.61	295.01	291.87	289.13	286.73	284.62	277.29	273.32	271.12
29000	338.78	330.94	324.25	318.51	313.56	309.27	305.54	302.29	299.45	296.97	294.78	287.19	283.08	280.81
30000	350.46	342.35	335.43	329.49	324.37	319.93	316.08	312.72	309.78	307.21	304.95	297.09	292.84	290.49
31000	362.14	353.77	346.61	340.48	335.18	330.60	326.61	323.14	320.11	317.45	315.11	307.00	302.60	300.17
32000	373.83	365.18	357.80	351.46	345.99	341.26	337.15	333.56	330.43	327.69	325.28	316.90	312.36	309.86
33000	385.51	376.59	368.98	362.44	356.81	351.93	347.69	343.99	340.76	337.93	335.44	326.80	322.12	319.54
34000	397.19	388.00	380.16	373.43	367.62	362.59	358.22	354.41	351.08	348.17	345.60	336.70	331.88	329.22
35000	408.87	399.41	391.34	384.41	378.43	373.26	368.76	364.84	361.41	358.41	355.77	346.61	341.64	338.90
36000	420.55	410.82	402.52	395.39	389.24	383.92	379.29	375.26	371.73	368.65	365.93	356.51	351.40	348.59
37000	432.24	422.24	413.70	406.37	400.06	394.58	389.83	385.68	382.06	378.89	376.10	366.41	361.16	358.27
38000	443.92	433.65	424.88	417.36	410.87	405.25	400.36	396.11	392.39	389.13	386.26	376.32	370.93	367.95
39000	455.60	445.06	436.06	428.34	421.68	415.91	410.90	406.53	402.71	399.37	396.43	386.22	380.69	377.63
40000	467.28	456.47	447.24	439.32	432.49	426.58	421.44	416.95	413.04	409.61	406.59	396.12	390.45	387.32
41000	478.96	467.88	458.42	450.31	443.30	437.24	431.97	427.38	423.36	419.85	416.76	406.02	400.21	397.00
42000	490.64	479.29	469.61	461.29	454.12	447.91	442.51	437.80	433.69	430.09	426.92	415.93	409.97	406.68
43000	502.33	490.71	480.79	472.27	464.93	458.57	453.04	448.23	444.01	440.33	437.09	425.83	419.73	416.37
44000	514.01	502.12	491.97	483.25	475.74	469.23	463.58	458.65	454.34	450.57	447.25	435.73	429.49	426.05
45000	525.69	513.53	503.15	494.24	486.55	479.90	474.11	469.07	464.67	460.81	457.42	445.64	439.25	435.73
46000	537.37	524.94	514.33	505.22	497.37	490.56	484.65	479.50	474.99	471.05	467.58	455.54	449.01	445.41
47000	549.05	536.35	525.51	516.20	508.18	501.23	495.19	489.92	485.32	481.29	477.75	465.44	458.78	455.10
48000	560.74	547.76	536.69	527.19	518.99	511.89	505.72	500.34	495.64	491.53	487.91	475.34	468.54	464.78
49000	572.42	559.18	547.87	538.17	529.80	522.56	516.26	510.77	505.97	501.77	498.07	485.25	478.30	474.46
50000	584.10	570.59	559.05	549.15	540.61	533.22	526.79	521.19	516.30	512.01	508.24	495.15	488.06	484.15
55000	642.51	627.65	614.96	604.07	594.67	586.54	579.47	573.31	567.92	563.21	559.06	544.67	536.86	532.56
60000	700.92	684.70	670.86	658.98	648.74	639.86	632.15	625.43	619.55	614.41	609.89	594.18	585.67	580.97
65000	759.33	741.76	726.77	713.90	702.80	693.18	684.83	677.55	671.18	665.61	660.71	643.69	634.47	629.39
70000	817.74	798.82	782.67	768.81	756.86	746.51	737.51	729.67	722.81	716.81	711.53	693.21	683.28	677.80
75000	876.15	855.88	838.58	823.73	810.92	799.83	790.19	781.79	774.44	768.01	762.36	742.72	732.09	726.22
80000	934.56	912.94	894.48	878.64	864.98	853.15	842.87	833.90	826.07	819.21	813.18	792.24	780.89	774.63
85000	992.97	970.00	950.39	933.56	919.04	906.47	895.55	886.02	877.70	870.41	864.00	841.75	829.70	823.04
90000	1051.38	1027.05	1006.29	988.47	973.10	959.79	948.22	938.14	929.33	921.61	914.83	891.27	878.50	871.46
95000	1109.79	1084.11	1062.20	1043.39	1027.16	1013.11	1000.90	990.26	980.96	972.81	965.65	940.78	927.31	919.87
100000	1168.19	1141.17	1118.10	1098.30	1081.22	1066.43	1053.58	1042.38	1032.59	1024.01	1016.47	990.30	976.11	968.29

TABLE 14
BETTERMENT (DEPRECIATION) GUIDE

Dwelling — Personal Property
Dwelling Items

Item	Years Average Life	Item	Years Average Life
Roofing		Cloth Awnings	4–5
Flat surface	10		
Built-up (3 layers of roll roofing)	10	Furnaces (including compressors	
Asphalt Composition Shingles	20	or motors)	
Wood Shingles	30	(Coal, Gas, Oil)	20
Metal	20		
		Equipment Pertaining to a Dwelling	
Painting and Decorating	3–5	Water Heater (Gas or Electric)	5–10
Exterior Painting	3–5	Well Pumps	5–10
Interior Painting	3–5	Sump Pumps	7–10

Personal Property

NOTE: Consideration should be given to the quality, use and maintenance when estimating the average life of personal property items.

Item	Years Average Life	Item	Years Average Life
Major Appliances		Rugs	
Stoves (Gas or Electric)	10–15	$5.95 per yard or less	7
Freezers	10–15	Over $5.95 to $9.95 per yard	10
Sewing Machines	10–20	Over $9.95 to $12.95 per yard	12
Refrigerators	10–15	Over $12.95 to $20.95 per yard	15
Window Air Conditioners		Draperies	5–10
(including compressors or motors)	7–10	Outdoor Equipment	
Portable Dishwashers	7–10	Push Mower	10
Automatic Washers	7–10	Power Mower	5–10
Automatic Dryers	7–10	Riding Mower	5–7
Small Appliances		Electric Edgers, Hedge Clippers,	
Electric Toasters	5–10	Trimmers, etc.	7–10
Electric Mixers	5–10	Tools	
Electric Can Openers, Knife		Power & Hand Tools	7–10
Sharpeners, Meat Slicers	5–10	Sports Equipment	
Electric Toothbrushes	5	Golf Clubs	10
TV Sets	8–10	Tennis Rackets	5
Picture Tubes	2–5	Tricycles	3
TV & Radio Antennas	6–10	Guns, Hand & Rifle	20
Radios		Baseball, Basketball, Football	
Portable or Transistor	5	and Similar Equipment	3
Console & Table Model	7–10	Bicycles	5–10
Stereos & Hi-Fi	7–10		
Vacuum Cleaners	7–10		
Electric Irons	5–7		

TABLE 15
HOMEOWNER'S INSURANCE RATES

ZONE I										ANNUAL PREMIUMS	
PROTECTION CLASS: 1–4											

	$50 ALL–PERIL DEDUCTIBLE						$100 ALL–PERIL DEDUCTIBLE					
	MASONRY OR MAS. VENEER			FRAME			MASONRY OR MAS. VENEER			FRAME		
	FORM			FORM			FORM			FORM		
AMOUNT	1	2	3	1	2	3	1	2	3	1	2	3
$ 5,000	41	47	48	41	48	49	37	43	44	37	44	45
7,000	43	49	50	43	49	51	39	45	46	39	45	46
8,000	44	50	51	44	50	52	40	45	46	40	45	47
10,000	45	51	53	45	52	54	41	46	48	41	47	49
12,000	46	53	54	46	54	55	42	48	49	42	49	50
14,000	49	56	57	49	56	58	45	51	52	45	51	53
15,000	50	57	58	50	58	59	45	52	53	45	53	54
16,000	52	59	61	52	60	62	47	54	55	47	55	56
17,000	54	61	62	54	62	63	49	55	56	49	56	57
18,000	55	63	64	55	64	65	50	57	58	50	58	59
19,000	58	65	66	58	65	66	53	59	60	53	59	60
20,000	59	66	68	59	67	69	54	60	62	54	61	63
21,000	61	69	70	61	70	71	55	63	64	55	64	65
22,000	63	71	72	63	71	73	57	65	66	57	65	66
23,000	65	73	74	65	74	75	59	66	67	59	67	68
24,000	68	76	78	68	78	79	62	69	71	62	71	72
25,000	72	80	82	72	81	83	65	73	75	65	74	75
26,000	75	84	85	75	85	86	68	76	77	68	77	78
27,000	78	87	89	78	89	90	71	79	81	71	81	82
28,000	81	91	92	81	93	94	74	83	84	74	85	86
29,000	84	93	95	84	95	96	76	85	86	76	86	87
30,000	86	97	98	86	99	100	78	88	89	78	90	91
31,000	90	101	103	90	103	104	82	92	94	82	94	95
32,000	94	105	107	94	107	108	85	95	97	85	97	98
33,000	97	109	111	97	111	112	88	99	101	88	101	102
34,000	101	113	115	101	115	117	92	103	105	92	105	106
35,000	104	116	118	104	118	119	95	105	107	95	107	108
36,000	107	120	122	107	122	123	97	109	111	97	111	112
37,000	111	124	126	111	126	128	101	113	115	101	115	116
38,000	114	128	130	114	130	131	104	116	118	104	118	119
39,000	118	132	134	118	134	136	107	120	122	107	122	124
40,000	122	136	138	122	138	140	111	124	125	111	125	127
42,000	129	144	146	129	146	148	117	131	133	117	133	135
44,000	136	152	154	136	154	156	124	138	140	124	140	142
46,000	143	160	163	143	163	165	130	145	148	130	148	150
48,000	150	168	171	150	171	173	136	153	155	136	155	157
50,000	158	177	179	158	179	182	144	161	163	144	163	165
60,000	194	217	220	194	221	223	176	197	200	176	201	203
70,000	230	257	261	230	262	264	209	234	237	209	238	240
80,000	266	297	301	266	304	305	242	270	274	242	276	277
90,000	302	337	342	302	346	347	275	306	311	275	315	316
$100,000	338	377	383	338	387	388	307	343	348	307	352	353
150,000	535	634	684	535	655	688	486	576	622	486	595	625
200,000	744	932	1042	744	964	1045	676	847	947	676	876	950
@10,000	39	48	54	39	50	54	35	44	49	35	45	49

TABLE 16
BASIC PREMIUM FOR AUTOMOBILE INSURANCE (SIX MONTHS)

Liability	Cost	Liability	Cost
10/ 20/10	$21.80	Collision (Medium-size car, $100 deductible)	
25/ 50/10	$24.40	1987 model	$46.80
50/100/10	$25.40	1986 and 1985	$39.80
100/300/50	$28.80	1984 and 1983	$35.20
Medical		1982 and older	$28.00
5,000	$ 3.40	Uninsured Motorist Coverage	
25,000	$ 6.60	10/ 20	$ 1.00
Comprehensive (Medium-size car, actual cash value)		25/ 50	$ 2.30
		100/300	$ 4.80
1987 model	$27.40		
1986 and 1985	$23.20		
1984 and 1983	$20.60		
1982 and older	$17.80		

TABLE 17
RATING FACTORS

Classification	Factor	Classification	Factor
Over age 25 married male or female		Single female under age 21	
less than 30 miles/week/work	1.10	less than 30 miles/week/work	1.95
more than 30 less than 100 miles/week/work	1.20	over 30 miles/week/work	2.15
more than 100 miles/week/work	1.35	Single female 21 to 24	
Under 21 married male		less than 30 miles/week/work	1.60
less than 30 miles/week/work	1.90	over 30 miles/week/work	1.85
over 30 miles/week/work	2.10	Single male under age 21	
21 or 22 married male		less than 30 miles/week/work	3.65
less than 30 miles/week/work	1.50	over 30 miles/week/work	3.95
more than 30 miles/week/work	1.70	Single male 21 to 25	
23 or 24 married male		less than 30 miles/week/work	2.90
less than 30 miles/week/work	1.25	over 30 miles/week/work	3.65
over 30 miles/week/work	1.45	Single male over age 25	
		less than 30 miles/week/work	1.65
		over 30 miles/week/work	1.90

TABLE 18
LIFE INSURANCE

Schedule of Insurance

The Amount payable per $1000 of Initial Face Amount will be determined at the corresponding Policy Year at death. Policy Year 1 begins on the Date of Issue, Policy Year 2 begins one year after the Date of Issue, etc.

Policy Year	Amount per $1000 of Initial Face Amount	Policy Year	Amount per $1000 of Initial Face Amount	Policy Year	Amount per $1000 of Initial Face Amount
1	$1000	6	$761	11	$438
2	958	7	704	12	361
3	913	8	643	13	278
4	865	9	579	14	191
5	815	10	511	15	99

TABLE 19
TABLE OF VALUES

Guaranteed Cash or Loan Value, Reduced Paid-up Insurance, Extended Term Insurance
Applicable to a Policy without Either Paid-up Additions or Dividend Accumulations and without Indebtedness
Values at end of years other than those shown will be quoted on request.

Years In Force	Age 20 Cash/Loan	Age 20 Paid-up	Age 20 ETI Yrs	Age 20 ETI Days	Age 21 Cash/Loan	Age 21 Paid-up	Age 21 ETI Yrs	Age 21 ETI Days	Age 22 Cash/Loan	Age 22 Paid-up	Age 22 ETI Yrs	Age 22 ETI Days	Age 23 Cash/Loan	Age 23 Paid-up	Age 23 ETI Yrs	Age 23 ETI Days	Age 24 Cash/Loan	Age 24 Paid-up	Age 24 ETI Yrs	Age 24 ETI Days	Years In Force
1/2	–	–	0	60	–	–	0	60	–	–	0	60	–	–	0	60	–	–	0	60	1/2
1	–	–	0	60	–	–	0	60	–	–	0	60	–	–	0	60	–	–	0	60	1
2	$1	$3	0	141	$1	$3	0	136	$1	$3	0	131	$1	$3	0	126	$1	$3	0	122	2
3	12	33	4	139	13	35	4	205	13	34	4	140	14	36	4	189	15	38	4	228	3
4	25	67	8	180	26	68	8	166	27	70	8	143	29	73	8	209	30	74	8	166	4
5	39	102	12	60	40	103	11	336	42	106	11	330	44	109	11	309	45	109	11	195	5
6	53	136	15	41	55	138	14	335	56	138	14	176	59	143	14	164	61	145	14	66	6
7	67	169	17	164	69	170	17	36	71	172	16	266	74	175	16	188	76	177	16	40	7
8	81	200	19	113	84	203	19	2	87	206	18	243	90	209	18	113	92	209	17	287	8
9	96	232	20	344	99	234	20	186	102	237	20	23	105	239	19	217	109	243	19	90	9
10	111	263	22	86	114	265	21	258	118	269	21	107	122	272	20	314	125	274	20	107	10
11	125	290	23	49	129	294	22	238	133	297	22	57	137	300	21	235	141	303	21	44	11
12	139	316	23	305	143	319	23	104	148	324	22	303	152	326	22	93	157	330	21	280	12
13	154	344	24	175	158	346	23	318	163	350	23	127	168	353	22	297	173	357	22	98	13
14	169	370	24	356	173	371	24	114	178	374	23	269	184	380	23	87	189	383	22	234	14
15	184	395	25	124	189	398	24	264	194	400	24	37	200	405	23	201	205	407	22	333	15
16	198	417	25	187	203	419	24	313	209	423	24	101	215	427	23	251	221	431	23	33	16
17	212	437	25	219	218	441	24	363	224	445	24	137	230	448	23	274	236	451	23	44	17
18	226	457	25	226	232	461	24	358	238	464	24	121	245	469	23	273	252	473	23	57	18
19	240	477	25	209	247	481	24	357	254	486	24	135	260	488	23	251	267	492	23	26	19
20	255	497	25	198	262	501	24	335	269	505	24	103	276	509	23	234	283	512	23	0	20
to Age 60	566	788	19	131	562	783	19	67	557	776	18	352	552	769	18	278	546	761	18	188	to Age 60
to Age 65	642	837	17	78	638	831	17	14	634	826	16	320	629	820	16	248	625	815	16	191	to Age 65

NONFORFEITURE FACTOR FOR EACH $1,000 OF FACE AMOUNT (See "Basis of Values" on page 7)

	Age 20 First 10 Years	Age 20 11th Through 15th Year	Age 21 First 10 Years	Age 21 11th Through 15th Year	Age 22 First 10 Years	Age 22 11th Through 15th Year	Age 23 First 10 Years	Age 23 11th Through 15th Year	Age 24 First 10 Years	Age 24 11th Through 15th Year
	$15.36	$14.19	$15.80	$14.58	$16.26	$15.00	$16.73	$15.43	$17.23	$15.89

Years In Force	Age 25 Cash/Loan	Age 25 Paid-up	Age 25 ETI Yrs	Age 25 ETI Days	Age 26 Cash/Loan	Age 26 Paid-up	Age 26 ETI Yrs	Age 26 ETI Days	Age 27 Cash/Loan	Age 27 Paid-up	Age 27 ETI Yrs	Age 27 ETI Days	Age 28 Cash/Loan	Age 28 Paid-up	Age 28 ETI Yrs	Age 28 ETI Days	Age 29 Cash/Loan	Age 29 Paid-up	Age 29 ETI Yrs	Age 29 ETI Days	Years In Force
1/2	–	–	0	60	–	–	0	60	–	–	0	60	–	–	0	60	–	–	0	60	1/2
1	–	–	0	60	–	–	0	60	$1	$3	0	112	$1	$3	0	107	$1	$3	0	102	1
2	$1	$3	0	117	$1	$3	0	112	2	5	0	213	2	5	0	203	3	7	0	290	2
3	16	40	4	258	17	41	4	278	18	43	4	291	19	45	4	295	20	46	4	293	3
4	31	75	8	115	33	78	8	143	34	79	8	78	35	80	8	4	37	83	8	4	4
5	47	112	11	155	49	114	11	104	50	114	10	342	52	116	10	276	54	118	10	203	5
6	63	146	13	325	65	148	13	213	67	150	13	95	70	153	13	29	72	155	12	264	6
7	79	180	15	308	82	183	15	202	84	184	15	39	87	187	14	285	90	190	14	160	7
8	95	212	17	144	98	215	16	363	102	219	16	253	105	221	16	94	108	223	15	296	8
9	112	245	18	274	116	249	18	133	119	251	17	310	123	254	17	157	127	257	17	2	9
10	129	277	19	303	133	280	19	129	137	283	18	317	141	286	18	135	146	290	17	349	10
11	145	305	20	213	149	308	20	16	154	312	19	213	158	314	19	10	163	318	18	199	11
12	161	332	21	64	166	336	20	242	171	340	20	53	176	343	19	224	181	346	19	29	12
13	178	360	21	259	183	364	21	53	188	366	20	209	193	369	19	364	199	374	19	177	13
14	194	385	22	15	200	390	21	185	205	392	20	326	211	396	20	126	217	400	19	289	14
15	211	411	22	125	217	415	21	280	223	419	21	68	229	422	20	218	235	425	20	3	15
16	227	434	22	176	233	437	21	319	239	441	21	94	246	445	20	257	252	448	20	31	16
17	242	454	22	177	249	459	21	333	256	463	21	121	262	466	20	251	269	470	20	37	17
18	258	475	22	180	265	480	21	326	272	483	21	104	279	487	20	247	287	492	20	44	18
19	274	496	22	163	282	501	21	321	289	504	21	91	297	509	20	245	304	512	20	14	19
20	291	517	22	150	298	520	21	278	306	525	21	60	314	529	20	207	322	533	19	353	20
to Age 60	540	752	18	98	535	745	18	23	528	735	17	288	522	727	17	203	515	717	17	105	to Age 60
to Age 65	620	808	16	119	615	801	16	48	610	795	15	343	605	788	15	278	599	781	15	200	to Age 65

NONFORFEITURE FACTOR FOR EACH $1,000 OF FACE AMOUNT (See "Basis of Values" on page 7)

	Age 25 First 10 Years	Age 25 11th Through 15th Year	Age 26 First 10 Years	Age 26 11th Through 15th Year	Age 27 First 10 Years	Age 27 11th Through 15th Year	Age 28 First 10 Years	Age 28 11th Through 15th Year	Age 29 First 10 Years	Age 29 11th Through 15th Year
	$17.75	$16.36	$18.29	$16.86	$18.85	$17.38	$19.44	$17.92	$20.06	$18.49

After the year for which a value is first shown, values as of any time during a policy year will be determined by the Company with allowance for the time elapsed in such year, and for any period in such year for which due premiums have been paid. However, if payment is made prior to the end of the period for which due premiums have been paid, the amount of such payment will be the Guaranteed Cash Value as of the end of that period less interest (at the effective rate of 5% per year) from the date of payment to the end of the period.

TABLE 20
ORDINARY LIFE (PER $1000)

Age At Issue	ANNUAL PREMIUMS					Years To Pay Up W/Divs.	Total Mo. Inc. At 65		Interest Adj. Cost Index	
	Life-M	Life-F	Non-Smokers	W.P.	A.D.B.		Male	Female	10 Yrs.	20 Yrs.
0	$ 7.77	$ 7.58		$ .20	$ .64	24	$15.24	$14.04	$ 3.46	$ 2.01
1	7.77	7.58		.20	.66	24	14.96	13.77	2.88	1.72
2	7.89	7.69		.21	.69	24	14.64	13.48	2.82	1.67
3	8.03	7.82		.21	.72	24	14.34	13.20	2.77	1.65
4	8.17	7.95		.22	.75	24	14.04	12.92	2.73	1.66
5	8.32	8.09		.22	.78	24	13.72	12.63	2.70	1.64
6	8.49	8.25		.23	.79	24	13.41	12.35	2.69	1.65
7	8.66	8.42		.23	.81	24	13.10	12.06	2.68	1.63
8	8.84	8.59		.24	.82	24	12.79	11.78	2.76	1.65
9	9.03	8.78		.24	.84	24	12.49	11.50	2.77	1.68
10	9.23	8.97		.25	.86	24	12.19	11.22	2.79	1.69
11	9.44	9.17		.25	.87	24	11.89	10.95	2.83	1.72
12	9.65	9.37		.26	.89	24	11.60	10.66	2.87	1.75
13	9.88	9.59		.26	.91	25	11.31	10.41	2.93	1.80
14	10.12	9.82		.27	.92	25	11.02	10.15	3.00	1.83
15	10.36	10.05		.28	.94	25	10.75	9.90	3.07	1.89
16	10.61	10.29		.28	.94	25	10.50	9.66	3.07	1.89
17	10.87	10.53		.29	.94	25	10.23	9.42	3.16	1.89
18	11.15	10.79		.30	.94	25	10.00	9.21	3.19	1.92
19	11.43	11.04		.31	.93	25	9.75	8.98	3.22	1.95
20	11.72	11.29	$ 11.42	.32	.91	25	9.51	8.76	3.25	1.96
21	12.04	11.58	11.72	.33	.90	25	9.31	8.57	3.23	2.00
22	12.37	11.88	12.02	.34	.89	25	9.09	8.37	3.30	2.02
23	12.72	12.20	12.35	.35	.88	25	8.88	8.17	3.31	2.06
24	13.08	12.53	12.68	.37	.87	25	8.67	7.98	3.41	2.11
25	13.46	12.87	13.03	.38	.88	25	8.46	7.79	3.45	2.18
26	13.91	13.28	13.46	.40	.88	25	8.29	7.63	3.54	2.25
27	14.38	13.70	13.92	.41	.88	25	8.11	7.46	3.56	2.38
28	14.88	14.15	14.40	.43	.89	25	7.93	7.30	3.70	2.47
29	15.39	14.61	14.89	.45	.90	25	7.75	7.13	3.85	2.64
30	15.93	15.10	15.42	.48	.91	25	7.57	6.97	3.95	2.77
31	16.50	15.61	15.97	.50	.92	24	7.39	6.81	4.06	2.95
32	17.09	16.13	16.53	.53	.93	24	7.23	6.66	4.26	3.14
33	17.72	16.69	17.14	.56	.94	24	7.05	6.49	4.43	3.37
34	18.37	17.26	17.77	.59	.96	24	6.87	6.32	4.62	3.59
35	19.06	17.86	18.43	.63	.97	24	6.69	6.16	4.84	3.89
36	19.79	18.50	19.13	.67	.98	24	6.50	5.99	5.13	4.23
37	20.57	19.19	19.89	.72	1.00	24	6.31	5.81	5.46	4.58
38	21.38	19.90	20.67	.77	1.01	24	6.12	5.64	5.82	5.00
39	22.22	20.64	21.48	.82	1.02	24	5.93	5.46	6.14	5.42
40	23.12	21.44	22.34	.88	1.04	24	5.72	5.27	6.59	5.93
41	24.05	22.26	23.24	.95	1.06	24	5.54	5.10	6.97	6.40
42	25.03	23.12	24.18	1.02	1.07	23	5.35	4.93	7.48	6.96
43	26.06	24.02	25.17	1.11	1.09	23	5.15	4.74	7.96	7.54
44	27.15	24.99	26.20	1.20	1.11	23	4.95	4.56	8.50	8.20
45	28.29	26.01	27.29	1.30	1.13	23	4.74	4.36	9.10	8.89
46	29.47	27.06	28.42	1.42	1.14	23	4.56	4.20	9.55	9.44
47	30.71	28.17	29.60	1.55	1.16	23	4.37	4.02	10.06	10.09
48	32.02	29.35	30.85	1.69	1.18	22	4.18	3.85	10.64	10.77
49	33.40	30.60	32.18	1.85	1.20	22	3.97	3.66	11.21	11.55
50	34.86	31.93	33.58	2.04	1.22	22	3.76	3.46	11.95	12.42
51	36.40	33.34	35.06	2.24	1.25	22	3.50	3.22	12.69	13.33
52	38.03	34.84	36.63	2.46	1.27	21	3.30	3.04	13.45	14.29
53	39.74	36.41	38.28	2.71	1.29	21	3.10	2.86	14.36	15.38
54	41.56	38.09	40.04	2.98	1.32	21	2.89	2.66	15.31	16.53
55	43.83	39.87	41.91	3.27	1.35	21	2.68	2.46	16.35	17.82
56	45.53	41.79	43.87	3.58	1.38	20	2.44	2.24	17.47	19.12
57	47.71	43.84	45.97	3.87	1.41	20	2.18	2.00	18.72	20.57
58	50.01	46.01	48.18	4.16	1.45	20	1.91	1.75	20.00	22.12
59	52.45	48.33	50.51	4.42	1.48	19	1.63	1.50	21.51	23.84
60	55.03	50.79	53.03		1.52	19	1.35	1.24	23.23	25.69
61	57.79	53.37	55.79		1.56	19	1.06	.97	24.93	27.64
62	60.71	56.08	58.71		1.59	19	.75	.69	26.87	29.74
63	63.81	58.96	61.81		1.64	18	.44	.40	28.99	32.02
64	67.09	62.04	65.09		1.68	18	.10	.10	31.29	34.52
65	70.57	65.30	68.57		1.72	18			33.71	37.18
66	74.35	68.86	72.35			18			36.45	40.10
67	78.34	72.62	76.34			17			39.33	43.23
68	82.55	76.59	80.55			17			42.42	46.54
69	86.99	80.78	84.99			17			45.75	50.08
70	91.66	85.20	89.66			17			49.30	53.82
71	96.80	90.08	94.80			16			53.06	
72	102.22	95.24	100.22			16			57.17	
73	107.95	100.70	105.95			16			61.59	
74	114.05	106.52	112.05			15			66.38	
75	120.57	112.76	118.57			15			71.67	

TABLE 21
PERCENTAGE METHOD INCOME
TAX WITHHOLDING TABLE

Payroll Period	One with-holding allowance
Weekly	$20.00
Biweekly	40.00
Semimonthly	43.33
Monthly	86.67
Quarterly	260.00
Semiannually	520.00
Annually	1,040.00
Daily or miscellaneous (each day of the payroll period) .	4.00

TABLE 22
TABLES FOR PERCENTAGE METHOD OF WITHHOLDING

If the Payroll Period With Respect to an Employee is Weekly

(a) SINGLE person—including head of household:

If the amount of wages is:		The amount of income tax to be withheld shall be:	
Not over $27 0			
Over—	But not over—		of excess over—
$27	—$84	. .12%	—$27
$84	—$185	. .$6.84 plus 15%	—$84
$185	—$292	. .$21.99 plus 19%	—$185
$292	—$440	. .$42.32 plus 25%	—$292
$440	—$556	. .$79.32 plus 30%	—$440
$556	—$663	. .$114.12 plus 34%	—$556
$663	. . . . .	. .$150.50 plus 37%	—$663

(b) MARRIED person—

If the amount of wages is:		The amount of income tax to be withheld shall be:	
Not over $48 0			
Over—	But not over—		of excess over—
$48	—$192	. .12%	—$48
$192	—$384	. .$17.28 plus 17%	—$192
$384	—$472	. .$49.92 plus 22%	—$384
$472	—$578	. .$69.28 plus 25%	—$472
$578	—$684	. .$95.78 plus 28%	—$578
$684	—$897	. .$125.46 plus 33%	—$684
$897	. . . . .	. .$195.75 plus 37%	—$897

If the Payroll Period With Respect to an Employee is Monthly

(a) SINGLE person—including head of household:

If the amount of wages is:		The amount of income tax to be withheld shall be:	
Not over $118 0			
Over—	But not over—		of excess over—
$118	—$364	. .12%	—$118
$364	—$800	. .$29.52 plus 15%	—$364
$800	—$1,267	. .$94.92 plus 19%	—$800
$1,267	—$1,908	. .$183.65 plus 25%	—$1,267
$1,908	—$2,411	. .$343.90 plus 30%	—$1,908
$2,411	—$2,871	. .$494.80 plus 34%	—$2,411
$2,871	. . . . .	. .$651.20 plus 37%	—$2,871

(b) MARRIED person—

If the amount of wages is:		The amount of income tax to be withheld shall be:	
Not over $208 0			
Over—	But not over—		of excess over—
$208	—$833	. .12%	—$208
$833	—$1,663	. .$75.00 plus 17%	—$833
$1,663	—$2,047	. .$216.10 plus 22%	—$1,663
$2,047	—$2,507	. .$300.58 plus 25%	—$2,047
$2,507	—$2,966	. .$415.58 plus 28%	—$2,507
$2,966	—$3,885	. .$544.10 plus 33%	—$2,966
$3,885	. . . . .	. .$847.37 plus 37%	—$3,885

And the wages are—		And the number of withholding allowances claimed is—										
At least	But less than	0	1	2	3	4	5	6	7	8	9	10
		The amount of income tax to be withheld shall be—										
$380	$390	$65	$60	$55	$50	$46	$41	$37	$33	$29	$26	$22
390	400	68	63	58	53	48	43	39	35	31	27	24
400	410	71	65	60	55	50	46	41	37	33	29	26
410	420	73	68	63	58	53	48	43	39	35	31	27
420	430	76	71	65	60	55	50	46	41	37	33	29
430	440	78	73	68	63	58	53	48	43	39	35	31
440	450	81	76	71	65	60	55	50	46	41	37	33
450	460	84	78	73	68	63	58	53	48	43	39	35
460	470	87	81	76	71	65	60	55	50	46	41	37
470	480	90	84	78	73	68	63	58	53	48	43	39
480	490	93	87	81	76	71	65	60	55	50	46	41
490	500	96	90	84	78	73	68	63	58	53	48	43
500	510	99	93	87	81	76	71	65	60	55	50	46
510	520	102	96	90	84	78	73	68	63	58	53	48
520	530	105	99	93	87	81	76	71	65	60	55	50
530	540	108	102	96	90	84	78	73	68	63	58	53
540	550	111	105	99	93	87	81	76	71	65	60	55
550	560	114	108	102	96	90	84	78	73	68	63	58
560	570	117	111	105	99	93	87	81	76	71	65	60
570	580	121	114	108	102	96	90	84	78	73	68	63
580	590	124	117	111	105	99	93	87	81	76	71	65
590	600	127	121	114	108	102	96	90	84	78	73	68
600	610	131	124	117	111	105	99	93	87	81	76	71
610	620	134	127	121	114	108	102	96	90	84	78	73
620	630	138	131	124	117	111	105	99	93	87	81	76
630	640	141	134	127	121	114	108	102	96	90	84	78
640	650	144	138	131	124	117	111	105	99	93	87	81
650	660	148	141	134	127	121	114	108	102	96	90	84
660	670	151	144	138	131	124	117	111	105	99	93	87
670	680	155	148	141	134	127	121	114	108	102	96	90
680	690	159	151	144	138	131	124	117	111	105	99	93
690	700	162	155	148	141	134	127	121	114	108	102	96
700	710	166	159	151	144	138	131	124	117	111	105	99
710	720	170	162	155	148	141	134	127	121	114	108	102
720	730	173	166	159	151	144	138	131	124	117	111	105
730	740	177	170	162	155	148	141	134	127	121	114	108
740	750	181	173	166	159	151	144	138	131	124	117	111
750	760	184	177	170	162	155	148	141	134	127	121	114
760	770	188	181	173	166	159	151	144	138	131	124	117
770	780	192	184	177	170	162	155	148	141	134	127	121
780	790	196	188	181	173	166	159	151	144	138	131	124
790	800	199	192	184	177	170	162	155	148	141	134	127
800	810	203	196	188	181	173	166	159	151	144	138	131
810	820	207	199	192	184	177	170	162	155	148	141	134
820	830	210	203	196	188	181	173	166	159	151	144	138
830	840	214	207	199	192	184	177	170	162	155	148	141
840	850	218	210	203	196	188	181	173	166	159	151	144
850	860	221	214	207	199	192	184	177	170	162	155	148
860	870	225	218	210	203	196	188	181	173	166	159	151
870	880	229	221	214	207	199	192	184	177	170	162	155
880	890	233	225	218	210	203	196	188	181	173	166	159
890	900	236	229	221	214	207	199	192	184	177	170	162
900	910	240	233	225	218	210	203	196	188	181	173	166
910	920	244	236	229	221	214	207	199	192	184	177	170
920	930	247	240	233	225	218	210	203	196	188	181	173
930	940	251	244	236	229	221	214	207	199	192	184	177
940	950	255	247	240	233	225	218	210	203	196	188	181
950	960	258	251	244	236	229	221	214	207	199	192	184
960	970	262	255	247	240	233	225	218	210	203	196	188
970	980	266	258	251	244	236	229	221	214	207	199	192
980	990	270	262	255	247	240	233	225	218	210	203	196
990	1,000	273	266	258	251	244	236	229	221	214	207	199
1,000	1,010	277	270	262	255	247	240	233	225	218	210	203
1,010	1,020	281	273	266	258	251	244	236	229	221	214	207
1,020	1,030	284	277	270	262	255	247	240	233	225	218	210
37 percent of the excess over $1,030 plus—												
$1,030 and over		286	279	271	264	257	249	242	234	227	220	212

TABLE 23 (cont.)
SINGLE PERSONS—MONTHLY PAYROLL PERIOD

And the wages are—		And the number of withholding allowances claimed is—										
At least	But less than	0	1	2	3	4	5	6	7	8	9	10
		The amount of income tax to be withheld shall be—										
$1,040	$1,080	$143	$127	$111	$96	$83	$69	$56	$43	$31	$19	$9
1,080	1,120	151	134	118	103	89	75	62	49	37	24	14
1,120	1,160	159	141	125	110	95	81	68	55	42	30	18
1,160	1,200	167	149	133	117	102	88	74	61	48	36	24
1,200	1,240	175	157	140	124	109	94	80	67	54	41	29
1,240	1,280	184	165	148	131	116	101	87	73	60	47	35
1,280	1,320	193	173	156	139	123	107	93	79	66	53	40
1,320	1,360	202	183	164	147	130	115	100	86	72	59	46
1,360	1,400	212	192	172	155	137	122	106	92	78	65	52
1,400	1,440	221	201	181	163	145	129	113	99	85	71	58
1,440	1,480	230	210	190	171	153	136	121	105	91	77	64
1,480	1,520	240	219	199	179	161	144	128	112	97	84	70
1,520	1,560	250	229	209	189	169	152	135	119	104	90	76
1,560	1,600	260	238	218	198	178	160	143	127	111	96	83
1,600	1,640	271	248	227	207	187	168	151	134	118	103	89
1,640	1,680	281	259	236	216	196	176	159	141	125	110	95
1,680	1,720	292	269	246	225	206	186	167	149	133	117	102
1,720	1,760	302	279	257	235	215	195	175	157	140	124	109
1,760	1,800	312	290	267	245	224	204	184	165	148	131	116
1,800	1,840	323	300	278	255	233	213	193	173	156	139	123
1,840	1,880	333	311	288	266	243	222	202	183	164	147	130
1,880	1,920	344	321	298	276	253	232	212	192	172	155	137
1,920	1,960	354	331	309	286	264	241	221	201	181	163	145
1,960	2,000	365	342	319	297	274	252	230	210	190	171	153
2,000	2,040	377	352	330	307	285	262	240	219	199	179	161
2,040	2,080	389	363	340	318	295	272	250	229	209	189	169
2,080	2,120	401	375	350	328	305	283	260	238	218	198	178
2,120	2,160	413	387	361	338	316	293	271	248	227	207	187
2,160	2,200	425	399	373	349	326	304	281	259	236	216	196
2,200	2,240	437	411	385	359	337	314	292	269	246	225	206
2,240	2,280	449	423	397	371	347	324	302	279	257	235	215
2,280	2,320	461	435	409	383	357	335	312	290	267	245	224
2,320	2,360	473	447	421	395	369	345	323	300	278	255	233
2,360	2,400	485	459	433	407	381	356	333	311	288	266	243
2,400	2,440	498	471	445	419	393	367	344	321	298	276	253
2,440	2,480	511	483	457	431	405	379	354	331	309	286	264
2,480	2,520	525	496	469	443	417	391	365	342	319	297	274
2,520	2,560	539	509	481	455	429	403	377	352	330	307	285
2,560	2,600	552	523	493	467	441	415	389	363	340	318	295
2,600	2,640	566	536	507	479	453	427	401	375	350	328	305
2,640	2,680	579	550	521	491	465	439	413	387	361	338	316
2,680	2,720	593	564	534	505	477	451	425	399	373	349	326
2,720	2,760	607	577	548	518	489	463	437	411	385	359	337
2,760	2,800	620	591	561	532	502	475	449	423	397	371	347
2,800	2,840	634	604	575	545	516	487	461	435	409	383	357
2,840	2,880	647	618	589	559	530	500	473	447	421	395	369
2,880	2,920	662	632	602	573	543	514	485	459	433	407	381
2,920	2,960	677	645	616	586	557	527	498	471	445	419	393
2,960	3,000	692	659	629	600	570	541	511	483	457	431	405
3,000	3,040	706	674	643	613	584	555	525	496	469	443	417
3,040	3,080	721	689	657	627	598	568	539	509	481	455	429
3,080	3,120	736	704	672	641	611	582	552	523	493	467	441
3,120	3,160	751	719	687	655	625	595	566	536	507	479	453
3,160	3,200	766	733	701	669	638	609	579	550	521	491	465
3,200	3,240	780	748	716	684	652	623	593	564	534	505	477
3,240	3,280	795	763	731	699	667	636	607	577	548	518	489
3,280	3,320	810	778	746	714	682	650	620	591	561	532	502
3,320	3,360	825	793	761	729	696	664	634	604	575	545	516
3,360	3,400	840	807	775	743	711	679	647	618	589	559	530
3,400	3,440	854	822	790	758	726	694	662	632	602	573	543
3,440	3,480	869	837	805	773	741	709	677	645	616	586	557
3,480	3,520	884	852	820	788	756	724	692	659	629	600	570
3,520	3,560	899	867	835	803	770	738	706	674	643	613	584
3,560	3,600	914	881	849	817	785	753	721	689	657	627	598
3,600	3,640	928	896	864	832	800	768	736	704	672	641	611
3,640	3,680	943	911	879	847	815	783	751	719	687	655	625
3,680	3,720	958	926	894	862	830	798	766	733	701	669	638
3,720	3,760	973	941	909	877	844	812	780	748	716	684	652
		37 percent of the excess over $3,760 plus—										
$3,760 and over		980	948	916	884	852	820	788	756	724	692	659

TABLE 23 (*cont.*)
MARRIED PERSONS—WEEKLY PAYROLL PERIOD

And the wages are–		And the number of withholding allowances claimed is–										
At least	But less than	0	1	2	3	4	5	6	7	8	9	10
		The amount of income tax to be withheld shall be–										
$490	$500	$75	$70	$66	$61	$57	$52	$48	$45	$41	$38	$34
500	510	78	73	68	63	59	55	50	47	43	39	36
510	520	80	75	70	66	61	57	52	48	45	41	38
520	530	83	78	73	68	63	59	55	50	47	43	39
530	540	85	80	75	70	66	61	57	52	48	45	41
540	550	88	83	78	73	68	63	59	55	50	47	43
550	560	90	85	80	75	70	66	61	57	52	48	45
560	570	93	88	83	78	73	68	63	59	55	50	47
570	580	95	90	85	80	75	70	66	61	57	52	48
580	590	98	93	88	83	78	73	68	63	59	55	50
590	600	101	95	90	85	80	75	70	66	61	57	52
600	610	103	98	93	88	83	78	73	68	63	59	55
610	620	106	101	95	90	85	80	75	70	66	61	57
620	630	109	103	98	93	88	83	78	73	68	63	59
630	640	112	106	101	95	90	85	80	75	70	66	61
640	650	115	109	103	98	93	88	83	78	73	68	63
650	660	117	112	106	101	95	90	85	80	75	70	66
660	670	120	115	109	103	98	93	88	83	78	73	68
670	680	123	117	112	106	101	95	90	85	80	75	70
680	690	126	120	115	109	103	98	93	88	83	78	73
690	700	129	123	117	112	106	101	95	90	85	80	75
700	710	132	126	120	115	109	103	98	93	88	83	78
710	720	136	129	123	117	112	106	101	95	90	85	80
720	730	139	132	126	120	115	109	103	98	93	88	83
730	740	142	136	129	123	117	112	106	101	95	90	85
740	750	146	139	132	126	120	115	109	103	98	93	88
750	760	149	142	136	129	123	117	112	106	101	95	90
760	770	152	146	139	132	126	120	115	109	103	98	93
770	780	155	149	142	136	129	123	117	112	106	101	95
780	790	159	152	146	139	132	126	120	115	109	103	98
790	800	162	155	149	142	136	129	123	117	112	106	101
800	810	165	159	152	146	139	132	126	120	115	109	103
810	820	169	162	155	149	142	136	129	123	117	112	106
820	830	172	165	159	152	146	139	132	126	120	115	109
830	840	175	169	162	155	149	142	136	129	123	117	112
840	850	179	172	165	159	152	146	139	132	126	120	115
850	860	182	175	169	162	155	149	142	136	129	123	117
860	870	185	179	172	165	159	152	146	139	132	126	120
870	880	188	182	175	169	162	155	149	142	136	129	123
880	890	192	185	179	172	165	159	152	146	139	132	126
890	900	195	188	182	175	169	162	155	149	142	136	129
900	910	199	192	185	179	172	165	159	152	146	139	132
910	920	202	195	188	182	175	169	162	155	149	142	136
920	930	206	199	192	185	179	172	165	159	152	146	139
930	940	210	202	195	188	182	175	169	162	155	149	142
940	950	213	206	199	192	185	179	172	165	159	152	146
950	960	217	210	202	195	188	182	175	169	162	155	149
960	970	221	213	206	199	192	185	179	172	165	159	152
970	980	225	217	210	202	195	188	182	175	169	162	155
980	990	228	221	213	206	199	192	185	179	172	165	159
990	1,000	232	225	217	210	202	195	188	182	175	169	162
1,000	1,010	236	228	221	213	206	199	192	185	179	172	165
1,010	1,020	239	232	225	217	210	202	195	188	182	175	169
1,020	1,030	243	236	228	221	213	206	199	192	185	179	172
1,030	1,040	247	239	232	225	217	210	202	195	188	182	175
1,040	1,050	250	243	236	228	221	213	206	199	192	185	179
1,050	1,060	254	247	239	232	225	217	210	202	195	188	182
1,060	1,070	258	250	243	236	228	221	213	206	199	192	185
1,070	1,080	262	254	247	239	232	225	217	210	202	195	188
1,080	1,090	265	258	250	243	236	228	221	213	206	199	192
1,090	1,100	269	262	254	247	239	232	225	217	210	202	195
1,100	1,110	273	265	258	250	243	236	228	221	213	206	199
1,110	1,120	276	269	262	254	247	239	232	225	217	210	202
1,120	1,130	280	273	265	258	250	243	236	228	221	213	206
1,130	1,140	284	276	269	262	254	247	239	232	225	217	210
		37 percent of the excess over $1,140 plus–										
$1,140 and over		286	278	271	263	256	249	241	234	226	219	212

TABLE 23 (*cont.*)
MARRIED PERSONS—MONTHLY PAYROLL PERIOD

And the wages are—		And the number of withholding allowances claimed is—										
At least	But less than	0	1	2	3	4	5	6	7	8	9	10
		The amount of income tax to be withheld shall be—										
$0	$212	$0	$0	$0	$0	$0	$0	$0	$0	$0	$0	$0
212	216	1	0	0	0	0	0	0	0	0	0	0
216	220	1	0	0	0	0	0	0	0	0	0	0
220	224	2	0	0	0	0	0	0	0	0	0	0
224	228	2	0	0	0	0	0	0	0	0	0	0
228	232	2	0	0	0	0	0	0	0	0	0	0
232	236	3	0	0	0	0	0	0	0	0	0	0
236	240	3	0	0	0	0	0	0	0	0	0	0
240	248	4	0	0	0	0	0	0	0	0	0	0
248	256	5	0	0	0	0	0	0	0	0	0	0
256	264	6	0	0	0	0	0	0	0	0	0	0
264	272	7	0	0	0	0	0	0	0	0	0	0
272	280	7	0	0	0	0	0	0	0	0	0	0
280	288	8	0	0	0	0	0	0	0	0	0	0
288	296	9	0	0	0	0	0	0	0	0	0	0
296	304	10	1	0	0	0	0	0	0	0	0	0
304	312	11	1	0	0	0	0	0	0	0	0	0
312	320	12	2	0	0	0	0	0	0	0	0	0
320	328	13	3	0	0	0	0	0	0	0	0	0
328	336	14	4	0	0	0	0	0	0	0	0	0
336	344	14	5	0	0	0	0	0	0	0	0	0
344	352	15	6	0	0	0	0	0	0	0	0	0
352	360	16	7	0	0	0	0	0	0	0	0	0
360	368	17	8	0	0	0	0	0	0	0	0	0
368	376	18	8	0	0	0	0	0	0	0	0	0
376	384	19	9	0	0	0	0	0	0	0	0	0
384	392	20	10	1	0	0	0	0	0	0	0	0
392	400	21	11	2	0	0	0	0	0	0	0	0
400	420	22	13	3	0	0	0	0	0	0	0	0
420	440	25	15	5	0	0	0	0	0	0	0	0
440	460	27	17	8	0	0	0	0	0	0	0	0
460	480	30	19	10	0	0	0	0	0	0	0	0
480	500	32	22	12	2	0	0	0	0	0	0	0
500	520	34	24	14	5	0	0	0	0	0	0	0
520	540	37	26	16	7	0	0	0	0	0	0	0
540	560	39	29	19	9	0	0	0	0	0	0	0
560	580	42	31	21	11	2	0	0	0	0	0	0
580	600	44	34	23	13	4	0	0	0	0	0	0
600	640	49	37	27	17	7	0	0	0	0	0	0
640	680	54	42	32	21	12	2	0	0	0	0	0
680	720	60	48	36	26	16	6	0	0	0	0	0
720	760	65	53	41	31	20	11	1	0	0	0	0
760	800	71	59	47	36	25	15	6	0	0	0	0
800	840	77	64	52	40	30	20	10	1	0	0	0
840	880	82	70	58	46	35	24	14	5	0	0	0
880	920	88	76	63	51	40	29	19	9	0	0	0
920	960	93	81	69	57	45	34	24	14	4	0	0
960	1,000	100	87	75	63	50	39	28	18	9	0	0
1,000	1,040	106	92	80	68	56	44	33	23	13	3	0
1,040	1,080	112	99	86	74	62	49	38	28	17	8	0
1,080	1,120	119	105	91	79	67	55	43	32	22	12	3
1,120	1,160	125	111	98	85	73	61	49	37	27	17	7
1,160	1,200	132	118	104	91	78	66	54	42	32	21	12
1,200	1,240	138	124	110	96	84	72	60	48	36	26	16
1,240	1,280	144	131	117	103	90	77	65	53	41	31	20
1,280	1,320	151	137	123	109	95	83	71	59	47	36	25
1,320	1,360	158	143	130	116	102	89	77	64	52	40	30
1,360	1,400	165	150	136	122	108	94	82	70	58	46	35
1,400	1,440	172	157	142	128	115	101	88	76	63	51	40
1,440	1,480	180	164	149	135	121	107	93	81	69	57	45
1,480	1,520	187	171	156	141	127	114	100	87	75	63	50
1,520	1,560	194	178	163	148	134	120	106	92	80	68	56
1,560	1,600	201	186	170	154	140	126	112	99	86	74	62
1,600	1,640	208	193	177	162	147	133	119	105	91	79	67
1,640	1,680	216	200	184	169	153	139	125	111	98	85	73
1,680	1,720	224	207	192	176	160	146	132	118	104	91	78
1,720	1,760	233	214	199	183	168	152	138	124	110	96	84
1,760	1,800	242	223	206	190	175	159	144	131	117	103	90
1,800	1,840	251	232	213	198	182	166	151	137	123	109	95
1,840	1,880	259	240	221	205	189	174	158	143	130	116	102
1,880	1,920	268	249	230	212	196	181	165	150	136	122	108
1,920	1,960	277	258	239	220	204	188	172	157	142	128	115
1,960	2,000	286	267	248	229	211	195	180	164	149	135	121
2,000	2,040	295	276	256	237	218	202	187	171	156	141	127

TABLE 24
FEDERAL INCOME TAX TABLES

Example: Mr. and Mrs. Green are filing a joint return. Their taxable income on line 16 of Form 1040A is $23,270. First, they find the $23,250-23,300 income line. Next, they find the column for married filing jointly and read down the column. The amount shown where the income line and filing status column meet is $3,706. This is the tax amount they must write on line 19a of Form 1040A.

At least	But less than	Single	Married filing jointly	Married filing separately	Head of a household
			Your tax is—		
→ 23,250	23,300	4,767	3,706	5,894	4,379
23,300	23,350	4,783	3,718	5,916	4,393
23,350	23,400	4,798	3,731	5,938	4,407

If 1040A, line 16, OR 1040EZ, line 7 is—		And you are—				If 1040A, line 16, OR 1040EZ, line 7 is—		And you are—				If 1040A, line 16, OR 1040EZ, line 7 is—		And you are—			
At least	But less than	Single	Married filing jointly	Married filing separately	Head of a house-hold	At least	But less than	Single	Married filing jointly	Married filing separately	Head of a house-hold	At least	But less than	Single	Married filing jointly	Married filing separately	Head of a house-hold
		Your tax is—						Your tax is—						Your tax is—			
0	1,700	0	0	0	0	**3,000**						5,500	5,550	452	256	549	410
1,700	1,725	0	0	a2	0	3,000	3,050	87	0	165	87	5,550	5,600	460	263	557	417
1,725	1,750	0	0	5	0	3,050	3,100	93	0	172	93	5,600	5,650	468	270	565	424
1,750	1,775	0	0	8	0	3,100	3,150	99	0	179	99	5,650	5,700	476	277	573	431
1,775	1,800	0	0	11	0	3,150	3,200	105	0	186	105	5,700	5,750	484	284	581	438
1,800	1,825	0	0	14	0	3,200	3,250	111	0	193	111						
1,825	1,850	0	0	17	0	3,250	3,300	117	0	200	117	5,750	5,800	492	291	589	445
1,850	1,875	0	0	20	0	3,300	3,350	123	0	207	123	5,800	5,850	500	298	597	452
1,875	1,900	0	0	23	0	3,350	3,400	129	0	214	129	5,850	5,900	508	305	605	459
1,900	1,925	0	0	26	0	3,400	3,450	136	c3	221	135	5,900	5,950	516	312	613	466
1,925	1,950	0	0	29	0	3,450	3,500	143	9	228	141	5,950	6,000	524	319	622	473
1,950	1,975	0	0	32	0	3,500	3,550	150	15	235	147	**6,000**					
1,975	2,000	0	0	35	0	3,550	3,600	157	21	242	153	6,000	6,050	532	326	631	480
2,000						3,600	3,650	164	27	249	159	6,050	6,100	540	333	641	487
2,000	2,025	0	0	38	0	3,650	3,700	171	33	256	165	6,100	6,150	548	340	650	494
2,025	2,050	0	0	41	0	3,700	3,750	178	39	263	171	6,150	6,200	556	347	660	501
2,050	2,075	0	0	44	0							6,200	6,250	564	354	669	508
2,075	2,100	0	0	47	0	3,750	3,800	185	45	270	177						
2,100	2,125	0	0	50	0	3,800	3,850	192	51	277	183	6,250	6,300	572	361	679	515
2,125	2,150	0	0	53	0	3,850	3,900	199	57	285	189	6,300	6,350	580	368	688	522
2,150	2,175	0	0	56	0	3,900	3,950	206	63	293	195	6,350	6,400	588	375	698	529
2,175	2,200	0	0	59	0	3,950	4,000	213	69	301	201	6,400	6,450	596	382	707	536
2,200	2,225	0	0	62	0	**4,000**						6,450	6,500	604	389	717	543
2,225	2,250	0	0	65	0	4,000	4,050	220	75	309	207						
2,250	2,275	0	0	68	0	4,050	4,100	227	81	317	213	6,500	6,550	612	396	726	550
2,275	2,300	0	0	71	0	4,100	4,150	234	87	325	219	6,550	6,600	621	403	736	558
2,300	2,325	b2	0	74	b2	4,150	4,200	241	93	333	225	6,600	6,650	629	410	745	566
2,325	2,350	5	0	77	5	4,200	4,250	248	99	341	231	6,650	6,700	638	417	755	574
2,350	2,375	8	0	80	8	4,250	4,300	255	105	349	237	6,700	6,750	646	424	764	582
2,375	2,400	11	0	83	11	4,300	4,350	262	111	357	243						
2,400	2,425	14	0	86	14	4,350	4,400	269	117	365	249	6,750	6,800	655	431	774	590
2,425	2,450	17	0	89	17	4,400	4,450	276	123	373	256	6,800	6,850	663	438	783	598
2,450	2,475	20	0	92	20	4,450	4,500	284	129	381	263	6,850	6,900	672	445	793	606
2,475	2,500	23	0	95	23	4,500	4,550	292	135	389	270	6,900	6,950	680	452	802	614
2,500	2,525	26	0	98	26	4,550	4,600	300	141	397	277	6,950	7,000	689	459	812	622
2,525	2,550	29	0	101	29	4,600	4,650	308	147	405	284	**7,000**					
2,550	2,575	32	0	104	32	4,650	4,700	316	153	413	291	7,000	7,050	697	466	821	630
2,575	2,600	35	0	107	35	4,700	4,750	324	159	421	298	7,050	7,100	706	473	831	638
2,600	2,625	38	0	110	38	4,750	4,800	332	165	429	305	7,100	7,150	714	480	840	646
2,625	2,650	41	0	113	41	4,800	4,850	340	171	437	312	7,150	7,200	723	487	850	654
2,650	2,675	44	0	116	44	4,850	4,900	348	177	445	319	7,200	7,250	731	494	859	662
2,675	2,700	47	0	119	47	4,900	4,950	356	183	453	326						
2,700	2,725	50	0	122	50	4,950	5,000	364	189	461	333	7,250	7,300	740	501	869	670
2,725	2,750	53	0	125	53	**5,000**						7,300	7,350	748	508	878	678
2,750	2,775	56	0	128	56	5,000	5,050	372	195	469	340	7,350	7,400	757	515	888	686
2,775	2,800	59	0	131	59	5,050	5,100	380	201	477	347	7,400	7,450	765	522	897	694
2,800	2,825	62	0	135	62	5,100	5,150	388	207	485	354	7,450	7,500	774	529	907	702
2,825	2,850	65	0	138	65	5,150	5,200	396	213	493	361						
2,850	2,875	68	0	142	68	5,200	5,250	404	219	501	368	7,500	7,550	782	536	916	710
2,875	2,900	71	0	145	71	5,250	5,300	412	225	509	375	7,550	7,600	791	543	926	718
2,900	2,925	74	0	149	74	5,300	5,350	420	231	517	382	7,600	7,650	799	550	935	726
2,925	2,950	77	0	152	77	5,350	5,400	428	237	525	389	7,650	7,700	808	558	945	734
2,950	2,975	80	0	156	80	5,400	5,450	436	243	533	396	7,700	7,750	816	566	954	742
2,975	3,000	83	0	159	83	5,450	5,500	444	249	541	403	7,750	7,800	825	574	964	750
												7,800	7,850	833	582	973	758
												7,850	7,900	842	590	983	766
												7,900	7,950	850	598	992	774
												7,950	8,000	859	606	1,002	782

Continued on next page

a If your taxable income is exactly $1,700, your tax is zero.   **c** If your taxable income is exactly $3,400, your tax is zero.
b If your taxable income is exactly $2,300, your tax is zero.

TABLE 24 (cont.)

If 1040A, line 16, OR 1040EZ, line 7 is— / **And you are—** / **Your tax is—**

At least	But less than	Single	Married filing jointly	Married filing separately	Head of a household
8,000					
8,000	8,050	867	614	1,012	790
8,050	8,100	876	622	1,023	798
8,100	8,150	884	630	1,034	806
8,150	8,200	893	638	1,045	814
8,200	8,250	901	646	1,056	822
8,250	8,300	910	654	1,067	830
8,300	8,350	918	662	1,078	838
8,350	8,400	927	670	1,089	846
8,400	8,450	935	678	1,100	854
8,450	8,500	944	686	1,111	862
8,500	8,550	953	694	1,122	870
8,550	8,600	962	702	1,133	878
8,600	8,650	972	710	1,144	886
8,650	8,700	981	718	1,155	894
8,700	8,750	991	726	1,166	903
8,750	8,800	1,000	734	1,177	913
8,800	8,850	1,010	742	1,188	923
8,850	8,900	1,019	750	1,199	933
8,900	8,950	1,029	758	1,210	943
8,950	9,000	1,038	766	1,221	953
9,000					
9,000	9,050	1,048	774	1,232	963
9,050	9,100	1,057	782	1,243	973
9,100	9,150	1,067	790	1,254	983
9,150	9,200	1,076	798	1,265	993
9,200	9,250	1,086	806	1,276	1,003
9,250	9,300	1,095	814	1,287	1,013
9,300	9,350	1,105	822	1,298	1,023
9,350	9,400	1,114	830	1,309	1,033
9,400	9,450	1,124	838	1,320	1,043
9,450	9,500	1,133	846	1,331	1,053
9,500	9,550	1,143	854	1,342	1,063
9,550	9,600	1,152	862	1,353	1,073
9,600	9,650	1,162	870	1,364	1,083
9,650	9,700	1,171	878	1,375	1,093
9,700	9,750	1,181	886	1,386	1,103
9,750	9,800	1,190	894	1,397	1,113
9,800	9,850	1,200	902	1,408	1,123
9,850	9,900	1,209	910	1,419	1,133
9,900	9,950	1,219	918	1,430	1,143
9,950	10,000	1,228	926	1,441	1,153
10,000					
10,000	10,050	1,238	934	1,452	1,163
10,050	10,100	1,247	942	1,463	1,173
10,100	10,150	1,257	950	1,475	1,183
10,150	10,200	1,266	958	1,487	1,193
10,200	10,250	1,276	966	1,500	1,203
10,250	10,300	1,285	974	1,512	1,213
10,300	10,350	1,295	982	1,525	1,223
10,350	10,400	1,304	990	1,537	1,233
10,400	10,450	1,314	998	1,550	1,243
10,450	10,500	1,323	1,006	1,562	1,253
10,500	10,550	1,333	1,014	1,575	1,263
10,550	10,600	1,342	1,022	1,587	1,273
10,600	10,650	1,352	1,030	1,600	1,283
10,650	10,700	1,361	1,038	1,612	1,293
10,700	10,750	1,371	1,046	1,625	1,303
10,750	10,800	1,380	1,054	1,637	1,313
10,800	10,850	1,391	1,062	1,650	1,323
10,850	10,900	1,402	1,070	1,662	1,333
10,900	10,950	1,413	1,078	1,675	1,343
10,950	11,000	1,424	1,086	1,687	1,353
11,000					
11,000	11,050	1,435	1,094	1,700	1,363
11,050	11,100	1,446	1,102	1,712	1,373
11,100	11,150	1,457	1,110	1,725	1,383
11,150	11,200	1,468	1,118	1,737	1,393
11,200	11,250	1,479	1,126	1,750	1,403
11,250	11,300	1,490	1,134	1,762	1,413
11,300	11,350	1,501	1,142	1,775	1,423
11,350	11,400	1,512	1,150	1,787	1,433
11,400	11,450	1,523	1,158	1,800	1,443
11,450	11,500	1,534	1,166	1,812	1,453
11,500	11,550	1,545	1,174	1,825	1,463
11,550	11,600	1,556	1,182	1,837	1,473
11,600	11,650	1,567	1,190	1,850	1,483
11,650	11,700	1,578	1,198	1,862	1,493
11,700	11,750	1,589	1,206	1,875	1,503
11,750	11,800	1,600	1,214	1,887	1,513
11,800	11,850	1,611	1,222	1,900	1,524
11,850	11,900	1,622	1,230	1,912	1,535
11,900	11,950	1,633	1,239	1,925	1,546
11,950	12,000	1,644	1,248	1,937	1,557
12,000					
12,000	12,050	1,655	1,258	1,950	1,568
12,050	12,100	1,666	1,267	1,962	1,579
12,100	12,150	1,677	1,277	1,975	1,590
12,150	12,200	1,688	1,286	1,987	1,601
12,200	12,250	1,699	1,296	2,000	1,612
12,250	12,300	1,710	1,305	2,012	1,623
12,300	12,350	1,721	1,315	2,026	1,634
12,350	12,400	1,732	1,324	2,040	1,645
12,400	12,450	1,743	1,334	2,055	1,656
12,450	12,500	1,754	1,343	2,069	1,667
12,500	12,550	1,765	1,353	2,084	1,678
12,550	12,600	1,776	1,362	2,098	1,689
12,600	12,650	1,787	1,372	2,113	1,700
12,650	12,700	1,798	1,381	2,127	1,711
12,700	12,750	1,809	1,391	2,142	1,722
12,750	12,800	1,820	1,400	2,156	1,733
12,800	12,850	1,831	1,410	2,171	1,744
12,850	12,900	1,842	1,419	2,185	1,755
12,900	12,950	1,853	1,429	2,200	1,766
12,950	13,000	1,864	1,438	2,214	1,777
13,000					
13,000	13,050	1,876	1,448	2,229	1,788
13,050	13,100	1,887	1,457	2,243	1,799
13,100	13,150	1,899	1,467	2,258	1,810
13,150	13,200	1,910	1,476	2,272	1,821
13,200	13,250	1,922	1,486	2,287	1,832
13,250	13,300	1,933	1,495	2,301	1,843
13,300	13,350	1,945	1,505	2,316	1,854
13,350	13,400	1,956	1,514	2,330	1,865
13,400	13,450	1,968	1,524	2,345	1,876
13,450	13,500	1,979	1,533	2,359	1,887
13,500	13,550	1,991	1,543	2,374	1,898
13,550	13,600	2,002	1,552	2,388	1,909
13,600	13,650	2,014	1,562	2,403	1,920
13,650	13,700	2,025	1,571	2,417	1,931
13,700	13,750	2,037	1,581	2,432	1,942
13,750	13,800	2,048	1,590	2,446	1,953
13,800	13,850	2,060	1,600	2,461	1,964
13,850	13,900	2,071	1,609	2,475	1,975
13,900	13,950	2,083	1,619	2,490	1,986
13,950	14,000	2,094	1,628	2,504	1,997
14,000					
14,000	14,050	2,106	1,638	2,519	2,008
14,050	14,100	2,117	1,647	2,533	2,019
14,100	14,150	2,129	1,657	2,548	2,030
14,150	14,200	2,140	1,666	2,562	2,041
14,200	14,250	2,152	1,676	2,577	2,052
14,250	14,300	2,163	1,685	2,591	2,063
14,300	14,350	2,175	1,695	2,606	2,074
14,350	14,400	2,186	1,704	2,620	2,085
14,400	14,450	2,198	1,714	2,635	2,096
14,450	14,500	2,209	1,723	2,649	2,107
14,500	14,550	2,221	1,733	2,664	2,118
14,550	14,600	2,232	1,742	2,678	2,129
14,600	14,650	2,244	1,752	2,693	2,140
14,650	14,700	2,255	1,761	2,707	2,151
14,700	14,750	2,267	1,771	2,722	2,162
14,750	14,800	2,278	1,780	2,736	2,173
14,800	14,850	2,290	1,790	2,751	2,184
14,850	14,900	2,301	1,799	2,765	2,195
14,900	14,950	2,313	1,809	2,780	2,206
14,950	15,000	2,324	1,818	2,795	2,217
15,000					
15,000	15,050	2,337	1,828	2,812	2,228
15,050	15,100	2,350	1,837	2,828	2,239
15,100	15,150	2,364	1,847	2,845	2,251
15,150	15,200	2,377	1,856	2,861	2,262
15,200	15,250	2,391	1,866	2,878	2,274
15,250	15,300	2,404	1,875	2,894	2,285
15,300	15,350	2,418	1,885	2,911	2,297
15,350	15,400	2,431	1,894	2,927	2,308
15,400	15,450	2,445	1,904	2,944	2,320
15,450	15,500	2,458	1,913	2,960	2,331
15,500	15,550	2,472	1,923	2,977	2,343
15,550	15,600	2,485	1,932	2,993	2,354
15,600	15,650	2,499	1,942	3,010	2,366
15,650	15,700	2,512	1,951	3,026	2,377
15,700	15,750	2,526	1,961	3,043	2,389
15,750	15,800	2,539	1,970	3,059	2,400
15,800	15,850	2,553	1,980	3,076	2,412
15,850	15,900	2,566	1,989	3,092	2,423
15,900	15,950	2,580	1,999	3,109	2,435
15,950	16,000	2,593	2,008	3,125	2,446
16,000					
16,000	16,050	2,607	2,019	3,142	2,458
16,050	16,100	2,620	2,030	3,158	2,469
16,100	16,150	2,634	2,041	3,175	2,481
16,150	16,200	2,647	2,052	3,191	2,492
16,200	16,250	2,661	2,063	3,208	2,504

Continued on next page

TABLE 24 (*cont.*)

If 1040A, line 16, OR 1040EZ, line 7 is—		Single	Married filing jointly	Married filing separately	Head of a household
At least	But less than				
		Your tax is—			
16,250	16,300	2,674	2,074	3,224	2,515
16,300	16,350	2,688	2,085	3,241	2,527
16,350	16,400	2,701	2,096	3,257	2,538
16,400	16,450	2,715	2,107	3,274	2,550
16,450	16,500	2,728	2,118	3,290	2,561
16,500	16,550	2,742	2,129	3,307	2,573
16,550	16,600	2,755	2,140	3,323	2,584
16,600	16,650	2,769	2,151	3,340	2,596
16,650	16,700	2,782	2,162	3,356	2,607
16,700	16,750	2,796	2,173	3,373	2,619
16,750	16,800	2,809	2,184	3,389	2,630
16,800	16,850	2,823	2,195	3,406	2,642
16,850	16,900	2,836	2,206	3,422	2,653
16,900	16,950	2,850	2,217	3,439	2,665
16,950	17,000	2,863	2,228	3,455	2,676
17,000					
17,000	17,050	2,877	2,239	3,472	2,688
17,050	17,100	2,890	2,250	3,488	2,699
17,100	17,150	2,904	2,261	3,505	2,711
17,150	17,200	2,917	2,272	3,521	2,722
17,200	17,250	2,931	2,283	3,538	2,734
17,250	17,300	2,944	2,294	3,554	2,745
17,300	17,350	2,958	2,305	3,571	2,757
17,350	17,400	2,971	2,316	3,587	2,768
17,400	17,450	2,985	2,327	3,604	2,780
17,450	17,500	2,998	2,338	3,620	2,791
17,500	17,550	3,012	2,349	3,637	2,803
17,550	17,600	3,025	2,360	3,653	2,814
17,600	17,650	3,039	2,371	3,671	2,826
17,650	17,700	3,052	2,382	3,691	2,837
17,700	17,750	3,066	2,393	3,710	2,849
17,750	17,800	3,079	2,404	3,730	2,860
17,800	17,850	3,093	2,415	3,749	2,872
17,850	17,900	3,106	2,426	3,769	2,883
17,900	17,950	3,120	2,437	3,788	2,895
17,950	18,000	3,133	2,448	3,808	2,906
18,000					
18,000	18,050	3,147	2,459	3,827	2,918
18,050	18,100	3,160	2,470	3,847	2,929
18,100	18,150	3,174	2,481	3,866	2,941
18,150	18,200	3,187	2,492	3,886	2,952
18,200	18,250	3,202	2,503	3,905	2,965
18,250	18,300	3,217	2,514	3,925	2,979
18,300	18,350	3,233	2,525	3,944	2,993
18,350	18,400	3,248	2,536	3,964	3,007
18,400	18,450	3,264	2,547	3,983	3,021
18,450	18,500	3,279	2,558	4,003	3,035
18,500	18,550	3,295	2,569	4,022	3,049
18,550	18,600	3,310	2,580	4,042	3,063
18,600	18,650	3,326	2,591	4,061	3,077
18,650	18,700	3,341	2,602	4,081	3,091
18,700	18,750	3,357	2,613	4,100	3,105
18,750	18,800	3,372	2,624	4,120	3,119
18,800	18,850	3,388	2,635	4,139	3,133
18,850	18,900	3,403	2,646	4,159	3,147
18,900	18,950	3,419	2,657	4,178	3,161
18,950	19,000	3,434	2,668	4,198	3,175

If 1040A, line 16, OR 1040EZ, line 7 is—		Single	Married filing jointly	Married filing separately	Head of a household
At least	But less than				
		Your tax is—			
19,000					
19,000	19,050	3,450	2,679	4,217	3,189
19,050	19,100	3,465	2,690	4,237	3,203
19,100	19,150	3,481	2,701	4,256	3,217
19,150	19,200	3,496	2,712	4,276	3,231
19,200	19,250	3,512	2,723	4,295	3,245
19,250	19,300	3,527	2,734	4,315	3,259
19,300	19,350	3,543	2,745	4,334	3,273
19,350	19,400	3,558	2,756	4,354	3,287
19,400	19,450	3,574	2,767	4,373	3,301
19,450	19,500	3,589	2,778	4,393	3,315
19,500	19,550	3,605	2,789	4,412	3,329
19,550	19,600	3,620	2,800	4,432	3,343
19,600	19,650	3,636	2,811	4,451	3,357
19,650	19,700	3,651	2,822	4,471	3,371
19,700	19,750	3,667	2,833	4,490	3,385
19,750	19,800	3,682	2,844	4,510	3,399
19,800	19,850	3,698	2,855	4,529	3,413
19,850	19,900	3,713	2,866	4,549	3,427
19,900	19,950	3,729	2,877	4,568	3,441
19,950	20,000	3,744	2,888	4,588	3,455
20,000					
20,000	20,050	3,760	2,899	4,607	3,469
20,050	20,100	3,775	2,910	4,627	3,483
20,100	20,150	3,791	2,921	4,646	3,497
20,150	20,200	3,806	2,932	4,666	3,511
20,200	20,250	3,822	2,943	4,685	3,525
20,250	20,300	3,837	2,956	4,705	3,539
20,300	20,350	3,853	2,968	4,724	3,553
20,350	20,400	3,868	2,981	4,744	3,567
20,400	20,450	3,884	2,993	4,763	3,581
20,450	20,500	3,899	3,006	4,783	3,595
20,500	20,550	3,915	3,018	4,802	3,609
20,550	20,600	3,930	3,031	4,822	3,623
20,600	20,650	3,946	3,043	4,841	3,637
20,650	20,700	3,961	3,056	4,861	3,651
20,700	20,750	3,977	3,068	4,880	3,665
20,750	20,800	3,992	3,081	4,900	3,679
20,800	20,850	4,008	3,093	4,919	3,693
20,850	20,900	4,023	3,106	4,939	3,707
20,900	20,950	4,039	3,118	4,958	3,721
20,950	21,000	4,054	3,131	4,978	3,735
21,000					
21,000	21,050	4,070	3,143	4,997	3,749
21,050	21,100	4,085	3,156	5,017	3,763
21,100	21,150	4,101	3,168	5,036	3,777
21,150	21,200	4,116	3,181	5,056	3,791
21,200	21,250	4,132	3,193	5,075	3,805
21,250	21,300	4,147	3,206	5,095	3,819
21,300	21,350	4,163	3,218	5,114	3,833
21,350	21,400	4,178	3,231	5,134	3,847
21,400	21,450	4,194	3,243	5,153	3,861
21,450	21,500	4,209	3,256	5,173	3,875
21,500	21,550	4,225	3,268	5,192	3,889
21,550	21,600	4,240	3,281	5,212	3,903
21,600	21,650	4,256	3,293	5,231	3,917
21,650	21,700	4,271	3,306	5,251	3,931
21,700	21,750	4,287	3,318	5,270	3,945

If 1040A, line 16, OR 1040EZ, line 7 is—		Single	Married filing jointly	Married filing separately	Head of a household
At least	But less than				
		Your tax is—			
21,750	21,800	4,302	3,331	5,290	3,959
21,800	21,850	4,318	3,343	5,309	3,973
21,850	21,900	4,333	3,356	5,329	3,987
21,900	21,950	4,349	3,368	5,348	4,001
21,950	22,000	4,364	3,381	5,368	4,015
22,000					
22,000	22,050	4,380	3,393	5,387	4,029
22,050	22,100	4,395	3,406	5,407	4,043
22,100	22,150	4,411	3,418	5,426	4,057
22,150	22,200	4,426	3,431	5,446	4,071
22,200	22,250	4,442	3,443	5,465	4,085
22,250	22,300	4,457	3,456	5,485	4,099
22,300	22,350	4,473	3,468	5,504	4,113
22,350	22,400	4,488	3,481	5,524	4,127
22,400	22,450	4,504	3,493	5,543	4,141
22,450	22,500	4,519	3,506	5,563	4,155
22,500	22,550	4,535	3,518	5,582	4,169
22,550	22,600	4,550	3,531	5,602	4,183
22,600	22,650	4,566	3,543	5,621	4,197
22,650	22,700	4,581	3,556	5,641	4,211
22,700	22,750	4,597	3,568	5,660	4,225
22,750	22,800	4,612	3,581	5,680	4,239
22,800	22,850	4,628	3,593	5,699	4,253
22,850	22,900	4,643	3,606	5,719	4,267
22,900	22,950	4,659	3,618	5,740	4,281
22,950	23,000	4,674	3,631	5,762	4,295
23,000					
23,000	23,050	4,690	3,643	5,784	4,309
23,050	23,100	4,705	3,656	5,806	4,323
23,100	23,150	4,721	3,668	5,828	4,337
23,150	23,200	4,736	3,681	5,850	4,351
23,200	23,250	4,752	3,693	5,872	4,365
23,250	23,300	4,767	3,706	5,894	4,379
23,300	23,350	4,783	3,718	5,916	4,393
23,350	23,400	4,798	3,731	5,938	4,407
23,400	23,450	4,814	3,743	5,960	4,421
23,450	23,500	4,829	3,756	5,982	4,435
23,500	23,550	4,846	3,768	6,004	4,450
23,550	23,600	4,863	3,781	6,026	4,466
23,600	23,650	4,881	3,793	6,048	4,482
23,650	23,700	4,898	3,806	6,070	4,498
23,700	23,750	4,916	3,818	6,092	4,514
23,750	23,800	4,933	3,831	6,114	4,530
23,800	23,850	4,951	3,843	6,136	4,546
23,850	23,900	4,968	3,856	6,158	4,562
23,900	23,950	4,986	3,868	6,180	4,578
23,950	24,000	5,003	3,881	6,202	4,594
24,000					
24,000	24,050	5,021	3,893	6,224	4,610
24,050	24,100	5,038	3,906	6,246	4,626
24,100	24,150	5,056	3,918	6,268	4,642
24,150	24,200	5,073	3,931	6,290	4,658
24,200	24,250	5,091	3,943	6,312	4,674
24,250	24,300	5,108	3,956	6,334	4,690
24,300	24,350	5,126	3,968	6,356	4,706
24,350	24,400	5,143	3,981	6,378	4,722
24,400	24,450	5,161	3,993	6,400	4,738
24,450	24,500	5,178	4,006	6,422	4,754

Continued on next page

TABLE 24 (cont.)

If 1040A, line 16, OR 1040EZ, line 7 is—		And you are—			
At least	But less than	Single	Married filing jointly	Married filing separately	Head of a household
		Your tax is—			
24,500	24,550	5,196	4,018	6,444	4,770
24,550	24,600	5,213	4,031	6,466	4,786
24,600	24,650	5,231	4,044	6,488	4,802
24,650	24,700	5,248	4,059	6,510	4,818
24,700	24,750	5,266	4,073	6,532	4,834
24,750	24,800	5,283	4,088	6,554	4,850
24,800	24,850	5,301	4,102	6,576	4,866
24,850	24,900	5,318	4,117	6,598	4,882
24,900	24,950	5,336	4,131	6,620	4,898
24,950	25,000	5,353	4,146	6,642	4,914
25,000					
25,000	25,050	5,371	4,160	6,664	4,930
25,050	25,100	5,388	4,175	6,686	4,946
25,100	25,150	5,406	4,189	6,708	4,962
25,150	25,200	5,423	4,204	6,730	4,978
25,200	25,250	5,441	4,218	6,752	4,994
25,250	25,300	5,458	4,233	6,774	5,010
25,300	25,350	5,476	4,247	6,796	5,026
25,350	25,400	5,493	4,262	6,818	5,042
25,400	25,450	5,511	4,276	6,840	5,058
25,450	25,500	5,528	4,291	6,862	5,074
25,500	25,550	5,546	4,305	6,884	5,090
25,550	25,600	5,563	4,320	6,906	5,106
25,600	25,650	5,581	4,334	6,928	5,122
25,650	25,700	5,598	4,349	6,950	5,138
25,700	25,750	5,616	4,363	6,972	5,154
25,750	25,800	5,633	4,378	6,994	5,170
25,800	25,850	5,651	4,392	7,016	5,186
25,850	25,900	5,668	4,407	7,038	5,202
25,900	25,950	5,686	4,421	7,060	5,218
25,950	26,000	5,703	4,436	7,082	5,234
26,000					
26,000	26,050	5,721	4,450	7,104	5,250
26,050	26,100	5,738	4,465	7,126	5,266
26,100	26,150	5,756	4,479	7,148	5,282
26,150	26,200	5,773	4,494	7,170	5,298
26,200	26,250	5,791	4,508	7,192	5,314
26,250	26,300	5,808	4,523	7,214	5,330
26,300	26,350	5,826	4,537	7,236	5,346
26,350	26,400	5,843	4,552	7,258	5,362
26,400	26,450	5,861	4,566	7,280	5,378
26,450	26,500	5,878	4,581	7,302	5,394
26,500	26,550	5,896	4,595	7,324	5,410
26,550	26,600	5,913	4,610	7,346	5,426
26,600	26,650	5,931	4,624	7,368	5,442
26,650	26,700	5,948	4,639	7,390	5,458
26,700	26,750	5,966	4,653	7,412	5,474
26,750	26,800	5,983	4,668	7,434	5,490
26,800	26,850	6,001	4,682	7,456	5,506
26,850	26,900	6,018	4,697	7,478	5,522
26,900	26,950	6,036	4,711	7,500	5,538
26,950	27,000	6,053	4,726	7,522	5,554
27,000					
27,000	27,050	6,071	4,740	7,544	5,570
27,050	27,100	6,088	4,755	7,566	5,586
27,100	27,150	6,106	4,769	7,588	5,602
27,150	27,200	6,123	4,784	7,610	5,618
27,200	27,250	6,141	4,798	7,632	5,634

If 1040A, line 16, OR 1040EZ, line 7 is—		And you are—			
At least	But less than	Single	Married filing jointly	Married filing separately	Head of a household
		Your tax is—			
27,250	27,300	6,158	4,813	7,654	5,650
27,300	27,350	6,176	4,827	7,676	5,666
27,350	27,400	6,193	4,842	7,698	5,682
27,400	27,450	6,211	4,856	7,720	5,698
27,450	27,500	6,228	4,871	7,742	5,714
27,500	27,550	6,246	4,885	7,764	5,730
27,550	27,600	6,263	4,900	7,786	5,746
27,600	27,650	6,281	4,914	7,808	5,762
27,650	27,700	6,298	4,929	7,830	5,778
27,700	27,750	6,316	4,943	7,852	5,794
27,750	27,800	6,333	4,958	7,874	5,810
27,800	27,850	6,351	4,972	7,896	5,826
27,850	27,900	6,368	4,987	7,918	5,842
27,900	27,950	6,386	5,001	7,940	5,858
27,950	28,000	6,403	5,016	7,962	5,874
28,000					
28,000	28,050	6,421	5,030	7,984	5,890
28,050	28,100	6,438	5,045	8,006	5,906
28,100	28,150	6,456	5,059	8,028	5,922
28,150	28,200	6,473	5,074	8,050	5,938
28,200	28,250	6,491	5,088	8,072	5,954
28,250	28,300	6,508	5,103	8,094	5,970
28,300	28,350	6,526	5,117	8,116	5,986
28,350	28,400	6,543	5,132	8,138	6,002
28,400	28,450	6,561	5,146	8,160	6,018
28,450	28,500	6,578	5,161	8,182	6,034
28,500	28,550	6,596	5,175	8,204	6,050
28,550	28,600	6,613	5,190	8,226	6,066
28,600	28,650	6,631	5,204	8,248	6,082
28,650	28,700	6,648	5,219	8,270	6,098
28,700	28,750	6,666	5,233	8,292	6,114
28,750	28,800	6,683	5,248	8,314	6,130
28,800	28,850	6,702	5,262	8,336	6,148
28,850	28,900	6,722	5,277	8,358	6,167
28,900	28,950	6,742	5,291	8,380	6,186
28,950	29,000	6,762	5,306	8,402	6,205
29,000					
29,000	29,050	6,782	5,320	8,424	6,224
29,050	29,100	6,802	5,335	8,446	6,243
29,100	29,150	6,822	5,349	8,468	6,262
29,150	29,200	6,842	5,364	8,490	6,281
29,200	29,250	6,862	5,378	8,512	6,300
29,250	29,300	6,882	5,393	8,534	6,319
29,300	29,350	6,902	5,407	8,556	6,338
29,350	29,400	6,922	5,422	8,578	6,357
29,400	29,450	6,942	5,436	8,600	6,376
29,450	29,500	6,962	5,451	8,622	6,395
29,500	29,550	6,982	5,465	8,644	6,414
29,550	29,600	7,002	5,480	8,666	6,433
29,600	29,650	7,022	5,494	8,688	6,452
29,650	29,700	7,042	5,509	8,710	6,471
29,700	29,750	7,062	5,523	8,732	6,490
29,750	29,800	7,082	5,538	8,754	6,509
29,800	29,850	7,102	5,552	8,776	6,528
29,850	29,900	7,122	5,567	8,798	6,547
29,900	29,950	7,142	5,582	8,820	6,566
29,950	30,000	7,162	5,599	8,842	6,585

If 1040A, line 16, OR 1040EZ, line 7 is—		And you are—			
At least	But less than	Single	Married filing jointly	Married filing separately	Head of a household
		Your tax is—			
30,000					
30,000	30,050	7,182	5,615	8,865	6,604
30,050	30,100	7,202	5,632	8,889	6,623
30,100	30,150	7,222	5,648	8,914	6,642
30,150	30,200	7,242	5,665	8,938	6,661
30,200	30,250	7,262	5,681	8,963	6,680
30,250	30,300	7,282	5,698	8,987	6,699
30,300	30,350	7,302	5,714	9,012	6,718
30,350	30,400	7,322	5,731	9,036	6,737
30,400	30,450	7,342	5,747	9,061	6,756
30,450	30,500	7,362	5,764	9,085	6,775
30,500	30,550	7,382	5,780	9,110	6,794
30,550	30,600	7,402	5,797	9,134	6,813
30,600	30,650	7,422	5,813	9,159	6,832
30,650	30,700	7,442	5,830	9,183	6,851
30,700	30,750	7,462	5,846	9,208	6,870
30,750	30,800	7,482	5,863	9,232	6,889
30,800	30,850	7,502	5,879	9,257	6,908
30,850	30,900	7,522	5,896	9,281	6,927
30,900	30,950	7,542	5,912	9,306	6,946
30,950	31,000	7,562	5,929	9,330	6,965
31,000					
31,000	31,050	7,582	5,945	9,355	6,984
31,050	31,100	7,602	5,962	9,379	7,003
31,100	31,150	7,622	5,978	9,404	7,022
31,150	31,200	7,642	5,995	9,428	7,041
31,200	31,250	7,662	6,011	9,453	7,060
31,250	31,300	7,682	6,028	9,477	7,079
31,300	31,350	7,702	6,044	9,502	7,098
31,350	31,400	7,722	6,061	9,526	7,117
31,400	31,450	7,742	6,077	9,551	7,136
31,450	31,500	7,762	6,094	9,575	7,155
31,500	31,550	7,782	6,110	9,600	7,174
31,550	31,600	7,802	6,127	9,624	7,193
31,600	31,650	7,822	6,143	9,649	7,212
31,650	31,700	7,842	6,160	9,673	7,231
31,700	31,750	7,862	6,176	9,698	7,250
31,750	31,800	7,882	6,193	9,722	7,269
31,800	31,850	7,902	6,209	9,747	7,288
31,850	31,900	7,922	6,226	9,771	7,307
31,900	31,950	7,942	6,242	9,796	7,326
31,950	32,000	7,962	6,259	9,820	7,345
32,000					
32,000	32,050	7,982	6,275	9,845	7,364
32,050	32,100	8,002	6,292	9,869	7,383
32,100	32,150	8,022	6,308	9,894	7,402
32,150	32,200	8,042	6,325	9,918	7,421
32,200	32,250	8,062	6,341	9,943	7,440
32,250	32,300	8,082	6,358	9,967	7,459
32,300	32,350	8,102	6,374	9,992	7,478
32,350	32,400	8,122	6,391	10,016	7,497
32,400	32,450	8,142	6,407	10,041	7,516
32,450	32,500	8,162	6,424	10,065	7,535
32,500	32,550	8,182	6,440	10,090	7,554
32,550	32,600	8,202	6,457	10,114	7,573
32,600	32,650	8,222	6,473	10,139	7,592
32,650	32,700	8,242	6,490	10,163	7,611
32,700	32,750	8,262	6,506	10,188	7,630

Continued on next page

TABLE 24 (*cont.*)

At least	But less than	Single	Married filing jointly	Married filing separately	Head of a household
		Your tax is—			
32,750	32,800	8,282	6,523	10,212	7,649
32,800	32,850	8,302	6,539	10,237	7,668
32,850	32,900	8,322	6,556	10,261	7,687
32,900	32,950	8,342	6,572	10,286	7,706
32,950	33,000	8,362	6,589	10,310	7,725
33,000					
33,000	33,050	8,382	6,605	10,335	7,744
33,050	33,100	8,402	6,622	10,359	7,763
33,100	33,150	8,422	6,638	10,384	7,782
33,150	33,200	8,442	6,655	10,408	7,801
33,200	33,250	8,462	6,671	10,433	7,820
33,250	33,300	8,482	6,688	10,457	7,839
33,300	33,350	8,502	6,704	10,482	7,858
33,350	33,400	8,522	6,721	10,506	7,877
33,400	33,450	8,542	6,737	10,531	7,896
33,450	33,500	8,562	6,754	10,555	7,915
33,500	33,550	8,582	6,770	10,580	7,934
33,550	33,600	8,602	6,787	10,604	7,953
33,600	33,650	8,622	6,803	10,629	7,972
33,650	33,700	8,642	6,820	10,653	7,991
33,700	33,750	8,662	6,836	10,678	8,010
33,750	33,800	8,682	6,853	10,702	8,029
33,800	33,850	8,702	6,869	10,727	8,048
33,850	33,900	8,722	6,886	10,751	8,067
33,900	33,950	8,742	6,902	10,776	8,086
33,950	34,000	8,762	6,919	10,800	8,105
34,000					
34,000	34,050	8,782	6,935	10,825	8,124
34,050	34,100	8,802	6,952	10,849	8,143
34,100	34,150	8,823	6,968	10,874	8,162
34,150	34,200	8,845	6,985	10,898	8,183
34,200	34,250	8,867	7,001	10,923	8,203
34,250	34,300	8,889	7,018	10,947	8,224
34,300	34,350	8,911	7,034	10,972	8,244
34,350	34,400	8,933	7,051	10,996	8,265
34,400	34,450	8,955	7,067	11,021	8,285
34,450	34,500	8,977	7,084	11,045	8,306
34,500	34,550	8,999	7,100	11,070	8,326
34,550	34,600	9,021	7,117	11,094	8,347
34,600	34,650	9,043	7,133	11,119	8,367
34,650	34,700	9,065	7,150	11,143	8,388
34,700	34,750	9,087	7,166	11,168	8,408
34,750	34,800	9,109	7,183	11,192	8,429
34,800	34,850	9,131	7,199	11,217	8,449
34,850	34,900	9,153	7,216	11,241	8,470
34,900	34,950	9,175	7,232	11,266	8,490
34,950	35,000	9,197	7,249	11,290	8,511
35,000					
35,000	35,050	9,219	7,265	11,315	8,531
35,050	35,100	9,241	7,282	11,339	8,552
35,100	35,150	9,263	7,298	11,364	8,572
35,150	35,200	9,285	7,315	11,388	8,593
35,200	35,250	9,307	7,333	11,413	8,613
35,250	35,300	9,329	7,352	11,437	8,634
35,300	35,350	9,351	7,372	11,462	8,654
35,350	35,400	9,373	7,391	11,486	8,675
35,400	35,450	9,395	7,411	11,511	8,695
35,450	35,500	9,417	7,430	11,535	8,716

At least	But less than	Single	Married filing jointly	Married filing separately	Head of a household
		Your tax is—			
35,500	35,550	9,439	7,450	11,560	8,736
35,550	35,600	9,461	7,469	11,584	8,757
35,600	35,650	9,483	7,489	11,609	8,777
35,650	35,700	9,505	7,508	11,633	8,798
35,700	35,750	9,527	7,528	11,658	8,818
35,750	35,800	9,549	7,547	11,682	8,839
35,800	35,850	9,571	7,567	11,707	8,859
35,850	35,900	9,593	7,586	11,731	8,880
35,900	35,950	9,615	7,606	11,756	8,900
35,950	36,000	9,637	7,625	11,780	8,921
36,000					
36,000	36,050	9,659	7,645	11,805	8,941
36,050	36,100	9,681	7,664	11,829	8,962
36,100	36,150	9,703	7,684	11,854	8,982
36,150	36,200	9,725	7,703	11,878	9,003
36,200	36,250	9,747	7,723	11,903	9,023
36,250	36,300	9,769	7,742	11,927	9,044
36,300	36,350	9,791	7,762	11,952	9,064
36,350	36,400	9,813	7,781	11,976	9,085
36,400	36,450	9,835	7,801	12,001	9,105
36,450	36,500	9,857	7,820	12,025	9,126
36,500	36,550	9,879	7,840	12,050	9,146
36,550	36,600	9,901	7,859	12,074	9,167
36,600	36,650	9,923	7,879	12,099	9,187
36,650	36,700	9,945	7,898	12,123	9,208
36,700	36,750	9,967	7,918	12,148	9,228
36,750	36,800	9,989	7,937	12,172	9,249
36,800	36,850	10,011	7,957	12,197	9,269
36,850	36,900	10,033	7,976	12,221	9,290
36,900	36,950	10,055	7,996	12,246	9,310
36,950	37,000	10,077	8,015	12,270	9,331
37,000					
37,000	37,050	10,099	8,035	12,295	9,351
37,050	37,100	10,121	8,054	12,319	9,372
37,100	37,150	10,143	8,074	12,344	9,392
37,150	37,200	10,165	8,093	12,368	9,413
37,200	37,250	10,187	8,113	12,393	9,433
37,250	37,300	10,209	8,132	12,417	9,454
37,300	37,350	10,231	8,152	12,442	9,474
37,350	37,400	10,253	8,171	12,466	9,495
37,400	37,450	10,275	8,191	12,491	9,515
37,450	37,500	10,297	8,210	12,515	9,536
37,500	37,550	10,319	8,230	12,540	9,556
37,550	37,600	10,341	8,249	12,564	9,577
37,600	37,650	10,363	8,269	12,589	9,597
37,650	37,700	10,385	8,288	12,613	9,618
37,700	37,750	10,407	8,308	12,638	9,638
37,750	37,800	10,429	8,327	12,662	9,659
37,800	37,850	10,451	8,347	12,687	9,679
37,850	37,900	10,473	8,366	12,711	9,700
37,900	37,950	10,495	8,386	12,736	9,720
37,950	38,000	10,517	8,405	12,760	9,741
38,000					
38,000	38,050	10,539	8,425	12,785	9,761
38,050	38,100	10,561	8,444	12,809	9,782
38,100	38,150	10,583	8,464	12,834	9,802
38,150	38,200	10,605	8,483	12,858	9,823
38,200	38,250	10,627	8,503	12,883	9,843

At least	But less than	Single	Married filing jointly	Married filing separately	Head of a household
		Your tax is—			
38,250	38,300	10,649	8,522	12,907	9,864
38,300	38,350	10,671	8,542	12,932	9,884
38,350	38,400	10,693	8,561	12,956	9,905
38,400	38,450	10,715	8,581	12,981	9,925
38,450	38,500	10,737	8,600	13,005	9,946
38,500	38,550	10,759	8,620	13,030	9,966
38,550	38,600	10,781	8,639	13,054	9,987
38,600	38,650	10,803	8,659	13,079	10,007
38,650	38,700	10,825	8,678	13,103	10,028
38,700	38,750	10,847	8,698	13,128	10,048
38,750	38,800	10,869	8,717	13,152	10,069
38,800	38,850	10,891	8,737	13,177	10,089
38,850	38,900	10,913	8,756	13,201	10,110
38,900	38,950	10,935	8,776	13,226	10,130
38,950	39,000	10,957	8,795	13,250	10,151
39,000					
39,000	39,050	10,979	8,815	13,275	10,171
39,050	39,100	11,001	8,834	13,299	10,192
39,100	39,150	11,023	8,854	13,324	10,212
39,150	39,200	11,045	8,873	13,348	10,233
39,200	39,250	11,067	8,893	13,373	10,253
39,250	39,300	11,089	8,912	13,397	10,274
39,300	39,350	11,111	8,932	13,422	10,294
39,350	39,400	11,133	8,951	13,446	10,315
39,400	39,450	11,155	8,971	13,471	10,335
39,450	39,500	11,177	8,990	13,495	10,356
39,500	39,550	11,199	9,010	13,520	10,376
39,550	39,600	11,221	9,029	13,544	10,397
39,600	39,650	11,243	9,049	13,569	10,417
39,650	39,700	11,265	9,068	13,593	10,438
39,700	39,750	11,287	9,088	13,618	10,458
39,750	39,800	11,309	9,107	13,642	10,479
39,800	39,850	11,331	9,127	13,667	10,499
39,850	39,900	11,353	9,146	13,691	10,520
39,900	39,950	11,375	9,166	13,716	10,540
39,950	40,000	11,397	9,185	13,740	10,561
40,000					
40,000	40,050	11,419	9,205	13,765	10,581
40,050	40,100	11,441	9,224	13,789	10,602
40,100	40,150	11,463	9,244	13,814	10,622
40,150	40,200	11,485	9,263	13,838	10,643
40,200	40,250	11,507	9,283	13,863	10,663
40,250	40,300	11,529	9,302	13,887	10,684
40,300	40,350	11,551	9,322	13,912	10,704
40,350	40,400	11,573	9,341	13,936	10,725
40,400	40,450	11,595	9,361	13,961	10,745
40,450	40,500	11,617	9,380	13,985	10,766
40,500	40,550	11,639	9,400	14,010	10,786
40,550	40,600	11,661	9,419	14,034	10,807
40,600	40,650	11,683	9,439	14,059	10,827
40,650	40,700	11,705	9,458	14,083	10,848
40,700	40,750	11,727	9,478	14,108	10,868
40,750	40,800	11,749	9,497	14,132	10,889
40,800	40,850	11,771	9,517	14,157	10,909
40,850	40,900	11,793	9,536	14,181	10,930
40,900	40,950	11,815	9,556	14,206	10,950
40,950	41,000	11,837	9,575	14,230	10,971

Continued on next page

TABLE 24 (*cont.*)

If 1040A, line 16, OR 1040EZ, line 7 is—		And you are—			
At least	But less than	Single	Married filing jointly	Married filing separately	Head of a household
		Your tax is—			
41,000					
41,000	41,050	11,859	9,595	14,255	10,991
41,050	41,100	11,881	9,614	14,279	11,012
41,100	41,150	11,903	9,634	14,304	11,032
41,150	41,200	11,925	9,653	14,328	11,053
41,200	41,250	11,947	9,673	14,353	11,073
41,250	41,300	11,969	9,692	14,377	11,094
41,300	41,350	11,991	9,712	14,402	11,114
41,350	41,400	12,013	9,731	14,426	11,135
41,400	41,450	12,035	9,751	14,451	11,155
41,450	41,500	12,057	9,770	14,475	11,176
41,500	41,550	12,081	9,790	14,500	11,196
41,550	41,600	12,106	9,809	14,524	11,217
41,600	41,650	12,131	9,829	14,549	11,237
41,650	41,700	12,156	9,848	14,573	11,258
41,700	41,750	12,181	9,868	14,598	11,278
41,750	41,800	12,206	9,887	14,622	11,299
41,800	41,850	12,231	9,907	14,647	11,319
41,850	41,900	12,256	9,926	14,671	11,340
41,900	41,950	12,281	9,946	14,696	11,360
41,950	42,000	12,306	9,965	14,720	11,381
42,000					
42,000	42,050	12,331	9,985	14,745	11,401
42,050	42,100	12,356	10,004	14,769	11,422
42,100	42,150	12,381	10,024	14,794	11,442
42,150	42,200	12,406	10,043	14,818	11,463
42,200	42,250	12,431	10,063	14,843	11,483
42,250	42,300	12,456	10,082	14,867	11,504
42,300	42,350	12,481	10,102	14,892	11,524
42,350	42,400	12,506	10,121	14,916	11,545
42,400	42,450	12,531	10,141	14,941	11,565
42,450	42,500	12,556	10,160	14,965	11,586
42,500	42,550	12,581	10,180	14,990	11,606
42,550	42,600	12,606	10,199	15,014	11,627
42,600	42,650	12,631	10,219	15,039	11,647
42,650	42,700	12,656	10,238	15,063	11,668
42,700	42,750	12,681	10,258	15,088	11,688
42,750	42,800	12,706	10,277	15,112	11,709
42,800	42,850	12,731	10,297	15,137	11,729
42,850	42,900	12,756	10,316	15,162	11,750
42,900	42,950	12,781	10,336	15,187	11,770
42,950	43,000	12,806	10,355	15,212	11,791
43,000					
43,000	43,050	12,831	10,375	15,237	11,811
43,050	43,100	12,856	10,394	15,262	11,832
43,100	43,150	12,881	10,414	15,287	11,852
43,150	43,200	12,906	10,433	15,312	11,873
43,200	43,250	12,931	10,453	15,337	11,893
43,250	43,300	12,956	10,472	15,362	11,914
43,300	43,350	12,981	10,492	15,387	11,934
43,350	43,400	13,006	10,511	15,412	11,955
43,400	43,450	13,031	10,531	15,437	11,975
43,450	43,500	13,056	10,550	15,462	11,996
43,500	43,550	13,081	10,570	15,487	12,016
43,550	43,600	13,106	10,589	15,512	12,037
43,600	43,650	13,131	10,609	15,537	12,057
43,650	43,700	13,156	10,628	15,562	12,078
43,700	43,750	13,181	10,648	15,587	12,098
43,750	43,800	13,206	10,667	15,612	12,119
43,800	43,850	13,231	10,687	15,637	12,139
43,850	43,900	13,256	10,706	15,662	12,160
43,900	43,950	13,281	10,726	15,687	12,180
43,950	44,000	13,306	10,745	15,712	12,201

If 1040A, line 16, OR 1040EZ, line 7 is—		And you are—			
At least	But less than	Single	Married filing jointly	Married filing separately	Head of a household
		Your tax is—			
44,000					
44,000	44,050	13,331	10,765	15,737	12,221
44,050	44,100	13,356	10,784	15,762	12,242
44,100	44,150	13,381	10,804	15,787	12,262
44,150	44,200	13,406	10,823	15,812	12,283
44,200	44,250	13,431	10,843	15,837	12,303
44,250	44,300	13,456	10,862	15,862	12,324
44,300	44,350	13,481	10,882	15,887	12,344
44,350	44,400	13,506	10,901	15,912	12,365
44,400	44,450	13,531	10,921	15,937	12,385
44,450	44,500	13,556	10,940	15,962	12,406
44,500	44,550	13,581	10,960	15,987	12,426
44,550	44,600	13,606	10,979	16,012	12,447
44,600	44,650	13,631	10,999	16,037	12,467
44,650	44,700	13,656	11,018	16,062	12,488
44,700	44,750	13,681	11,038	16,087	12,510
44,750	44,800	13,706	11,057	16,112	12,535
44,800	44,850	13,731	11,077	16,137	12,559
44,850	44,900	13,756	11,096	16,162	12,584
44,900	44,950	13,781	11,116	16,187	12,608
44,950	45,000	13,806	11,135	16,212	12,633
45,000					
45,000	45,050	13,831	11,155	16,237	12,657
45,050	45,100	13,856	11,174	16,262	12,682
45,100	45,150	13,881	11,194	16,287	12,706
45,150	45,200	13,906	11,213	16,312	12,731
45,200	45,250	13,931	11,233	16,337	12,755
45,250	45,300	13,956	11,252	16,362	12,780
45,300	45,350	13,981	11,272	16,387	12,804
45,350	45,400	14,006	11,291	16,412	12,829
45,400	45,450	14,031	11,311	16,437	12,853
45,450	45,500	14,056	11,330	16,462	12,878
45,500	45,550	14,081	11,350	16,487	12,902
45,550	45,600	14,106	11,369	16,512	12,927
45,600	45,650	14,131	11,389	16,537	12,951
45,650	45,700	14,156	11,408	16,562	12,976
45,700	45,750	14,181	11,428	16,587	13,000
45,750	45,800	14,206	11,447	16,612	13,025
45,800	45,850	14,231	11,468	16,637	13,049
45,850	45,900	14,256	11,490	16,662	13,074
45,900	45,950	14,281	11,512	16,687	13,098
45,950	46,000	14,306	11,534	16,712	13,123
46,000					
46,000	46,050	14,331	11,556	16,737	13,147
46,050	46,100	14,356	11,578	16,762	13,172
46,100	46,150	14,381	11,600	16,787	13,196
46,150	46,200	14,406	11,622	16,812	13,221
46,200	46,250	14,431	11,644	16,837	13,245
46,250	46,300	14,456	11,666	16,862	13,270
46,300	46,350	14,481	11,688	16,887	13,294
46,350	46,400	14,506	11,710	16,912	13,319
46,400	46,450	14,531	11,732	16,937	13,343
46,450	46,500	14,556	11,754	16,962	13,368
46,500	46,550	14,581	11,776	16,987	13,392
46,550	46,600	14,606	11,798	17,012	13,417
46,600	46,650	14,631	11,820	17,037	13,441
46,650	46,700	14,656	11,842	17,062	13,466
46,700	46,750	14,681	11,864	17,087	13,490
46,750	46,800	14,706	11,886	17,112	13,515
46,800	46,850	14,731	11,908	17,137	13,539
46,850	46,900	14,756	11,930	17,162	13,564
46,900	46,950	14,781	11,952	17,187	13,588
46,950	47,000	14,806	11,974	17,212	13,613

If 1040A, line 16, OR 1040EZ, line 7 is—		And you are—			
At least	But less than	Single	Married filing jointly	Married filing separately	Head of a household
		Your tax is—			
47,000					
47,000	47,050	14,831	11,996	17,237	13,637
47,050	47,100	14,856	12,018	17,262	13,662
47,100	47,150	14,881	12,040	17,287	13,686
47,150	47,200	14,906	12,062	17,312	13,711
47,200	47,250	14,931	12,084	17,337	13,735
47,250	47,300	14,956	12,106	17,362	13,760
47,300	47,350	14,981	12,128	17,387	13,784
47,350	47,400	15,006	12,150	17,412	13,809
47,400	47,450	15,031	12,172	17,437	13,833
47,450	47,500	15,056	12,194	17,462	13,858
47,500	47,550	15,081	12,216	17,487	13,882
47,550	47,600	15,106	12,238	17,512	13,907
47,600	47,650	15,131	12,260	17,537	13,931
47,650	47,700	15,156	12,282	17,562	13,956
47,700	47,750	15,181	12,304	17,587	13,980
47,750	47,800	15,206	12,326	17,612	14,005
47,800	47,850	15,231	12,348	17,637	14,029
47,850	47,900	15,256	12,370	17,662	14,054
47,900	47,950	15,281	12,392	17,687	14,078
47,950	48,000	15,306	12,414	17,712	14,103
48,000					
48,000	48,050	15,331	12,436	17,737	14,127
48,050	48,100	15,356	12,458	17,762	14,152
48,100	48,150	15,381	12,480	17,787	14,176
48,150	48,200	15,406	12,502	17,812	14,201
48,200	48,250	15,431	12,524	17,837	14,225
48,250	48,300	15,456	12,546	17,862	14,250
48,300	48,350	15,481	12,568	17,887	14,274
48,350	48,400	15,506	12,590	17,912	14,299
48,400	48,450	15,531	12,612	17,937	14,323
48,450	48,500	15,556	12,634	17,962	14,348
48,500	48,550	15,581	12,656	17,987	14,372
48,550	48,600	15,606	12,678	18,012	14,397
48,600	48,650	15,631	12,700	18,037	14,421
48,650	48,700	15,656	12,722	18,062	14,446
48,700	48,750	15,681	12,744	18,087	14,470
48,750	48,800	15,706	12,766	18,112	14,495
48,800	48,850	15,731	12,788	18,137	14,519
48,850	48,900	15,756	12,810	18,162	14,544
48,900	48,950	15,781	12,832	18,187	14,568
48,950	49,000	15,806	12,854	18,212	14,593
49,000					
49,000	49,050	15,831	12,876	18,237	14,617
49,050	49,100	15,856	12,898	18,262	14,642
49,100	49,150	15,881	12,920	18,287	14,666
49,150	49,200	15,906	12,942	18,312	14,691
49,200	49,250	15,931	12,964	18,337	14,715
49,250	49,300	15,956	12,986	18,362	14,740
49,300	49,350	15,981	13,008	18,387	14,764
49,350	49,400	16,006	13,030	18,412	14,789
49,400	49,450	16,031	13,052	18,437	14,813
49,450	49,500	16,056	13,074	18,462	14,838
49,500	49,550	16,081	13,096	18,487	14,862
49,550	49,600	16,106	13,118	18,512	14,887
49,600	49,650	16,131	13,140	18,537	14,911
49,650	49,700	16,156	13,162	18,562	14,936
49,700	49,750	16,181	13,184	18,587	14,960
49,750	49,800	16,206	13,206	18,612	14,985
49,800	49,850	16,231	13,228	18,637	15,009
49,850	49,900	16,256	13,250	18,662	15,034
49,900	49,950	16,281	13,272	18,687	15,058
49,950	50,000	16,306	13,294	18,712	15,083

GLOSSARY

GLOSSARY

Accelerated cost recovery system (ACRS) depreciation   A depreciation method in which all depreciable assets are placed in one of four categories. These categories contain percentages which are used to depreciate the asset.

Accidental death benefit   This life insurance feature allows the beneficiary to receive twice the face amount of the policy in the event the insured dies in an accident. Also called double indemnity.

Acid test ratio   Quick assets ratio.

Add-on interest   Interest which is added on to a loan at the time the loan is made.

Addend   One of the numbers being added in an addition problem. For example, both 2 and 3 are addends in $2 + 3 = 5$.

Amortized loans   Loans extending over a long time period in which all payments are equal.

Annual percentage rate (APR)   The effective interest rate paid when you borrow money.

Annuity   Equal payments of money over time.

Annuity due   An annuity in which payments are made at the beginning of a time period.

Arithmetic mean   See average.

Assessed value   The value of property used to determine the amount of property taxes.

Average   A number which is representative of a set of data. It is obtained by adding the numbers and dividing by the number of addends.

Balance sheets   A statement on which assets and liabilities are listed which provide a financial picture of the company.

Bank statement   A record periodically sent to a depositor by his or her bank which helps to determine whether the bank's records and the depositor's records of an account agree.

Banker's 360-day method   Method used to compute simple interest which assumes a year has 360 days and the exact number of days from one date to another is used.

Bond   A certificate which indicates indebtedness of a company or governmental entity to the public.

Celsius   The base unit of normal temperature measurement in the metric system. Scientific measurement of temperature in the metric system is done using degrees Kelvin.

Centi   A prefix which means one hundredth. For example, a centimeter is one hundredth of a meter.

Centigrade   See Celsius.

Chain discount   Additional discounts given by manufacturers to retailers to move their products quickly.

Check record book   An attachment which accompanies a checkbook and is used to record checks written and deposits made.

Co-insurance   Insurance where the policyholder and the company both pay certain amounts for a covered loss.

Commission   A pay plan in which pay is determined on the basis of sales made.

Common multiple   A number which is a multiple of two or more numbers. For example, 24 is a multiple of both 3 and 4 so 24 is a common multiple of 3 and 4.

Compound interest   Interest paid on principal and previously earned interest.

Current ratio   The ratio of current assets to current liabilities.

Current yield   The annual interest for a bond divided by its current market price.

Deci   A prefix which means one tenth. For example, a decimeter is one tenth of a meter.

Decimal equivalent   An equivalent way of expressing a fraction. For example, $\frac{2}{5}$ has a decimal equivalent 0.4.

Decimal notation   Writing a number using a decimal point. For example, 0.456.

Deka   A prefix which means ten. For example, a dekameter is 10 meters.

Denominator   The bottom number in a fraction. For example, 7 is the denominator in $\frac{4}{7}$.

Deposit slip   A slip used to deposit currency, checks, and coins in a savings institution.

Depreciation   The decrease in value of an asset which distributes its cost less salvage value over its estimated useful life.

Difference   The answer to a subtraction problem. For example, 5 is the difference in $9 - 4 = 5$.

Differential piecework plan   A pay plan in which employees are paid an increased rate per unit as the number of units produced increases.

Discount   The amount a lender deducts from a note at the time a loan is made.

Dividend   The number being divided in a division problem. For example, 28 is the dividend in $28 \div 4 = 7$.

Dividends   Money or additional stock paid to stockholders of a company.

Divisor   The number by which we divide. For example, 4 is the divisor in $28 \div 4 = 7$.

Double declining-balance method   A depreciation method in which certain assets are depreciated at two times the straight-line rate of depreciation.

Double indemnity   See accidental death benefit.

Draw   An amount paid to an employee who is on a commission basis. This amount is an advance paid against potential earnings and is reduced if the sales used to determine earnings are not met.

Effective interest rate   The equivalent annual interest rate. For example, $1000 invested at 8% compounded quarterly would grow to $1082.43 in one year. The effective interest rate is 8.243%.

Exact (accurate) interest method   Method used to compute simple interest which assumes a year has 365 days and the exact number of days from one date to another is used.

Exponential notation   Writing a number using exponents. For example, in exponential notation 8 is expressed as 2^3.

Factors   Numbers that are multiplied together. Therefore, 4 and 6 are factors of 24 since $4 \times 6 = 24$.

Fahrenheit   The base unit of temperature measurement in the American measurement system.

Fraction   A number which may be written as the quotient of two numbers. For example, $\frac{1}{3}$ is a fraction.

Fractional equivalent   An equivalent way of expressing a decimal. For example, 0.2 has a fractional equivalent $\frac{1}{5}$.

Future value   The amount which an investment today will become at some future date. For example, $1171.66 is the future value of $1000 compounded quarterly at 8% for 2 years.

Gross earnings   The amount of money earned before deductions.

Gross profit   The amount obtained when the cost of goods sold is subtracted from net sales.

Hecto   A prefix which means one hundred. For example, a hectometer is 100 meters.

Horizontal analysis   Method used to compare figures for two or more time intervals.

Income statement   A statement which shows how much a business made or lost.

Individual Retirement Accounts   Accounts in which individuals may deposit money for use later, usually during retirement. The amount deposited and the earnings on this amount are not taxed until the money is withdrawn.

Installment plan   Paying for goods and services over a period of time.

Interest   Money paid for the use of money.

Interest bearing note   A note in which the borrower gets the amount listed on the note.

Interest rate   The interest expressed as a percent.

Interpolation   Method used to find a value between two entries in a table.

Inventory   A method used by businesses to count and price their goods.

Keogh Plans   Accounts in which individuals who qualify deposit money for use later, usually during retirement. The amount deposited and the earnings on this amount are not taxed until the money is withdrawn.

Kilo   A prefix which means one thousand. For example, a kilometer is 1000 meters.

Least common denominator (LCD)   The least common multiple of the denominators. For example, 12 is the LCD when adding $\frac{1}{4}$ and $\frac{5}{6}$.

Least common multiple (LCM)   The smallest number that is a multiple of two or more numbers. For example, 12 is the LCM of 4 and 6.

Levy   A figure obtained by dividing the amount of money needed in the budget by the total assessed value of property within the governmental boundary.

Liter   The metric unit of capacity (volume). It is one cubic decimeter.

Major fraction rule   A method used to compute sales tax in which any fraction of a cent less than one-half is disregarded whereas for any fraction greater than or equal to one-half a penny is added.

Markdown   The difference between the regular price and the sale price of merchandise.

Markup   The difference between the selling price and the cost of an article to a retailer.

Mass   A quantity of matter. It is measured on a balance scale and always stays the same.

Matures   Date at which a bond is paid off.

Mean   See average.

Median   The middle amount in a set of numbers.

Merchant's Rule   A method used to apply partial payments toward the principal of a loan.

Meter   The basic unit of length in the metric system. It is roughly the distance from your nose to your fingertip when your arm is outstretched to your side and your head faces forward.

Method of complements   A method used to find the net price when several discounts are given.

Metric system   A numbering system which is based on the number 10.

Mill   A method of expressing the property tax rate. A mill is one thousandth of a dollar.

Milli   A prefix which means one thousandth. For example, a millimeter is one thousandth of a meter.

Minuend   The number being subtracted from in a subtraction problem. For example, 9 is the minuend in $9 - 4 = 5$.

Mixed numeral   Writing a number as a whole number and a fraction between 0 and 1. For example, $25\frac{1}{4}$ is a mixed numeral.

Mode   The number which appears most often in a set of numbers.

Money market mutual funds   Investment companies which pool (put together money from many investors) money to purchase large denomination savings instruments.

Multiple   A number is a multiple of another if it can be written as the product of the other and a nonzero number. For example, 18 is a multiple of 2 since $18 = 2 \times 9$.

Multiplicand   The number being multiplied. For example, 6 is the multiplicand in $4 \times 6 = 24$.

Multiplier   The number by which we multiply. For example, 4 is the multiplier in $4 \times 6 = 24$.

Net deposit   Amount actually deposited.

Net income   The amount remaining after all deductions.

Net pay   The amount of pay an employee receives after deductions.

Net profit   Net income.

Net profit ratio   The quotient of net profit and net sales.

Net sales   Revenue from the sale of goods less returns and adjustments.

Nominal (published) rate of interest   The published rate of interest. For example, if $1000 is invested at 8% compounded quarterly then 8% is the nominal rate of interest.

Noninterest bearing note   The amount a borrower obtains is the amount remaining after interest is first deducted.

Numerator   The top number in a fraction. For example, 4 is the numerator in $\frac{4}{7}$.

Odd lots   Stock sales other than round lots.

Operating margin of profit   The quotient of the operating profit and net sales.

Ordinary annuity   An annuity in which payments are made at the end of a time period.

Override   A pay plan in which a supervisor is paid a commission on sales and, in addition, a commission on sales of those supervised.

Par value   The basic value of a bond.

Payee   The person or business who is to be paid. For example, on a check the payee is the person or business to whom the amount on the check is to be paid.

Percent $n\%$ means $n/100$ or $n \times \frac{1}{100}$ or $n \times 0.01$. For example, 5% means $\frac{5}{100}$ or $5 \times \frac{1}{100}$ or 5×0.01.

Percentage method   A method used to determine income tax withheld from pay.

Permanent insurance   Type of life insurance which provides benefits without regard to the date when the insured dies.

Piecework plan   A pay plan in which employees are paid for the number of units they produce.

Premiums   Money paid by a policyholder to an insurance company for coverage.

Present value   The amount which when invested now will result in a certain amount at some future date.

Present value of an annuity   Sum of the present value of each of the payments into an annuity.

Price-earnings ratio   The price of a share of stock divided by the earnings per share.

Principal   The amount borrowed.

Proceeds   The amount the borrower receives.

Product   The answer to a multiplication problem. For example, 24 is the product in $4 \times 6 = 24$.

Promissory note   A document which specifies the borrower, amount of money borrowed, the interest rate and the time before the note must be repaid to the lender.

Property taxes   A tax imposed by local governments on real estate and personal property to pay for schools and other governmental services.

Proportion   An equation showing that two numbers are proportional. For example, $\frac{2}{3} = \frac{4}{6}$.

Proportional   Two pairs of numbers having the same ratio are said to be proportional. For example, 3,4 and 6,8.

Quick assets ratio   The ratio of current assets less inventories to current liabilities.

Quota   A sales goal which if exceeded will result in additional compensation for an employee.

Quotient   The answer to a division problem. For example, 7 is the quotient in $28 \div 4 = 7$.

Rate   A ratio which compares two different kinds of measures. For example, coffee was recently selling for $4.12 per pound, the ratio of dollars to pounds is 4.12 to 1 and this ratio is a rate.

Ratio   Comparison of two or more numbers. For example, the ratio of the number of quarts of ice cream eaten annually by the average Southener in comparison with the average New Englander is 11 to 22.

Reciprocals   Numbers whose product is 1. For example, $\frac{4}{5}$ and $\frac{5}{4}$ are reciprocals since their product is 1

Reconciling   The process of comparing the bank statement with the check record.

Regular time   Working time up to and including 40 hours a week.

Repeating decimals   Decimal numbers that do not terminate. For example, $5.4\overline{32}$.

Replacement cost   The present value of a house less the value of the land and basement.

Revenue   The amount of money from sales.

Revolving credit plan   A charge account in which amounts for new purchases are added to existing amounts owed.

Round lots   Stock sales in multiples of 100.

Rounding   Writing a number using fewer nonzero digits. For example, rounding 34.63 to the tenths position is 34.6.

Rule of 78   A method used to determine the interest rebate when a loan is repaid early.

Sales taxes   Taxes imposed on goods and services by state and local governments.

Salvage value   See trade-in value.

Selling price   The agreed upon price in a stock transaction.

Series discount   See chain discount.

Simple interest   Interest paid on only the principal for the entire time of the loan.

Straight-line method   A depreciation method in which the value of an asset is divided equally over its useful life.

Straight piecework plan   A pay plan in which employees are paid a fixed amount for each unit they produce.

Subtrahend   The number being subtracted in a subtraction problem. For example, 4 is the subtrahend in 9 − 4 = 5.

Sum   The answer to an addition problem. For example, 5 is the sum in 2 + 3 = 5.

Sum-of-the-years'-digits method   A depreciation method which allows larger amounts of depreciation in early years and smaller amounts in later years.

Take-home pay   See net pay.

Tax shelters   Investments which defer some tax liability until a later time.

Term insurance   Type of life insurance which provides benefits only when an insured dies.

Trade discount   The discount given to a retailer by a manufacturer or wholesaler.

Trade-in value   The value of something after it has been completely depreciated.

United States Rule   A method used to apply partial payments toward the principal of a loan.

Universal life   Type of life insurance which provides protection at death and savings at a higher rate than in other policies.

Vertical analysis   A method used to analyze financial statements in which the percent of net sales for each entry on the income statement is determined.

Wage bracket method   A method used to determine income tax withheld from pay.

Weight   A force exerted by gravitation. It varies with the distance of the object from the center of the planetary body.

Working capital   The difference between total current assets and current liabilities.

Yield   The percent the yearly monetary dividend is of the price of a share of the stock.

Yield on purchase price   The annual interest for a bond divided by its total cost.

ANSWERS

ANSWERS

CHAPTER 0

Margin Exercises, pp. 2–4

1. 1560.76   **2.** 1096.12   **3.** 468.81   **4.** 82,250
5. 214,130   **6.** 49   **7.** 198.81

Review Test, Chapter 0, pp. 5–6

1. 148.6   **2.** 107.5   **3.** 76.6   **4.** 185.5   **5.** 572.5
6. 1900.6   **7.** 1440.3   **8.** 1277.8   **9.** 193   **10.** 176
11. 480.5   **12.** 1125.57   **13.** 892.55   **14.** 1548.54
15. 1997.59   **16.** 1807.20   **17.** 39.7   **18.** 55.8   **19.** 23.5
20. 34.5   **21.** 110.18   **22.** 448.42   **23.** 343.06
24. 390.25   **25.** 631.3   **26.** 4149.03   **27.** 2518.7
28. 1139.77   **29.** 1912.42   **30.** 4896.6   **31.** 9468.1
32. 1843.25   **33.** 30,114   **34.** 96,530   **35.** 49,416
36. 42,777   **37.** 44,280   **38.** 144,207   **39.** 17,217.8
40. 38,022.5   **41.** 13,246.92   **42.** 36,350.19   **43.** 14,580
44. 170,810   **45.** 10,120   **46.** 129,917.1   **47.** 65   **48.** 98
49. 65   **50.** 57   **51.** 68   **52.** 19   **53.** 8.4   **54.** 2.6
55. 17.8   **56.** 29.8   **57.** 64   **58.** 343   **59.** 19.4481
60. 104.8576   **61.** 128   **62.** 2187   **63.** 390,625
64. 5,764,801

CHAPTER 1

Margin Exercises, Section 1.1, pp. 8–10

1. Two hundred twenty million, four hundred fifty-six
thousand, two hundred three   **2.** eighty-eight   **3.** 10,787
4. 14,944   **5.** 8258   **6.** 478   **7.** 90   **8.** 779   **9.** 1236
10. 3387   **11.** 4585   **12.** 5315 kWh   **13.** $741

Exercise Set 1.1, pp. 11–12

1. Thirteen
3. Fifty-six thousand, seven hundred eighty-nine
5. 1110   **7.** 1010   **9.** 11,114   **11.** 17,647   **13.** 78,341
15. 123,229   **17.** 2256   **19.** 14,444   **21.** 395   **23.** 408
25. 185   **27.** 431   **29.** 301   **31.** 5674   **33.** 33,293
35. 446 kWh   **37.** $16,266   **39.** $5314   **41.** 429,278 cars
43. 5508 books   **45.** $28,789,088   **47.** 141,301 (increase)
49. 2697 metric tons

Margin Exercises, Section 1.2, pp. 13–16

1. 33,423   **2.** 425,034   **3.** 263,948   **4.** 50,122,408
5. 29,468   **6.** 3923 R 1   **7.** 560   **8.** $4742
9. 217 bottles; 3 oz   **10.** $1088

Exercise Set 1.2, pp. 17–18

1. 61,632   **3.** 78,144   **5.** 184,832   **7.** 94,554
9. 675,360   **11.** 8,042,027   **13.** 109,989   **15.** 23,050,584
17. 24 R 15   **19.** 32 R 16   **21.** 46   **23.** 116 R 9
25. 900   **27.** 25 R 7   **29.** 7   **31.** 185 R 129
33. 2072 miles   **35.** $384   **37.** $28,477,128   **39.** $4272
41. $156   **43.** $5000   **45.** Fourteen thousand, five hundred
eighty-three   **47.** 1696

Margin Exercises, Section 1.3, pp. 19–20

1. $\frac{5}{8}$ **2.** $\frac{2}{3}$ **3.** $\frac{3}{4}$ **4.** $\frac{4}{6}$ **5.** $\frac{1}{6}$ **6.** $\frac{3}{19}; \frac{4}{19}$ **7.** $8\frac{1}{8}$

8. $4\frac{3}{4}$ **9.** $5\frac{9}{16}$ **10.** $\frac{7}{3}$ **11.** $\frac{31}{8}$ **12.** $\frac{164}{15}$

Exercise Set 1.3, pp. 21–22

1. $\frac{2}{3}$; $\frac{1}{3}$ **3.** $\frac{2200}{8760}$ **5.** $\frac{2}{5}$ **7.** $18\frac{8}{9}$ **9.** $59\frac{11}{12}$ **11.** $1\frac{4}{5}$

13. $2\frac{3}{8}$ **15.** $4\frac{7}{10}$ **17.** $9\frac{1}{6}$ **19.** $57\frac{5}{6}$ **21.** $8\frac{79}{100}$ **23.** $\frac{4}{3}$

25. $\frac{37}{5}$ **27.** $\frac{93}{10}$ **29.** $\frac{9944}{100}$ **31.** $\frac{134}{9}$ **33.** $\frac{40,693,237}{8910}$

35. $\frac{147}{10}$ **37.** $\frac{373}{15}$ **39.** Impossible **41.** 0 **43.** 6569

45. 56

Margin Exercises, Section 1.4, pp. 23–26

1. $\frac{2}{3}$ **2.** 6 **3.** $25\frac{1}{2}$ **4.** $\frac{4}{3}$ **5.** $\frac{5}{6}$ **6.** $\frac{8}{15}$ **7.** $2\frac{5}{8}$ **8.** $\frac{1}{64}$

9. $1\frac{1}{3}$ **10.** $33\frac{1}{3}$ pounds **11.** $192\frac{1}{2}$ miles **12.** 800 jars

13. 20 miles per gallon

Exercise Set 1.4, pp. 27–28

1. $\frac{1}{3}$ **3.** $\frac{10}{27}$ **5.** 15 **7.** 90 **9.** 6 **11.** 12 **13.** $4\frac{1}{4}$

15. $35\frac{91}{100}$ **17.** 84 **19.** $\frac{1}{2}$ **21.** $\frac{4}{5}$ **23.** $3\frac{3}{8}$ **25.** $\frac{3}{7}$

27. 35 **29.** 1 **31.** $\frac{2}{3}$ **33.** $\frac{1}{6}$ **35.** 2 **37.** $1\frac{37}{68}$

39. $1\frac{14}{59}$ **41.** $\frac{7}{30}$ **43.** $4\frac{1}{2}$ **45.** $13\frac{3}{5}$ **47.** $3662\frac{1}{2}$

49. 96 miles **51.** 6,368,440 students

53. 30 miles per gallon **55.** 440 miles **57.** 8 pounds

59. 32,026 **61.** $\frac{1681}{37}$

Margin Exercises, Section 1.5, pp. 29–34

1. 60 **2.** 42 **3.** 15 **4.** $\frac{2}{3}$ **5.** $26\frac{1}{3}$ **6.** $\frac{23}{24}$ **7.** $20\frac{17}{24}$

8. $\frac{2}{3}$ **9.** $\frac{2}{3}$ **10.** $8\frac{2}{3}$ **11.** $\frac{11}{63}$ **12.** $6\frac{17}{24}$ **13.** $2\frac{3}{8}$

14. $48\frac{1}{8}$ **15.** $17\frac{1}{12}$ yd **16.** $18\frac{7}{8}$ **17.** $22\frac{3}{4}$ gallons

Exercise Set 1.5, pp. 35–36

1. 63 **3.** 15 **5.** 72 **7.** 315 **9.** 12 **11.** 12 **13.** 16

15. 8 **17.** $\frac{5}{18}$ **19.** $1\frac{1}{2}$ **21.** $12\frac{5}{8}$ **23.** $19\frac{2}{5}$ **25.** $\frac{1}{24}$

27. $\frac{3}{5}$ **29.** $5\frac{3}{4}$ **31.** $14\frac{3}{8}$ **33.** $61\frac{3}{8}$ **35.** $23\frac{7}{15}$ lb

37. $55\frac{5}{8}$ **39.** $6\frac{9}{16}$ inches **41.** $3\frac{7}{12}$ hr

43. 7,103,260 students

Margin Exercises, Section 1.6, pp. 37–42

1. Eighteen and forty-nine hundredths
2. Six hundred forty-five thousandths
3. Twelve and five ten-thousandths
4. Eighteen and $\frac{49}{100}$ dollars

5. Two thousand, three hundred forty-six and $\frac{76}{100}$ dollars

6. $\frac{568}{1000}$ **7.** $\frac{23}{10}$ **8.** $\frac{8904}{100}$ **9.** $18\frac{3}{10}$ **10.** $7\frac{3019}{10,000}$

11. 4.131 **12.** 0.4131 **13.** 5.73 **14.** 14.57 **15.** 22.07

16. 3.019 **17.** 7.6783 **18.** 284.455 **19.** 268.63

20. 27.676 **21.** 64.683 **22.** 99.59 **23.** 239.883

24. 7695¢ **25.** 14¢ **26.** $.95 **27.** $7.95 **28.** $2388.18

29. $1931.55

Exercise Set 1.6, pp. 43–44

1. Thirty-four and eight hundred ninety-one thousandths
3. Nine hundred three ten-thousandths

5. Three hundred twenty-six and $\frac{48}{100}$ dollars **7.** $\frac{67}{100}$ dollars

9. $\frac{49}{10}$ **11.** $\frac{59}{100}$ **13.** $\frac{20,007}{10,000}$ **15.** $\frac{78,898}{10}$ **17.** $18\frac{46}{100}$

19. $4\frac{13}{1000}$ **21.** $234\frac{5}{10}$ **23.** $5\frac{4111}{10,000}$ **25.** 0.1

27. 0.0001 **29.** 307.9 **31.** 9.999 **33.** 0.0039

35. 0.00001 **37.** 6.014 **39.** 126.8 **41.** 444.94

43. 390.617 **45.** 155.724 **47.** 63.79 **49.** 32.234

51. 26.835 **53.** 47.91 **55.** 1.9193 **57.** 8995¢ **59.** 45¢

61. $.95 **63.** $1.79 **65.** $3843.22 **67.** 39,595.3

69. 1022.6 **71.** 6.4° **73.** $31\frac{1}{5}$ **75.** $2\frac{1}{4}$

Margin Exercises, Section 1.7, pp. 45–48

1. 5.868 **2.** 0.5868 **3.** 51.53808 **4.** 48.9 **5.** 15.82
6. 1.28 **7.** 17.95 **8.** 856 **9.** 0.85 **10.** $0.\overline{6}$ **11.** $7.\overline{63}$
12. $117.75 **13.** 32 miles per gallon

Exercise Set 1.7, pp. 49–50

1. 9.968 **3.** 386.104 **5.** 179.5 **7.** 0.1894 **9.** 15.288
11. 527.28 **13.** 1.40756 **15.** 3.60558 **17.** 2.3 **19.** 5.2
21. 0.023 **23.** 18.75 **25.** 660 **27.** $1.\overline{18}$ **29.** $145.15
31. $100.38 **33.** $1.08 **35.** 538 bushels

37. 26 miles per gallon **39.** 879 **41.** $\frac{109}{8}$

Margin Exercises, Section 1.8, pp. 51–52

1. 2.8 **2.** 13.9 **3.** 7.0 **4.** 7.83 **5.** 34.68 **6.** 0.03
7. 0.943 **8.** 8.004 **9.** 43.112 **10.** 37.401
11. 7459.355 **12.** 7459.35 **13.** 7459.4 **14.** 7459
15. 7460 **16.** 17.5 miles per gallon **17.** $.35

Exercise Set 1.8, pp. 53–54

1. 745.07; 745.1; 745; 750; 700 **3.** 6780.51; 6780.5; 6781; 6780; 6800 **5.** $17.99; $18 **7.** $346.08; $346 **9.** $17

11. $190   **13.** 12.3457; 12.346; 12.35; 12.3; 12
15. 31.9 miles per gallon   **17.** $4.89   **19.** $6.08
21. $11,786   **23.** 832 chickens   **25.** .530; .353; .560; .470
27. $5.55   **29.** $.35

23. 1310.796   **25.** 1259.712   **27.** 4   **29.** 15   **31.** 1
33. 1   **35.** 1   **37.** 1   **39.** 383   **41.** 1091   **43.** 1400
45. 27   **47.** 1166.2   **49.** 2136   **51.** $51\frac{11}{20}$ **53.** $8\frac{4}{5}$

Margin Exercises, Section 1.9, pp. 55–56

1. 5^3 **2.** 5^5 **3.** $(1.08)^2$ **4.** 10,000   **5.** 512   **6.** 1.331
7. 5   **8.** 43   **9.** 5.8   **10.** 1   **11.** 1   **12.** 1843   **13.** 83
14. 1880   **15.** 305   **16.** 34,279.2

Exercise Set 1.9, pp. 57–58

1. 3^4 **3.** 10^5 **5.** 1^8 **7.** 25   **9.** 59,049   **11.** 100
13. 1   **15.** 5.29   **17.** 0.008   **19.** 416.16   **21.** $\frac{9}{64}$

Review Test, Chapter 1, pp. 59–60

1. 12,974   **2.** 4111   **3.** $103,759   **4.** 3648   **5.** 209
6. $485   **7.** $\frac{17}{3}$ **8.** $4\frac{5}{12}$ **9.** $\frac{1}{8}$ **10.** 4   **11.** $11,112.50
12. 160 pounds   **13.** $14\frac{7}{12}$ **14.** $\frac{1}{12}$ **15.** $99\frac{1}{8}$ **16.** $\frac{678}{100}$
17. 18.95   **18.** 86.0298   **19.** 9.342   **20.** $3010.65
21. 430.8   **22.** 55.6   **23.** $8250   **24.** 34.1
25. 15.2 miles per gallon   **26.** 1.1236   **27.** 929

CHAPTER 2

Margin Exercises, Section 2.1, pp. 62–64

1. For example, 6 and 3, 40 and 20, 100 and 50   **2.** $\frac{3}{2}$ **3.** $\frac{7}{11}$
4. $\frac{0.189}{3.4}$, or $\frac{189}{3400}$ **5.** $\frac{9}{3}$ **6.** $\frac{5928}{22,800}$ **7.** $\frac{4}{7\frac{2}{3}}$ **8.** 14   **9.** 9
10. 5   **11.** 12   **12.** $\frac{3}{10}$ **13.** 1100   **14.** 4   **15.** 14.5
16. $18,000; $9000; $4500   **17.** $600,000

Exercise Set 2.1, pp. 65–66

1. $\frac{4}{5}$ **3.** $\frac{0.4}{12}$, or $\frac{4}{120}$ **5.** $\frac{2}{12}$ **7.** 45   **9.** 12   **11.** 10
13. 20   **15.** 5   **17.** 18   **19.** 22   **21.** 28   **23.** $9\frac{1}{3}$
25. $2\frac{8}{9}$ **27.** 40 km/hr   **29.** 11 m/sec   **31.** 25; $\frac{1}{25}$
33. $\frac{623}{1000}$ gal/ft²   **35.** $1,400,000; $875,000; $350,000
37. $133\frac{1}{3}$ miles   **39.** about 25 radios   **41.** 650 miles
43. 780,000 kg   **45.** $2\frac{1}{4}$ **47.** 10   **49.** 1   **51.** 28.3

Margin Exercises, Section 2.2, pp. 67–72

1. $\frac{90}{100}$; $90 \times \frac{1}{100}$; 90×0.01 **2.** $\frac{3.4}{100}$; $3.4 \times \frac{1}{100}$; 3.4×0.01
3. $\frac{100}{100}$; $100 \times \frac{1}{100}$; 100×0.01 **4.** 0.34   **5.** 0.789
6. 0.1208   **7.** 24%   **8.** 347%   **9.** 100%   **10.** 40%
11. 25%   **12.** 87.5%   **13.** 57%   **14.** 76%   **15.** $\frac{3}{5}$
16. $\frac{13}{400}$ **17.** $\frac{2}{3}$ **18.** $\frac{5}{6}$, $\frac{3}{8}$; 0.2, 0.375; 20%, $83.\overline{3}$% or $83\frac{1}{3}$%

19. $12\% \times 50 = n$ **20.** $n = 40\% \times \$60$ **21.** $\$45 = 20\% \times n$
22. $120\% \times n = 60$ **23.** $16 = n\% \times 40$
24. $n\% \times \$9600 = \$7104$ **25.** 24   **26.** $35.20   **27.** 225
28. $50   **29.** 40%   **30.** 12.5%

Exercise Set 2.2, pp. 73–74

1. $\frac{80}{100}$; $80 \times \frac{1}{100}$; 80×0.01 **3.** $\frac{12.5}{100}$; $12.5 \times \frac{1}{100}$;
12.5×0.01 **5.** 0.18   **7.** 0.789   **9.** 0.01   **11.** 4.25
13. 78%   **15.** 101.5%   **17.** 56.2%   **19.** 80%   **21.** 19%
23. 150%   **25.** 12.5%   **27.** 60%   **29.** 6.3%   **31.** 22.2%
33. 104.5%   **35.** 57.5%   **37.** $\frac{3}{5}$ **39.** $\frac{1}{8}$ **41.** $\frac{5}{6}$ **43.** $\frac{34}{25}$
45. $\frac{7}{20}$ **47.** $n = 41\% \times 89$ **49.** $89 = n\% \times 100$
51. $13 = 25\% \times n$ **53.** 90   **55.** 45   **57.** 24%   **59.** 50%
61. 88   **63.** 20   **65.** 780 miles

Margin Exercises, Section 2.3, pp. 75–80

1. $3900   **2.** $88   **3.** 14%   **4.** 9%   **5.** 3.5%
6. $22,890   **7.** $13.41

Exercise Set 2.3, pp. 81–82

1. $4800   **3.** $367.50   **5.** 87.5%   **7.** 8%; 92%; 600
9. 804 people   **11.** 7%   **13.** 2051 consumers   **15.** 9%
17. $35,100   **19.** 4%   **21.** $4836.21   **23.** 3.8%   **25.** 300
27. 160

Review Test, Chapter 2, pp. 83–84

1. 2 to 1   **2.** 2.24   **3.** 26 to 1   **4.** $5.61   **5.** 0.874
6. 31%   **7.** 95%   **8.** $\frac{19}{200}$ **9.** 15.52   **10.** $1500
11. 78.4%   **12.** $132   **13.** $737   **14.** $18, 286.10
15. 8%   **16.** 7.4%   **17.** $1.00

CHAPTER 3

Margin Exercises, Section 3.1, pp. 86–88

1. $240 **2.** $1.00 **3.** 15% **4.** $180 **5.** $75.11 **6.** $665

Exercise Set 3.1, pp. 89–90

1. $65.00 **3.** $510.00 **5.** $225.00 **7.** $6.75 **9.** 17%
11. 12.75% **13.** 11% **15.** $7000 **17.** $1900
19. $6576.92 **21.** $1500 **23.** $168.02 **25.** $322.43
27. $128.78 **29.** $1610 **31.** $852 **33.** $1775 **35.** $1\frac{5}{24}$
37. 434

Margin Exercises, Section 3.2, pp. 91–94

1. $18.26 **2.** $15.45 **3.** $9.33 **4.** $9.59 **5.** $20.97
6. $28.11

Exercise Set 3.2, pp. 95–96

1. $5.00 **3.** $72.00 **5.** $106.67 **7.** $16.13 **9.** $20.71
11. $89.35 **13.** $66.78 **15.** $16.44 **17.** $18.33
19. $172.90 **21.** $22,898.96 **23.** $33.48 **25.** $17.44
27. $15,002.05 **29.** 4.45 **31.** 16

Margin Exercises, Section 3.3, pp. 97–100

1. $1.35 **2.** $9.27 **3.** $1.33 **4.** $60.11

Exercise Set 3.3, pp. 101–102

1. $612.50 **3.** $312.38 **5.** $517.00 **7.** $504.47
9. $115.31 **11.** $42.39 **13.** $16.47 **15.** $604.11
17. $308.10 **19.** $509.92 **21.** $497.56 **23.** $113.73
25. $5.12 **27.** $9.58 **29.** 2.5%

Margin Exercises, Section 3.4, pp. 103–108

1. $32.32 **2.** $24.18 **3.** $12,682.42; $2682.42
4. $327.60 **5.** $462.73 **6.** $1175.46 **7.** $27.09
8. $36.66 **9.** $973.52 **10.** $973.60

Exercise Set 3.4, pp. 109–110

1. $30.38 **3.** $98.00 **5.** $231.84 **7.** $40.40 **9.** $51.01
11. $1061.21; $61.21 **13.** $609.54 **15.** $53.82
17. $429.50 **19.** $6312.39 **21.** $1.73 **23.** $4.38
25. $5.57 **27.** 1 to 6

Margin Exercises, Section 3.5, pp. 111–112

1. 8.77% **2.** 13.37%, 13.42%; 13% compounded
semiannually earns more.

Exercise Set 3.5, pp. 113–114

1. 5.09% **3.** 8.24% **5.** 12.55% **7.** 5.06% **9.** 8%
11. 12.36% **13.** 7.79% **15.** 9.96% **17.** 6.92%
19. 9.38%, 9.58%; $9\frac{1}{4}$% compounded quarterly earns more.
21. 10.75%, 10.92%; $10\frac{1}{2}$% compounded quarterly earns more.
23. 14.93%, 15.03%; $14\frac{1}{2}$% compounded semiannually earns
more. **25.** 9.38%, 9.73%; $9\frac{1}{2}$% compounded semiannually
earns more. **27.** 0.06 **29.** 2.5

Margin Exercises, Section 3.6, pp. 115–116

1. $4701.15 **2.** $7323.24 **3.** $5383.77

Exercise Set 3.6, pp. 117–118

1. $4909.65 **3.** $7435.55 **5.** $12,548.24 **7.** $2192.07
9. $4891.53 **11.** $2308.33 **13.** $915.41 **15.** $1825.64
17. $3069.57 **19.** $\frac{4}{5}$ **21.** 0.021

Review Test, Chapter 3, pp. 119–120

1. $675.00 **2.** 8% **3.** $60,000 **4.** $1100.00 **5.** $32.73
6. $19.93 **7.** $24.84 **8.** $200.70 **9.** $28.28
10. $192.52 **11.** $3038.77 **12.** $17,091.40 **13.** $2.52
14. $1.59 **15.** 8.24% **16.** 10.51%, 10.38%; $10\frac{1}{4}$%
compounded semiannually earns more. **17.** $20,102.60
18. $15,357.92

CHAPTER 4

Margin Exercises, Section 4.1, pp. 122–128

1.

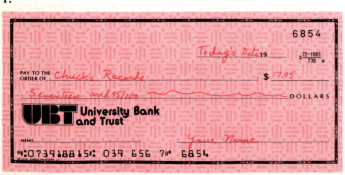

2. (a)

(c)

For deposit only
Your name

(b)

Pay to the order of
Joe Banks

your name

3. 43 51334; $43.10
4. Solo's Concrete; $2.89
5. $728.17
6. $276.00
7. $3101.03
8. $281.67

Exercise Set 4.1, pp. 129–132

1.

```
                                              6855
                              Today's Date 19 ___  x 72-1881/739 ®
PAY TO THE
ORDER OF  Ferber's                    $ 29.99 ___
Twenty-nine and 99/100 ~~~~~~~~~~~~~  DOLLARS
UBT University Bank
    and Trust
MEMO ___                    Your Name ___
⑆073918815⑆ 039 656 7⑈ 6855
```

3.

```
                                              6857
                              Today's Date 19 ___  x 72-1881/739 ®
PAY TO THE
ORDER OF  Jay Haus                    $ 19.25 ___
Nineteen and 25/100 ~~~~~~~~~~~~~  DOLLARS
UBT University Bank
    and Trust
MEMO ___                    Your Name ___
⑆073918815⑆ 039 656 7⑈ 6857
```

5.

Your Name

7.

Pay to the order
of Jim Felbo
Your name

9. 40 041 8; $7.50
11. Jo Pyle; $14.87   **13.** $530.76
15. $950.23   **17.** $634.99
19. $113.47   **21.** $925.08
23. $941.83   **25.** $3206.52
27. $3051.12
29. $1061.21; $61.21

Margin Exercises, Section 4.2, pp. 133–136

1. New balance = $583.88 + $459.69 − $10.00 = $1033.57   **2.** $514.48

3.

① LIST YOUR OUTSTANDING CHECKS BELOW

CHECK NUMBER	PAYEE	AMOUNT
		$ 62.17
		45.82
TOTAL CHECKS OUTSTANDING (ENTER ON LINE 4)		$ 107.99

THIS FORM IS PROVIDED TO HELP YOU BALANCE YOUR BANK STATEMENT

② BALANCE YOUR ACCOUNT BELOW

1 STATEMENT BALANCE	$ 456.85
2 ADD DEPOSITS NOT CREDITED ON THIS STATEMENT	$ 167.98
	$
	$
3 SUB TOTAL	$ 624.83
SUBTRACT 4 CHECKS OUTSTANDING	$ 107.99
5 BALANCE	$ 516.84

③

CHECKBOOK BALANCE	$ 516.84
LESS BANK CHARGES	$ —
CHECK BOOK BALANCE	$ 516.84

④ IF YOUR ACCOUNT DOES NOT BALANCE -

1. COMPARE CANCELLED CHECKS TO YOUR STATEMENT.
2. COMPARE DEPOSIT RECEIPTS TO YOUR CHECKBOOK AND STATEMENT.
3. SORT CANCELLED CHECKS BY CHECK NUMBER OR DATE ISSUED AND COMPARE THEM TO YOUR CHECKBOOK.
4. CHECK ALL ADDITIONS AND SUBTRACTIONS IN YOUR CHECKBOOK.
5. BE SURE THAT ALL BANK CHARGES HAVE BEEN DEDUCTED FROM YOUR CHECKBOOK.

⑤ REPORT ANY DIFFERENCE TO THE AUDITING DEPARTMENT.

4. Adjusted statement balance = $635.98 + $78.19 − $176.32 = $537.85; adjusted check balance = $539.53 − $1.68 = $537.85

Exercise Set 4.2, pp. 137–138

1. $572.54   **3.** $339.69   **5.** $20.00   **7.** $19.85   **9.** $61.40   **11.** $215.53

13. ①

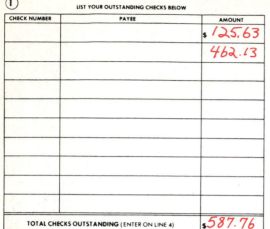

LIST YOUR OUTSTANDING CHECKS BELOW

CHECK NUMBER	PAYEE	AMOUNT
		$ 125.63
		462.13
TOTAL CHECKS OUTSTANDING (ENTER ON LINE 4)		$ 587.76

THIS FORM IS PROVIDED TO HELP YOU BALANCE YOUR BANK STATEMENT

②

BALANCE YOUR ACCOUNT BELOW

1. STATEMENT BALANCE	$ 403.09
2. ADD DEPOSITS NOT CREDITED ON THIS STATEMENT	$ 525.48
	$
	$
3. SUB TOTAL	$
SUBTRACT 4. CHECKS OUTSTANDING	$ 587.76
5. BALANCE	$ 340.81

③

CHECKBOOK BALANCE	$ 340.81
LESS BANK CHARGES	$ —
CHECK BOOK BALANCE	$ 340.81

④ **IF YOUR ACCOUNT DOES NOT BALANCE -**

1. COMPARE CANCELLED CHECKS TO YOUR STATEMENT.
2. COMPARE DEPOSIT RECEIPTS TO YOUR CHECKBOOK AND STATEMENT.
3. SORT CANCELLED CHECKS BY CHECK NUMBER OR DATE ISSUED AND COMPARE THEM TO YOUR CHECKBOOK.
4. CHECK ALL ADDITIONS AND SUBTRACTIONS IN YOUR CHECKBOOK.
5. BE SURE THAT ALL BANK CHARGES HAVE BEEN DEDUCTED FROM YOUR CHECKBOOK.

⑤ **REPORT ANY DIFFERENCE TO THE AUDITING DEPARTMENT.**

14. ①

LIST YOUR OUTSTANDING CHECKS BELOW

CHECK NUMBER	PAYEE	AMOUNT
		$ 189.01
TOTAL CHECKS OUTSTANDING (ENTER ON LINE 4)		$ 189.01

THIS FORM IS PROVIDED TO HELP YOU BALANCE YOUR BANK STATEMENT

②

BALANCE YOUR ACCOUNT BELOW

1. STATEMENT BALANCE	$ 613.48
2. ADD DEPOSITS NOT CREDITED ON THIS STATEMENT	$
	$
	$
3. SUB TOTAL	$
SUBTRACT 4. CHECKS OUTSTANDING	$ 189.01
5. BALANCE	$ 424.47

③

CHECKBOOK BALANCE	$ 424.47
LESS BANK CHARGES	$ —
CHECK BOOK BALANCE	$ 424.47

④ **IF YOUR ACCOUNT DOES NOT BALANCE -**

1. COMPARE CANCELLED CHECKS TO YOUR STATEMENT.
2. COMPARE DEPOSIT RECEIPTS TO YOUR CHECKBOOK AND STATEMENT.
3. SORT CANCELLED CHECKS BY CHECK NUMBER OR DATE ISSUED AND COMPARE THEM TO YOUR CHECKBOOK.
4. CHECK ALL ADDITIONS AND SUBTRACTIONS IN YOUR CHECKBOOK.
5. BE SURE THAT ALL BANK CHARGES HAVE BEEN DEDUCTED FROM YOUR CHECKBOOK.

⑤ **REPORT ANY DIFFERENCE TO THE AUDITING DEPARTMENT.**

Answers

15. ①

LIST YOUR OUTSTANDING CHECKS BELOW

CHECK NUMBER	PAYEE	AMOUNT
		$ 51.23
		79.96
TOTAL CHECKS OUTSTANDING (ENTER ON LINE 4)		$ 131.19

THIS FORM IS PROVIDED TO HELP YOU BALANCE YOUR BANK STATEMENT

②

BALANCE YOUR ACCOUNT BELOW

1. STATEMENT BALANCE	$ 737.22
2. ADD DEPOSITS NOT CREDITED ON THIS STATEMENT	$ 159.17
	$
	$
3. SUB TOTAL	$
SUBTRACT 4. CHECKS OUTSTANDING	$ 131.19
5. BALANCE	$ 765.20

③

CHECKBOOK BALANCE	$ 765.92
LESS BANK CHARGES	$ 0.72
CHECK BOOK BALANCE	$ 765.20

④ **IF YOUR ACCOUNT DOES NOT BALANCE -**

1. COMPARE CANCELLED CHECKS TO YOUR STATEMENT.
2. COMPARE DEPOSIT RECEIPTS TO YOUR CHECKBOOK AND STATEMENT.
3. SORT CANCELLED CHECKS BY CHECK NUMBER OR DATE ISSUED AND COMPARE THEM TO YOUR CHECKBOOK.
4. CHECK ALL ADDITIONS AND SUBTRACTIONS IN YOUR CHECKBOOK.
5. BE SURE THAT ALL BANK CHARGES HAVE BEEN DEDUCTED FROM YOUR CHECKBOOK.

⑤ REPORT ANY DIFFERENCE TO THE AUDITING DEPARTMENT.

---

16. ①

LIST YOUR OUTSTANDING CHECKS BELOW

CHECK NUMBER	PAYEE	AMOUNT
		$ 91.15
TOTAL CHECKS OUTSTANDING (ENTER ON LINE 4)		$ 91.15

THIS FORM IS PROVIDED TO HELP YOU BALANCE YOUR BANK STATEMENT

②

BALANCE YOUR ACCOUNT BELOW

1. STATEMENT BALANCE	$ 418.62
2. ADD DEPOSITS NOT CREDITED ON THIS STATEMENT	$
	$
	$
3. SUB TOTAL	$
SUBTRACT 4. CHECKS OUTSTANDING	$ 91.15
5. BALANCE	$ 327.47

③

CHECKBOOK BALANCE	$ 329.02
LESS BANK CHARGES	$ 1.55
CHECK BOOK BALANCE	$ 327.47

④ **IF YOUR ACCOUNT DOES NOT BALANCE -**

1. COMPARE CANCELLED CHECKS TO YOUR STATEMENT.
2. COMPARE DEPOSIT RECEIPTS TO YOUR CHECKBOOK AND STATEMENT.
3. SORT CANCELLED CHECKS BY CHECK NUMBER OR DATE ISSUED AND COMPARE THEM TO YOUR CHECKBOOK.
4. CHECK ALL ADDITIONS AND SUBTRACTIONS IN YOUR CHECKBOOK.
5. BE SURE THAT ALL BANK CHARGES HAVE BEEN DEDUCTED FROM YOUR CHECKBOOK.

⑤ REPORT ANY DIFFERENCE TO THE AUDITING DEPARTMENT.

17. ①

LIST YOUR OUTSTANDING CHECKS BELOW

CHECK NUMBER	PAYEE	AMOUNT
		$ 42.63
		115.95
TOTAL CHECKS OUTSTANDING (ENTER ON LINE 4)		$ 158.58

➡️

THIS FORM IS PROVIDED TO HELP YOU BALANCE YOUR BANK STATEMENT

②

BALANCE YOUR ACCOUNT BELOW

1. STATEMENT BALANCE		$ 823.41
ADD 2. DEPOSITS NOT CREDITED ON THIS STATEMENT		$ 426.83
		$
		$
3. SUB TOTAL		$ 1250.24
SUBTRACT 4. CHECKS OUTSTANDING		$ 158.58
5. BALANCE		$ 1091.66

③

CHECKBOOK BALANCE		$ 1091.66
LESS BANK CHARGES		$
CHECK BOOK BALANCE		$ 1091.66

④ IF YOUR ACCOUNT DOES NOT BALANCE -

1. COMPARE CANCELLED CHECKS TO YOUR STATEMENT.
2. COMPARE DEPOSIT RECEIPTS TO YOUR CHECKBOOK AND STATEMENT.
3. SORT CANCELLED CHECKS BY CHECK NUMBER OR DATE ISSUED AND COMPARE THEM TO YOUR CHECKBOOK.
4. CHECK ALL ADDITIONS AND SUBTRACTIONS IN YOUR CHECKBOOK.
5. BE SURE THAT ALL BANK CHARGES HAVE BEEN DEDUCTED FROM YOUR CHECKBOOK.

⑤ REPORT ANY DIFFERENCE TO THE AUDITING DEPARTMENT.

---

18. ①

LIST YOUR OUTSTANDING CHECKS BELOW

CHECK NUMBER	PAYEE	AMOUNT
		$
		215.85
		463.21
TOTAL CHECKS OUTSTANDING (ENTER ON LINE 4)		$ 679.06

➡️

THIS FORM IS PROVIDED TO HELP YOU BALANCE YOUR BANK STATEMENT

②

BALANCE YOUR ACCOUNT BELOW

1. STATEMENT BALANCE		$ 1050.31
ADD 2. DEPOSITS NOT CREDITED ON THIS STATEMENT		$ 325.50
		$ 463.75
		$
3. SUB TOTAL		$ 1839.56
SUBTRACT 4. CHECKS OUTSTANDING		$ 679.06
5. BALANCE		$ 1160.50

③

CHECKBOOK BALANCE		$ 1162.85
LESS BANK CHARGES		$ 2.35
CHECK BOOK BALANCE		$ 1160.50

④ IF YOUR ACCOUNT DOES NOT BALANCE -

1. COMPARE CANCELLED CHECKS TO YOUR STATEMENT.
2. COMPARE DEPOSIT RECEIPTS TO YOUR CHECKBOOK AND STATEMENT.
3. SORT CANCELLED CHECKS BY CHECK NUMBER OR DATE ISSUED AND COMPARE THEM TO YOUR CHECKBOOK.
4. CHECK ALL ADDITIONS AND SUBTRACTIONS IN YOUR CHECKBOOK.
5. BE SURE THAT ALL BANK CHARGES HAVE BEEN DEDUCTED FROM YOUR CHECKBOOK.

⑤ REPORT ANY DIFFERENCE TO THE AUDITING DEPARTMENT.

Answers

19. ①

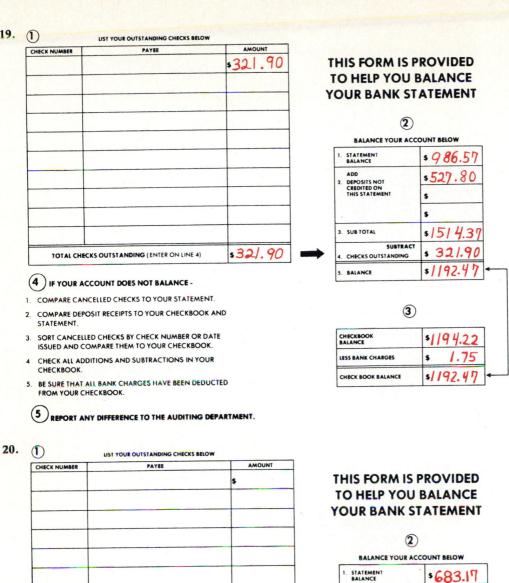

LIST YOUR OUTSTANDING CHECKS BELOW

CHECK NUMBER	PAYEE	AMOUNT
		$321.90
TOTAL CHECKS OUTSTANDING (ENTER ON LINE 4)		$321.90

**THIS FORM IS PROVIDED
TO HELP YOU BALANCE
YOUR BANK STATEMENT**

②

BALANCE YOUR ACCOUNT BELOW

1. STATEMENT BALANCE	$986.57
2. ADD DEPOSITS NOT CREDITED ON THIS STATEMENT	$527.80
	$
	$
3. SUB TOTAL	$1514.37
SUBTRACT 4. CHECKS OUTSTANDING	$321.90
5. BALANCE	$1192.47

③

CHECKBOOK BALANCE	$1194.22
LESS BANK CHARGES	$1.75
CHECK BOOK BALANCE	$1192.47

④ **IF YOUR ACCOUNT DOES NOT BALANCE –**

1. COMPARE CANCELLED CHECKS TO YOUR STATEMENT.
2. COMPARE DEPOSIT RECEIPTS TO YOUR CHECKBOOK AND STATEMENT.
3. SORT CANCELLED CHECKS BY CHECK NUMBER OR DATE ISSUED AND COMPARE THEM TO YOUR CHECKBOOK.
4. CHECK ALL ADDITIONS AND SUBTRACTIONS IN YOUR CHECKBOOK.
5. BE SURE THAT ALL BANK CHARGES HAVE BEEN DEDUCTED FROM YOUR CHECKBOOK.

⑤ **REPORT ANY DIFFERENCE TO THE AUDITING DEPARTMENT.**

20. ①

LIST YOUR OUTSTANDING CHECKS BELOW

CHECK NUMBER	PAYEE	AMOUNT
		$
TOTAL CHECKS OUTSTANDING (ENTER ON LINE 4)		$

**THIS FORM IS PROVIDED
TO HELP YOU BALANCE
YOUR BANK STATEMENT**

②

BALANCE YOUR ACCOUNT BELOW

1. STATEMENT BALANCE	$683.17
2. ADD DEPOSITS NOT CREDITED ON THIS STATEMENT	$648.26
	$
	$
3. SUB TOTAL	$1331.43
SUBTRACT 4. CHECKS OUTSTANDING	$0
5. BALANCE	$1331.43

③

CHECKBOOK BALANCE	$1331.43
LESS BANK CHARGES	$0
CHECK BOOK BALANCE	$1331.43

④ **IF YOUR ACCOUNT DOES NOT BALANCE –**

1. COMPARE CANCELLED CHECKS TO YOUR STATEMENT.
2. COMPARE DEPOSIT RECEIPTS TO YOUR CHECKBOOK AND STATEMENT.
3. SORT CANCELLED CHECKS BY CHECK NUMBER OR DATE ISSUED AND COMPARE THEM TO YOUR CHECKBOOK.
4. CHECK ALL ADDITIONS AND SUBTRACTIONS IN YOUR CHECKBOOK.
5. BE SURE THAT ALL BANK CHARGES HAVE BEEN DEDUCTED FROM YOUR CHECKBOOK.

⑤ **REPORT ANY DIFFERENCE TO THE AUDITING DEPARTMENT.**

21. 673 high school student leaders

Margin Exercises, Section 4.3, pp. 139–140

1. $372.33 **2.** $299.29 **3.** 9.98% **4.** 8.26% **5.** 10.16% **6.** $10,019.14

Exercise Set 4.3, pp. 141–142

1. $460.13 **3.** $460.25 **5.** $276.87 **7.** 9.22% **9.** 9.08% **11.** $15,032.56 **13.** $15,031.47 **15.** $15,030.35 **17.** $15.00 **19.** 1.05

Review Test, Chapter 4, pp. 143–146

1.

2. (a) *Your Name*   (b) *For deposit only Your Name*   (c) *Pay to The order of Kleeber's Your Name*

3. 037 614 0; $14.27 **4.** Everhoff's $4.75 **5.** $433.53 **6.** $685.86 **7.** $109.62 **8.** $1422.08 **9.** $1214.02

10.

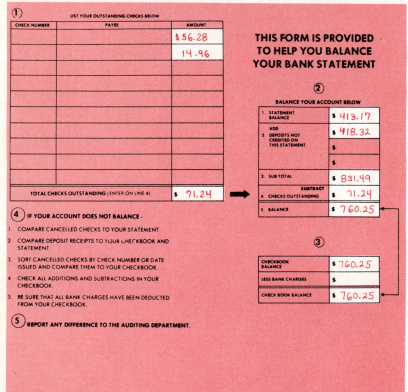

11.

① LIST YOUR OUTSTANDING CHECKS BELOW		
CHECK NUMBER	PAYEE	AMOUNT
		85.96
TOTAL CHECKS OUTSTANDING (ENTER ON LINE 4)		$85.96

THIS FORM IS PROVIDED TO HELP YOU BALANCE YOUR BANK STATEMENT

② **BALANCE YOUR ACCOUNT BELOW**

1. STATEMENT BALANCE	$	487.50
2. ADD DEPOSITS NOT CREDITED ON THIS STATEMENT	$	49.24
	$	
	$	
3. SUB TOTAL	$	536.74
4. SUBTRACT CHECKS OUTSTANDING	$	85.96
5. BALANCE		450.78

③

CHECKBOOK BALANCE	$	454.23
LESS BANK CHARGES	$	3.45
CHECK BOOK BALANCE	$	450.78

④ **IF YOUR ACCOUNT DOES NOT BALANCE -**

1. COMPARE CANCELLED CHECKS TO YOUR STATEMENT.
2. COMPARE DEPOSIT RECEIPTS TO YOUR CHECKBOOK AND STATEMENT.
3. SORT CANCELLED CHECKS BY CHECK NUMBER OR DATE ISSUED AND COMPARE THEM TO YOUR CHECKBOOK.
4. CHECK ALL ADDITIONS AND SUBTRACTIONS IN YOUR CHECKBOOK.
5. BE SURE THAT ALL BANK CHARGES HAVE BEEN DEDUCTED FROM YOUR CHECKBOOK.

⑤ **REPORT ANY DIFFERENCE TO THE AUDITING DEPARTMENT.**

12. $363.35
13. $293.03
14. $5010.98

CHAPTER 5

Margin Exercises, Section 5.1, pp. 148–152

1. $60.00   **2.** October 3   **3.** $1980; $4020   **4.** $10.65; $589.35   **5.** $714.28   **6.** $8116.88

Exercise Set 5.1, pp. 153–154

1. 33.00   **3.** $40.41   **5.** $540.00   **7.** $214.50   **9.** Oct. 3   **11.** Feb. 10   **13.** Nov. 29   **15.** $770; $2730   **17.** $140.65; $4671.26   **19.** $15.53; $734.47   **21.** $15; $435   **23.** $4.40; $888.10   **25.** $4545.45   **27.** $4736.84   **29.** $2577.32   **31.** $6463.29   **33.** $4803.36   **35.** 8.24%

Margin Exercises, Section 5.2, pp. 156–160

1. $816.18   **2.** $1143.61   **3.** $1619.34   **4.** $804.07   **5.** $1530.28

Exercise Set 5.2, pp. 161–162

1. 152; $295.56; $154.44; $4845.56   **3.** 99; $186.55; $433.06; $4412.50   **5.** $3813.56   **7.** 93; $112.11; 0; $4000.00   **9.** 66; $68.76; 0; $3456.77   **11.** $4101.35   **13.** $6400   **15.** 270; $25.20; $265.20; $5583.65   **17.** $4559.81; 0   **19.** $757.88   **21.** 272; $8.20; $108.20; $4331.80   **23.** 86; $1.30; $51.30; $3548.43   **25.** $3966.77   **27.** $\frac{4}{5}$ **29.** $3\frac{3}{8}$

Margin Exercises, Section 5.3, pp. 163–168

1. $6.35   **2.** $8.12   **3.** $14.78   **4.** $73,368.19   **5.** $7.12   **6.** $9.09   **7.** $16.55   **8.** $32,865.85   **9.** $600   **10.** $1000   **11.** $940   **12.** $30,000   **13.** $22,500   **14.** $27,500   **15.** $540,585.20   **16.** $20,000   **17.** $15,000   **18.** $30,000   **19.** $5760   **20.** $6000   **21.** 36000   **22.** $796,083.48

Exercise Set 5.3, pp. 169–170

1. $19.34   **3.** $2687.04   **5.** $3061.13   **7.** $7346.71   **9.** $4386.52   **11.** $4408.90   **13.** $4391.59   **15.** $52,638.21   **17.** $39,309   **19.** $540,585   **21.** $767,042   **23.** $1,532,183   **25.** $2,421,625   **27.** $122,799.02   **29.** $99,151.56   **31.** $21,538.44   **33.** $468.93

Margin Exercises, Section 5.4, pp. 171–174

1. $3.60   **2.** $4.56   **3.** $5.65   **4.** $10,814.33   **5.** $4.04   **6.** $5.11   **7.** $6.33   **8.** $2614.55

Exercise Set 5.4, pp. 175–176

1. $82,449.25   **3.** $113.004.46   **5.** $28,701.38   **7.** $1969.64   **9.** $98,500   **11.** $1164.20   **13.** $32,298.80

15. $34,006.79   **17.** $23,469.00   **19.** $21,286.01
21. $16,608.16   **23.** $13,447.92   **25.** $1250.44
27. $7670.74   **29.** $1092.73, $92.73

Review Test, Chapter 5, pp. 177–178

1. $78.75   **2.** Sept. 4   **3.** $231; $3969   **4.** $1235.00
5. $1234.14   **6.** $9183.39   **7.** $2377.31
8. $1,291,653.90   **9.** $62,822.56   **10.** $10,630.72
11. $2957   **12.** $31,309.70

CHAPTER 6

Margin Exercises, Section 6.1, pp. 180–184

1. $663.08   **2.** 10.25%   **3.** 12.75%   **4.** 12.36%
5. 10.79%

Exercise Set 6.1, pp. 185–186

1. $4075.36   **3.** $18,600.00   **5.** 16%   **7.** $15\frac{1}{4}$%   **9.** 13%
11. 17%   **13.** 21.46%   **15.** 10.92%   **17.** 33.80%
19. 14.98%   **21.** 14.52%   **23.** $1455.83   **25.** 8.24%

Margin Exercises, Section 6.2, pp. 187–190

1. $249.10   **2.** $644.44   **3.** $637.08   **4.** $503.68; $98,754
5. $674.00; $13.25; $59,898.05
6. $523.50; $25.35; $59.803.25

Exercise Set 6.2, pp. 191–192

1. $42.14   **3.** $42.24   **5.** $126.40   **7.** $122.10
9. $839.41   **11.** $920.98   **13.** $666.53; $20.72; $59,225.98
15. $500.97; $47.88; $57,205.57   **17.** $16.96   **19.** 312

Margin Exercises, Section 6.3, pp. 193–198

1. $307.89   **2.** $34.47   **3.** 19.50%   **4.** $80   **5.** $12.19
6. $26.70   **7.** $17.56   **8.** $527.20

Exercise Set 6.3, pp. 199–200

1. $65; $23.54; 12%   **3.** $8\frac{1}{2}$%; $33.12; $15\frac{1}{2}$%
5. 9%; $432; 16%   **7.** $450; $21.19; 12%
9. $600; 8%; $14\frac{3}{4}$%   **11.** $32.00   **13.** $19.00   **15.** $47.60
17. $51.66   **19.** $58.23   **21.** $8.60   **23.** $13.85
25. $151.40   **27.** $966.15   **29.** $438.31   **31.** $1580.65
33. $18,059.97

Margin Exercises, Section 6.4, pp. 201–204

1. $6.54   **2.** $9.98   **3.** $258.94   **4.** $30.00   **5.** $240.00
6. $489.23   **7.** $6.23

Exercise Set 6.4, pp. 205–208

1. $5.20; $378.72; $16.00   **3.** $424.35
5. $9.26; $312.37; $101.75; $640.84
7. $7.81; $525.29; $500.28; $24.38; $524.66

Review Test, Chapter 6, pp. 209–210

1. $946.00   **2.** 13%   **3.** 12.30%   **4.** $145.41
5. $653.72; $33.53; $58,075.12   **6.** $1144.00   **7.** 13%
8. $46.00   **9.** $8.72   **10.** $371.28   **11.** $10.81
12. $4.11; $277.38; $244.48; $274.16   **13.** $131,394.95
14. $290,265.84

CHAPTER 7

Margin Exercises, Section 7.1, pp. 212–214

1. $2919.75   **2.** $33,030   **3.** $2805.25   **4.** $32,520

Exercise Set 7.1, pp. 215–216

1. $6960   **3.** $1606.50   **5.** $11,870   **7.** $12,020
9. $133,875   **11.** $3626   **13.** $6902.50   **15.** $6982.50
17. $23,700   **19.** $4\frac{1}{2}$ **21.** 40

Margin Exercises, Section 7.2, pp. 217–218

1. 7.8%   **2.** 11.0%   **3.** 11.6   **4.** 6.4

Exercise Set 7.2, pp. 219–220

1. 7.6%   **3.** 4.5%   **5.** 9.0%   **7.** 4.4%   **9.** 13.0
11. 7.0   **13.** 10.0   **15.** $31.15   **17.** $190.49

Margin Exercises, Section 7.3, pp. 221–224

1. $2080   **2.** $18,157.50   **3.** 15.0%   **4.** 13.3%

Exercise Set 7.3, pp. 225–226

1. $2017.50   **3.** $2150   **5.** $9775   **7.** $14,687.50
9. $9250   **11.** 11.9%   **13.** 11.0%   **15.** 15.1%   **17.** 9.3%
19. 11.7%   **21.** 7.5%   **23.** Sept. 2   **25.** 1605.90

Review Test, Chapter 7, pp. 227–228

1. $4296.75   **2.** $5710   **3.** $4128.25   **4.** $5540
5. 3.1%   **6.** 13.0   **7.** $2961.25   **8.** $17,115   **9.** 6.4%
10. 8.6%   **11.** 11.0%   **12.** 13.6%

Answers

CHAPTER 8

Margin Exercises, Section 8.1, pp. 230–236

1. $45.00 **2.** $464.00 **3.** $65,000 **4.** $10,000
5. $6617.65
6. up to $24,000 for contents; up to $9600 for living expenses
7. $560 **8.** $127 **9.** $129 **10.** $1011

Exercise Set 8.1, pp. 237–238

1. $850.00 **3.** $150.00 **5.** $612.00 **7.** $45,000
9. $5000 **11.** $4090.91 **13.** up to $18,500 for contents;
up to $7400 for living expenses **15.** $560 **17.** $306
19. $78 **21.** $115 **23.** $230 **25.** $219.50
27. $1045 **29.** $525

Margin Exercises, Section 8.2, pp. 239–242

1. $100,000 **2.** $2435 **3.** $3632 **4.** $3250 **5.** $600
6. $21 **7.** $1868 **8.** $402.34

Exercise Set 8.2, pp. 243–244

1. (a) $6250; (b) $100,000 **3.** (a) 0; (b) $238
5. (a) $3679; (b) $5000 **7.** (a) 0; (b) $5675
9. (a) $100; (b) $3446 **11.** (a) 0; (b) $275,000

13. (a) $2000; (b) $50,000 **15.** (a) 0; (b) $4200
17. (a) 0; (b) $317 **19.** (a) $500; (b) $280
21. $875,876.50 **23.** $176.72 **25.** $193.50 **27.** $287.66
29. $306.14 **31.** $148.17 **33.** $3700

Margin Exercises, Section 8.3, pp. 245–250

1. $20,265 **2.** $5330 **3.** 23 years, 251 days **4.** $12,930
5. $302.00 **6.** $305.00 **7.** $348.30
8. (a) $26.54; (b) $318.48

Exercise Set 8.3, pp. 251–252

1. $28,880 **3.** $20,440 **5.** $84,835 **7.** $5160
9. $1085 **11.** 20 years, 247 days **13.** 22 years, 86 days
15. $56,070 **17.** $30,440 **19.** $405.30 **21.** $402.00
23. $313.75 **25.** $119.26, $447.04 **27.** $80.27 **29.** 25%

Review Test, Chapter 8, pp. 253–254

1. $4687.50 **2.** $1800 **3.** $220 **4.** $3500 **5.** $100,000
6. $2450 **7.** $389.36 **8.** $36,675 **9.** $6440
10. $30,000 for 19 years, 213 days **11.** $40,050
12. $1002.40 **13.** $510.80 **15.** $415.20

CHAPTER 9

Margin Exercises, Section 9.1, pp. 256–258

1. 4¢ **2.** 3¢ **3.** $28.36 **4.** $10,626.00 **5.** $7393.27

Exercise Set 9.1, pp. 259–260

1. 3¢ **3.** 5¢ **5.** 3¢ **7.** $7.50 **9.** $2001.14
11. $49.50 **13.** $252.00 **15.** $6465.71 **17.** $9425.00
19. $145.38 **21.** $11.60; $301.55 **23.** $229.99; 3%
25. $25.73

Margin Exercises, Section 9.2, pp. 261–262

1. $22,360 **2.** 12.457 mills **3.** $111.11

Exercise Set 9.2, pp. 263–264

1. $31,247.50 **3.** $37,125 **5.** $37,440 **7.** 4.15 mills
9. 1.22% **11.** $689.51 **13.** $614.35 **15.** $307.35
17. 15.09 mills **19.** $10,250

Review Test, Chapter 9, pp. 265–266

1. $1.49 **2.** $9482.69 **3.** $594.95 **4.** $34,875
5. 10.579 mills **6.** $1246.19

CHAPTER 10

Margin Exercises, Section 10.1, pp. 268–270

1. $3880 **2.** $2103 **3.** $5367 **4.** $2092
5. The loss was $346.

Exercise Set 10.1, pp. 271–272

1. $1233 **3.** $669 **5.** $2204 **7.** $2417 **9.** $957
11. $8613 **13.** $2252 **15.** $1855
17. Gross profit = $5245.81; The loss was $454.06
19. $20,455.20

Margin Exercises, Section 10.2, pp. 273–276

1. $105,000 − ($80,000 + $2000 + $19,000) = $4000
2. $140,000 − ($102,000 + $5000 + $24,000) = $9000
3. $4000 + $1500 = $5500 **4.** $9000 + $4000 = $13,000
5. $5500 − $3500 = $2000 **6.** $13,000 − $3500 = $9500
7. (0.15)($2000) = $300 **8.** $2000 − $300 = $1700
9. $9500 − $1400 = $8100 **10.** 1.6% **11.** 1%
12. 26.3% increase

Exercise Set 10.2, pp. 277–278

1. 1987: 11,000; 23,000; 17,000; 14,450
1986: 3,000; 11,000; 5,000; 4,250
3. 17.5; 11.1; −20; 4.8; 4.2   **5.** 1987: 5.7%; 22.3%; 20%
1986: 2.0%; 22.5%   **7.** $4529.75

Margin Exercises, Section 10.3, pp. 279–284

1. $5200 + $9800 + $20,000 + $43,000 = $78,000
2. $7000 + $13,000 + $28,000 + $41,000 = $89,000
3. $6000 + $45,000 + $11,000 + $1500 = $63,500
4. $6000 + $48,000 + $14,000 + $2000 = $70,000
5. $63,500 − $11,500 = $52,000
6. $70,000 − $14,000 = $56,000
7. $78,000 + $52,000 + $1000 + $1000 = $132,000
8. $89,000 + $56,000 + $2000 + $1000 = $148,000
9. $21,000 + $9000 + $2000 + $1000 = $33,000
10. $25,000 + $8000 + $6700 + $1300 = $41,000
11. $33,000 + $35,000 = $68,000
12. $41,000 + $35,000 = $76,000
13. $33,000 + $9000 + $22,000 = $64,000
14. $33,000 + $9000 + $30,000 = $72,000
15. $68,000 + $64,000 = $132,000
16. $76,000 + $72,000 = $148,000   **17.** 2.4 to 1
18. 1.7 to 1

Exercise Set 10.3, pp. 285–286

1. $120,000; $142,000; $126,000; $251,000   **3.** $77,000
5. 1.7 to 1   **7.** $81,990.98

Review Test, Chapter 10, pp. 287–290

1. $4813   **2.** $4461   **3.** $40,000, 19.5; $45,000, 22.0%;
$30,000; $25,400, 12.4%   **4.** 12.5%; 16.7%; 25.0%; 24.4%
5. 11.1%   **6.** 10.7%   **7.** $152,000; $171,000; $153,000;
$336,000   **8.** $104,000; $164,000; $172,000; $336,000
9. $48,000   **10.** 1.5 to 1   **11.** 0.86 to 1

CHAPTER 11

Margin Exercises, Section 11.1, pp. 292–294

1. $413   **2.** $122.49   **3.** $516   **4.** 20%   **5.** $75.06

Exercise Set 11.1, pp. 295–296

1. $34.49   **3.** $1569.40   **5.** $35.00   **7.** $31.48
9. $629.99   **11.** $13.83   **13.** 20%   **15.** 40%
17. $410.64   **19.** $585.29   **21.** 265,160

Margin Exercises, Section 11.2, pp. 297–300

1. $39.52   **2.** $39.52   **3.** 28%   **4.** 29.6%, $2923.00
5. 19.0%; 19.2%. The second discount is better.
6. $136.36   **7.** $787.12

Exercise Set 11.2, pp. 301–302

1. $223.40   **3.** $18.99   **5.** $10.56   **7.** $33.72   **9.** $20.79
11. 24%   **13.** 17.9%   **15.** $47.71
17. 22.7%; 23.2%. The second discount is better.
19. 25.6%; 26.5%. The second discount is better.
21. $1428.28   **23.** $3926.75   **25.** $5829.54
27. $12,310.72

Margin Exercises, Section 11.3, pp. 303–306

1. $1250.00   **2.** $27,595   **3.** $11,900
4. $15,041.15 (FIFO); $12,978.40 (LIFO); $14,015.92
(weighted ave.)   **5.** $12,232.80 (FIFO); $10,170.05 (LIFO);
$11,231.41 (weighted ave.)

Exercise Set 11.3, pp. 307–308

1. $420.00   **3.** $11,000.00   **5.** $598.75   **7.** $584.10
9. $1968.00   **11.** $873.00   **13.** $354.00   **15.** $460.00
17. $18,009.10   **19.** $7500   **21.** $40,936   **23.** $53,573
25. $15,745.10   **27.** $14,977.76   **29.** $2321.60
31. $2459.90   **33.** $1692.56   **35.** $3690.75
37. $3205.72; $405.72

Review Test, Chapter 11, pp. 309–310

1. $33   **2.** 25%   **3.** $39.96   **4.** 23.5%
5. $19\frac{1}{4}$%; 19%. The first discount is better.   **6.** $1562.29
7. $1978.00   **8.** $23,134   **9.** $776.55   **10.** $374.75

CHAPTER 12

Margin Exercises, Section 12.1, pp. 312–314

1. $7100; $1420; 20%

2.

Year	Rate of depreciation	Annual depreciation	Value	Total depreciation
0			$8700	
1	$\frac{1}{5}$ or 20%	$1420	7280	$1420
2	20%	1420	5860	2840
3	20%	1420	4440	4260
4	20%	1420	3020	5680
5	20%	1420	1600	7100

Exercise Set 12.1, pp. 315–316

1. (a) $6000; (b) $1500   **3.** (a) $450; (b) $56.25
5. (a) $50,000; (b) $1500

7.

Year	Rate of depreciation	Annual depreciation	Value	Total depreciation
0			$8000	
1	$\frac{1}{4}$ or 25%	$1500	6500	$1500
2	25%	1500	5000	3000
3	25%	1500	3500	4500
4	25%	1500	2000	6000

9.

Year	Rate of depreciation	Annual depreciation	Value	Total depreciation
0			$450	
1	$\frac{1}{8}$ or 12.5%	$56.25	393.75	$ 56.25
2	12.5%	56.25	337.50	112.50
3	12.5%	56.25	281.25	168.75
4	12.5%	56.25	225.00	225.00
5	12.5%	56.25	168.75	281.25
6	12.5%	56.25	112.50	337.50
7	12.5%	56.25	56.25	393.75
8	12.5%	56.25	0	450.00

11. $1500, $1500, $48,500; $3000, $1500, $47,000   **13.** $630

3.

Year	Rate of depreciation	Annual depreciation	Value	Total depreciation
0			$2500	
1	$\frac{2}{6}$ or $33\frac{1}{3}$%	$833.33	1666.67	$ 833.33
2	$33\frac{1}{3}$%	555.56	1111.11	1388.89
3	$33\frac{1}{3}$%	370.37	740.74	1759.26
4	$33\frac{1}{3}$%	246.91	493.83	2006.17
5	$33\frac{1}{3}$%	164.61	329.22	2170.78
6	$33\frac{1}{3}$%	109.74	219.48	2280.52

5.

Year	Rate of depreciation	Annual depreciation	Value	Total depreciation
0			$5400	
1	$\frac{2}{5}$ or 40%	$2160	3240	$2160
2	40%	1296	1944	3456
3	40%	777.60	1166.40	4233.60
4		166.40	1000.00	4400.00
5		0	1000.00	4400.00

7. $3750, $\frac{3}{80}$ or 3.75%, $96,250; $3609.38, $\frac{3}{80}$ or 3.75%, $92,640.62   **9.** $47.44

Margin Exercises, Section 12.2, pp. 317–318

1.

Year	Rate of depreciation	Annual depreciation	Value	Total depreciation
0			$8700	
1	$\frac{2}{5}$ or 40%	$3480	5220	$3480
2	40%	2088	3132	5568
3	40%	1252.80	1879.20	6820.80
4		279.20	1600	7100
5		0	1600	7100

Exercise Set 12.2, pp. 319–320

1.

Year	Rate of depreciation	Annual depreciation	Value	Total depreciation
0			$8000	
1	$\frac{2}{4}$ or 50%	$4000	4000	$4000
2	50%	2000	2000	6000
3		0	2000	6000
4		0	2000	6000

Margin Exercises, Section 12.3, pp. 321–322

1. (a) $\frac{5}{15}, \frac{4}{15}, \frac{3}{15}, \frac{2}{15}, \frac{1}{15}$; (b) $2366.67, $6333.33; $1893.33, $4440.00; $1420.00, $3020.00

2.

Year	Rate of depreciation	Annual depreciation	Value	Total depreciation
0			$8700	
1	$\frac{5}{15}$	$2366.67	6333.33	$2366.67
2	$\frac{4}{15}$	1893.33	4440.00	4260.00
3	$\frac{3}{15}$	1420.00	3020.00	5680.00
4	$\frac{2}{15}$	946.67	2073.33	6626.67
5	$\frac{1}{15}$	473.33	1600.00	7100.00

Exercise Set 12.3, pp. 323–324

1. $\frac{4}{10}, \frac{3}{10}, \frac{2}{10}, \frac{1}{10}$ **3.** $\frac{8}{36}, \frac{7}{36}, \frac{6}{36}, \frac{5}{36}, \frac{4}{36}, \frac{3}{36}, \frac{2}{36}, \frac{1}{36}$

5.

Year	Rate of depreciation	Annual depreciation	Value	Total depreciation
0			$8000	
1	$\frac{4}{10}$	$2400	5600	$2400
2	$\frac{3}{10}$	1800	3800	4200
3	$\frac{2}{10}$	1200	2600	5400
4	$\frac{1}{10}$	600	2000	6000

7.

Year	Rate of depreciation	Annual depreciation	Value	Total depreciation
0			$450	
1	$\frac{8}{36}$	$100	350	$100.00
2	$\frac{7}{36}$	87.50	262.50	187.50
3	$\frac{6}{36}$	75.00	187.50	262.50
4	$\frac{5}{36}$	62.50	125.00	325.00
5	$\frac{4}{36}$	50.00	75.00	375.00
6	$\frac{3}{36}$	37.50	37.50	412.50
7	$\frac{2}{36}$	25.00	12.50	437.50
8	$\frac{1}{36}$	12.50	0	450.00

9. $\frac{25}{325}$, $6153.85, $73,846.15; $\frac{24}{325}$, $5907.69, $67,938.46

11. 52.6%

Margin Exercises, Section 12.4, pp. 325–326

1.

Year	Rate of depreciation	Annual depreciation	Value	Total depreciation
0			$300,000	
1	25%	$ 75,000	225,000	$ 75,000
2	38%	114,000	111,000	189,000
3	37%	111,000	0	300,000

2.

Year	Rate of depreciation	Annual depreciation	Value	Total depreciation
0			$200,000	
1	15%	$30,000	170,000	$ 30,000
2	22%	44,000	126,000	74,000
3	21%	42,000	84,000	116,000
4	21%	42,000	42,000	158,000
5	21%	42,000	0	200,000

Exercise Set 12.4, pp. 327–328

1.

Year	Rate of depreciation	Annual depreciation	Value	Total depreciation
0			$15,000	
1	25%	$3,750	11,250	$ 3,750
2	38%	5,700	5,550	9,450
3	37%	5,550	0	15,000

3.

Year	Rate of depreciation	Annual depreciation	Value	Total depreciation
0			$210,000	
1	15%	$31,500	178,500	$ 31,500
2	22%	46,200	132,300	77,700
3	21%	44,100	88,200	121,800
4	21%	44,100	44,100	165,900
5	21%	44,100	0	210,000

5.

Year	Rate of depreciation	Annual depreciation	Value	Total depreciation
0			$130,000	
1	8%	$10,400	119,600	$ 10,400
2	14%	18,200	101,400	28,600
3	12%	15,600	85,800	44,200
4	10%	13,000	72,800	57,200
5	10%	13,000	59,800	70,200
6	10%	13,000	46,800	83,200
7	9%	11,700	35,100	94,900
8	9%	11,700	23,400	106,600
9	9%	11,700	11,700	118,000
10	9%	11,700	0	130,000

7. $1699.15

Review Test, Chapter 12, pp. 329–330

1.

Year	Rate of depreciation	Annual depreciation	Value	Total depreciation
0			$8500	
1	$\frac{1}{5}$ or 20%	$1700	6800	$1700
2	20%	1700	5100	3400
3	20%	1700	3400	5100
4	20%	1700	1700	6800
5	20%	1700	0	8500

2.

Year	Rate of depreciation	Annual depreciation	Value	Total depreciation
0			$8500	
1	$\frac{2}{5}$ or 40%	$3400	5100	$3400
2	40%	2040	3060	5440
3	40%	1224	1836	6664
4	40%	734.40	1101.60	7398.40
5	40%	440.64	660.96	7839.04

3. $\frac{5}{15}, \frac{4}{15}, \frac{3}{15}, \frac{2}{15}, \frac{1}{15}$

4.

Year	Rate of depreciation	Annual depreciation	Value	Total depreciation
0			$8500	
1	$\frac{5}{15}$	$2833.33	5666.67	$2833.33
2	$\frac{4}{15}$	2266.67	3400	5100
3	$\frac{3}{15}$	1700	1700	6800
4	$\frac{2}{15}$	1133.33	566.67	7933.33
5	$\frac{1}{15}$	566.67	0	8500

5.

Year	Rate of depreciation	Annual depreciation	Value	Total depreciation
0			$8500	
1	15%	$1275	7225	$1275
2	22%	1870	5355	3145
3	21%	1785	3570	4930
4	21%	1785	1785	6715
5	21%	1785	0	8500

CHAPTER 13

Margin Exercises, Section 13.1, pp. 332–334

1. $23.55 **2.** $23.05 **3.** 52% **4.** $45.15 **5.** $11.11

Exercise Set 13.1, pp. 335–336

1. $1899 **3.** $79.00 **5.** $20.07 **7.** $39.19 **9.** $8550
11. 37% **13.** 48% **15.** $8203.80 **17.** $7788
19. $81.44 **21.** $375.00 **23.** $5.93 **25.** $2840
27. 89,000

Margin Exercises, Section 13.2, pp. 337–340

1. 34% **2.** $174 **3.** $86.94 **4.** $9.75

Exercise Set 13.2, pp. 341–342

1. 21% **3.** 40% **5.** 40% **7.** 38% **9.** $49.00

11. $23.32 **13.** $42.31 **15.** $587.65 **17.** $22.86
19. $181.97 **21.** $27.47 **23.** 36, $12.12 **25.** $25.77

Margin Exercises, Section 13.3, pp. 343–346

1. $6.00 **2.** $4.60 **3.** $5591.30 **4.** 29% **5.** 57%

Exercise Set 13.3, pp. 347–348

1. $41.50 **3.** $191.50 **5.** $136.80 **7.** $96.75 **9.** $7.00
11. $210.00 **13.** $299.00 **15.** $103.53 **17.** 19%
19. 25% **21.** 11% **23.** 25% **25.** $1061.21; $61.21

Review Test, Chapter 13, pp. 349–350

1. $17.95 **2.** 35% **3.** $120.40 **4.** $25.00 **5.** 31%
6. $199.92 **7.** $11.21 **8.** $544.62 **9.** $1347.50
10. $178.50 **11.** 17% **12.** 50%

CHAPTER 14

Margin Exercises, Section 14.1, pp. 352–354

1. $100.05 **2.** $407.68 **3.** $426.79 **4.** $60.00
5. $28.99 **6.** $433.88

Exercise Set 14.1, pp. 355–356

1. $240.00 **3.** $200.00 **5.** $250.00 **7.** $242.00
9. $562.65 **11.** $363.00 **13.** $396.18 **15.** $535.00
17. $396.00 **19.** $255.00 **21.** $530.58 **23.** $525.72
25. $\approx$ 4.65 million businesses

Margin Exercises, Section 14.2, pp. 357–362

1. $196.15 **2.** $369.23 **3.** $1250.00 **4.** $1416.67
5. $70,000 **6.** $410.00 **7.** $3980.00 **8.** $232.00
9. $1110.00 **10.** $61.00 above draw **11.** $130.00 below
draw **12.** $663.07

Exercise Set 14.2, pp. 363–364

1. $2426.67, $29,120 **3.** $1300, $15,600 **5.** $319.85,
$693.00 **7.** $384.62, $833.33 **9.** $6090.00
11. $1600.00 **13.** $192.00 **15.** $347.00 **17.** $671.00
19. $632.10 **21.** 6.0%

Margin Exercises, Section 14.3, pp. 365–368

1. $151.04 **2.** $115 **3.** $1764.85 **4.** $3031.60
5. $160.49 **6.** $5166

Exercise Set 14.3, pp. 369–370

1. $177.05 **3.** $103.34 **5.** $175 **7.** $103 **9.** $1700.27
11. $3031.60 **13.** $1944.80 **15.** $5215.20 **17.** $4182
19. $5702.76 **21.** 0.9944

Margin Exercises, Section 14.4, pp. 371–374

1. $263.61 **2.** $3300; $2345.05 **3.** 13:30 (1:30 p.m.); 38 **4.** $351.12; $52.26; $8.83; $21.24 **5.** $312.03

Exercise Set 14.4, pp. 375–376

1.

WEEKLY TIME TICKET

EMPLOYEE'S NAME: DANA GARNER NO. ___ WEEK ENDING: JULY 24 19 87

JOB NAME OR NO.	KIND OF WORK DONE	S	M	T	W	T	F	S	HRS.	RATE	AMOUNT	
36824	ASSEMBLY		3	4	1.7	2	5		15.7	13.50	211	95
47895	MAINTENANCE	2.4	1.8	5.4	3.3	0.6			13.5	13.50	182	25
18462	TROUBLESHOOTING	0.9	1.1		1.8	1.8			5.6	13.50	75	60
49183	PRESS WORK	1.7	1.1	0.9	0.9	0.6			5.2	13.50	70	20
	Total Regular Time	8	8	8	8	8			40		540	00
	Total Overtime											

APPROVED: a p T'

WITHHOLD 63.00 | S.D.I. | F.I.C.A. 38.61 | STATE WH. | SAVINGS 18.75 | Total Earnings 540 00 | Total Deductions 120 36

4K 409 Rediform Date Paid 7/27/87 Check No. 2395 NET PAY 419 64

3.

WEEKLY TIME TICKET

EMPLOYEE'S NAME: STANLEE OTT NO. ___ WEEK ENDING: JULY 24 19 87

JOB NAME OR NO.	KIND OF WORK DONE	S	M	T	W	T	F	S	HRS.	RATE	AMOUNT	
47895	MAINTENANCE	0.5	1.5	2.2	3	2.5			9.7	14.50	140	65
18263	WELDING	1.2	3.2	5.1	0.6	3.1			13.2	14.50	191	40
18462	TROUBLESHOOTING	5.1	1.7	0.2	0.7	1.6			9.3	14.50	134	85
49183	PRESS WORK		1.6	0.4	0.5	0.4			2.9	14.50	42	05
62171	GLAZING	1.2		0.1	3.2	0.4			4.9	14.50	71	05
	Total Regular Time	8	8	8	8	8			40		580	00
	Total Overtime											

APPROVED: a p T'

WITHHOLD 88.00 | S.D.I. | F.I.C.A. 41.47 | STATE WH. | INS. 20.50 | Total Earnings 580 00 | Total Deductions 149 97

4K 409 Rediform Date Paid 7/27/87 Check No. 2397 NET PAY 430 03

5.

PAYROLL JOURNAL SHEET NO. ___

WORK WEEK, BEGINS—DAY: MONDAY TIME OF DAY: ___ DATE OF PAYMENT: July 27, 1987

EMPLOYEE'S NAME	EXEMPTIONS FED.	STATE	S	M	T	W	T	F	S	TOTAL HOURS	REGULAR RATE OF PAY	AT REGULAR RATE FOR TOTAL HOURS WORKED (1)	EXTRA FOR OVERTIME (1)	OTHER WAGES (ROOM, BOARD, ETC.) (2)	TOTAL WAGES	F.O.A.B. TAX	FED. WITH-HOLDING TAX	STATE WITH-HOLDING TAX	SAV	CONT	INS	TOTAL DEDUCTIONS	NET CASH WAGES PAID
DANA GARNER (M)				8	8	8	8	8		40	13.50/hr.	540 00			540 00	38 61	63 00		18 75			120 36	419 64
DALE FAKRAR (S)				8	8	8	8	8		40	15.95/hr.	630 00			630 00	45 05	127 00				5 50	177 55	452 45
STANLEE OTT (M)				8	8	8	8	8		40	14.50/hr.	580 00			580 00	41 47	88 00				20 50	149 97	430 03
TRACEY STOLTZ (S)				8	8	8	8	8		40	12.25/hr.	490 00			490 00	35 04	90 00					125 04	364 97

7. $21.90 **9.** $15.57 **11.** $1044.93 **13.** $602

Margin Exercises, Section 14.5, pp. 377–384

1. (3) $20,475.00, (4) $15.00, (5) $20,460.00, (7) $19,460.00, (9) $3,589.00, (10) $421.00
2. (10) $37,130.00, (11) $75.00, (12) $37,055, (14) $37,040, (15) $2000.00, (16) $35,040.00, (18) $8300.00, (19a) $7,265.00, (20) $7,265.00, (21) $1,035.00

Exercise Set 14.5, pp. 385–388

1. (3) $14,850.00, (5) $14,835.00, (7) $13,835.00, (9) $2060.00, (10) $280.00
3. (10) $48,400.00, (12) $48,230.00, (14) $48,210.00, (15) $4,000.00, (16) $44,210.00, (18) $8,271.00, (19a) $10,843.00, (20) $10,843.00, (22) $2572.0 **5.** $298,667.86

Review Test, Chapter 14, pp. 389–392

1. $157.50 **2.** $37.20 **3.** $454.58 **4.** $600.00 **5.** $340.38 **6.** $5940.00 **7.** $478.59 **8.** $38.14 **9.** $115.00
10. $3003.00 **11.** $5166 **12.** $554.05 **13.** $405.60 **14.** $24.54 **15.** (3) $24,890, (5) $24,865, (7) $23,865, (9) $4968,
(10) $232.00 **16.** (10) $27,670.00, (12) $27,558.00, (14) $27,538.00, (15) $3000.00, (16) $24,538.00, (18) $3540.00,
(19a) $4018.00, (20) $4018.00, (22) $478.00

Margin Exercises, Section 15.1, pp. 394–396

1. 85   **2.** 64.9   **3.** 80   **4.** $8771.44   **5.** 30   **6.** $17,750
7. 17   **8.** 18   **9.** 17   **10.** 37.5   **11.** 7   **12.** 88
13. 201,203

Exercise Set 15.1, pp. 397–398

1. 22; 23.5; 25   **3.** 18; 15; 15   **5.** $8.20; $8.55; $9.40
7. 3; 3; 1, 2, 3, 4, 5   **9.** $1.67   **11.** 41   **13.** $19,230
15. 82; 81; 81   **17.** 137.438; 137.625; $134\frac{1}{8}$, or 134.125
19. 182   **21.** 90   **23.** $3.73

Margin Exercises, Section 15.2, pp. 399–400

1.
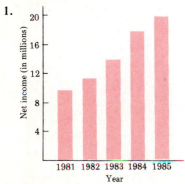

2.
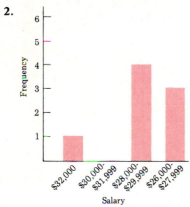

Exercise Set 15.2, pp. 401–402

1.
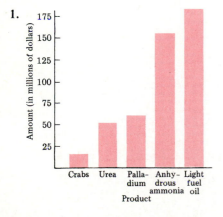

3.
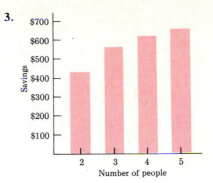

5.
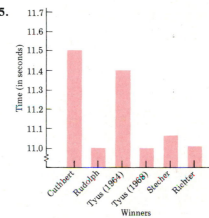

7.
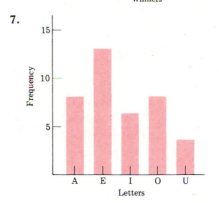

9. $267

Margin Exercises, Section 15.3, pp. 403–406

1.
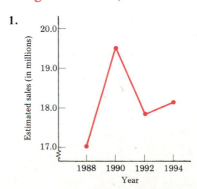

2.

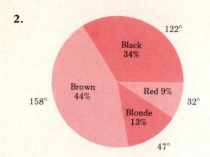

Exercise Set 15.3, pp. 407–410

1.

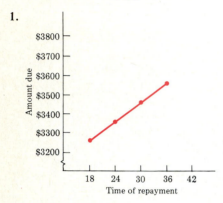

3.

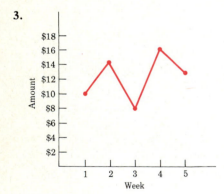

5.

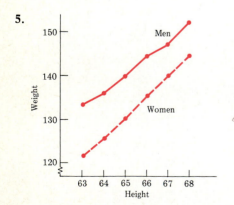

7.

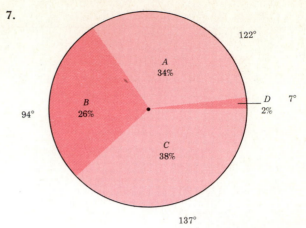

9.

	Angle
Pacific	55°
West	20°
Central	89°
South	59°
Atlantic	58°
Northeast	79°

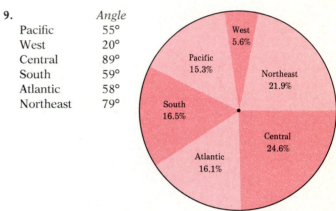

11.

Manufacturer	Angle
GM	205°
Ford	85°
Chrysler	48°
VW	4°
Amer. Motors	5°
Honda	8°
Nissan	4°

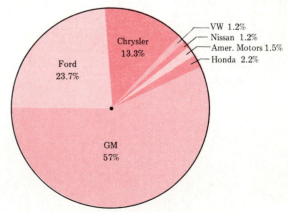

13. 37.7%

Review Test, Chapter 15, pp. 411–412

1. 52; 48.5; 45   **2.** $1.925; $1.845; $1.89

3.

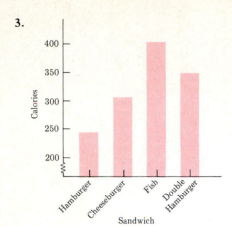

5.

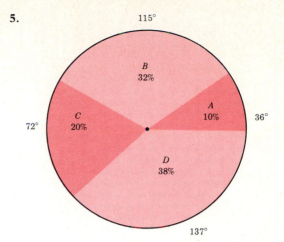

4.

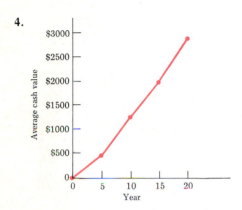

6.

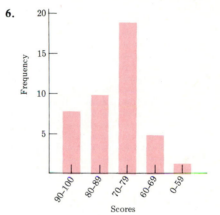

APPENDIX

Margin Exercises—Appendix, pp. 414–418

1. 0.7106   **2.** 299,700   **3.** 0.5689   **4.** 730   **5.** 840
6. 7.66   **7.** 8300   **8.** 0.2094   **9.** 21   **10.** 678.8
11. −4°C   **12.** 0°C   **13.** 68°F   **14.** −8°F

Exercises—Appendix, pp. 419–420

1. (a) 1000; (b) 0.001   **3.** (a) 100; (b) 0.01   **5.** (a) 0.001;

(b) 1000   **7.** 7800   **9.** 0.87   **11.** 7.801   **13.** 0.06555
15. 799,900   **17.** 7.88   **19.** 311   **21.** 0.1   **23.** 100,000
25. 450   **27.** 130   **29.** 0.00014   **31.** 0.688   **33.** 1000;
1000   **35.** 96,000   **37.** 0.069   **39.** 0.000703   **41.** 8012
43. 1000   **45.** 10   **47.** 0.01   **49.** 100   **51.** 25,000
53. 0.789   **55.** 705   **57.** 0.57   **59.** 7.89   **61.** 7.8
63. 70,000   **65.** 0.4   **67.** 0.0034   **69.** 1000   **71.** 149°F
73. 59°F   **75.** 87.08°F   **77.** 60°C   **79.** 15°C   **81.** 1000°C

INDEX

Accelerated Cost Recovery System (ACRS), 325–326
Accidental death benefit, 249
Accountants, 1, 311
Accounts payable, 282
Accounts receivable, 280
Accrued expenses payable, 282
Accumulated retained earnings, 283–284
Accurate interest method, 93, 95
Acid test ratio, 284
ACRS; see Accelerated Cost Recovery System
Add-on interest, 193–194
  annual percentage rate for, 193–194
Addition
  with calculator, 2
  of decimals, 39
  of fractions, 30–31
  of whole numbers, 8–9
Administration
  business, 267
  expenses of, 274
  of personal trust, 255
Advertising, 61
Annual percentage rate (APR), 180–186
  for add-on interest, 193–194
  finance charge and, 180
  finding, 180–183
  formula for estimating, 184
  table of, 194
Annuities, 163–176
  Individual Retirement Accounts as, 166–167
  ordinary, 163–164, 171–173
  present value of, 171–176

Annuities due, 164–166
  present value of, 173–174
Approximate time interest
  360-day, 94, 97–98
  365-day, 94, 98–101
Arithmetic mean, 394–395
Assessed value, 261
Assets
  current, 279
  fixed, 280
  quick asset ratio and, 284
Automobile insurance, 239–244
  amount of loss payable by, 239–241
  cost of, 242
Averages, 394–395

Balance
  of bank statement, 133–134
  of checking account, 126–127
  declining, depreciation and, 317–320, 325
Balance sheets, 279–286
  analyzing, 284
Bank cards, 202–204
Bank statement, 133–138
  reconciling with check record, 134–136
  verifying balance on, 133–134
Banker's 360-day method of interest computation, 91–93
Bar graphs, 399
Bayless, James R., 147
Bond(s), 221–226, 282–283
  buying, 222
  commission on, 222
  current yield on, 223
  interest on, 274–275

Bond listings, 221
Business administration, 267
Business consultants, 179
Business owner's fire insurance, 230–231
Butters, Mary Anne, 61

Calculator
  operation of, 2–4
  simplification of exponential expressions using, 56
Capacity, in metric system, 415–416
Capital, working, 284
Capital stock, 283
Capital surplus, 283
Carucci, Ray, 267
Cash, 279
Cash discounts, 299–300
Cash value of life insurance, 246–247
Celcius scale, 417–418
Centigrade scale, 417–418
Certified public accountants (CPAs), 1, 311
Chain discounts, 297
Charge(s)
  deferred, 281
  finance, 180
  interest; see Interest
Charge cards, 201–208
  revolving credit and, 201–202
Check(s), 122–138
  how to endorse, 123
  how to write, 122
  information on, 123–124
  payee and check amount on, 125
Check record book, 126–127

Checking account
  balancing, 126–127
  deposit slip and, 128
  reconciling bank statement with
    check record and, 133–138
Circle graphs, 404–406
Coinsurance, 232
Commission(s), 359–364
  on bonds, 222
  earnings and, 359–362
  on stocks, 213–214
Commission overtime, 362
Common multiple, 29
Common stock, 283
Complements, discounts and, 297
Compound interest, 103–110
  continuous, 108
  daily, 107–108
  formula for, 104
  solving problems with, 103
  tables for, 105–106
Cost(s)
  accelerated recovery system for,
    325–326
  of automobile insurance, 242
  dealer, 340
  of homeowner's insurance, 234–236
  of goods in inventory, 303–304
  of life insurance, 248–250
  markup as percentage of, 332–333
  retailer, 332, 334
  of sales, 273
  see also Expense(s)
Cost of goods sold, 273, 304
CPAs; see Certified public accountants
Credit
  installment, 180–210
  revolving, 201–202
Credit cards, 201–208
Current assets, 279
Current liabilities, 282
Current ratio, 284
Current yield on bonds, 223

Daily compound interest, 107–108
Daryanani, Michael, 331
Data processing, 121, 393
Dealer cost, 340
Decimal(s), 37–50
  addition with, 39
  converting from fractions to, 38–39
  converting from percent to, 67
  converting to fractions from, 38
  converting to percent from, 68
  division of, 46–47
  multiplication with, 45
  repeating, 47

subtraction with, 40
  word names and, 37
Decimal equivalents, 70
Declining-balance method for
  depreciation, 317–320, 325
Deferred charges, 281
Dennis, Daniel, 311
Denominator, 19
  least common, 29–30
Deposit, net, 41–42
Deposit slip, 128, 132
Depreciation, 274, 280, 312–328
  accelerated cost recovery system
    and, 325–328
  declining-balance method for,
    317–320, 325
  defined, 312
  straight-line method for, 312–316,
    325
  sum-of-the-years'-digits method for,
    321–324, 325
  tax, 325–328
Depreciation fractions, 321
Dickerson, Barbara, 121
Differential piecework plan, 354
Disability waiver of premium, 250
Discount(s), 292–302
  cash, 299–300
  chain, 297
  method of complements and, 297
  on notes, 148–152
  series, 297
  trade, 292–293
Discount rate(s), 293–294
  changing several to single rate, 298
  comparing, 298–299
Dividend (division), 14
Dividends on stock, 217
Division
  of decimals, 46–47
  of fractions, 23–25
  using calculator, 4
  of whole numbers, 14–15
  by zero, 20
Divisor, 14
Double declining-balance method for
  depreciation, 317–320, 325
Double indemnity, 249
Draw, 361

Earnings; see Payroll
Effective interest rates, 111–114
Employees withholding
  for income taxes, 365–366
  for social security taxes, 367–368
Endorsement of checks, 123
Equations, translation to, 70–71

Equivalents, decimal and fractional, 70
Exact interest method, 93
Expense(s)
  accrued, 282
  operating, 273
  selling and administrating, 274
  see also Cost(s)
Exponent(s), 55–58
  one as, 55
  using calculator, 4
  zero as, 55–56
Exponential expressions
  evaluating, 55–56
  simplification of, 56
Exponential notation, 55
Extended term coverage, 247

Fahrenheit scale, 417–418
Farrel, Maria Gamboa, 1
Federal income tax, 377–388
  depreciation and, 325–326
  Form 1040A and, 382–384
  Form 1040EZ and, 377–381
  on income statement, 275
  withholding for, 365–366
Federal income tax payable, 282
Federal Insurance Contributions Act
  (FICA), 367–368
FICA taxes, 367–368
FIFO; see First In, First Out method
Finance charges, 180
Financial consultants, 211
Fire insurance, 230–231
First In, First Out (FIFO) method, 305
Fixed assets, 280
Form 1040A, 382–384
Form 1040EZ, 377–381
Fraction(s), 19–36
  addition using, 30–31
  converting from decimals to, 38
  converting from percent to, 69–70
  converting to decimals from, 38–39
  converting to percent from, 68–69
  depreciation, 321
  division using, 23–25
  multiplication using, 23
  simplification using, 23
  subtraction using, 31–32
Fractional equivalents, 70
Frequency distributions, 400
Future value, 116

Goods sold, cost of, 273, 304
Graphs
  bar, 399

circle, 404–406
line, 403
Gross earnings, 352–353
Gross profit, 268
 calculating, 306

Homeowner's insurance, 231–236
 cost of, 234–236
Horizontal analysis, 276
Hsia, Ho Ming, 7

Income
 net, 269–270
 see also Payroll
Income statements, 173–178
 analyzing, 275–276
Income tax; *see* Federal income tax
Individual Retirement Accounts
 (IRAs), 166–167
Installment credit, 180–210
 final payment for, 198
 interest on, 195–196
 interest refund and, 197
Insurance
 automobile; *see* Automobile
 insurance
 business owner's, 230–231
 fire, 230–231
 homeowner's; *see* Homeowner's
 insurance
 life; *see* Life insurance
 reduced paid up, 247–248
Insurance agents, 229
Intangibles, 281
Interest, 86, 193–200
 add-on, 193–194
 amount of monthly payment for,
 88, 189–190
 banker's method of computation of,
 91–93
 on bonds, 274–275
 compound; *see* Compound interest
 on installment plan purchases,
 195–196
 refund of, 197
 on savings accounts, 139
 simple; *see* Simple interest
Interest rate(s), 86
 comparing, 112, 114
 effective, 111–114
 finding, 87
 nominal, 111–114
Interpolation, 235
Inventory(ies), 280, 303–308
 cost of goods and, 303–304
 cost of goods sold and, 304

gross profit and, 306
 valuation of, 305–306
IRAs; *see* Individual Retirement
 Accounts

Kaufman, Barton L., 229
Keogh Plans, 166, 168, 170

Last In, First Out (LIFO) method, 305
Least common denominator (LCD),
 29–30, 35
Least common multiple (LCM), 29, 35
Length, in metric system, 414–415
Levy, 261
Liabilities
 current, 282
 long-term, 282
Life insurance, 245–252
 agents for, 229
 amount of coverage under, 245–246
 cash value of, 246–247
 cost of, 248–250
 extended term coverage and, 247
 reduced paid up coverage and,
 247–248
 types of, 245
LIFO; *see* Last In, First Out method
Line graphs, 403
Liter, 415–416
Loan(s)
 amortized, 188
 see also Note(s)
Loan officers, 147
Long-term liabilities, 282

Major fraction rule, 256–257
Management
 of restaurant, 291
 of small business, 7
Markdown, 343–348
 as percentage of sale price, 345–346
 sale price and, 344–345
Marketable securities, 279
Marketing, 61
Markup, 332
 as percentage of cost, 332–333
 as percentage of selling price,
 337–338
Mass, in metric system, 416–417
Maturity, of bond, 221
McCord, Elizabeth, 255
Mean, 394–395
Measurements, metric, 414–420
Medians, 396
Merchandising, 331

Merchant's Rule, for partial payment
 of notes, 158–160
Meter, 414–415
Method of complements, 297
Metric system, 414–420
Mixed numerals, 20
Modes, 396
Money market mutual funds, 140
Monthly payments, 187–189
Multiple, least common, 29
Multiplicand, 13
Multiplication
 of decimals, 45
 of fractions, 23
 using calculator, 3
 of whole numbers, 13
Multiplier, 13
Mutual funds, 140

Net deposit, 41–42
Net income, 269–270
Net pay, 371
Net profit, 269–270, 275
Net profit ratio, 276
Net sales, 268, 273
Nominal interest rate, 111–114
Note(s), 148–154
 due date of, 148–149
 interest bearing and noninterest
 bearing, 148
 interest due on, 148
 partial payment of, 155–162
Notes payable, 282
Numbers
 mixed, 20
 whole; *see* Whole numbers
 word names for, 8, 37
Numerator, 19

Odd lots, 214
One as exponent, 55
Operating expenses, 273
Operating margin of profit, 275–276
Ordinary annuity, 163–164
 present value of, 171–173
Overtime
 commission and, 362
 piecework earnings and, 354

Paid up coverage, 247–248
Par value, 221
Payment(s), 187–192
 amount of interest in, 88, 90
 by check, 122–138
 final, 198

Payment(s) (*continued*)
  interest and principal portions of, 189–190
  monthly, 187–189
Payroll, 352–376
  computerized, 372–374
  differential piecework earnings and, 354
  federal withholding and, 365–368
  gross earnings and, 352–353
  hourly and piecework wages and, 352–356
  net pay and, 371
  overtime piecework earnings and, 354
  social security tax and, 367–368
  straight piecework earnings and, 353
Payroll journal, 372
Payroll supervisors, 351
P/E; *see* Price-earnings ratio
Percent, 62
  converting from decimals to, 68
  converting from fractions to, 68–69
  converting to decimals from, 67
  converting to fractions from, 69–70
  increase or decrease in, 77–80
  problem solving with, 70–71, 75–82
  see also Annual percentage rate; Interest rate(s)
Percentage method for federal withholding, 365
Permanent insurance, 245
Personal trust administrators, 255
Piecework plan, 353
Place value, 8
Power; *see* Exponent(s)
Premium(s), 230
  disability waiver of, 250
  interpolation and, 235
Prepayments, 281
Present value, 115–118
  of annuity due, 173–174
  finding without a table, 116
  of ordinary annuity, 171–173
Price-earnings ratio (P/E), 217–218
Pricing, 332–336, 337–348
  dealer cost and, 340
  markdown and, 343–348
  markup and; *see* Markup
  retailer cost and, 332, 334
  selling price and, 339
  see also Sale price
Principal, 86
  amount of monthly payment for, 189–190
  finding, 87–88
Proceeds, on notes, 149–152, 153–154
Product, 13

Profit
  gross, 268
  net, 269–270, 275
  operating margin of, 275–276
Promissory note; *see* Notes
Property tax, 261–264
  amount of tax and, 262
  assessed value and, 261
  tax rate and, 261
Proportion, 62–63
Published interest rate, 111–114

Quick assets ratio, 284
Quotient, 14

Raising to a power; *see* Exponent(s)
Rate(s), 63
  annual percentage; *see* Annual percentage rate
  discount; *see* Discount rate(s)
  interest; *see* Interest rate(s)
  tax, on property, 261
Ratio(s), 62
  acid test, 284
  current, 284
  net profit, 276
  profit-earnings, 217–218
  proportion and, 62
  quick assets, 284
  rate as, 63
Realtors, 85
Reciprocals, 23
Reconciling bank statement with check record, 134–136, 138
Reduced paid up coverage, 247–248
Regular time, 352
Replacement cost, 232–233
Restaurant management, 7
Retailer cost, 332, 334
Retained earnings, accumulated, 283–284
Revenue(s), 268
Revolving credit plan, 201–202
Riders, on insurance policies, 248
Round lots, 214
Rounding, 51–54
Rule of 78, 197

Salary, 357–359
  amount on pay and, 357–359
Sale(s)
  cost of, 273, 274
  determining, 258
  net, 268, 273
  of stocks, 214

Sale price, 339, 344–345
  markdown as percentage of, 345–346
Sales tax, 256–260
  determining sales and, 258
  finding, 256–257
Salvage value, 312
Savings accounts, 139
  interest on, 139, 141
Schnicke, Clarence W., 211
Self-employed persons tax, 368
Selling and administrating expenses, 274
Selling price; *see* Pricing; Sale price
Series discounts, 297
Simple interest, 86–102
  amount in payment, 88
  amount paid back and, 88
  banker's 360-day method for computation of, 91–93
  exact interest method of computation of, 93
  finding, 86–87
  finding principal and, 87–88
  finding rate of, 87
  tables for, 97–102
  360-day, approximate time method of computing, 94
  365-day, approximate time method of computing, 94
Simplification
  of exponential expressions, 56
  using fractional notation, 23
Single rate equivalent of several discount rates, 298
Social Security taxes, 367–368
Stanford, Alma, 351
Stock exchange, 212
Stock exchange quotations, 212
Stock(s), 212–220, 283
  buying, 212–213
  capital, 283
  commission on, 213–214
  common, 283
  price-earnings ratio of, 217–218
  selling, 214
  yield of, 217
Stockbrokers, 211
Straight piecework earnings, 353
Straight-line method for depreciation, 312–316, 325
Subtraction
  of decimals, 40
  of fractions, 31–32
  using calculator, 3
  of whole numbers, 9–10
Sum-of-the-years'-digits method for depreciation, 321–324, 325

Take-home pay, 371
Tax
    income; *see* Federal income tax
    property; *see* Property tax
    sales; *see* Sales tax
    social security, 367–368
Tax rate, on property, 261
Tax shelters, 166
Taylor, Henry M., 179
Teletype operators, 393
Temperature in metric system,
    417–418
Term insurance, 245
Theodorou, Dixie Chavis, 291
360-day, approximate time interest, 94
    tables for, 97–98
365-day, approximate time interest, 94
    tables for, 98–101
Trade discount, 292–293

Trade-in value, 312
Translation to equations, 70–71, 75
Trust administrators, 255

United States Rule, for partial
    payment of notes, 155–157, 161
Universal life insurance, 245

Venezia, Toni, 393
Vertical analysis, 276

Wage(s); *see* Payroll
Wage bracket method, for federal
    withholding, 366
Weight in metric system, 416–417
Weighted average method, 305
Whole numbers, 8–18
    addition of, 8–9

dividing decimals by, 46
division of, 14–15
multiplication of, 13
subtraction of, 9–10
Wignall, Patty Sanchez, 85
Withholding of federal tax, 365–368
Word names
    for decimals, 37
    for numbers, 8
Working capital, 284

Yield, 217
    on bonds, 223–224
    current, 223
    on purchase price, 224

Zero
    dividing by, 20
    as exponent, 55–56

EP67X